S0-EWI-154

BLACK 01
BOOK 02

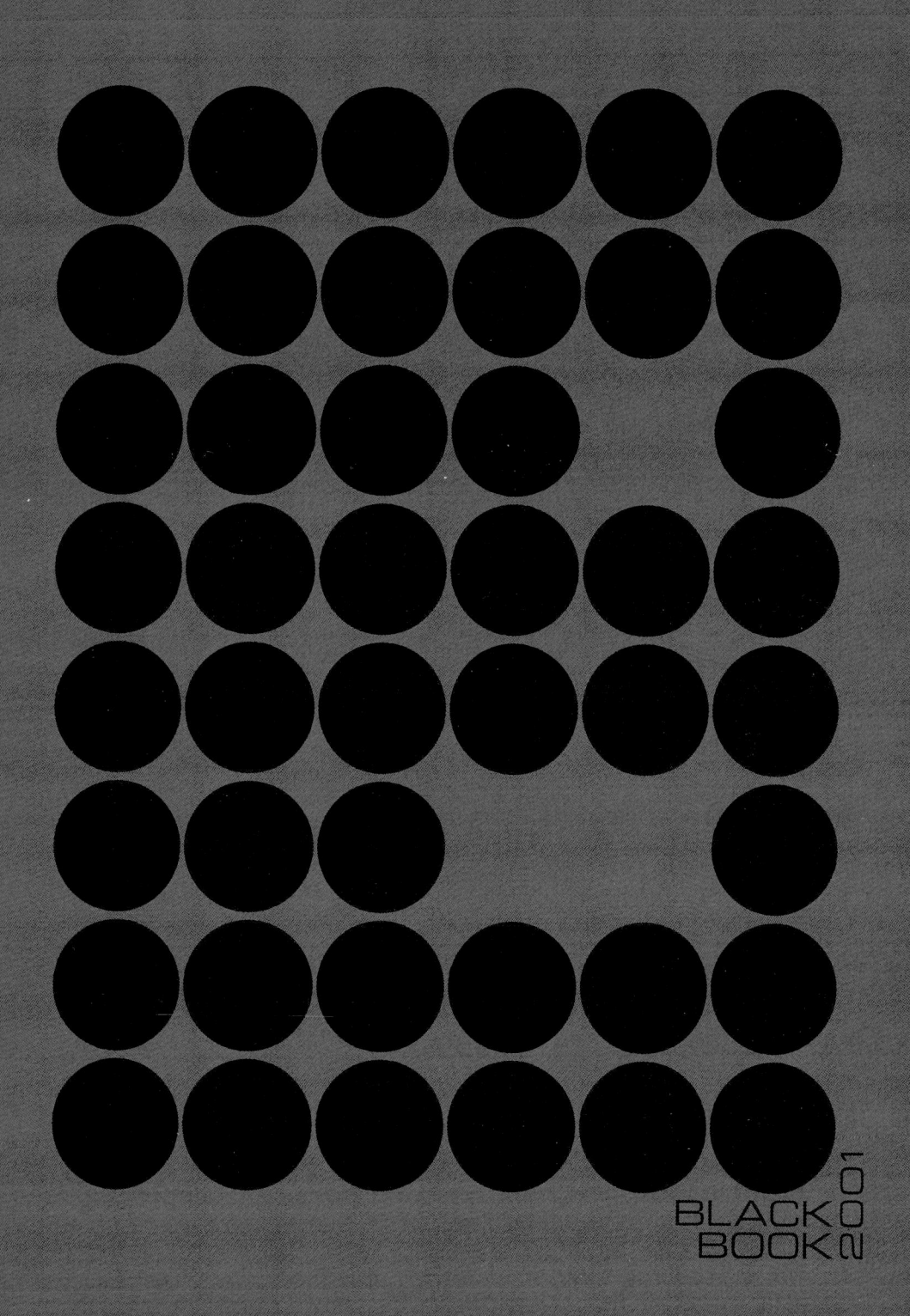

BLACK BOOK PHOTOGRAPHY 2001
portfolio edition

Black Book Photography is distributed in the U.S. by
The Black Book.

The Black Book
10 Astor Place, Sixth Floor
New York, N.Y. 10003
Tel: 212.539.9800/800.841.1246
Fax: 212.539.9801
HYPERLINK http://www.BlackBook.com

THE BLACK BOOK
& BLACK BOOK PHOTOGRAPHY

are trademarks of
Black Book Marketing Group Inc.
ISBN 0-942454-73-1
ISSN 1094-0499
©2001 Black Book Marketing Group Inc.
All rights reserved. We are not
responsible for errors or omissions.

All of the artwork contained in
this publication, reproduced
here with permission from the artist,
is the property of the artist and may be
protected by prior copyright. No art shown
in this publication may be reproduced
in any form without first obtaining
the permission of the artist.

Outside the U.S. contact:

RotoVision S.A.
7 rue du Bugnon
1299 Crans
Switzerland
Tel: 41 22 776 05 11
Fax: 41 22 776 08 89

SALES OFFICE

RotoVision S.A. Sheridan House
112-116 Western Road
Hove
East Sussex BN3 1DD
England
Tel: 44 1273 727268
Fax: 44 1273 727269
E-Mail: BRIANM @ ROTOVISION.COM

A subsidiary of BrandEra.com

Black Book Photography 2001 Designed by ink&co

Printed in Italy by Mondadori Printing, Verona
Special thanks to Enrico Bighin for his expertise and dedication

black book 2001

THE BLACK BOOK

PRESIDENT & PUBLISHER
Christina Holbrook
Executive Assistant
Valerie Frasca

PRODUCTION

Production Manager
Tracy Russek
Production Coordinators
Alan Haverly, Cathy Citarella, Wendy Weinberg
Traffic & Graphic Coordinators
Keith Werwa, Frances Matteo

Photography
Michael Mazzola 212.539.9826
Jason Brenner 212.539.9836
Illustration
Alison Curry 212.686.1440

Marketing Associate & AR100 Project Manager
Tosca Marcy

Photography
Jean Burnstine 888.619.9541
Illustration
Adrian Johnson 847.713.2439

Photography
Nancy McEntegart 800.841.1246

Photography
Debra Weiss 800.841.1246
Illustration
Lenore Cymes 800.841.1246
Sales Administration Coordinator
Maggie Kenny 800.658.7427

ACCOUNTING
Controller
Leighton Watson
Senior Accounting Coordinator
Farida Dhanji
Junior Accountant/Office Manager
Natalie Bousigard-Hyde

CIRCULATIONS & LISTINGS
Circulation & Listings Manager
Patricia Cassidy
Listings Coordinator
Linda Novak
Circulation Assistant
Anjon Moore

WEBSITE
Multimedia Manager
Alexandra Nevins
Web Coordinator
Felix Serrano

ADMINISTRATION
Receptionist
Anny Mejia
Quality Control
Gil Sembrano

LISTINGS A-Z

A

John Acurso 738-739
AKA Reps, Inc. 466-467
Carlos Alejandro 458-459
Robin Anderson 444-445
Randy Anderson Studio 498-499
Jeffrey Apoian 213-215
Aresu/Goldring Studio 382-383
Paul Armbruster 440-441
Alison Armstrong 697
Jim Arndt 530-531
Paul Audia 540
Christopher Ayers 740-741
Deborah Ayerst Artists Agent 618-619

B

Baartman Photography 596
Robert Bacall Representatives 247-257
Quentin Bacon 121, 146-147
Jorg Badura 50, 64-65
Chris Bailey 262-263, 541
Joel Baldwin 50, 78-79
Jacques Barbey 750-751
Ellen Barnes 620-623
Melanie Eve Barocas 302-303
John Barrett 360-361
Peter Barrett 486-487
Wendy Barrows 368-369
Sue Barton Represents 474-475, 480-481
David Bashaw 200-201
Rick Becker Studios, Inc. 340-341
Butch Belair 28-29

Steve Belkowitz 242-243
Bender & Bender 756-757
David Bentley 600-601
Howard Berman 424-425
Bernstein & Andriulli, Inc. 120-159
Andrew D. Bernstein Associates 718-719
Dennis Blachut 387, 392-393
Barry Blackman 765
Rick Bolen 624-625
Lou Bopp 256-257
Charlie Borland 664-665
Robert Bossi 322-325
Barbara Bowman 510-511
Richard Bradbury 100, 108-109, 769
Michael Brian 94-95
Thomas Broening 748-749
Steve Bronstein 422-423
Doug Brown Artist Management 387-395
Raphael Buchler 181
Jan Bugher 592-593
Rick Burda 186-187
Desmond Burdon 224-225, 541
Jeffrey Burke 696-697
Robert Burke 520-521
Burke/Triolo Productions 696-697
Tom Burkhart 563, 702-703
Burns Auto Parts 590-591
Kimberly Butler 326-327

C

Fabrizio Cacciatore 246
Marilyn Cadenbach 404-409
Caesar Photo Design 694-695
Ian Campbell 331-333
Teri Campbell 534-535
Marianne Campbell Associates 314-315
Elise Caputo & Associates Ltd. 213-223
Marc Carter 722-723
Marge Casey & Associates 343-351, 742-743
Judy Casey, Inc. 304-305
Mike Caspar 432-433
Bill Charles Represents 274-279
Chris Cheetham 30-31
Paul Christensen 348-349
Clare Agency (Clare O'Dea) 314-315
Clor Photography & Imaging 764
Stewart Charles Cohen 506-507
Terry Collier 336-337
Benton Collins 270-271
Chris Collins Studio 46-47
Colin Cooke 248-249
Ryann Cooley 488-489
Angela Coppola 386
Tony Cordoza 384-385
Richard Corman 50, 62-63
Dan Couto 226-227
Marnie Crawford Samuelson 244-245
Creative Management 16-21, 536-537, 682-683
Crosby Stills 522
Lee Crum 387, 390-391
Scott Cunningham 396-397

D

Damon Productions, Inc. 640-641
Patrick Darby 670-671
Hasnain Dattu 166-167, 331
Cameron Davidson 510-511
Brooke Davis 644-645
Davo Photographic 760-761
Peggy Day 562, 658-659
Deddens & Deddens 702-703
Katrina Deleon 468-469
Ric Deliantoni 712-713
Tony Demin 472-473
Walt Denson 644-645
Klaxonnez/Anne Desrochers 272-273
Robin Dictenberg 228-239
David Dimicco 410-411
Bill Diodato 446-447
Vincent Dixon 229, 232-233
Don Dixon & Avner Levona 100, 106-107, 768
Alan Dockery 613
Kevin Dodge 490-491
Tony D'Orio 598-599
Thomas Drew 560-561, 767
Dublin Productions 596-597
Francoise Dubois/Dennis Represents 718-719
Miki Duisterhof 121, 138-139

E

Dana Edmunds 734-735
Heather Elder 614-615
Lisa Ellison, Artist Representative 676-677
Lauren Elvers 270-271

Envoy Creative Consultants 374-379
Robert Epstein 8-9
Rhoni Epstein Artists' Management 706-707
Jim Erickson 682-683
Darryl Estrine 32-33
Steve Ewert 541, 544-545

F

Ron Fehling 272-273
Brad Feinknopf 558-559
Georg Fischer 50, 68-69
James Flanagan 212
Jim Flynn 460-461
Marili Forastieri 178
Chip Forelli Studio, Inc. 306-307
Ken Frantz 532-533
Hunter Freeman 614-615
Wolfgang Freithof 162-163
Paula Friedland Studio, Inc. 548-549
Rafael Fuchs 100, 112-113
Eric Futran 573

G

Bruno Gaget 182-183
David Gardiner 312-313
Kurt Gardner 285, 288-289
Michele Gastl 320-321
Didier Gault 179
Marlaina Gayle 430-431
Gregory Gaymont 556
Joe Gibbs 638-639

John Gillan Photography, Inc. 505
Michael Ginsburg & Associates 27-39
Keith Glassman 358-359
Globus Brothers 372-373
Rolph Gobits 50, 60-61
Barry Goldring 382-383
Andy Goodwin 538-539
Chris Gordaneer 48-49, 331
Steve Gottlieb 213, 216-217
Gozo 470-471
Michael Grecco Photography, Inc. 66-467
Beth Green Studios, Inc. 26
Jill Greenberg 304-305
Timothy Greenfield-Sanders 50, 56-57
Simon Griffiths 496-497
Steve Grubman Photography, Inc. 602-603
Lorentz Gullachsen 192-193

H

Philip Habib 204-207
Holly Hahn & Company (H2 + Co.) 570-571, 576-577
Stuart Hall 121, 152-155
Hamilton Gray 466-467
Giles Hancock 387
Acey Harper 646-647
Michael Hart 516-517
Eric Haselton 493
Hashi Studio, Inc. 50, 82-83
The Hawkins Group 498-499, 516-517
Tim Hawley 697

Olive Head 12-13
Gregory Heisler 121, 156-159
Cynthia Held 470-471
Steve Hellerstein Studio, Inc. 168-175
Steve Henke 574-575
Greg Hinsdale 402-403
Ruedi Hofmann 50, 74-75
Steve Hogben 508
Robert Holley 728-729
Alex Hong 438-439
Denise Hopkins 552-553
Rob Howard 202-203
Vic Huber 692-693
William Huber 406-409
Kelvin Hudson 387, 394-395
Hurewitz Creative Partners 598-599
Terry Husebye 700-701

I

Icon Digital Imaging 410-411
Mike Iezzi 764
James Imbrogno 578-579
Michael Indresano 258-259
Walter Iooss 50, 66-67

J

Edward Jacoby 450-451
Theresa Jae 505
Bruce James 696-697
David Joel 557
Susan Johann 318-319

Don Johnston 563, 568-569
Spencer Jones 278-279
William Jones 732-733
Joyce Photography, Inc. 594-595

K

Kalman & Pabst Photo Group 771
Vincent Kamin & Associates 644-645
George Kamper 285, 298-299
Carol Kaplan Studio, Inc. 196-199
Catherine Karnow 668-669
Dirk Karsten 42-43
George Kavanagh 308-309
Scott Keith 494-495
Robert Kent 213, 218-219
Josh Kessler 34-35
Greg Kinch 430-431
Bevil Knapp 509
Karl Knize 588-589
Palma Kolansky Studio 266-267
Korman + Company 100-113, 768-770
KSC 284-299
Karen Kuehn 208-209
Eric Kulin 454-455

L

Mir Lada 762-763
John Lair Studio 586-587
Mark Laita 229, 236-237
David Lamb 176
Joe Lampi 597

Lamprecht & Bennett 320-321

Rob Lang 356-357

Peter Langone 474-475, 480-481

Joel Larson 344-345

Robert Latorre 500-501

Mark Lee 378-379

Albert Leggett 529

Thomas K. Leighton 354-355

Peter Leverman Photography, Inc. 14-15

Liz Li 192-195

Mel Lindstrom 660-663

Joe Lombardo (KSC) 284-285

Lars Lonninge 285, 292-293

Kent Lund 760-761

Britt Lundquist 252-253

M

Richard Mack Photography Ltd. 546-547

Larry Maglott 342

Brian Mahany 654-655

Michael Mahovlich 210-211

Nicola Majocchi 50, 54-55

Dominique Malaterre 300-301

Daniel Malka 190-191

Tom Maloney 697

Tim Mantoani 636-637

Frank Marchese 114-115

Mariano 328-329

Paul Markow/Markow Southwest, Inc. 690-691

Joe McBride 744-745

Steven McDonald 550-551

James McEntee 98-99

Judith McGrath & Associates 224-225, 262-265, 541-545

Robert Mead Associates 42-43, 554-555

Lisa Means 502-503

Wild Bill Melton 452-453

Frank Meo 636-637

Eric Meola 50, 90-91

Meoli Studio 552-553

Scott Meyer 16-19

Bill Miles 121, 148-151

Susan Miller Represents 262-265

Doug Mindell 268-269

Martin Mistretta 194-195

Russell Monk 160-161, 331

Scott Montgomery 688-689

Simon Mooney 312-313

John Morrison 686-687

Will Mosgrove 708-709

Dennis Mosner 213, 220-221

Francesco Mosto 320-321

Joseph Mulligan 40-41

Dennis Murphy 350-351

James T. Murray 22-25

Stan Musilek, Inc. 618-619

N

Willie Nash 164-165

Anthony Nex 706-707

Nancy Ney 464-465

Mark Niederman 334-335
Niwa Studio, Inc. 444-445
Marc Norberg Studio, Inc. 580-581
Todd Norwood 180

O

Dennis O'Clair 398-399
John O'Conner 330
Glenn Oakley 656-657
John Offenbach 50, 58-59
Tim Olive 518-519
Roseanne Olson 726-727
Martijn Oort 404-405
Orbit Representation 226-227
Craig Orsini/Orsini, Inc. 364-367
John Owens Studio 116-119

P

Jackie Page 472-475, 480-481
Lee Page 44-45
Tim Pannell 746-747
David Papas 680-681
Michael Paras 352-353
Gary Parker 720-721
Andrew Parsons 184-185
Allan Penn 240-241
Victor John Penner 20-21
Bryan F. Peterson 310-311
Grant Peterson 274-275
Keith Philpott 584-585
Carlo Pieroni 100, 110-111, 770

Judd Pilosoff Inc. 346-347
George Pizzo Photography 563-565
Michael Pohuski 434-435
Todd Powell 285, 290-291
Greg Premru 316-317

Q

Ed Quinn 362-363

R

Peter Rad 387
David Radler 285, 296-297
Jon Ragel 276-277
Aaron Rapoport 714-715
K. Ray 264-265
Darran Rees 387-389
Repfile, Inc. 488-489, 552-553
Carolyn Somlo/Reptile Artists Agent 602-603
Aaron Rezny 414
Ted Rice 590-591
Philipp Scholz Rittermann 684-685
Michelle Roache Management Services 480-481
Lew Robertson 697
The Roland Group 434-435
Rosa + Rosa Studio, Inc. 36-37
Uli Rose 50, 80-81
Howard Rosenberg 628-631
Philip Rostron 442-443, 766
Kate Roth 536-537
John Rusnak 213, 222-223
John Russell 704-705

S

James Salzano 314-315
Sampsel & Preston 730-731
Chris Sanders 38-39
Sandro 16-19
Robb Scharetg 648-653
Frank Schiefelbein 572
Charles Schiller 96-97
Kevin R. Schochat 306-309
Michael Schoenfeld 254-255
Chris Schrameck 742-743
John Schulz 616-617
Schumann & Co. 578-579
Jeff Sciortino 576-577
Freda Scott, Inc. 644-645
Pete Seaward 121, 140-141
Greg Sellentin Productions 204-209
Dave Shafer 492
Karen Shell 724-725
Stephen Sherman 420-421
David Shopper 462-463
Zubin Shroff 456-457
Jay Silverman Productions 672-675
Mark Silverstein 736-737
George Simhoni 229-231, 331
Charlie Simokaitis 541-543
Chip Simons 634-635
Evan Sklar 121, 134-135
Dave Slagle 448-449
Brian Smith 482-483
Gil Smith 666-667
Maureen M. Smith 422-427

Ron Baxter Smith 188-189
Anthony Snyder 285, 294-295
Souders Studios 678-679
Southlight Associates 486-487
Dick Spahr 592-593
Stephen Spartana 376-377
Andy Spreitzer 418-419
Daniela Stallinger 121, 124-127
Shelly Steichen 692-693
Chris Stein 438-439
David Harry Stewart 100, 102-105
John Still 758-759
Simon Stock 229, 234-235
Stockland Martel 50-91
Maggie Storck 648-653
Tom Strand Studio 582-583
Jeremiah Sullivan & Associates 710-711
Kevin Summers 121, 144-145

T

Michel Tcherevkoff 370-371
Team Russell 704-705
Rocky Thies 412-413
Leen Thijsse 50, 86-89
Steve Thompson 264-265
Steve Thornton 512-513
Tilt, Inc. 300-301
Lorraine Triolo 696-697
Helen Trotman 10-11
Doug Truppe 8-9, 114-115

Danny Turner 514-515
Kate Turning 285-287

U

U3-Agents For The Visual Arts 562-569, 702-703
Randel Urbauer 642-643
Utopia The Agency 177-187

V

Rob Van Petten 12-13
Nick Vedros 554-555
Chris Vincent 415
Vue Represents 464-465

W

Paul Wakefield 121, 136-137
Teri Walderman 188-189
Douglas E. Walker 632-633
We're Jammin' 100, 106-107, 768
Uli Weber 121, 132-133
Mark Weidman 280-283
Christine Cain Weidner 380-381
Ken Weingart 338-339
Debra Weiss 632-633
Randy Wells 698-699
Bob Werre 504
Graham Westmoreland 229, 238-239
Westside Studio 48-49, 160-161, 166-167, 230-231, 331-333

Glen Wexler Studio 626-627
Greg Whitaker 570-571
Ross Whitaker 250-251
Bill White 260-261
Dan White 604-605
Timothy White 50, 72-73
White Light Images, Inc. 493
Mark Wieland 374-375
Stephen Wilkes 121, 128-131
John Wilkes Studio 400-401
Byll Williams 676-677
Jimmy Williams Productions 484-485
Bret Wills 426-427
Bruce Wolf 50, 84-85
Troy Wood 566-567
Angela Woods Agency 102-105
Ashton Worthington 428-429

Y

Sam Yocum 716-717

Z

Z Agency 540
Lesley Zahara - Zahara Productions 48-49
Jodie Zeitler 598-599
Oded Zeldin 436-437
Michael Zeppetello 50, 70-71
David Zimmerman Studio, Inc. 92-93, 416-417
Roy Zipstein 121, 142-143
Luca Zordan 50, 76-77

NORTHEAST

AKA Reps, Inc. 466-467

Carlos Alejandro 458-459

Robin Anderson 444-445

Jeffrey Apoian 213-215

Aresu/Goldring Studio 382-383

Paul Armbruster 440-441

Robert Bacall Representatives 247-257

Quentin Bacon 146-147

Jorg Badura 64-65

Chris Bailey 262-263, 541

Joel Baldwin 78-79

Melanie Eve Barocas 302-303

Wendy Barrows 368-369

Sue Barton Represents 474-475, 480-481

David Bashaw 200-201

Rick Becker Studios, Inc. 340-341

Butch Belair 28-29

Steve Belkowitz 242-243

Howard Berman 424-425

Bernstein & Andriulli Inc. 120-159

Dennis Blachut 387, 392-393

Lou Bopp 256-257

Robert Bossi 322-325

Richard Bradbury 100-101, 108-109, 769

Michael Brian 94-95

Steve Bronstein 422-423

Doug Brown Artist Management 387-395

Kathy Bruml 96-97

Raphael Buchler 181

Rick Burda 186-187

Desmond Burdon 224-225, 541

Kimberly Butler 326-327

Fabrizio Cacciatore 246

Marilyn Cadenbach 404-409

Ian Campbell 331-333

Marianne Campbell Associates 314-315, 708-709

Elise Caputo & Associates Ltd. 213-223

Marge Casey & Associates 343-351, 742-743

Judy Casey, Inc. 304-305

Bill Charles Represents 274-277

Chris Cheetham 30-31

Paul Christensen 348-349

Clare Agency 314-315

Terry Collier 336-337

Benton Collins 270-271

Chris Collins Studio 46-47

Colin Cooke 248-249

Angela Coppola 386

Tony Cordoza 384-385

Richard Corman 62-63

Dan Couto 226-227

Marnie Crawford Samuelson 244-245

Creative Management/Michael Ash 16-21, 682-683

Lee Crum 387, 390-391

Scott Cunningham 396-397

Hasnain Dattu 166-167, 331

Katrina DeLeon 468-469

Tony Demin 472-473

Robin Dictenberg 228-239

Bill Diodato 446-447

Vincent Dixon 228-229, 232-233

Don Dixon & Avner Levona 100-101, 106-107, 768

Miki Duisterhof 138

Lauren Elvers 270-271

Marion Enste-Jaspers 238-239

Envoy Creative Consultants 374-379

Robert Epstein 8-9

Darryl Estrine 32-33

Ron Fehling 272-273

Randi Fiat & Associates 16-21, 190-191, 536-537

Georg Fischer 68-69

James Flanagan 212

Jim Flynn 460-461

Marili Forastieri 178

Chip Forelli Studio, Inc. 306-307

Wolfgang Freithof 162-163

Rafael Fuchs 100-101, 112-113

Bruno Gaget 182-183

David Gardiner 312-313

Kurt Gardner 284-285, 288-289

Michele Gastl 320-321

Didier Gault 179

Marlaina Gayle 430-431

Paola Giavedoni 210-211

Michael Ginsburg & Associates 27-39

Keith Glassman 358-359

Globus Brothers 372-373

Rolph Gobits 60-61

Barry Goldring 382-383

Chris Gordaneer 48-49, 331

Steve Gottlieb 213, 216-217

Gozo 470-471

Michael Grecco Photography, Inc. 466-467

Beth Green Studios, Inc. 26

Jill Greenberg 304-305

Timothy Greenfield-Sanders 56-57

Lorentz Gullachsen 192-193

Philip Habib 204-207

Stuart Hall 152-155

Hamilton Gray 466-467

Giles Hancock 387

Joel Harlib Associates, Inc. 44-45

Hashi Studio, Inc. 82-83

Olive Head 2-13

Gregory Heisler 156-159

Cynthia Held 470-471

Steve Hellerstein Studio, Inc. 168-175

Greg Hinsdale 402-403

Ruedi Hofmann 74-75

Alex Hong 438-439

Lisa Howard 202-203

Rob Howard 202-203

William Huber 406-409

Kelvin Hudson 387, 394-395

Hurewitz Creative Partners 240-241, 598-599

Michael Indresano 258-259

Walter Iooss 66-67

Edward Jacoby 450-451

Susan Johann 318-319

Spencer Jones 278-279

George Kamper 284-285, 298-299

Carol Kaplan Studio, Inc. 196-199

Dirk Karsten 42-43

George Kavanagh 308-309

Robert Kent 213, 218-219

Josh Kessler 34-35

Greg Kinch 430-431

Klaxonnez/Anne Desrochers 272-273

Palma Kolansky Studio 266-267

Korman + Company 100-105, 108-113, 768-770

KSC 284-299

Karen Kuehn 208-209

Eric Kulin 454-455

Mark Laita 228-229, 236-237

David Lamb 176

Lamprecht & Bennett 320-321

Rob Lang 356-357

Peter Langone 474-475, 480-481

Joel Larson 344-345

Mark Lee 378-379

Thomas K. Leighton 354-355

Peter Leverman Photography, Inc. 14-15

Samantha Lewin 370-371

Liz Li 192-195

Lars Lonninge 284-285, 292-293

Britt Lundquist 252-253

Larry Maglott 342

Michael Mahovlich 210-211

Nicola Majocchi 54-55

Dominique Malaterre 300-301

Daniel Malka 90-191

Frank Marchese 114-115
Mariano 328-329
James McEntee 98-99
Judith McGrath & Associates 224-225, 262-265, 541-545
Robert Mead Associates 42-43, 554-555
Bill Melton 452-453
Eric Meola 90-91
Scott Meyer 16-19
Bill Miles 148-151
Susan Miller Represents 262-265
Doug Mindell 268-269
Martin Mistretta 194-195
Russell Monk 160-161, 331
Simon Mooney 312-313
Dennis Mosner 213, 220-221
Francesco Mosto 320-321
Joseph Mulligan 40-41
Dennis Murphy 350-351
James T. Murray 22-25
Willie Nash 164-165
Nancy Ney 464-465
Mark Niederman Photography 334-335
Niwa Studio, Inc. 444-445
Todd Norwood 180
Dennis O'Clair 398-399

John O'Conner 330
O'Gorman/Schramm 200-201
John Offenbach 58-59
Martijn Oort 404-405
Orbit Representation 226-227
Craig Orsini/Orsini, Inc. 364-367
John Owens Studio 116-119
Jackie Page 472-475, 480-481
Lee Page 44-45
Michael Paras 352-353
Andrew Parsons 184-185
Allan Penn 240-241
Victor John Penner 20-21
Bryan F. Peterson 310-311
Grant Peterson 274-275
Carlo Pieroni 100-101, 110-111, 770
Judd Pilossof, Inc. 346-347
Joseph Piscitelli 116-119
Michael Pohuski 434-435
Todd Powell 284-285, 290-291
Greg Premru 316-317
Ed Quinn 362-363
Peter Rad 387
David Radler 284-285, 296-297
Jon Ragel 276-277
K. Ray 264-265

Darran Rees 387-389

Aaron Rezny 414

Michelle Roache Management Services 98-99, 474-475, 480-481

The Roland Group 434-435

Rosa + Rosa Studio, Inc. 36-37

Uli Rose 80-81

Philip Rostron 442-443, 766

John Rusnak 222-223

Dario Sacramone 400-401

James Salzano 314-315

Chris Sanders 38-39

Sandro 16-19

Charles Schiller 96-97

Kevin R. Schochat 306-309

Michael Schoenfeld 254-255

Pete Seaward 140-141

Greg Sellentin Productions 204-209, 260-261

Stephen Sherman 420-421

David Shopper 462-463

Zubin Shroff 456-457

George Simhoni 228-231, 331

Evan Sklar 134-135

Dave Slagle 448-449

Maureen M. Smith 422-427

Ron Baxter Smith 188-189

Anthony Snyder 284-285, 294-295

Stephen Spartana 376-377

Andy Spreitzer 418-419

Daniela Stallinger 124-127

Chris Stein 438-439

David Harry Stewart 100-105

Simon Stock 228-229, 234-235

Stockland Martel 50-91

Kevin Summers 144-145

Michel Tcherevkoff 370-371

Rocky Thies 412-413

Leen Thijsse 86-89

Steve Thompson 264-265

Tilt, Inc. 300-301

Helen Trotman 10-11

Doug Truppe 8-9, 114-115

Kate Turning 284-287

Utopia The Agency 177-187

Rob Van Petten 12-13

Chris Vincent 415

VUE Represents 464-465

Paul Wakefield 136-137

Teri Walderman 188-189

Michael Walz 196-199

We're Jammin' 100-101, 106-107, 768

Uli Weber 132-133

Mark Weidman 280-283

Christine Cain Weidner 380-381

Ken Weingart 338-339

Graham Westmoreland 228-229, 238-239

Westside Studio 48-49, 160-161, 166-167, 230-231, 331-333

Ross Whitaker 250-251

Bill White 260-261

Timothy White 72-73

Mark Wieland 374-375

Stephen Wilkes 130-131

John Wilkes Studio 400-401

Bret Wills 426-427

Bruce Wolf 84-85

Angela Woods Agency 102-105

Ashton Worthington 428-429

Lesley Zahara – Zahara Productions 48-49, 686-687

Jodie Zeitler 236-237, 598-599

Oded Zeldin 436-437

Michael Zeppetello 70-71

David Zimmerman Studio, Inc. 92-93, 416-417

Roy Zipstein 142-143

Luca Zordan 76-77

ANNA SUI

Robert Epstein

FILM/DIGITAL PHOTOGRAPHER

REPRESENTED BY:
Doug Truppe
212-685-1223
www.robepstein.com

HELEN TROTMAN | PHOTOGRAPHY
212 625 3871

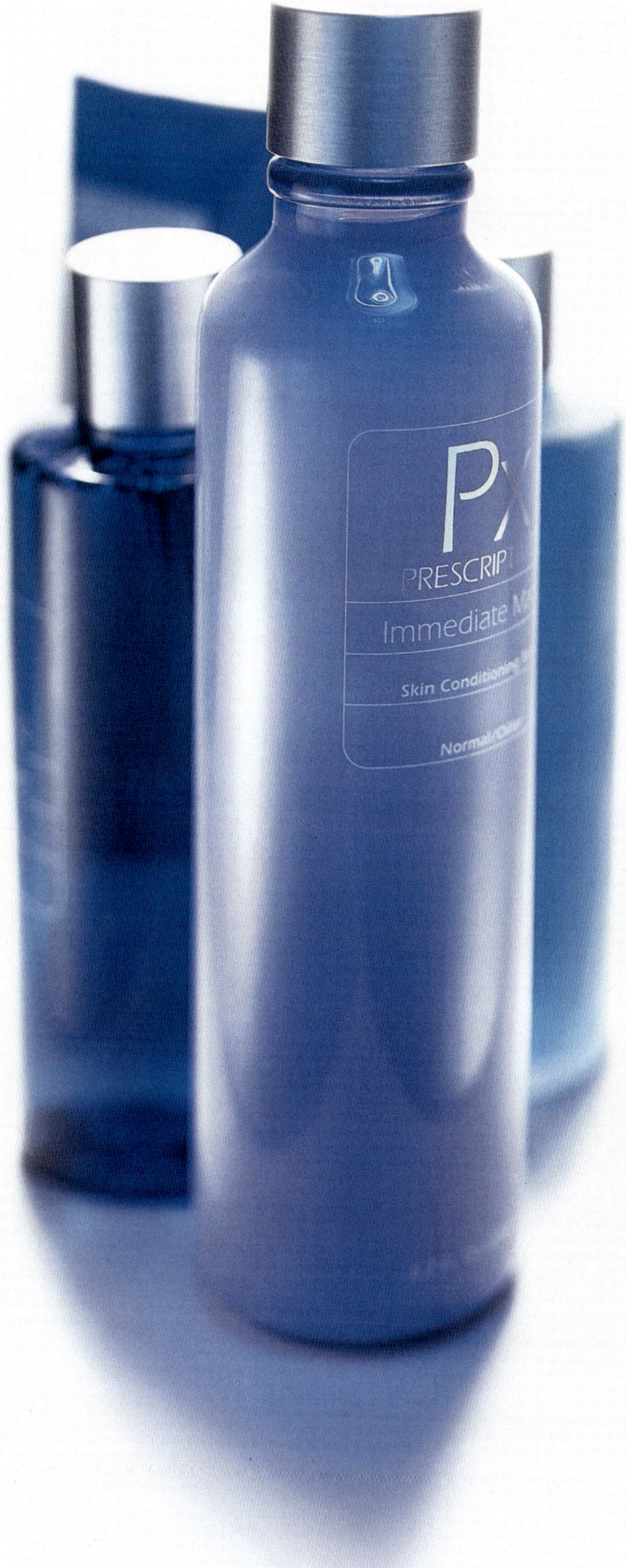
PRESCRIP
Immediate M
Skin Conditioning
Normal/Oily

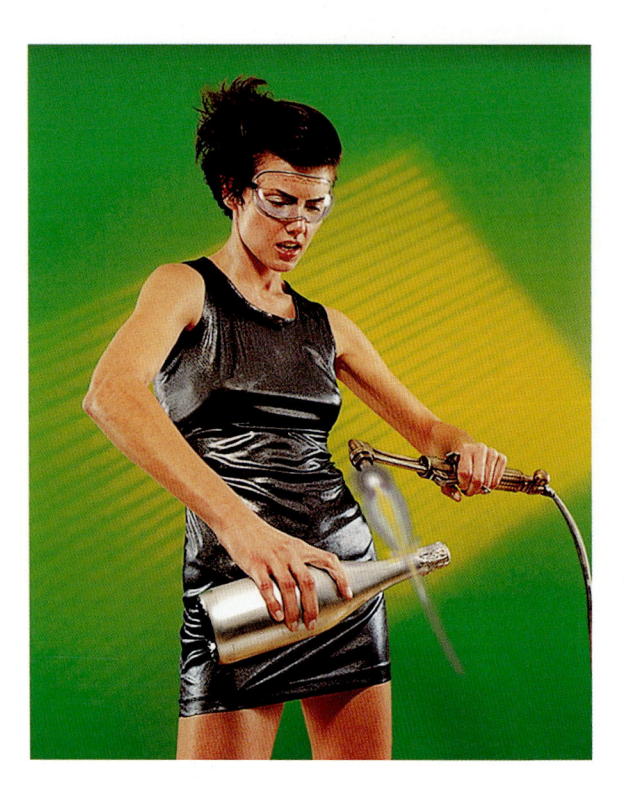

represented by Olive Head (212) 580-3323

(212) 869-2190

Rob Van Petten

www.robvanpetten.com

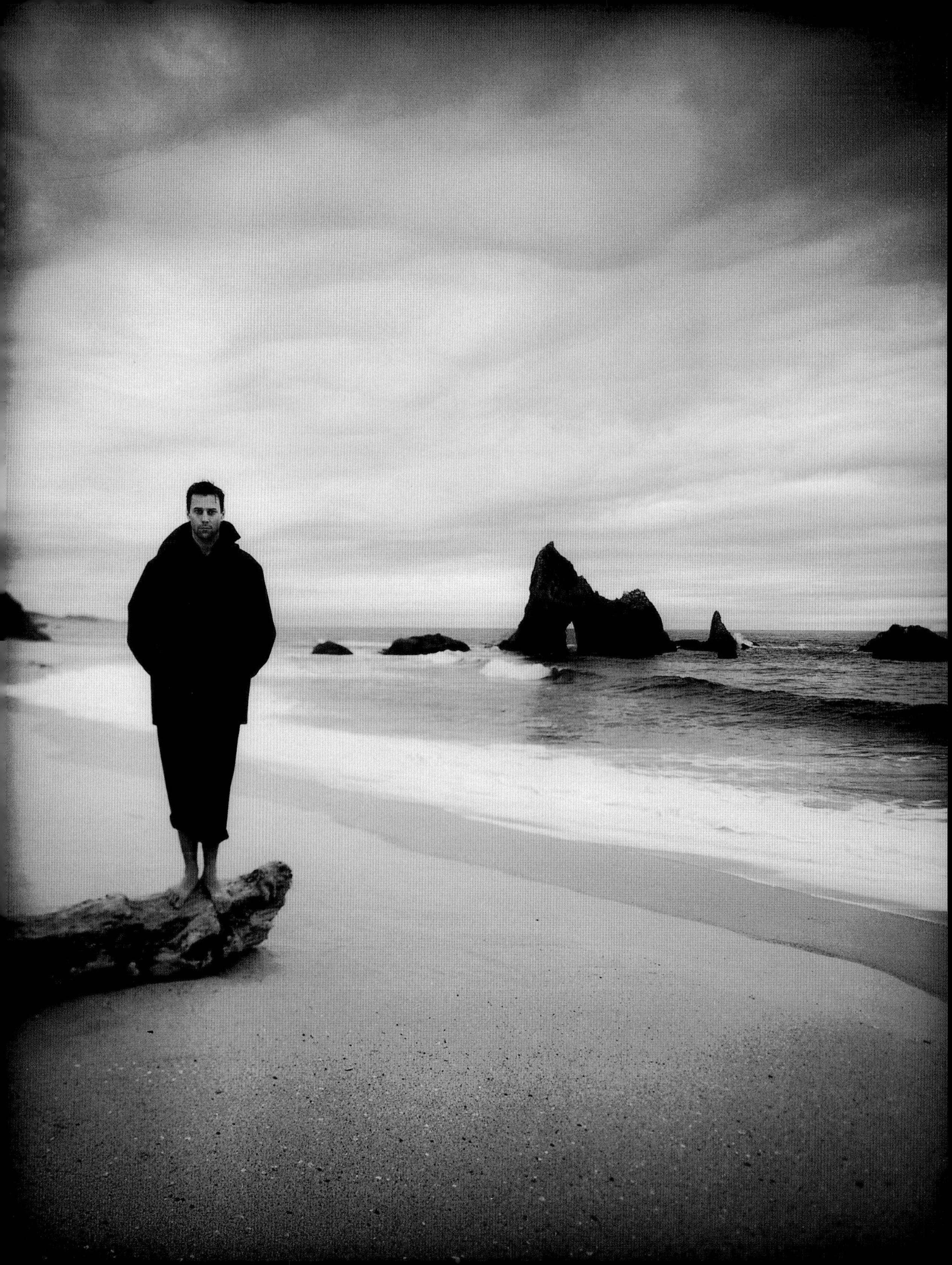

Peter Leverman

1 800 851 4524
www.peterleverman.com

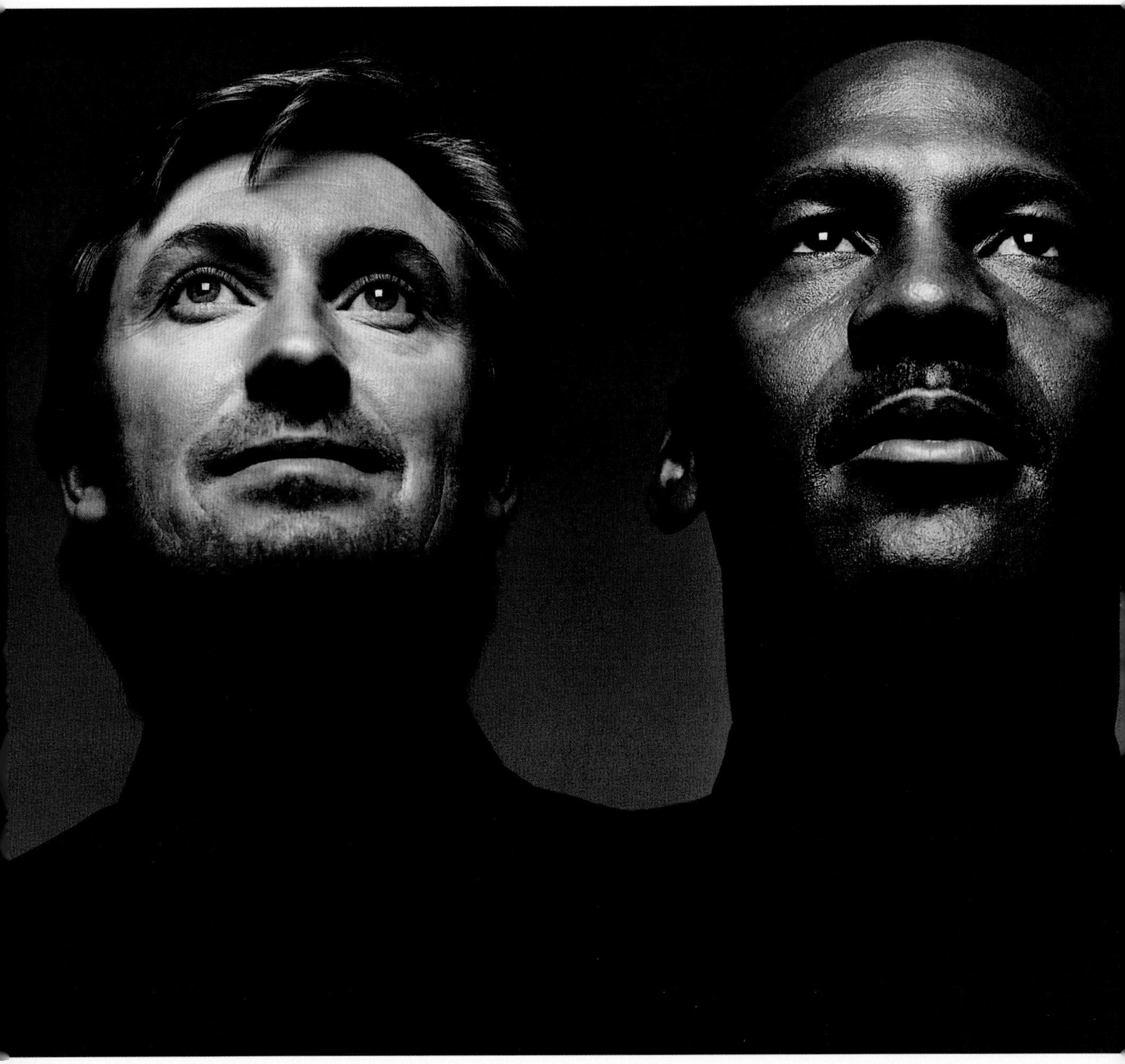

SANDRO
PHOTOGRAPHY

www.sandrofilm.com

Courtesy: mvp.com

Represented by:

CMP
Michael Ash & Estelle Leeds
212.655.6500

CMP Midwest
Randi Fiat
312.329.9800

CMP West Coast
Stephanie Menuez
415.460.6571

CMP Los Angeles
Scott Meyer
310.449.0085

SANDRO
PHOTOGRAPHY

www.sandrofilm.com

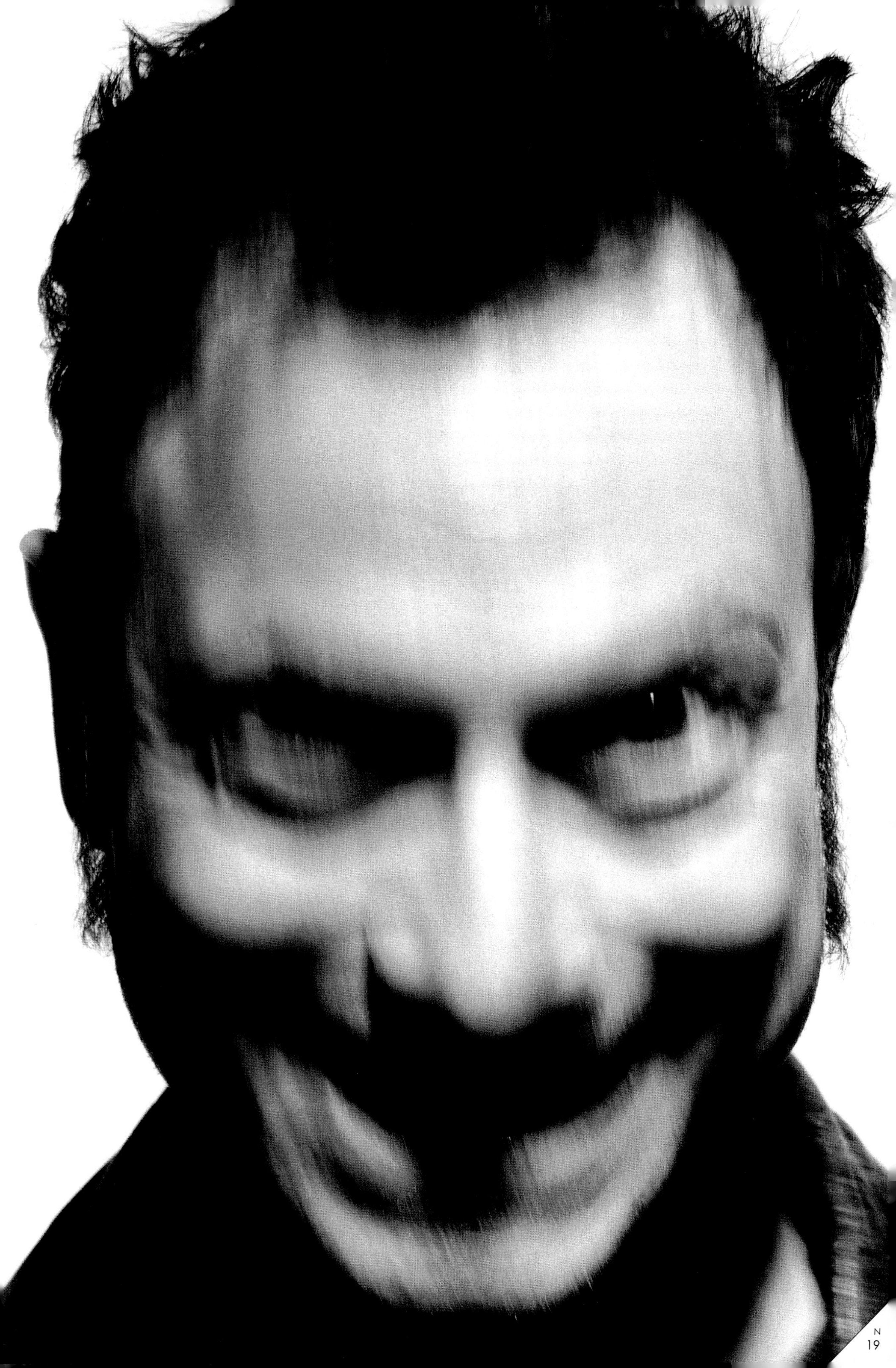

KING'S
BARBICID
REG. U. S. PAT. OFF.
The Approved
GERMICIDE & DISINFEC

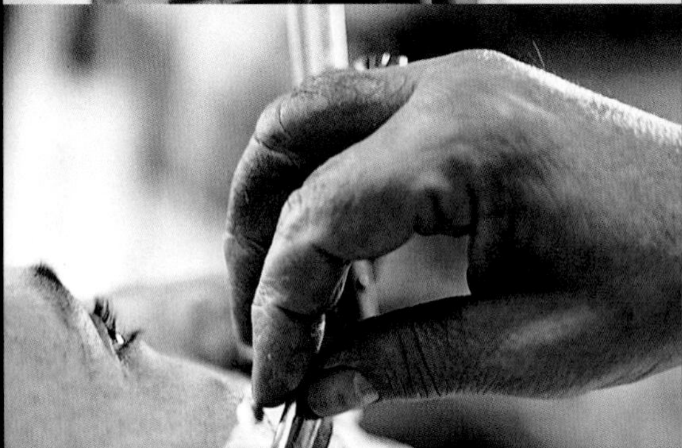

LOOK-BETTER
FEEL-BETTER
TRY-FRANK'S
BARBER-
-SHOP-

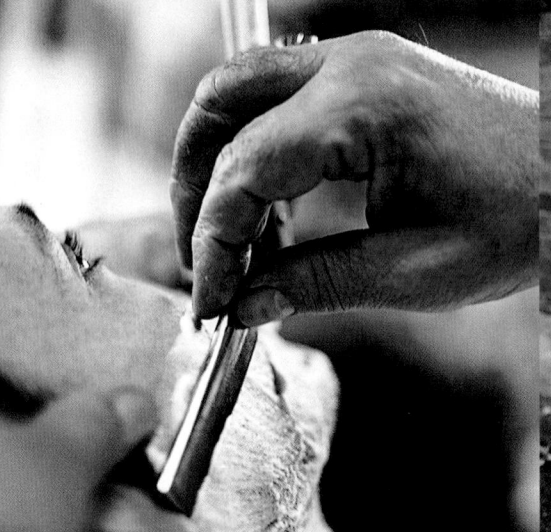

CREATIVE MANAGEMENT PARTNERS
east **michael ash** t **212.655.6500**
midwest **randi fiat** t **312.329.9800**
west **stephanie menuez** t **415.460.6571**

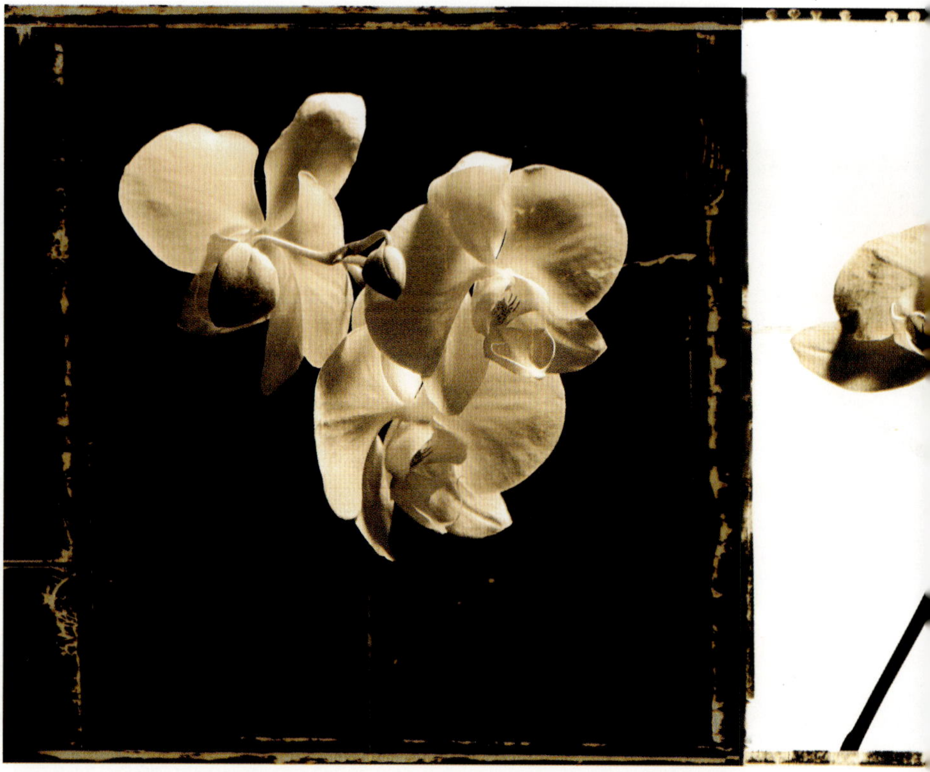

t murray photography 62 west 45th street nyc 212 997 4499 www.jamestmurray.com

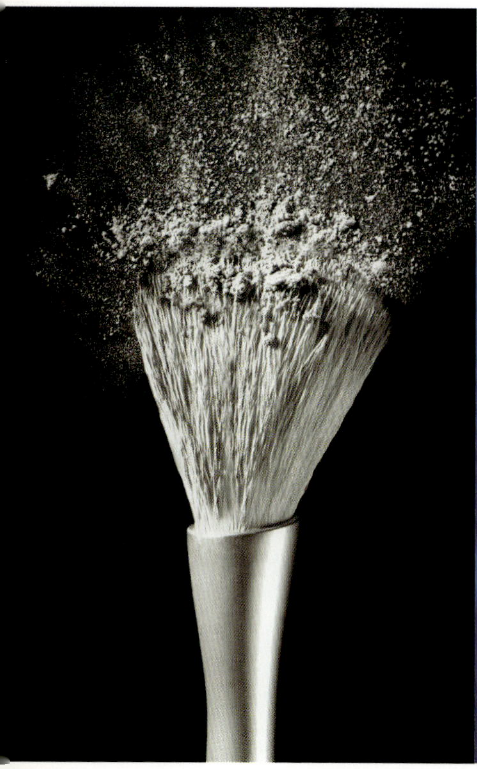

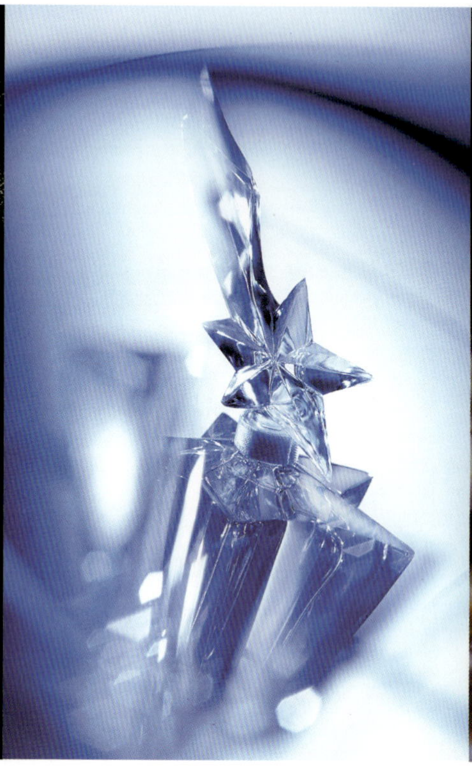

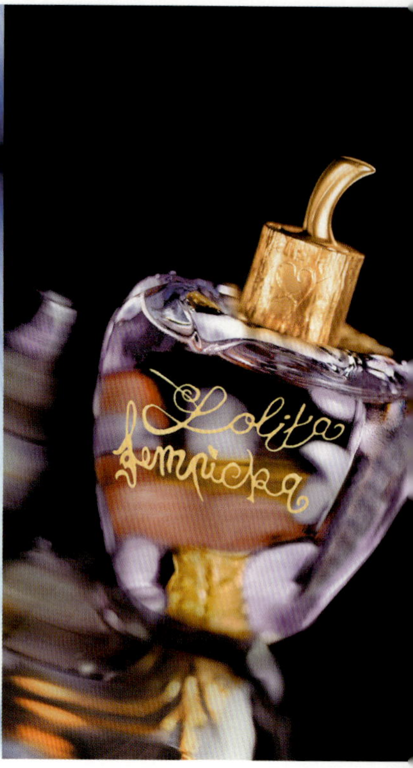
Lolita
Lempicka

www.jamestmurray.com

design: the dot group inc www.dot-ny.com

Beth Green STUDIOS

(212) 580-1928
www.bethgreen.com

MICHAEL GINSBURG REPRESENTS

Butch Belair • *Karen Capucilli* • Chris Cheetham
Darryl Estrine • Joshua Kessler • *Doug Rosa* • Chris Sanders

tel 212 679-8881 *fax* 212 679-2053 *email* mginsburg@mindspring.com

Butch Belair is represented by Michael Ginsburg (212) 679-8881

Client: Steve Madden / Art Direction: Tom Kane

Butch Belair is represented by Michael Ginsburg (212) 679-8881

www.chrischeetham.com

Drivetime 94.9fm   94.9FM **BBC** LONDON LIVE
London as you've never heard it

New Kellogg's
Special K red berries.
Delicious whole raspberries,
sliced strawberries and cherries.

Bosch hat das Handy
für Pendler entwickelt

BOSCH

Represented by Michael Ginsburg Telephone (212) 679 8881 Fax (212) 679 2053

(TOP ROW LEFT TO RIGHT) VANITY FAIR'S E-ESTABLISHMENT; SCOTT BLUM buy.com, MARK CUBAN digital yahoo, ELLEN SIMINOFF yahoo, CHRISTOS COTSAKOS e-trade, JOSEPH PARK kozmo.com, ELLEN HANCOCK exodus communications, JONATHON NELSON organic, CRAIG KANARICK razorfish, JEFFREY DACHIS razorfish, CANDICE CARPENTER ivillage, DA... CASE Chase HSQ, ANN WINBLAD hummer winblad venture partners, HALSEY MINOR cnet, SCOTT KURNIT about.com, MARY MEEKER morgan stanley dean witter JAY WALKER pricelin...

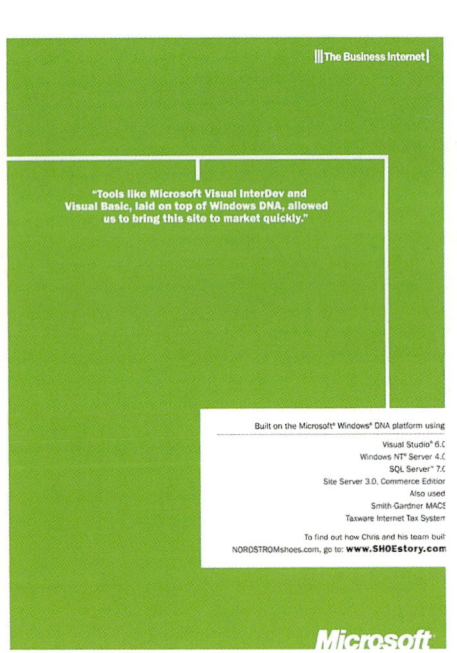

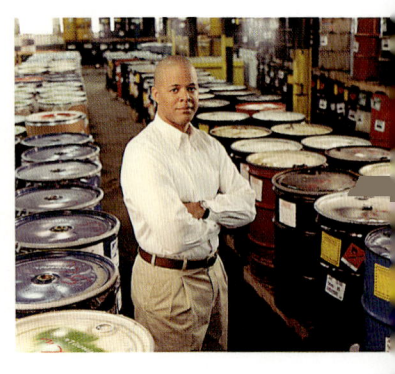

Chris Dressler, Senior Program Manager, NORDSTROMshoes.com

"So the challenge here was knowing the speed of how quickly we had to bring shoe vendors online."

"We went from 6 to 10 to 20 vendors and we're continuing down that road."

"So how do we rapidly do the development to make all this happen?"

The Business Internet

"Tools like Microsoft Visual InterDev and Visual Basic, laid on top of Windows DNA, allowed us to bring this site to market quickly."

Built on the Microsoft® Windows® DNA platform using
Visual Studio® 6.0
Windows NT® Server 4.0
SQL Server™ 7.0
Site Server 3.0, Commerce Edition
Also used
Smith Gardner MACS
Taxware Internet Tax System

To find out how Chris and his team built NORDSTROMshoes.com, go to: **www.SHOEstory.com**

Microsoft

David Warthen, Chief Technology Officer, Ask Jeeves

"One of our biggest challenges was to take something that's really hard to build – natural language Web querying – and disguise the complexities to make it easy to use."

"In the past, we were focused on developing the core question-answering technology."

"Now we're expanding to provide solutions to a multitude of businesses and need to scale accordingly."

DARRYL ESTRINE
photography

NY ph (212) 780.0026
LA ph (213) 694.0503

Represented by **Michael Ginsburg**
PH (212) 679.8881

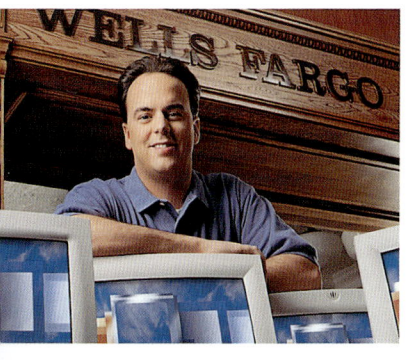

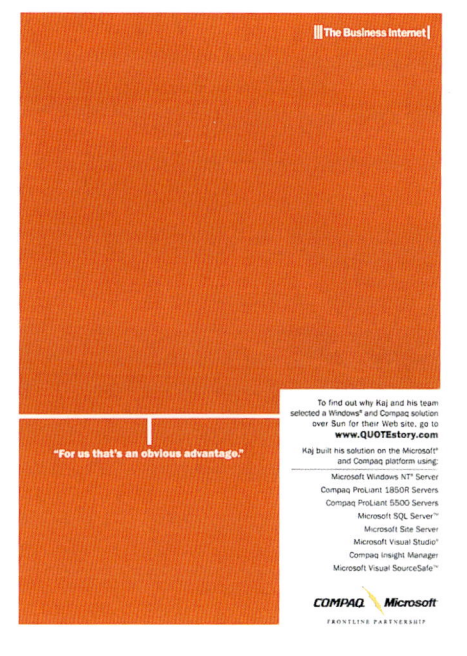

joshua kessler   represented by michael ginsburg 212.679.8881

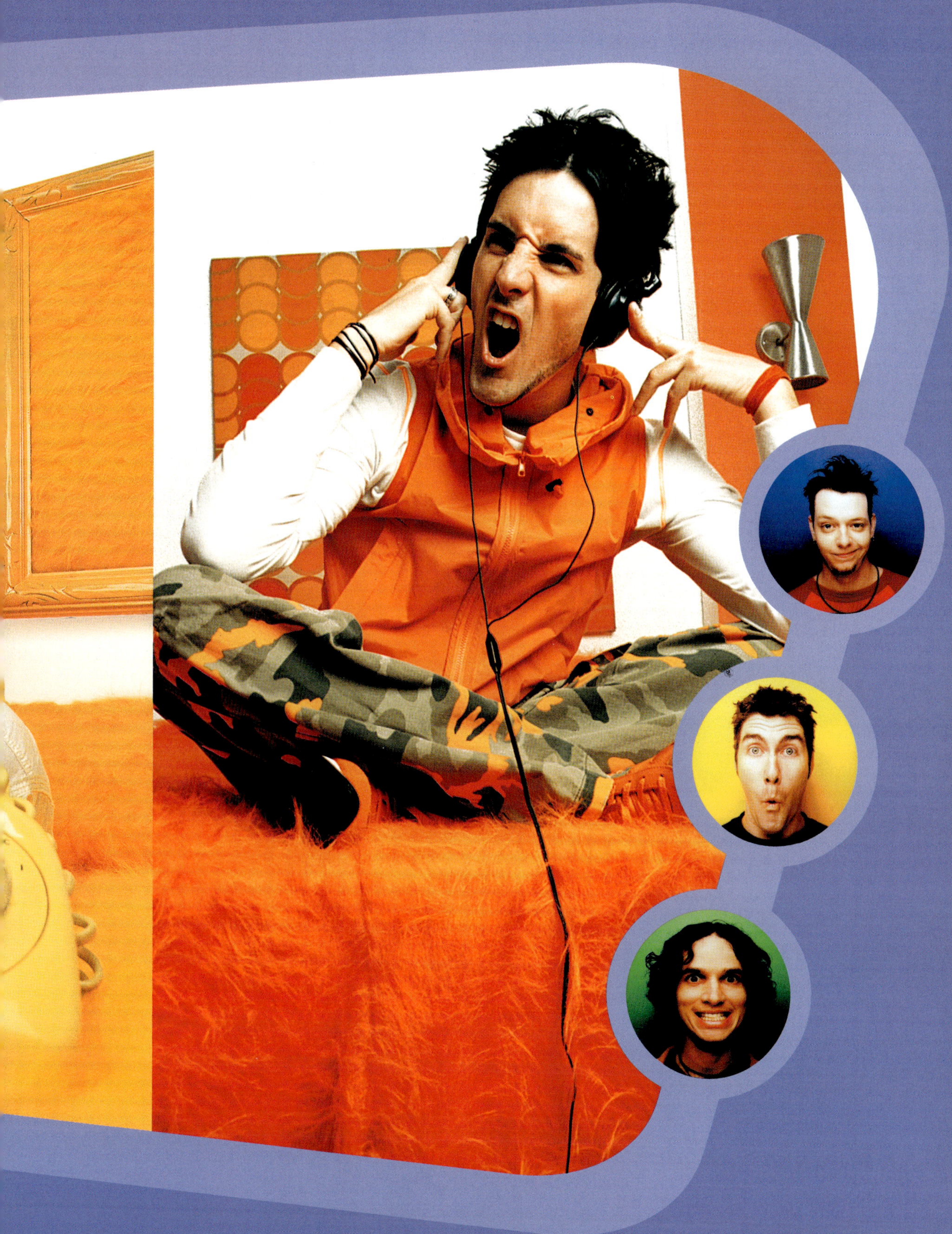

studio
t 212 366 4898

rosa+**rosa** inc

represented by michael ginsburg

t 212 679 8881
f 212 679 2053

doug rosa
photography

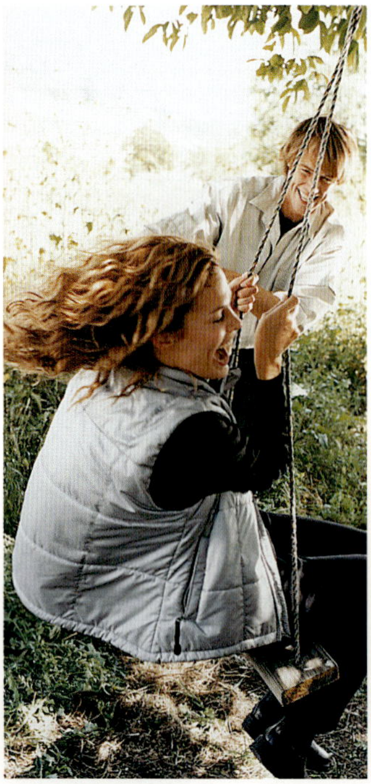
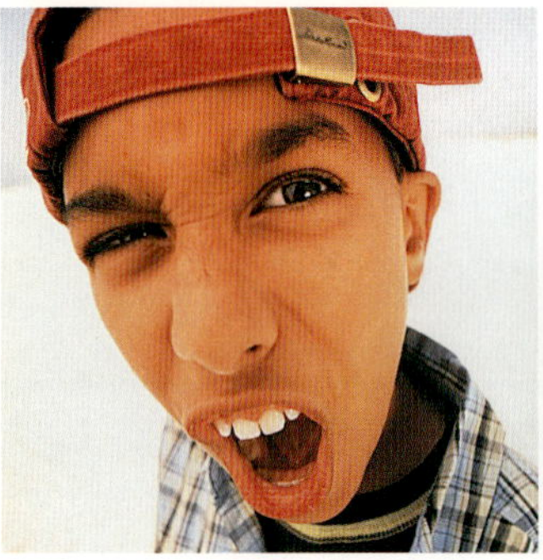
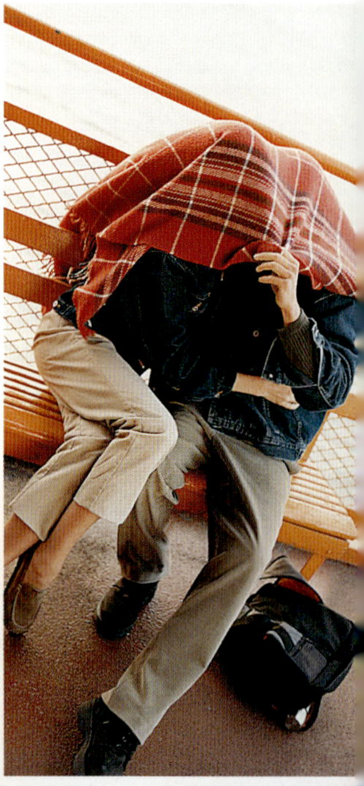
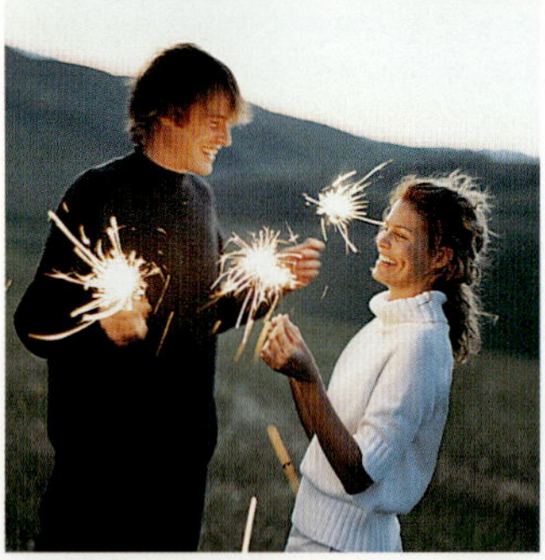
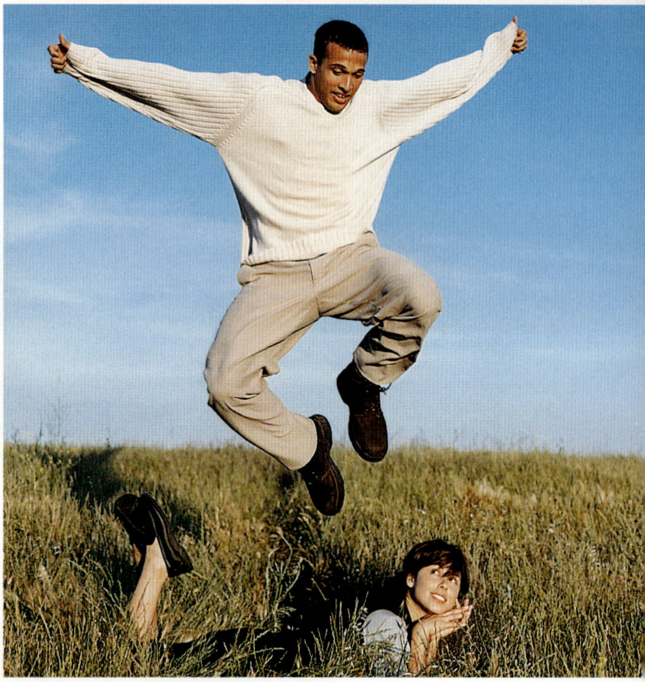
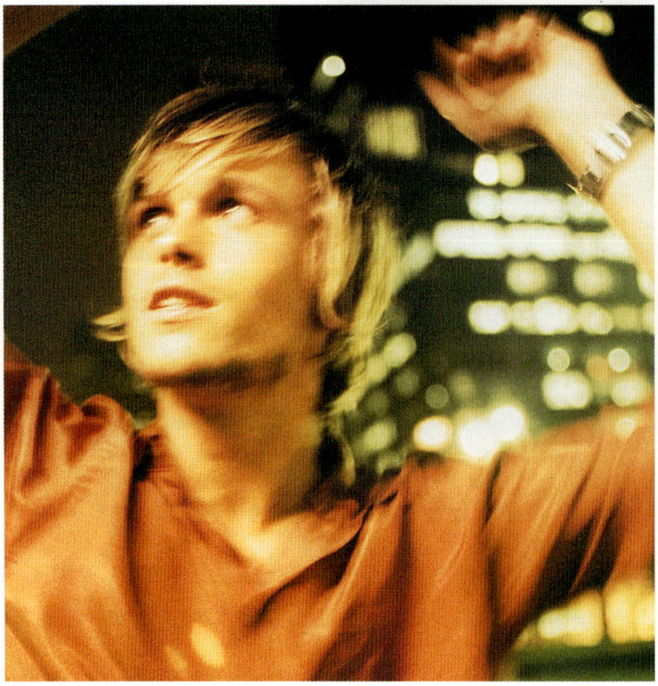
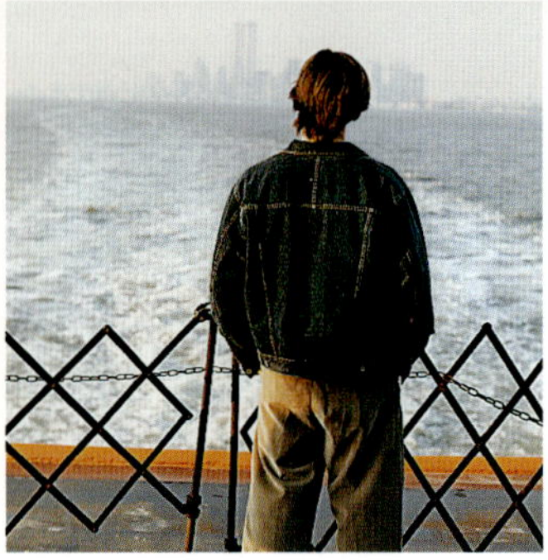

chris sanders

REPRESENTED BY
MICHAEL GINSBURG
212 679 8881

73 SPRING STREET #502
NEW YORK CITY 10012
PH 212 343 0003
FAX 212 343 0087
WWW.CHRIS-SANDERS.COM

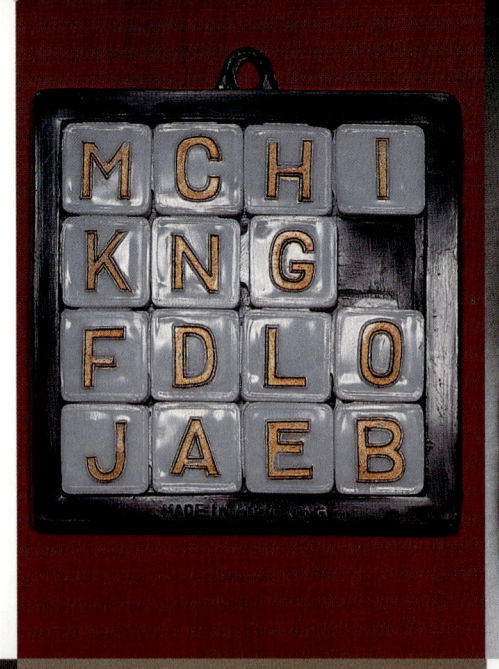

p 212 620 6110
f 212 620 6113

joseph mulligan

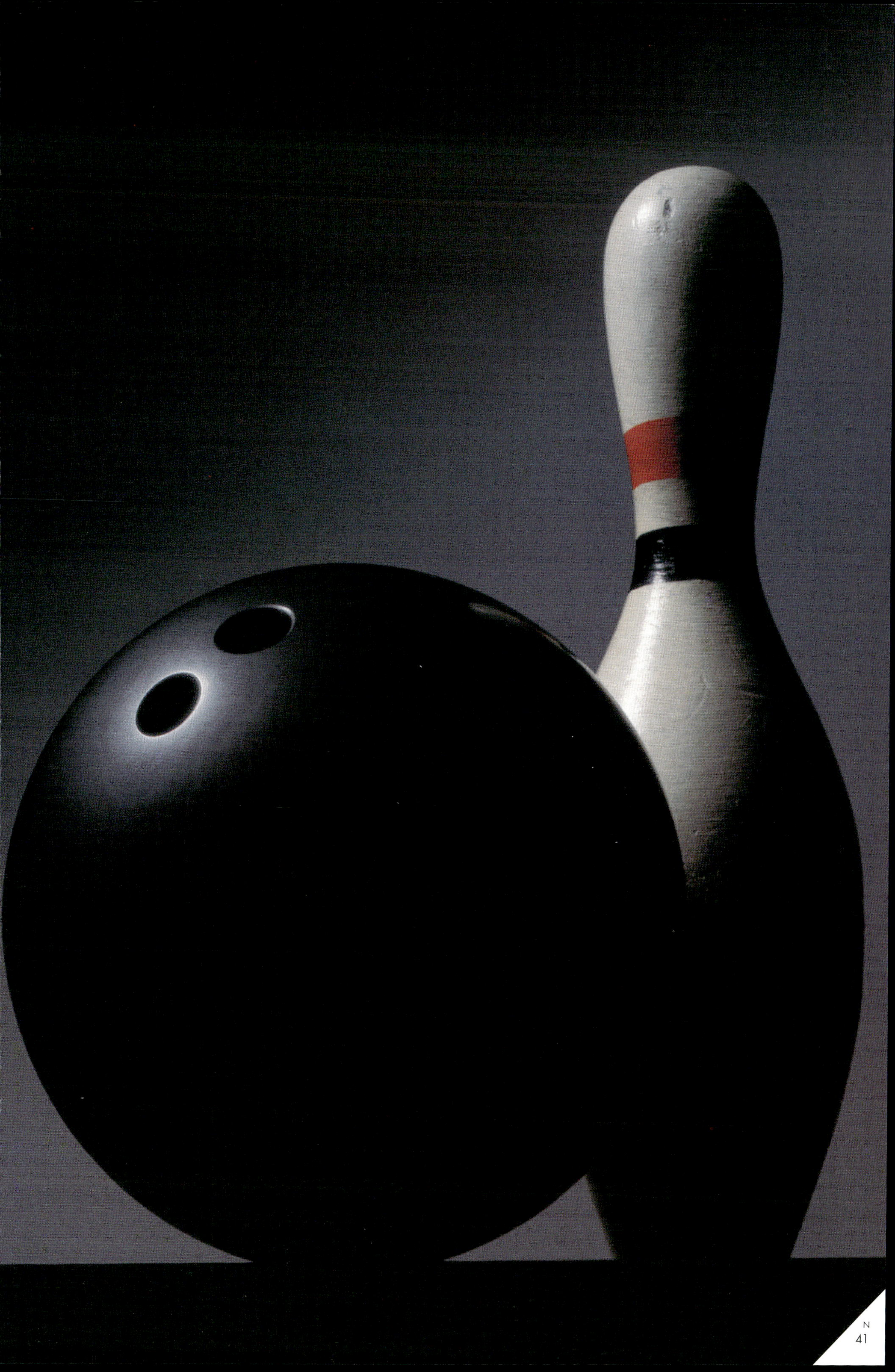

DIRK KARSTEN

REPRESENTED BY ROBERT MEAD ASSOCIATES • 800.717.1994 • NYC 212.688.7474
WWW.DIRKKARSTEN.COM

LEE PAGE · 68 THOMAS STREET · NEW YORK CITY · 212-233-2227 · www.leepage.com

LEE PAGE · NEW YORK CITY · 212-233-2227 · www.leepage.com

CHRIS COLLINS

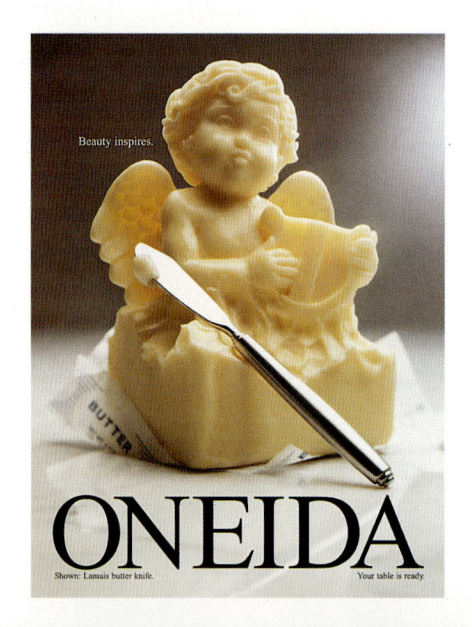

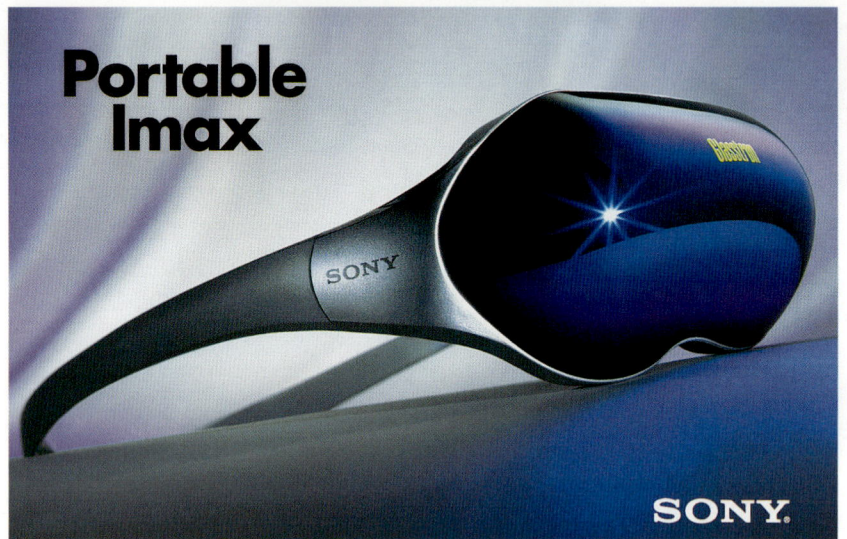

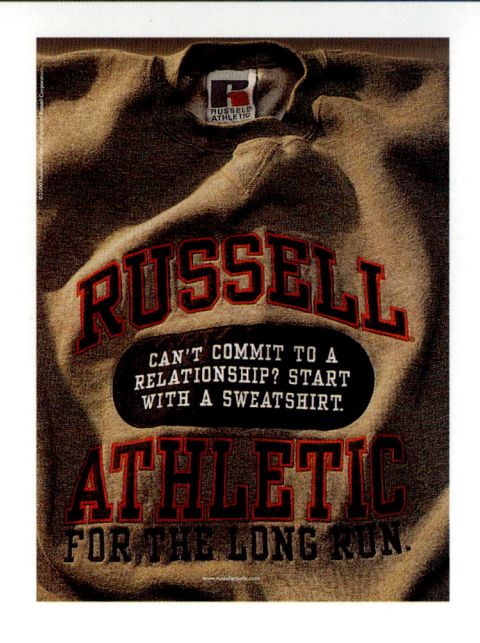

ONEIDA
Beauty inspires.
Shown: Lamais butter knife. Your table is ready.

Portable Imax
SONY.

RUSSELL ATHLETIC
CAN'T COMMIT TO A RELATIONSHIP? START WITH A SWEATSHIRT.
FOR THE LONG RUN.

35 WEST 20TH STREET NYC 10011 212.633.1670 FAX 212.727.1518

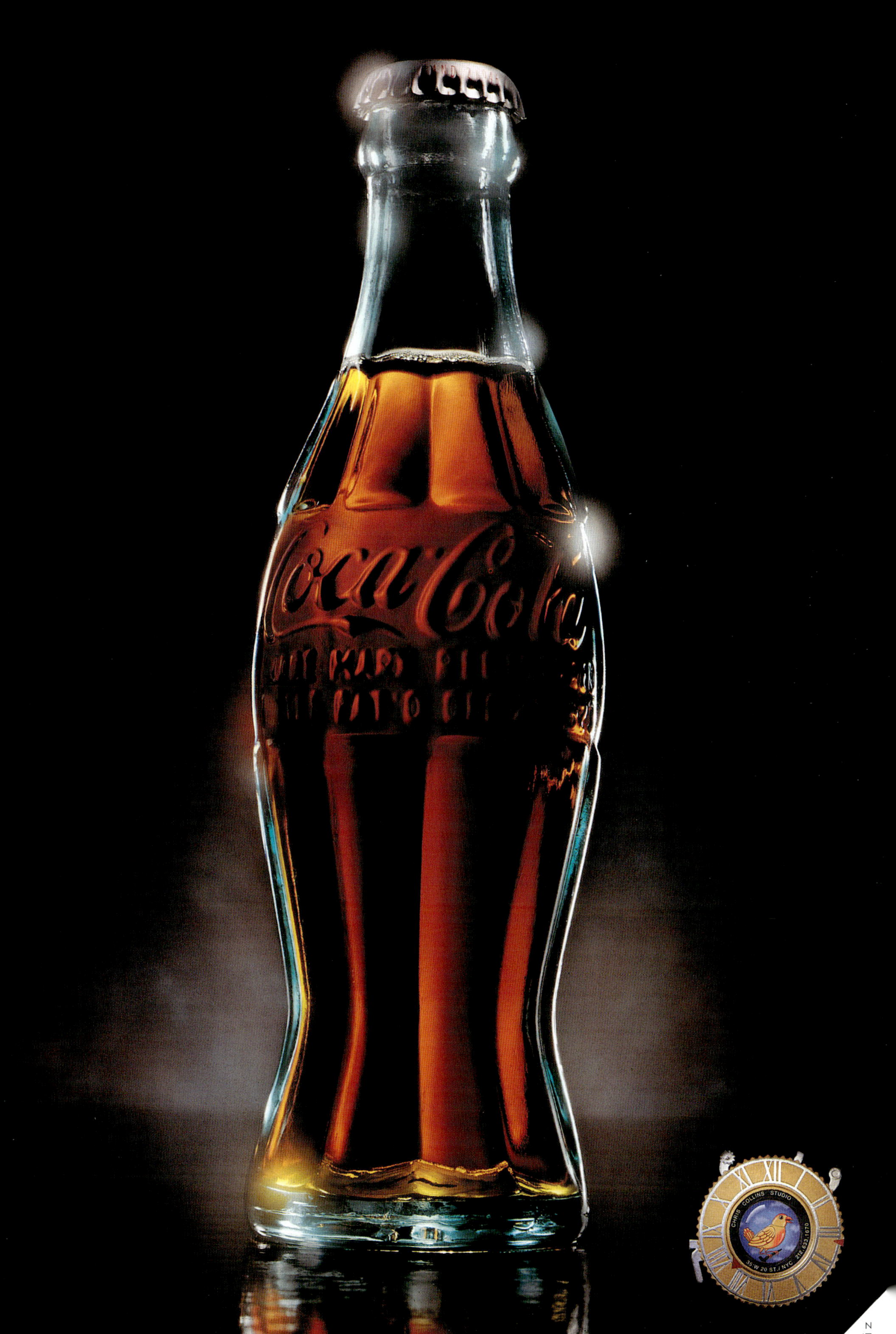
Coca-Cola
CHRIS COLLINS STUDIO
35 W 20 ST./NYC 212.633.1670

chris
gordaneer

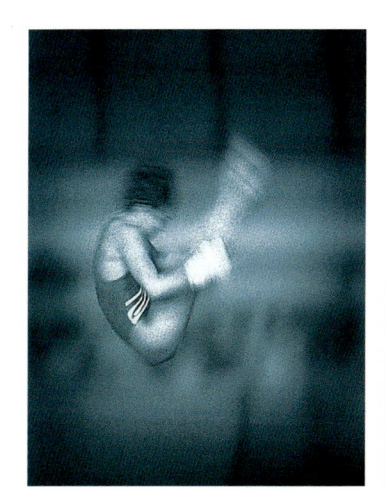

REPRESENTED BY WESTSIDE STUDIO

TEL (416) 535-1955 FAX (416) 535-0118

representing photographers

Jorg Badura
Joel Baldwin
Richard Corman
Georg Fischer
Rolph Gobits
Timothy Greenfield-Sanders
Hashi
Ruedi Hofmann
Walter Iooss
Nadav Kander
Dean Karr
Nicola Majocchi
Toni Meneguzzo
Eric Meola
John Offenbach
Uli Rose
Leen Thijsse
Timothy White
Michael Wirth
Bruce Wolf
Michael Zeppetello
Luca Zordan

WALTER IOOSS 
JORG BADURA
TIMOTHY WHITE 
DEAN KARR
RUEDI HOFMANN 
BRUCE WOLF

NADAV KANDER

TIMOTHY GREENFIELD SANDERS

MICHAEL ZEPPETELLO

STOCKLAND MARTEL
stocklandmartel.com

(SM)

5 Union Square West
New York, NY 10003
tel. 212.727.1400
fax. 212.727.9459
stocklandmartel.com

TONI MENEGUZZO

LUCA ZORDAN

HASHI

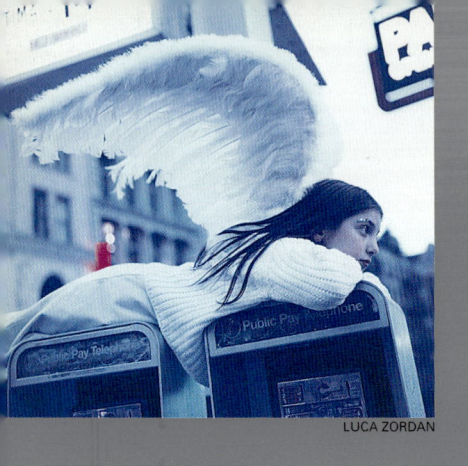

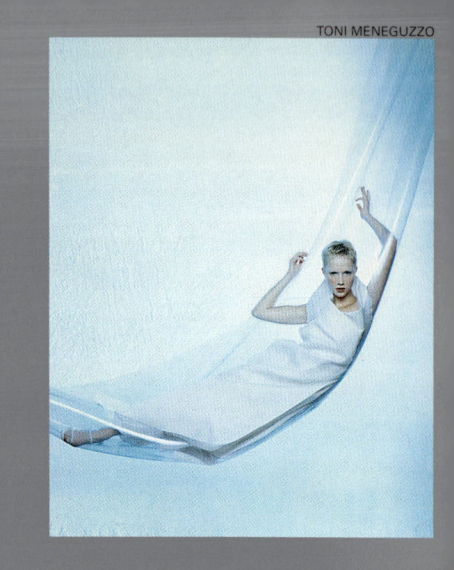

MICHAEL WIRTH

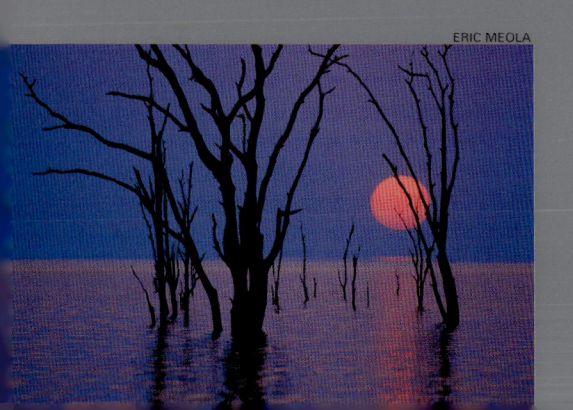

ULI ROSE

NICOLA MAJOCCHI

ERIC MEOLA

JOEL BALDWIN

ROLPH GOBITS

RICHARD CORMAN

LEEN THIJSSE

STOCKLAND MARTEL
stocklandmartel.com

5 Union Square West
New York, NY 10003
tel. 212.727.1400
fax. 212.727.9459
stocklandmartel.com

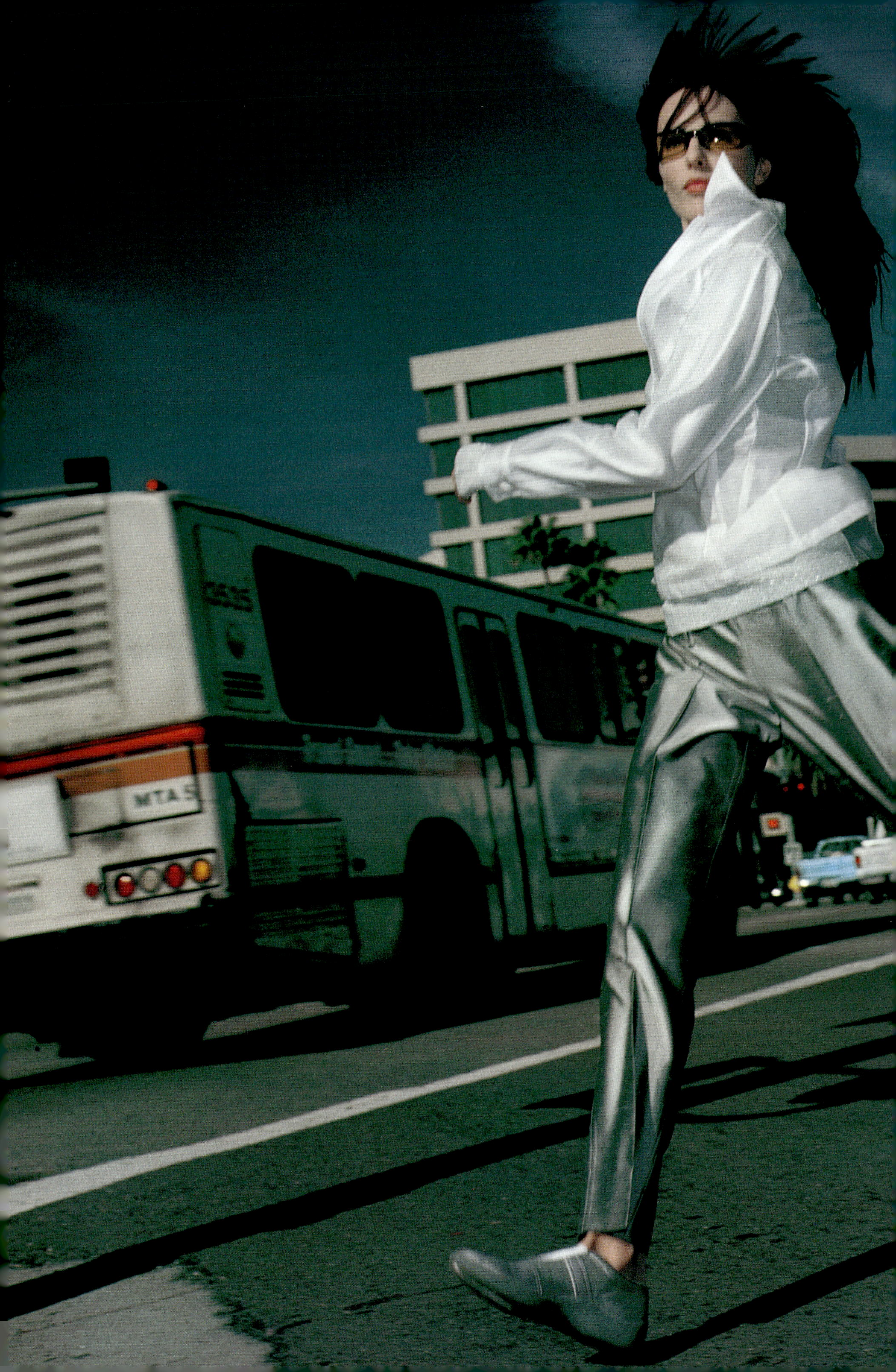
MTA

Nicola Majocchi
Stockland Martel
5 Union Square West, New York, NY 10003
tel. 212.727.1400 fax. 212.727.9459
stocklandmartel.com

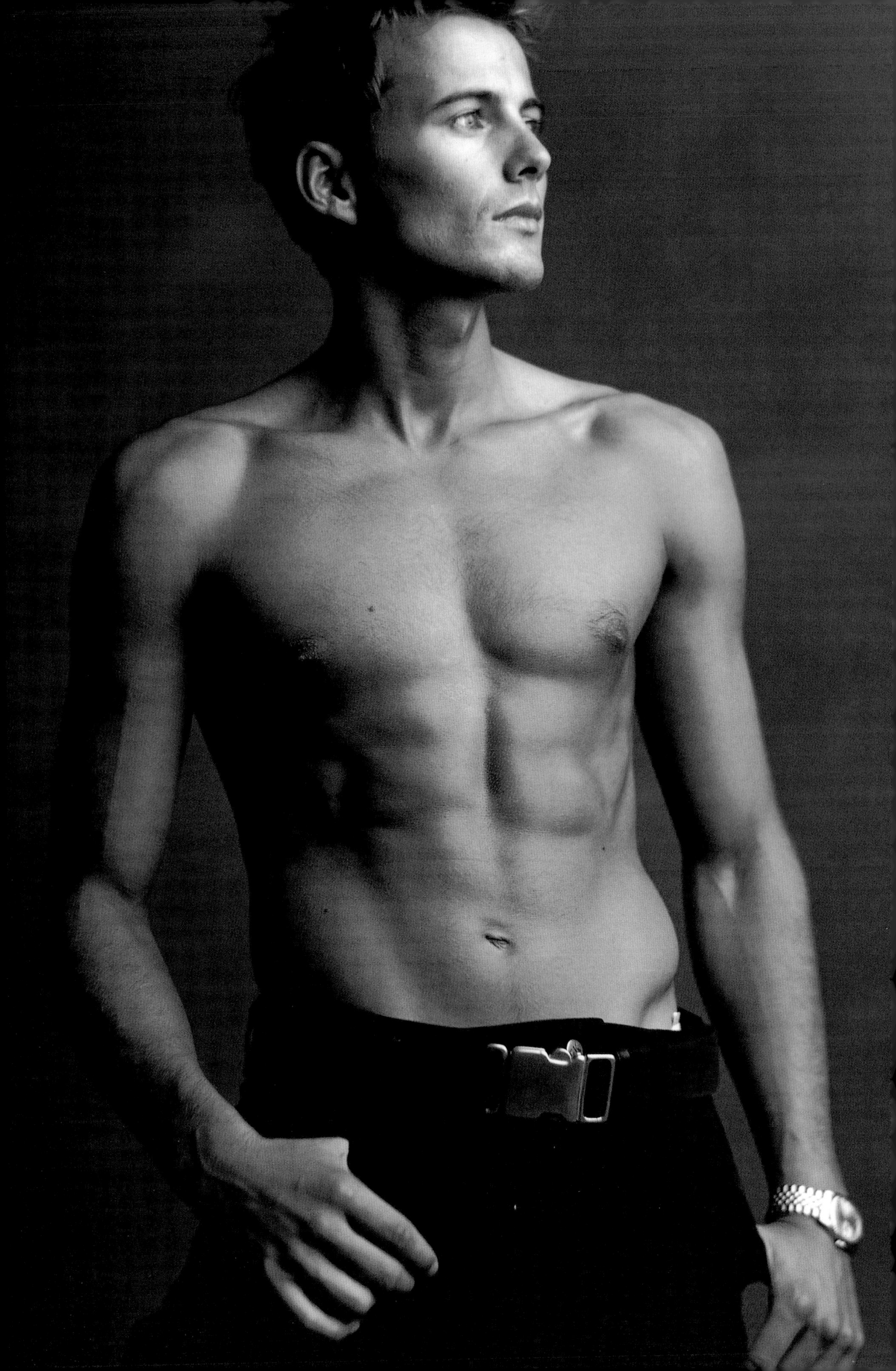

Timothy Greenfield-Sanders
greenfield-sanders.com

Stockland Martel
5 Union Square West, New York, NY 10003
tel. 212.727.1400 fax. 212.727.9459
stocklandmartel.com
Film reel available

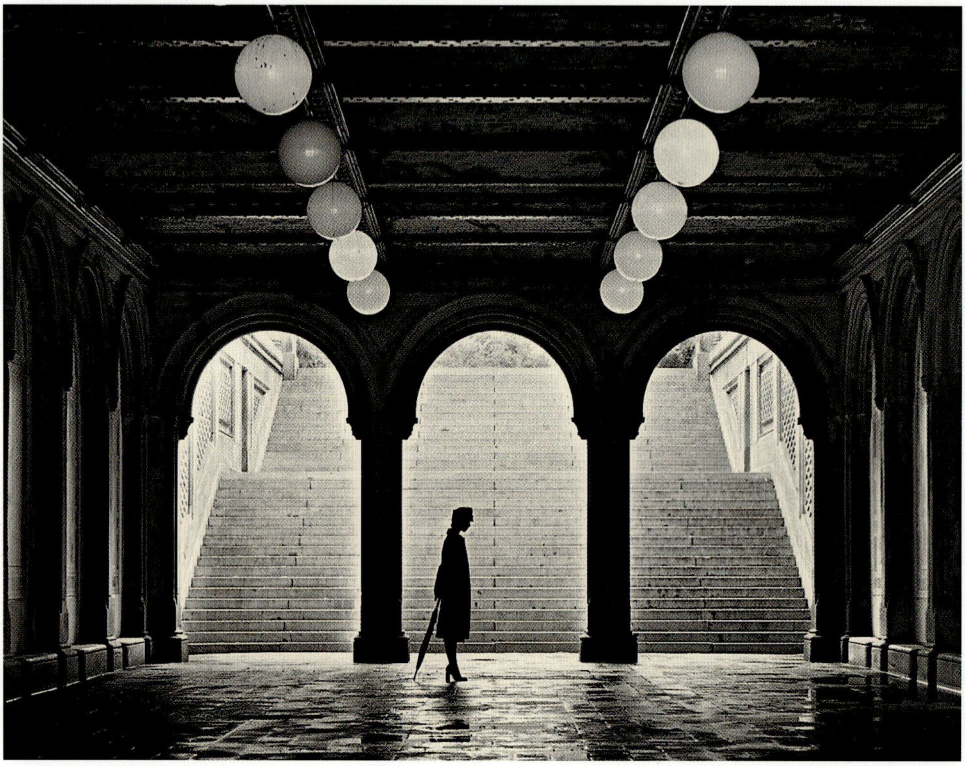

John Offenbach

Stockland Martel
5 Union Square West, New York, NY 10003
tel. 212.727.1400 fax. 212.727.9459
stocklandmartel.com

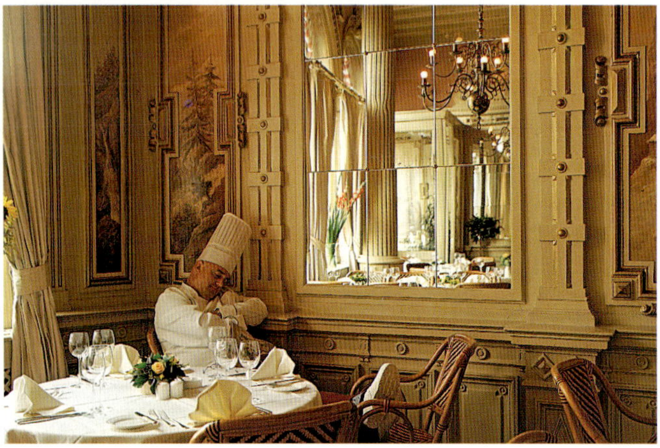

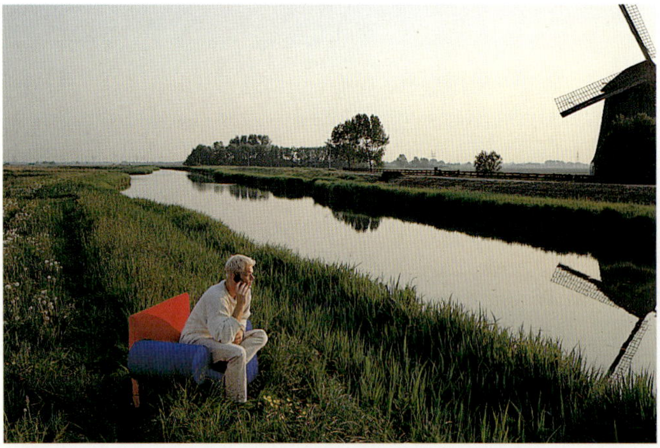

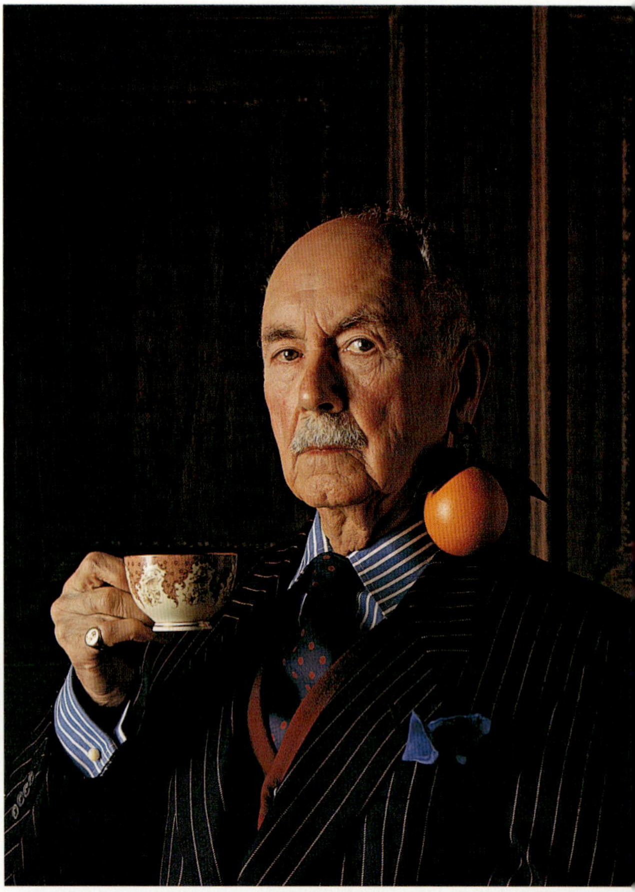

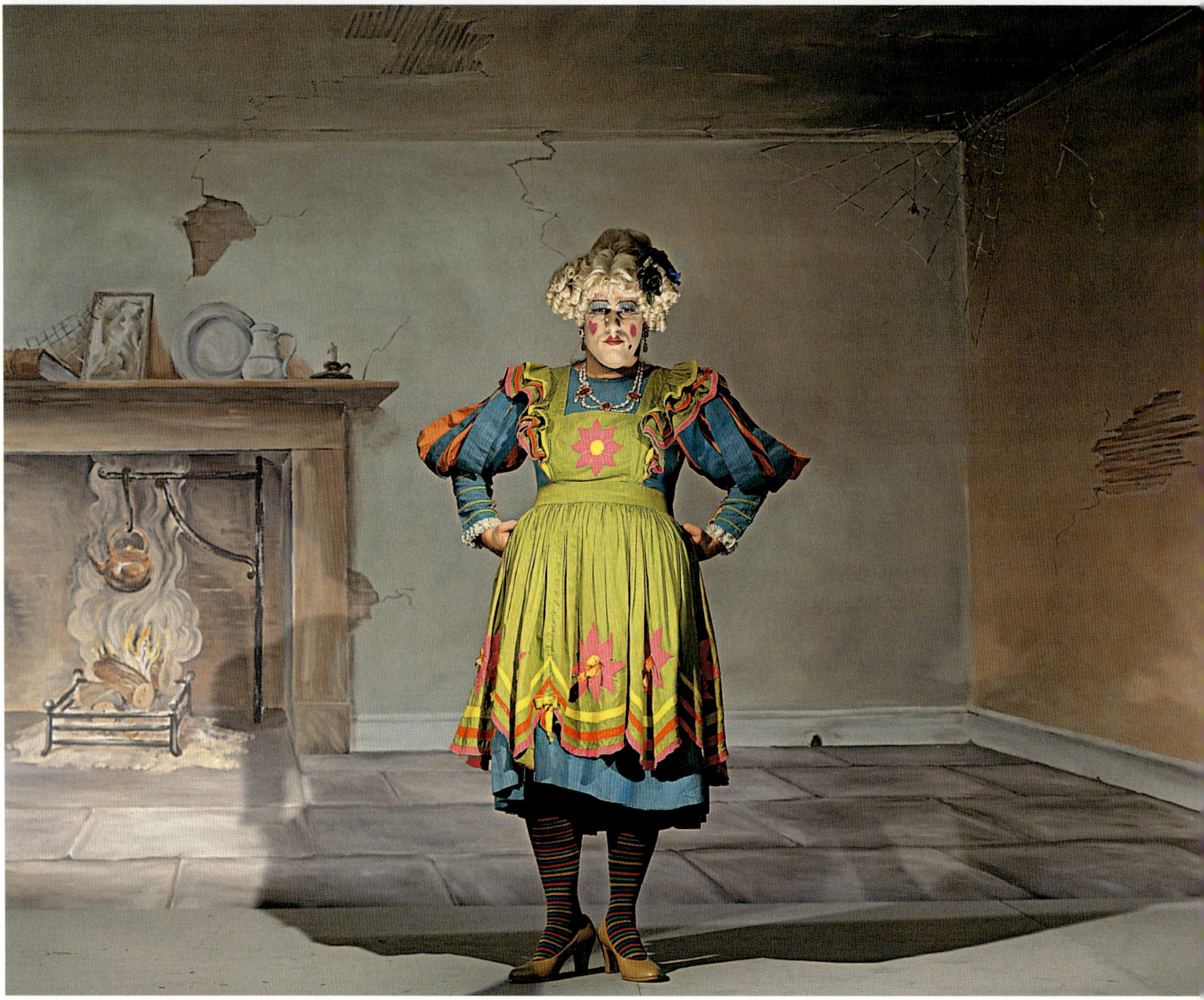

Rolph Gobits

Stockland Martel
5 Union Square West, New York, NY 10003
tel. 212.727.1400 fax. 212.727.9459
stocklandmartel.com

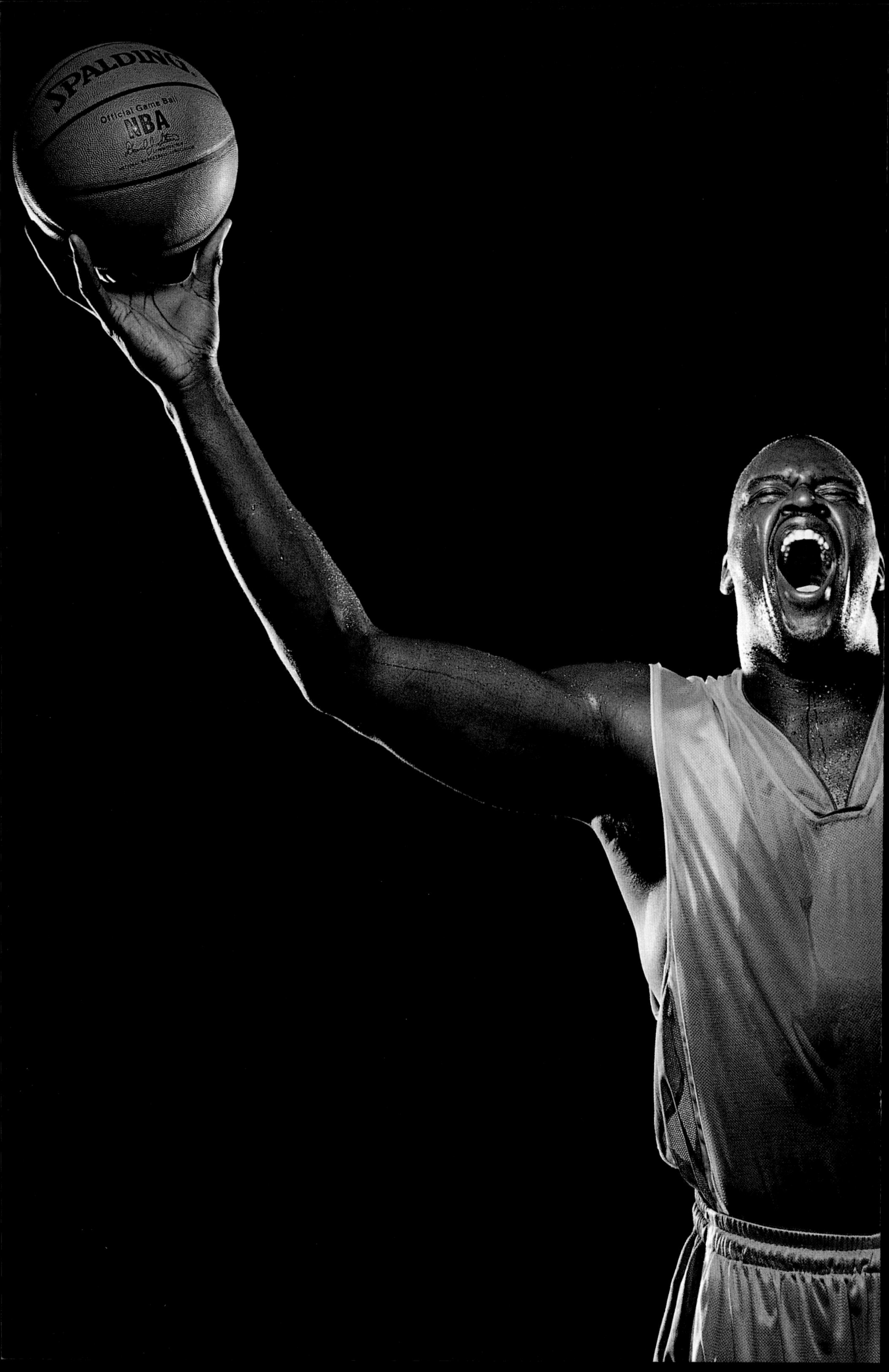
SPALDING
Official Game Ball
NBA

Richard Corman
richardcorman.com

Stockland Martel
5 Union Square West, New York, NY 10003
tel. 212.727.1400 fax. 212.727.9459
stocklandmartel.com

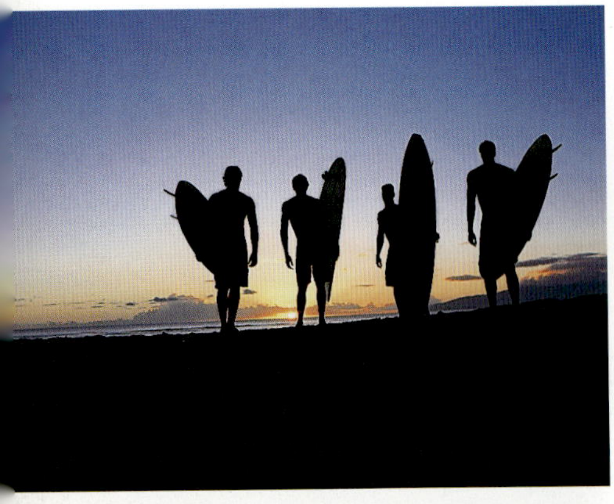
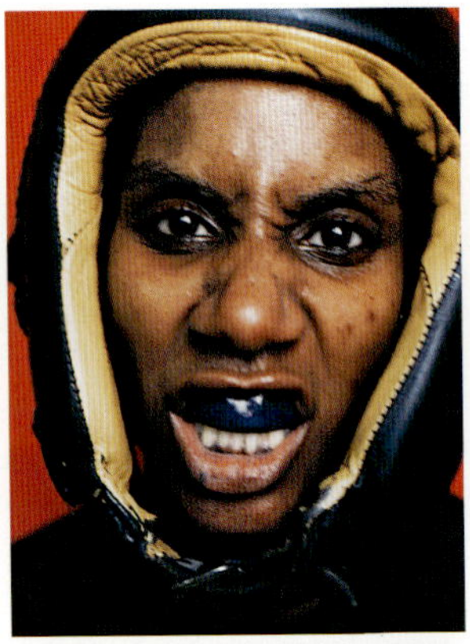
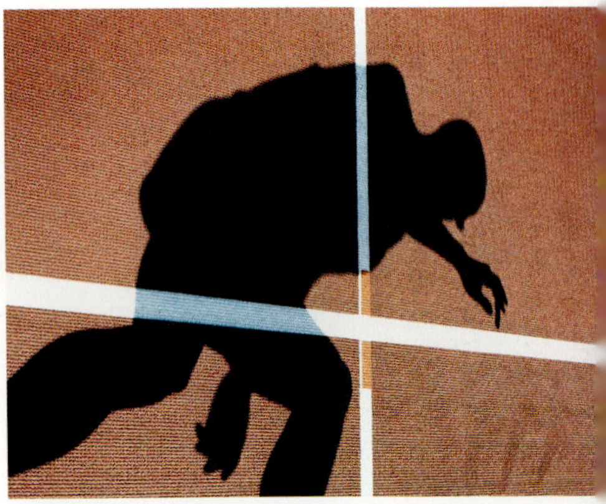
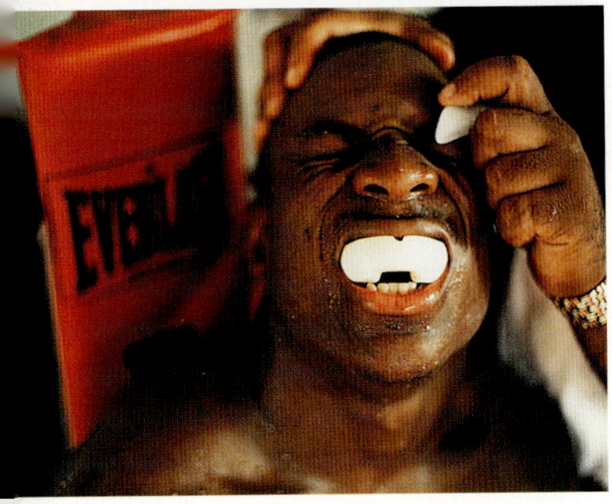
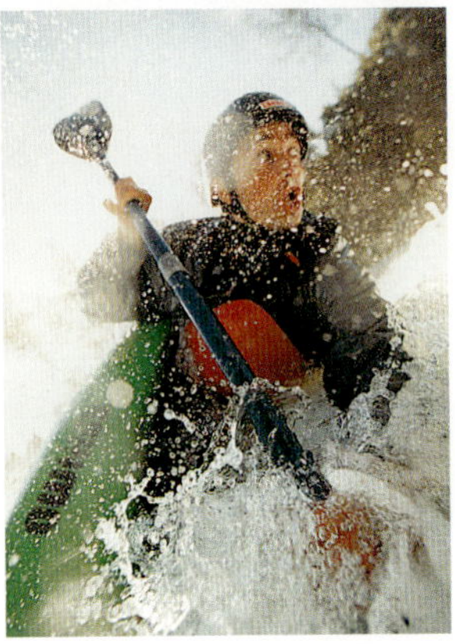
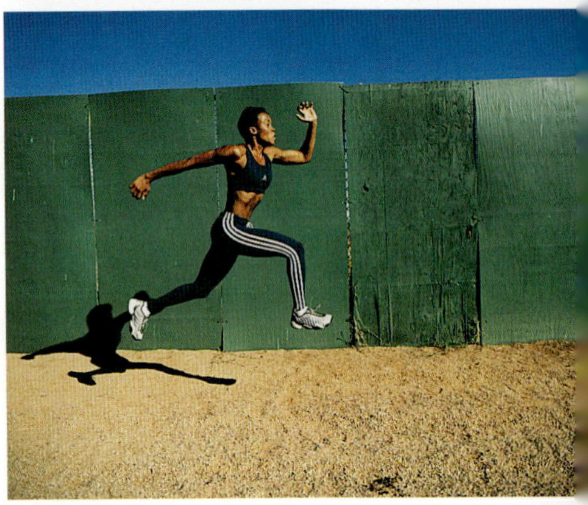

JORG BADURA
jorgbadura.com

Stockland Martel
5 Union Square West, New York, NY 10003
tel. 212.727.1400 fax. 212.727.9459
stocklandmartel.com
Film reel available

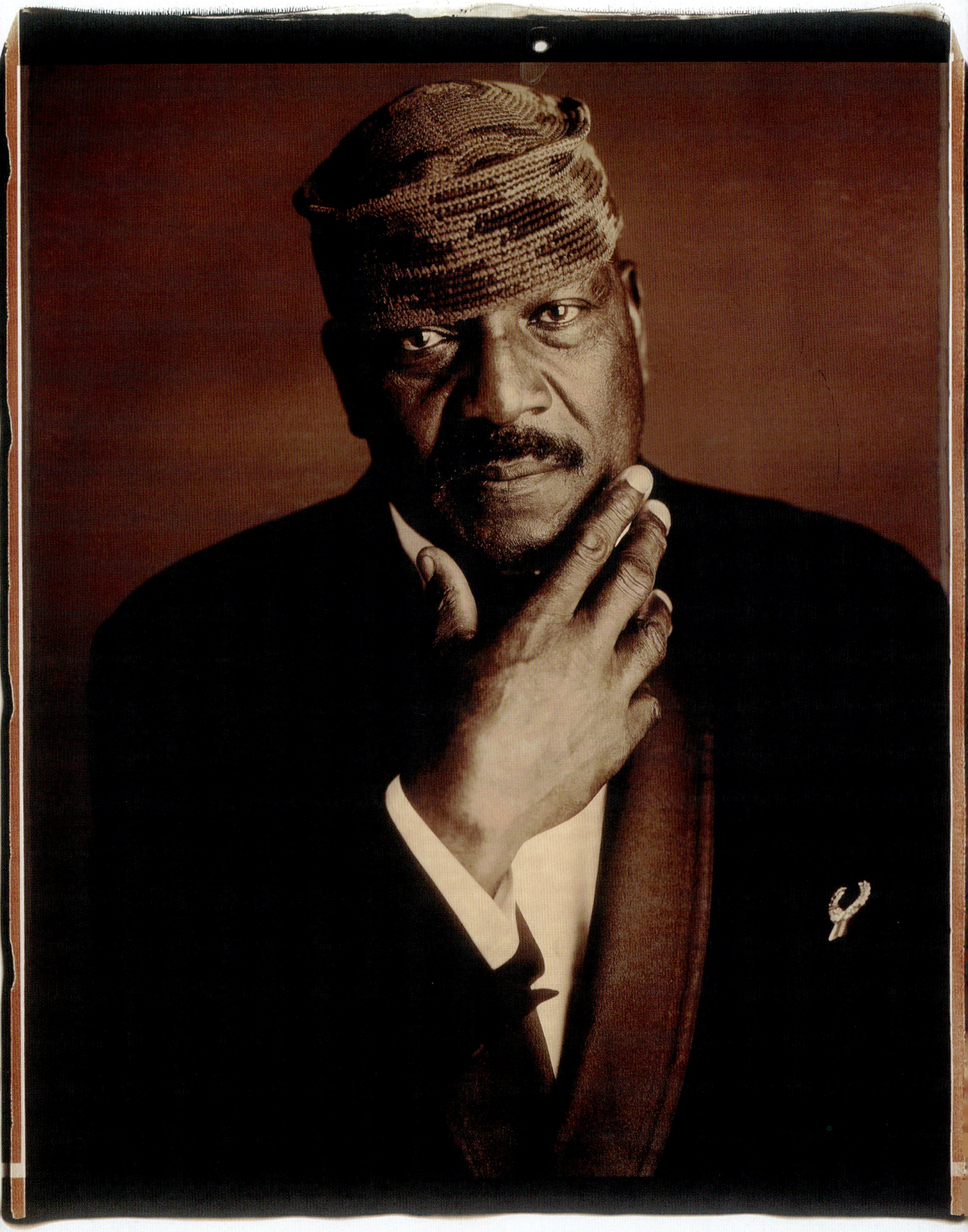

Jim Brown

Walter Iooss

Stockland Martel
5 Union Square West, New York, NY 10003
tel. 212.727.1400 fax. 212.727.9459
stocklandmartel.com

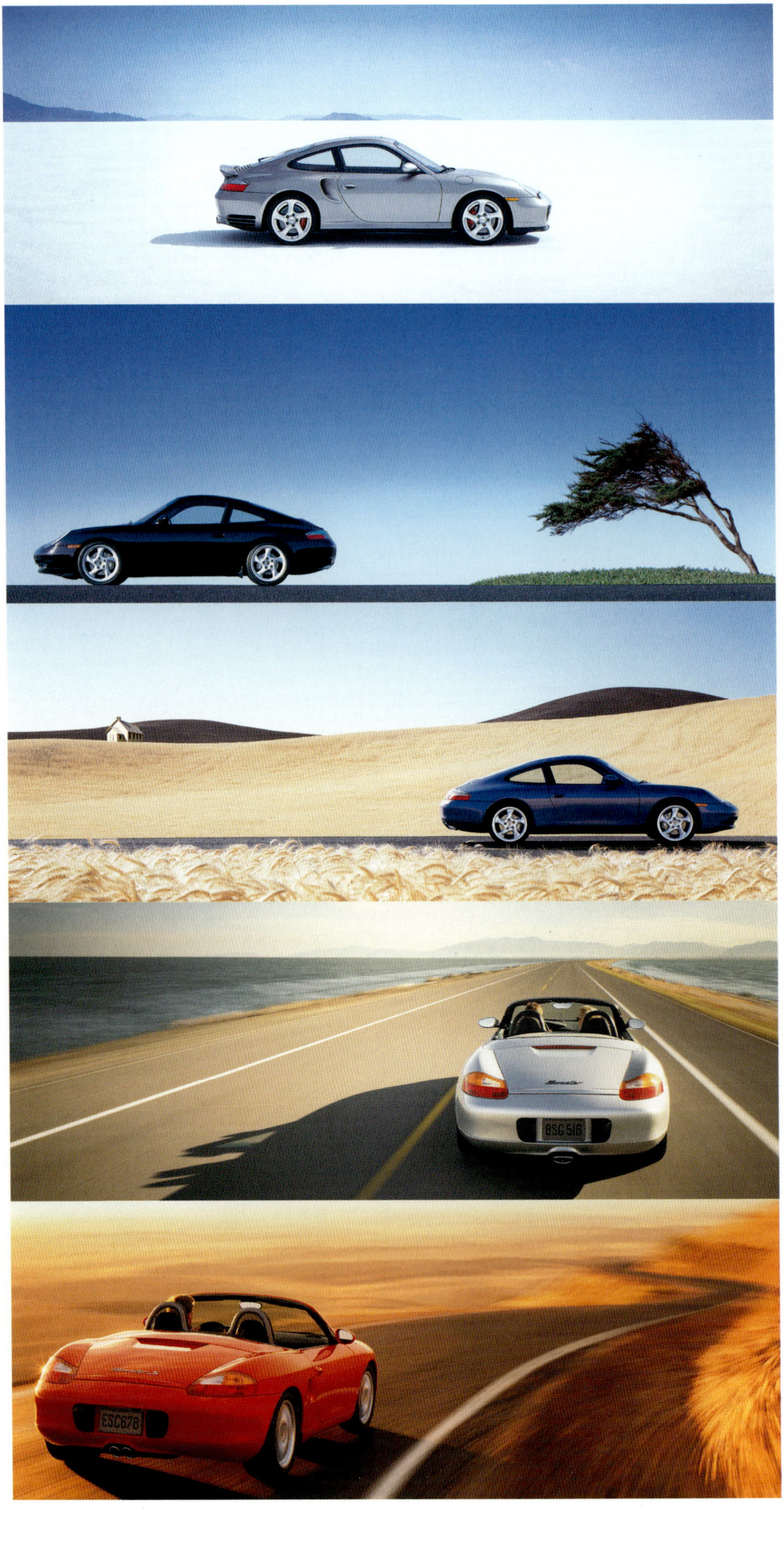
BSG 516
ESC678

Georg Fischer
georg-fischer.com

Stockland Martel (SM)
5 Union Square West, New York, NY 10003
tel. 212.727.1400 fax. 212.727.9459
stocklandmartel.com

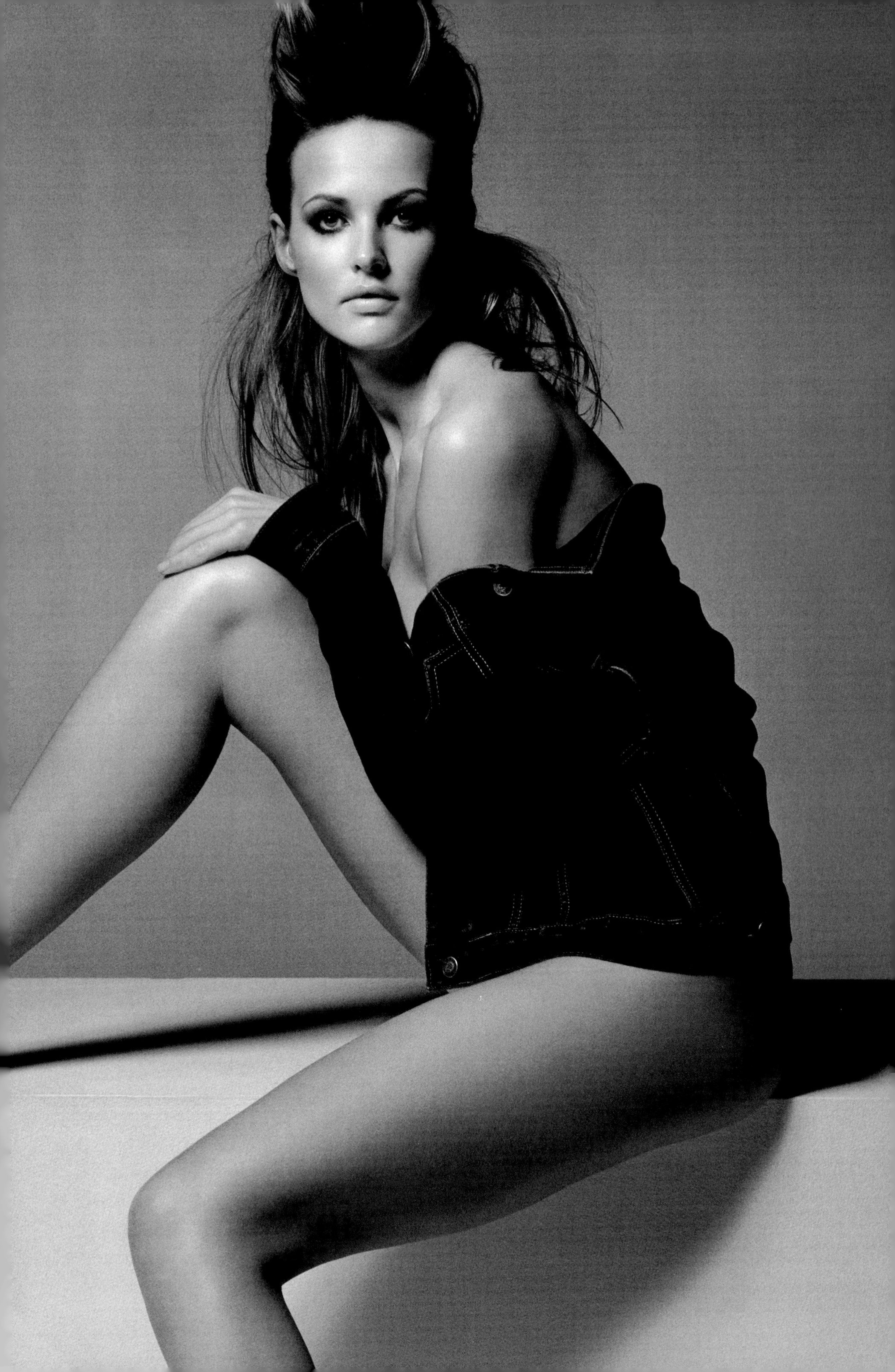

Michael Zeppetello
zeppetello.com

Stockland Martel
5 Union Square West, New York, NY 10003
tel. 212.727.1400 fax. 212.727.9459
stocklandmartel.com
Film reel available

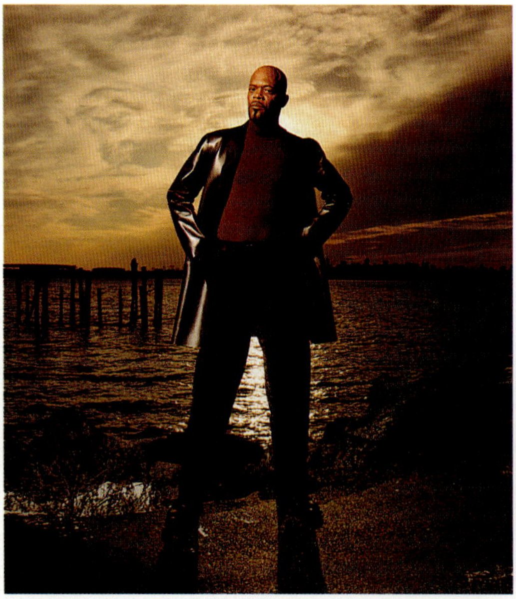
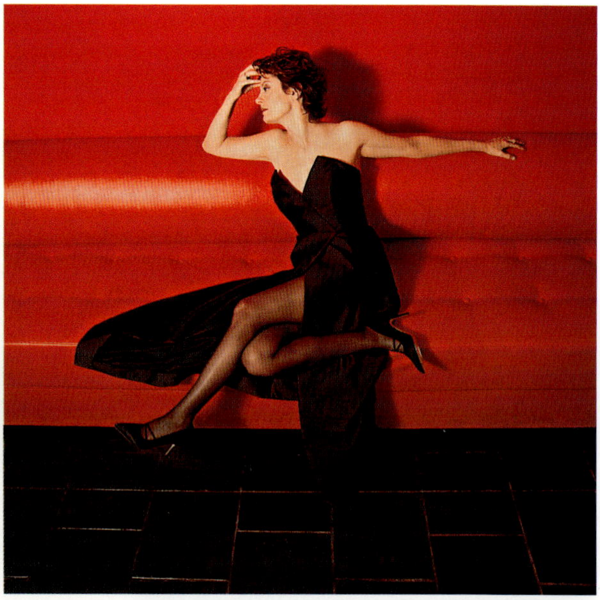
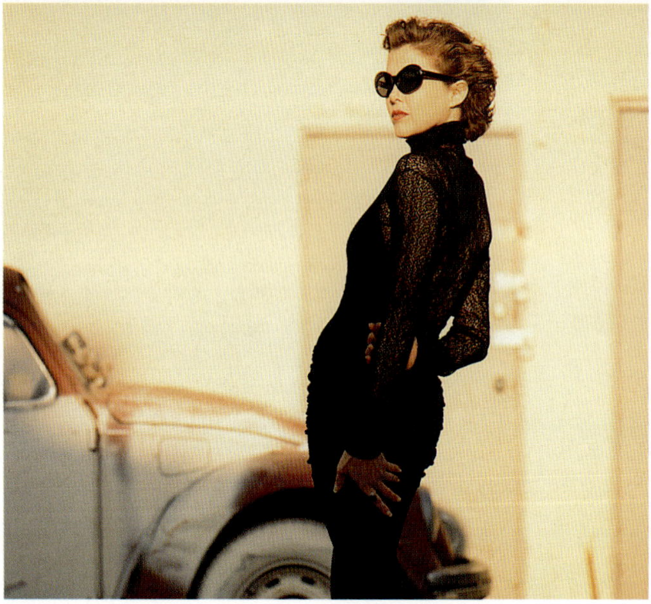
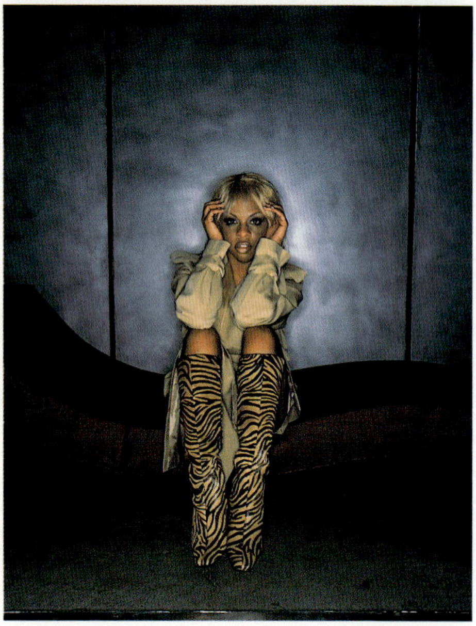

Timothy White
timothywhite.com

Stockland Martel
5 Union Square West, New York, NY 10003
tel. 212.727.1400 fax. 212.727.9459
stocklandmartel.com
Film reel available

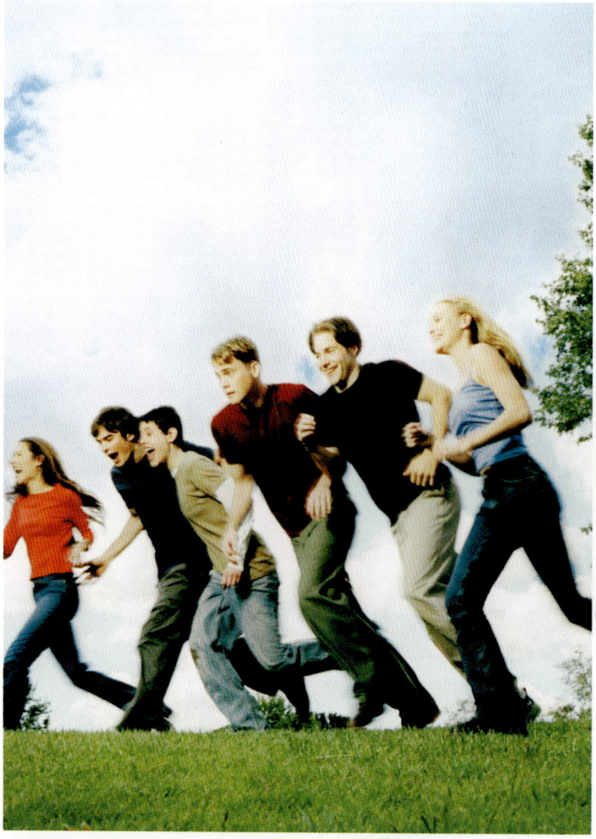
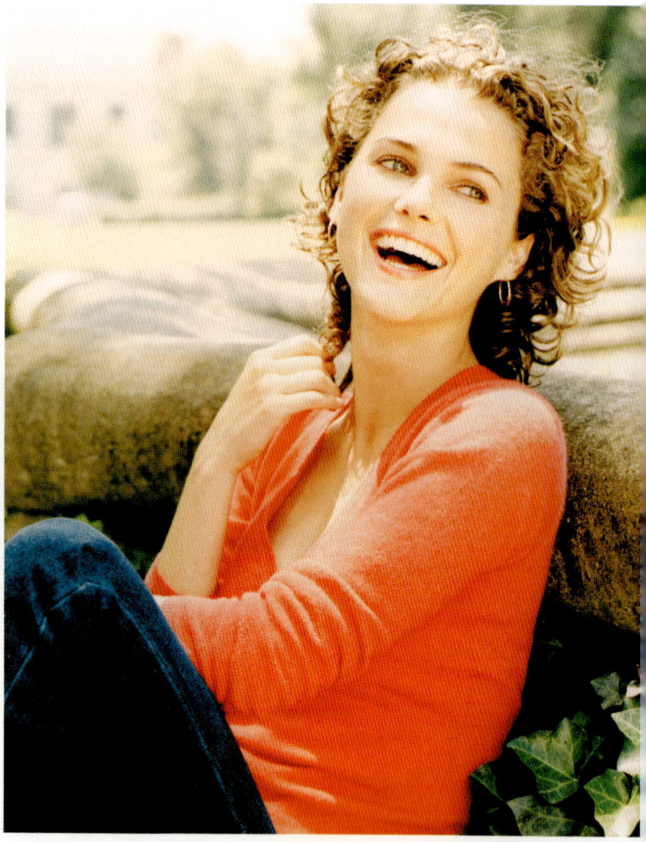
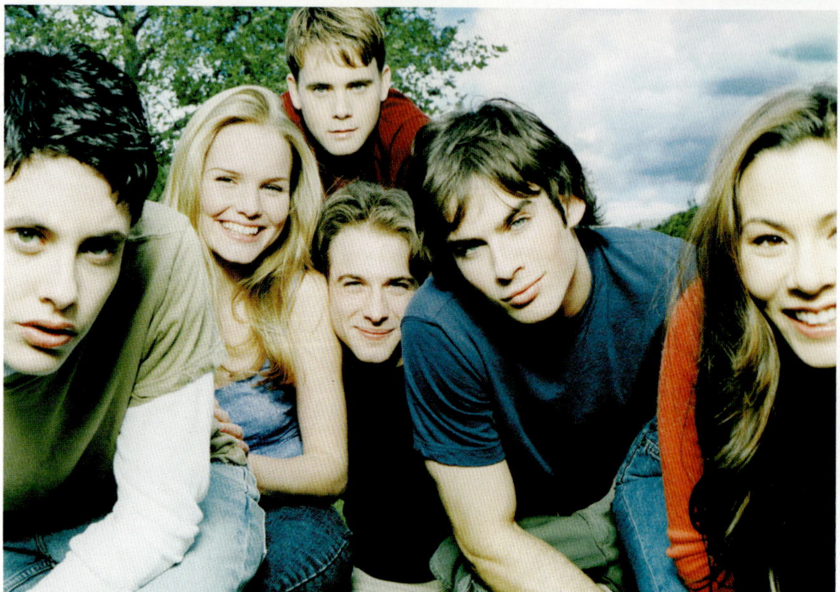
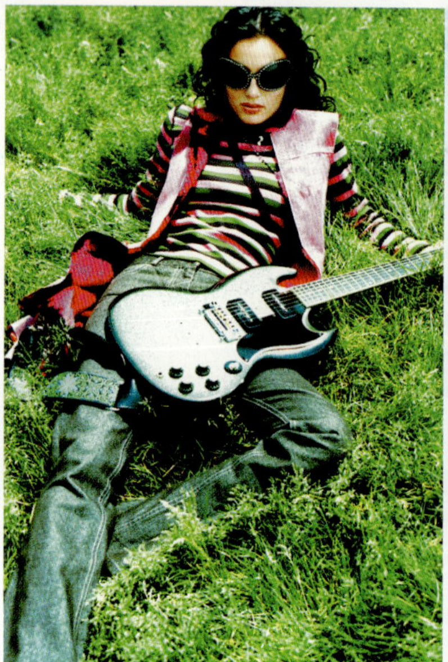

Ruedi Hofmann
Stockland Martel
5 Union Square West, New York, NY 10003
tel. 212.727.1400 fax. 212.727.9459
stocklandmartel.com
Film reel available

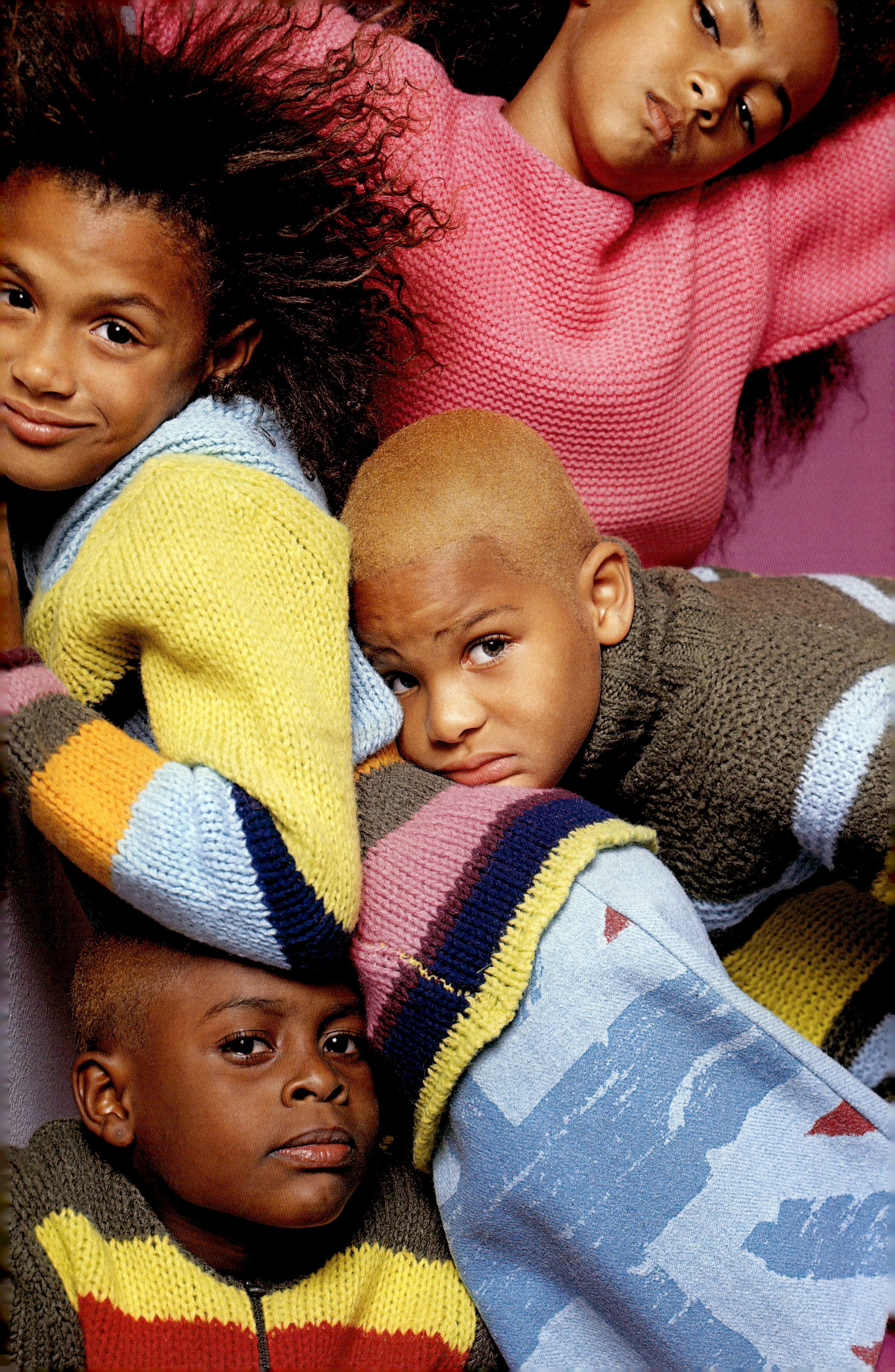

Luca Zordan
Stockland Martel
5 Union Square West, New York, NY 10003
tel. 212.727.1400 fax. 212.727.9459
stocklandmartel.com

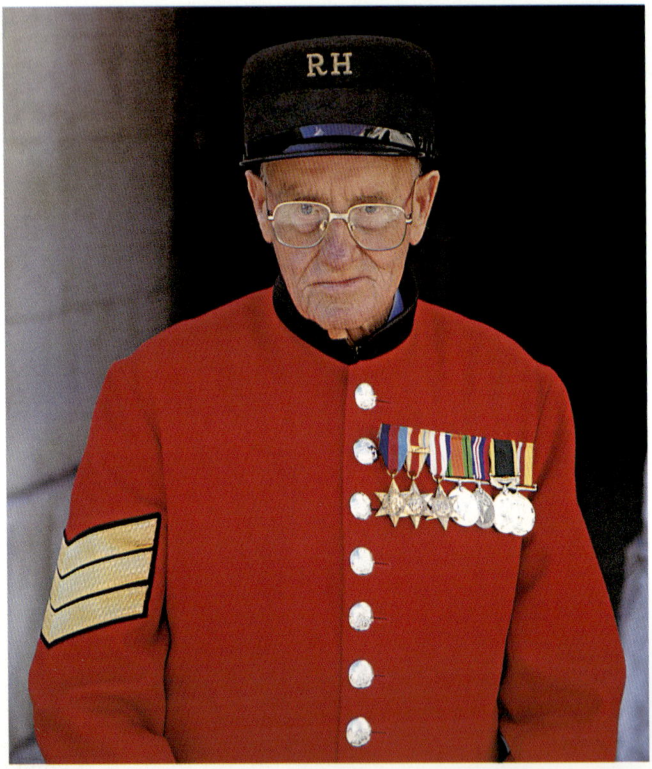
RH
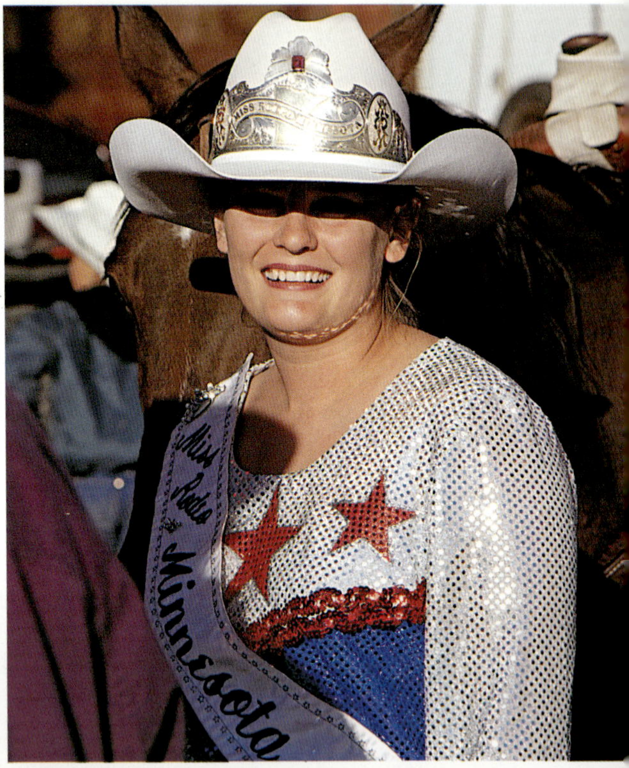
Miss Rodeo
Minnesota
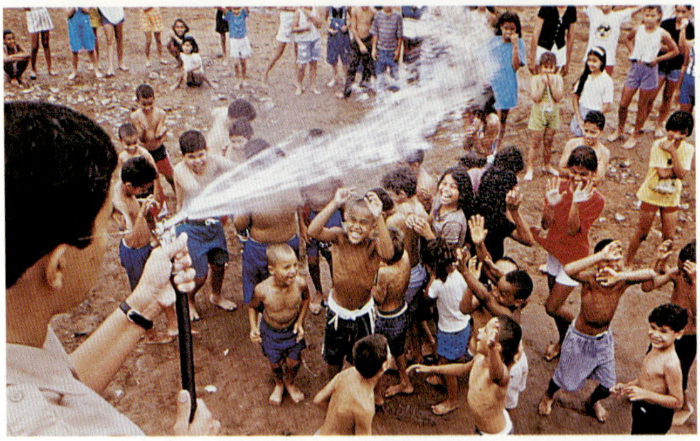
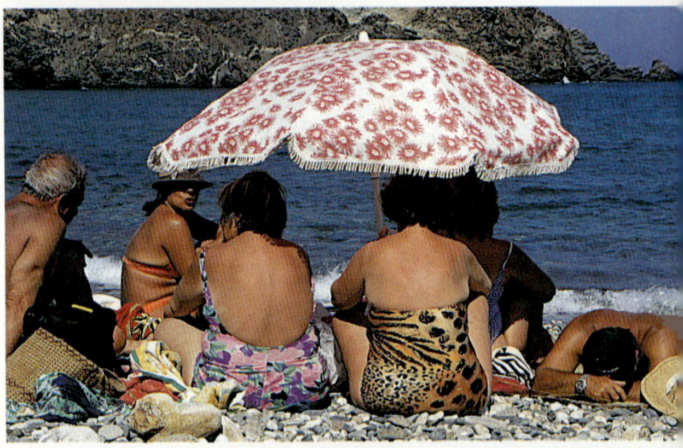
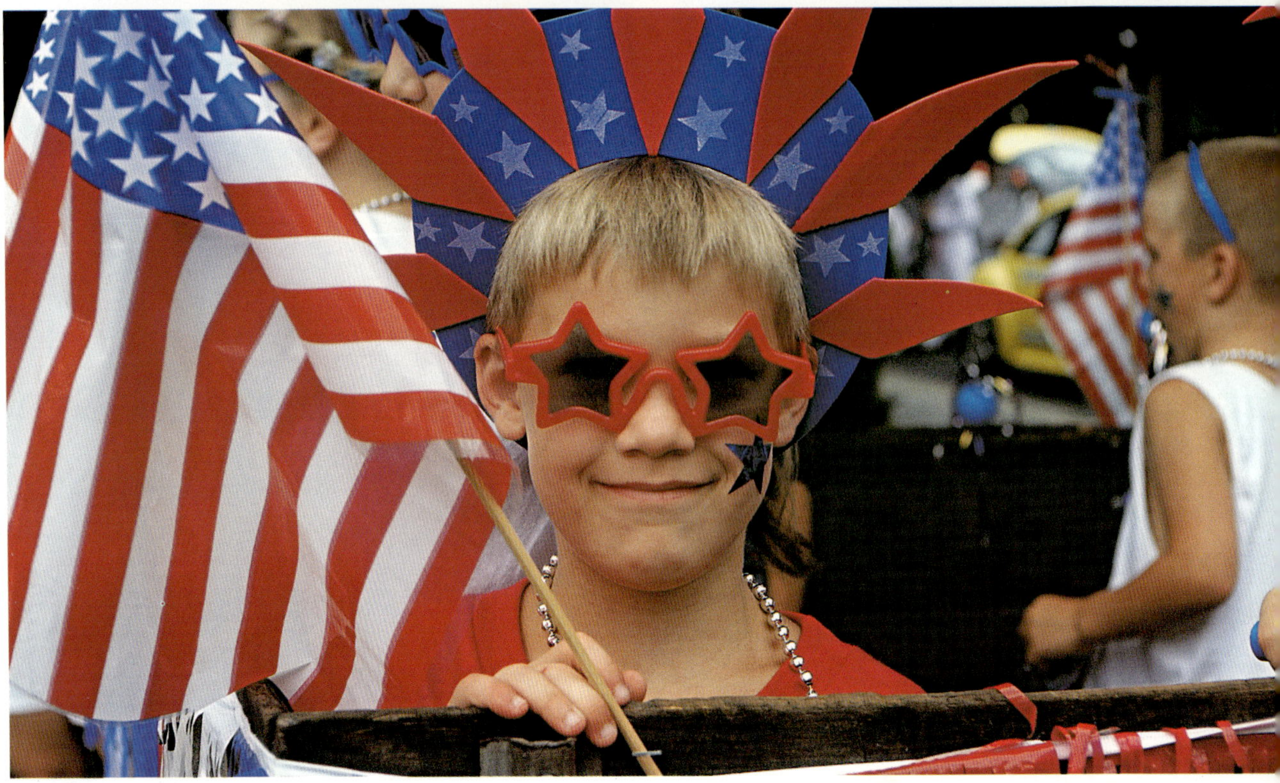

Joel Baldwin
joelbaldwin.com
Stockland Martel
5 Union Square West, New York, NY 10003
tel. 212.727.1400 fax. 212.727.9459
stocklandmartel.com

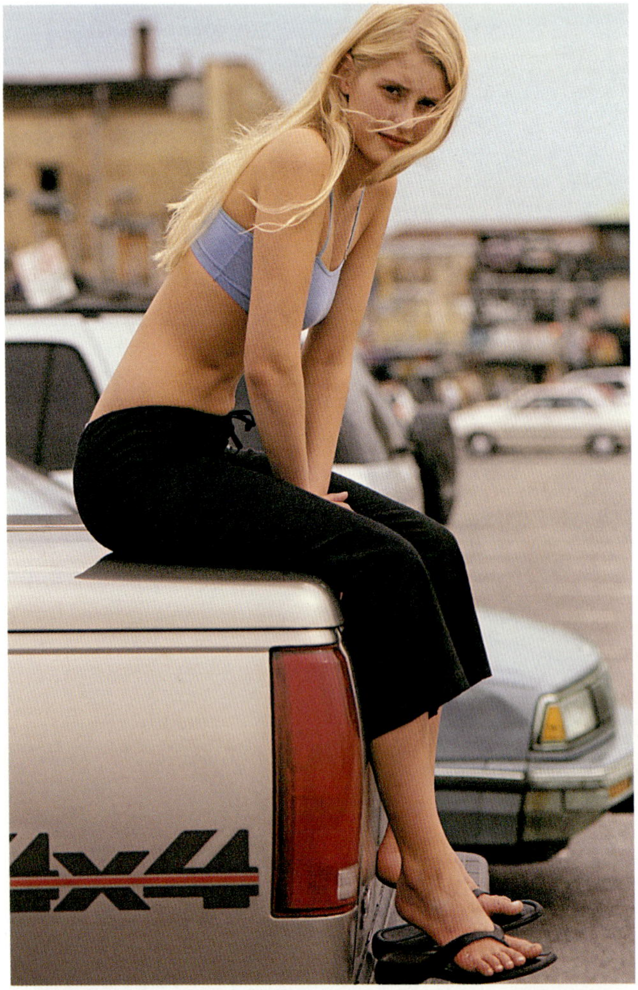
4x4

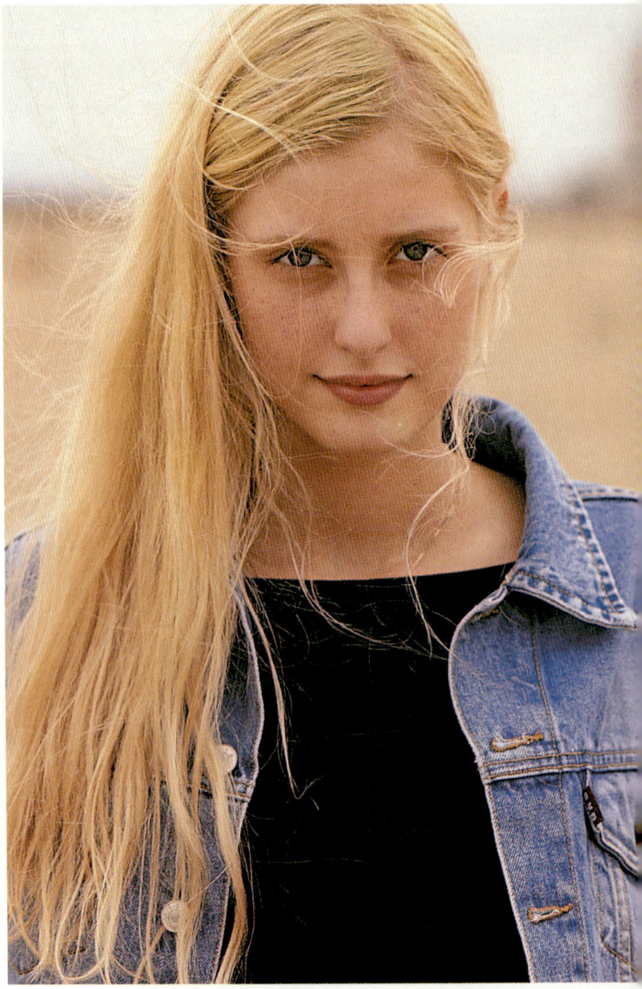

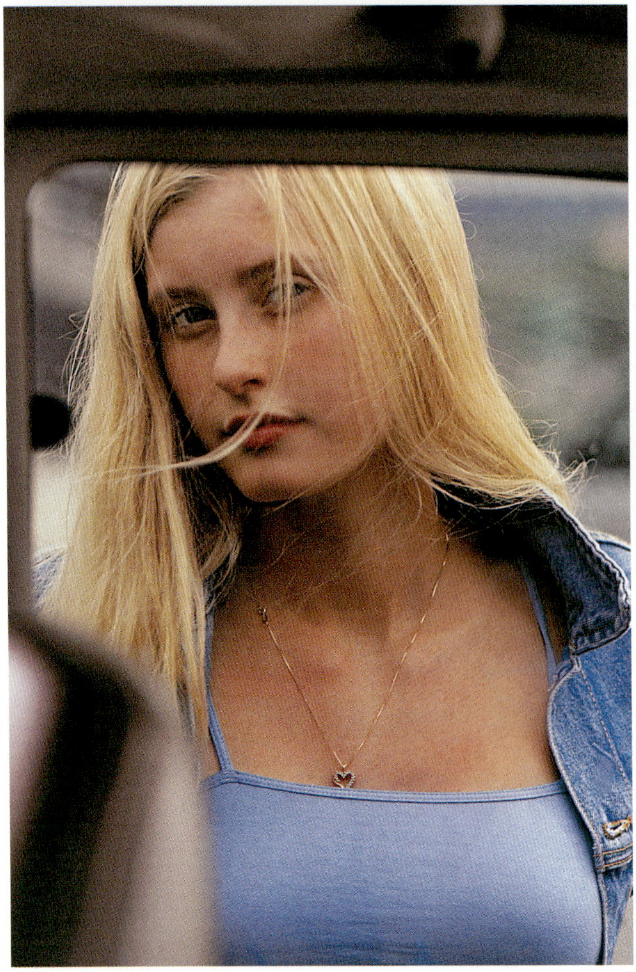

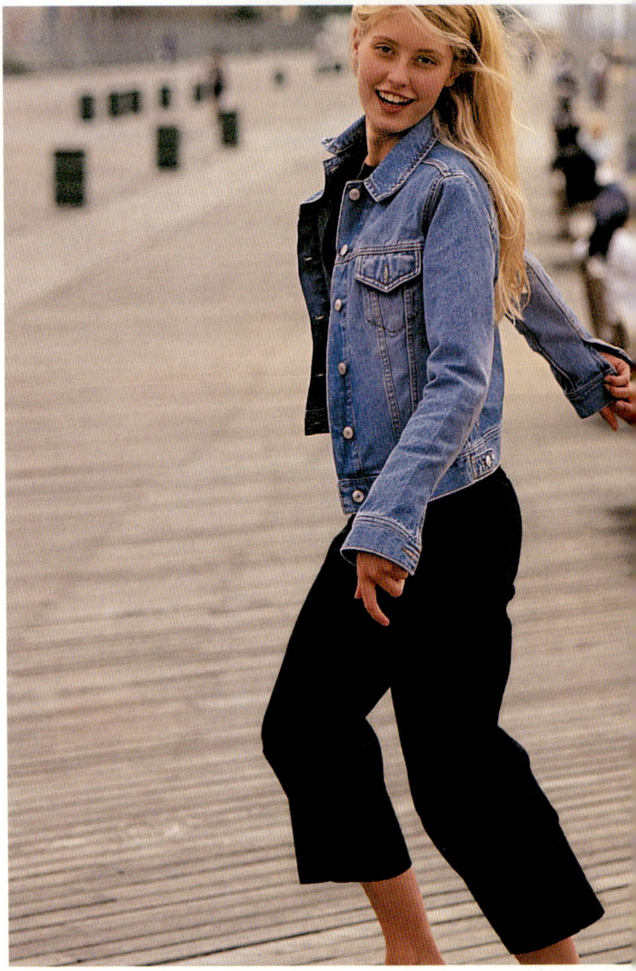

Uli Rose
ulirose.com

Stockland Martel
5 Union Square West, New York, NY 10003
tel. 212.727.1400 fax. 212.727.1950
stocklandmartel.com

©HASHI

©HASHI

Hashi

Hashi Studio, Inc.
tel. 212.532.5584
fax. 212.532.5711
www.hashistudio.com

Stockland Martel
5 Union Square West, New York, NY 10003
tel. 212.727.1400 fax. 212.727.9459
stocklandmartel.com
Film reel available

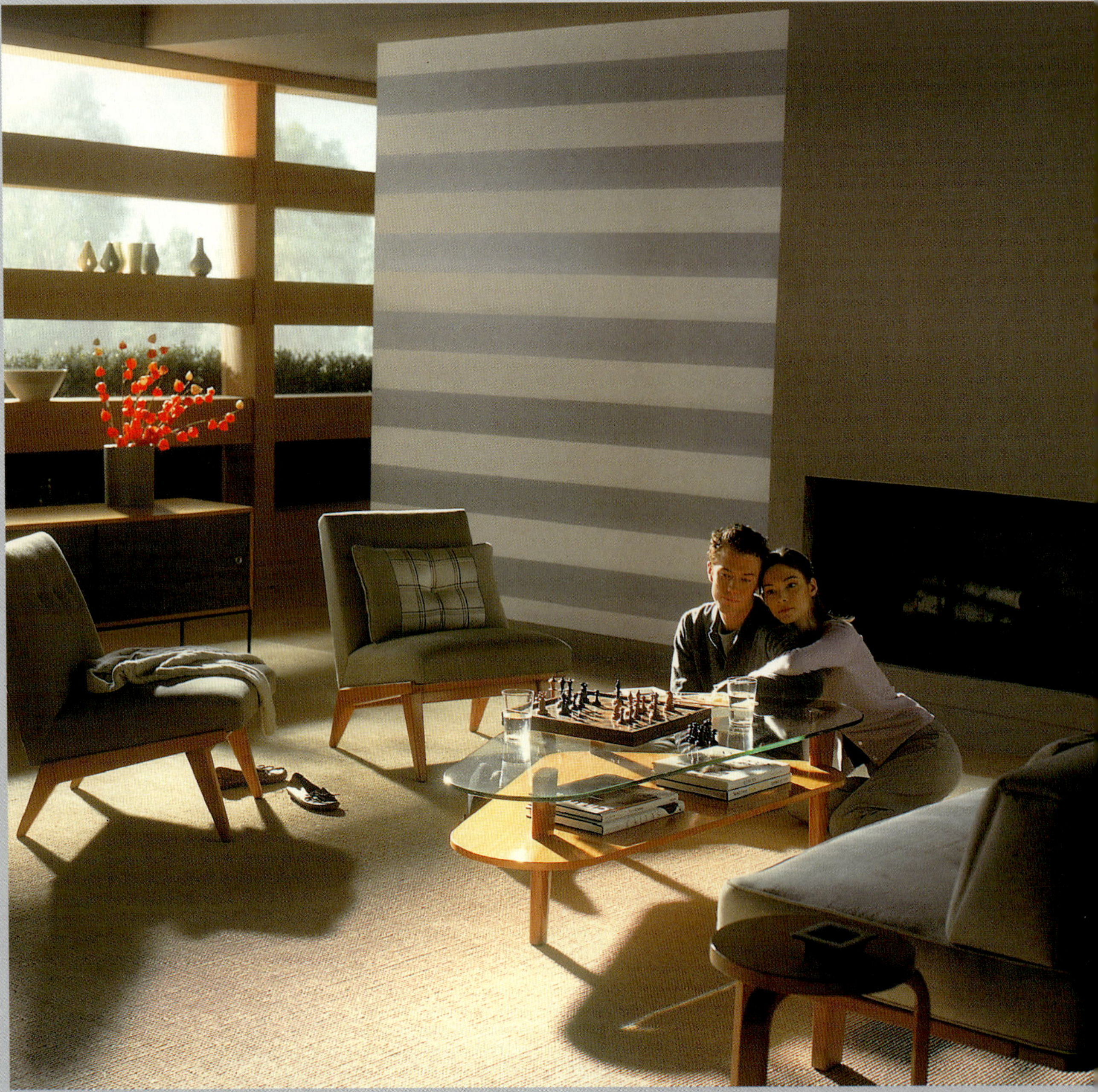

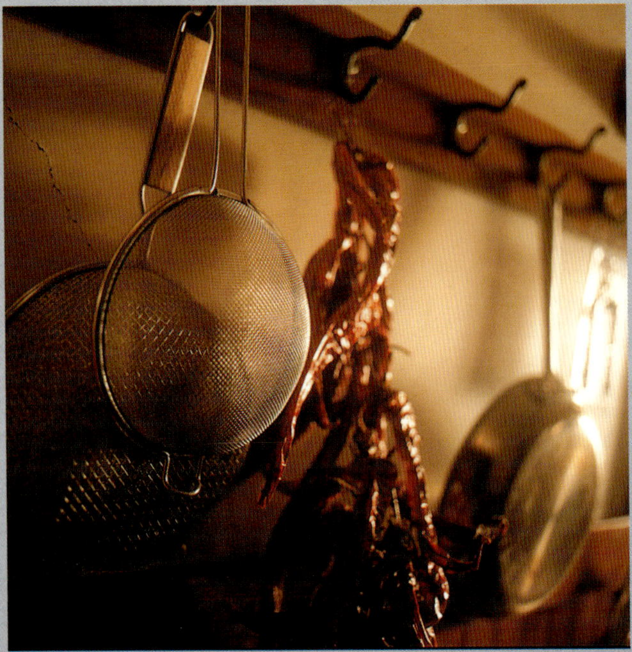

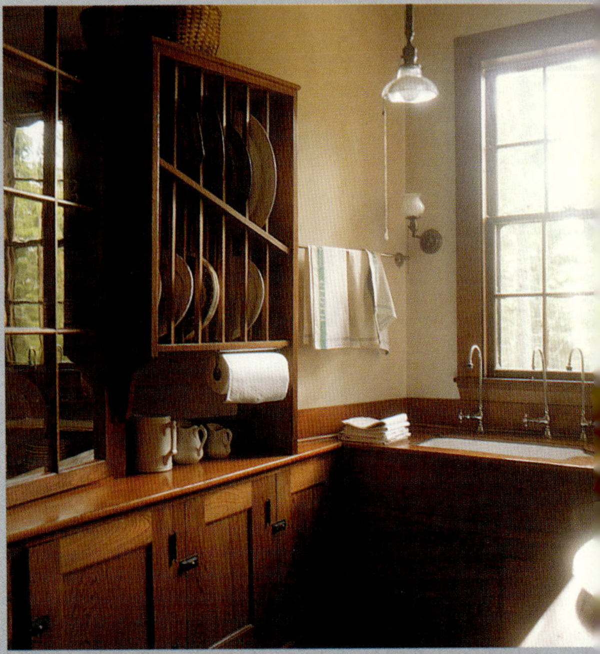

BRUCE WOLF
2 1 2 . 6 3 3 . 6 6 6 0

Stockland Martel
5 Union Square West, New York, NY 10003
tel. 212.727.1400 fax. 212.727.9459
stocklandmartel.com
Film reel available

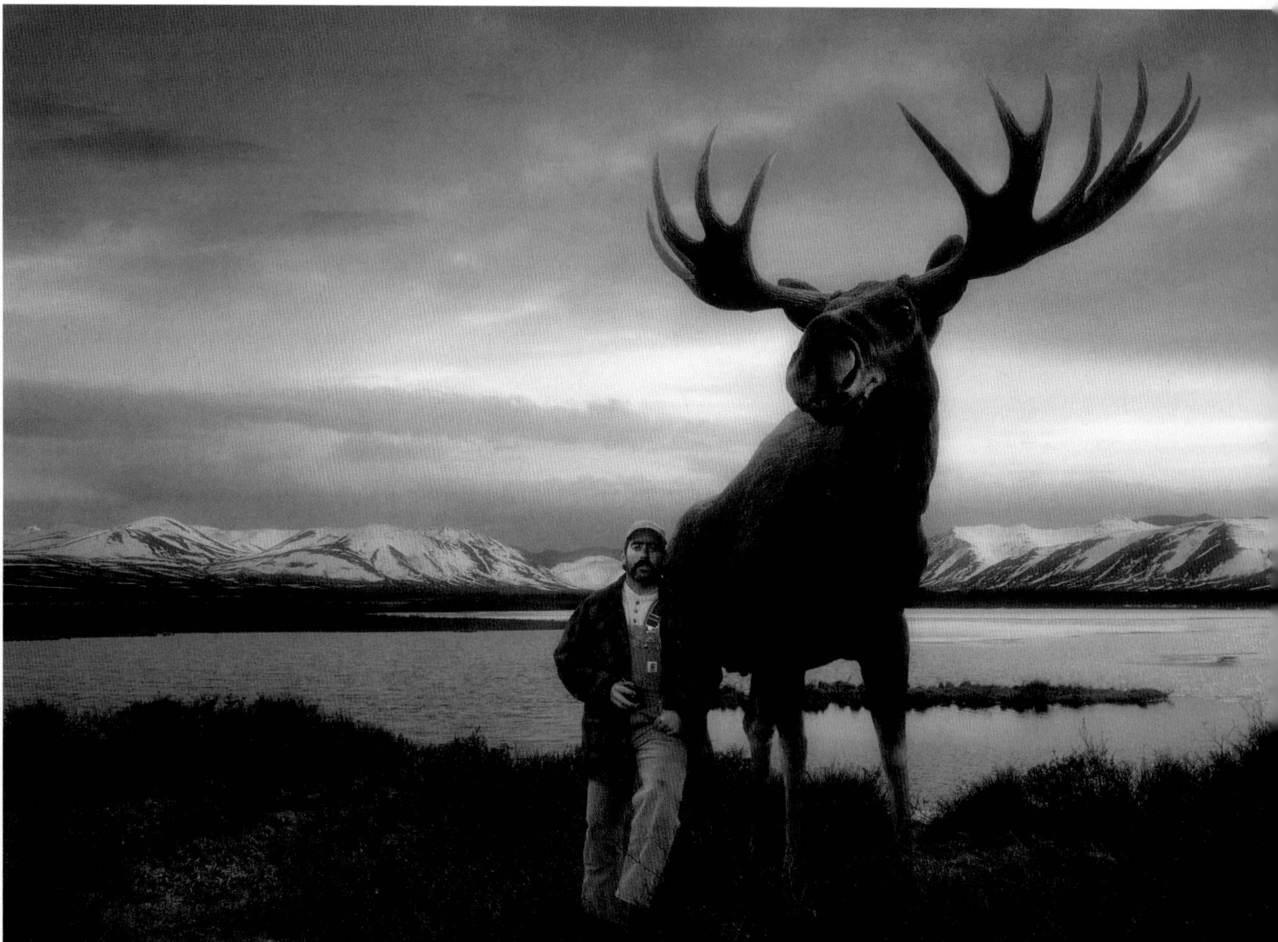

Leen Thijsse
leenthijsse.com
Stockland Martel
5 Union Square West, New York, NY 10003
tel. 212.727.1400 fax. 212.727.9459
stocklandmartel.com
Film reel available

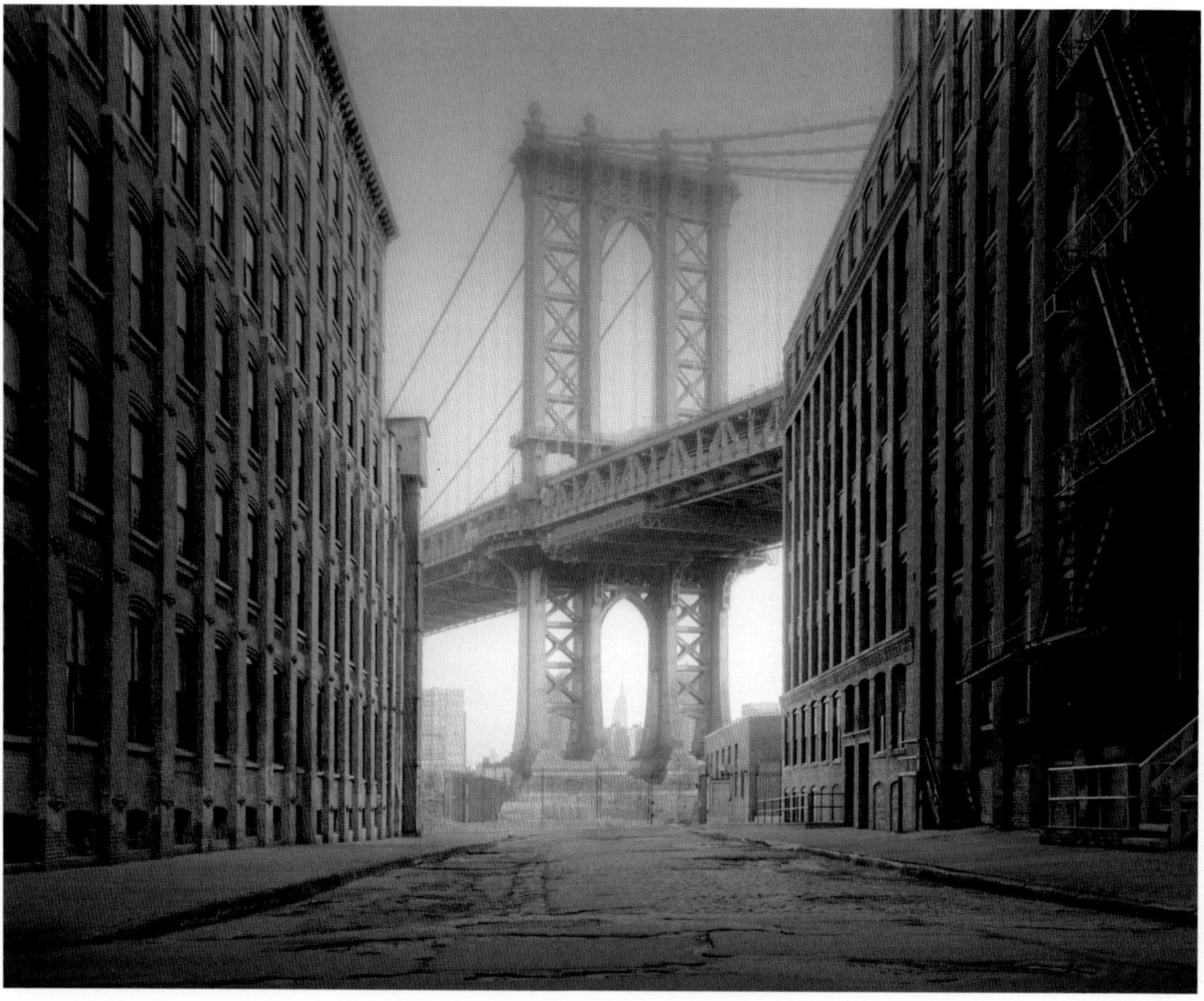

Leen Thijsse
leenthijsse.com

Stockland Martel
5 Union Square West, New York, NY 10003
tel. 212.727.1400 fax. 212.727.9459
stocklandmartel.com
Film reel available

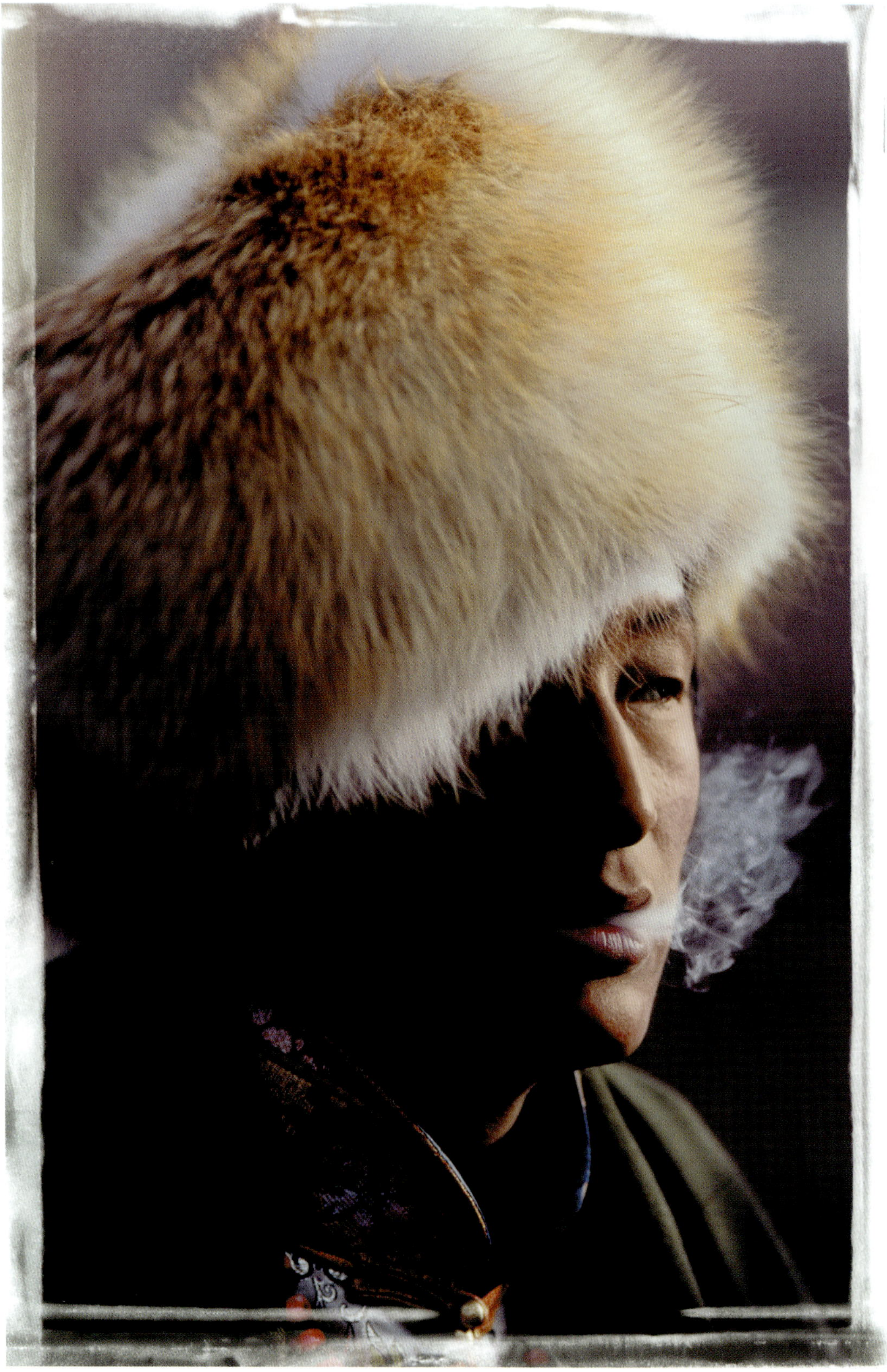

Eric Meola

Stockland Martel
5 Union Square West, New York, NY 10003
tel. 212.727.1400 fax. 212.727.9459
stocklandmartel.com

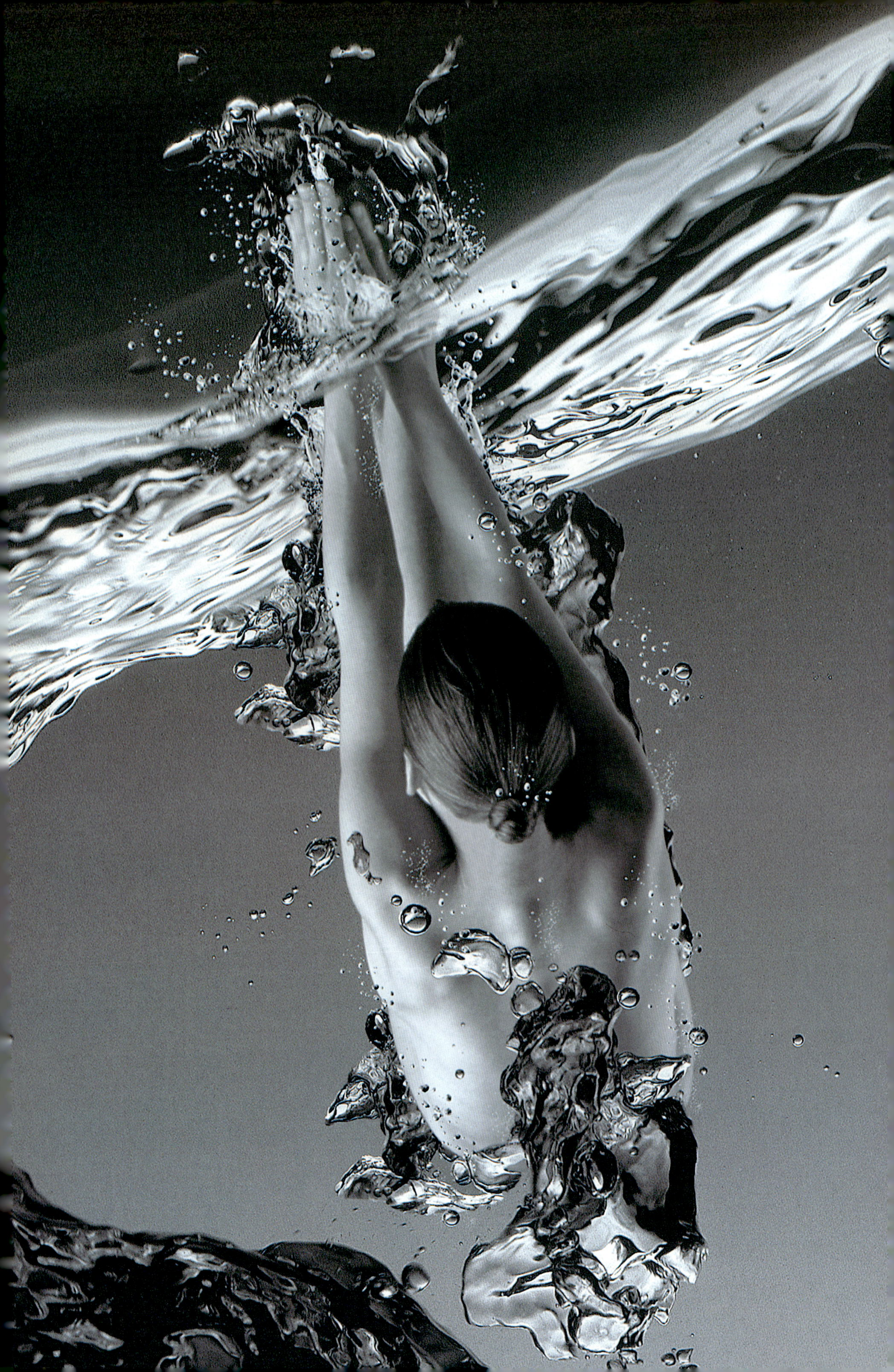

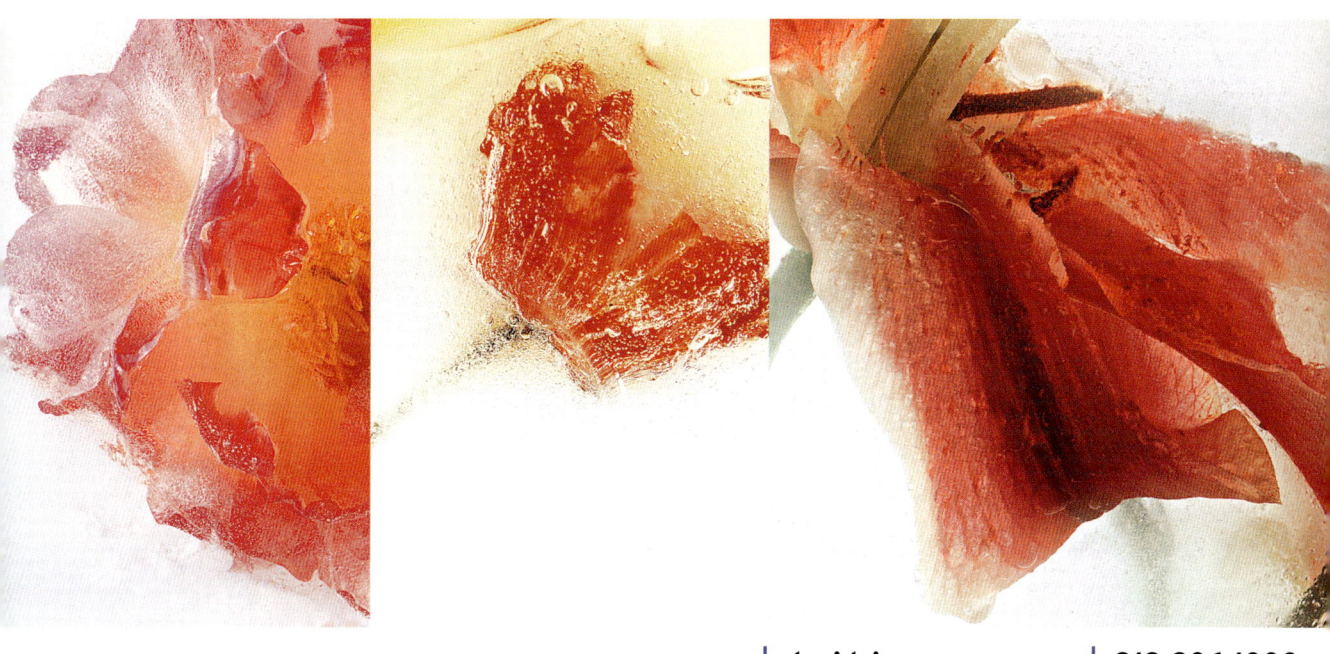

ZIMMERMAN | davidzimmerman.com | 212.206.1000

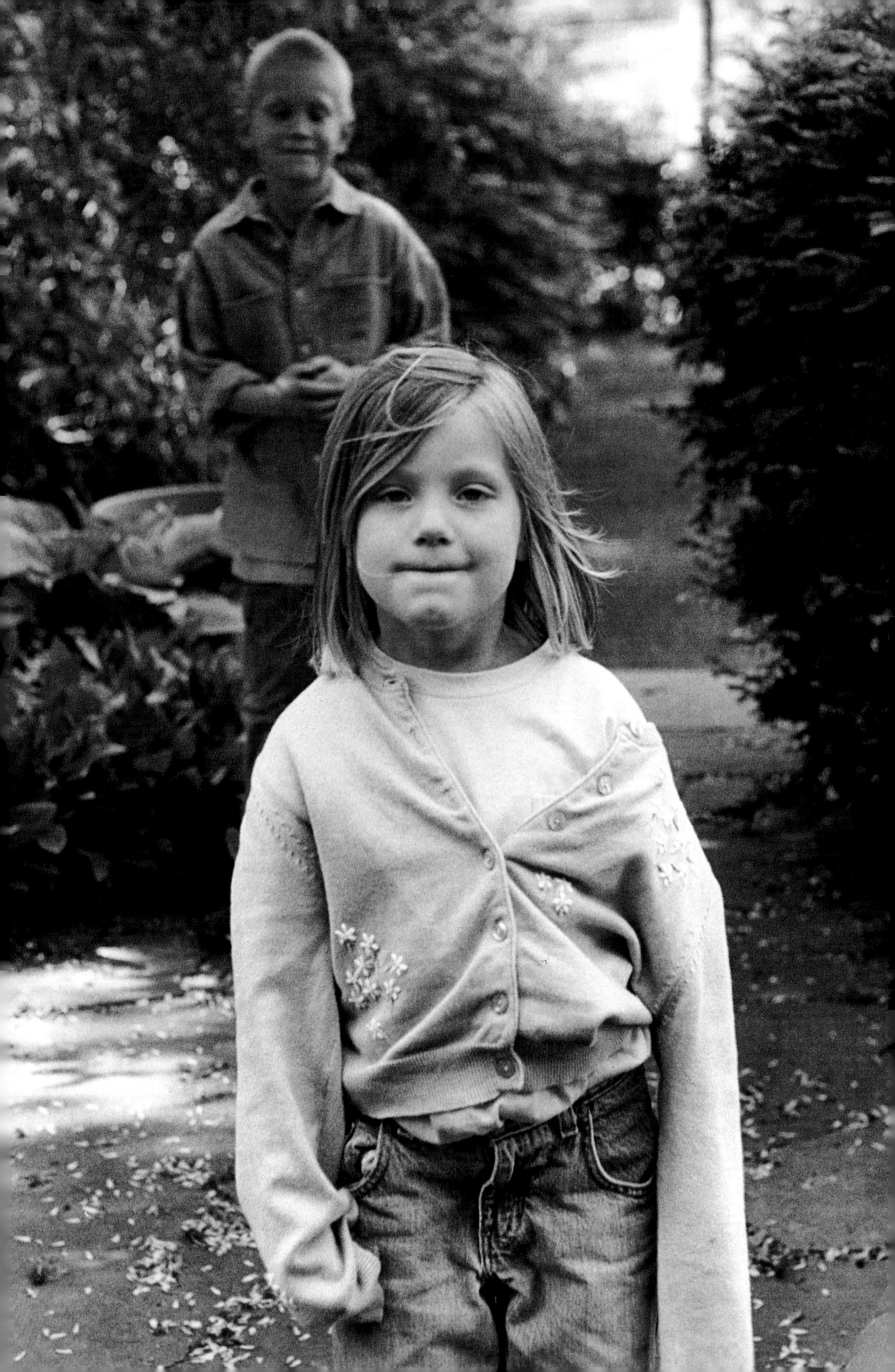

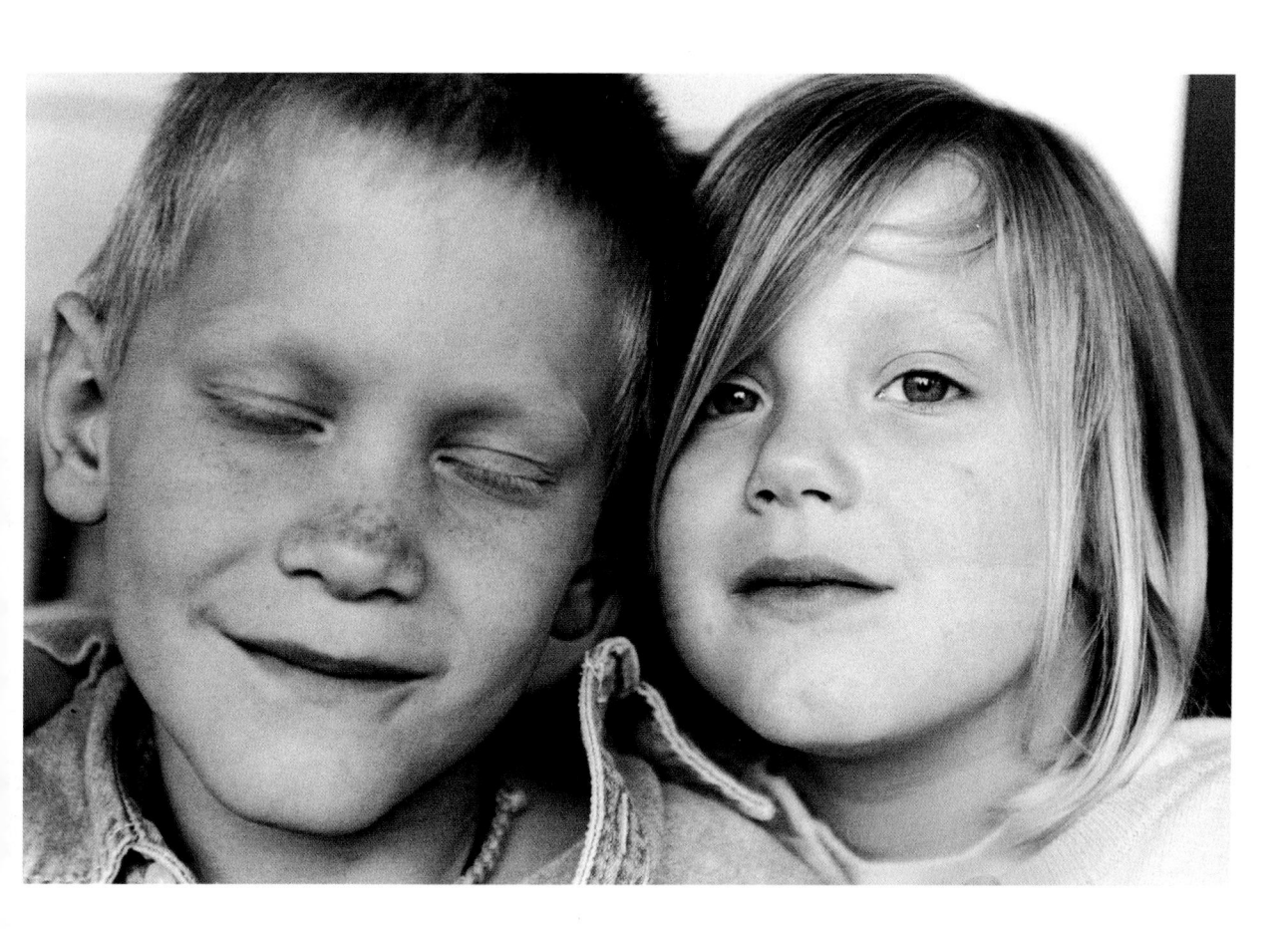

MICHAEL BRIAN PHOTOGRAPHY   9 1 4 . 2 4 2 . 8 8 9 4

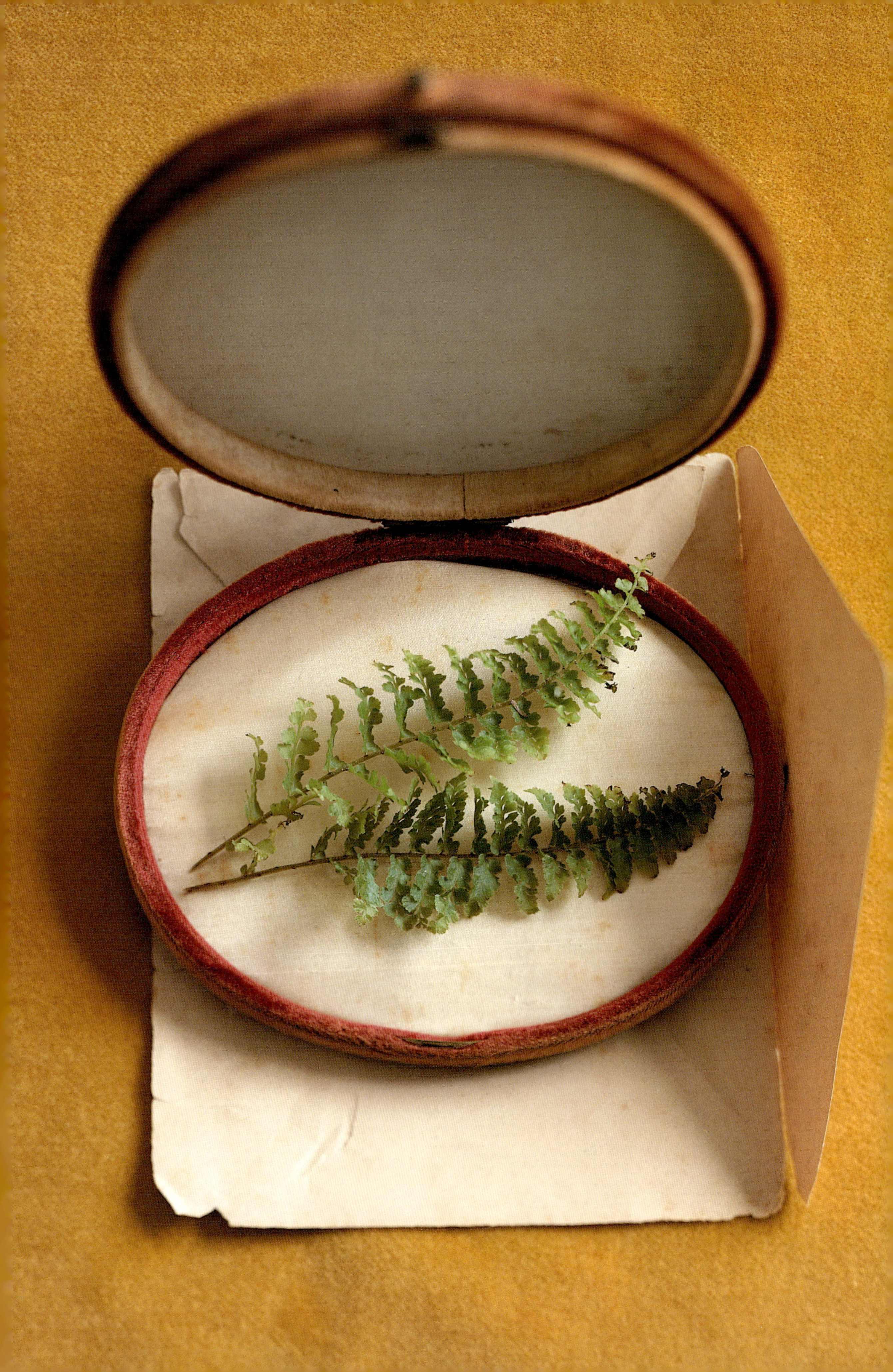

CHARLES SCHILLER PHOTOGRAPHY   151 WEST 19TH STREET   NEW YORK   NY   10011   212.620.6104

< J a m e s M c E n t e e >

> N Y C | 2 1 2 | 7 3 4 | 1 5 5 9 <

> w w w . j a m e s m c e n t e e . c o m <

> www.jamesmcentee.com

NYC | 212 | 734 | 1559 < > FLA | 954 | 565 | 0178

< JamesMcEntee >

> clients...
American Express
Burlington CoatFactory
Donzi Boats
Electronic Media
Florida Lottery
Guess Home
Grupo Taca Airlines
JC Penney
Muvico

Regal Cruises
Red Herring
Ryder Trucks
The Industry Standard
Unversoul Circus
WNBA- Miami Sol

korman + company

we're jammin'

carlo pieroni

david harry stewart

rafael fuchs

richard bradbury

agents : alison korman + patricia muzikar
kormanandcompany.com   west: 626.583.1442   east: 212.402.2450

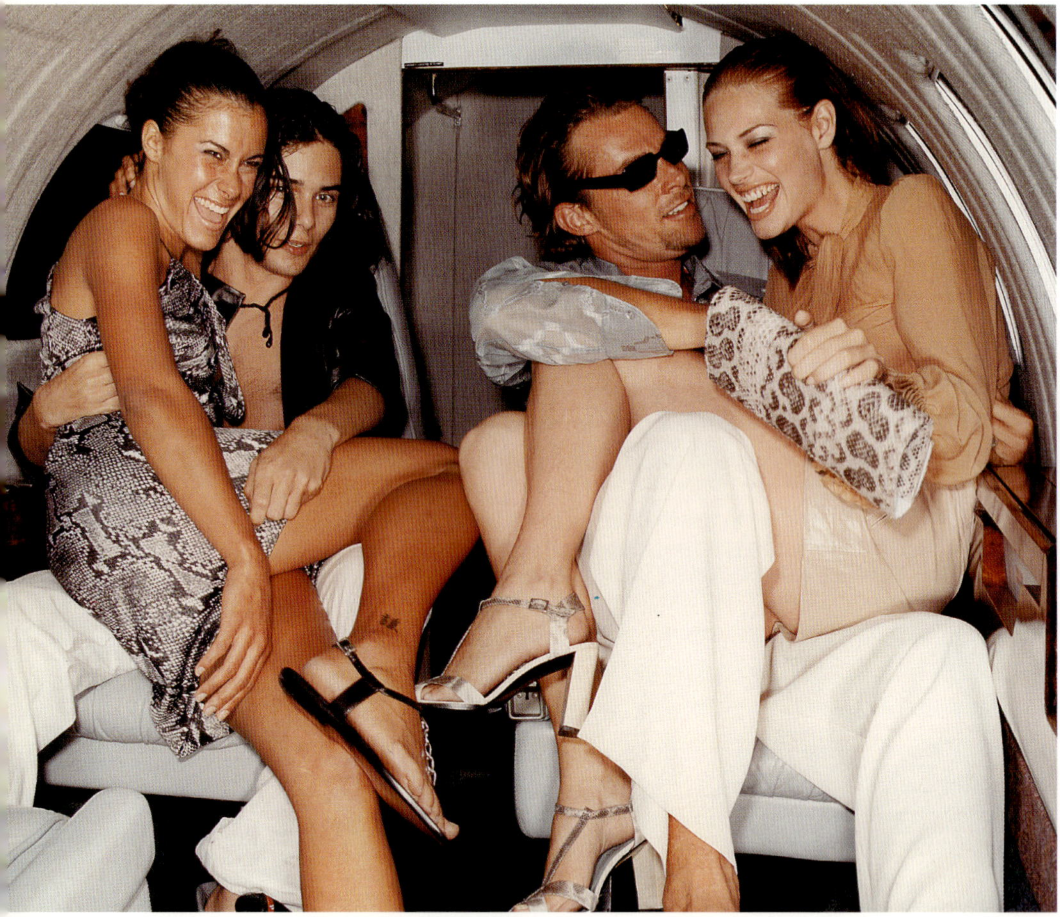

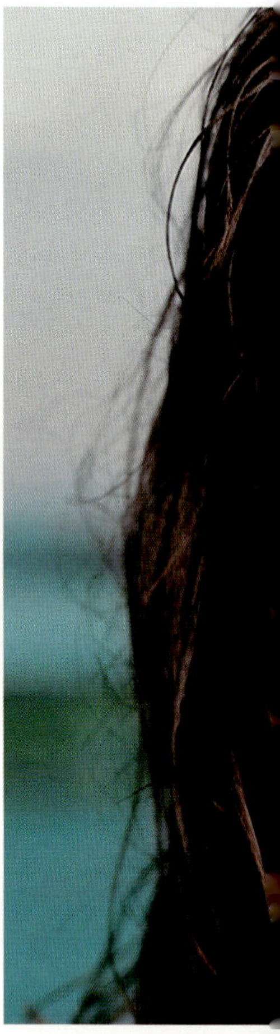

AVID HARR

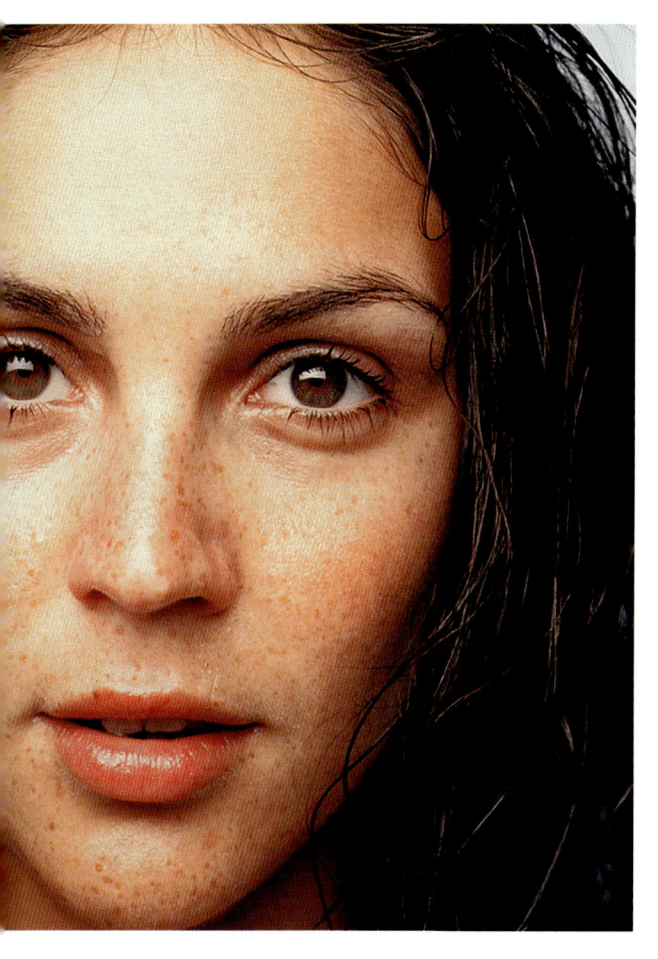

DAVID HARRY STEWART 666 GREENWICH STREET PH#8 NYC 10014
STUDIO: 212 242 0457 FAX: 212 242 0637
WWW.DHSTEWART.COM
REPRESENTATION: USA—KORMAN+COMPANY
EAST: 212 402 2450 WEST: 626 583 1442
UK—ANGELA WOODS: 0171 284 3417

korman + company

RY STEWAR

DAVID HARRY STEWART 666 GREENWICH STREET PH#8 NYC 10014
STUDIO: 212 242 0457 FAX: 212 242 0637
WWW.DHSTEWART.COM
REPRESENTATION: USA–KORMAN+COMPANY
EAST: 212 402 2450   WEST: 626 583 1442
UK–ANGELA WOODS: 0171 284 3417

korman + company

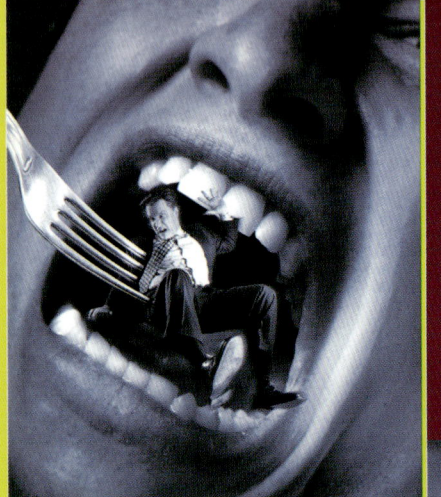

WE'RE JAMMIN'

TradeCast.com Campaign

WE'RE JAMMIN',
team of Photographer Don Dixon
and Digital Artist Avner Levona
STUDIO: (416) 465-3634
www.were-jammin.com

represented by
KORMAN + COMPANY

korman + company

EAST: (212) 402-2450
WEST: (626) 583-1442

Award-Winning 25th Anniversary Poster
The Toronto International Film Festival

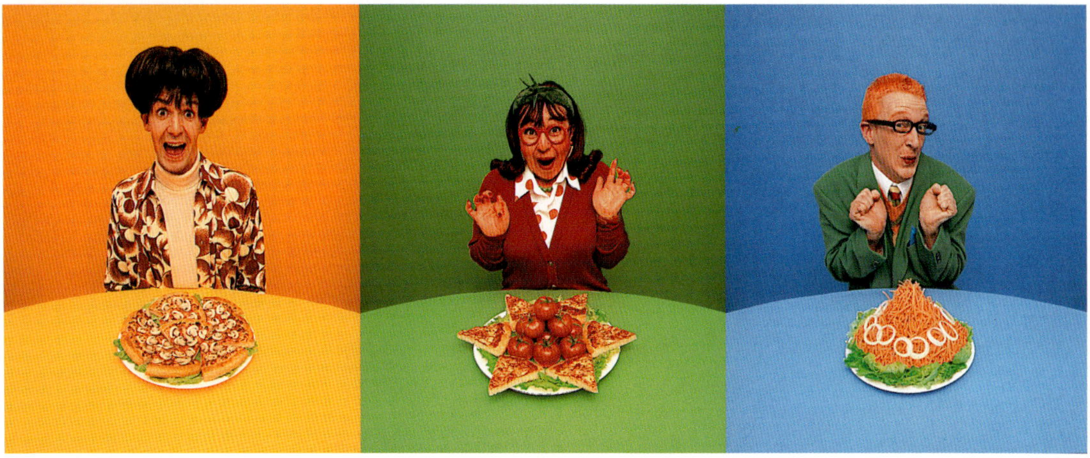

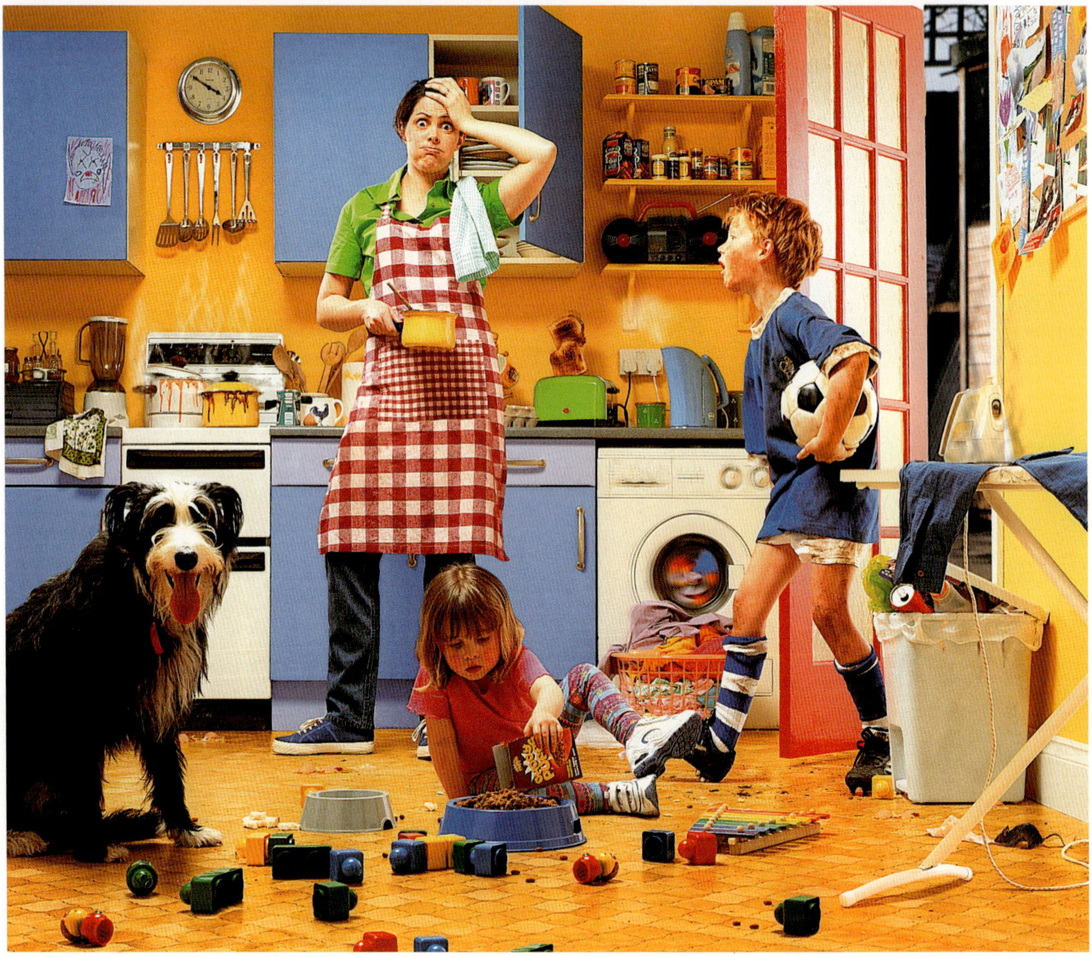

Richard Bradbury

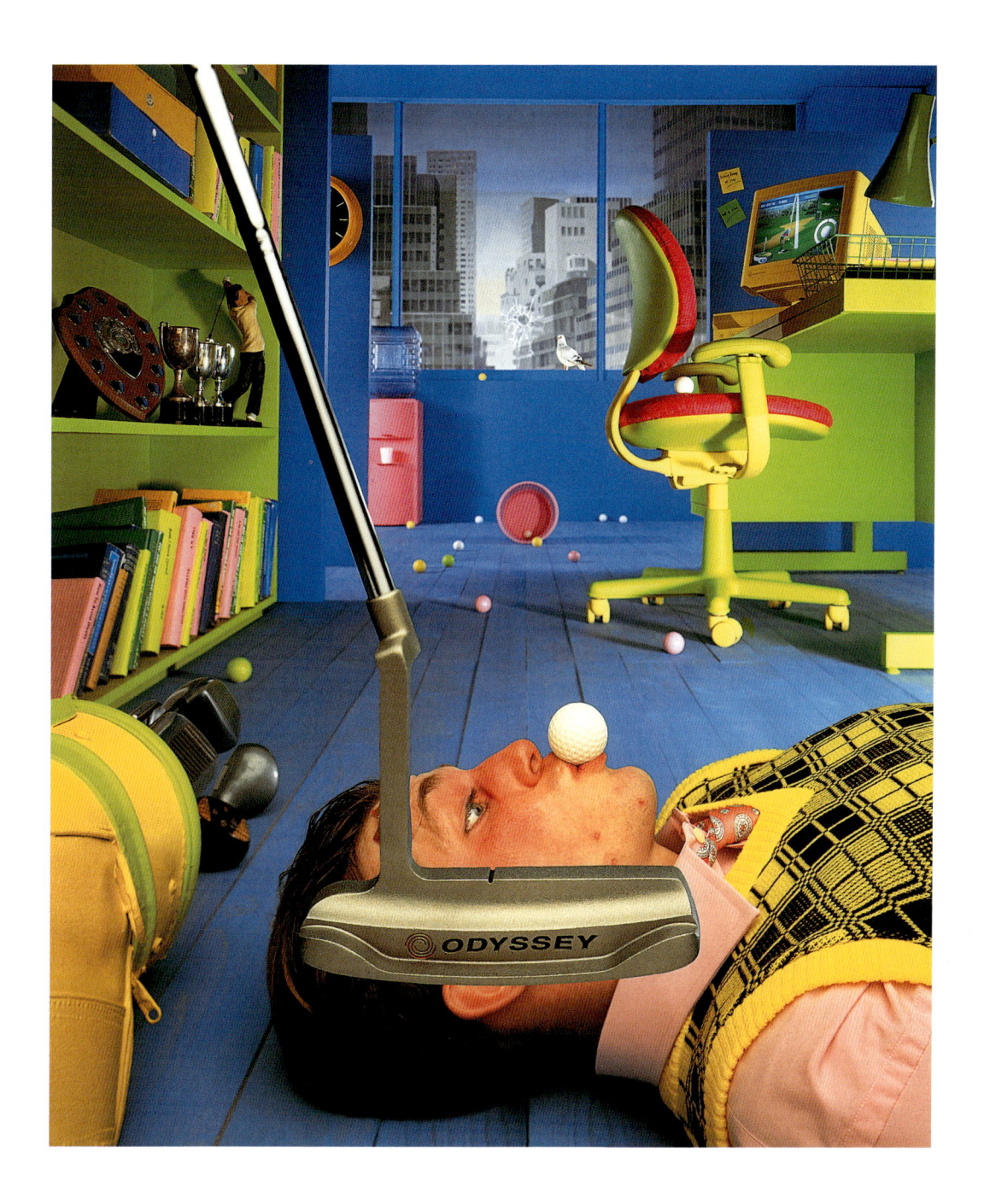

Photography & image manipulation

Representation:
US: Korman + Company
East: 212 402 2450
West: 626 583 1442

UK: Stan Cripps
+44 20 8838 0520

www.rbradbury.com

korman + company

represented

in the United States, Canada, Mexico by

korman + company

East Coast   212.402.2450
West Coast   626.583.1442

in France by Eskimo (+33) 06.16.23.28.66

in Italy by Kim Arena (+39) 02.70.10.67.75

carlo pieroni

www.carlopieroni.com
e-mail: cp@carlopieroni.com

rafael Fuchs

korman + company

REPRESENTED BY
KORMAN+COMPANY
EAST 212 402 2450
WEST 626 583 1442

RAFAEL FUCHS PHOTOGRAPHY 212 529 0518

represented by Doug Truppe
212 685 1223

Frank Marchese Photography

www.frankmarchese.com

John Owens

tel (617)330-1498 fax (617)345-1070
www.johnowens.com

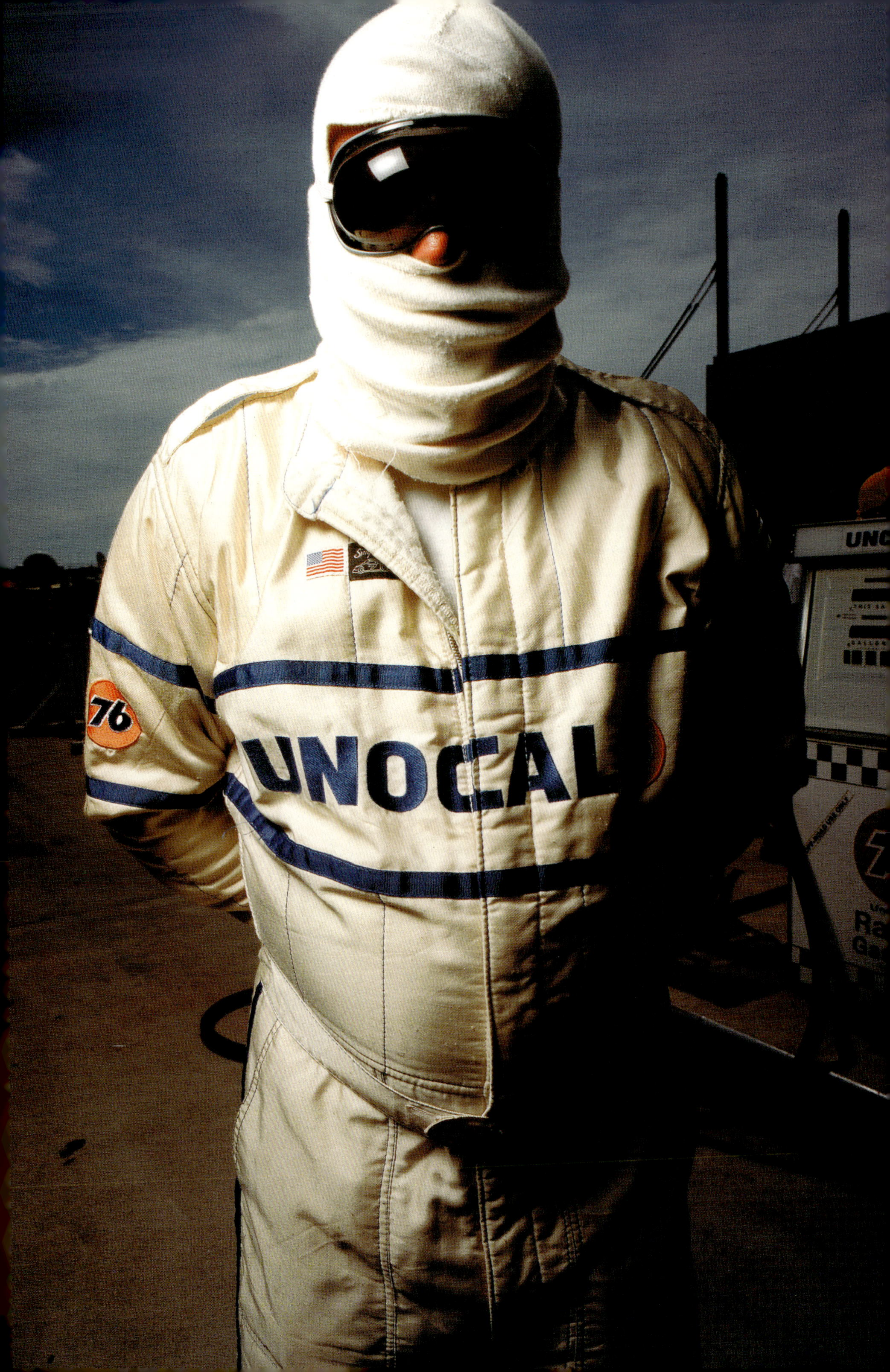
76
UNOCAL

JOHN OWENS

tel (617)330-1498 fax (617)345-1070

www.johnowens.com

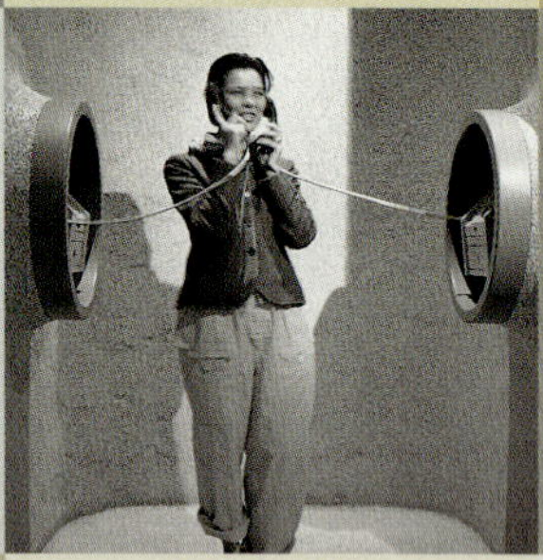

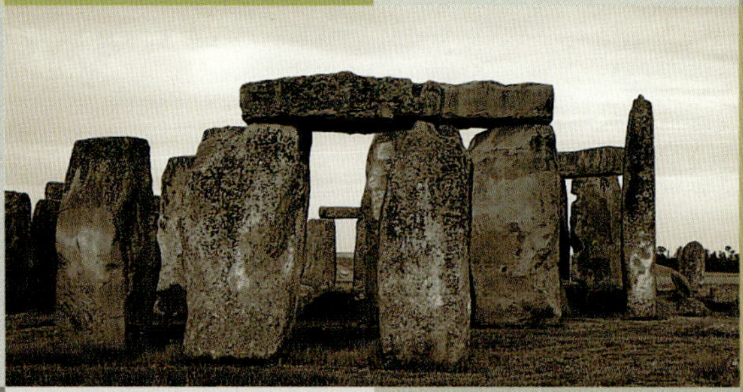

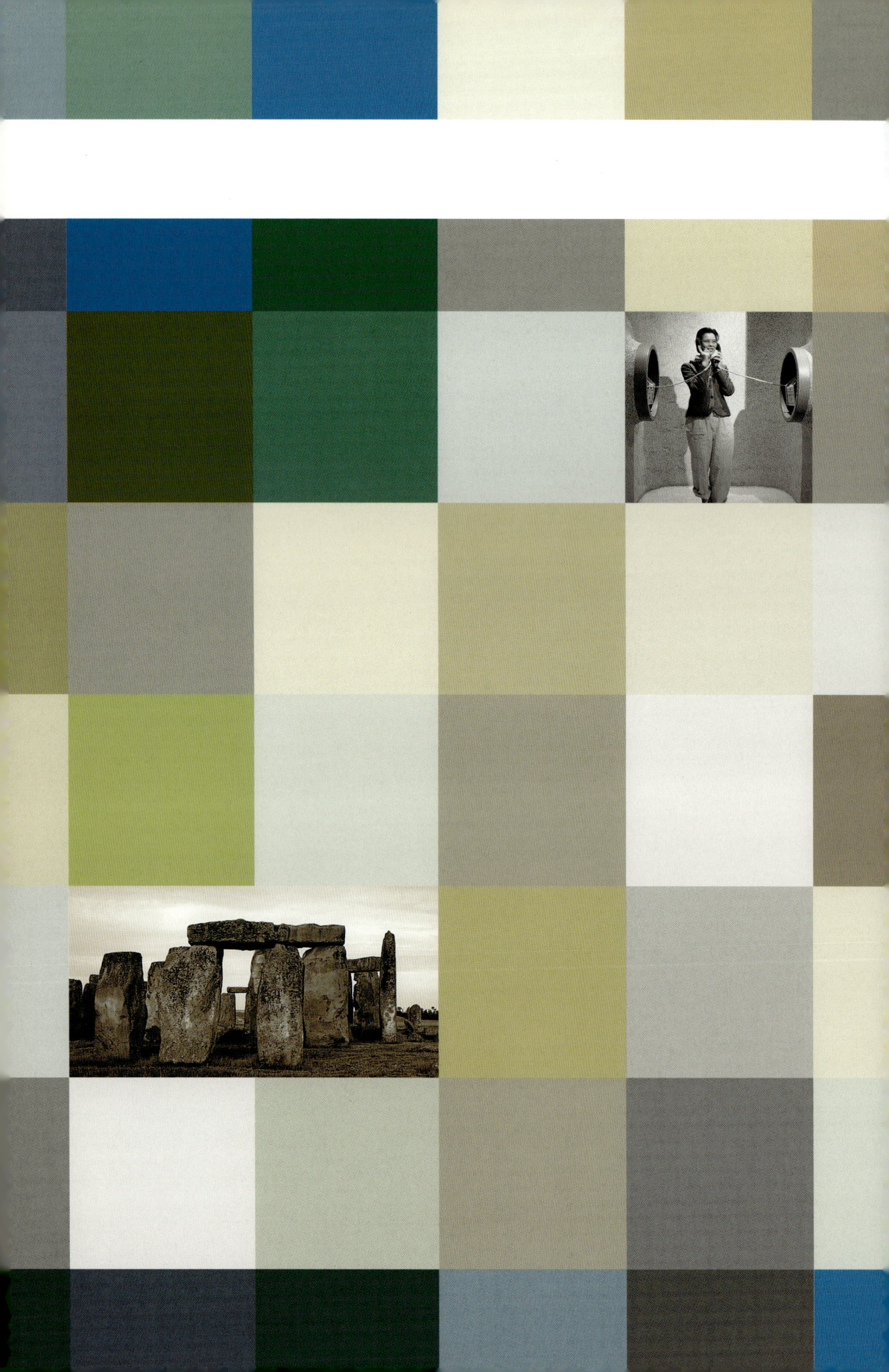

BERNSTEIN & ANDRIULLI
PHONE> 212.682.1490   WEB> WWW.BA-REPS.COM

A REPRESENTS

QUENTIN BACON
NICK BARRATTA
GRANT DELIN
MIKI DUISTERHOF
ANDREW FRENCH
BRETT FROOMER
STUART HALL
GREGORY HEISLER
BOB HIEMSTRA
THIBAULT JEANSON
BILL MILES
PETE SEAWARD
EVAN SKLAR
DANIELA STALLINGER
KEVIN SUMMERS
PAUL WAKEFIELD
ULI WEBER
CATHERINE WESSEL
STEVEN WHITE
STEPHEN WILKES
ROY ZIPSTEIN

BERNSTEIN & ANDRIULLI
PHONE> 212.682.1490   WEB> WWW.BA-REPS.COM

A REPRESENTS

QUENTIN BACON
NICK BARRATTA
GRANT DELIN
MIK DUIJSTERHOF
ANDREW FRENCH
BRETT FROOMER
STUART HALL
GREGORY HEISLER
BOB HIEMSTRA
THIBAULT JEANSON
BILL MILES
PETE SEAWARD
EVAN SKLAR
DANIELA STALLINGER
KEVIN SUMMERS
SAUL WAKEFIELD
ULI WEBER
CATHERINE WESSEL
STEVEN WHITE
STEPHEN WILKES
ROY ZIPSTEIN

DANIELA STALLINGER

REPRESENTED BY **BERNSTEIN & ANDRIULLI**
PHONE> 212.682.1490   WEB> WWW.BA-REPS.COM

DANIELA STALLINGER

BERNSTEIN & ANDRIULLI
REPRESENTED BY
PHONE> 212.682.1490   WEB> WWW.BA-REPS.COM

STEPHEN WILKES

REPRESENTED BY BERNSTEIN & ANDRIULLI
PHONE> 212.682.1490   WEB> WWW.BA-REPS.COM

STEPHEN WILKES

BERNSTEIN & ANDRIULLI
REPRESENTED BY
PHONE> 212.682.1490   WEB> WWW.BA-REPS.COM

ULI WEBER.COM

BERNSTEIN & ANDRIULLI
PHONE> 212.682.1490 WEB> WWW.BA-REPS.COM

EVAN SKLAR

REPRESENTED BY **BERNSTEIN & ANDRIULLI**
PHONE> 212.682.1490   WEB> WWW.BA-REPS.COM

PAUL WAKEFIELD

BERNSTEIN & ANDRIULLI
PHONE> 212.682.1490   WEB> WWW.BA-REPS.COM

MIKI DUISTERHOF

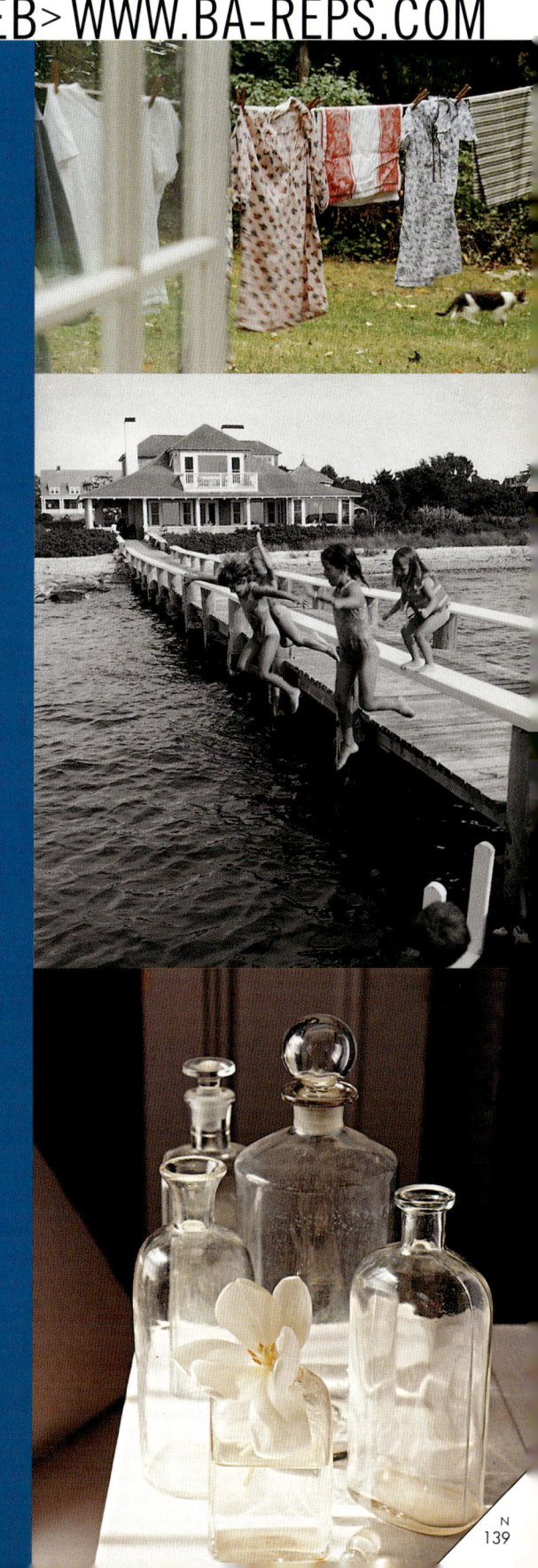

BERNSTEIN & ANDRIULLI

REPRESENTED BY
PHONE> 212.682.1490   WEB> WWW.BA-REPS.COM

PETE SEAWARD

REPRESENTED BY **BERNSTEIN & ANDRIULLI**
PHONE> 212.682.1490   WEB> WWW.BA-REPS.COM

ROY ZIPSTEIN

BERNSTEIN & ANDRIULLI
PHONE> 212.682.1490   WEB> WWW.BA-REPS.COM

KEVIN SUMMERS

Worried about dark shadows? Unhealthy complexion? Fading looks? On a pack a day you certainly should be. we'd like to reassure you that you're just being paranoid. You're skin, despite the 4000 toxins in every cigarette you smoke, is still dewy and radiant. Your eyes, despite the poisonous effect of smoke, are still clear and bright. We'd like to reassure you, but we can't. Be afraid. Be very afraid. **Quitline 0800 002200**

REPRESENTED BY BERNSTEIN & ANDRIULLI
PHONE> 212.682.1490   WEB> WWW.BA-REPS.COM

QUENTIN BACON

BERNSTEIN & ANDRIULLI
REPRESENTED BY
PHONE> 212.682.1490   WEB> WWW.BA-REPS.COM

BILL MILES

BERNSTEIN & ANDRIULLI
PHONE> 212.682.1490   WEB> WWW.BA-REPS.COM

BILL MILES

REPRESENTED BY **BERNSTEIN & ANDRIULLI**
PHONE> 212.682.1490   WEB> WWW.BA-REPS.COM

STUART HALL

BERNSTEIN & ANDRIULLI
REPRESENTED BY
PHONE> 212.682.1490 WEB> WWW.BA-REPS.COM

STUART HALL

BERNSTEIN & ANDRIULLI
REPRESENTED BY
PHONE> 212.682.1490   WEB> WWW.BA-REPS.COM

GREGORY HEISLER

REPRESENTED BY **BERNSTEIN & ANDRIULLI**
PHONE> 212.682.1490   WEB> WWW.BA-REPS.COM

GREGORY HEISLER

REPRESENTED BY **BERNSTEIN & ANDRIULLI**
PHONE> 212.682.1490   WEB> WWW.BA-REPS.COM

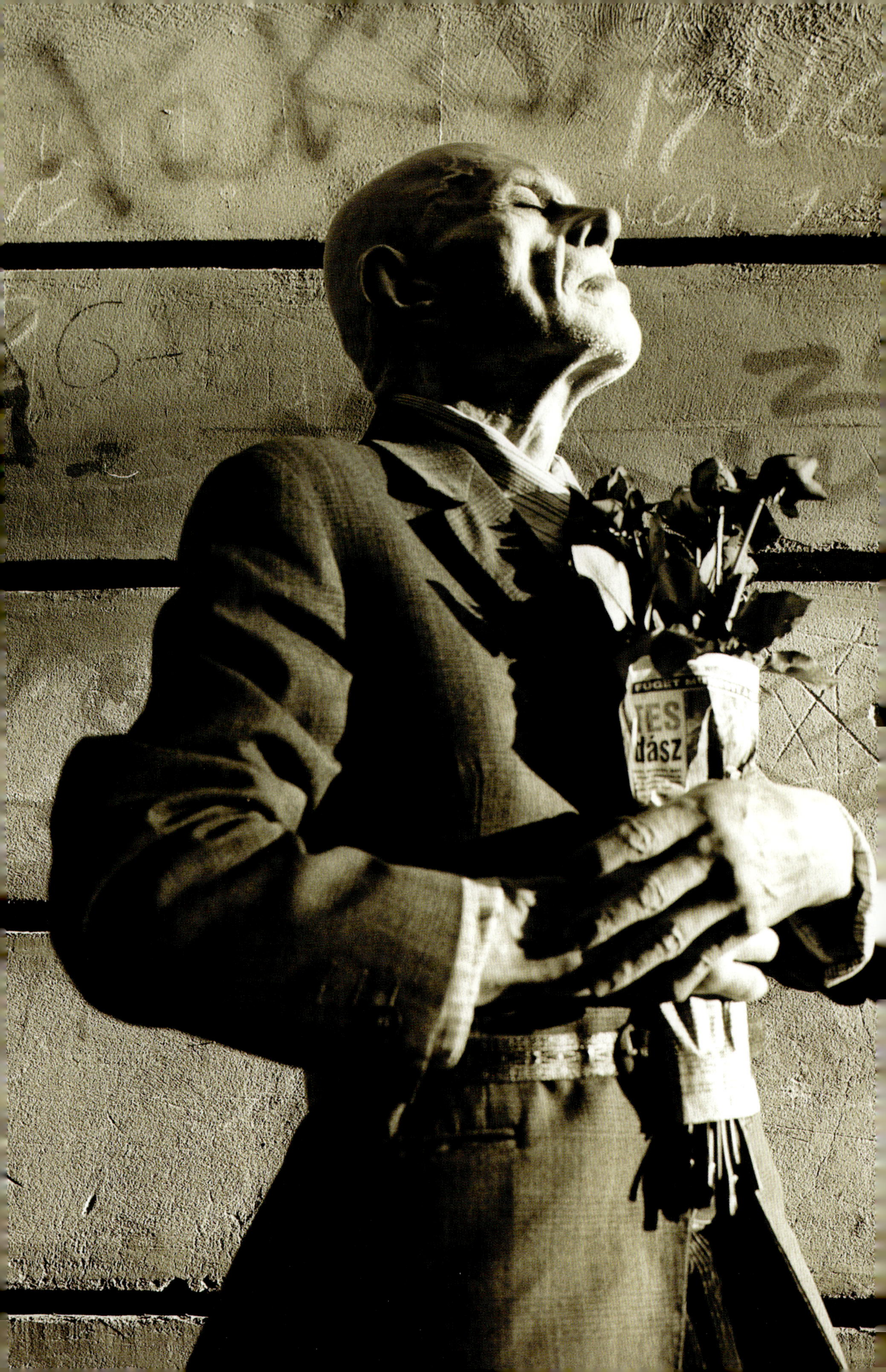

RUSSELL MONK

REPRESENTED BY WESTSIDE STUDIO • TELEPHONE: 416.535.1955

FACSIMILE: 416.535.0118 • E-MAIL: MONKMAN@INTERLOG.COM

WEB: WWW.RUSSELLMONK.COM • ABLE TO SEE IN COLOR AS WELL

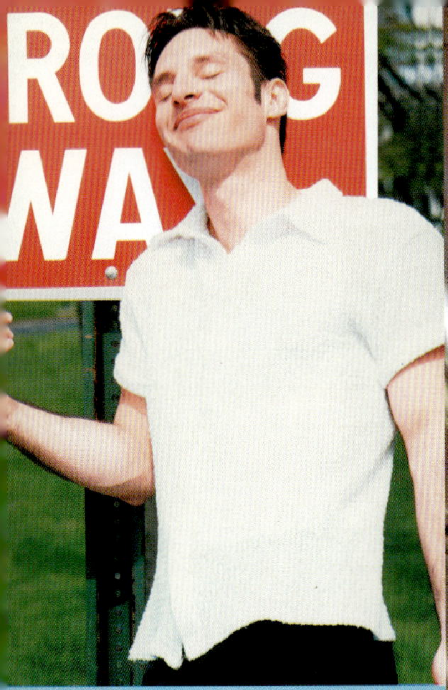

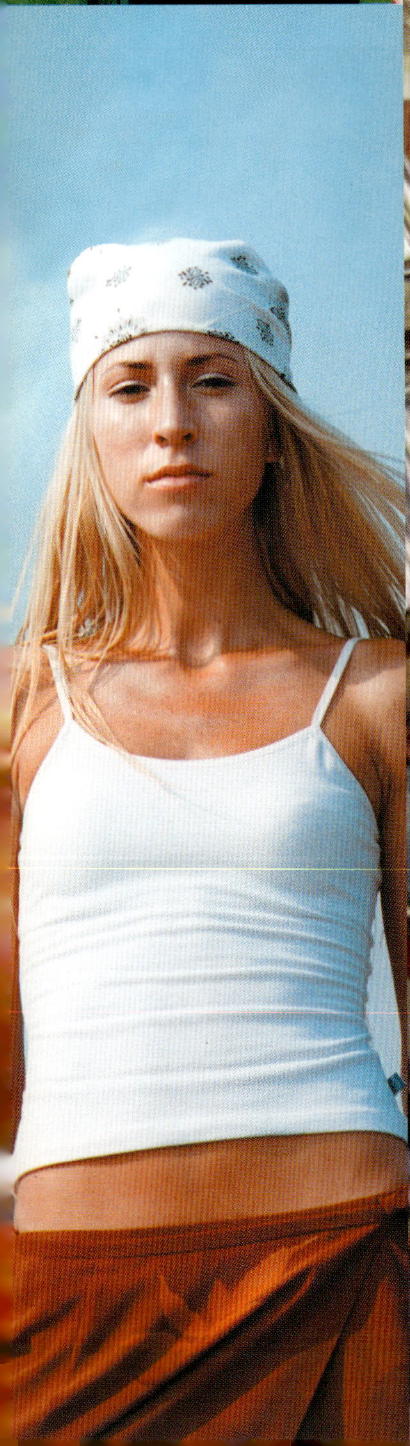

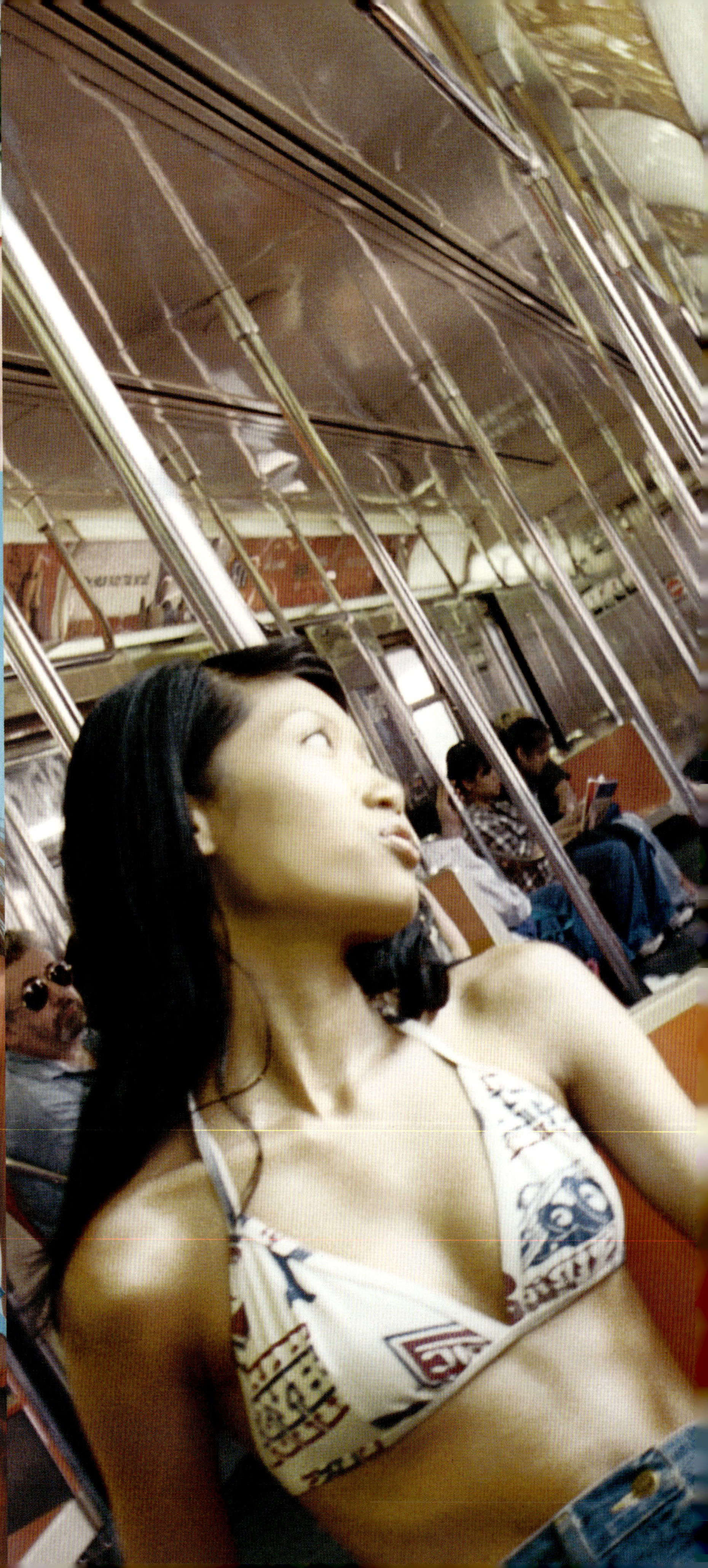

wolfgang freithof

212 724 1790
www.wfx.net

WILLIE NASH PHOTOGRAPHY

212 WEST 29 STREET N.Y.C. 212 594-7175

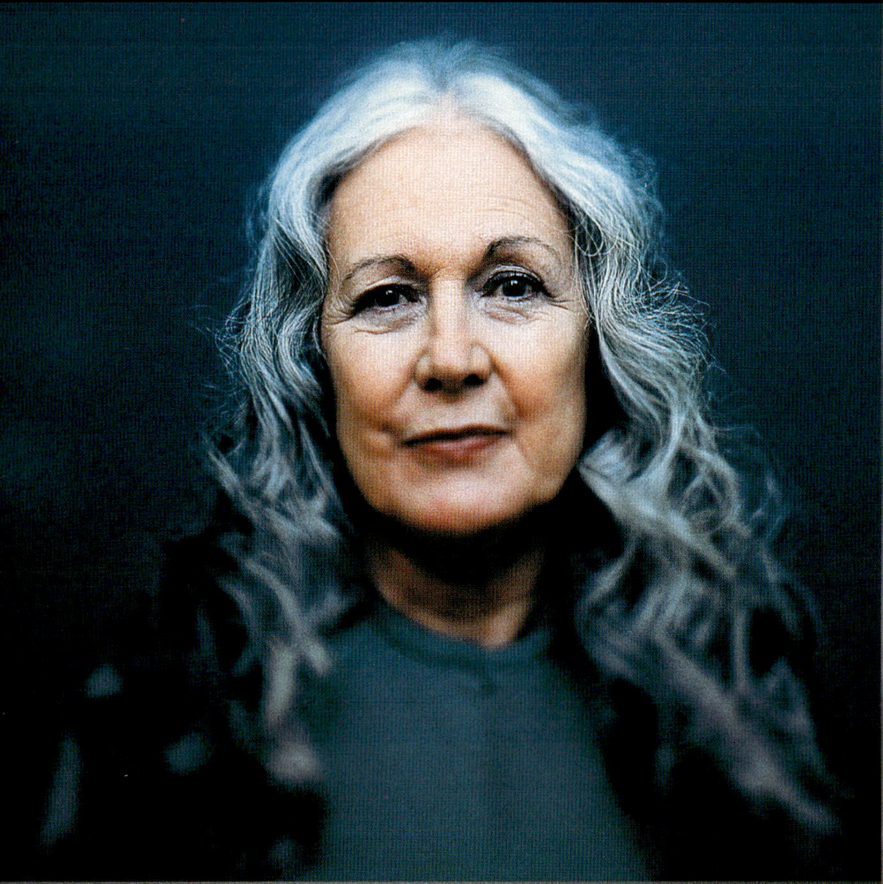

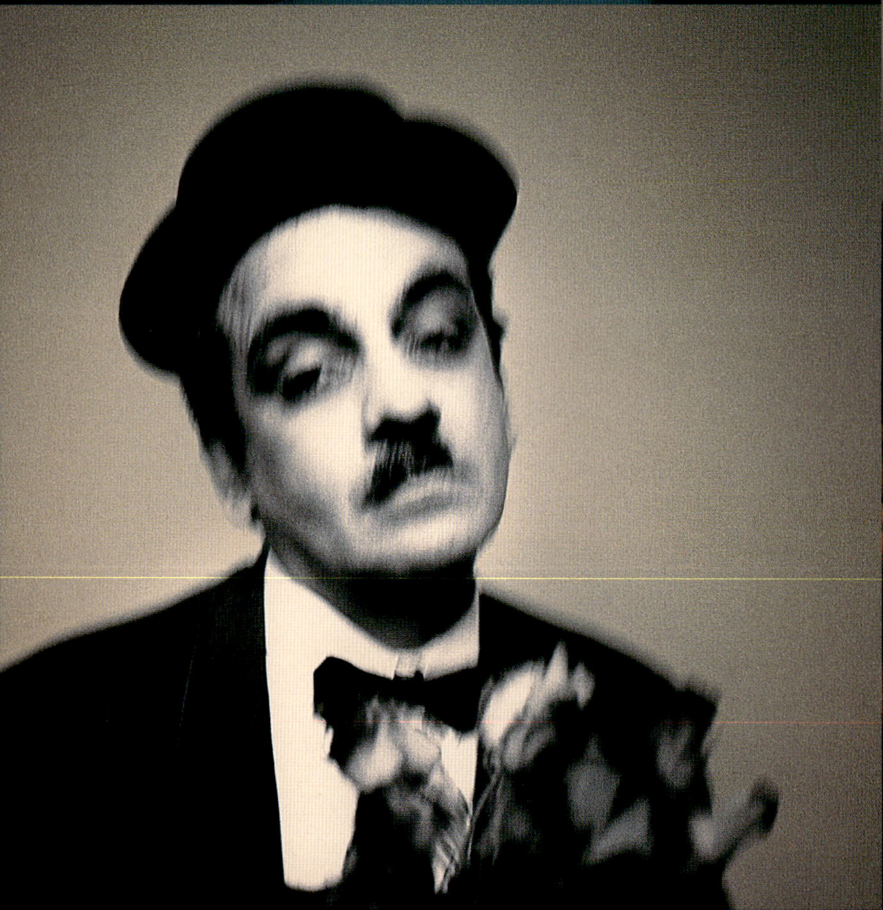

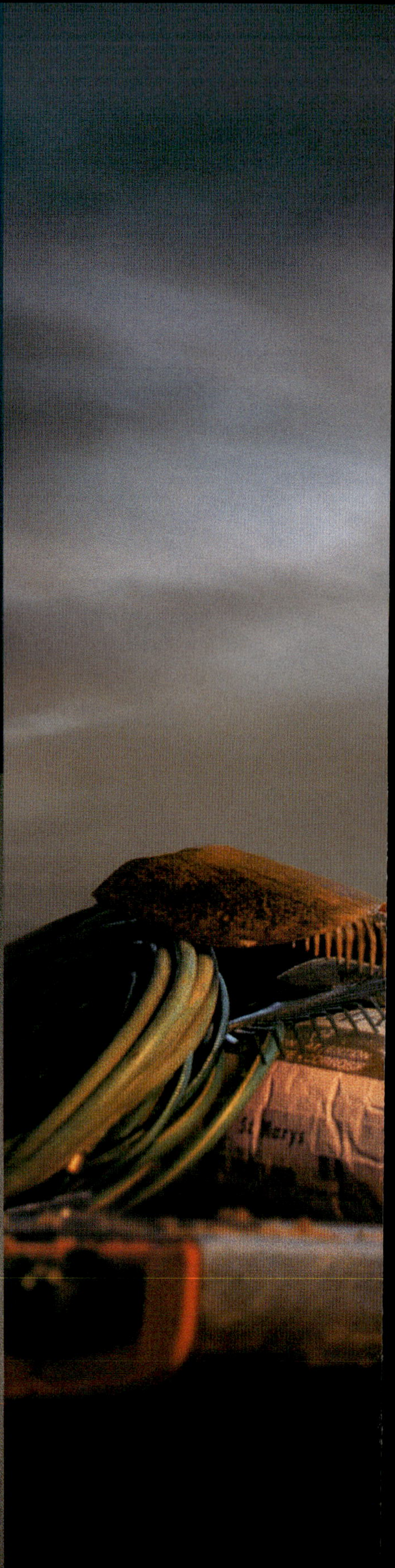

represented by westside studio 416-535-1955 DATTU.COM

INTEL CAMPAIGN, DSW Partners, CD: Jeff Begley, AD: Steve Cardon

CANON ELPH CAMPAIGN, Grey Advertising, AD: Dios Lagos

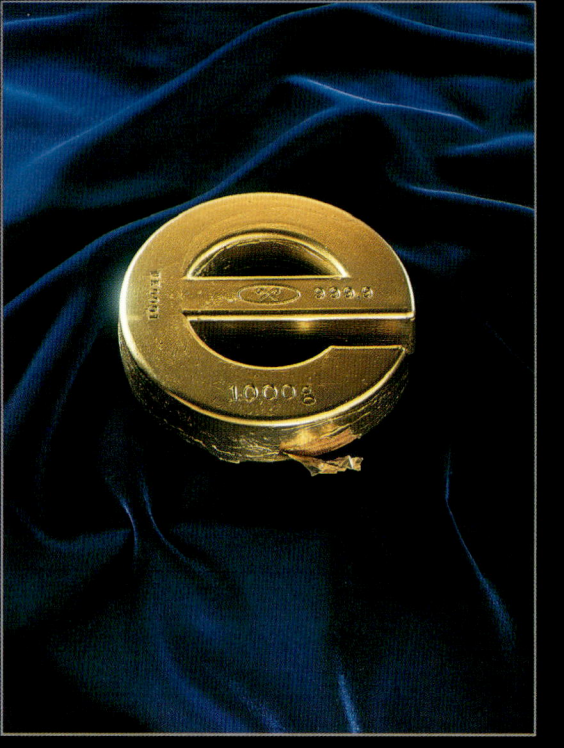

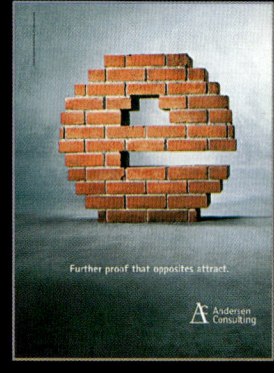

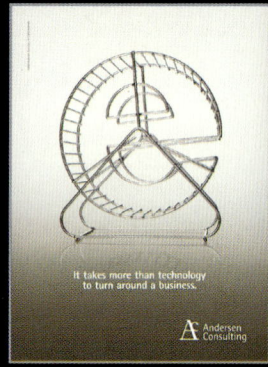

ANDERSEN CONSULTING CAMPAIGN, Young and Rubicam, AD: Michael Brenneke

H

DEBEERS DIAMONDS CAMPAIGN, J. Walter Thompson, CD: Ed Evangelista, CW: Erick Izo

THIS CHRISTMAS
CUPID
TRADES IN HIS BOW FOR A BAZOOKA

De Beers
A DIAMOND IS FOREVER

WHAT ARE YOU WAITING FOR, THE YEAR 3000?

De Beers

AND THE WINNER IN THE CATEGORY OF MALE IN A ROMANTIC ROLE IS

(YOUR NAME HERE)

De Beers
A DIAMOND IS FOREVER

IF YOU THINK THIS ISN'T THE YEAR FOR DIAMONDS YOU'RE IN FOR A LONG MILLENNIUM

THE THREE-STONE ANNIVERSARY RING

De Beers
A DIAMOND IS FOREVER

LUCKY STRIKE CAMPAIGN , Bates USA, AD: Mark Finely

H

Steve Hellerstein

Ask for Mia Choi or Marie Hall / T: 212.645.0508 / www.hellerstein.com

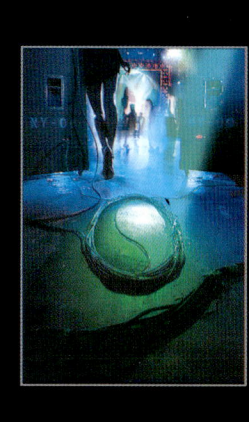

SALEM CAMPAIGN, West Wayne, Inc., AD: Taylor Crawford

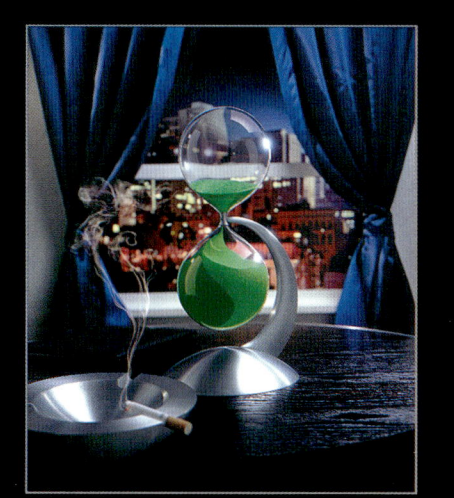

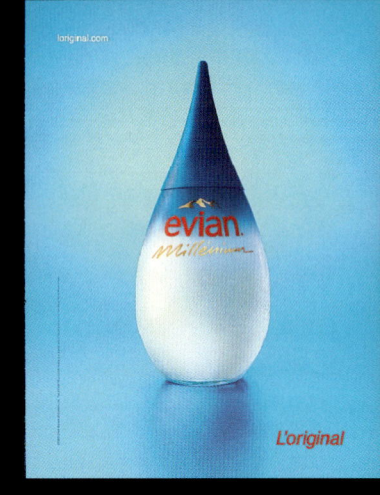

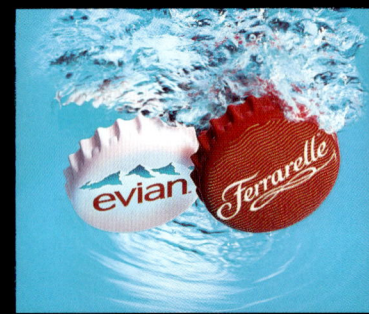

EVIAN CAMPAIGN, Messner Vetere Berger McNamee, CD: Guy Sesse, AD: John Tumelty

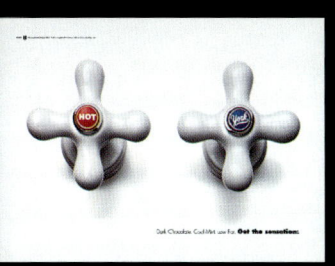

Dark Chocolate. Cool Mint. Low Fat. **Get the sensation.**

YORK CAMPAIGN, DDB Needham, CD: Tony Romero

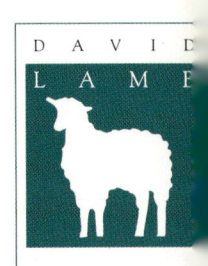

800 836 9258 | davidlambphotography.com | mary@davidlambphotography.com

DAVID LAMB

Representing   Photographers • Hair • Make-Up • Stylists

utopia

12 west end avenue new york, ny 10023 tel 212 • 634 • 9280 fax 212 • 634 • 9288 http://www.utopianyc.com

Marili Forastieri
Photography

utopia
http://www.utopianyc.com   12 west end avenue new york, ny 10023 tel 212 • 634 • 9280 fax 212 • 634 • 9288

Didier Gault
Photography

utopia

www.utopianyc.com 12 west end avenue new york, ny 10023 tel 212 • 634 • 9280 fax 212 • 634 • 9288

Todd Norwood
Photography

utopia

http://www.utopianyc.com 12 west end avenue new york, ny 10023 tel 212 • 634 • 9280 fax 212 • 634 • 9288

Raphael Buchler
Photography

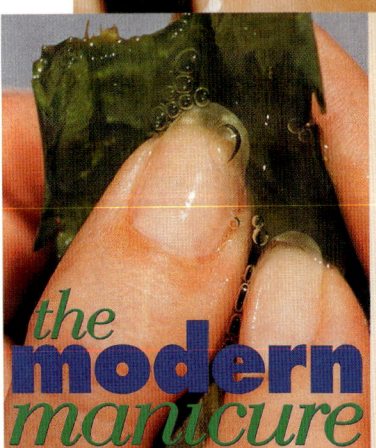

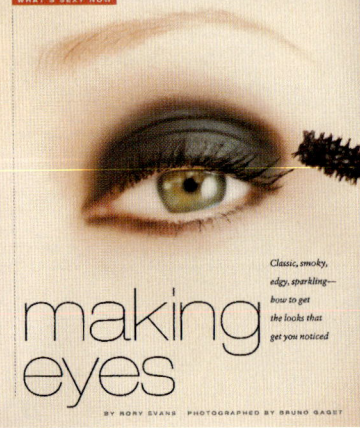

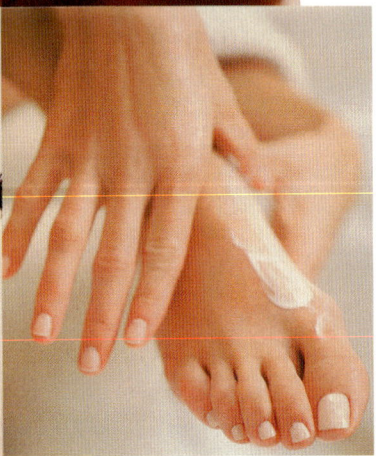

Bruno Gaget
Photography

utopia

http://www.utopianyc.com   12 west end avenue new york, ny 10023 tel 212 • 634 • 9280 fax 212 • 634 • 9288

Walk This Way

Wearing a suit is about strutting your stuff. Words of wisdom from those who do.

"Style comes from the streets, the heart and the soul. It's an expression of who we are. Sometimes spiritual, sometimes sexual, sometimes political."

—BILLE WOODRUFF, director

Bruno Gaget
Photography

utopia

12 west end avenue new york, ny 10023 tel 212 • 634 • 9280 fax 212 • 634 • 9288

http://www.utopianyc.com

utopia
http://www.utopianyc.com

andrew parsons photographer
12 west end avenue new york, ny 10023 tel 212•634•9280 fax 212•634•9288

© 2000 The California Fluid Milk Processor Advisory Board.

got milk?

NOKIA
9:30
NOKIA
5100 Series
Menu
C
1
2abc
3def
4ghi
5jkl
6mno
7pqrs
8tuv
9wxyz
*+
0
#

rick burda

212.971.9455

represented by

utopia

www.utopianyc.com
tel 212.634.9280

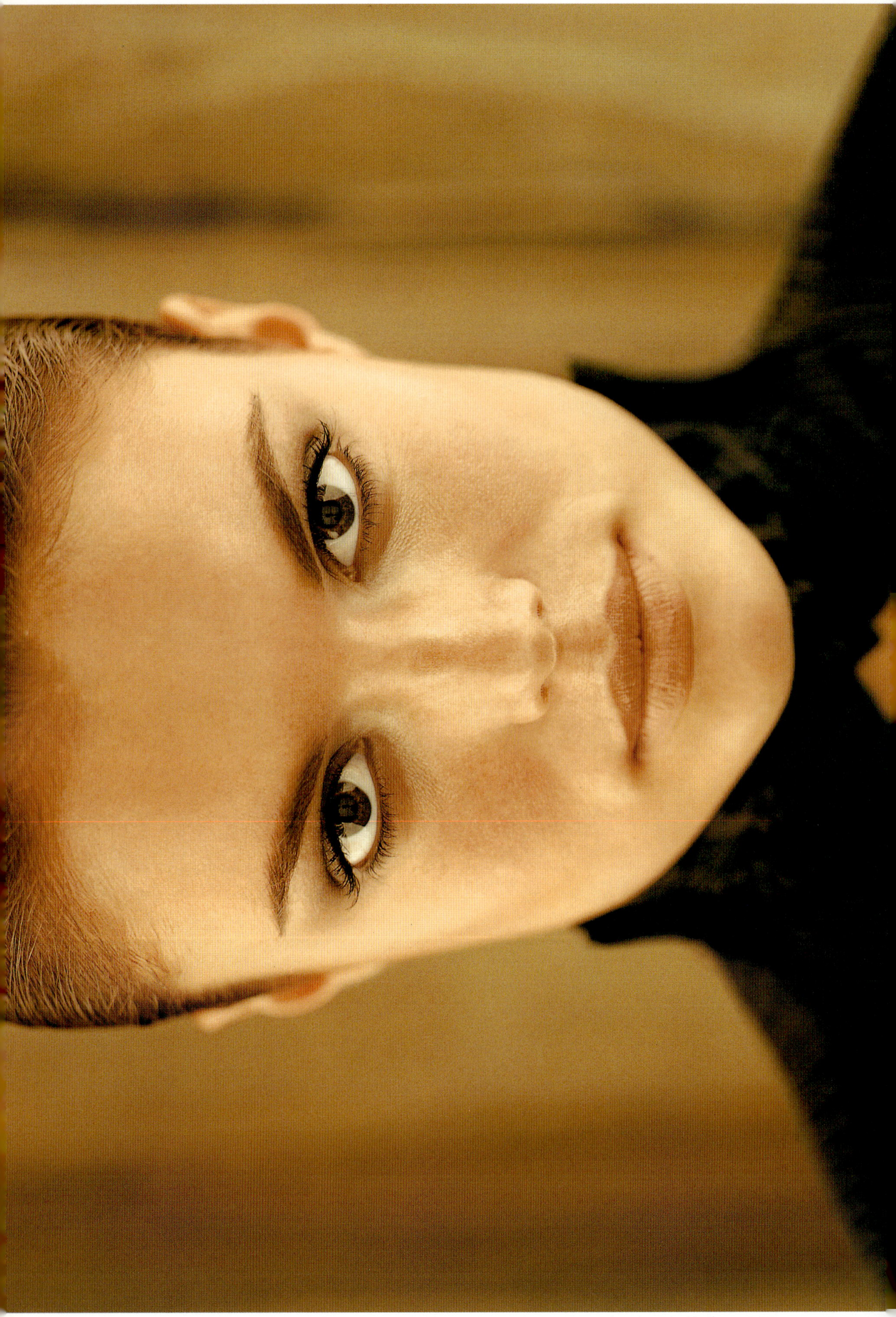

RON BAXTER SMITH

(TORONTO)
416 972 6500

REPRESENTED BY TERI WALDERMAN
1 800 720 1144

(NEW YORK)
212 343 0132

REEL AVAILABLE UPON REQUEST | WWW.RONBAXTERSMITH.COM

Daniel Malka 905.709.9544 / U.S. Agent Randi Fiat 312.329.9800

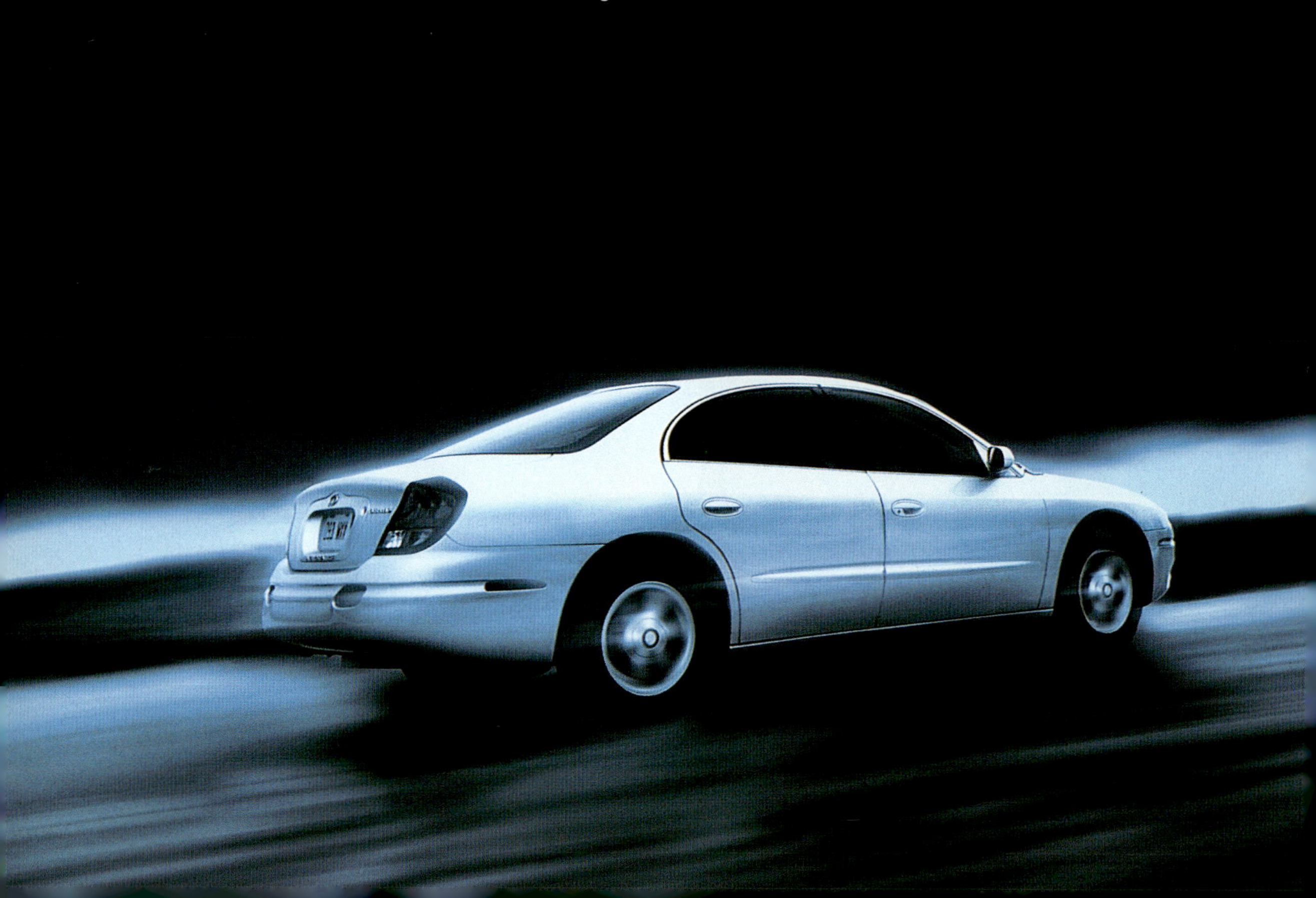

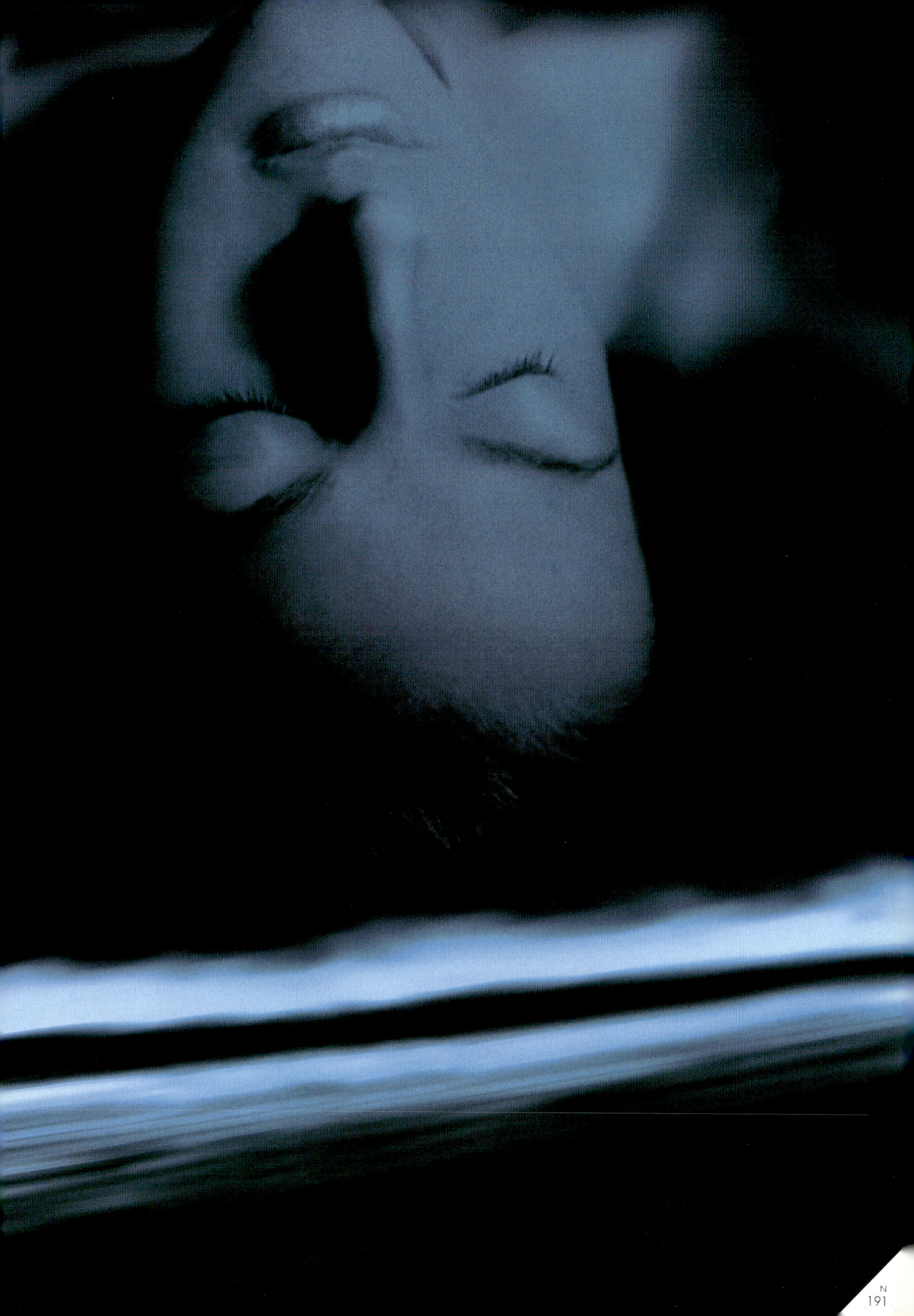

Landscape or portrait?

Lorentz Gullachsen
Represented by Liz-Li 212 889 7067
www.gullachsen.com

Martin Mistretta Inc.
www.martinmistretta.com
Represented By: Liz Li
Phone: 212.889.7067

Martin Mistretta Inc.
www.martinmistretta.com
Represented By: Liz Li
Phone: 212.889.7067

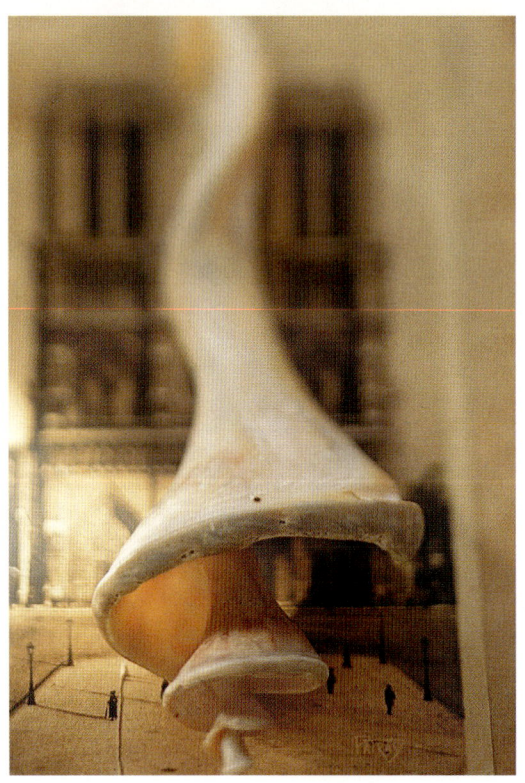

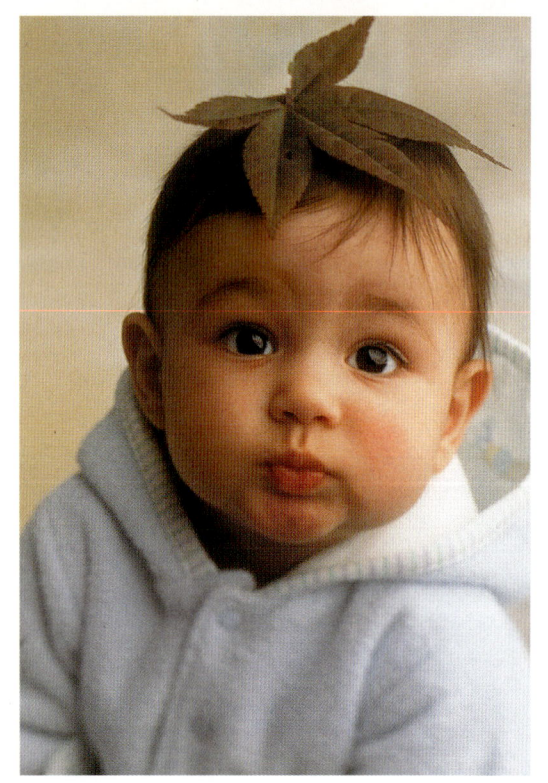

Kaplan

CAROL KAPLAN STUDIO INC • BOSTON, MA 617·426·1131

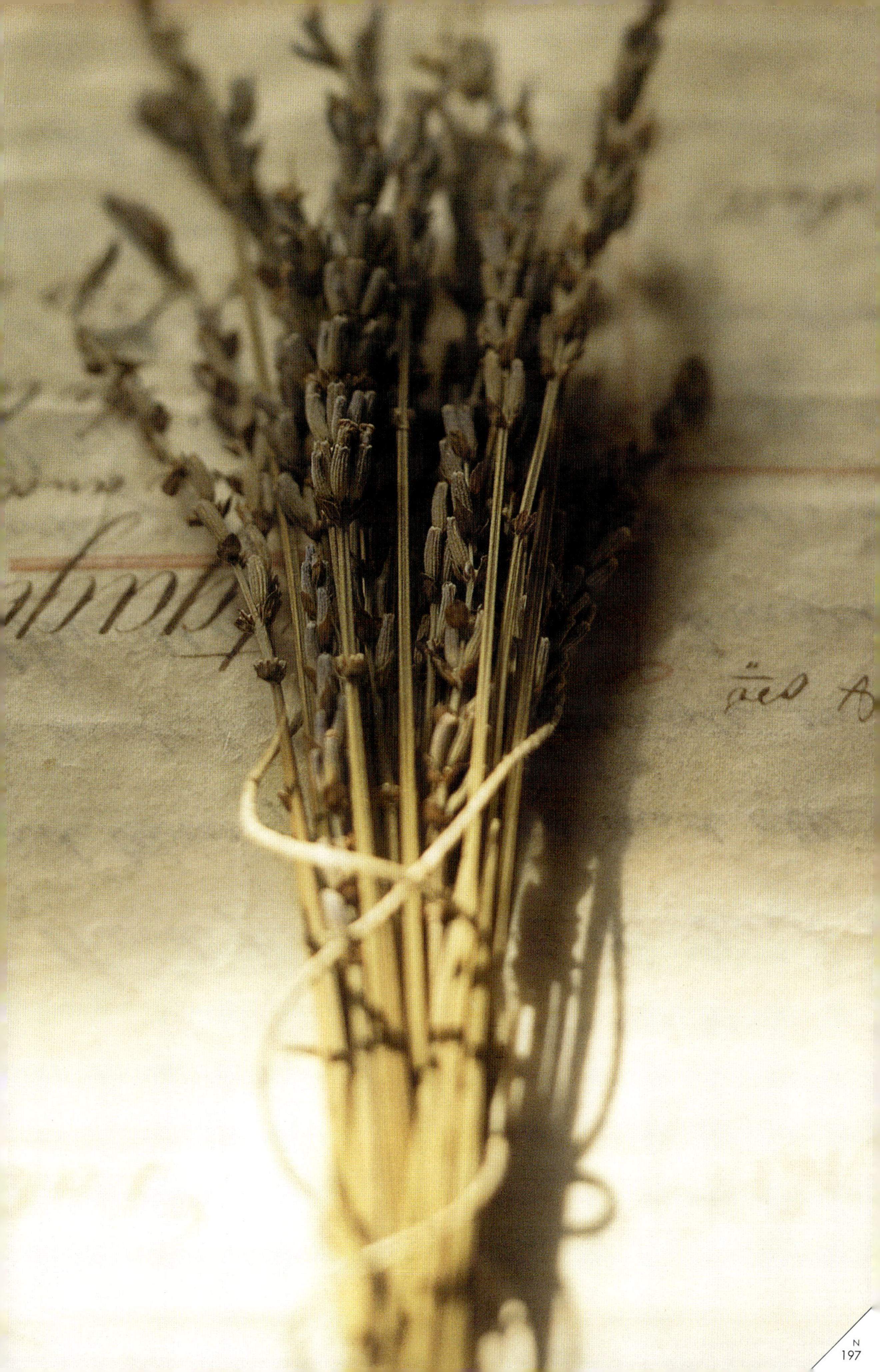

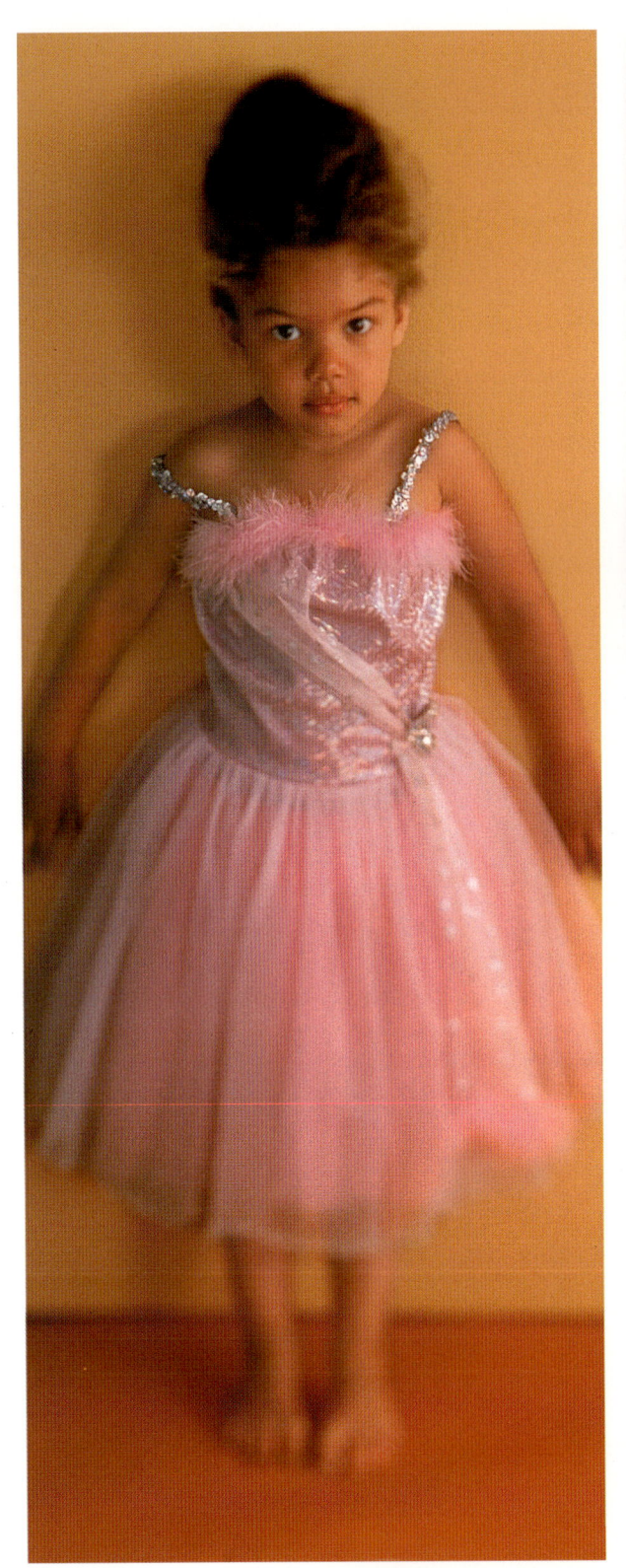

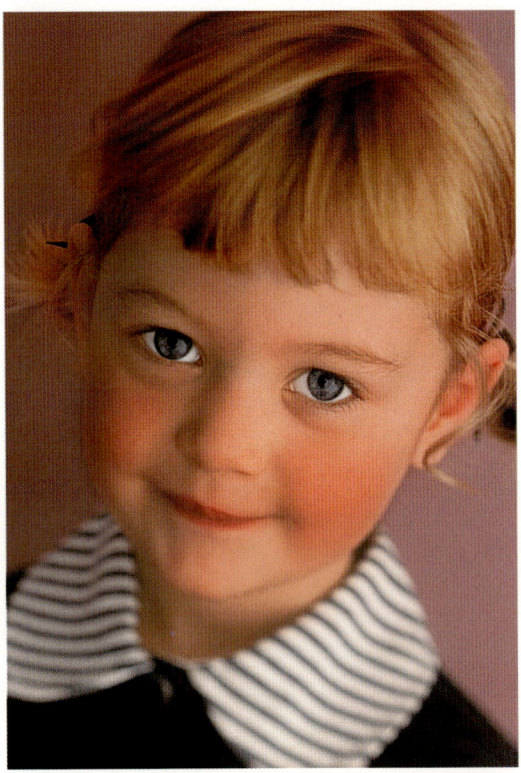

Kaplan

CAROL KAPLAN STUDIO INC ♦ BOSTON, MA 617·426·1131

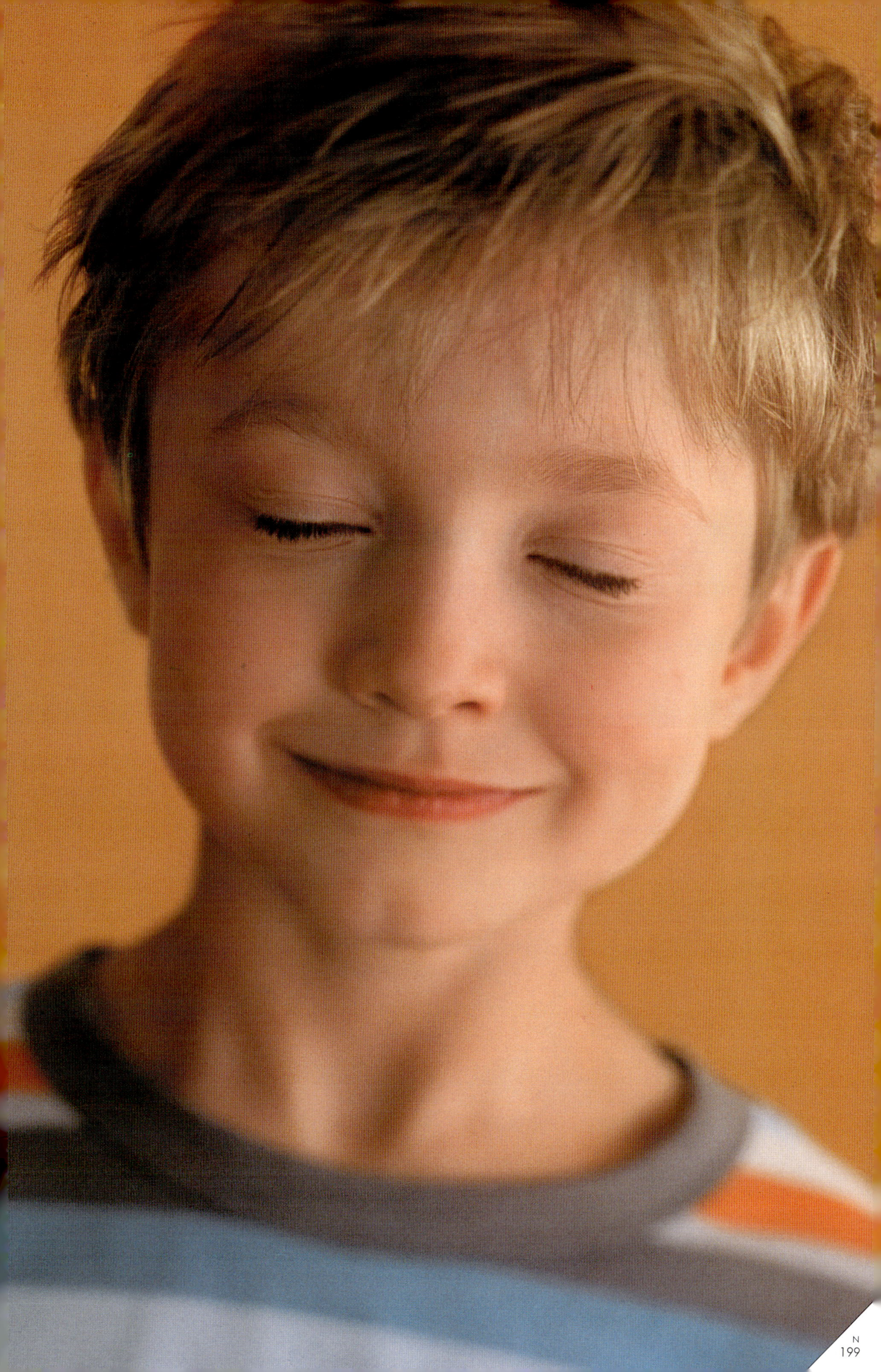

david bashaw studio
(212) 675 6313
davidbashaw.com

VOX
IMPORTED FROM
DISTILLED FIVE TIMES
VOX
FROM
ALCOHOL BY VOLUME (80 PROOF)

ROB HOWARD   REPRESENTED BY LISA HOWARD TEL 212/863-2340

N
203

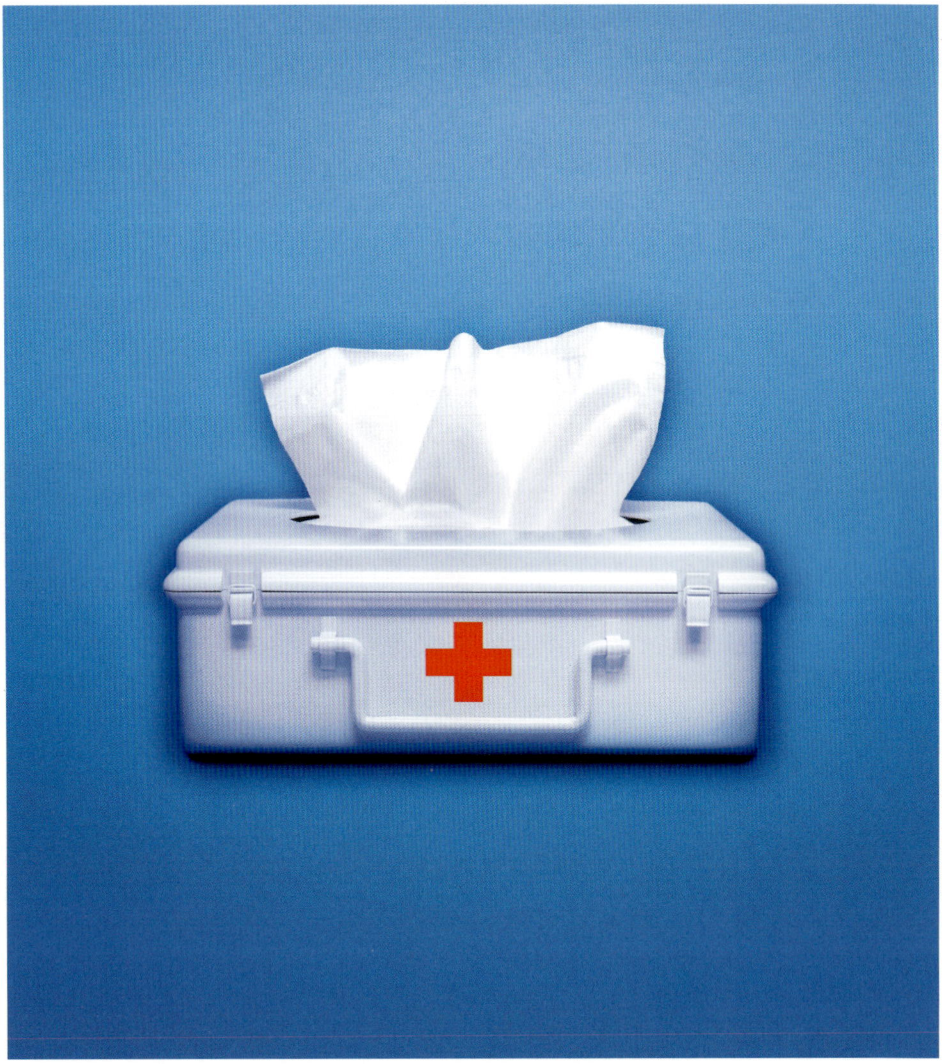

philip habib

AGENT **GREG SELLENTIN** T 212.736.0488   F 212.736.0032

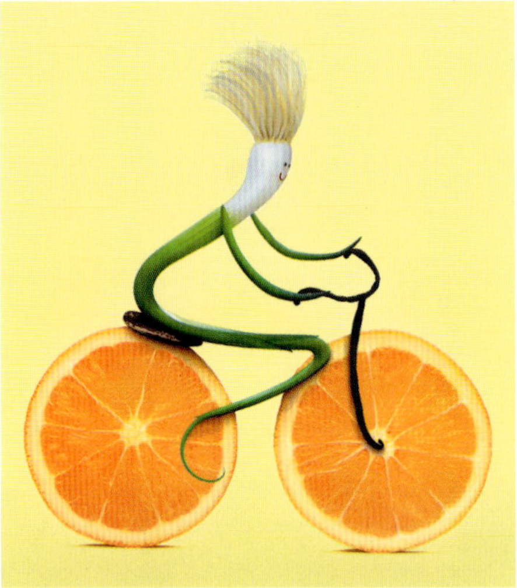

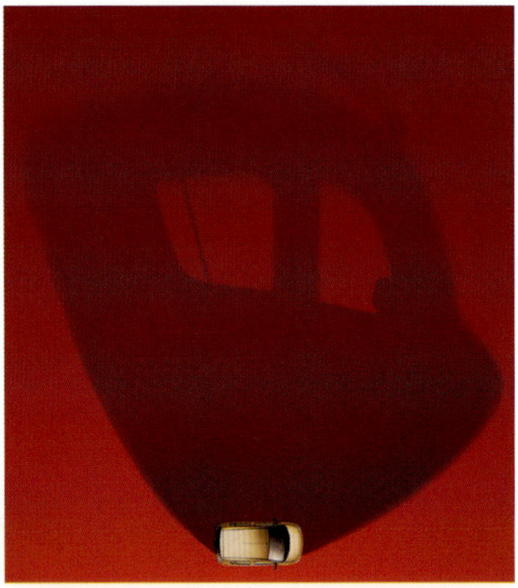

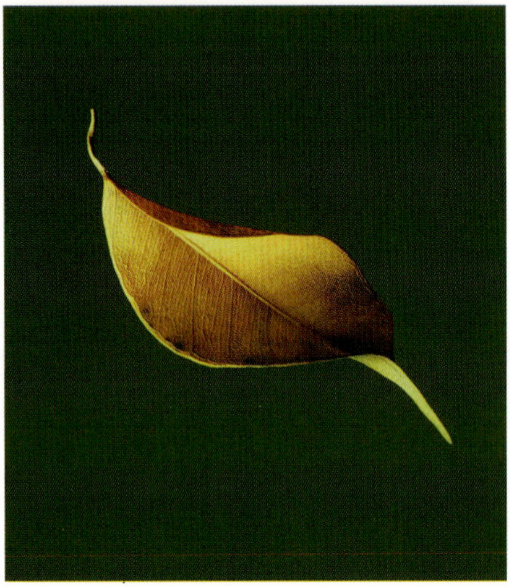

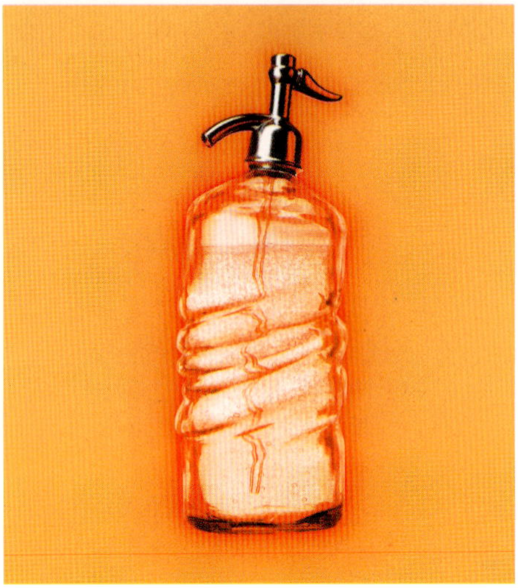

philip habib

AGENT **GREG SELLENTIN** T 212.736.0488   F 212.736.0032

"teenage sex talk" mastercard

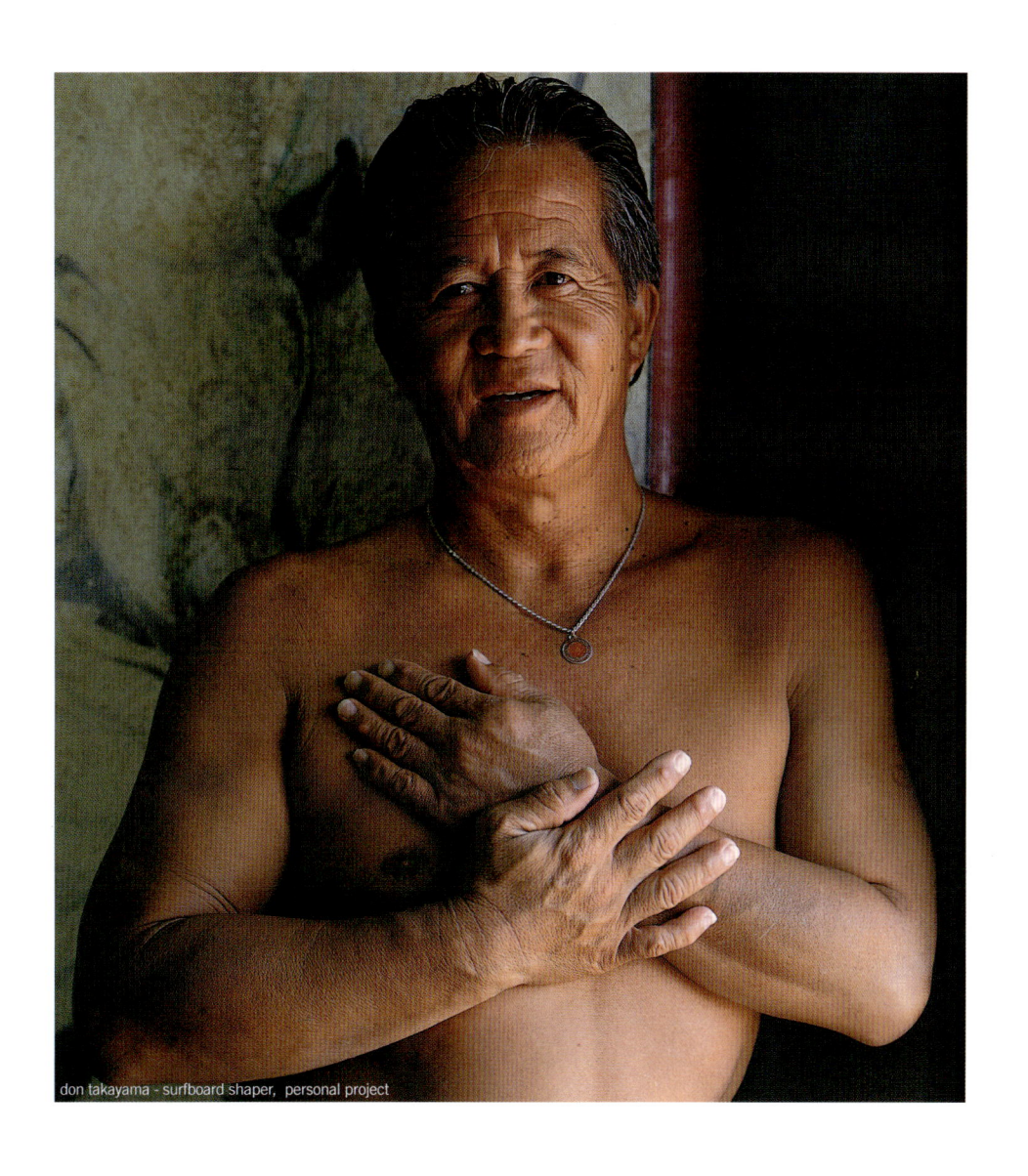

don takayama - surfboard shaper, personal project

karen kuehn

AGENT **GREG SELLENTIN** T 212.736.0488   F 212.736.0032

MICHAEL MAHOVLICH
PHOTOGRAPHY

REPRESENTED BY
Paola Giavedoni
1.416.588.0326
www.mmphotos.com
Now providing
digital services.

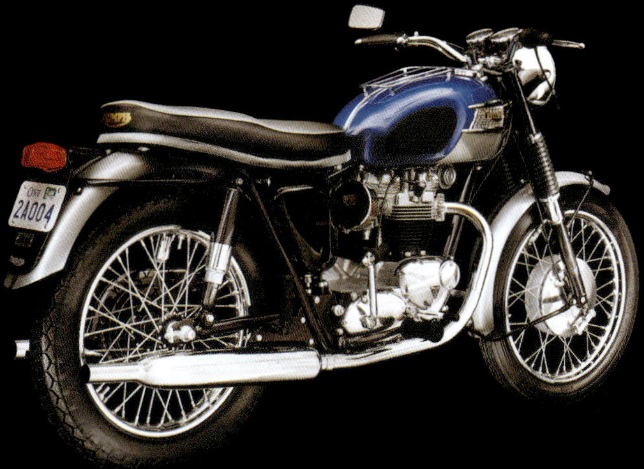

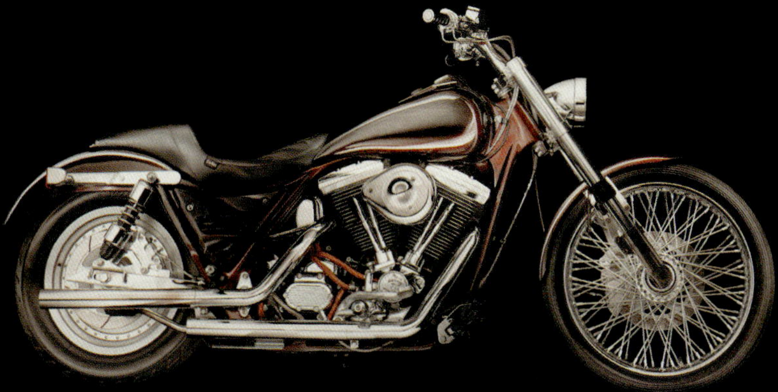

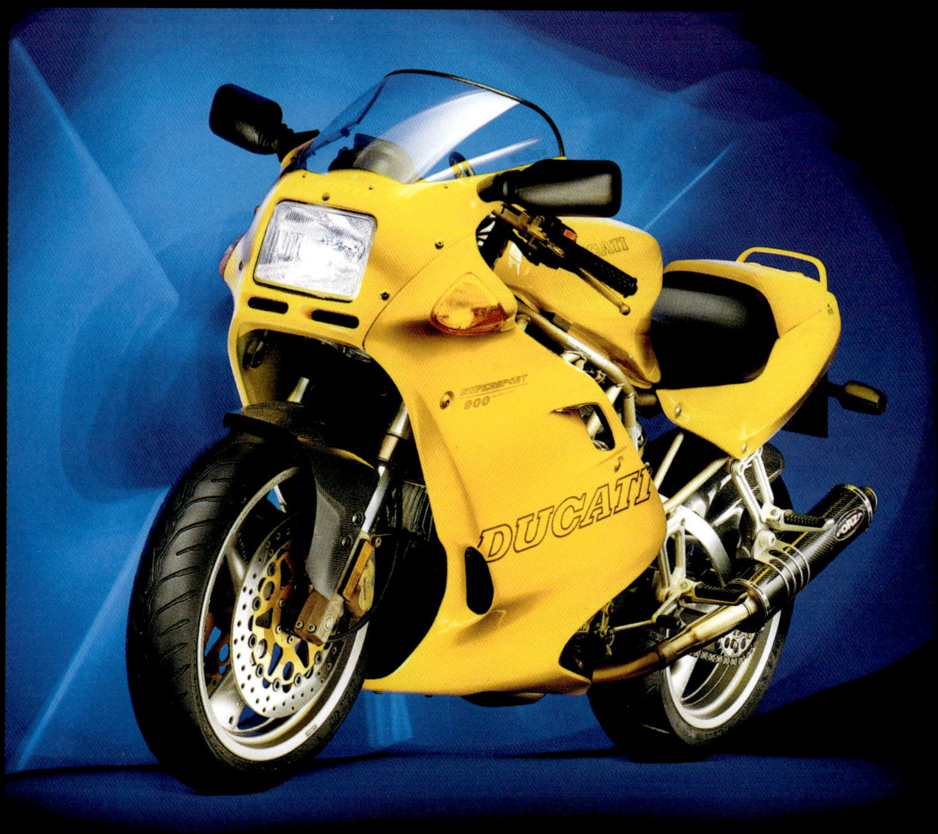
DUCATI

Elise

Elise Caputo & Associates represents

tel 212.725.0503 • fax 212.683.4673 • www.elisecaputo.com

uty, Fashion, Still Life — Jeffrey Apoian

hitecture, Corporate, People — Steve Gottlieb

d, Still Life — Robert Kent

nals, Kids, Still Life — Dennis Mosner

ion, Portraiture, Stories — John Rusnak

Jeffrey Apoian

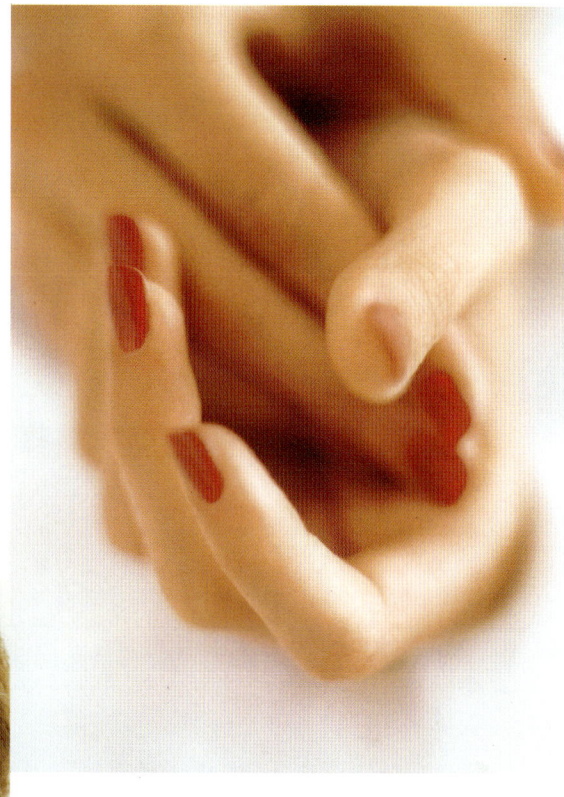

NYC Studio • 212.431.5513
www.jeffreyapoian.com • reel available
Represented by Elise Caputo • 212.725.0503

STEVE GOTTLIEB

800 453 3383 • www.gottliebphoto.com
Represented by Elise Caputo 212 725 0503

ROBERT KENT

NYC Studio • 212.290.5368
Represented by Elise Caputo • 212.725.0503

ROBERT KENT

NYC Studio • 212.290.5368
Represented by Elise Caputo • 212.725.0503

Dennis Mosner

37 West 37th Street, New York Tel 212.730.7180
Represented by Elise Caputo Tel 212.725.0503 Fax 212.683.4673

Dennis Mosner

37 West 37th Street, New York Tel 212.730.7180
Represented by Elise Caputo Tel 212.725.0503 Fax 212.683.4673

JOHN RUSNAK
NYC Studio • 212.861.0213
Represented by Elise Caputo • 212.725.0503

JOHN RUSNAK

NYC Studio • 212.861.0213
Represented by Elise Caputo • 212.725.0503

Desmond Burdon
www.dburdon.com
Represented by Judith McGrath 312 944 5116 - 212 569 1955

Desmond Burdon

Desmond Burdon
www.dburdon.com
Represented by Judith McGrath 312 944 5116 - 212 569 1955

dan couto   represented by orbit (416) 429-2840

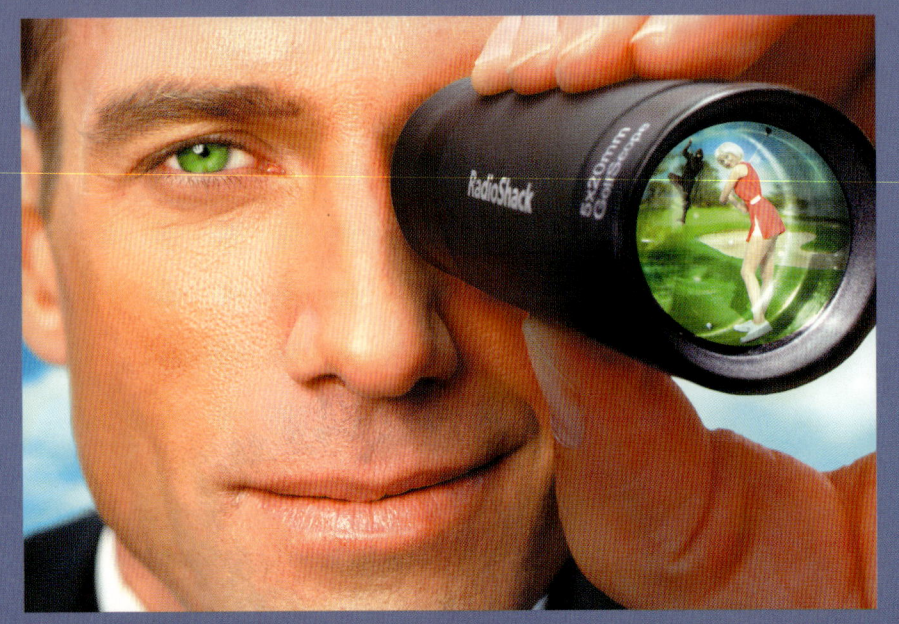

represented by orbit (416) 429-2840   couto dan

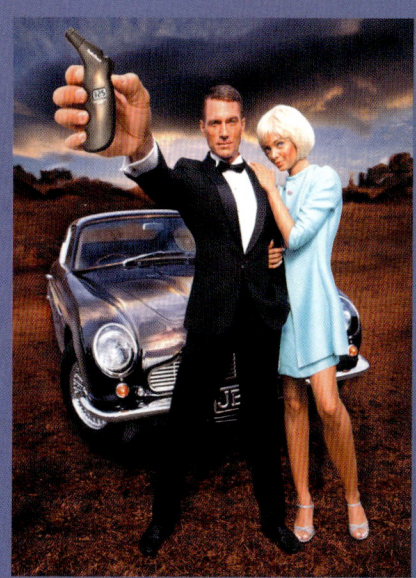

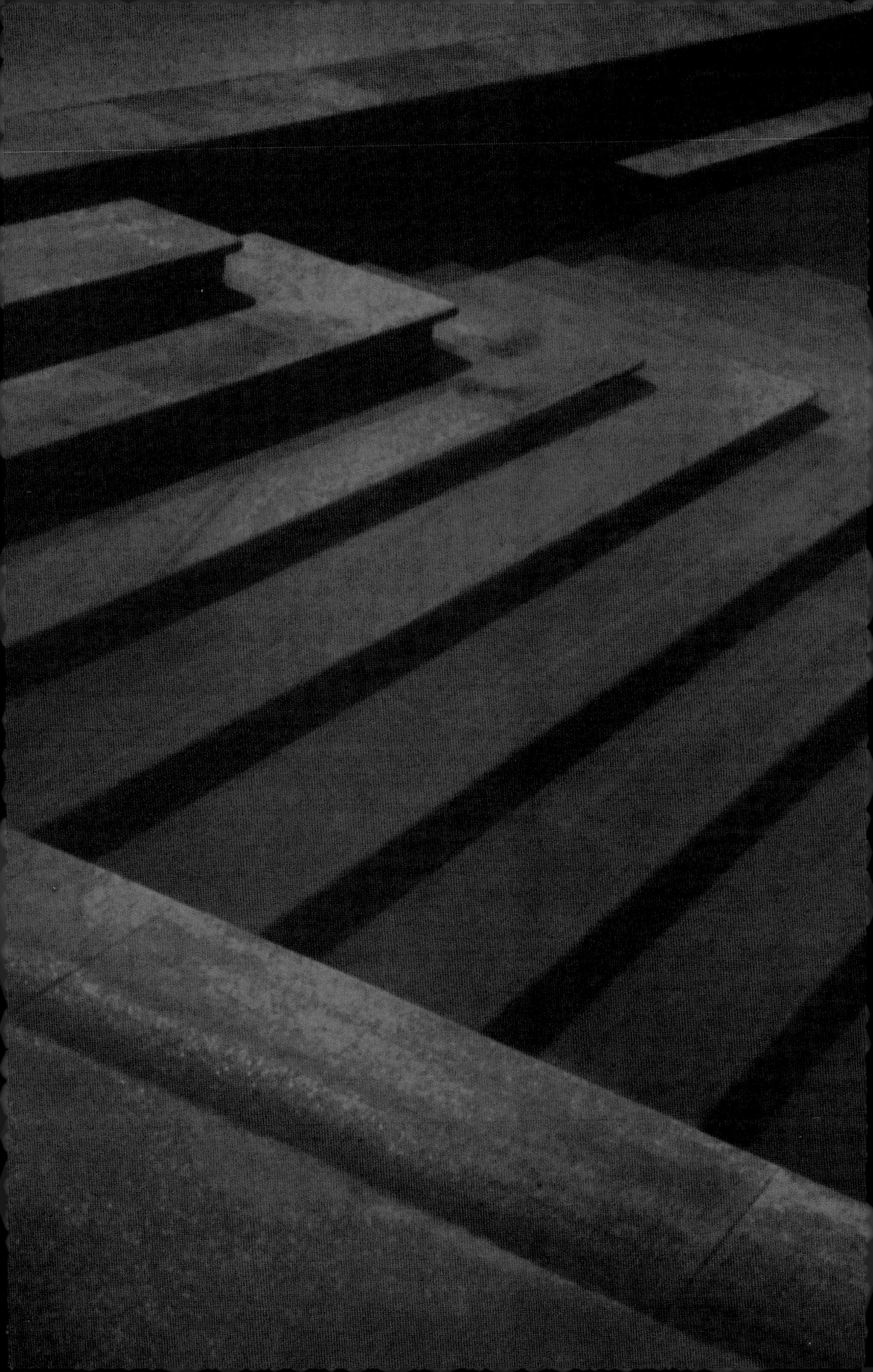

ROBIN DICTENBERG REPRESENTS
VINCENT DIXON JOHN HUET GRAHAM FORD MARK LAITA
348 WEST 11TH STREET APT 2B NEW YORK CITY 10014 T 212 620 0995 F 212 620 0128
ANDI FELLMAN GEORGE SIMHONI SIMON STOCK GRAHAM WESTMORELAND
PHOTOGRAPH JOHN HUET

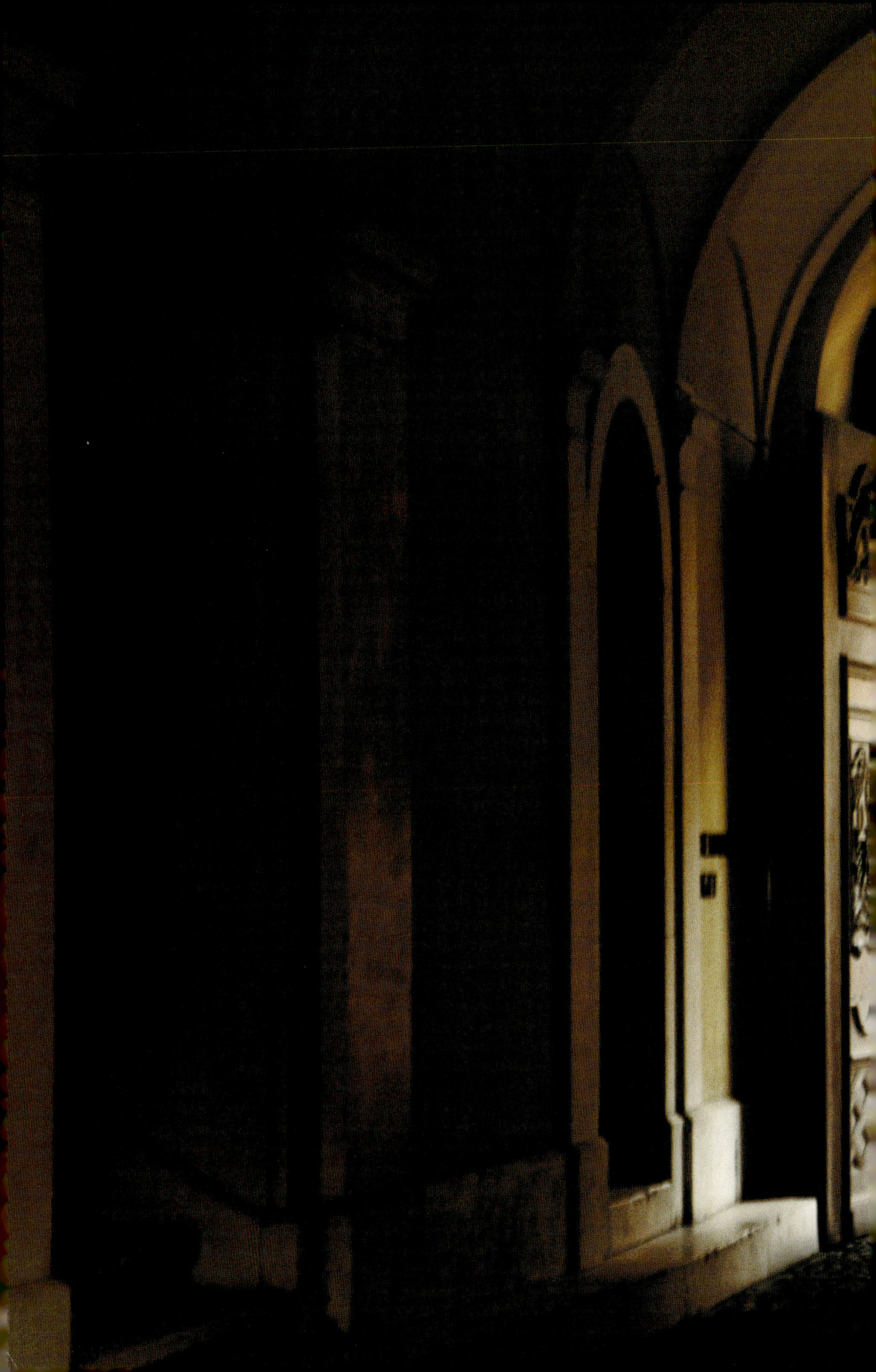

GEORGE SIMHONI
T 416 535 1955   WWW.WESTSIDESTUDIO.COM
REPRESENTED BY ROBIN DICTENBERG   1 212 620 0995 F 212 620 0128

VINCENT DIXON

REPRESENTED BY ROBIN DICTENBERG T 212 620 0995 F 212 620 0128

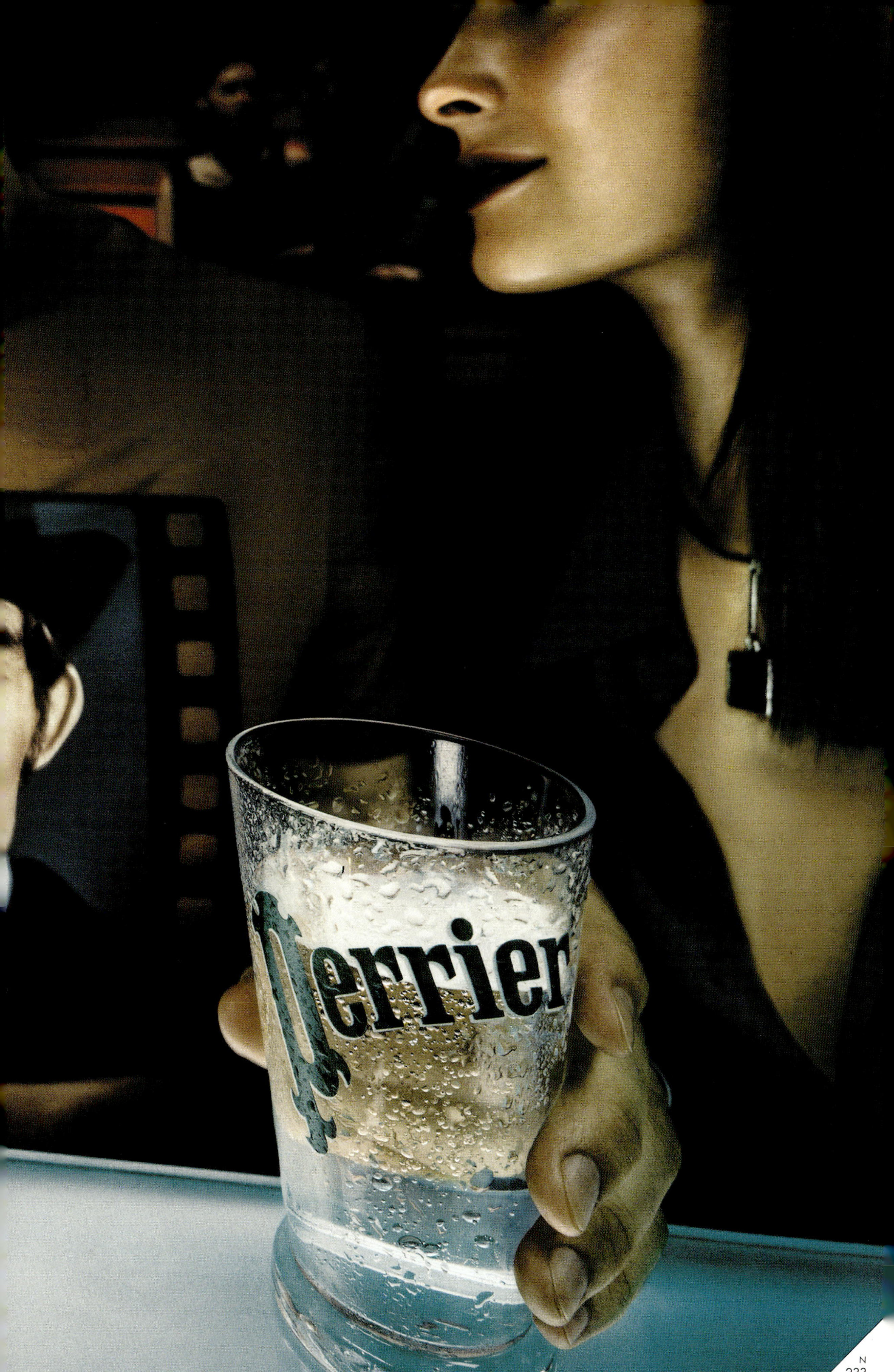
Perrier

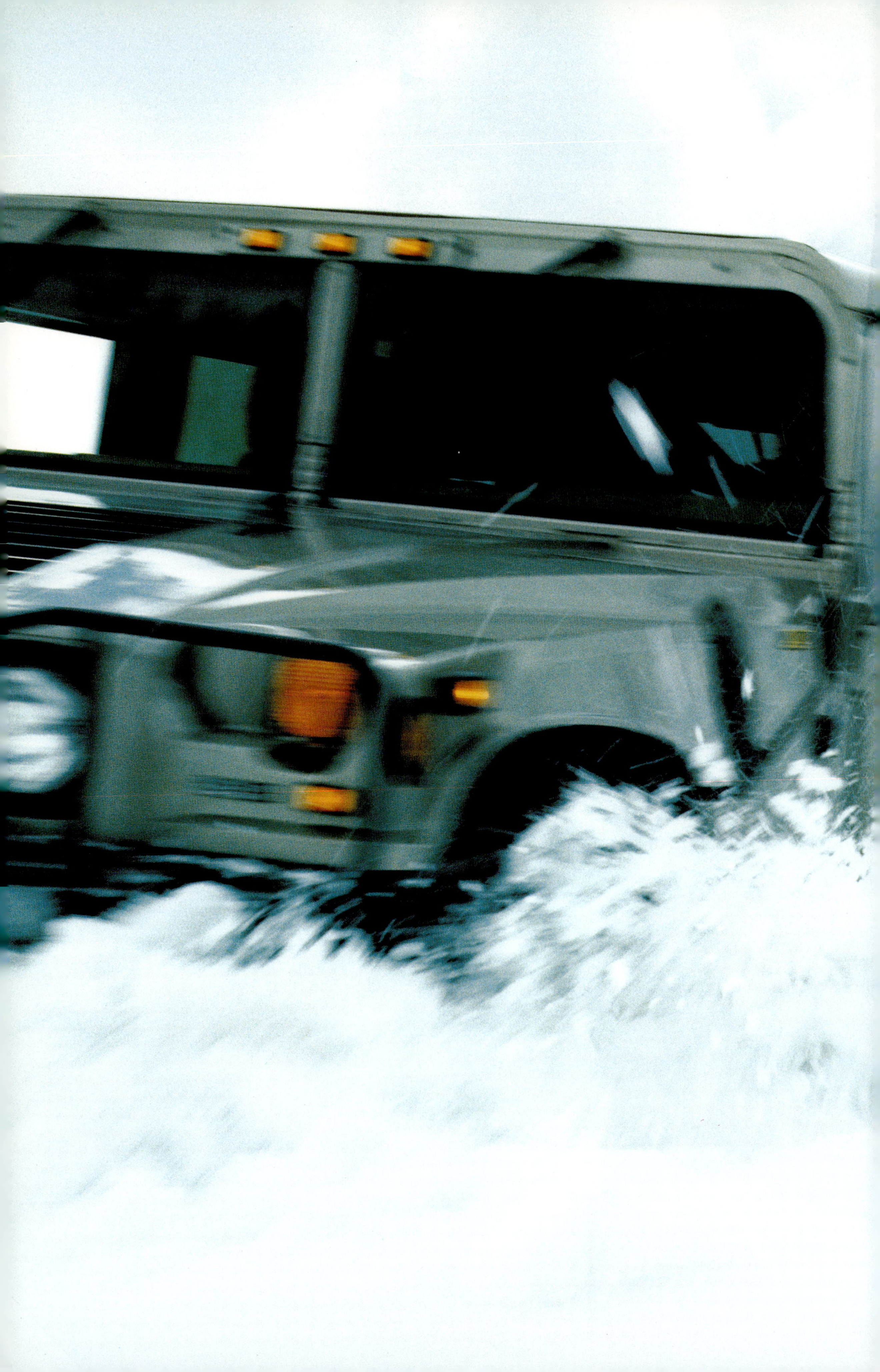

SIMON STOCK

REPRESENTED BY ROBIN DICTENBERG T 212 620 0995 F 212 620 0128

LAITA

mark laita photography   212 228 4880   NY robin dictenberg   212 620 0995   CHI jodie zeitler   312 222

LAITA mark laita photography   212 228 4880   NY robin dictenberg   212 620 0995   CHI jodie zeitler   312 222 0504

Graham Westmoreland Photography

WEST

Represented in America by Robin Dictenberg · tel. 212 620 0995, fax. 212 620 0128.

MORE

In London by Horton Stevens · tel. (44) 20 7582 0082, fax. (44) 20 7582 0001.

LAND

In Germany by Marion Enste Jaspers · tel. (40) 49 22 22 26, fax. (40) 49 22 10 62.

Agency FCB Worldwide Client Chrysler PT Cruiser

Art Directed by Tim Teegarden, Paul Szary and John Scully

Post Production by Saddington and Baynes London · tel. (44) 20 7833 3032.

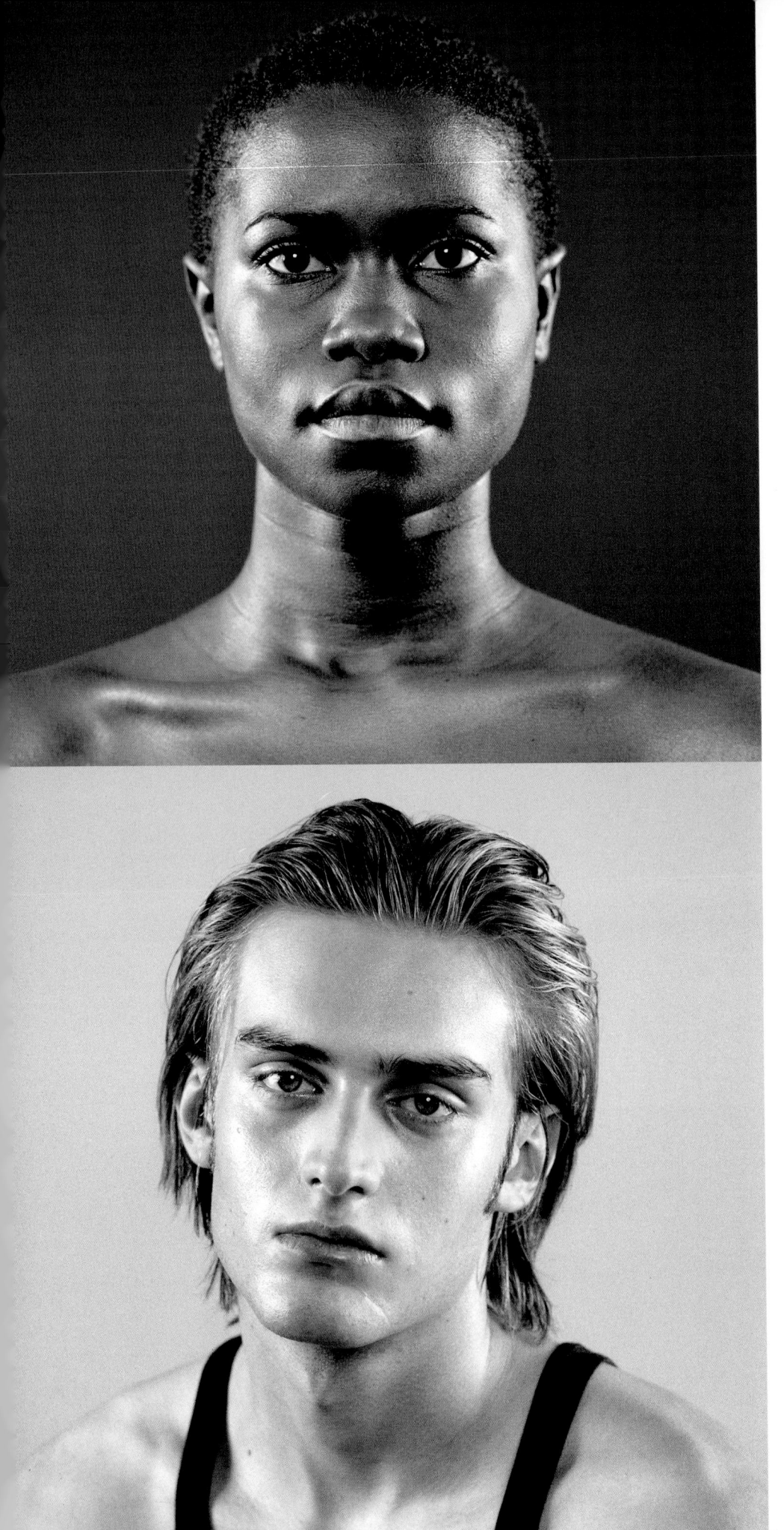

ALLAN PENN PHOTOGRAPHY TEL:617.423.1776 FAX:617.423.9257 WWW.ALLANPENN.COM

PENN

STEVE BELKOWITZ, PHOTOGRAPHER
PHILADELPHIA 215.629.1802   NEW YORK 212.719.9306

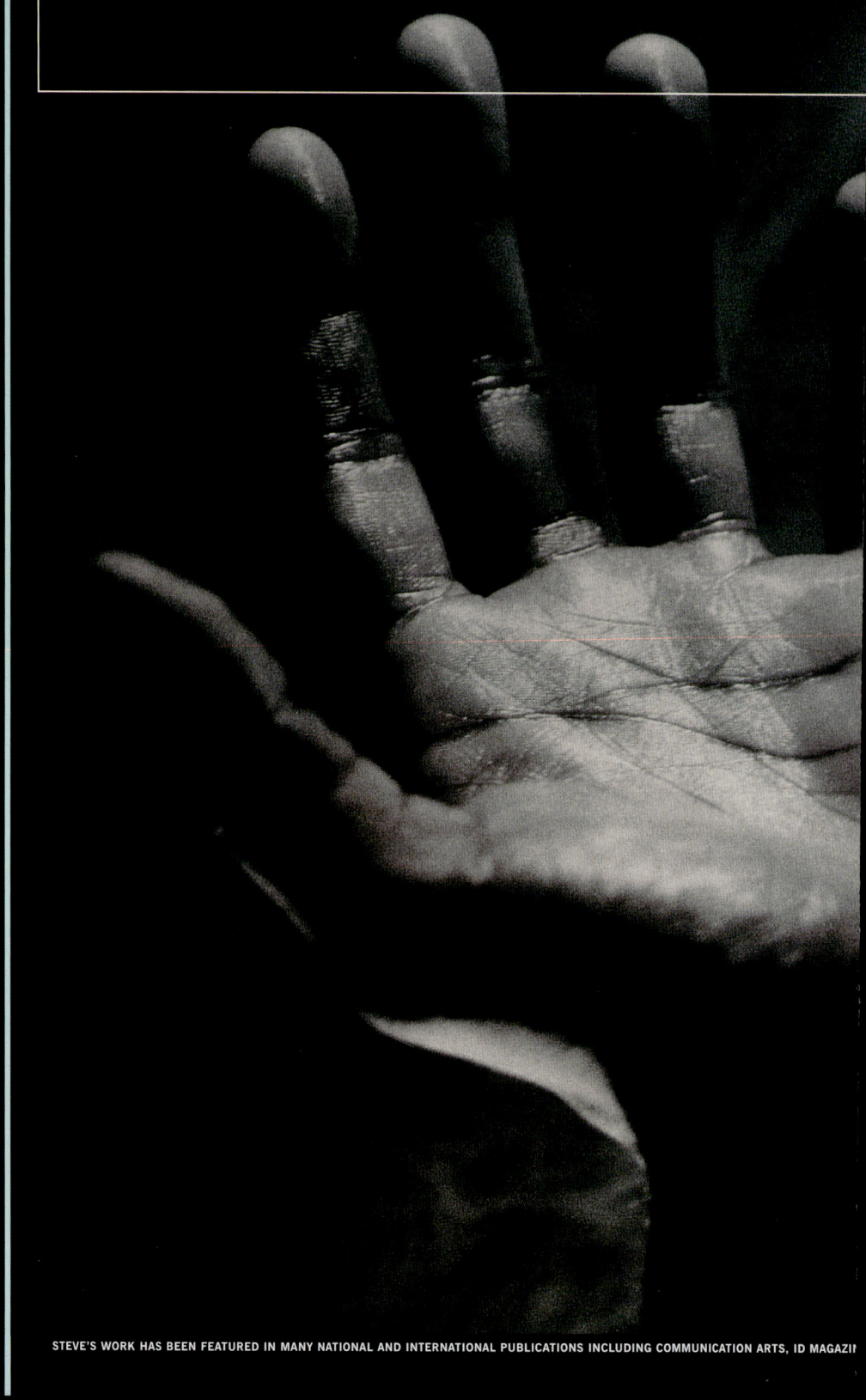

STEVE'S WORK HAS BEEN FEATURED IN MANY NATIONAL AND INTERNATIONAL PUBLICATIONS INCLUDING COMMUNICATION ARTS, ID MAGAZI

B"H

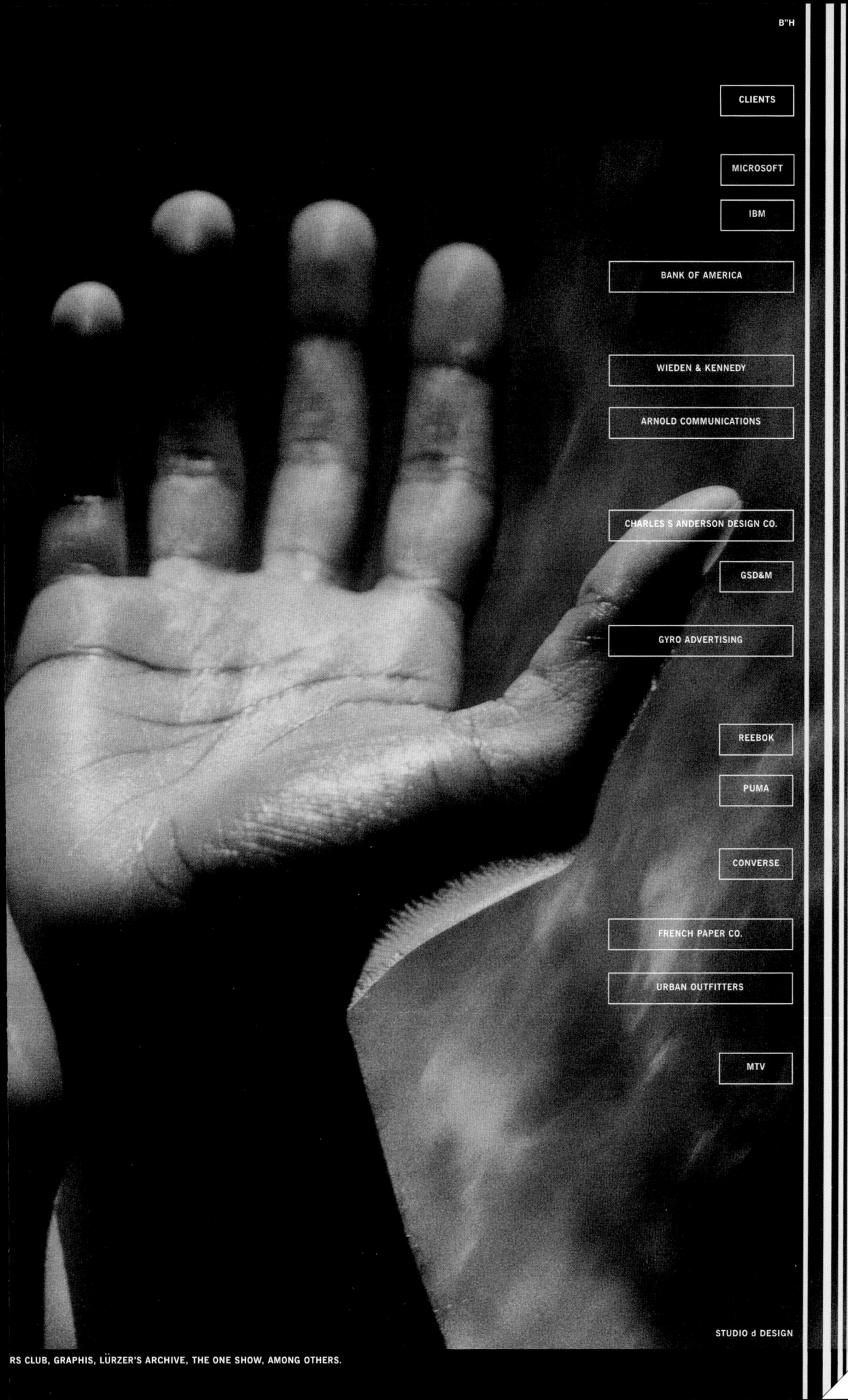

CLIENTS

MICROSOFT

IBM

BANK OF AMERICA

WIEDEN & KENNEDY

ARNOLD COMMUNICATIONS

CHARLES S ANDERSON DESIGN CO.

GSD&M

GYRO ADVERTISING

REEBOK

PUMA

CONVERSE

FRENCH PAPER CO.

URBAN OUTFITTERS

MTV

STUDIO d DESIGN

RS CLUB, GRAPHIS, LÜRZER'S ARCHIVE, THE ONE SHOW, AMONG OTHERS.

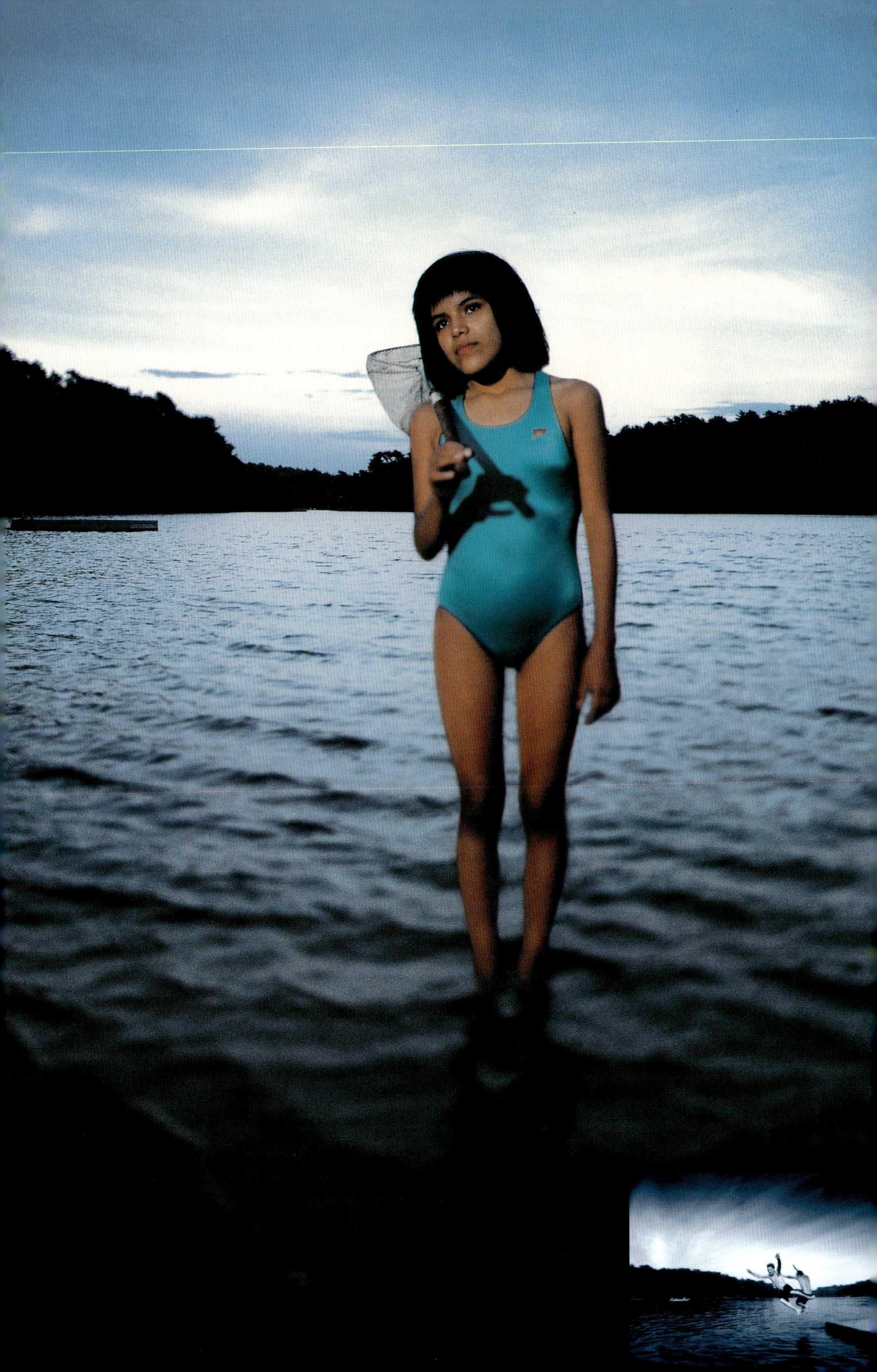

BOSTON
PICTURE
GROUP, INC.
BOSTON
MA

CRAWFORD@SHORE.NET
WWW.MCRAWFORDSAMUELSON.COM
617.524.0003

MARNIE CRAWFORD SAMUELSON

fabrizio

CACCIATORE

617.331.5340

www.cacciaphoto.com

robert **bacall**
representative

rBr

robert bacall
representative
212.695.1729
rob@bacall.com
www.bacall.com

COLIN COOKE

REPRESENTED BY ROBERT BACA[LL]
212.695.172
WWW.BACALL.COM/COL

food stylist: Nir Ada

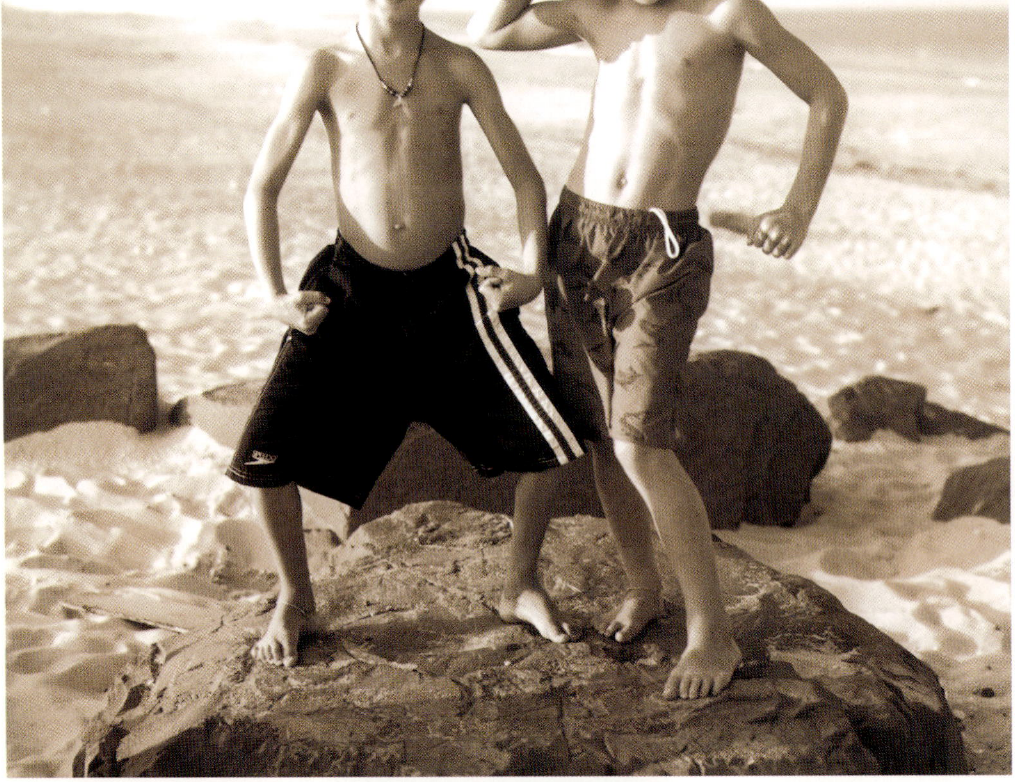
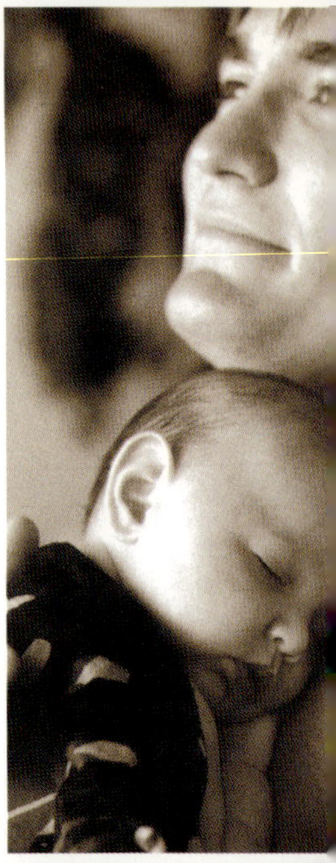
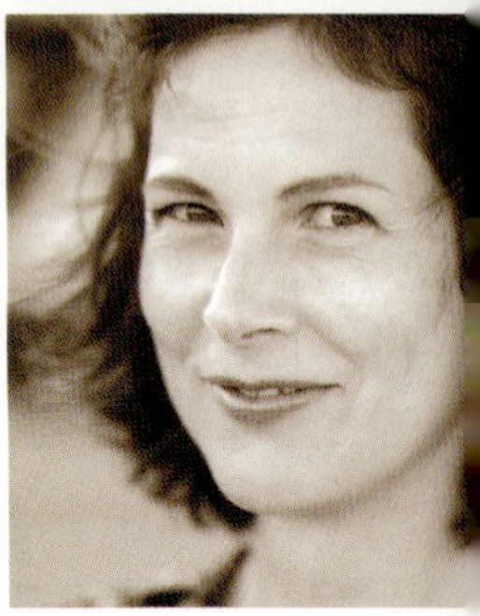
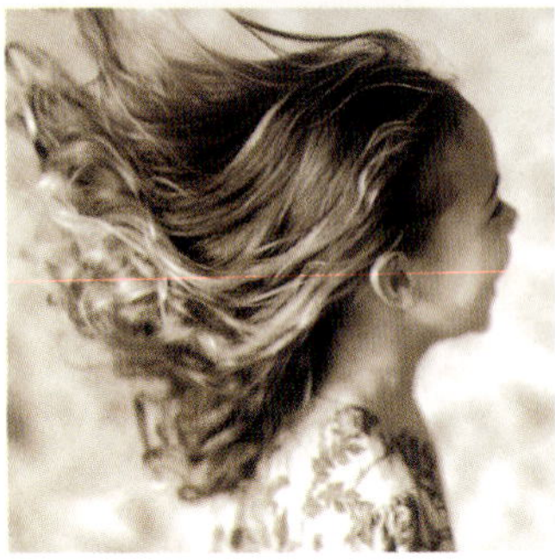
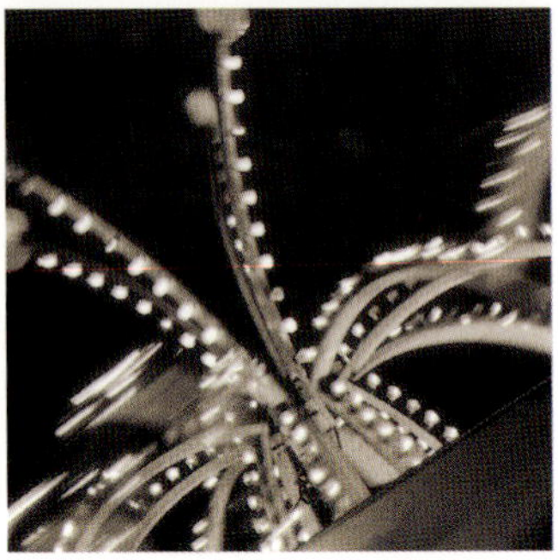
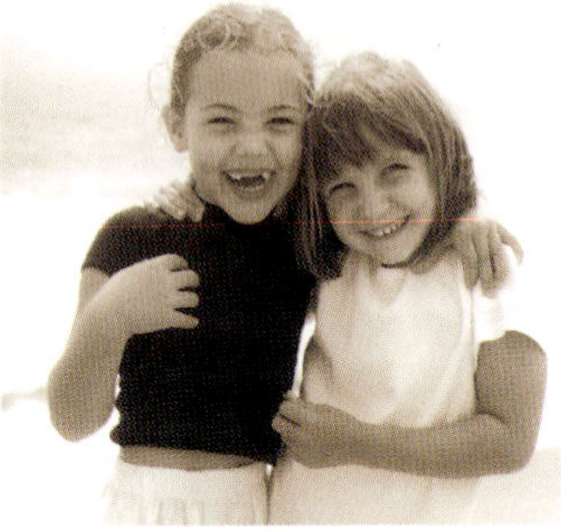
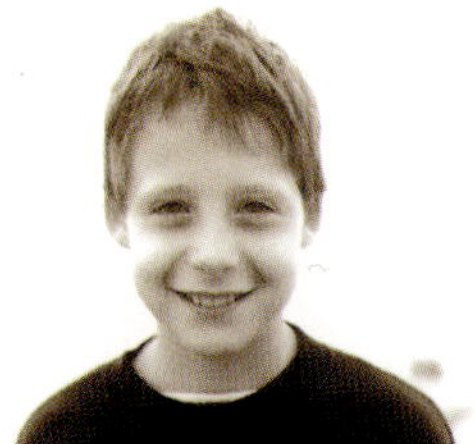
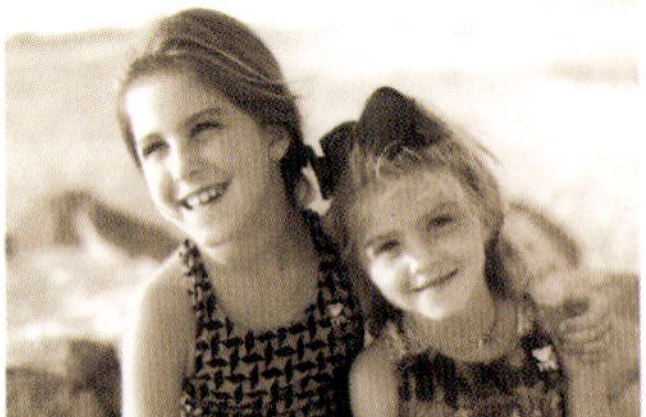
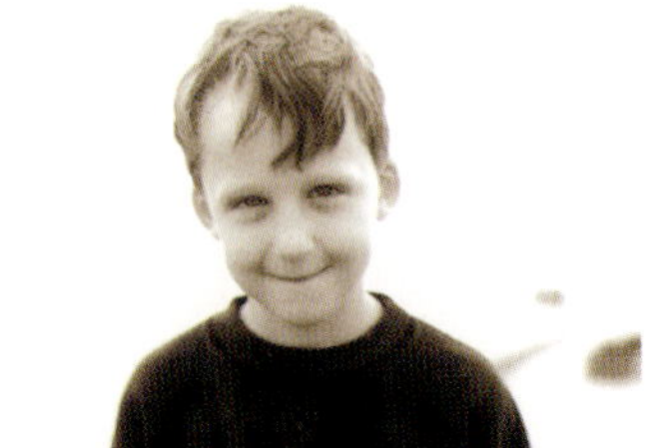
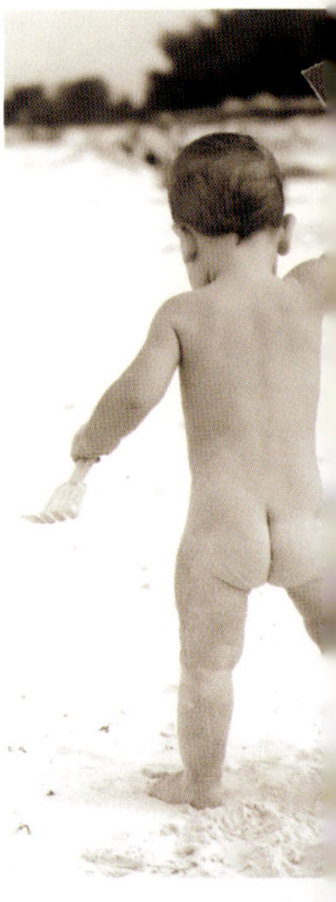
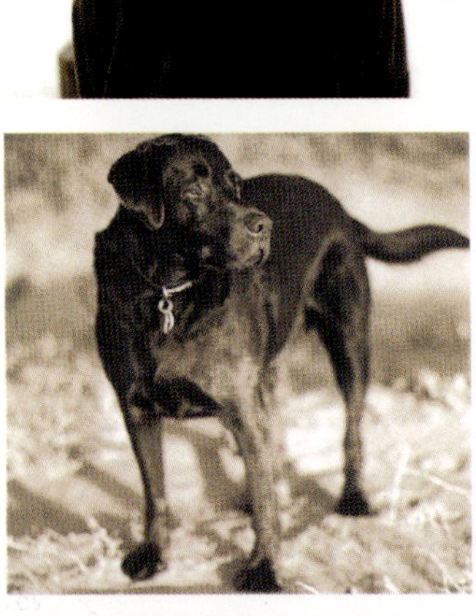
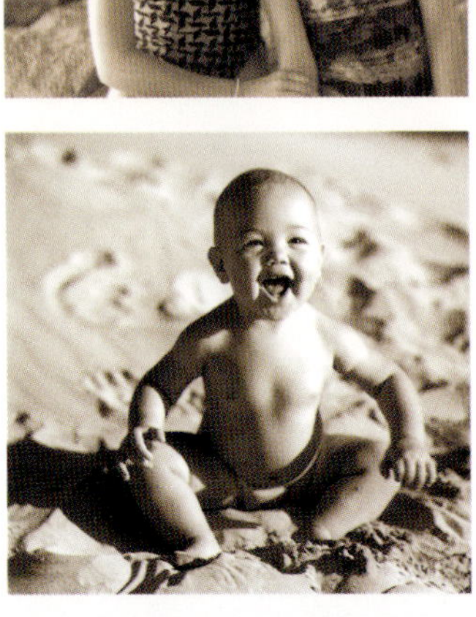
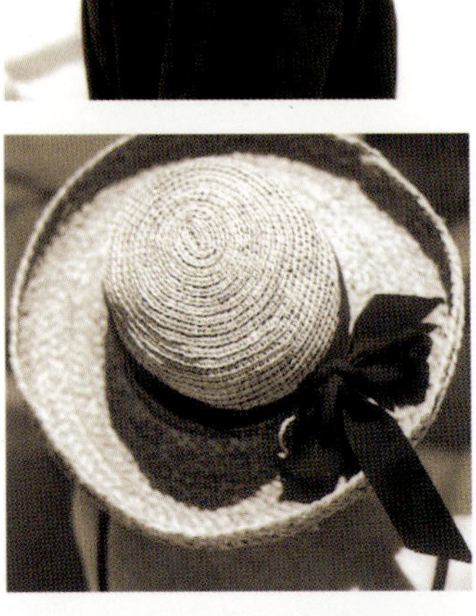

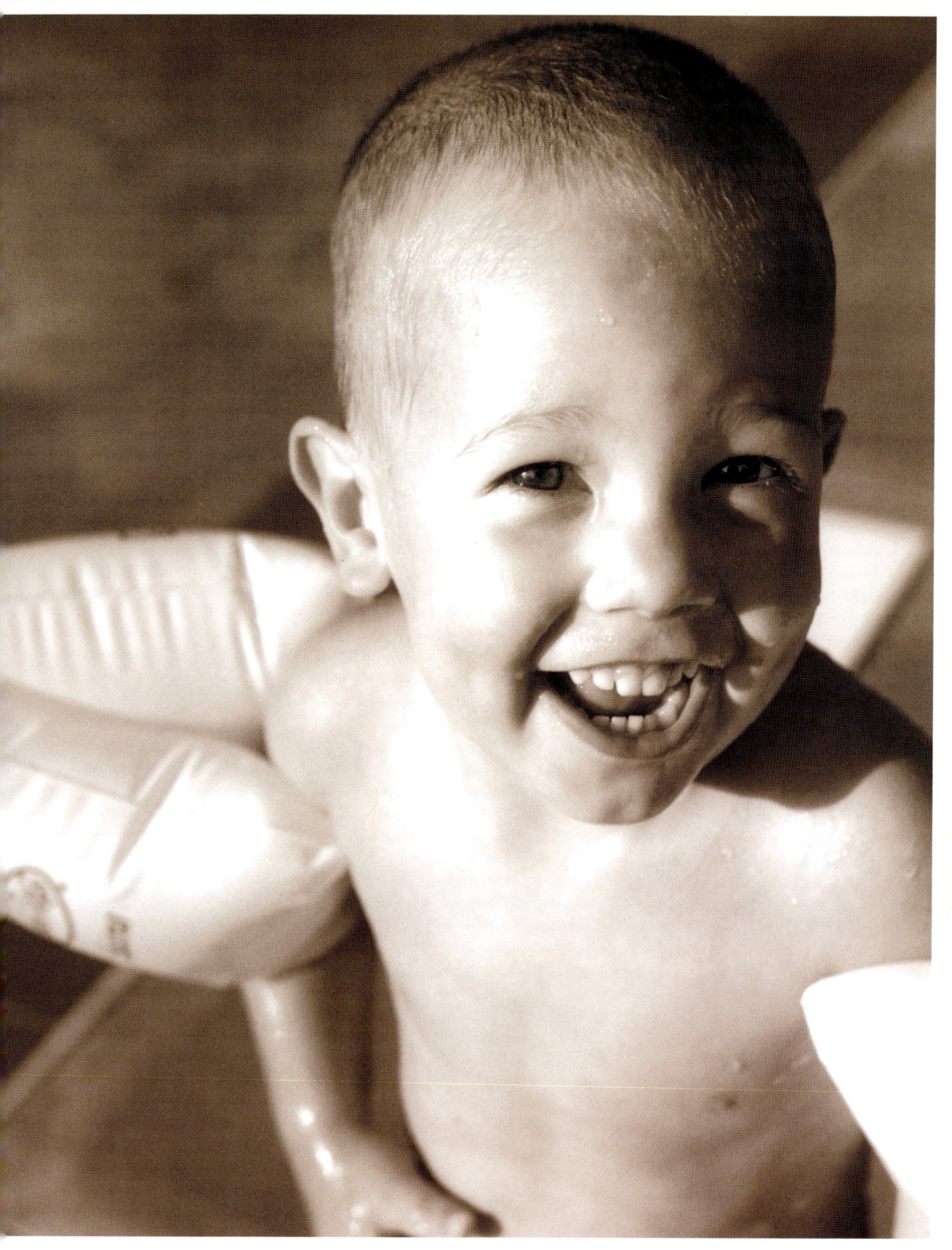

Ross Whitaker

212) 279-2600   www.rosswhitaker.com   Rep. Robert Bacall (212) 695-1729

britt lundquist

rBr | robert bacall
representative
212.695.1729
rob@bacall.com
www.bacall.com

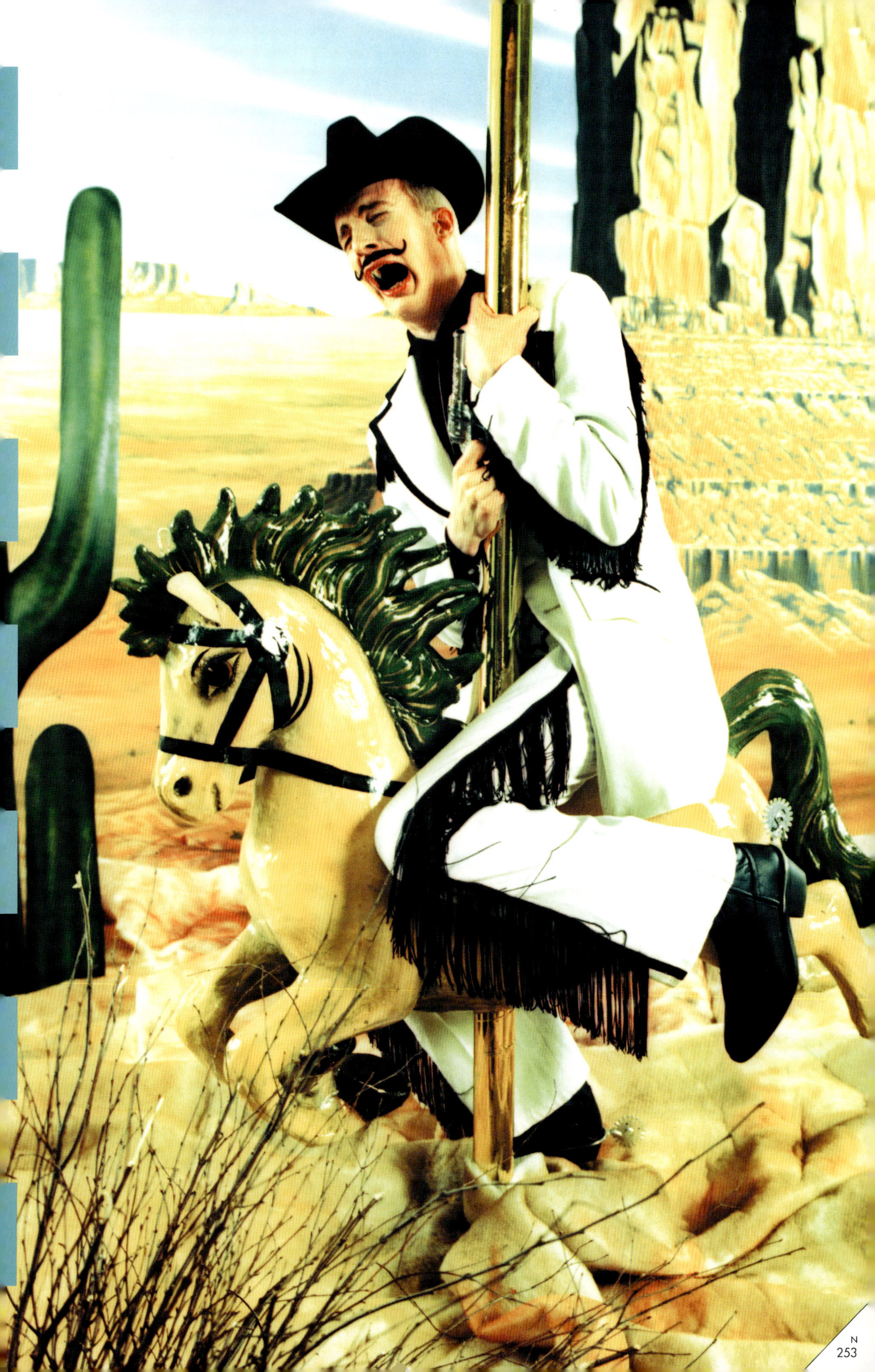

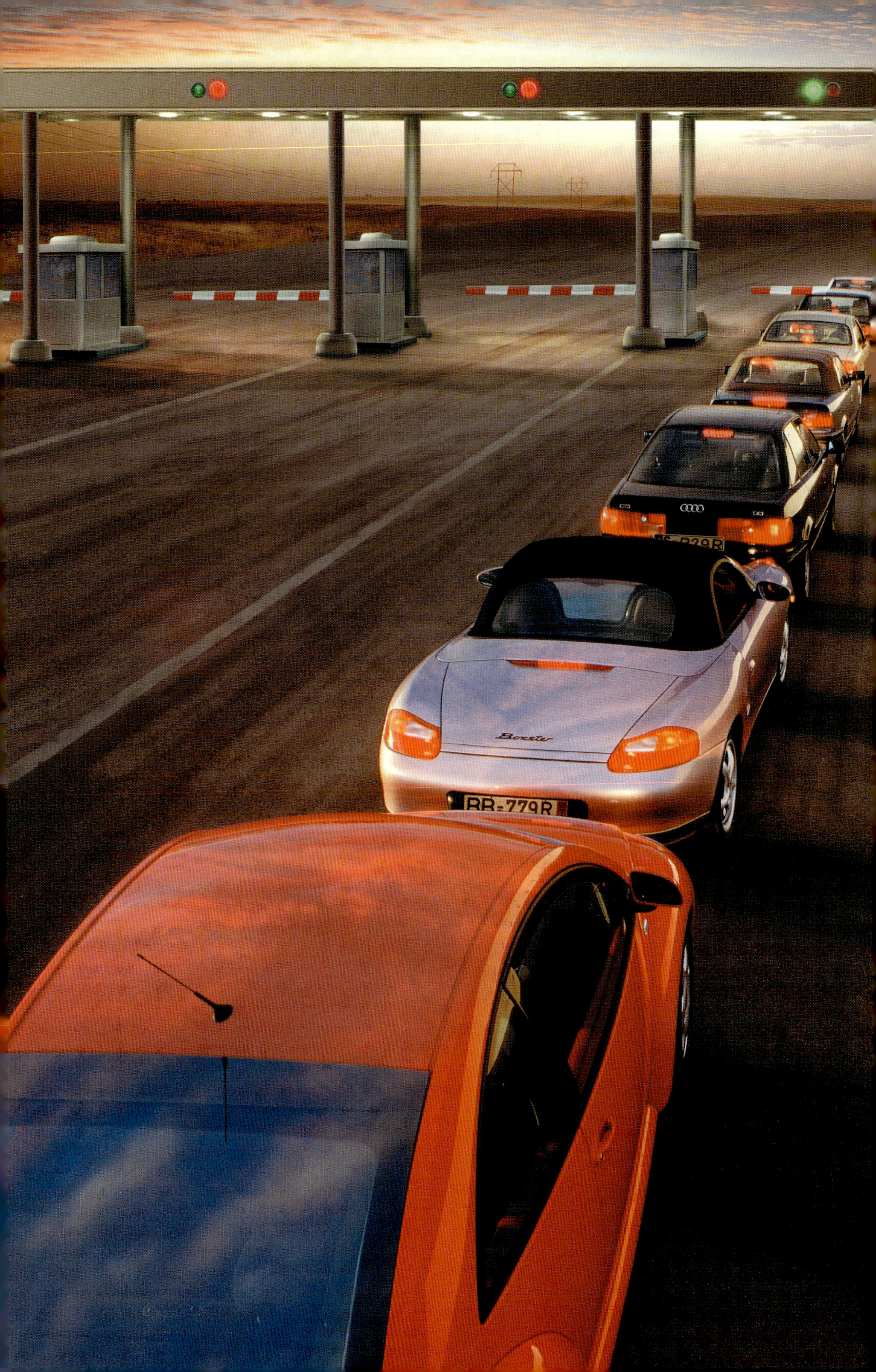
Boxster
BB-779R

MICHAEL SCHOENFELD

rBr | robert bacall
representative
212.695.1729
rob@bacall.com
www.bacall.com

what's your favorite possession?

Lou Bōpp   NYC 212.598.1170   St. Louis 314.962.6769   bopp@loubopp.com   www.loubopp.com

Lou Bōpp NYC 212.598.1170 St. Louis 314.962.6769 bopp@loubopp.com www.loubopp.com

Lawyer

Michael Indresano Photography • 617.269.2400 • www.indresano.com

r Garciaparra

BILL WHITE

628 Broadway
Suite 302
New York, NY 10012

T: 212 533.4195
F: 212 533.4465

Oh Oh!

SWINGS BOTH WAYS

MIXING IS FUN!

imix.com

BEWARE: BLUE MOON'S SMOOTHNESS MAY FOOL YOU

The PT Cruiser ranges in price from $16,000 to $19,995.* For info, call 1.800.CHRYSLER or visit www.chrysler.com.
CHRYSLER
ENGINEERED TO BE GREAT CARS

The PT Cruiser ranges in price from $16,000 to $19,995.* For info, call 1.800.CHRYSLER or visit www.chrysler.com.
CHRYSLER

BAILEY

ADVERTISING PHOTOGRAPHY : STUDIO & LOCATION

AGENCY: BARKER RAISTON, LONDON. CLIENT: SAAB. AD: JULIAN SCOTT.

Steve THOMPSON

Represented by
SUSAN MILLER, JENNIFER MIN
212.427.9600

LONDON Steve Thompson +44 20 8298 1950
MIDWEST Judy McGrath 312.944.5116
WEST K. Ray 310.453.0053

AGENCY: J. WALTER THOMPSON. **CLIENT:** SHELL OIL. **AD:** CANDY PETERSON.

AGENCY: J. WALTER THOMPSON. **CLIENT:** SHELL OIL. **AD:** CANDY PETERSON.

AGENCY: J. WALTER THOMPSON. **CLIENT:** SHELL OIL. **AD:** CANDY PETERSON.

PHOTOGRAPHER **PALMA KOLANSKY** 212-727-73
18 WEST 23rd STREET NY NY 10010 PALMAKOLANSKY.CO

OTOGRAPHER **PALMA KOLANSKY** 212-727-7300
WEST 23RD STREET NY NY 10010   PALMAKOLANSKY.COM

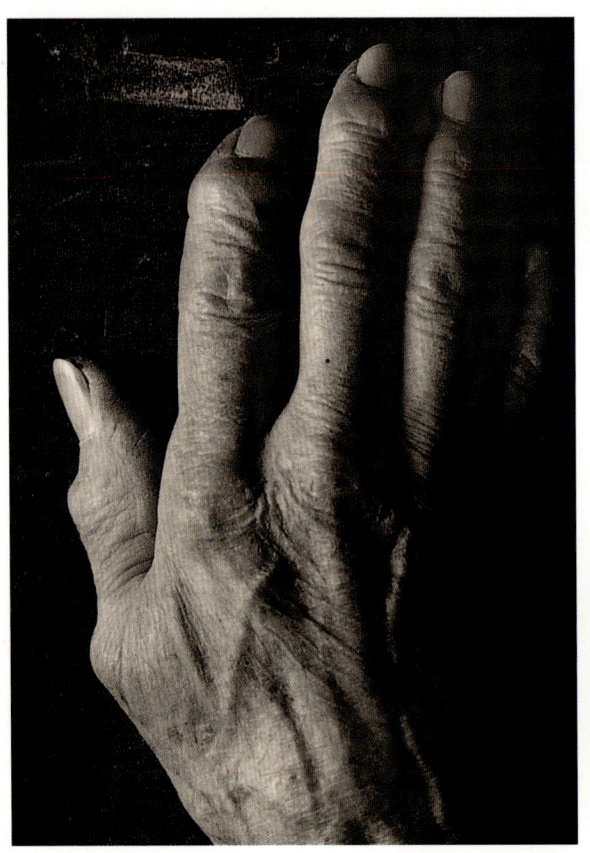

Doug Mindell

617.951.0077 dougmindell.com

Doug Mindell

617.951.0077 dougmindell.com

B

studio 212 242 3099

BENTON COLLINS

www.bentoncollins.com

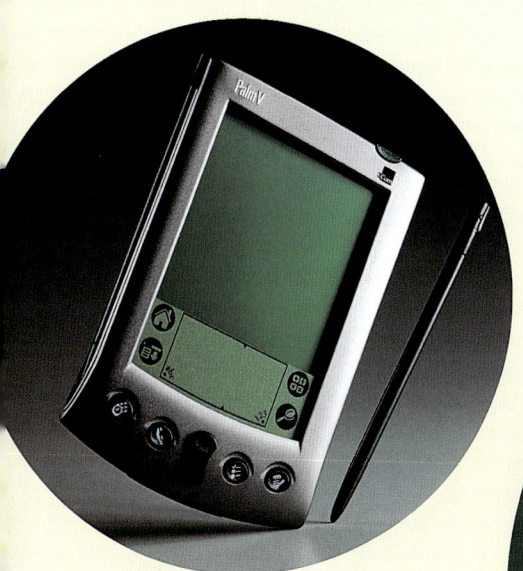

Represented by Lauren Elvers
212 924 9211

R
ron Fehling

represented by
Anne Desrochers

telephone 416.538.9183   fax 416.534.0430   studio 416.962.7795

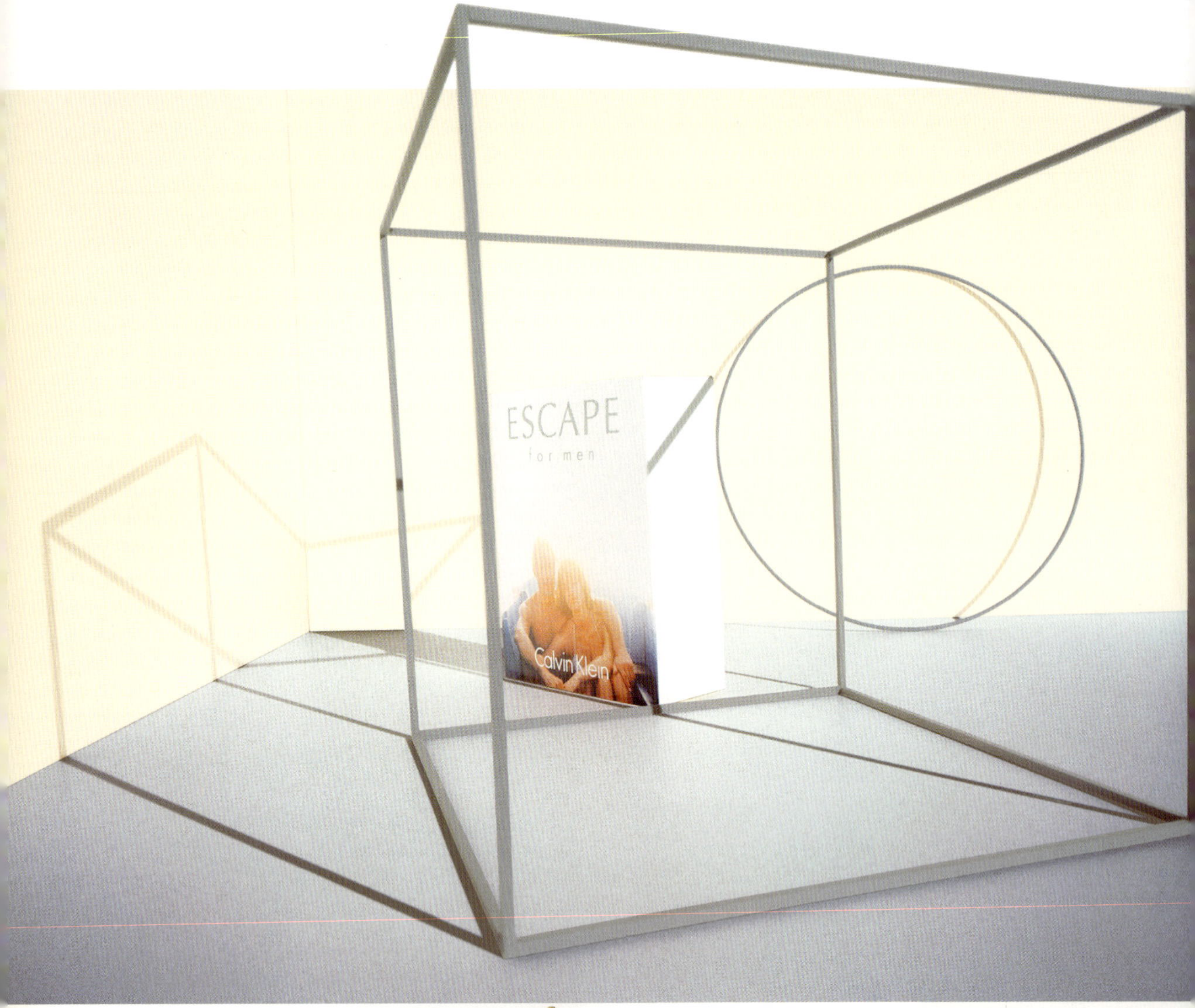

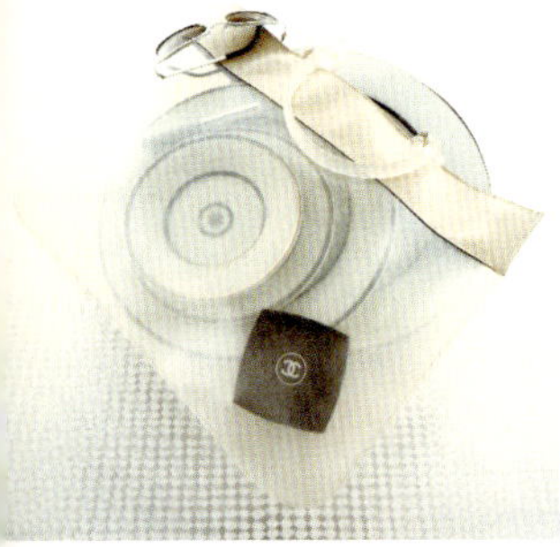

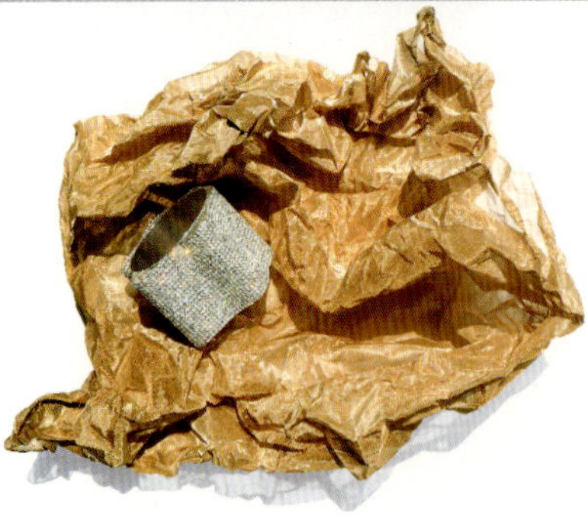

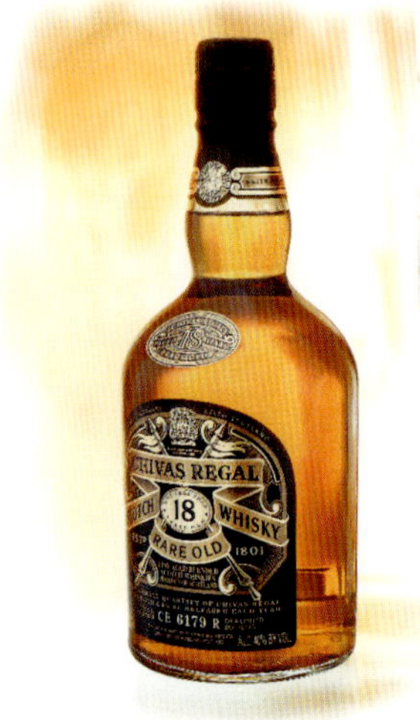

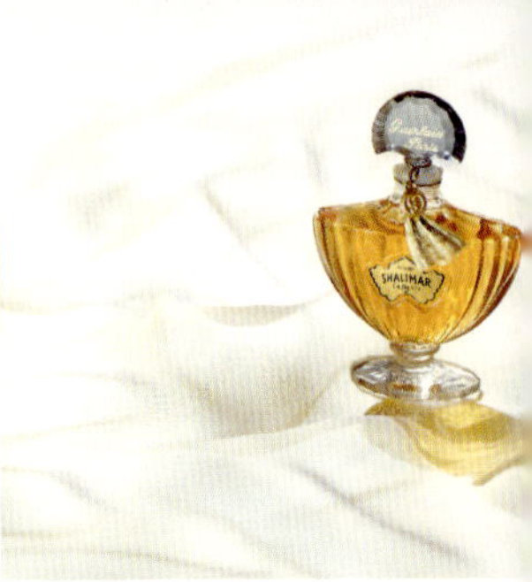

Grant Peterson

BILL CHARLES INC.
ARTIST REPRESENTATIVES
TEL 212.965.1465   FAX 212.965.9235
WWW.BILLCHARLES.COM

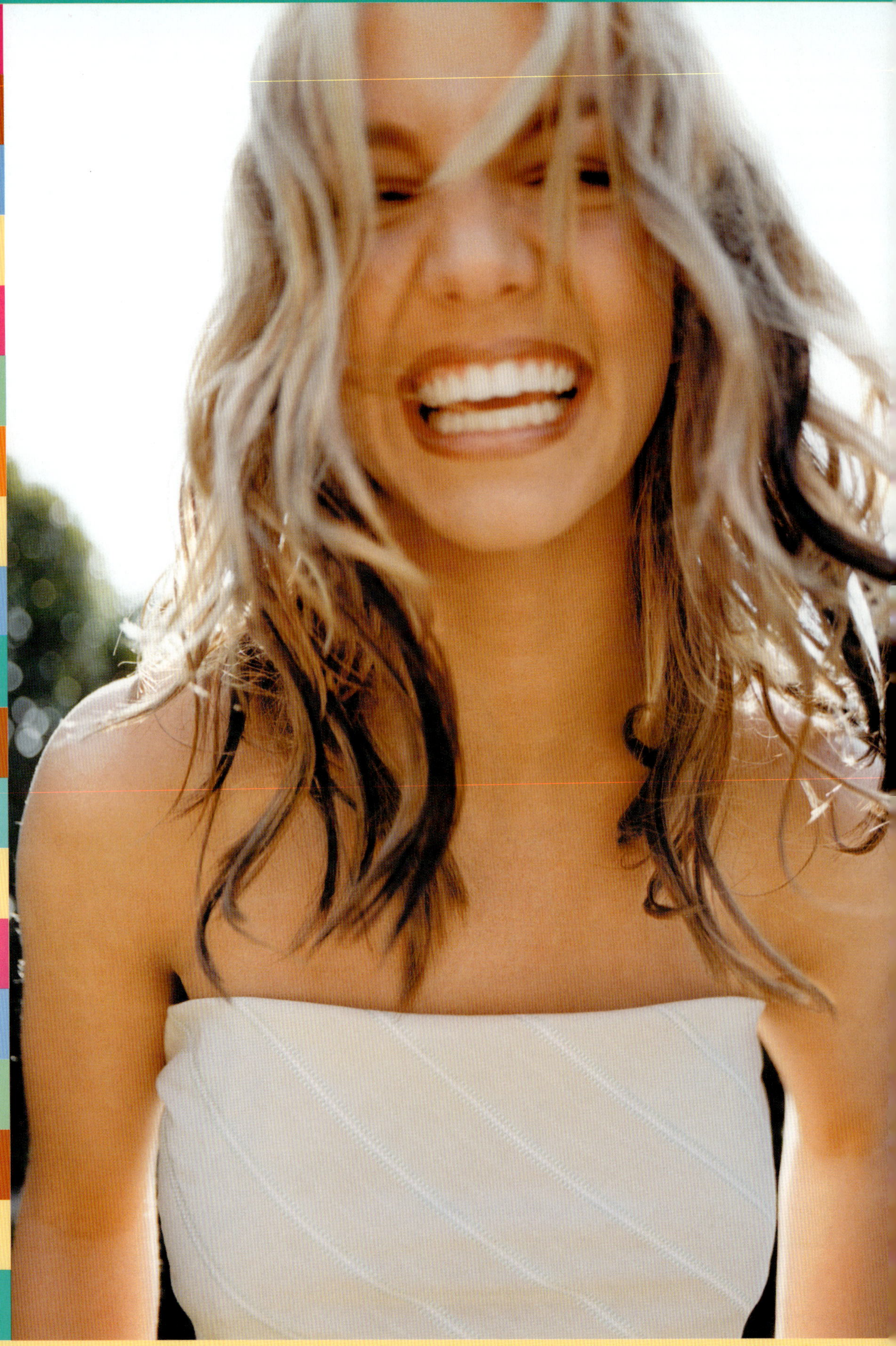

Jon Ragel

BILL CHARLES INC. Artist Representatives
tel   212.965.1465   fax   212.965.9235
www.billcharles.com

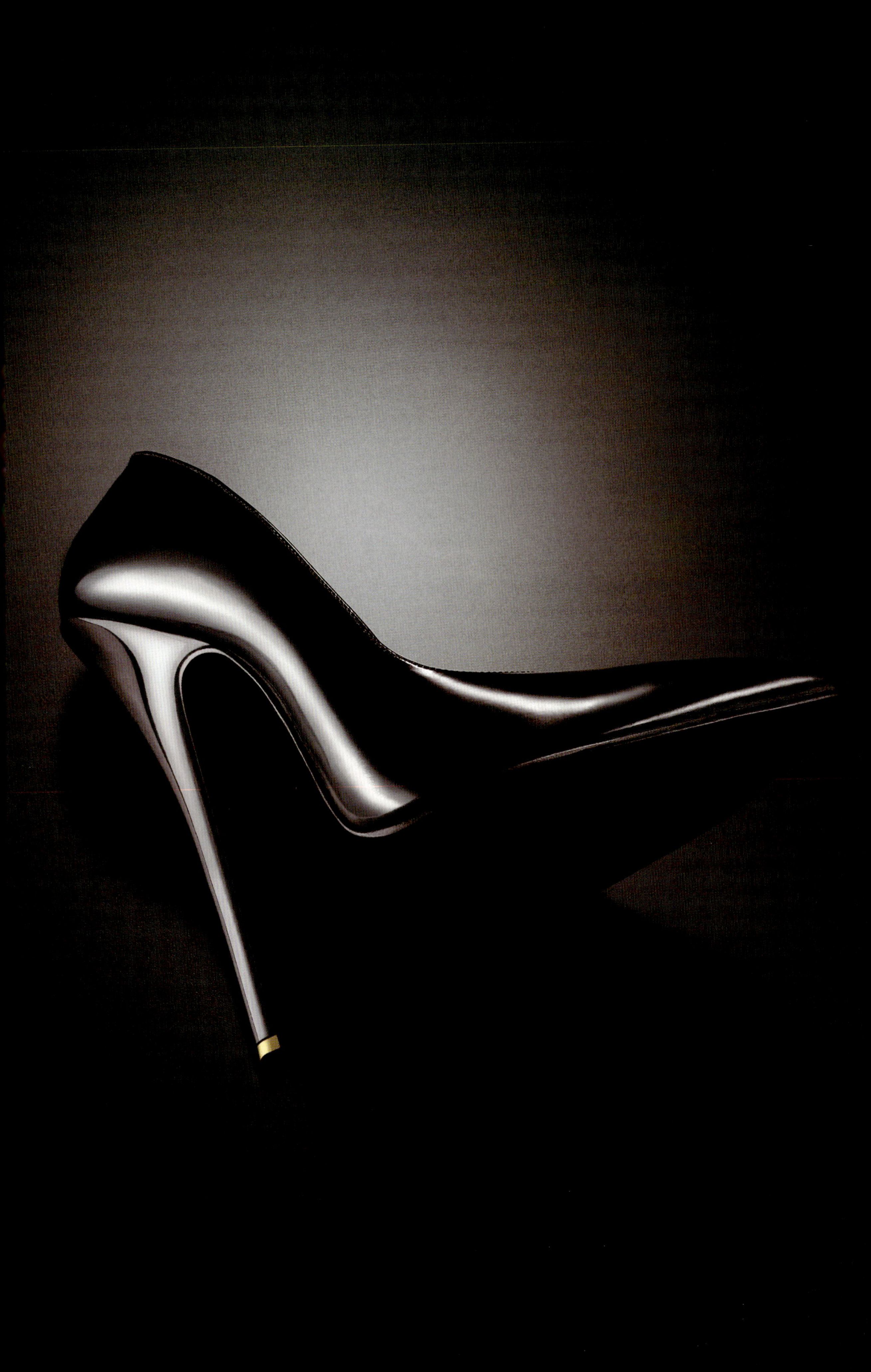

SPENCER JONES

BILL CHARLES INC. ARTIST REPRESENTATIVES
tel 212.965.1465 fax 212.965.9235 www.billcharles.com

H. MARK WEIDMAN

WWW.WEIDMANPHOTO.COM
TEL +1 610 388 9818

H. MARK WEIDMAN

WWW.WEIDMANPHOTO.COM

TEL +1 610 388 9818

KSC

Joe Lombardo
represents

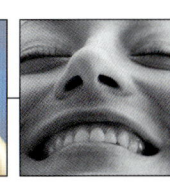

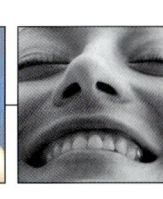

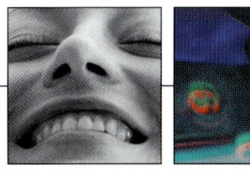

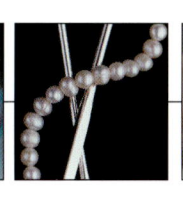

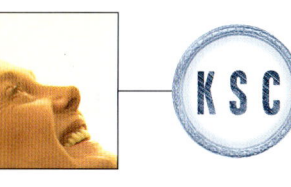

kate turning · kurt gardner · todd powell · lars lonninge · anthony snyder · david radler · george kamper

KSC

VIRGIN

KSC *represents*

kate turning

phone: 212 627 7171 — 800 950 7006
www.KSCreps.com www.turningpix.com
West Coast: 310 278 9060

KSC *represents*

kurt gardner

phone: 212 627 7171 – 800 950 7006
www.KSCreps.com

KSC *represents*

todd powell

phone: 212 627 7171 – 800 950 7006
www.KSCreps.com
studio: 970 668 2280

KSC *represents*

lars lönninge

phone: 212 627 7171 – 800 950 7006
www.KSCreps.com   **www.**lonninge.com
Studio: 212 627 0100

KSC *represents*

anthony snyder

phone: 212 627 7171 – 800 950 7008
www.KSCreps.com   www.anthonysnyder.com/photography
Studio: 212 352 3357

KSC *represents*

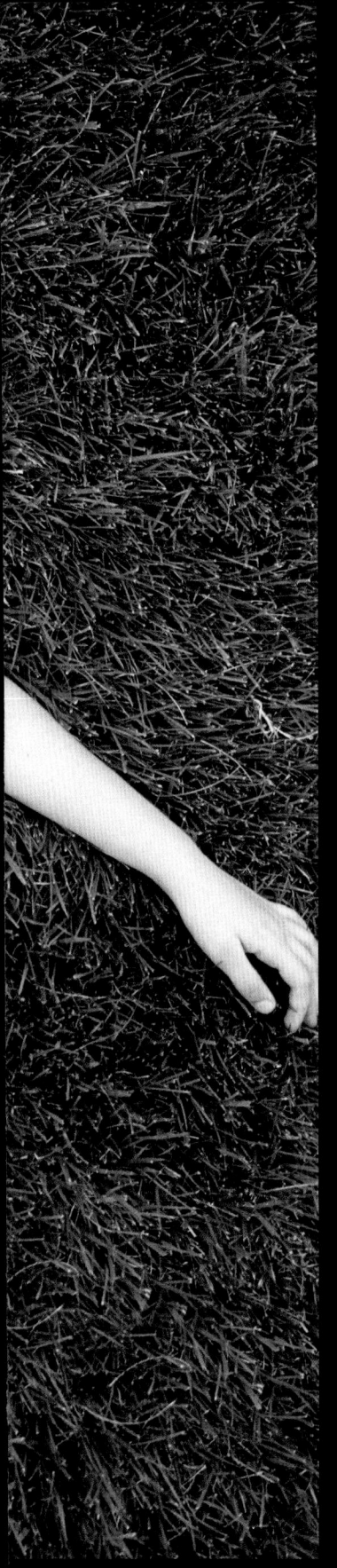

david radler

phone: 212 627 7171 – 800 950 7006
www.davidradler.com
Studio: 800 851 2734

KSC *represents*

george kamper

phone: 212 627 7171   800 950 7006
www.KSCreps.com
studio: 212 627 3157

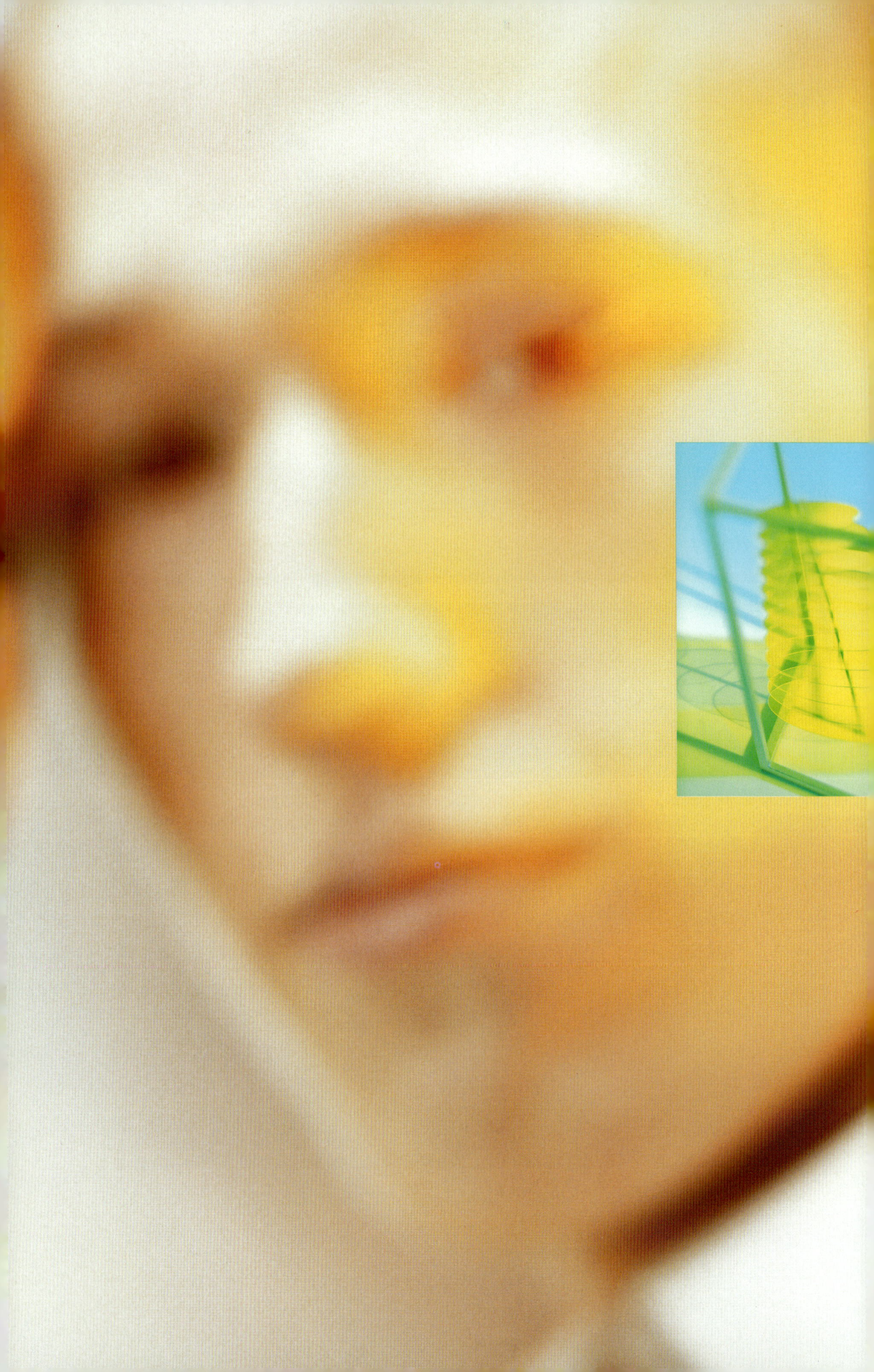

dominique malaterre
téléphone 514 844 0294
e mail zinc@tilt.ca

TILT
INC

MELANIE EVE BAROCAS

THAILAND

Aetna · Agfa · AIG · American Express · Apple · AT&T · Blue Cross Blue Shield · Bristol Meyers Squibb · Champion · Compaq · Danskin · Dupont · Fannie Mae · Fidelity · Fleet · Ford · General Electric · Glaxo · General Motors · Grolier · Houghton Miflin · IBM · International Paper · Kimberly Clark · Mercedes Benz · MCI · Microsoft · Mobil · New Line Cinema · Nordic Track · Pfizer · Phillip Morris · Proctor & Gamble · Prudential · Saab · Texaco · Timex · Toyota · Western Union · Whirlpool · United Technologies · Xerox

www.barocas.com   email: melanie@barocas.com   fax: 203 457-0022   tel: 203 457-1717

MELANIE EVE BAROCAS

THAILAND

EDEN, A black and white photography book,
winner of sixteen international awards,
spanning fifteen years of documentary work from Siberia to Cuba,
Africa to Central America.
To order a copy contact Melanie Eve Barocas.

www.barocas.com   email: melanie@barocas.com   fax: 203 457-0022   tel: 203 457-1717

jill greenberg studio 212 594 5624 www.manipulator.c

represented by **judy casey** 212 228 750

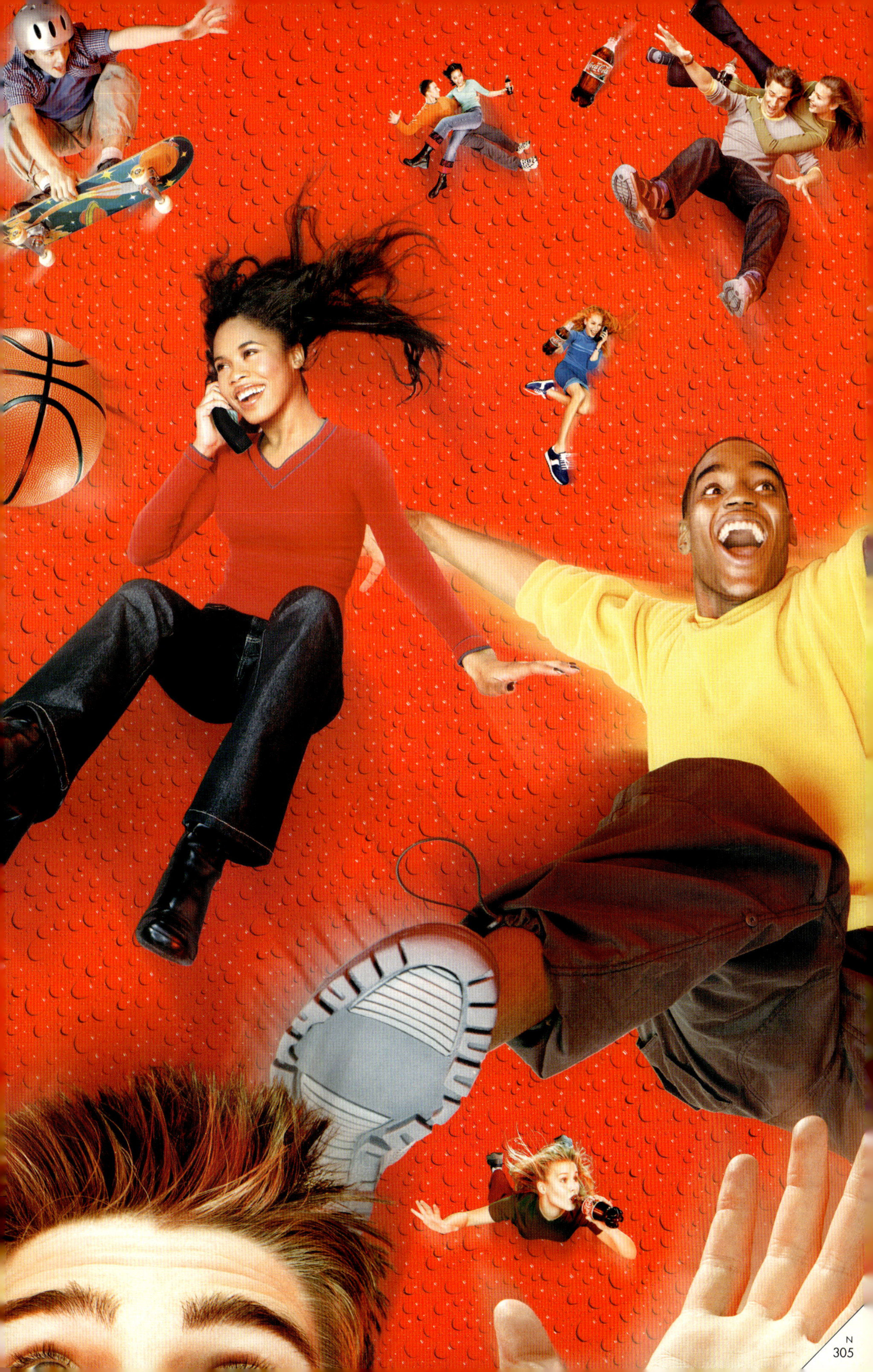

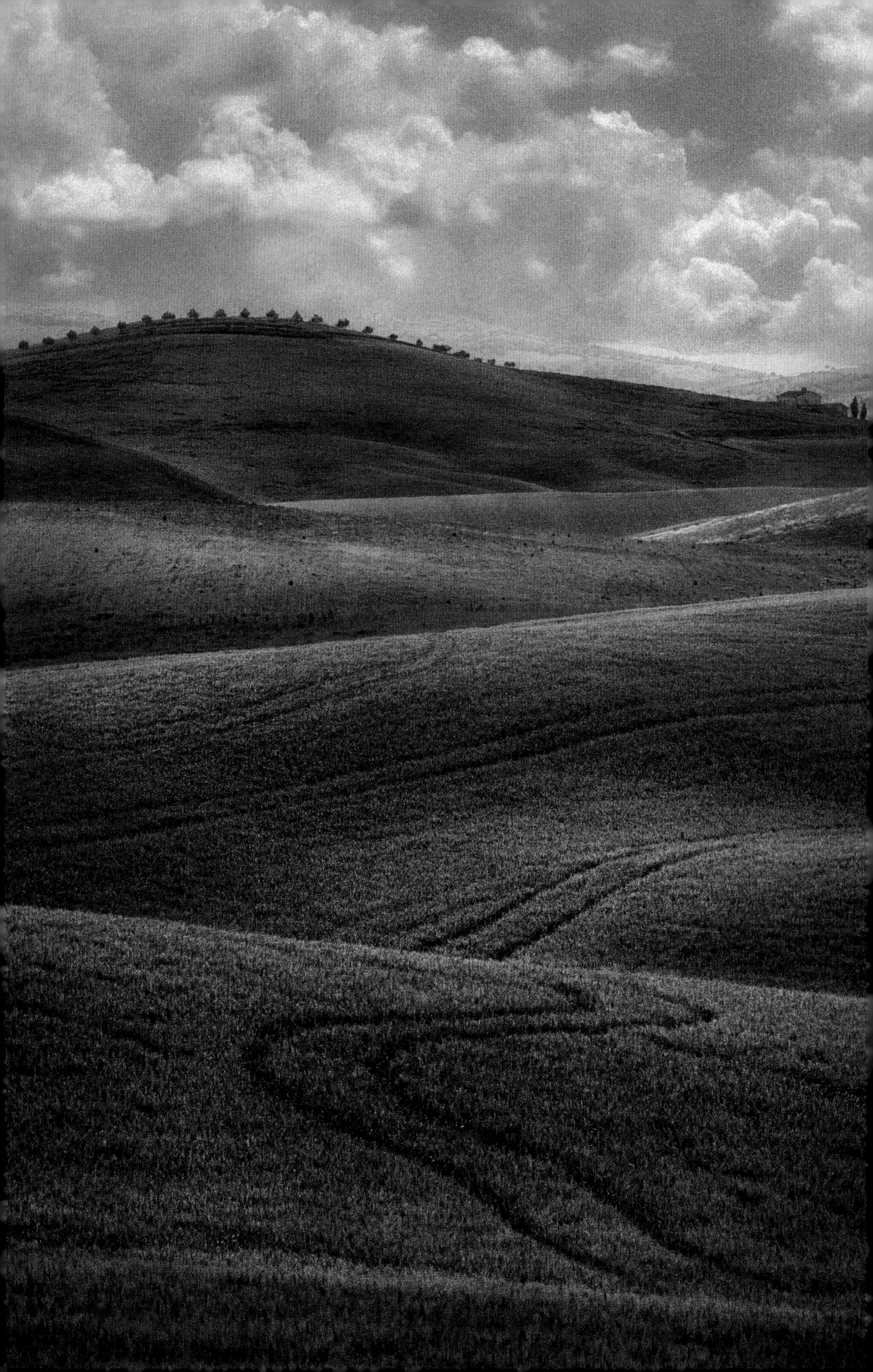

C h i p F o r e l l i

AGENT Kevin R. Schochat 212.633.8750 www.kevinschochat.com
STUDIO 212.564.1835 www.chipforelli.com

DOCTORS WITHOUT BORDERS AGENCY: TBWA/CHIAT/DAY

AGENT Kevin R. Schochat   TEL 212.633.8750   FAX 212.633.8960   www.kevinschochat.com

GEORGE KAVANAGH

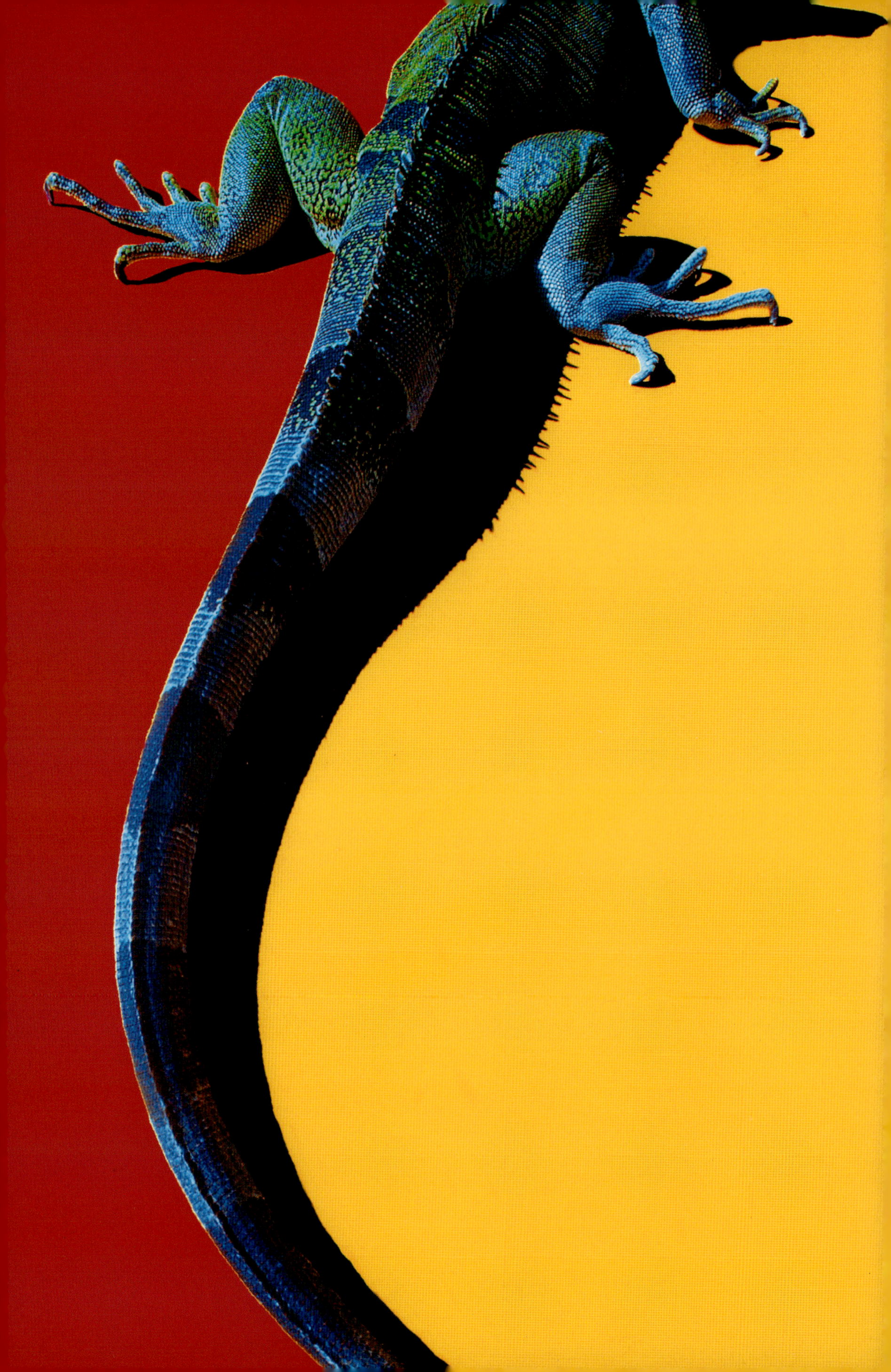

BRYAN F. PETERSON

PHOTOGRAPHY

mooney photo

ACROBATS / PHYSIOSPORT / OGILVY, LONDON

CHEETAH / AUDI / BBH, LONDON

TAKE YOUR COAT / UMBRO / D'ARCY, LONDON

REPRESENTED
BY DAVID GARDINER

EUROPE
Apartment B
21 Endlesham Rd
London SW12 8JX
T. +44(0)20 8675 3055
F. +44(0)20 8675 3440
E. gardiner@dircon.co.uk

USA
Tania Kimche
137 5th Avenue
11th Floor
New York NY 10010
T. 212 529 3556
F. 212 353 0831
E. TaniKim@aol.com

WAY / NIKE / GOODBY SILVERSTEIN, SAN FRANCISCO

RAIN / TOYOTA / SAATCHI & SAATCHI, LONDON

'ARCY, LONDON

LAWSUIT / AIG / OGILVY, NEW YORK

BODENFORS, GOTHENBURG

see an online portfolio and showreel, go to

www.mooney-photo.co.uk

James Salzano

REPRESENTED ON THE EAST COAST BY
CLARE O'DEA 212.968.7185
ON THE WEST COAST BY
MARIANNE CAMPBELL ASSOCIATES 415.433.0353
OR VISIT SALZANOPHOTO.COM

CLAUDIA KRETSCHMAN, TRI-ATHLETE. WALL STREET JOURNAL.
©2000 JAMES SALZANO.

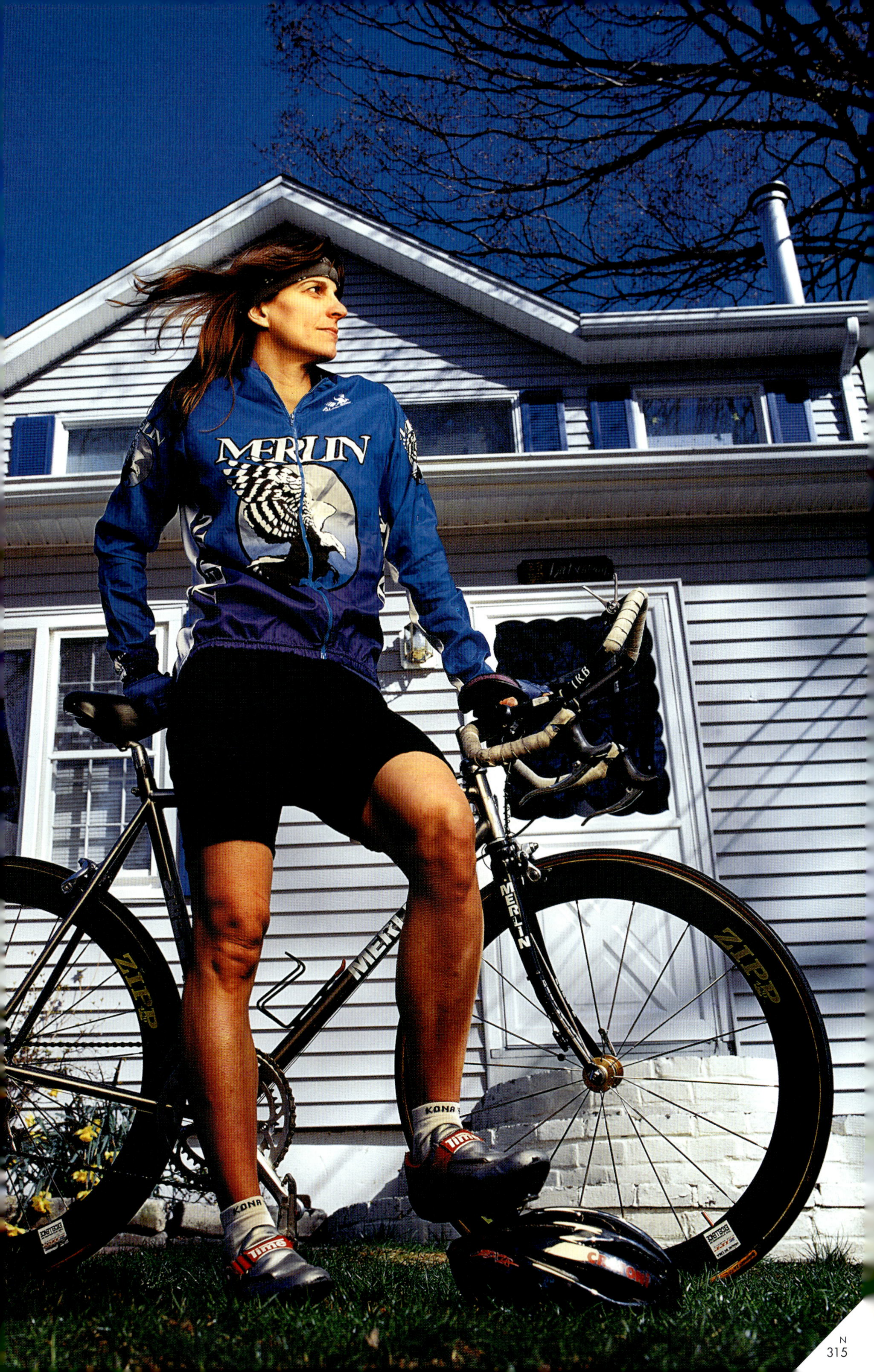
MERLIN
ZIPP
KONA

Greg Premru Photography

348 Congress Street

Boston, MA 02210

617.451.7770 *studio*

www.gregpremru.com

617.451.7770

GREG PREMRU
PHOTOGRAPHY
Architectural & Interior

www.gregpremru.com

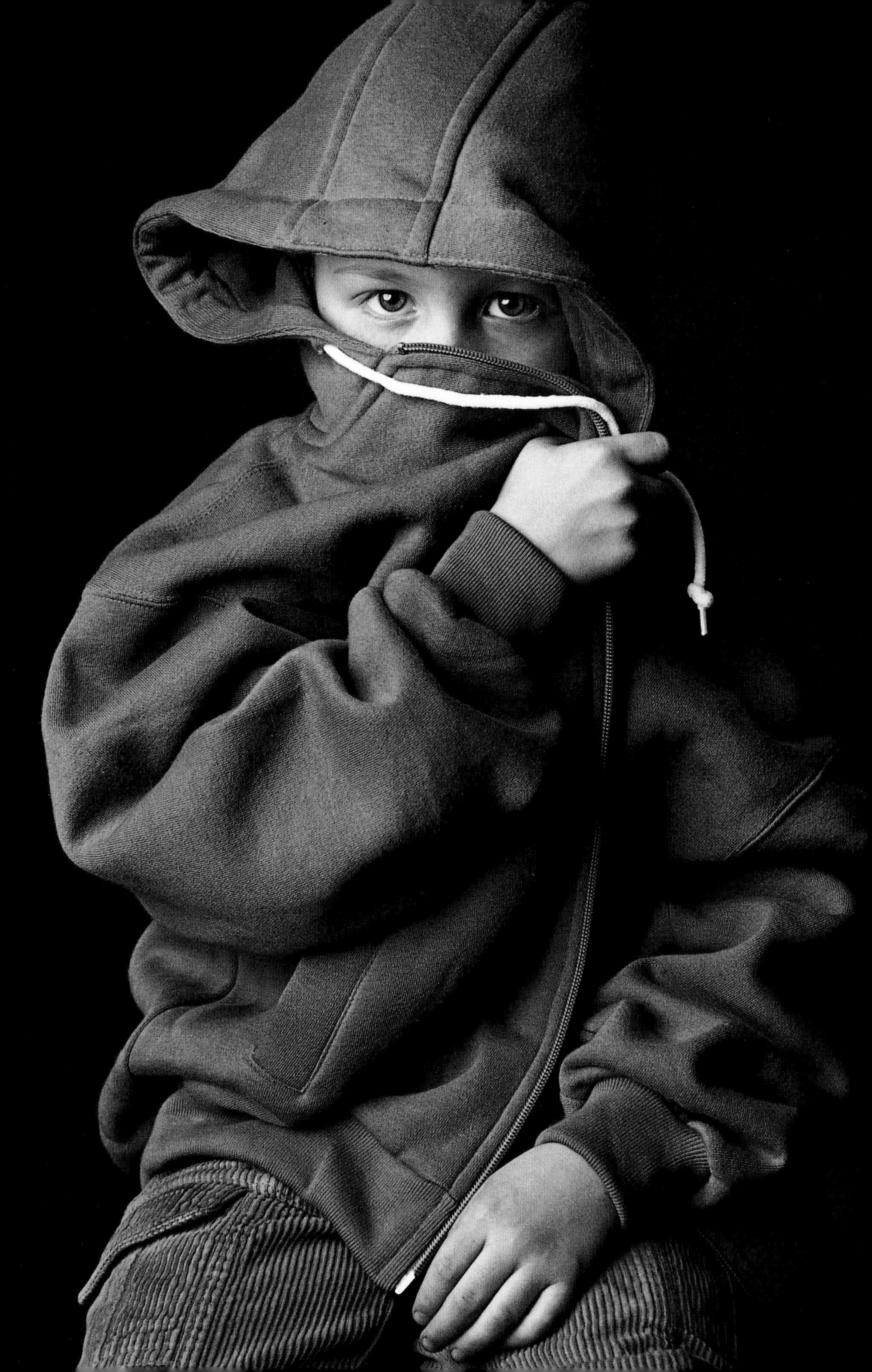

SUSAN JOHANN

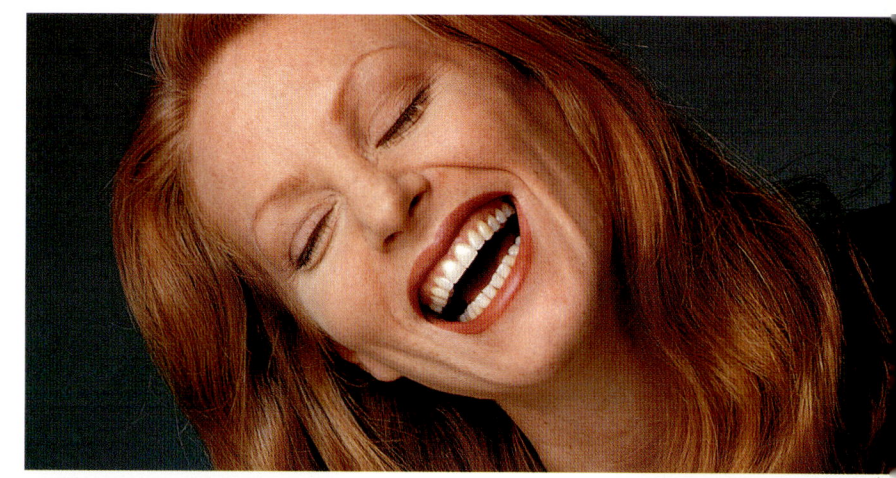

212.941.4151

Michele Gastl

photography

Represented by
Lamprecht and Bennett Inc.

212 533 3900 Fax 533 4191

200 Park Avenue South Suite 1
New York New York 10003

FRANCESCO MOSTO photography represented by LAMPRECHT & BENNETT 212.5333900

603-431-7366

verybossi@aol.com

ROB BOSSI

ROB BOSSI

603-431-7366

verybossi@aol.com

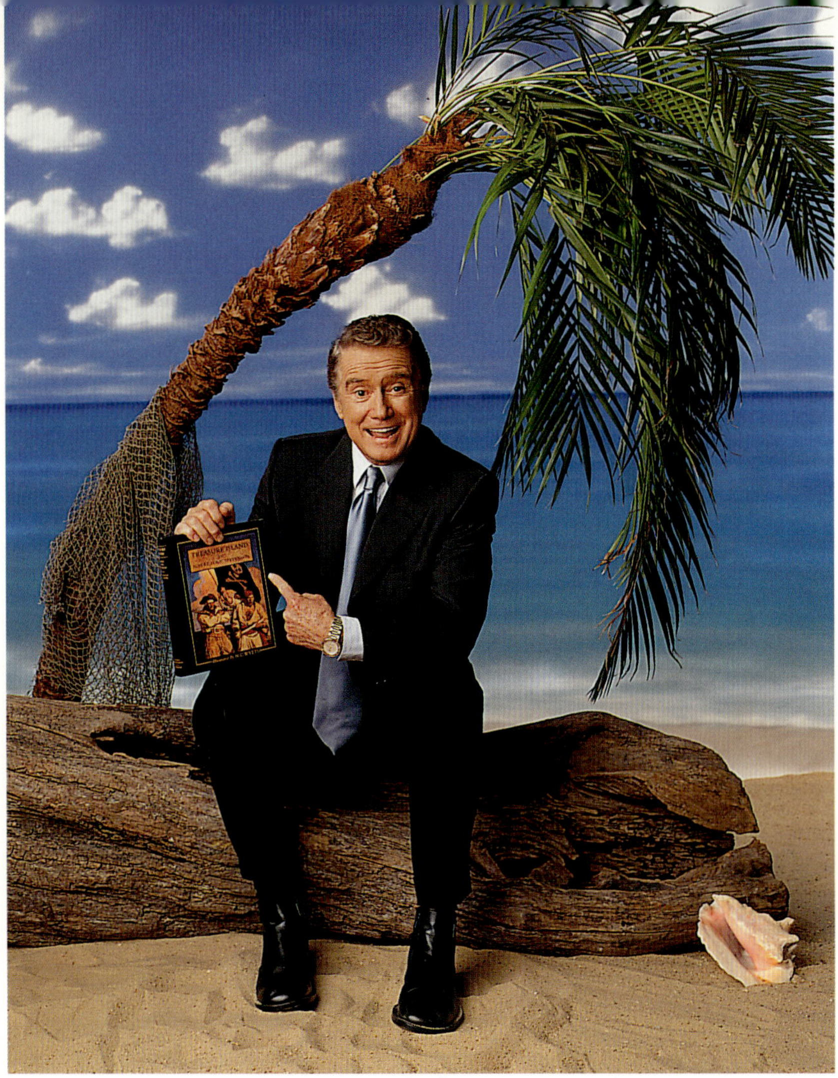

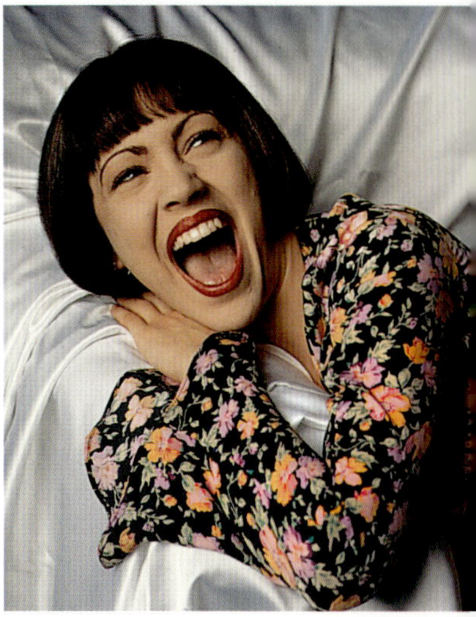

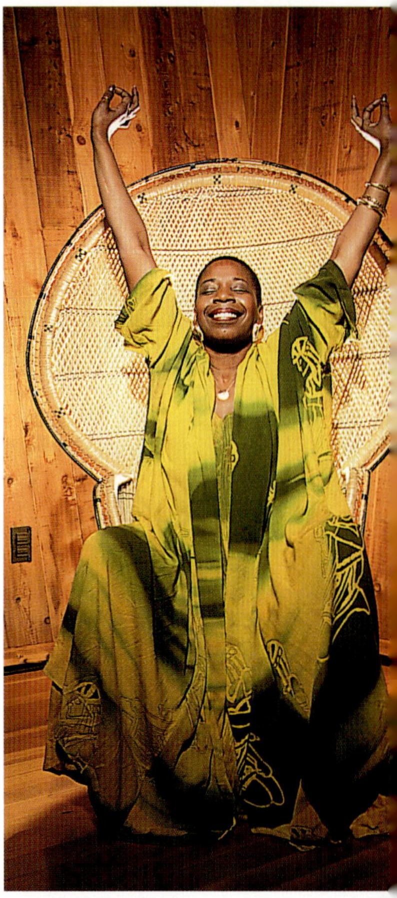

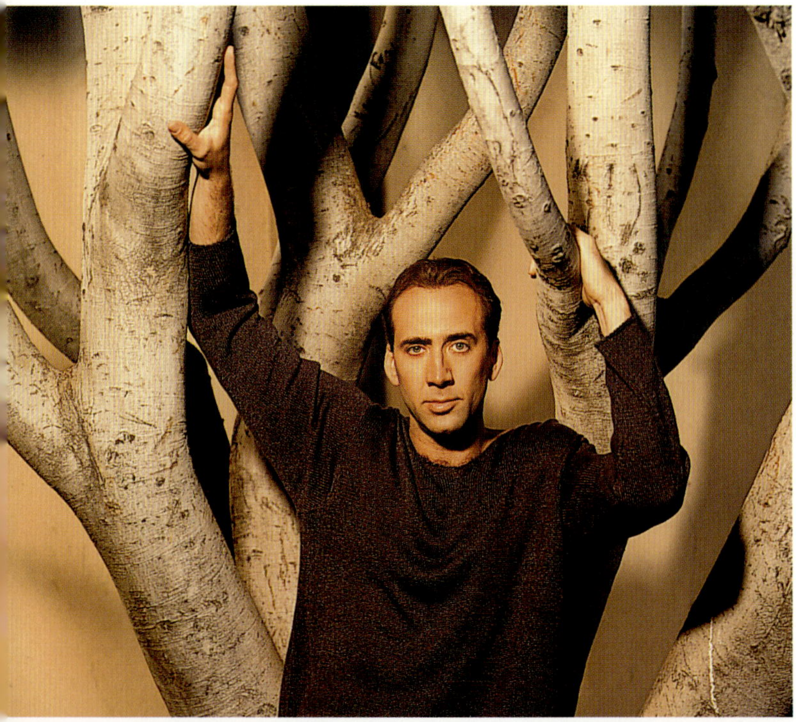

Kimberly Butler Photography

212.768.2924 / 800.793.3026
www.kimberlybutler.com
KBu6@aol.com

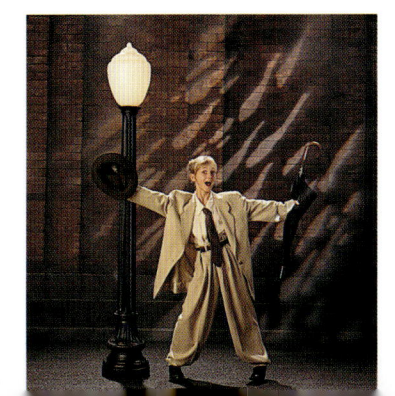

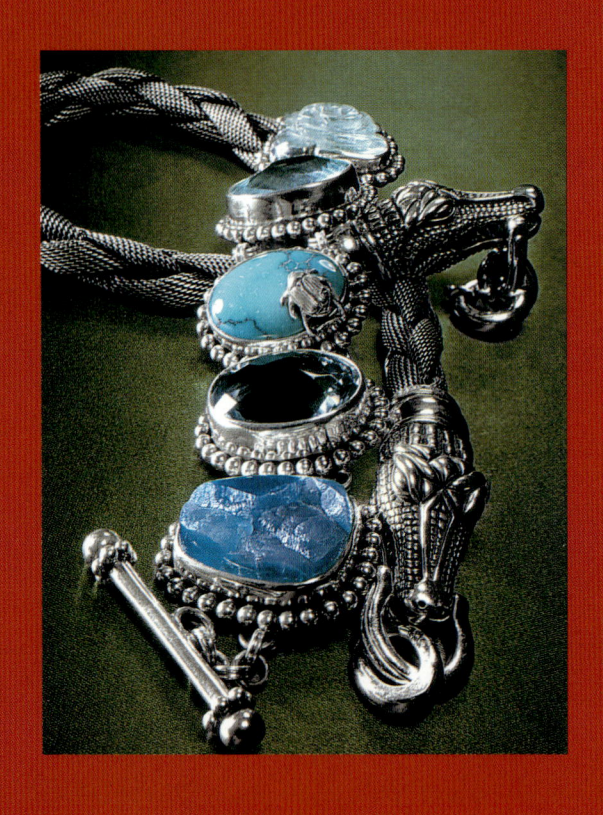

mariano : 212.645.7115

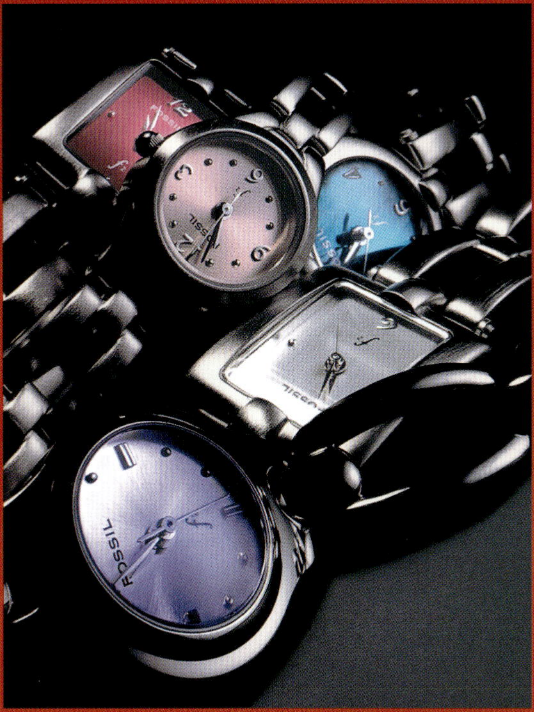
FOSSIL

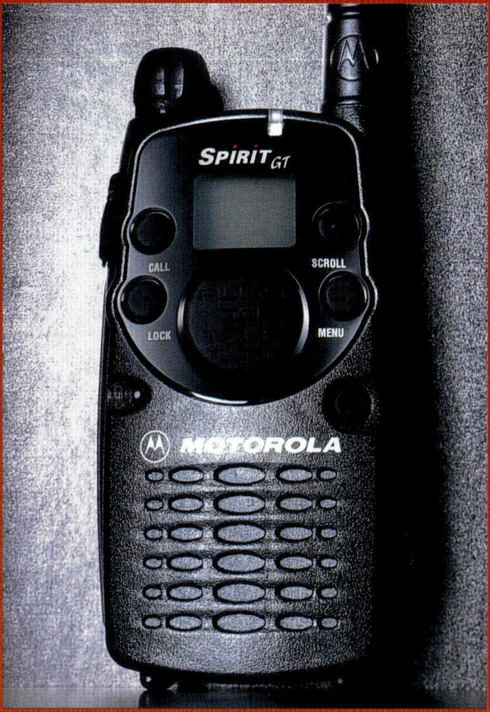
SPIRIT GT
CALL
SCROLL
LOCK
MENU
MOTOROLA

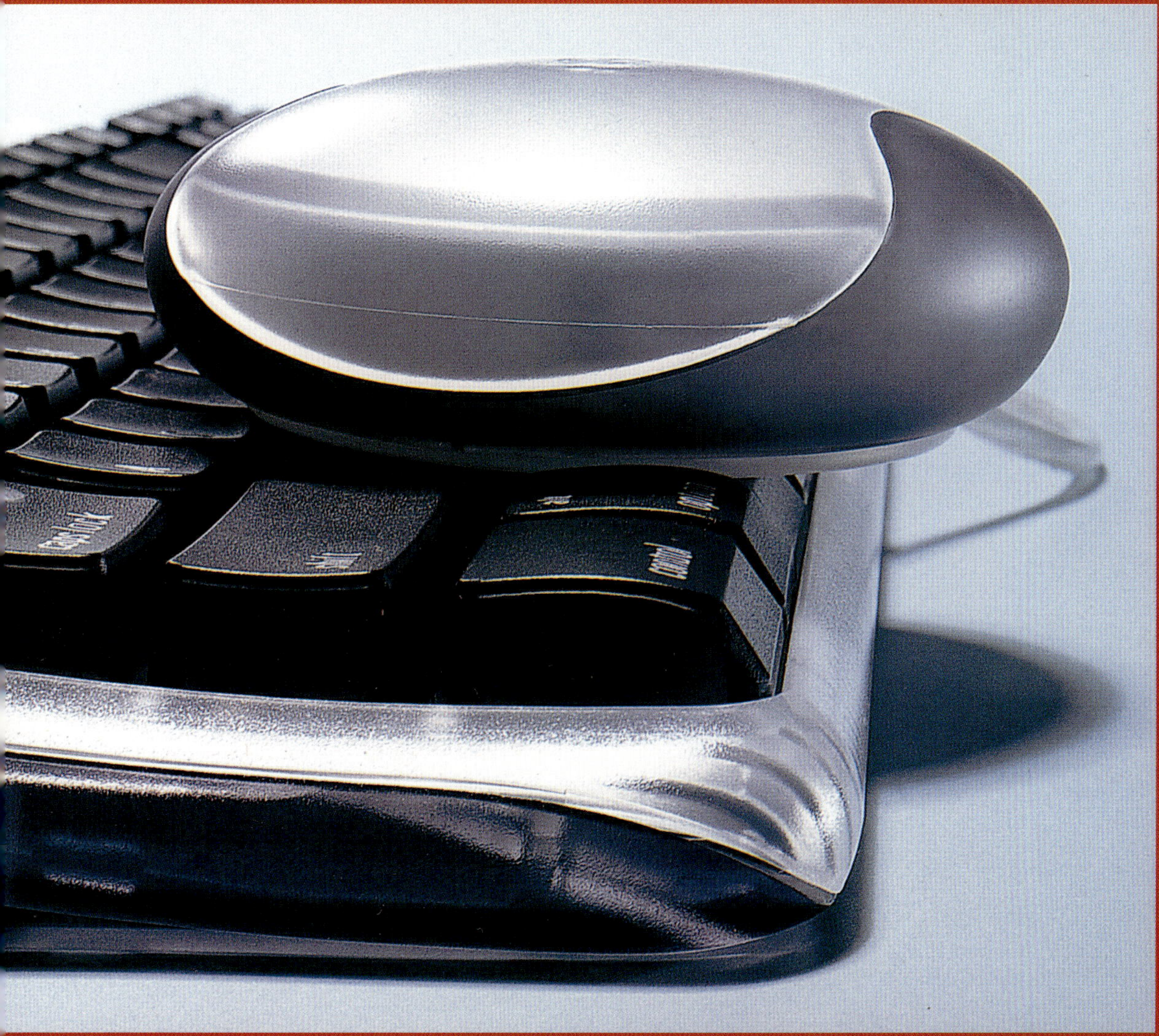

John O'Connor

PHONE - 917-318-9689
HTTP://CELTICASTLEPHOTOGRAPHY.COM

RUSSELL MONK
GEORGE SIMHONI
HASNAIN DATTU
IAN CAMPBELL
CHRIS GORDANEER

IAN CAMPBELL REPRESENTED BY WESTSIDE STUDIO

TEL 416 535 1955   FAX 416 535 0118   www.iancampbellphotography.com

Reeves Gabrels – Musician

MARK NIEDERMAN PHOTOGRAPHY

Valisa Fischer – Art Director

119 W 25th St.
Suite 1101
New York, NY 10001

TERRY COLLIER
WAHOOZ STILLS AND MOTION PICTURES INC. 1-800-615-7115

TERRY COLLIER
WAHOOZ STILLS AND MOTION PICTURES INC. 1-800-615-7115

KEN WEINGART

PHOTOGRAPHY

212 979 8978
www.kenweingart.com
800 754 9792
New York Los Angeles

KEN WEINGART

PHOTOGRAPHY

212 979 8978
www.kenweingart.com
800 754 9792
New York Los Angeles

RICK BECKER

500 Broadway   New York NY 10012   tel 212.925.3974
rickbecker@earthlink.net   www.rickbeckerstudios.com

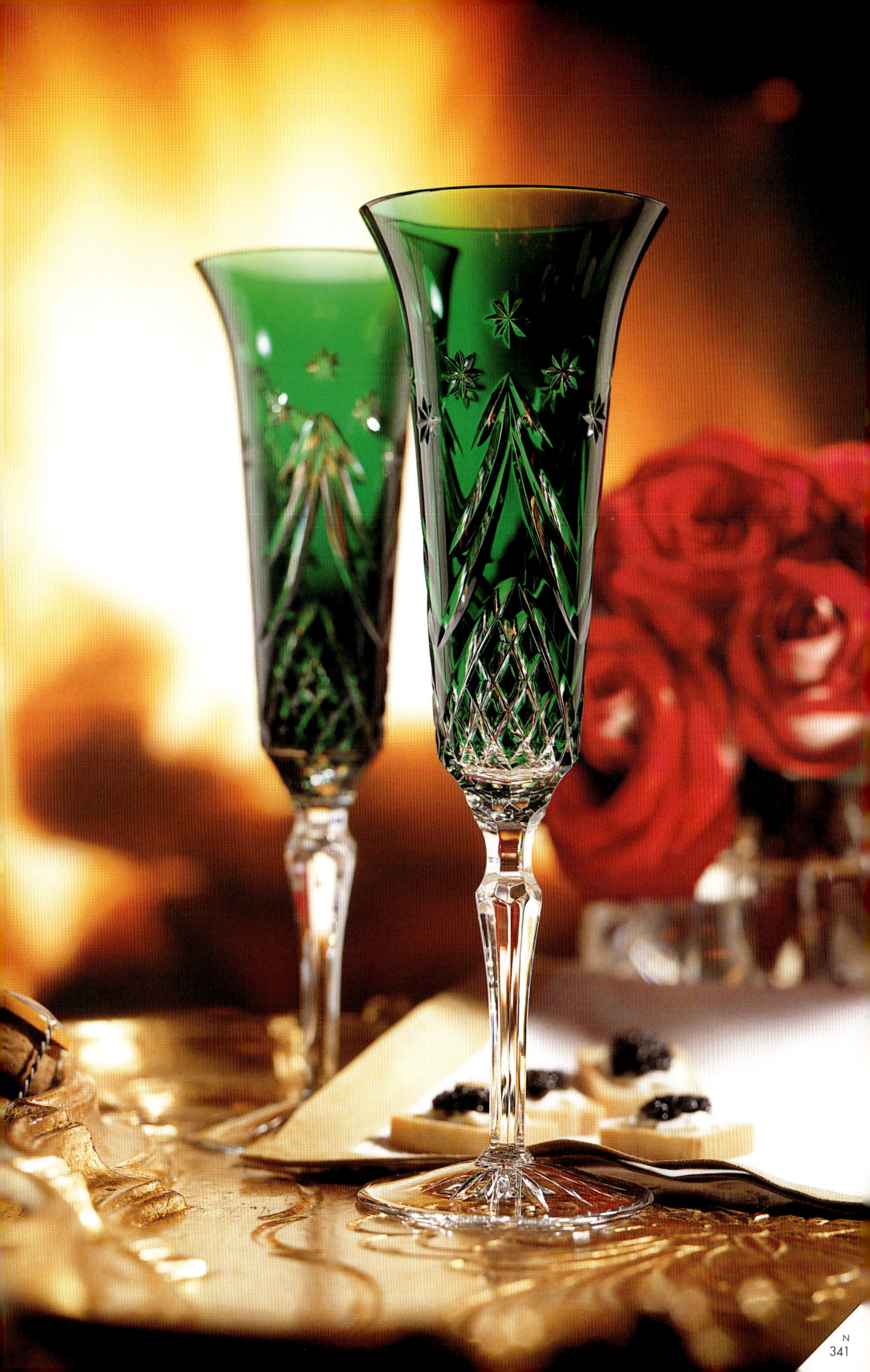

LM/P

Larry Maglott Photography

t / f 508.785.2712

http://www.larrymaglott.com

MARGE CASEY & ASSOCIATES   150 WEST 28TH STREET, SUITE 1803
NEW YORK, NEW YORK 10001   PHONE 212 929-3757   FAX 212 929-8611
WEB WWW.MARGECASEY.COM

JOEL LARSON PHOTOGRAPHY
Phone 612.332.2670

Represented by:
Marge Casey & Associates
Phone 212.929.3757

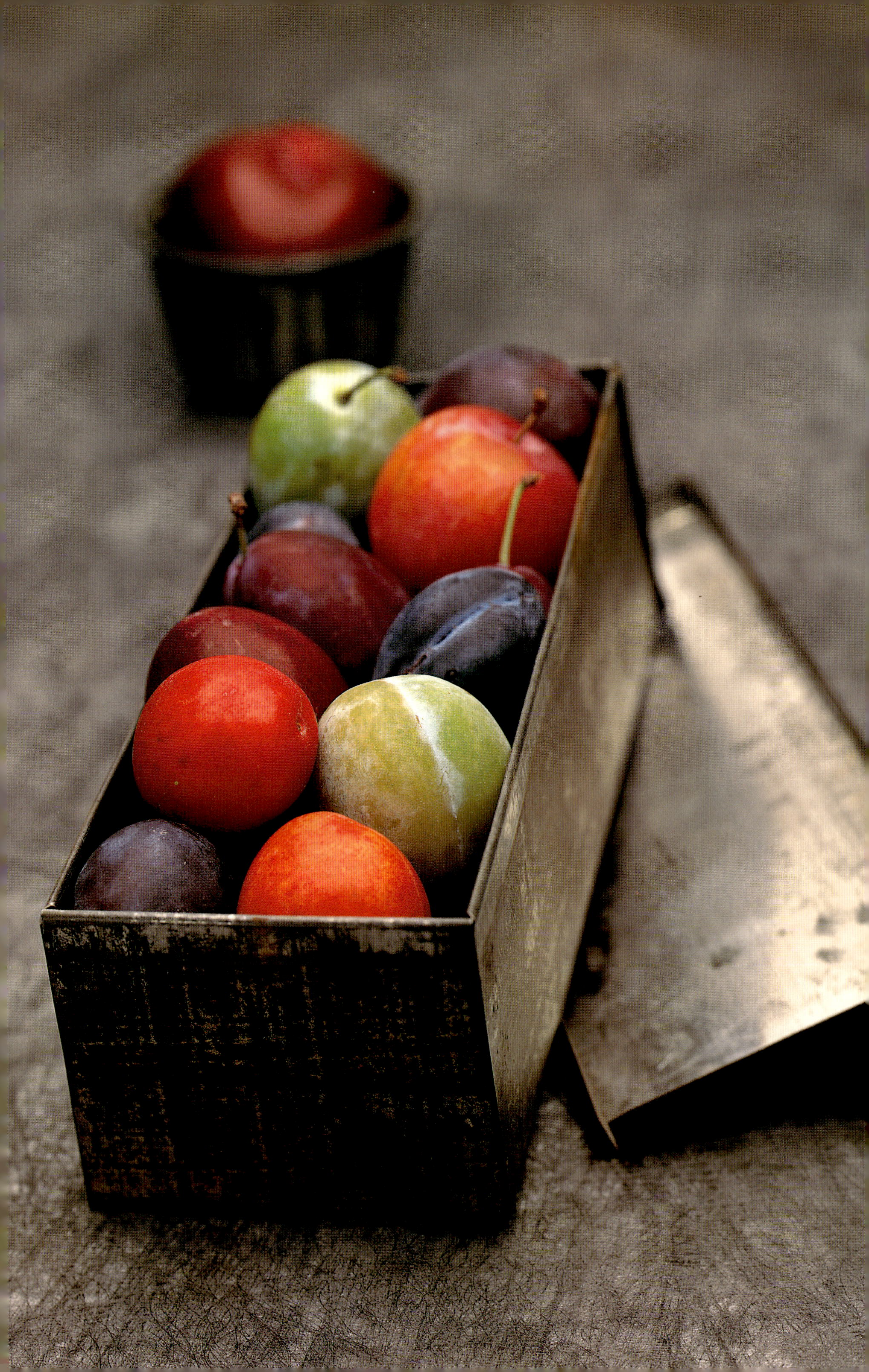

JUDD PILOSSOF

Contact:
Marge Casey & Associates (212) 929-3757

Paul Christensen

Worldwide Representation By
Marge Casey & Associates
Phone (212) 929.3757   www.paulchristensen.com

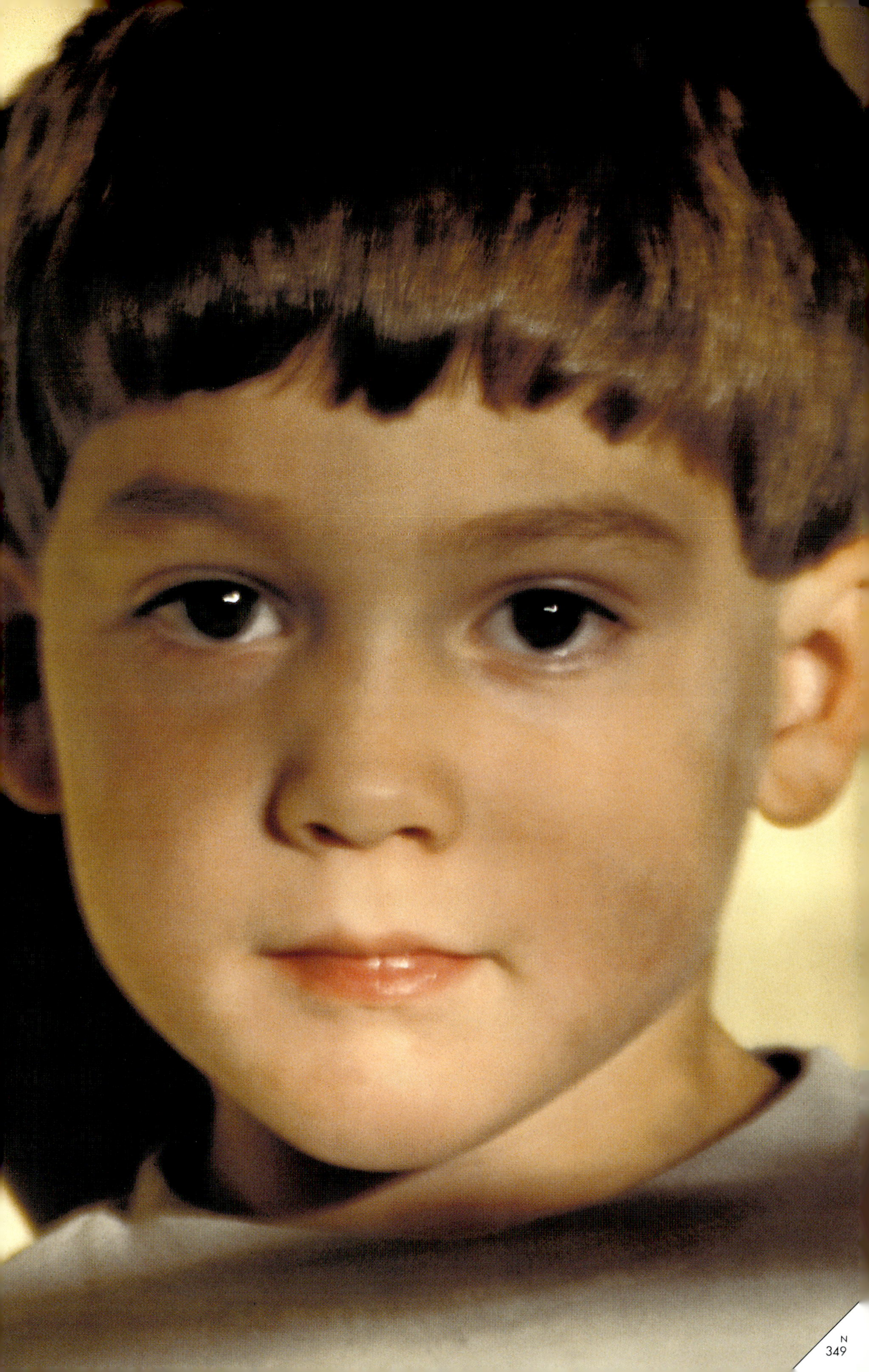

Dennis Murphy is represented by Marge Casey & Associates
212 929 3757   studio 214 651 7516

dmurphyphoto.com   margecasey.com

Murphy

Marge Casey & Associates

TELEPHONE: 212.736.7835 FACSIMILE: 212.736.0387
PARAS@PARASPHOTOGRAPHY.COM WWW.PARASPHOTOGRAPHY.COM

MICHAEL PARAS
PHOTOGRAPHY

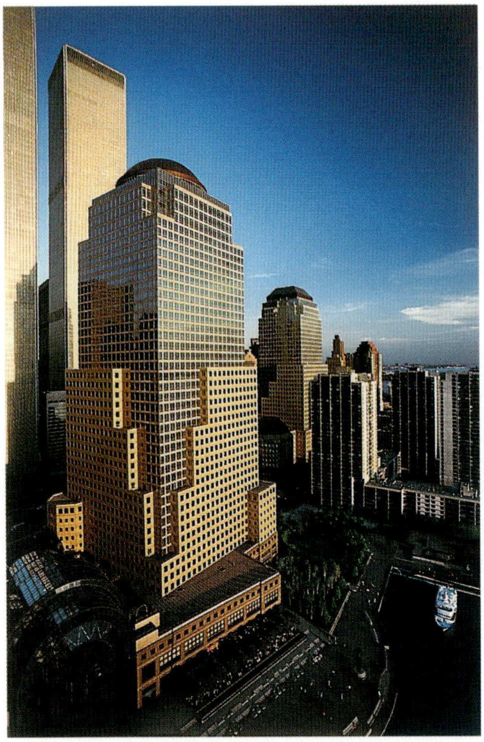
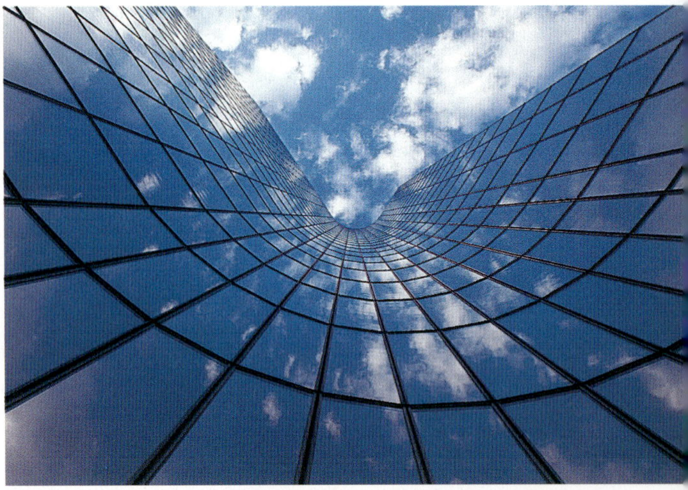
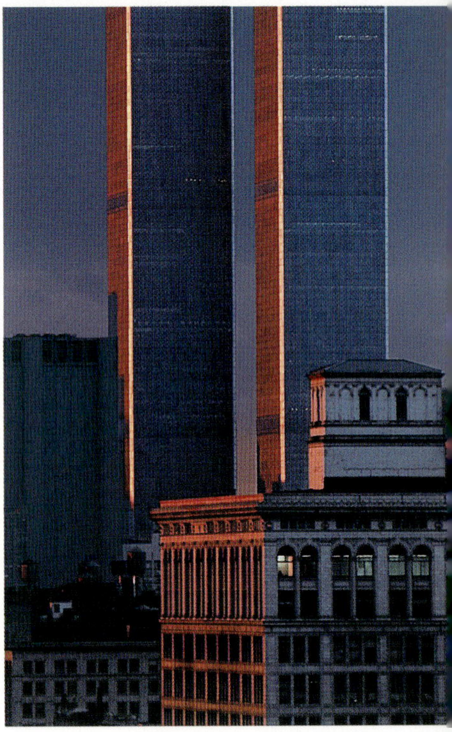
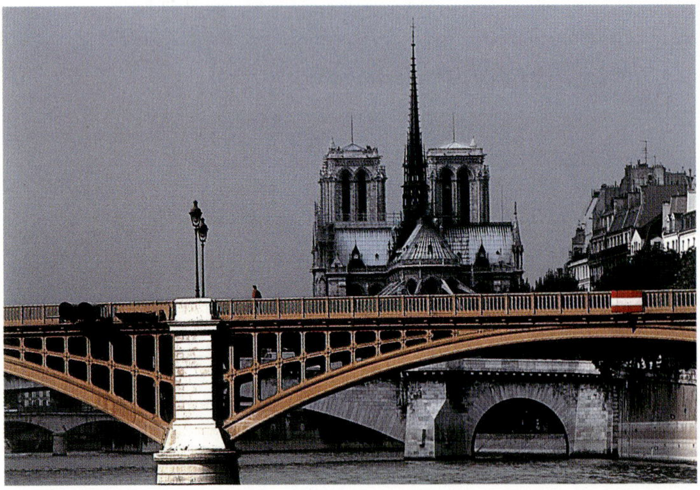

Thomas K. Leighton   212.370.1835

ROB LANG 212 595 2217

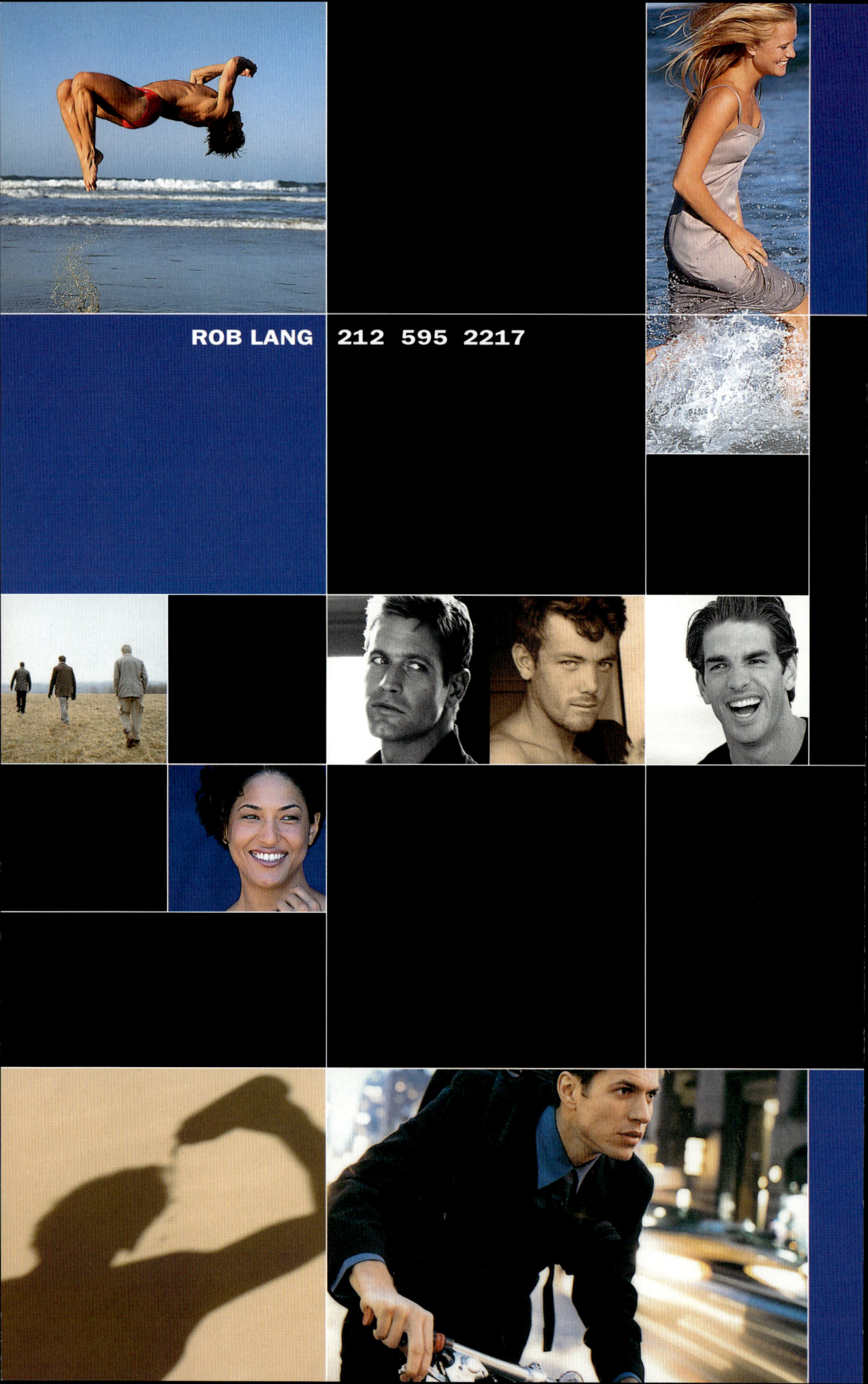

www.roblangphoto.com

ROB LANG   212 595 2217

represented by Lise Hintze 631 689 7054

Keith Glassman
212 353 1214

212 353 1214
Glassman

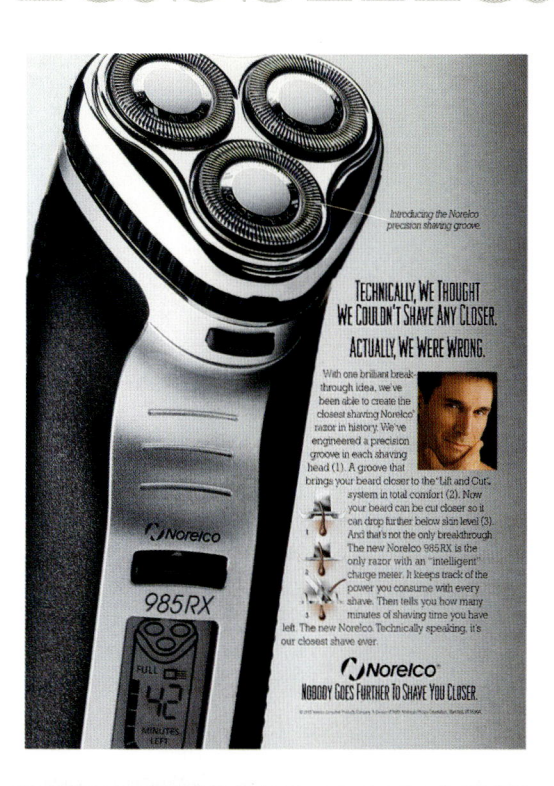

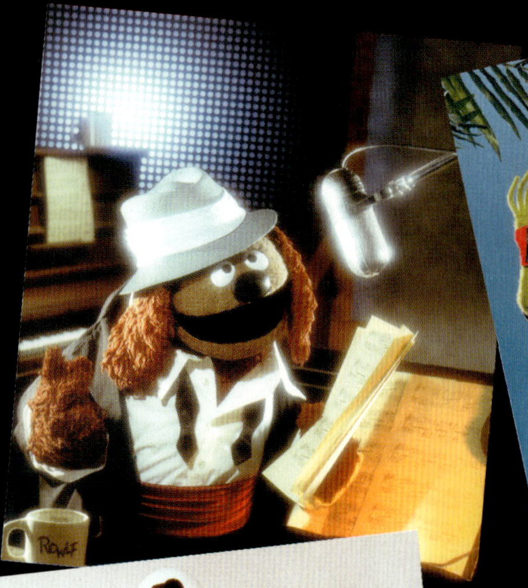

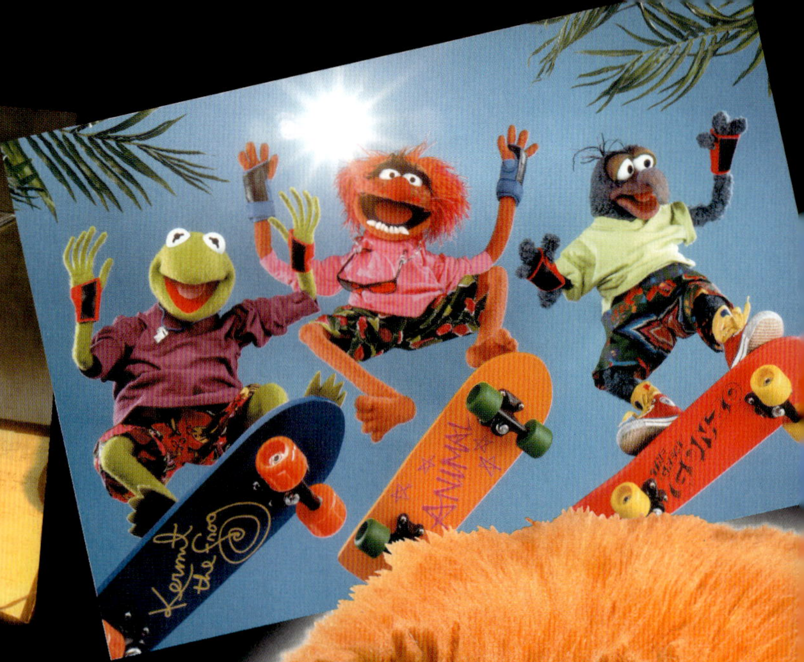
Kermit the Frog

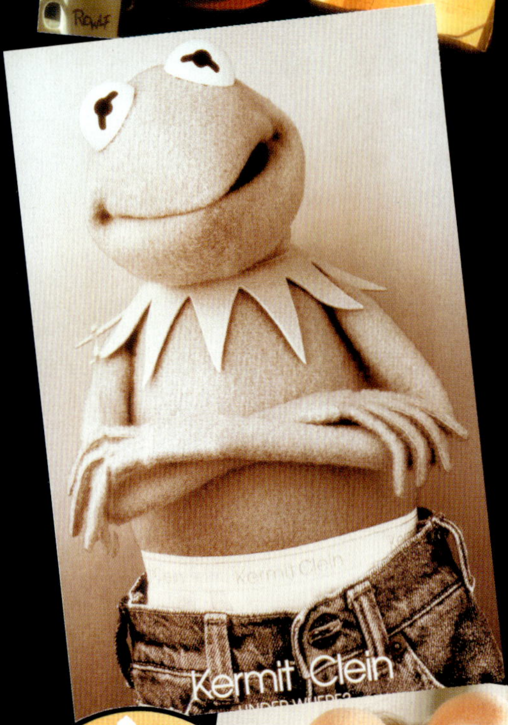
Kermit Clein
Kermit Clein

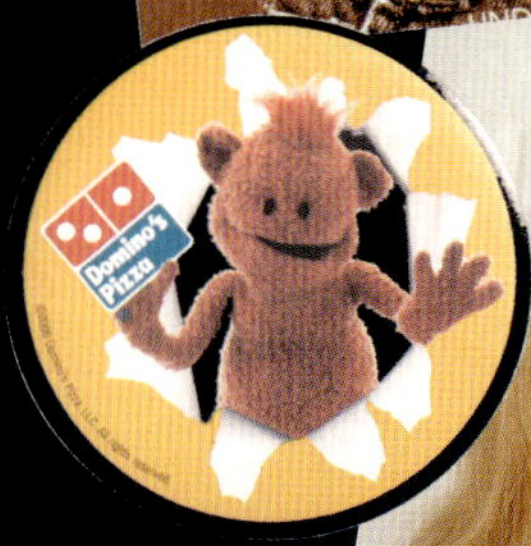
Domino's Pizza

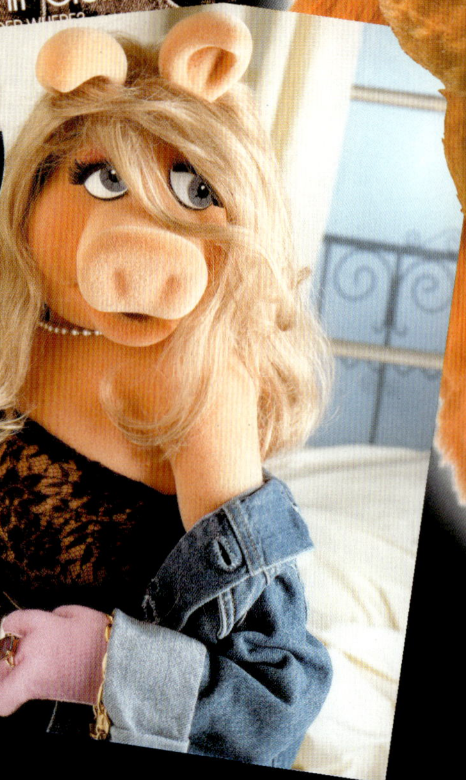

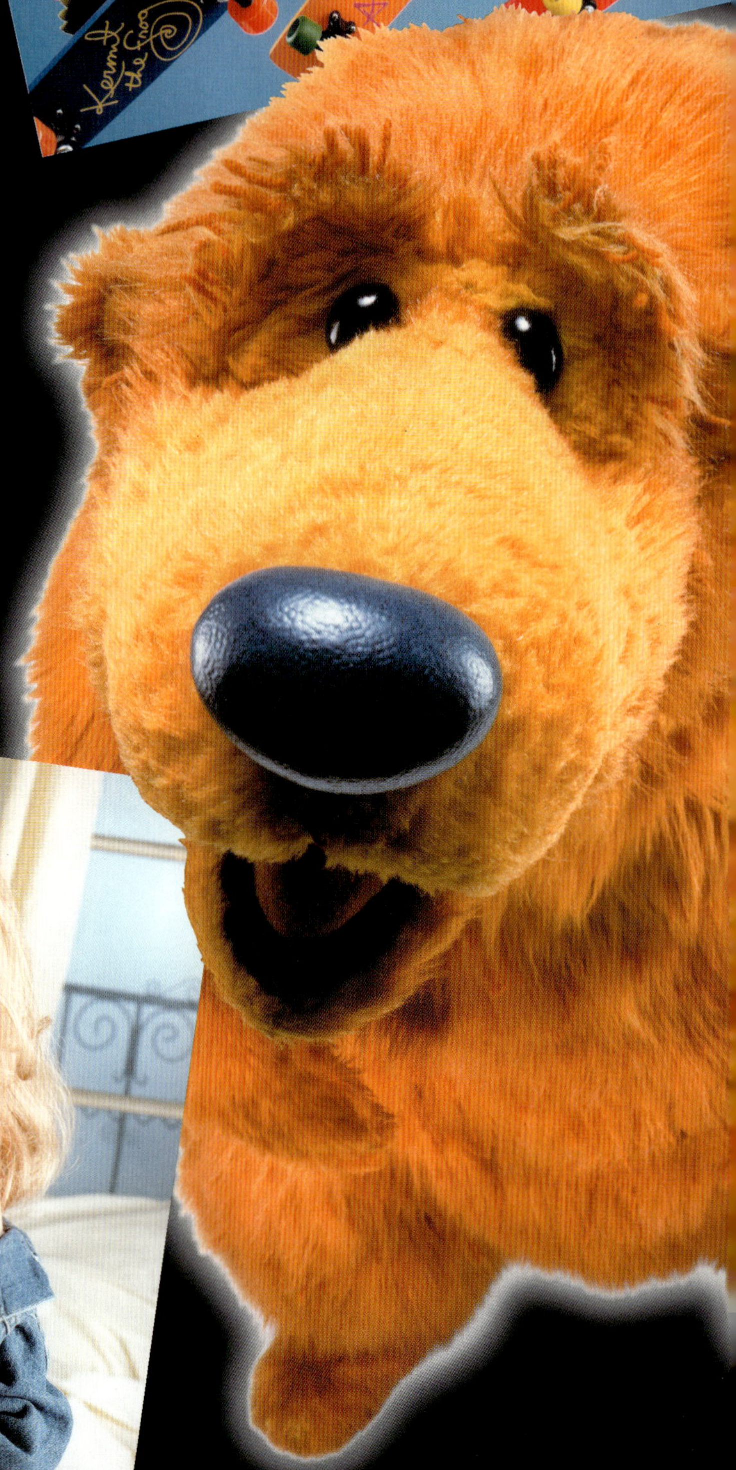

CELEBRITY PORTRAITURE

got milk?

JOHN E. BARRETT

www.johnebarrettphoto.com • NYC: 212-749-3613 • Cell: 917-539-9365

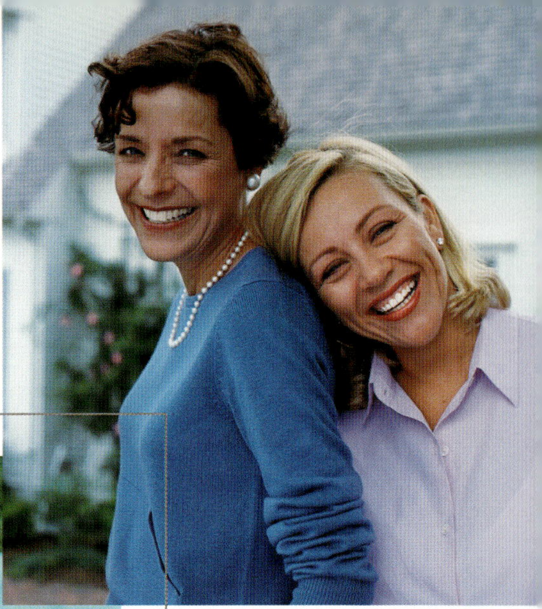

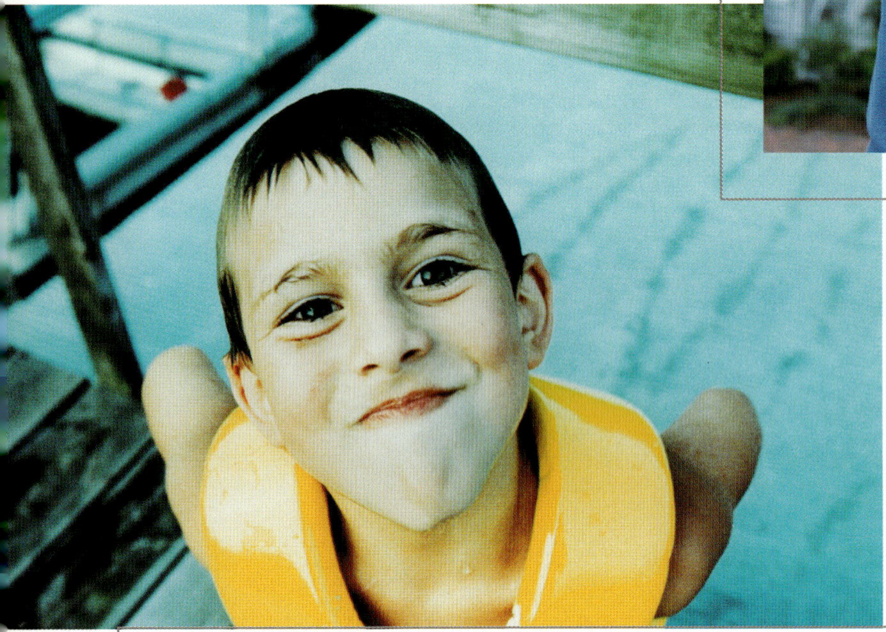

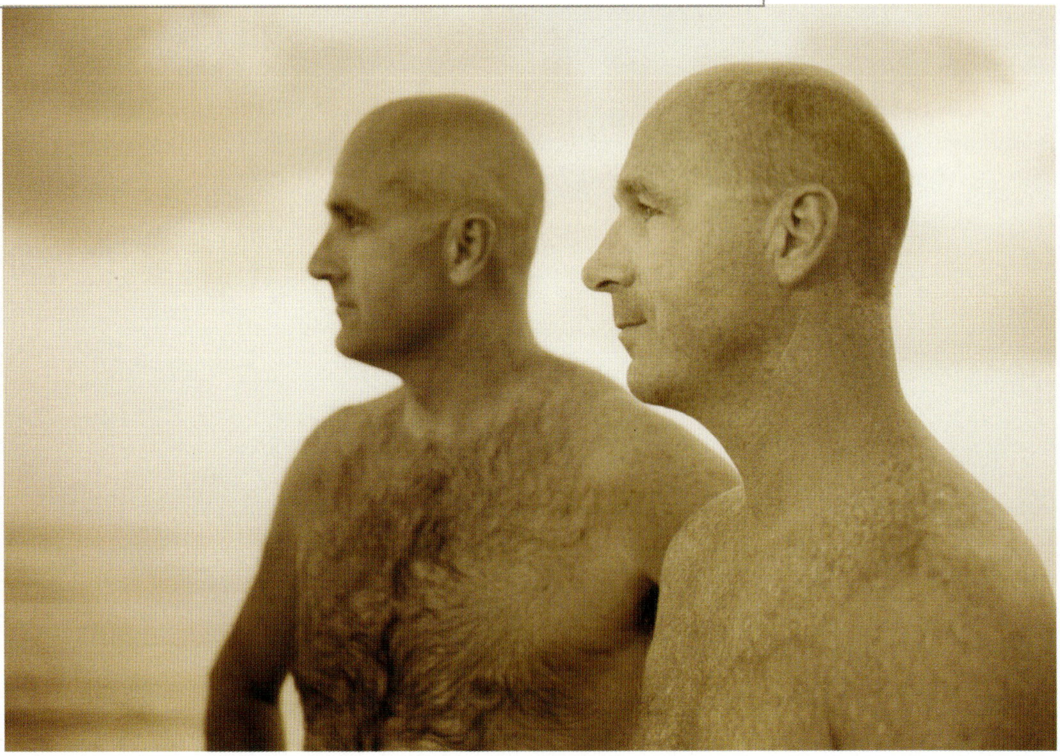

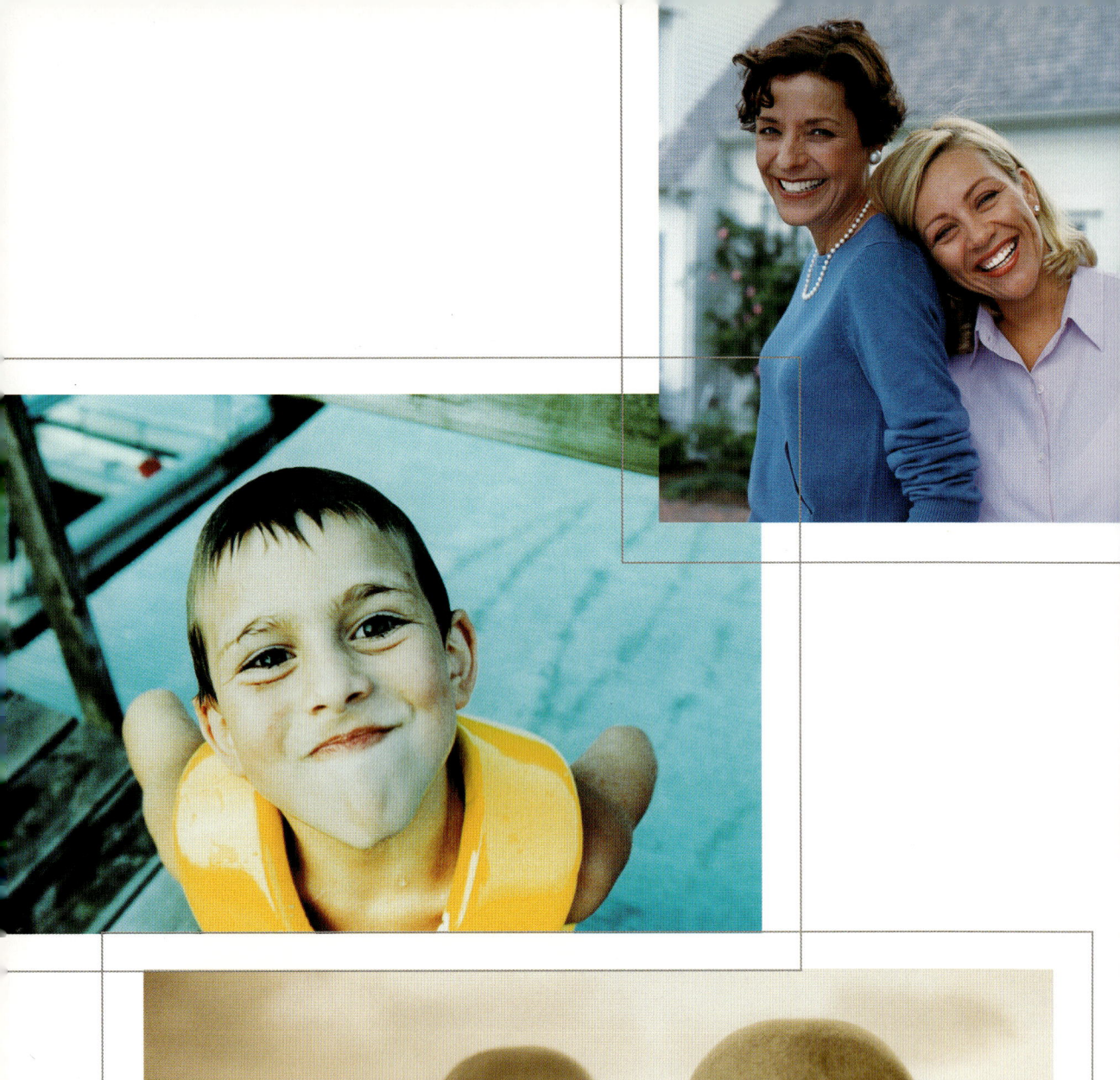

ed|quinn| photography

781.736.1761

ORSINI
PHOTOGRAPHER
www.orsini-photo.com

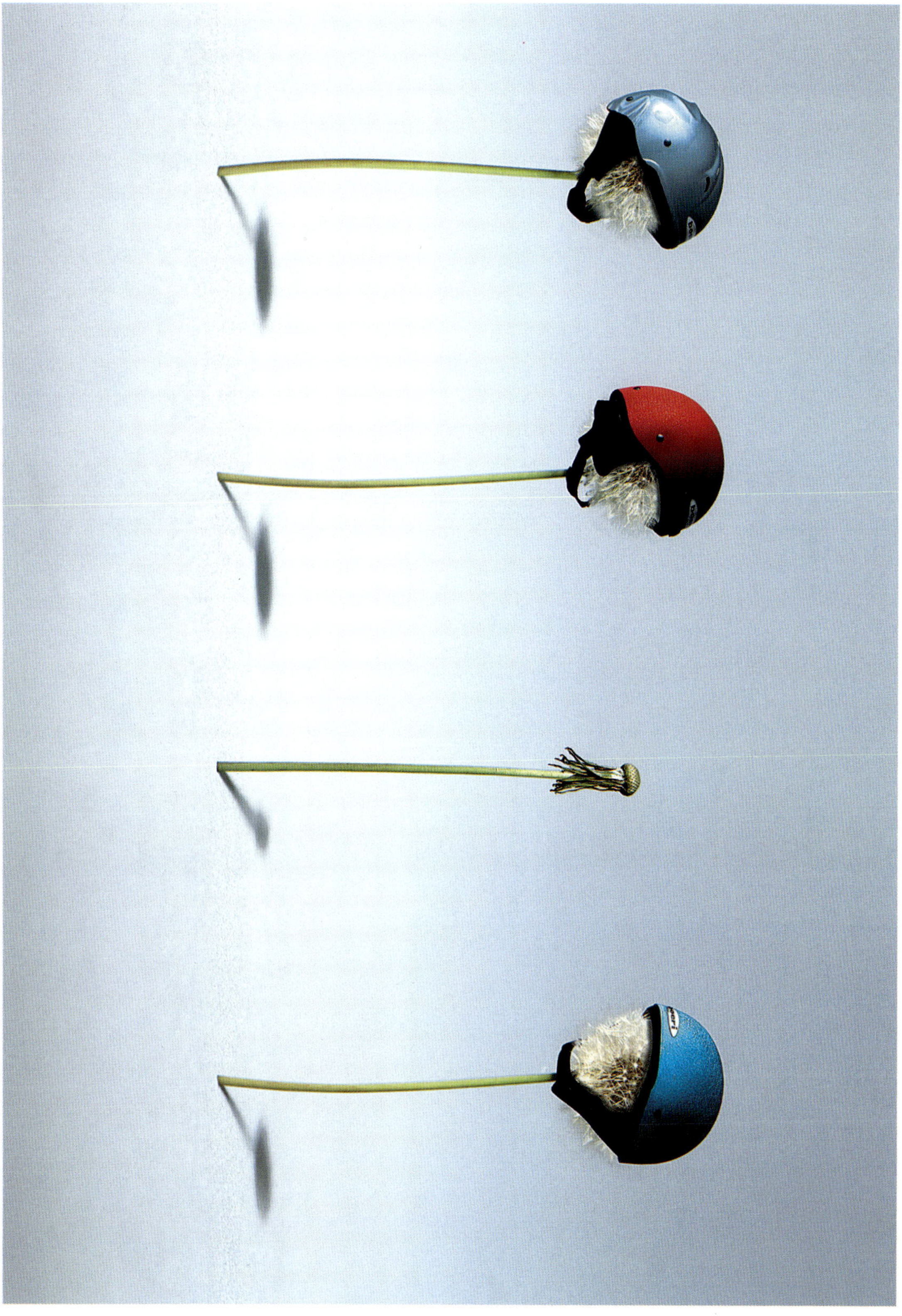

O 354 CONGRESS STREET BOSTON, MA 02210
617-357-6082 www.orsini-photo.com

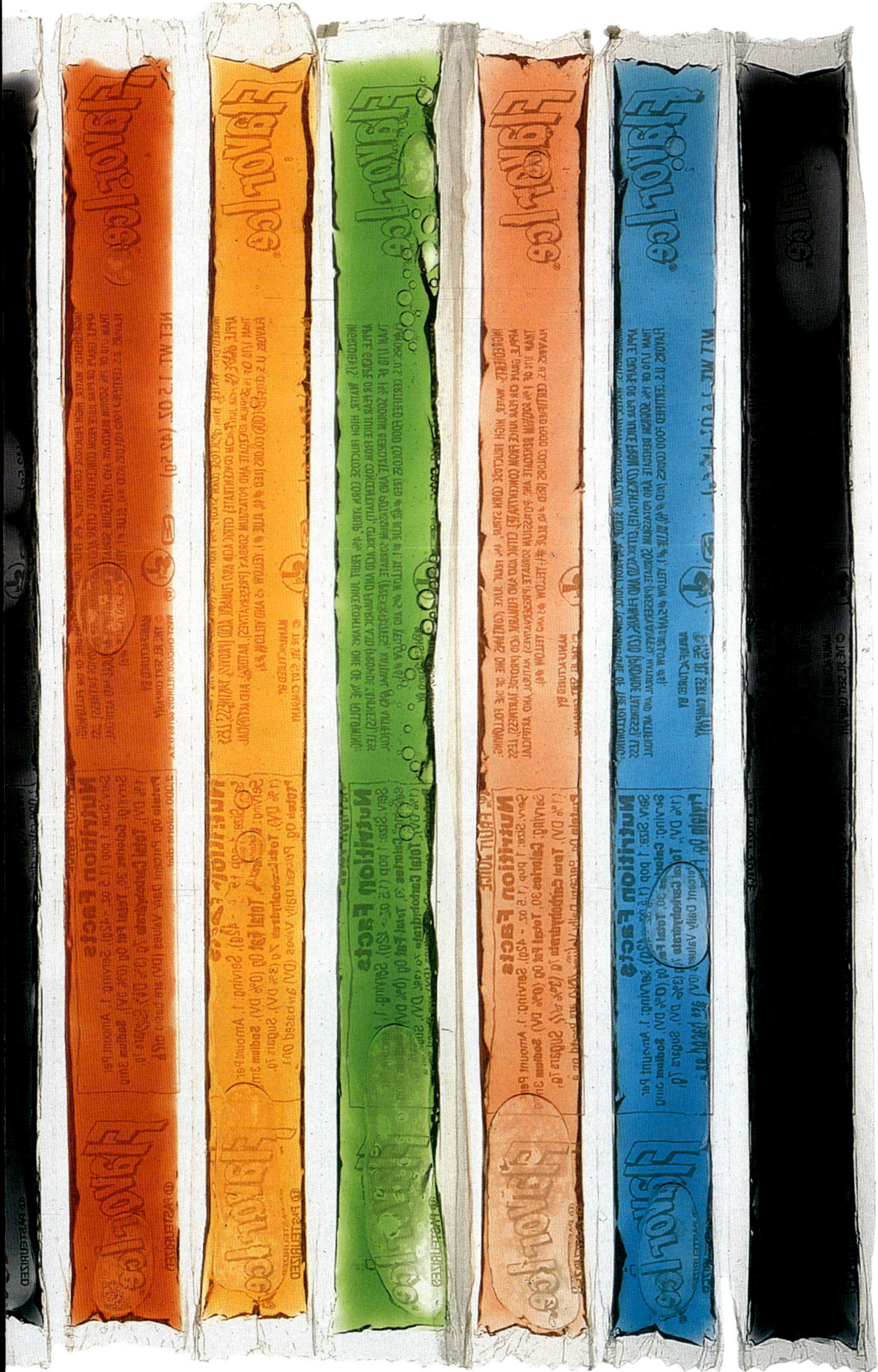

Wendy Barrows

photography
212 685 0799

Ben Katchor, MacArthur fellow

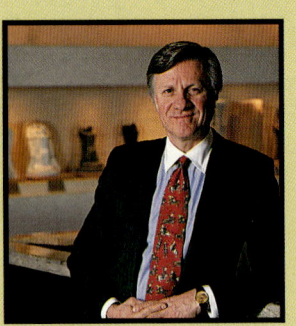

**Peter DaPuzzo, Co-President,
Cantor Fitzgerald & Co.**

**James Cear, SVP, Mellon Private Asset
Management**

Clients Include:
American Express
The American Stock Exchange
Bayer Corp.
Chase Manhattan Bank
Dow Jones Inc.
The Dreyfus Corp.
The Federal Reserve Bank of NY
Morgan Stanley Dean Witter
Pfizer, Inc.
Praxair, Inc
TIAA/CREF
UPS

**Camy Vazifdar,
VP Public Relations,
Instinet Corp.**

Richard Parsons, President, Time Warner Inc.

Wendy Barrows

photography
212 685 0799

Judy Lotas, partner, Lotas Minard Patton McIver, Inc.

find*fresh*

@

www.tcherevkoff.com

michel tcherevkoff studio 212.229.1733

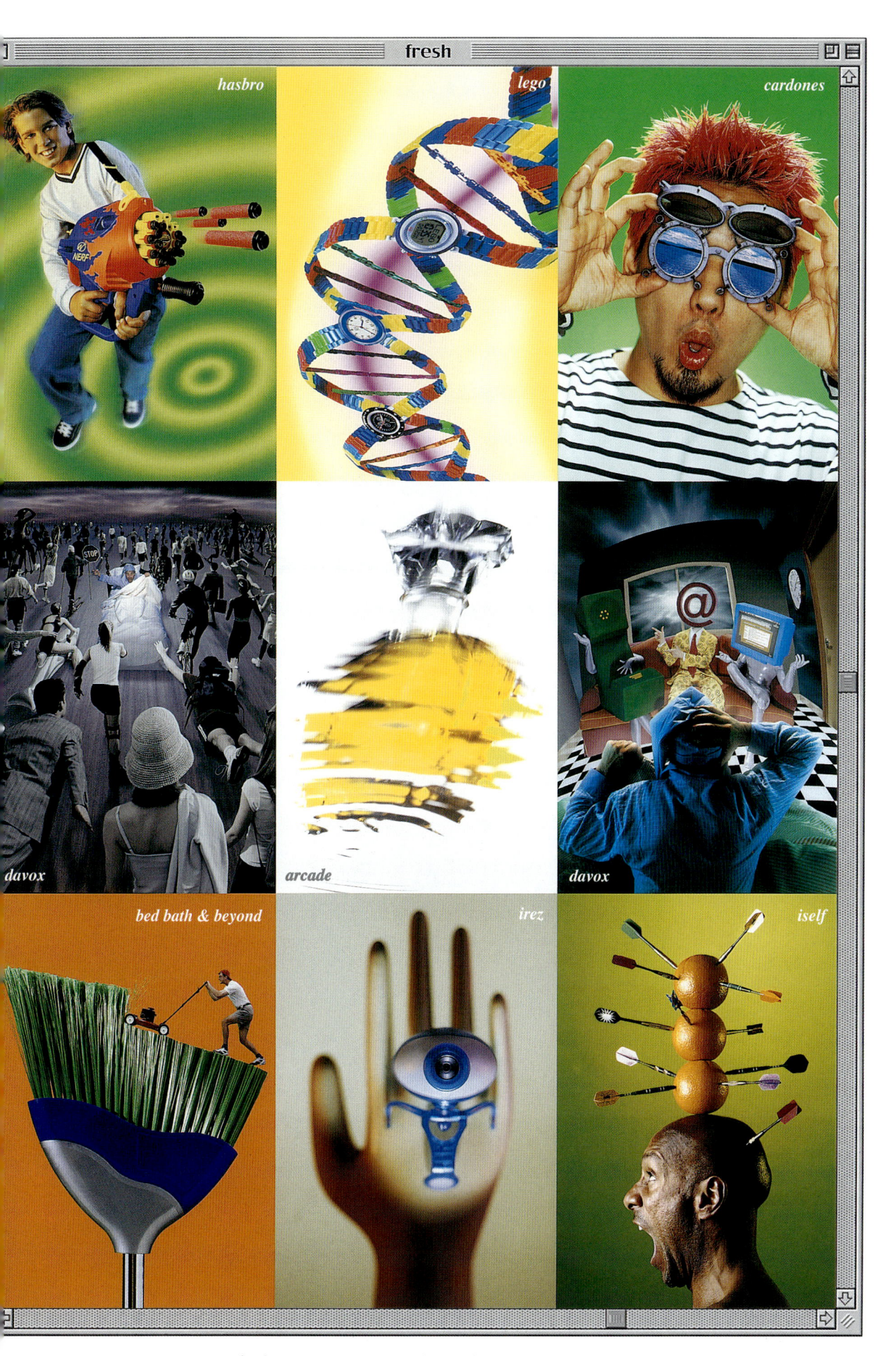

represented by samantha lewin 212.228.5530

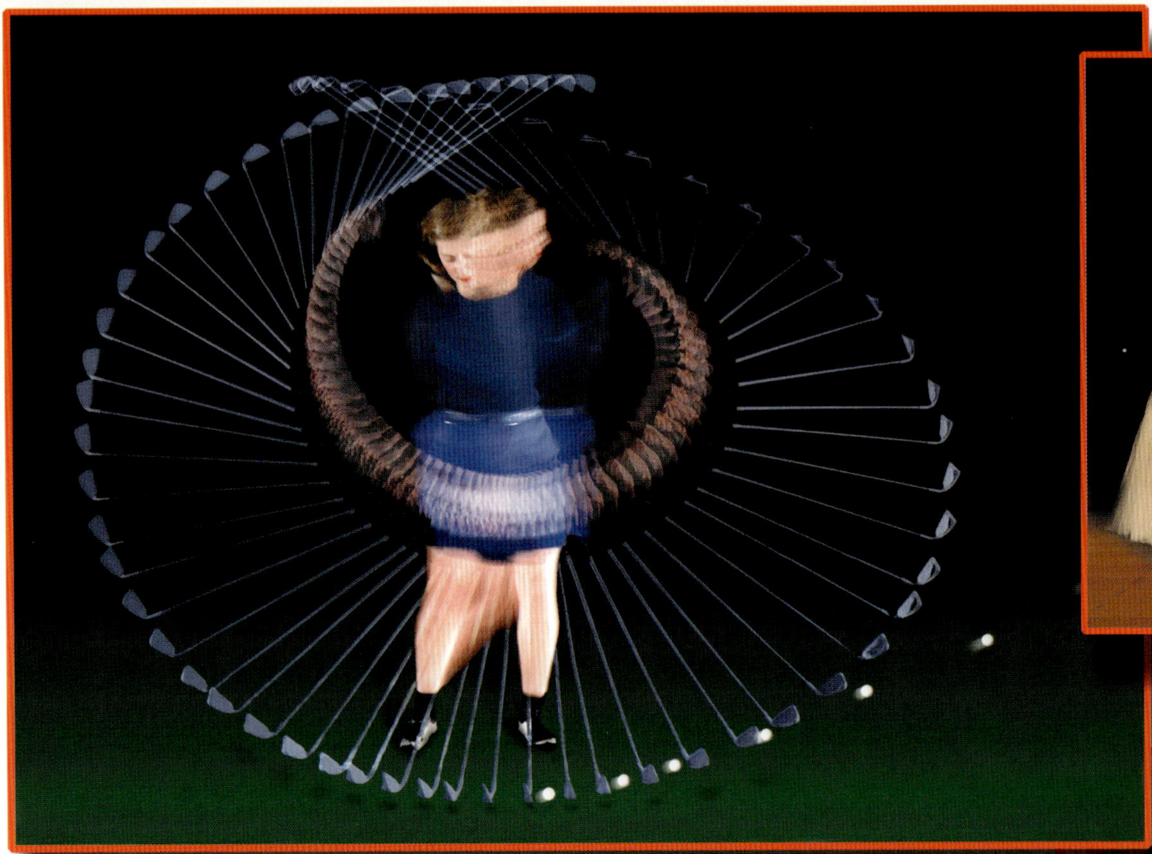
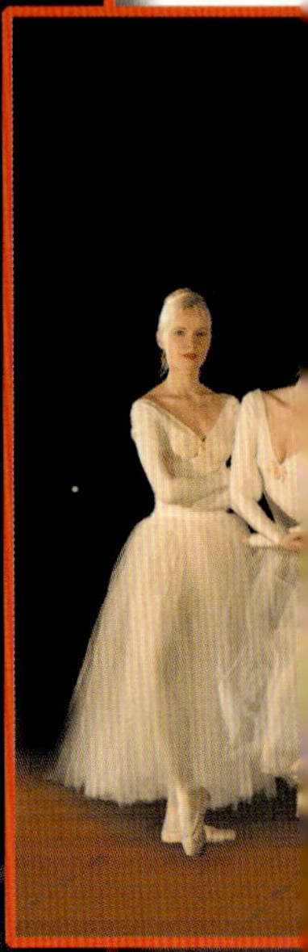
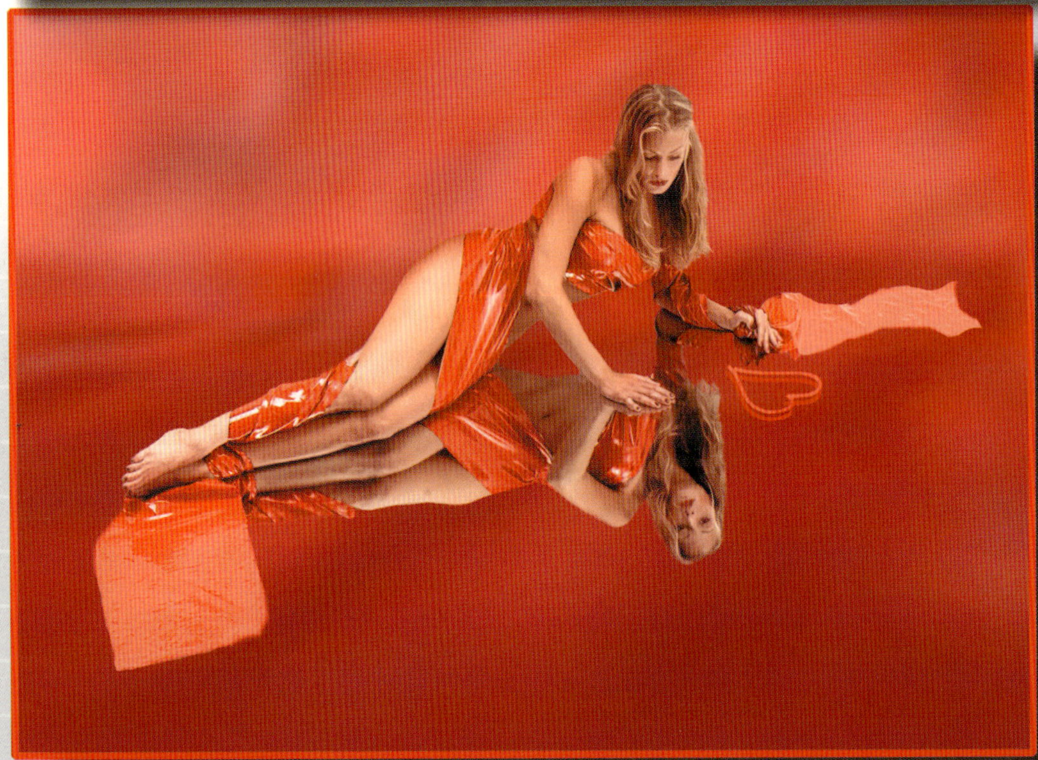
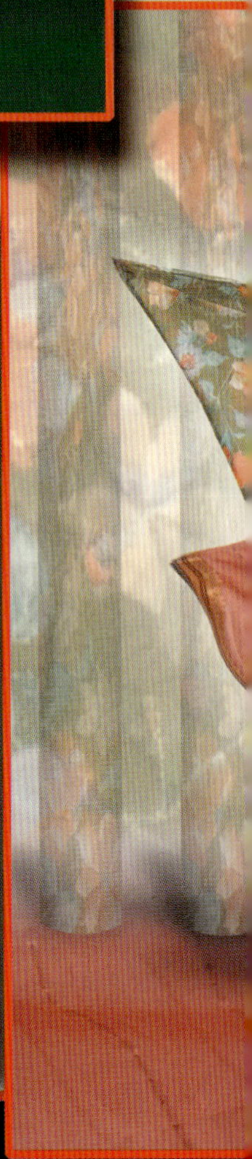
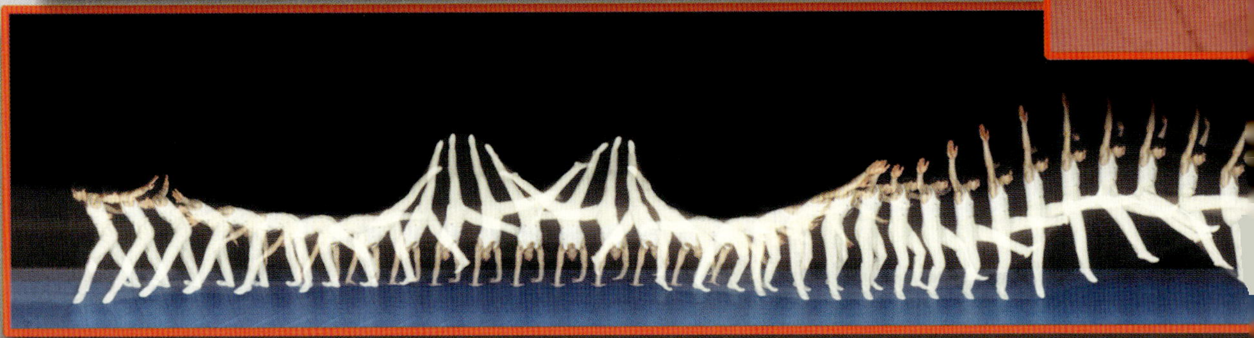

THE GLOBUS BROTHERS

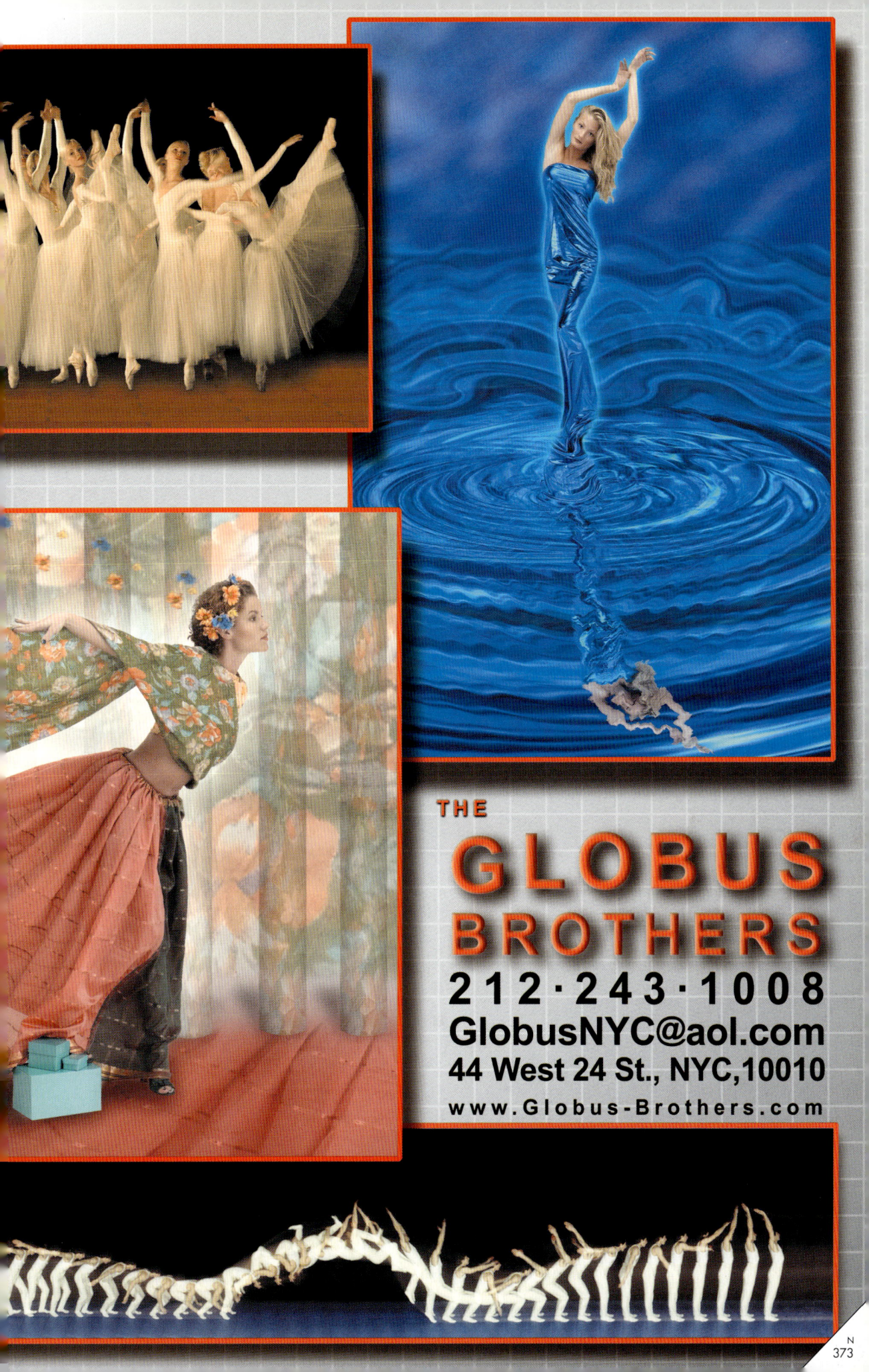

212·243·1008
GlobusNYC@aol.com
44 West 24 St., NYC, 10010
www.Globus-Brothers.com

MARK WIELAND

3 0 1 . 6 0 8 . 3 9 3 9

envoy
CREATIVE CONSULTANTS

represented by envoy creative consultants • 1.800.853.686

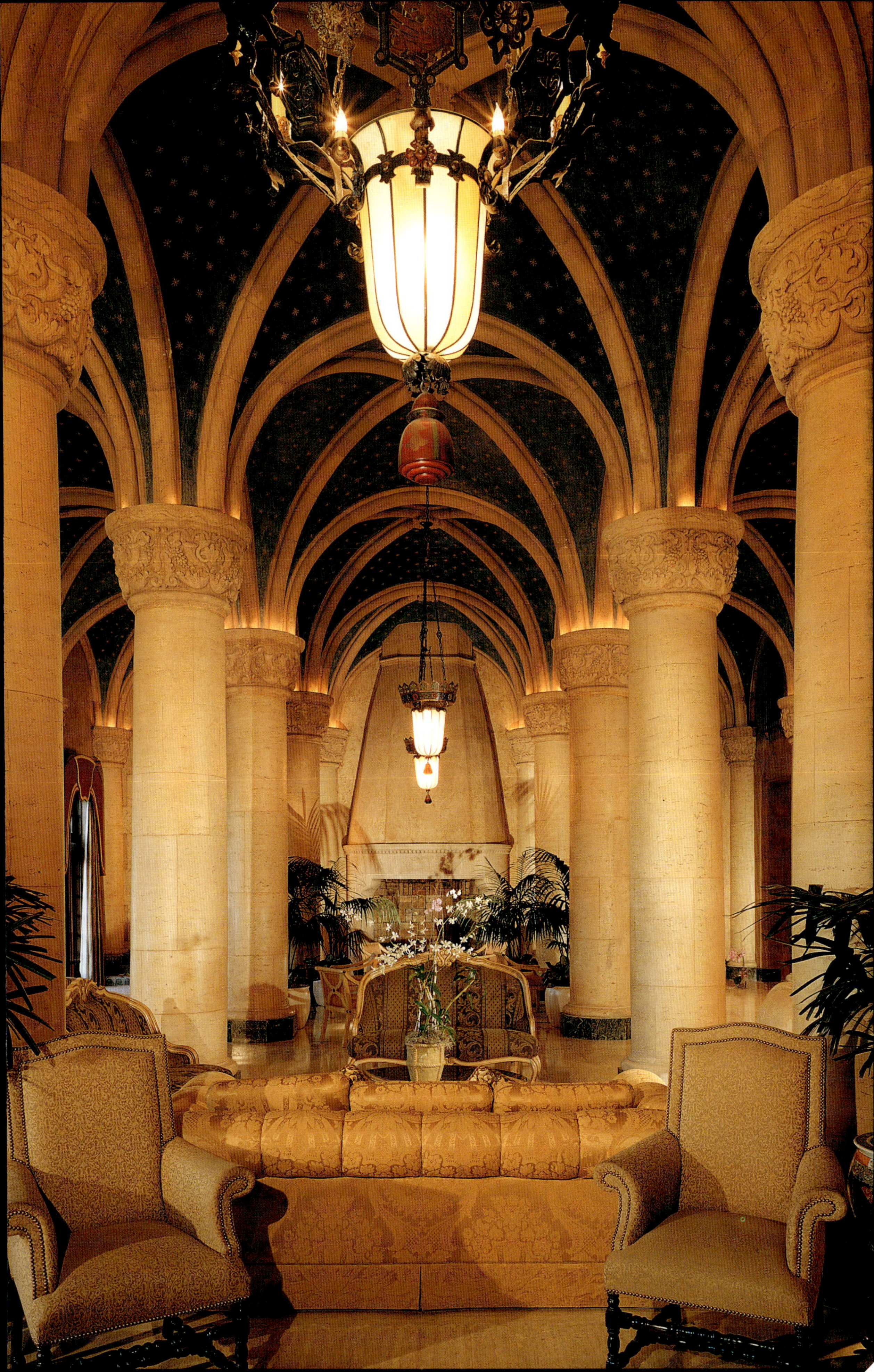

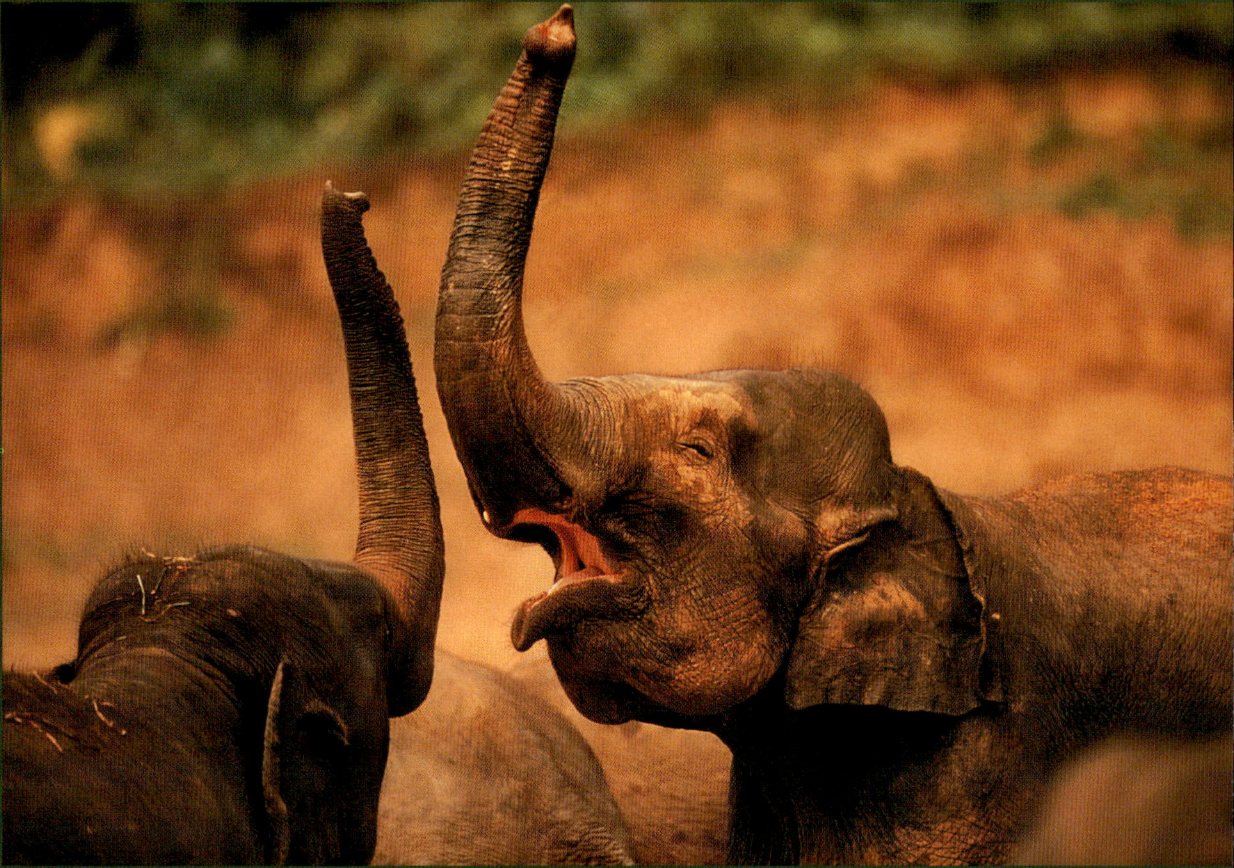

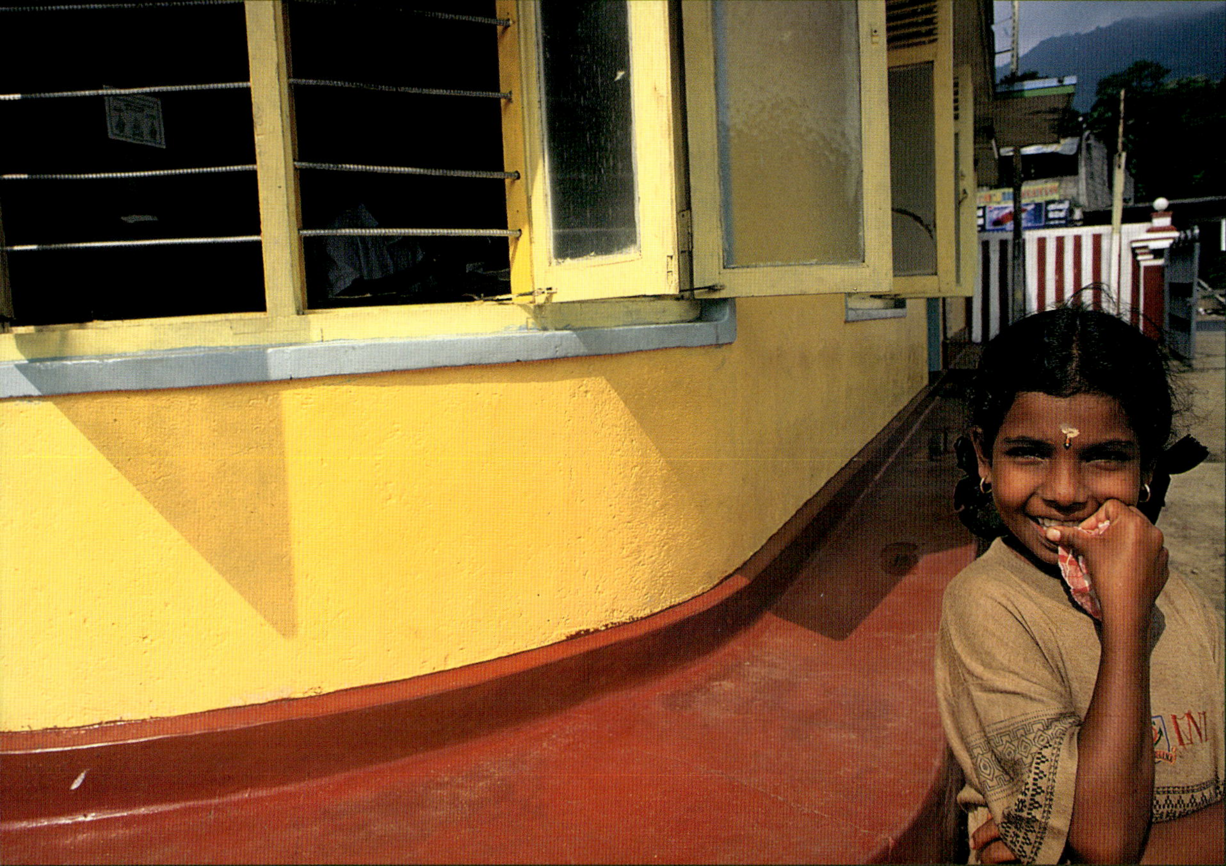

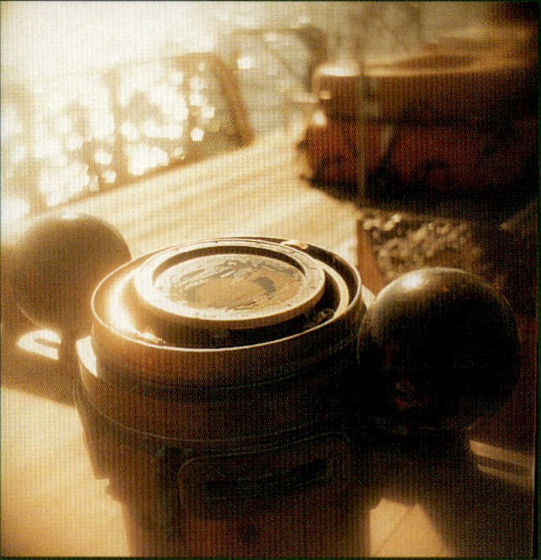
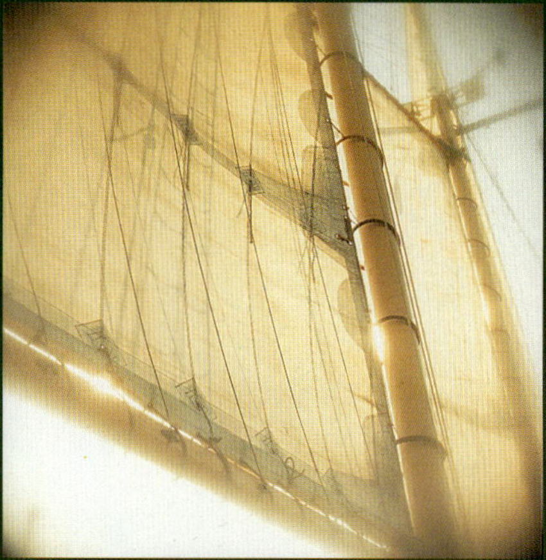
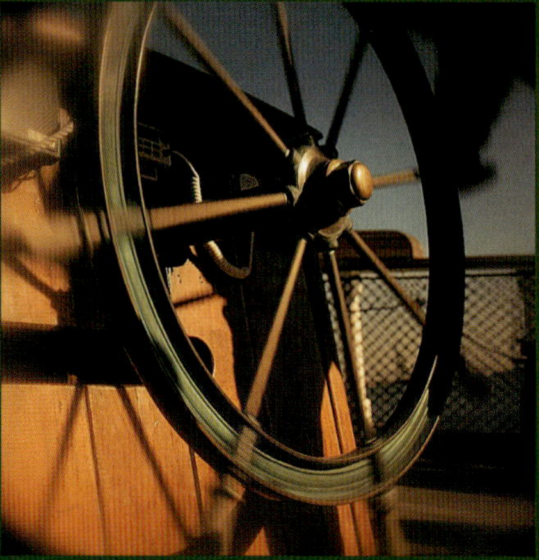
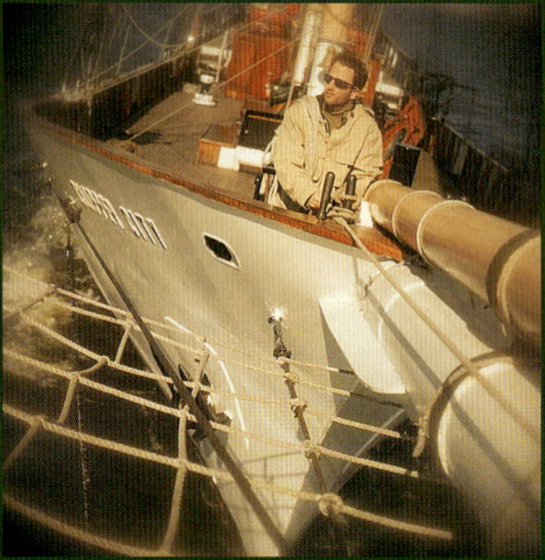
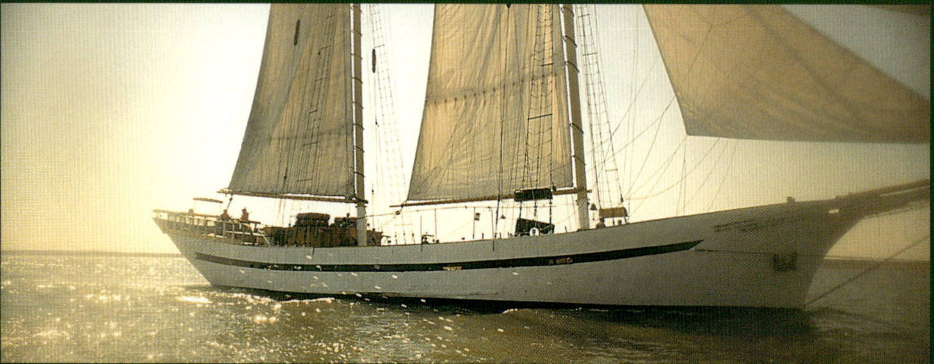

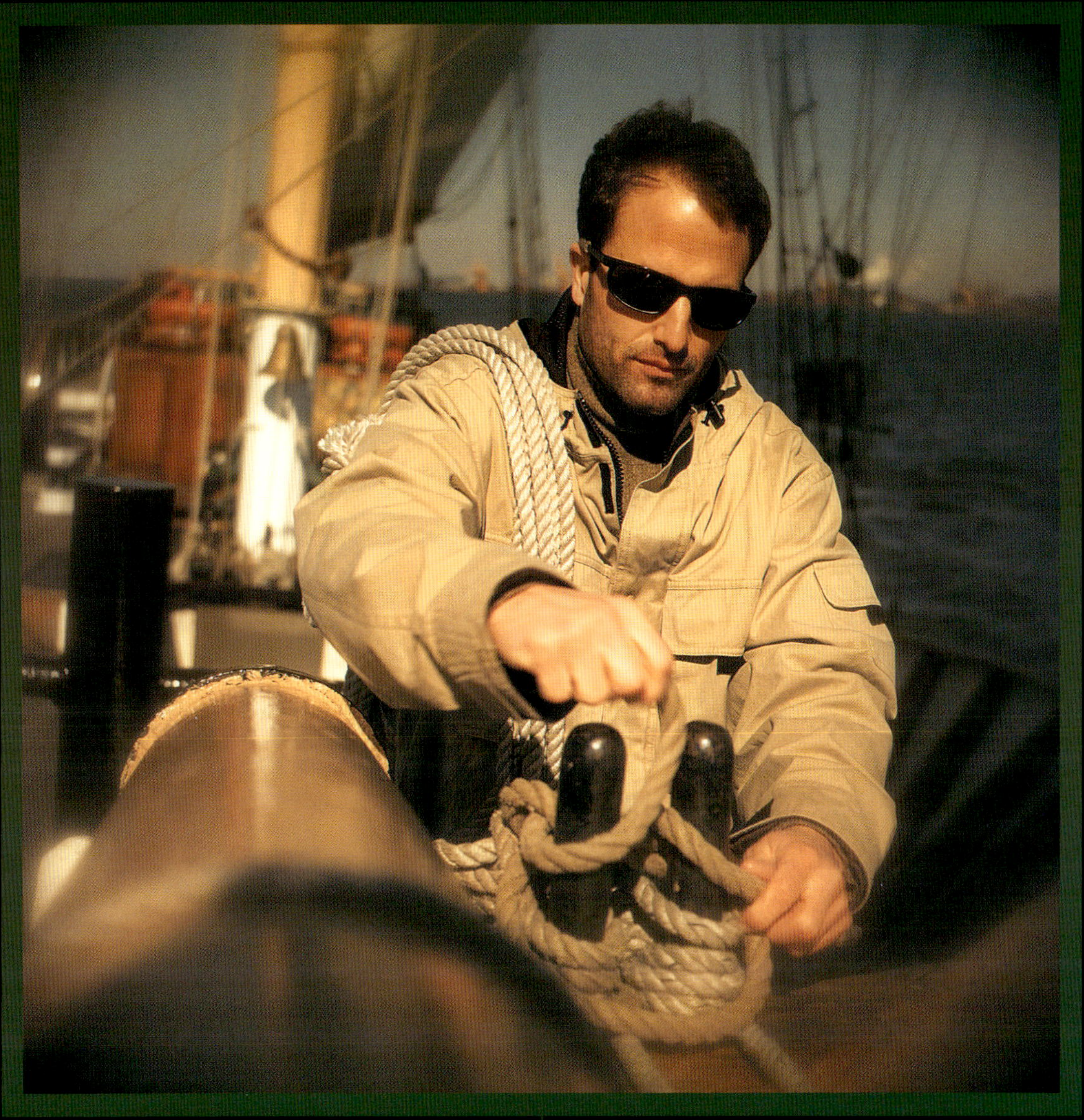

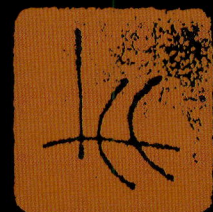

- Christine Cain Weidner -

(212) 349-6354

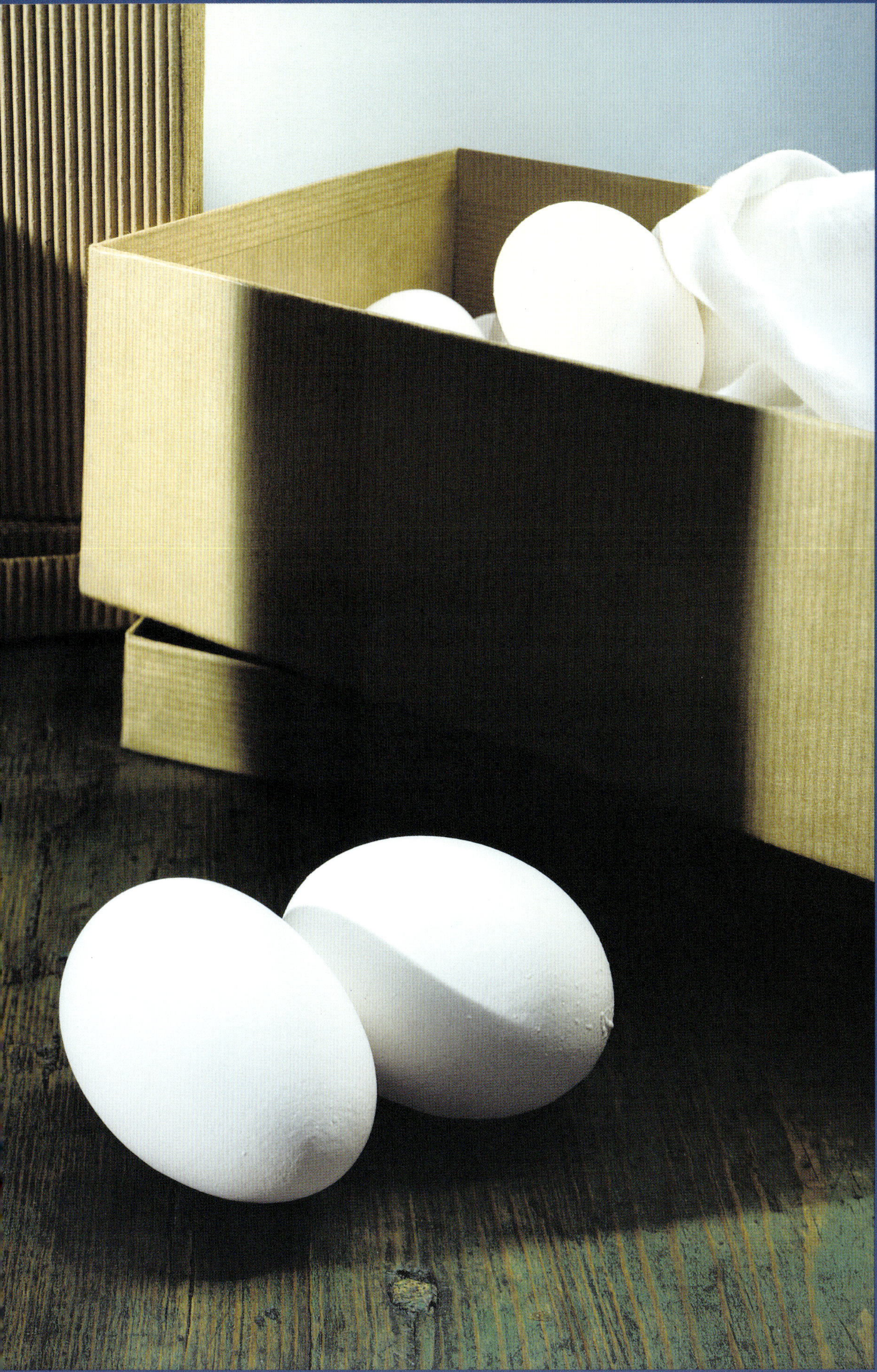

paul aresu represented by barry goldring

telephone: 212.604.0606   website: www.paularesu.com

TONY CORDOZA   PHOTOGRAPHER   212.689.4077   WWW.TONYCORDOZA.COM

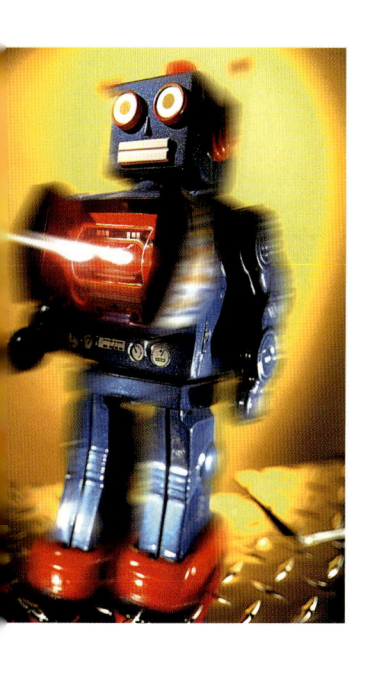

TONY CORDOZA   PHOTOGRAPHER   212.689.4077   WWW.TONYCORDOZA.COM

angela coppola

423 WEST BROADWAY, BOSTON, MA 02127
PHONE 617.268.3303 FAX 617.268.3536
WWW.ANGELACOPPOLA.COM

REPRESENTING

DENNIS BLACHUT

LEE CRUM

GILES HANCOCK

KELVIN HUDSON

PETER RAD

DARRAN REES

db

DOUG BROWN artist management

865 First Avenue Suite 5A NYC 10017   Tel 212 935 4242   Fax 212 935 4344

DARRAN REES

REPRESENTED BY DOUG BROWN ARTIST MANAGEMENT 212 935 4242

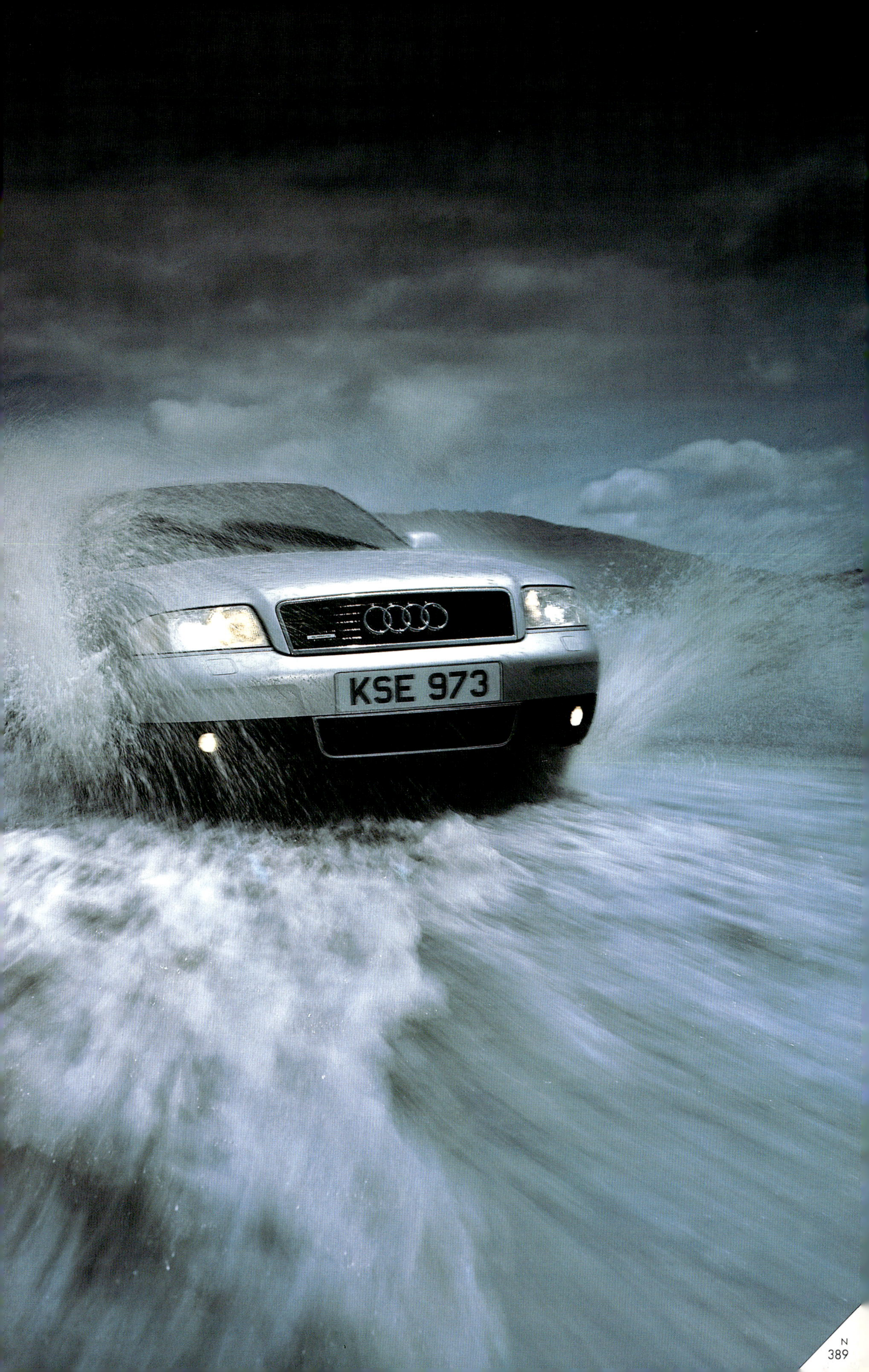
KSE 973

lee crum @ doug brown artist management   212.935.4242   leecrum.com lee crum @ doug brown artist management   212.935.4242   leecrum.com

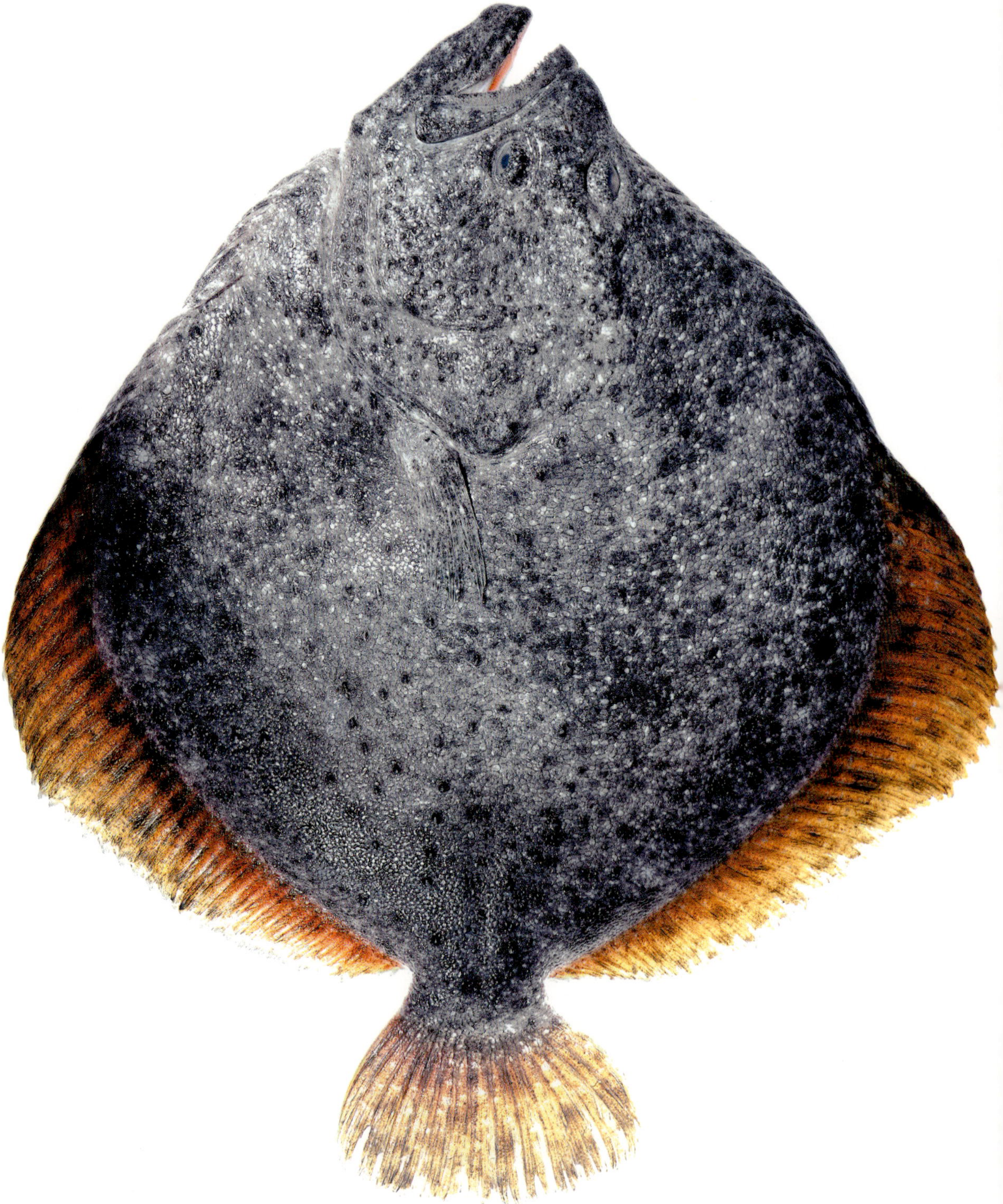

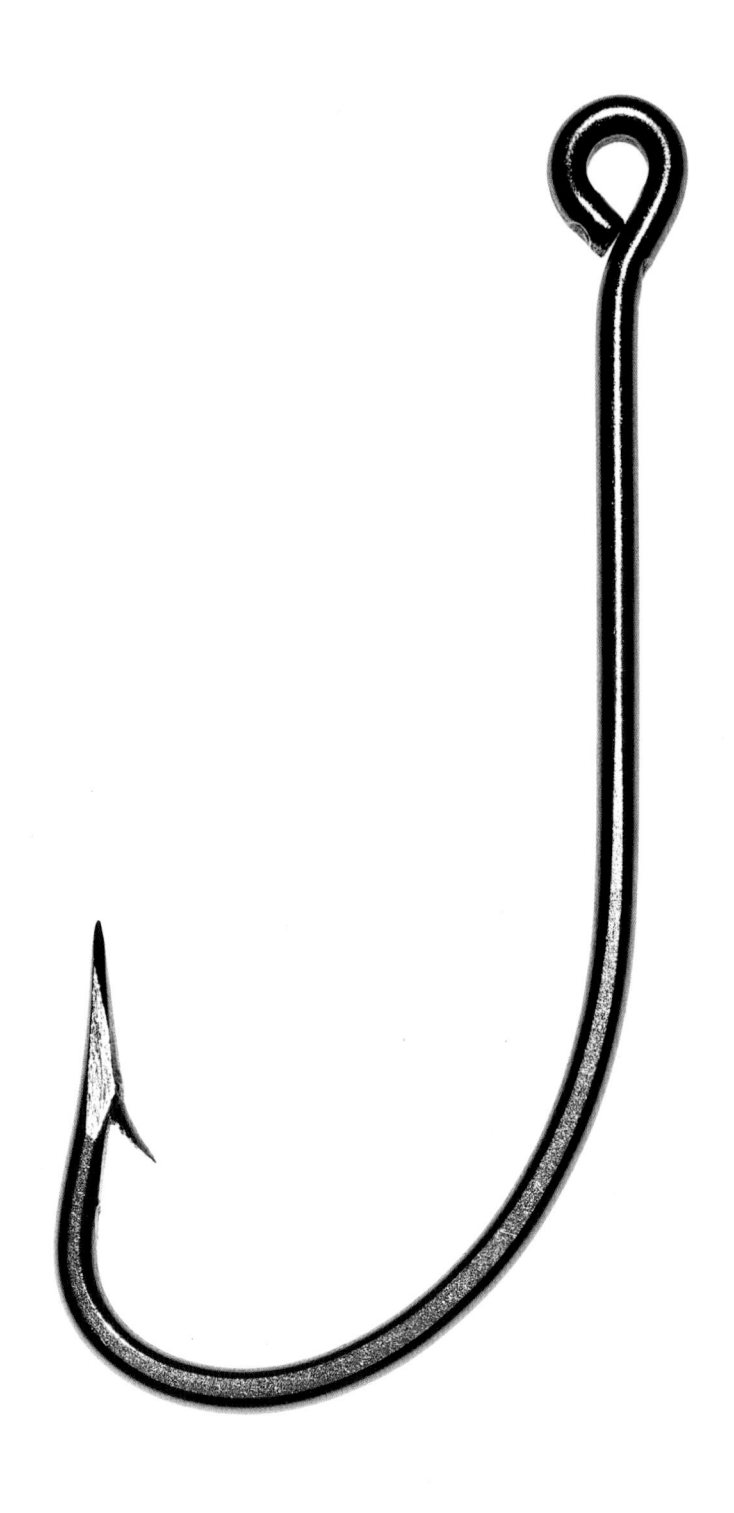

dennis blachut
represented by doug brown artist management
212 935 4242

True to the original.
Realism that would impress a sand crab. Stunning detail.
Printouts that are most like your original photos.
The new hp DeskJet 970C.
Invent, create and inspire for just $399*
For more information, visit hp.com/go/original.
hp
invent

hp
invent
True to the original.
Capture life's vibrant colors.
Discover the nuances of light and shadow.
Printouts that are most like your original photos.
The new hp DeskJet 970C.
Invent, create and inspire for just $399*
hp.com/go/original.

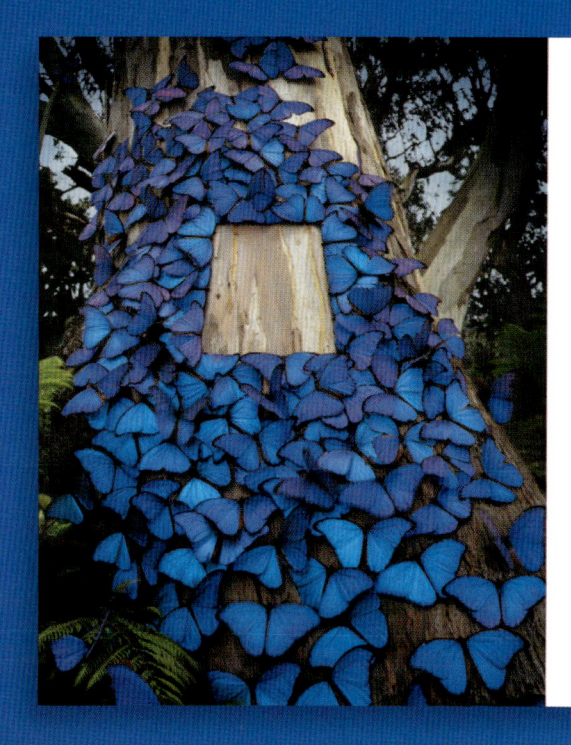

KELVIN HUDSON

REPRESENTED BY DOUG BROWN ARTIST MANAGEMENT

212 935 4242

SCOTT CUNNINGHAM

888 607-9681 • 212 633-9125

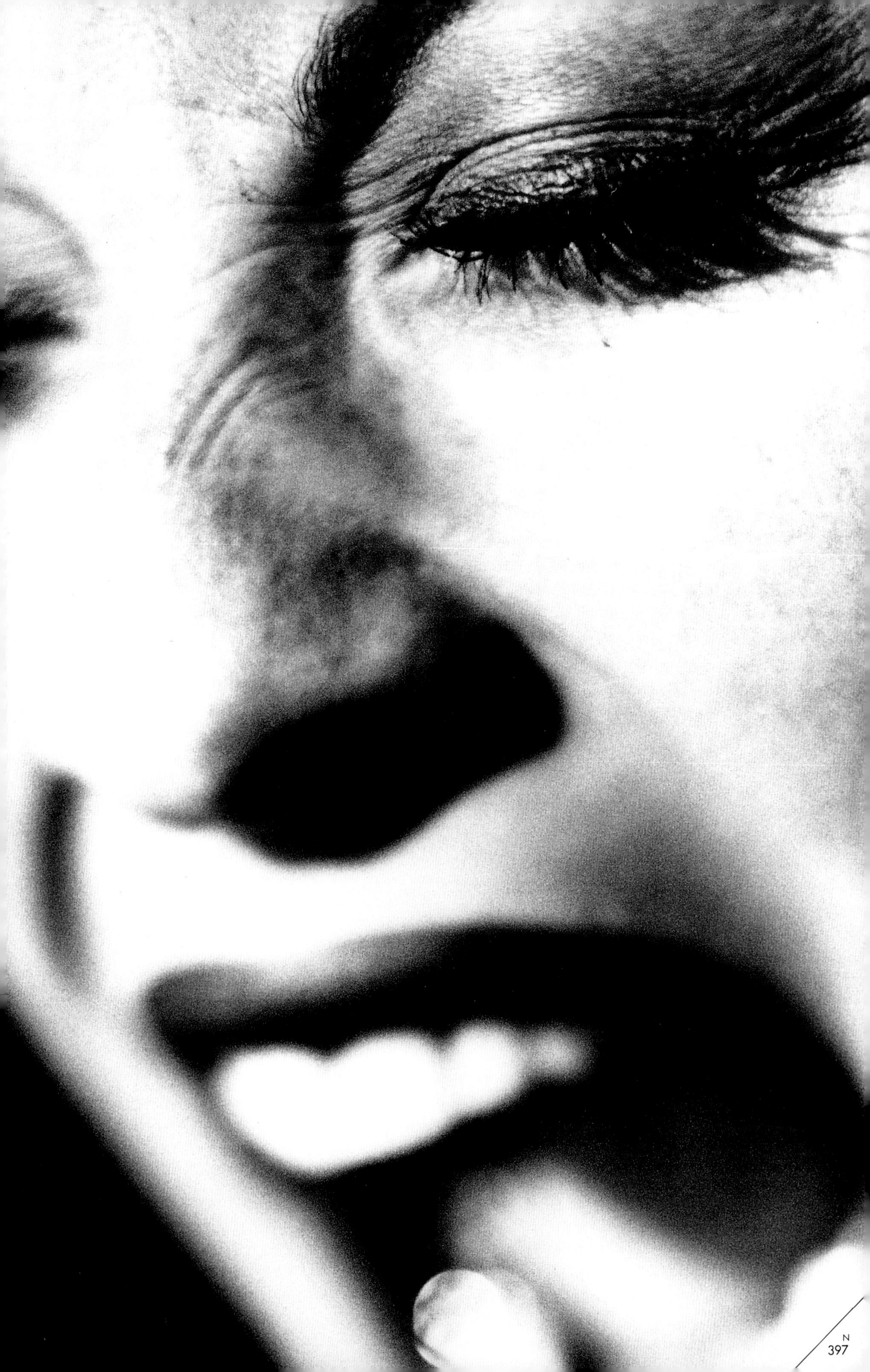

DENNIS O'CLAIR   631 598 3546

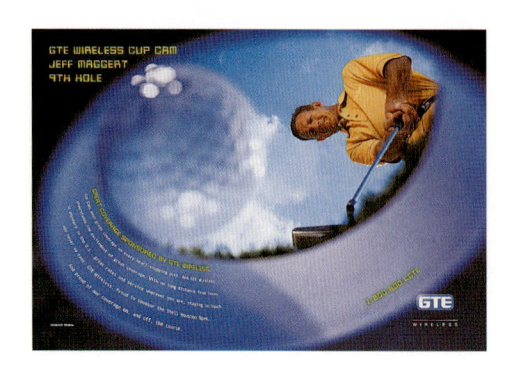

DENNIS O'CLAIR   631 598 3546

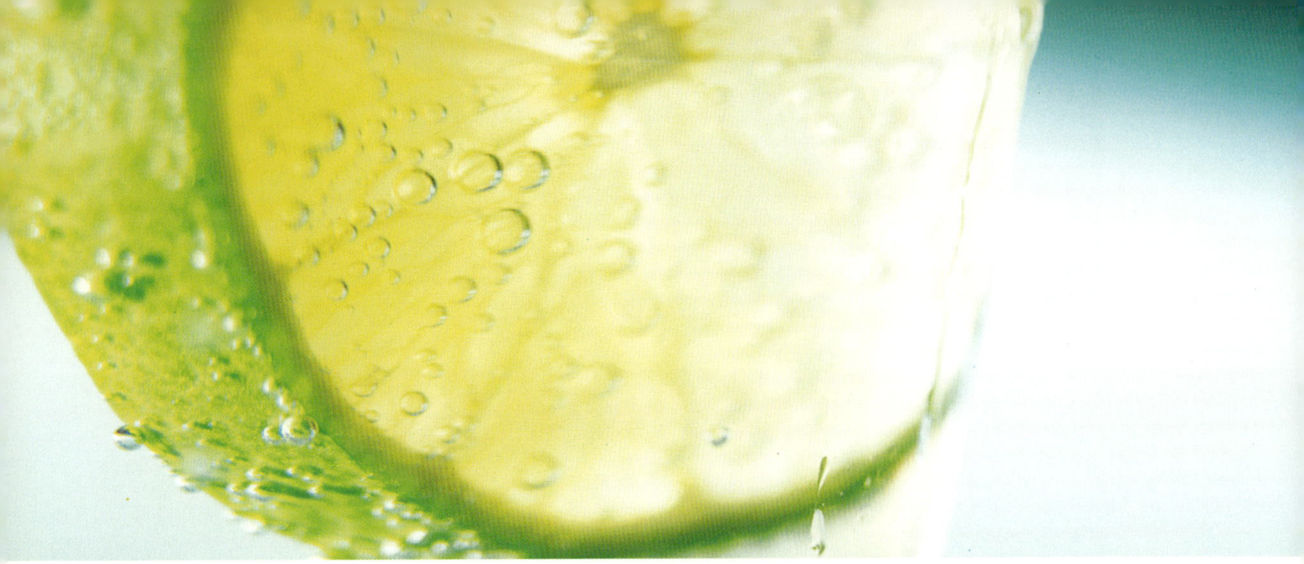

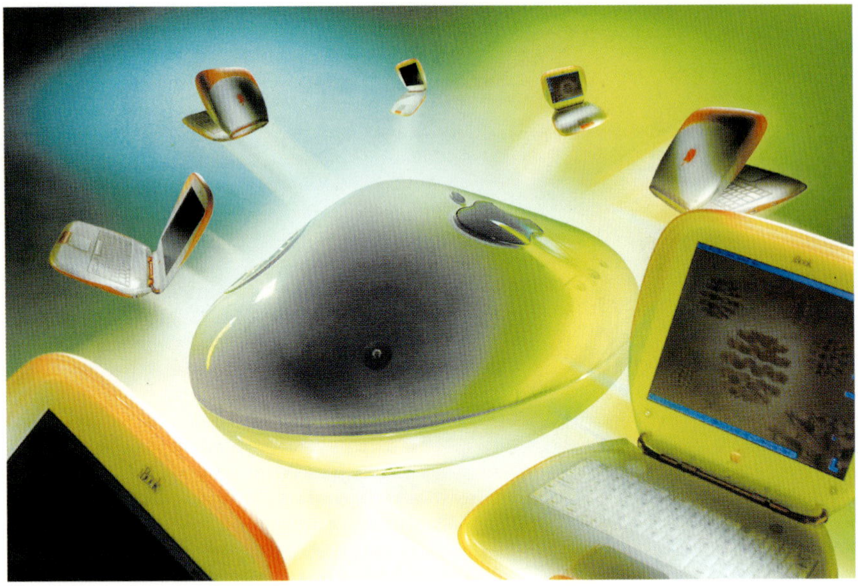

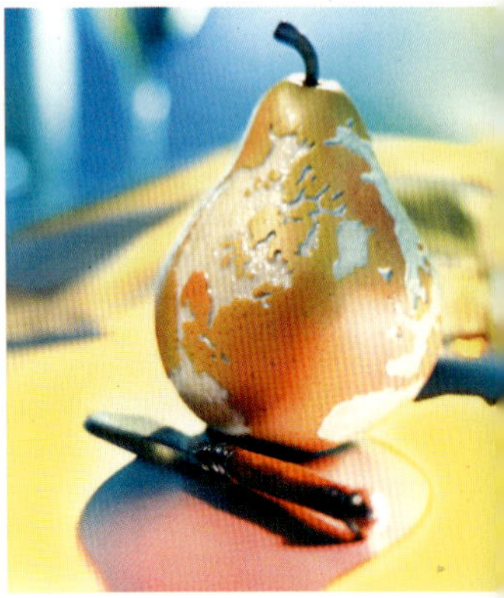

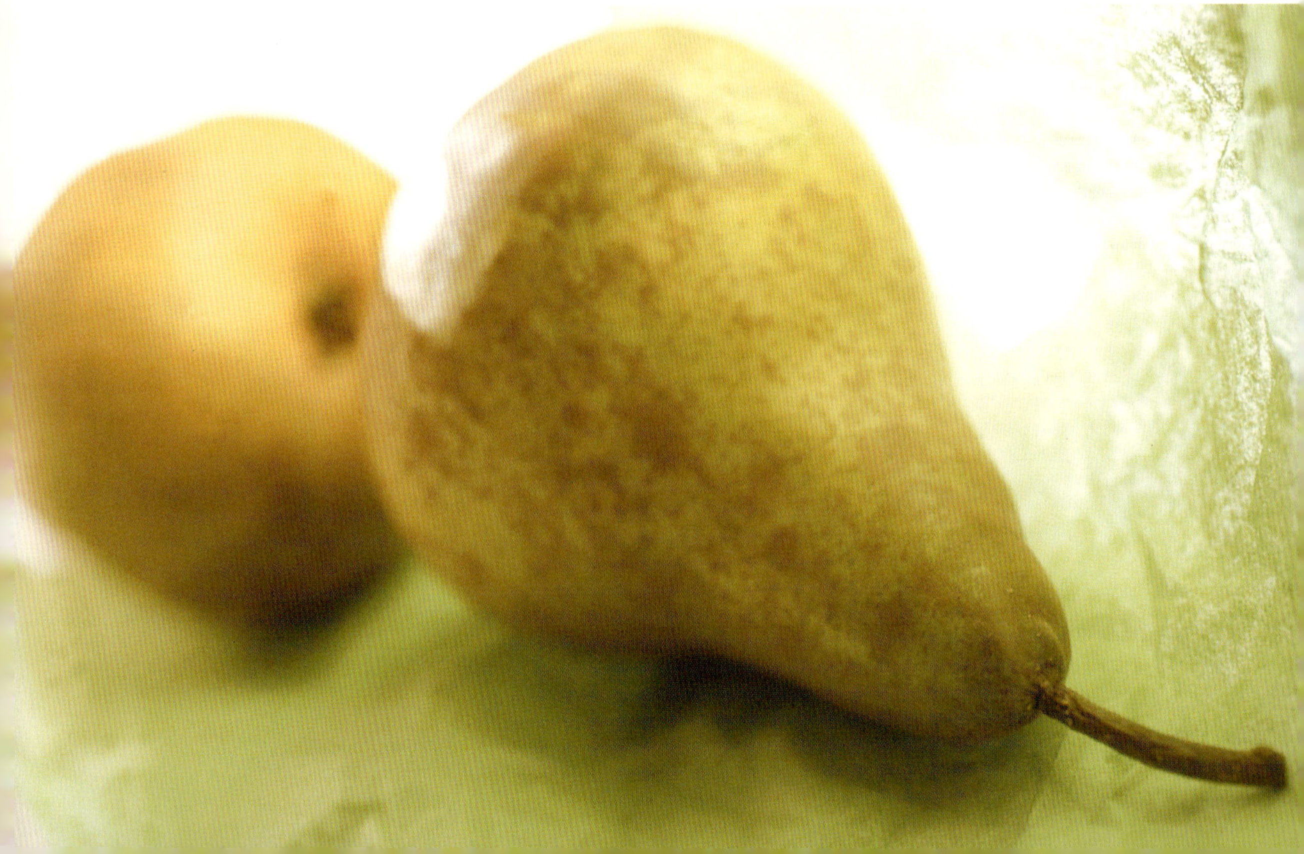

John Wilkes Studio
212-645-1110
www.johnwilkesstudio.com

GREG HINSDALE PHOTOGRAPHY / REPRESENTED BY DIANA BASTIDAS / 212.777.1112 / WWW.GREGHINSDALE.COM

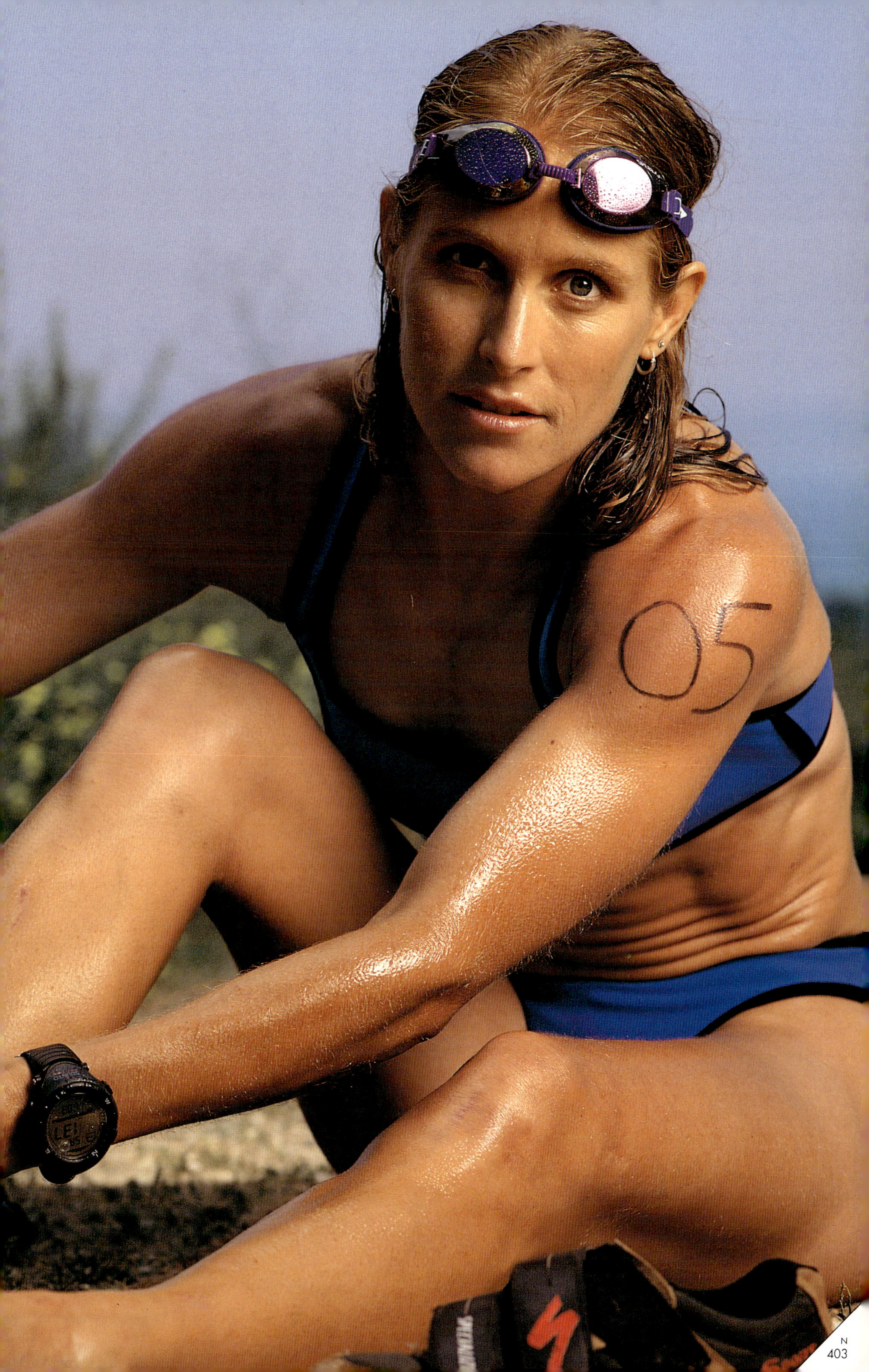

MARTIJN OORT

MARILYN CADENBACH ASSOCIATES
617.868.2004 / www.cadenbach.com

WILLIAM HUBER

Youth Smoking Prevention Campaign ~ Philip Morris

represented by Marilyn Cadenbach Associates
617-868-2004   www.cadenbach.com

represented by Marilyn Cadenbach Associates
617-868-2004   www.cadenbach.com

Ads for Chopin Vodka ~ Warsaw, Poland

WILLIAM HUBER

photography > retouching > web imaging > archiving

ⓘ

icon digital imaging

david dimicco > photographer > > > > >

212.685.1191   www.icondigital.com

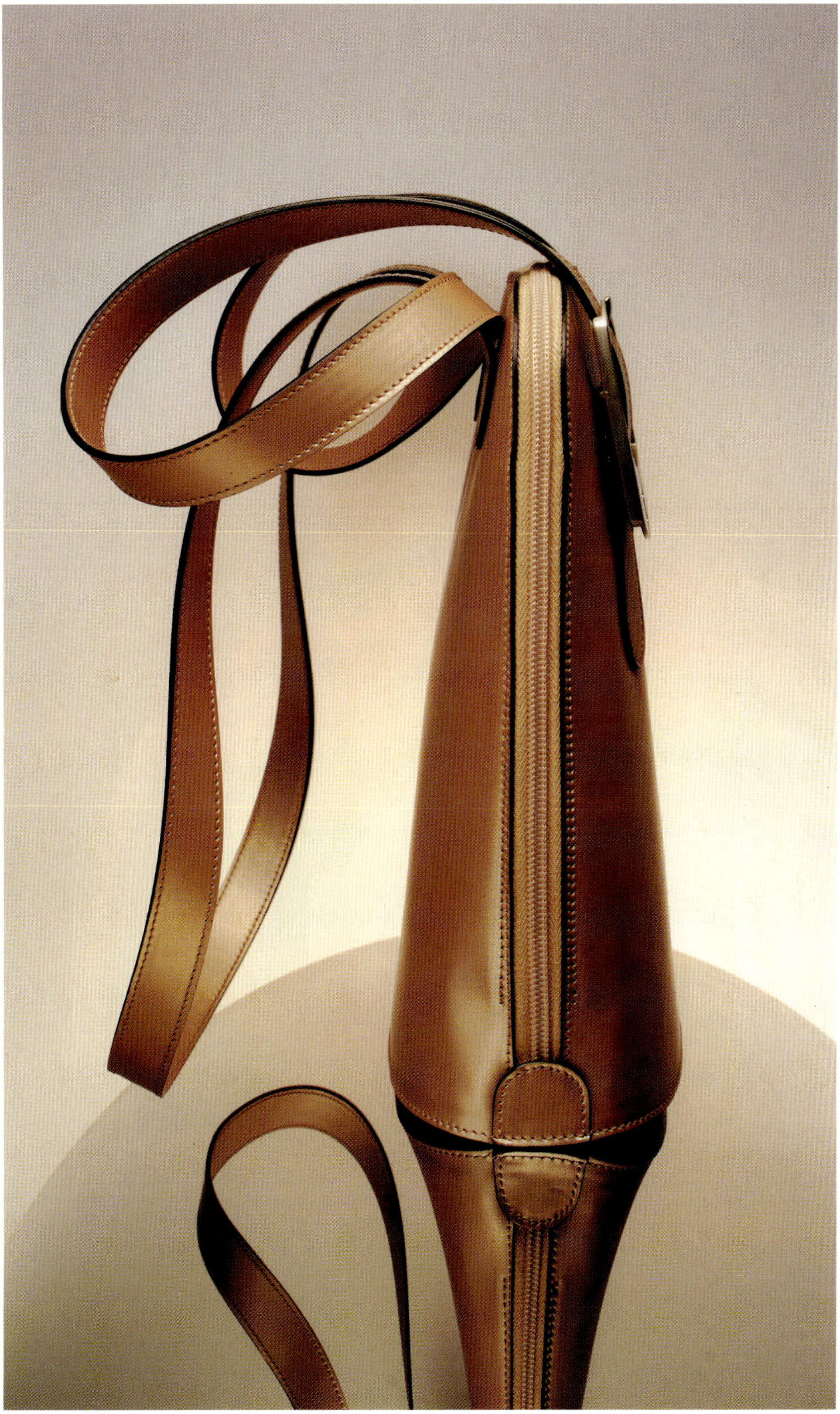

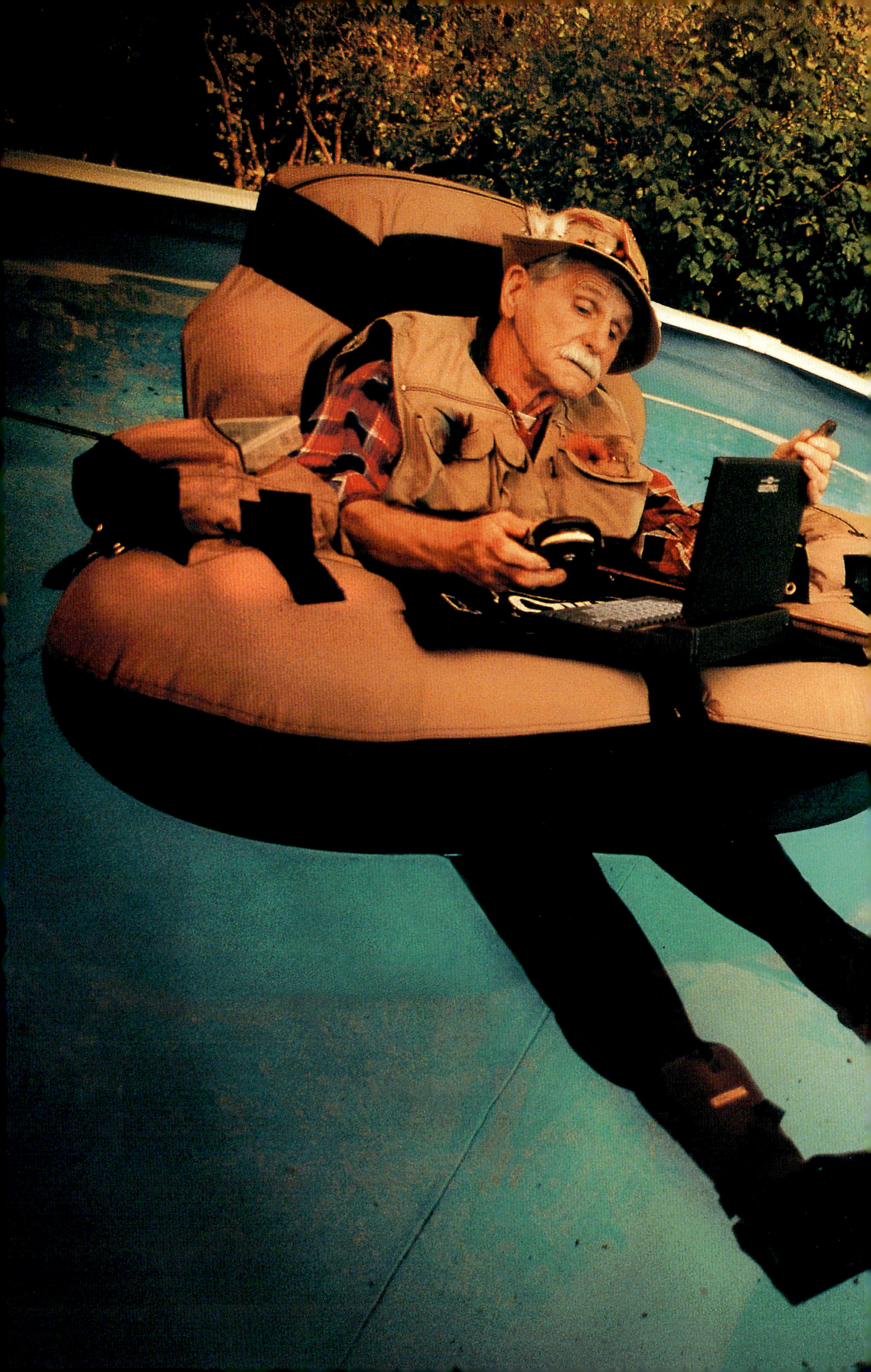

Rocky Thies TEL 617 269 2211
840 SUMMER STREET BOSTON MASSACHUSETTS 02127
WWW.ROCKYTHIES.COM
© 2000 Rocky Thies

REZNY

PHOTOGRAPHY BY AARON REZNY

VOICE: 212 691 1894
FAX: 212 691 1685
EMAIL: AaronRezny@aol.com
WEBSITE: www.cris.com/~rezny

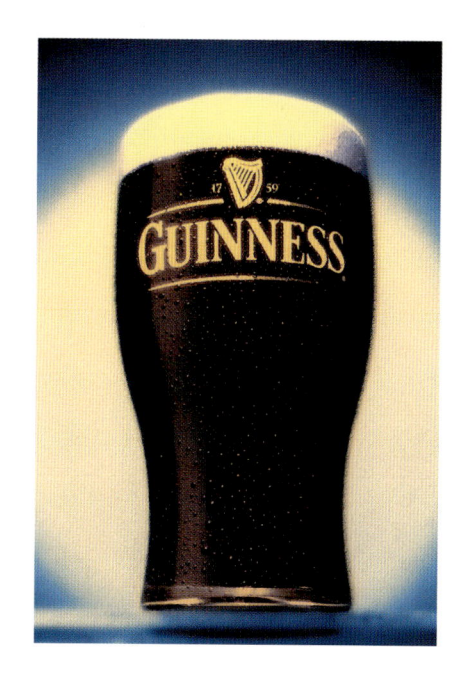

VINCENT

PHOTOGRAPHY BY CHRIS VINCENT

VOICE: 212 691 1894
FAX: 212 691 1685
EMAIL: cvphoto@cris.com
WEBSITE: www.cris.com/~cvphoto

ZIMMERMAN | davidzimmerman.com | 212.206.1000

417

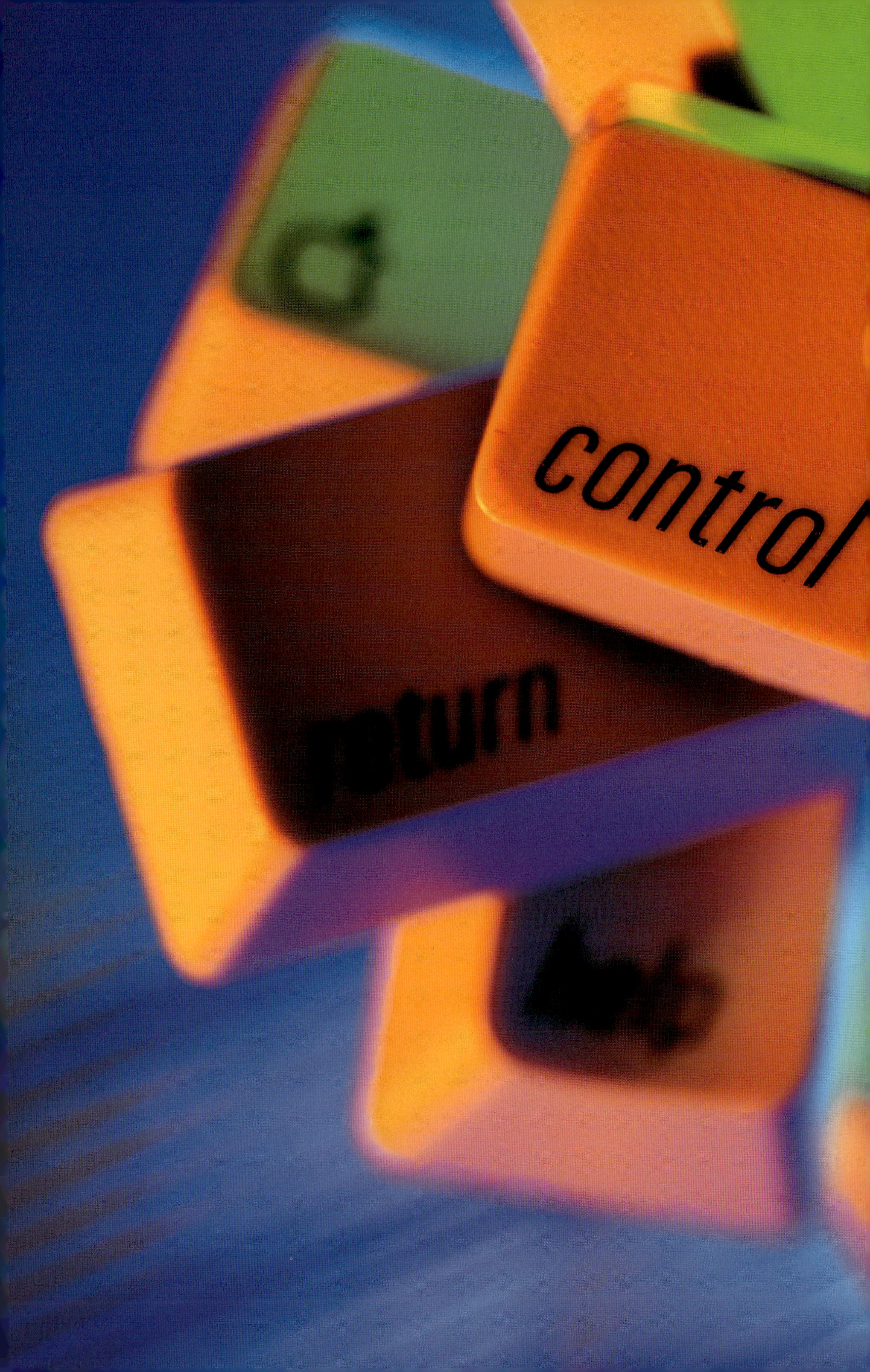
control
return

Spreitzer

Andy Spreitzer Photography
112 West 31st Street
New York, NY 10001
Phone: 212.967.9011
Fax: 212.967.8993
E-mail: info@spreitzerphotography.com
Url: www.spreitzerphotography.com

STEPHEN SHERMAN PHOTOGRAPH

617.542.1496 Voice   617.542.2537 Fax   www.shermanphoto.com

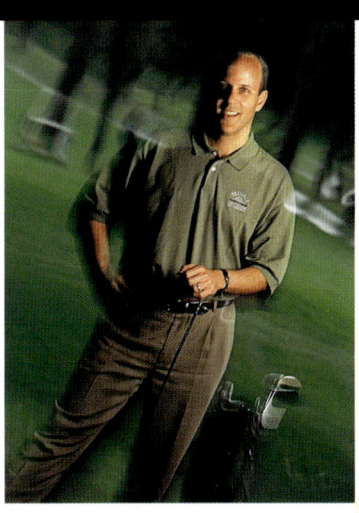

Bronstein Berman Wills
Represented by Maureen M. Smith
Tel 212 925 2999 Fax 212 925 3799 www.bbwstudio.com

Steve Bronstein

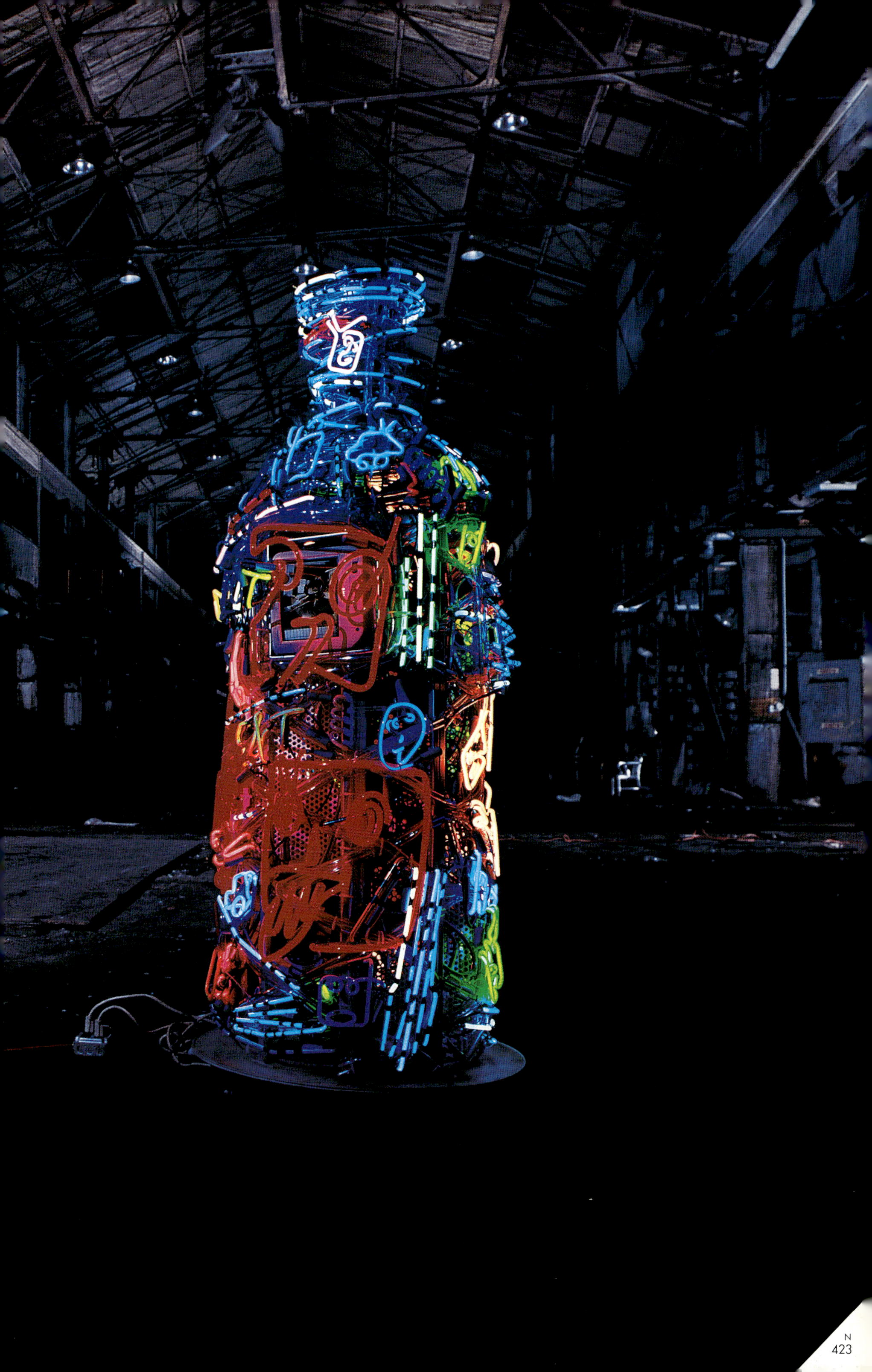

Howard

Berman

Bronstein Berman Wills

Represented by Maureen M. Smith Tel 212 925 2999 Fax 212 925 3799 www.bbwstudio.com

Bronstein Berman Wills
Represented by Maureen M. Smith
Tel 212 925 2999　Fax 212 925 3799　www.bbwstudio.com

Bret Wills

ASHTON WORTHINGTON   > 212.207.5155   > 1032 AVENUE OF THE AMERICAS > NUMBER 4

EW YORK > NEW YORK > 10018 > E ASHTON@ASHTONOGRAPHY.COM > WEB WWW.ASHTONOGRAPHY.COM real light...

real life

Greg Kinch → 212.988.5210
represented by Marlaina Gayle → 212.822.8510
→ www.kinch.com

Greg Kinch
photography

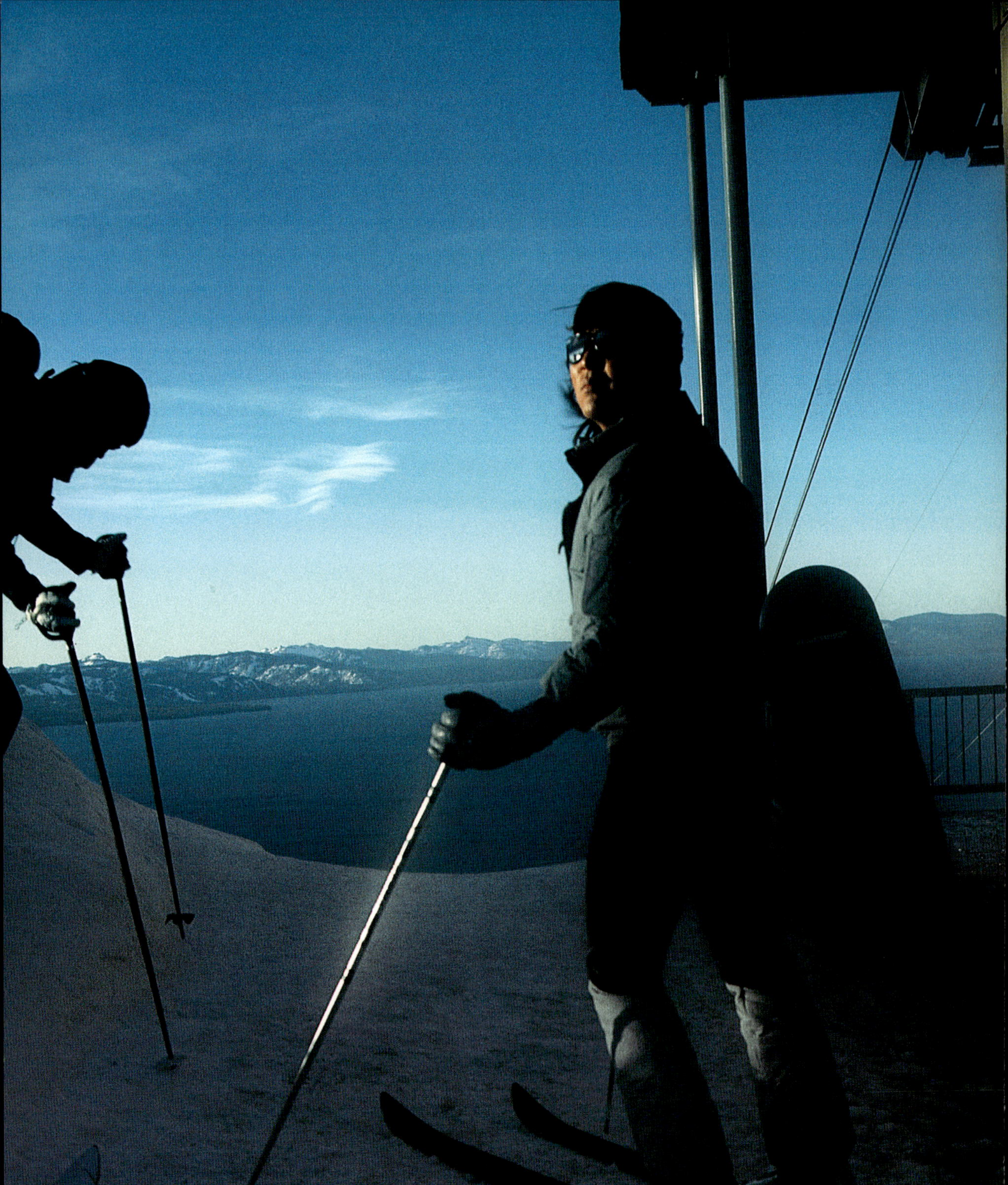

Mike Casper
Ithaca, New York
607-257-5349
www.casperphoto.com

PŌ′HÜ′SKI

Pohuski cooks.

Michael Pohuski   Print & Film   1.410.962.5404

Represented by The Roland Group   1.301.718.7955

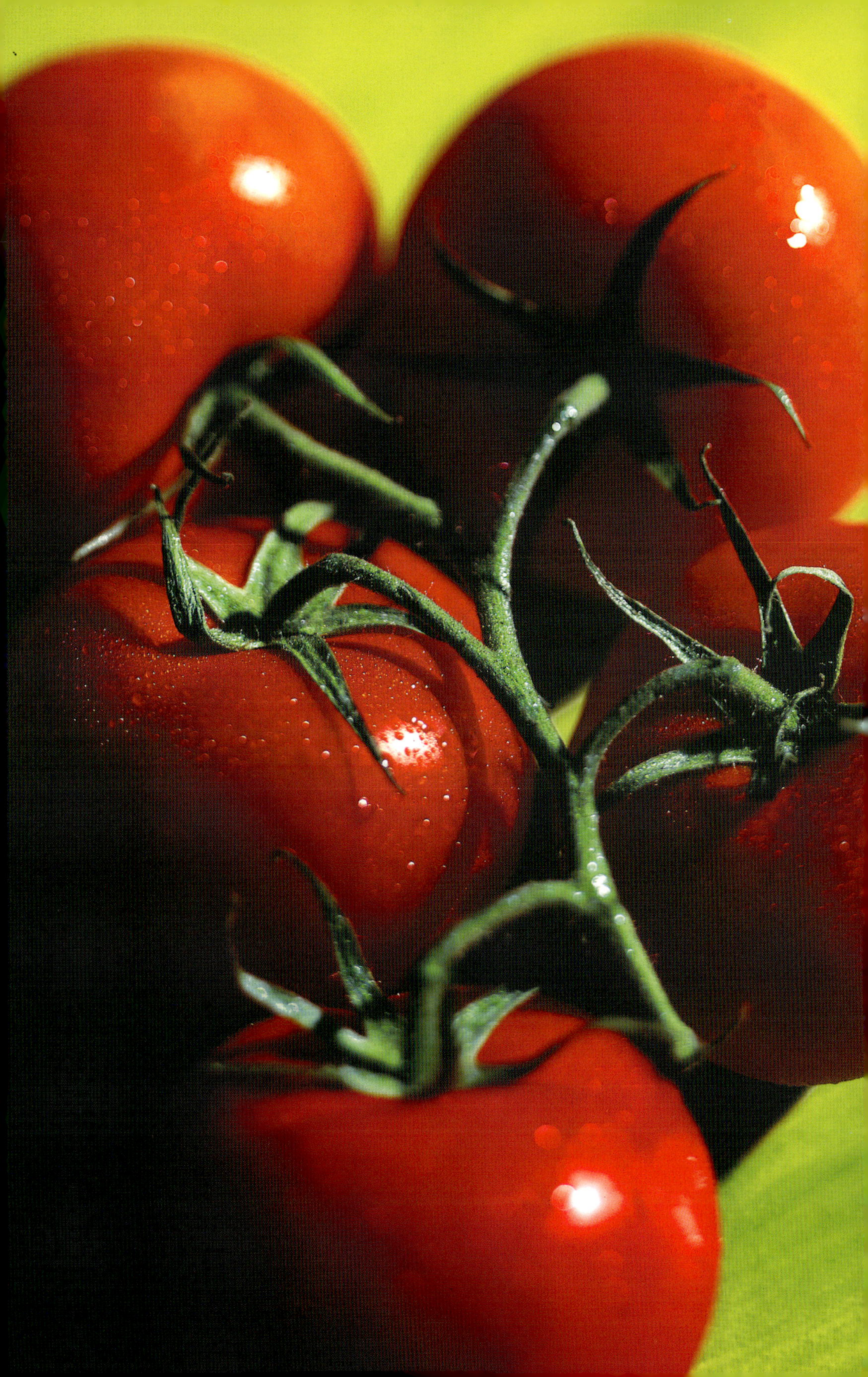

Zeldin

NEW YORK CITY

212.696.9647

WWW.ODEDZELDIN.C

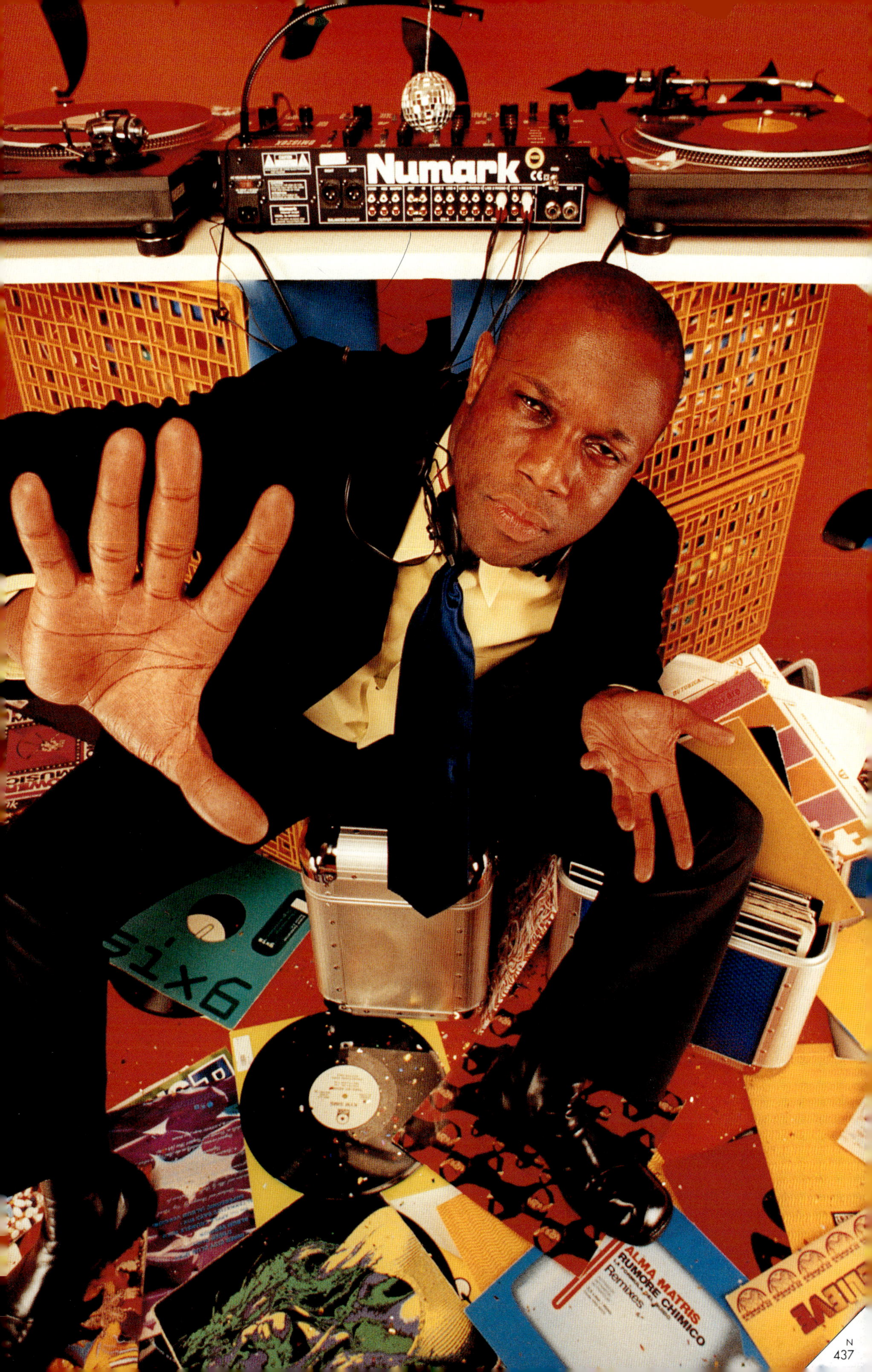
Numark
ALMA MATRIS
RUMORE CHIMICO
Remixes

chris stein digital & film photography

represented by alex hong t 212.620.0295

Brooks Brothers
ESTABLISHED 1818
Brooks Brothers
ESTABLISHED 1818
Brooks Brothers
SPECIAL ORDER
Brooks Brothers
ESTABLISHED 1818
Brooks Brothers
ESTABLISHED 1818
Brooks Brothers
ESTABLISHED 1818

Paul Ar

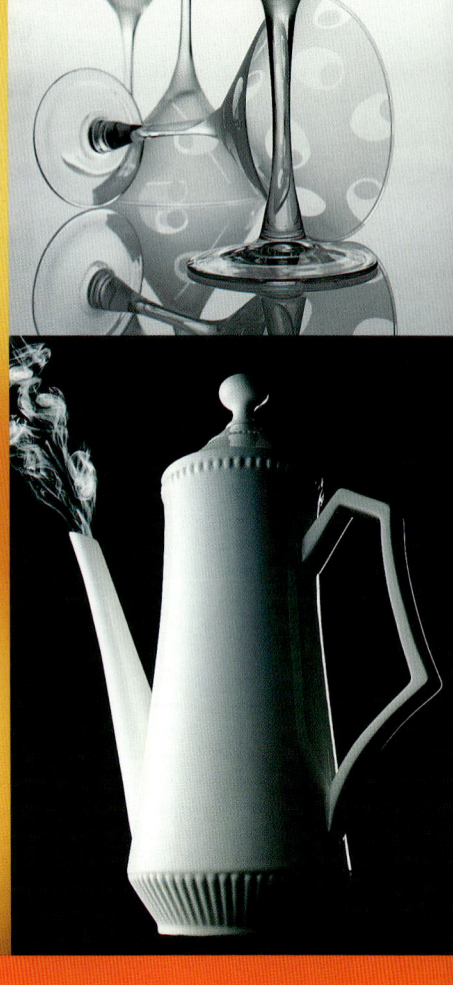

bruster

150 west 28th street #1201 NYC 10001 212-691-8107

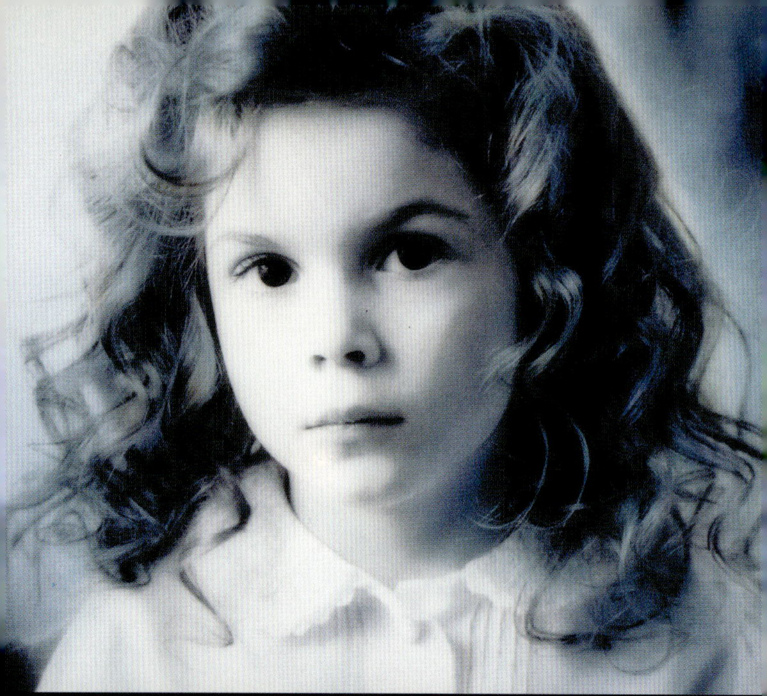

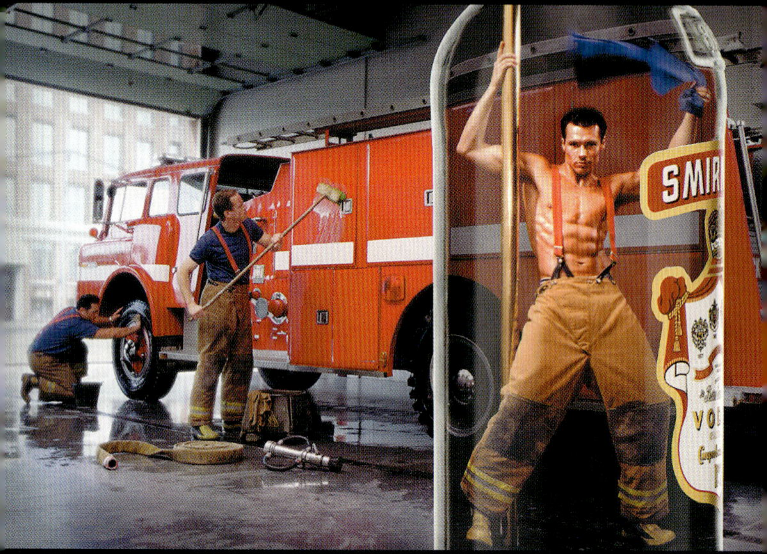
SMIR

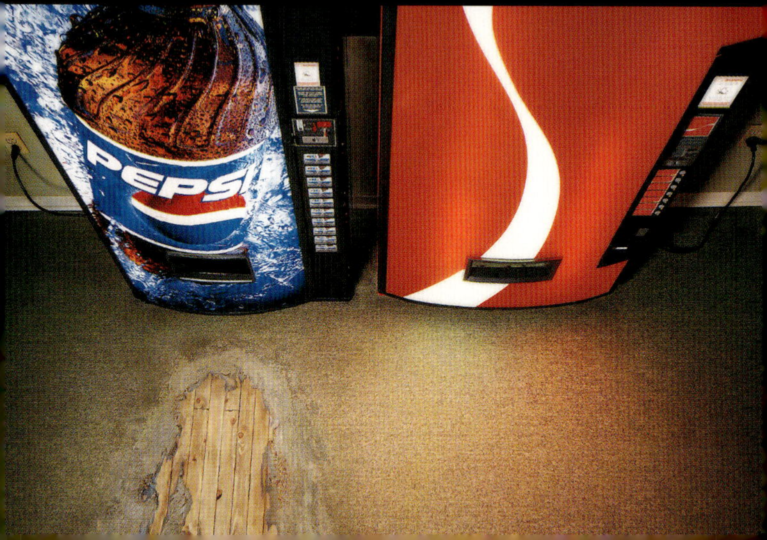
PEPSI

PHILIP ROSTRON

Instil Productions

Photography & Digital Imaging

Tel: 416 596 6587 • Fax: 416 596 8649

instil@interlog.com • www.instilproductions.com

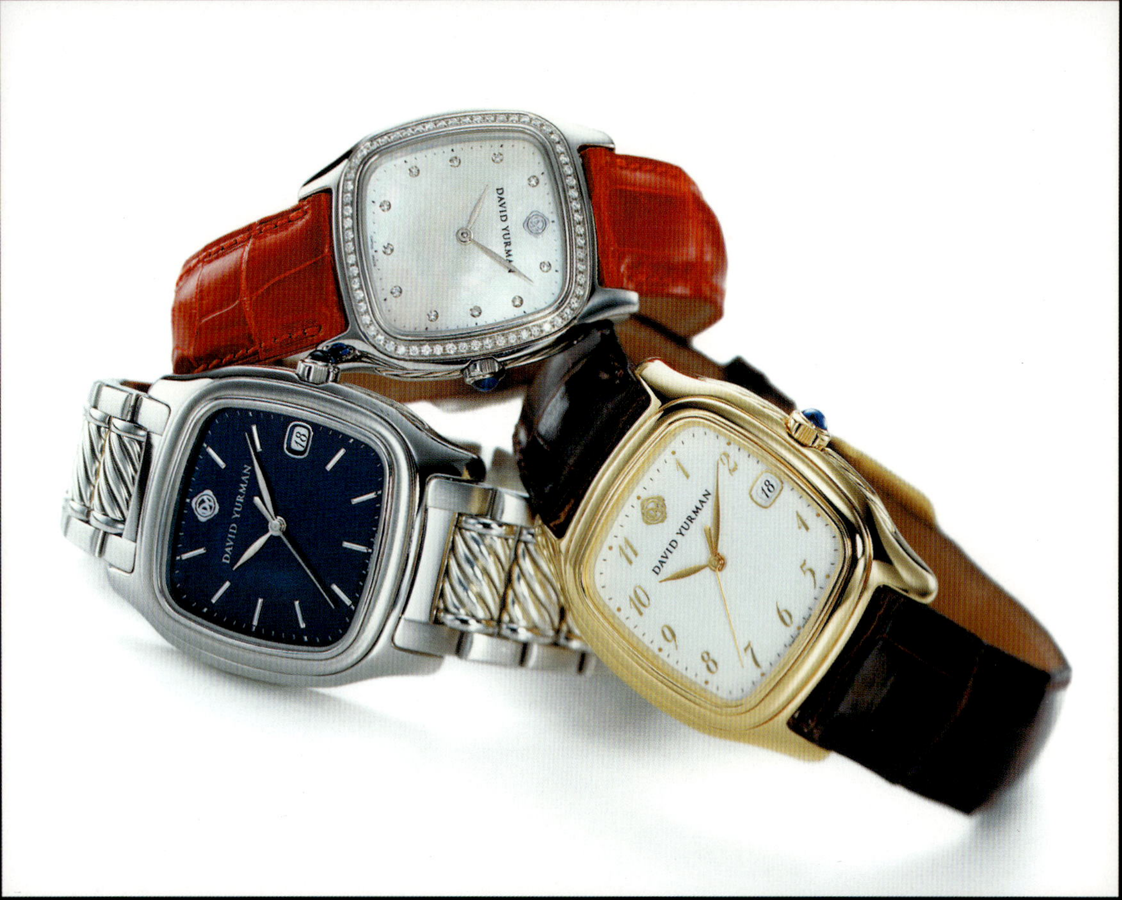

DAVID YURMAN
DAVID YURMAN
DAVID YURMAN

NIWA STUDIO INC 5 EAST 16 STREET NEW YORK NY 10003
REPRESENTED BY ROBIN ANDERSON 212 627 4608 WWW.NIWASTUDIO.COM

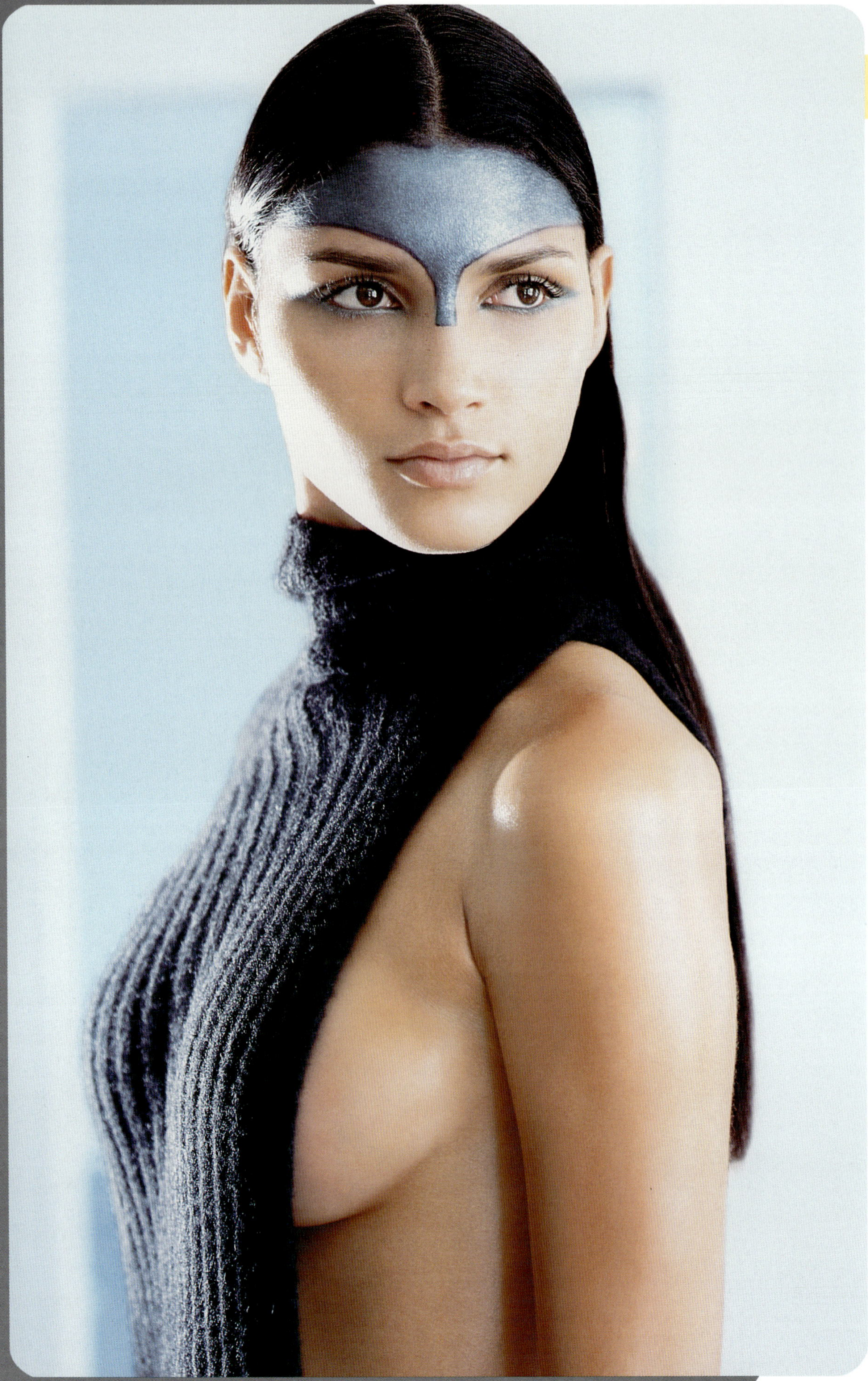

433 west 34th nyc ny 10001 tel. 212 563 1724

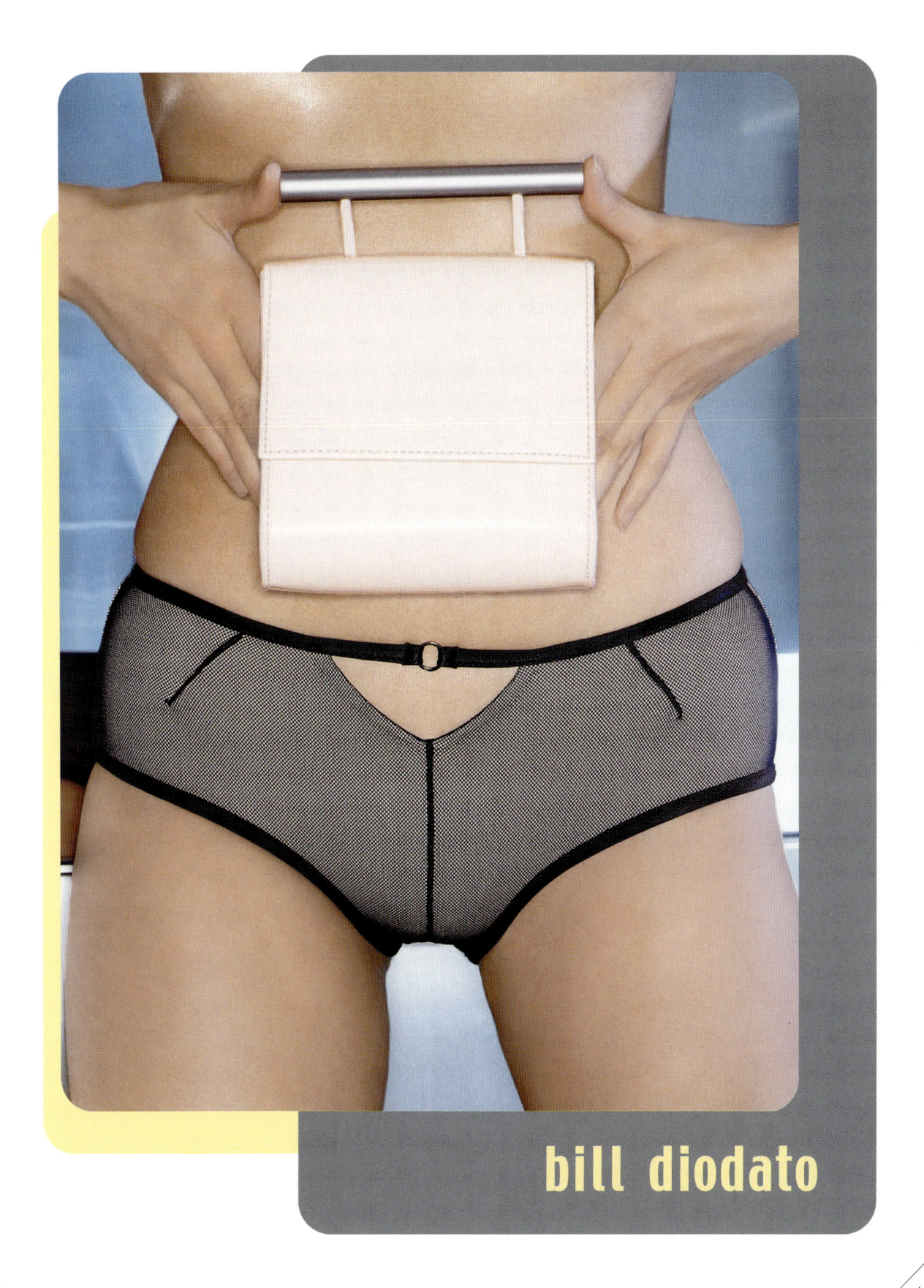

bill diodato

ABSOLUT
Country of Sweden
VODKA
This superb vodka
was distilled from grain grown
in the rich fields of southern Sweden.
It has been produced at the famous
old distilleries near Åhus
in accordance with more than
400 years of Swedish tradition.
Vodka has been sold under the name
Absolut since 1879.
40% ALC./VOL. (80 PROOF) 750 ML.
IMPORTED
BY THE ABSOLUT COMPANY
A DIVISION OF V&S VIN&SPRIT AB

DAVE SLAGLE PHOTOGRAPHY • 306 W 38TH STREET NEW YORK, NY 10018 • 212 268 3030

108 Mt. Vernon Street
Boston, MA 02108-1228
Tel: 617.723.4896

call for
client list • samples
or visit
www.archi-medias-jacoby.c

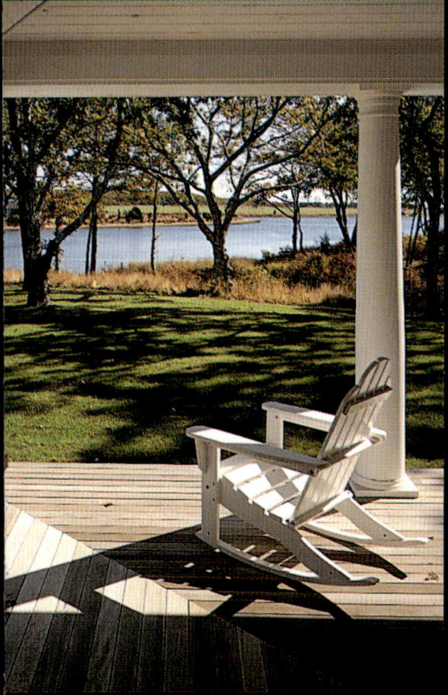
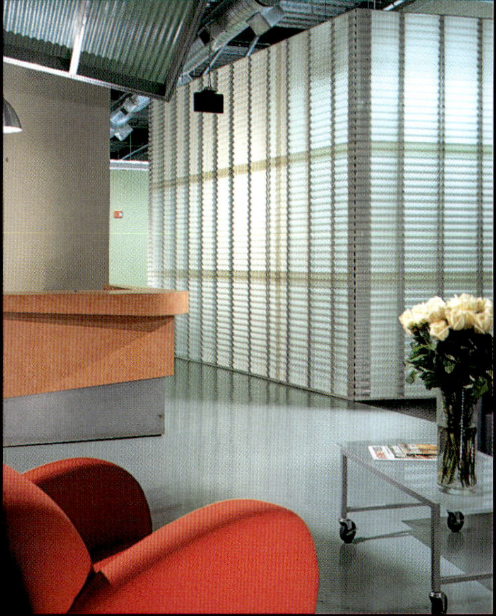
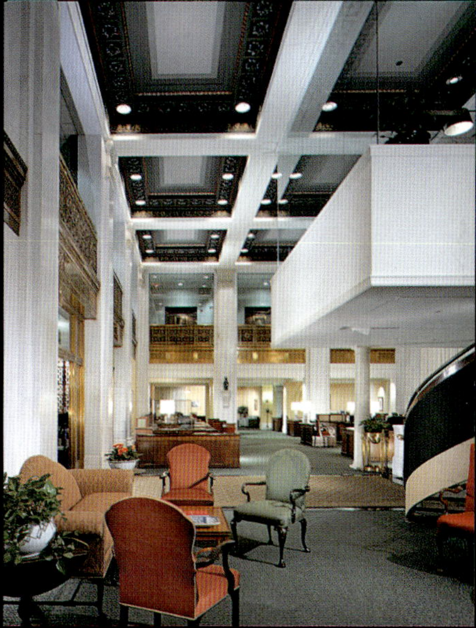

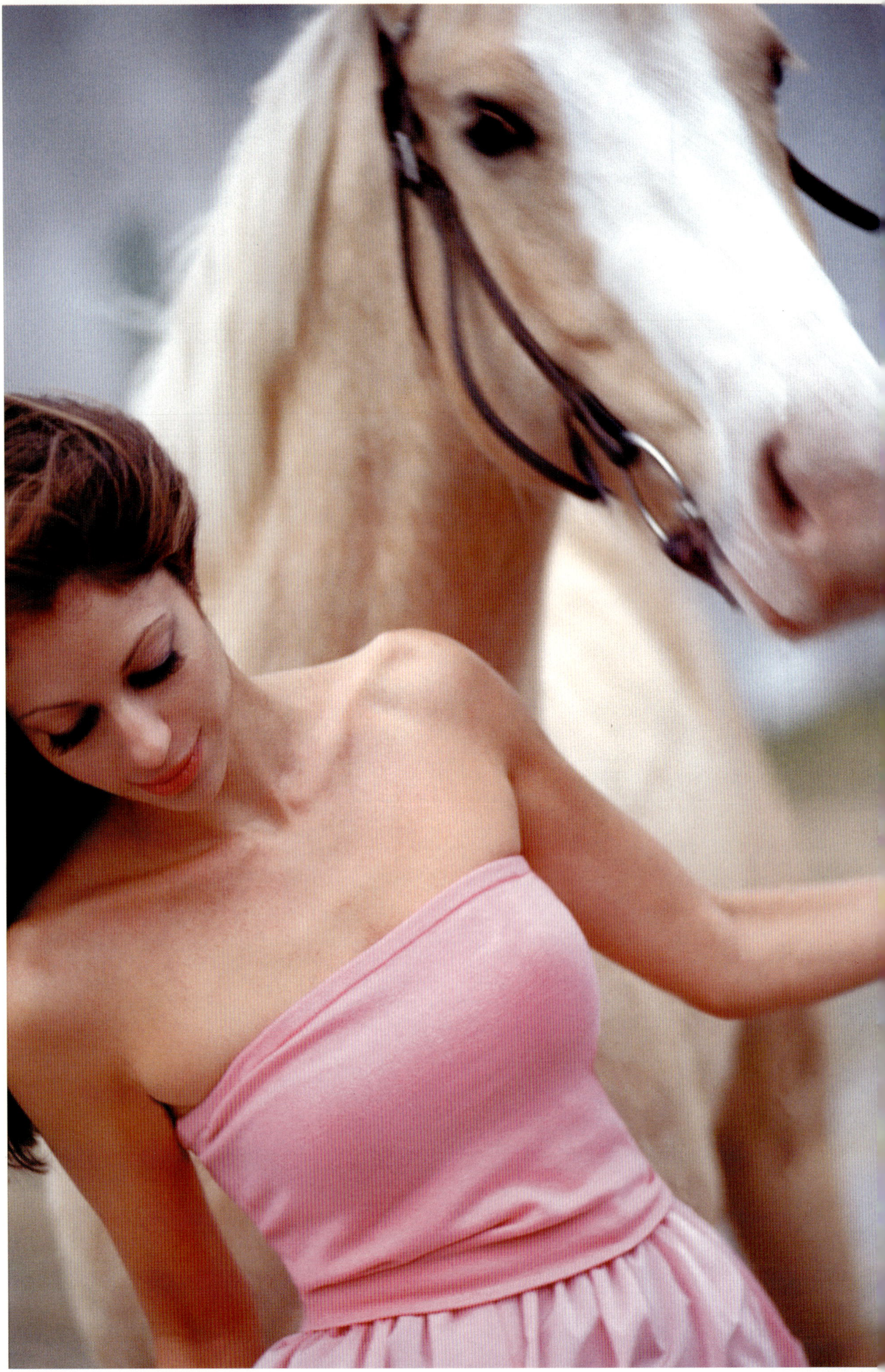

Wild Bill Melton   800 527 0119   www.wildbillstudios.com

ERIC KULIN

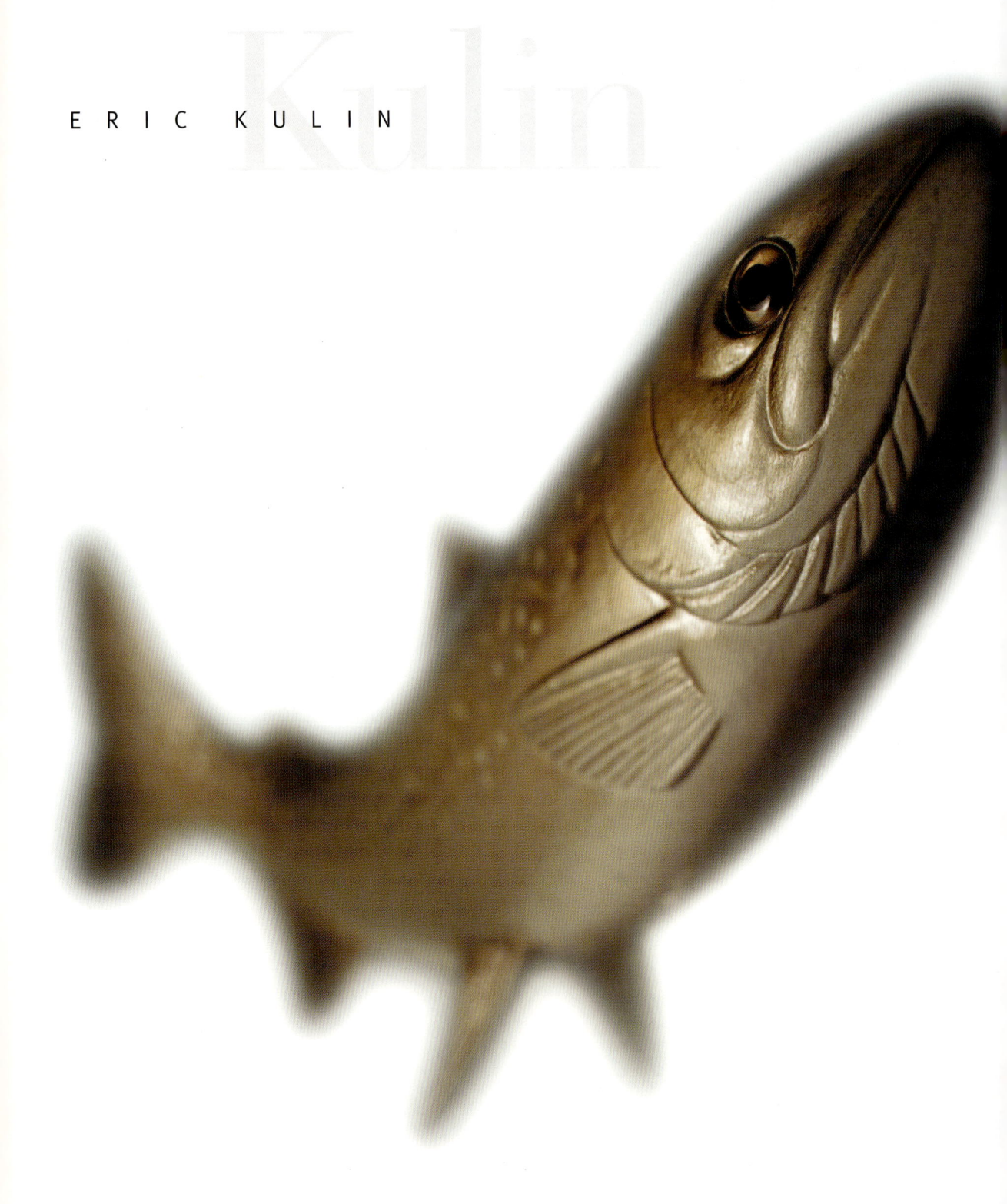

tel 617 269 5500 fax 617 269 6698 e-mail kulinphoto@aol.com

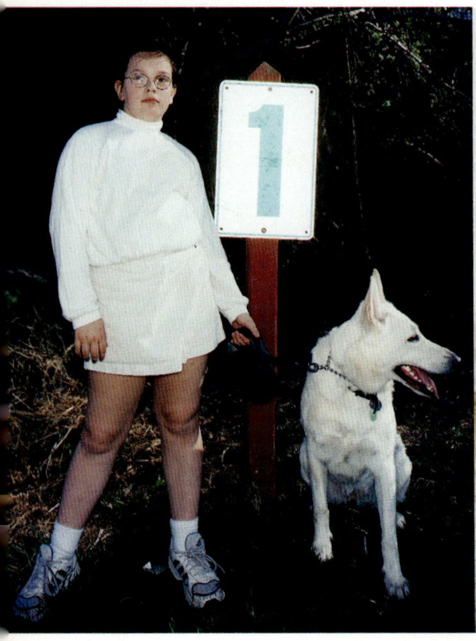
1
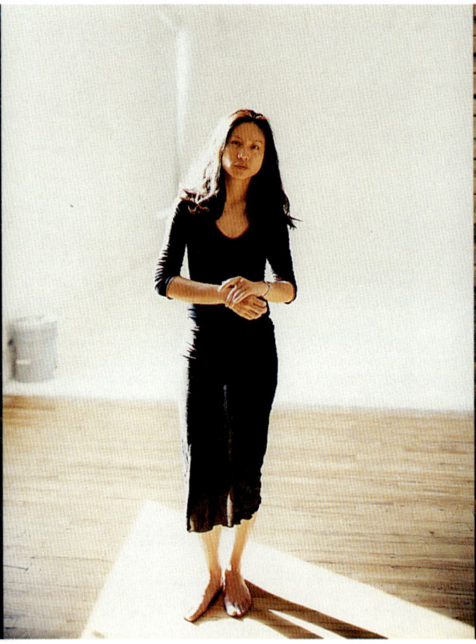
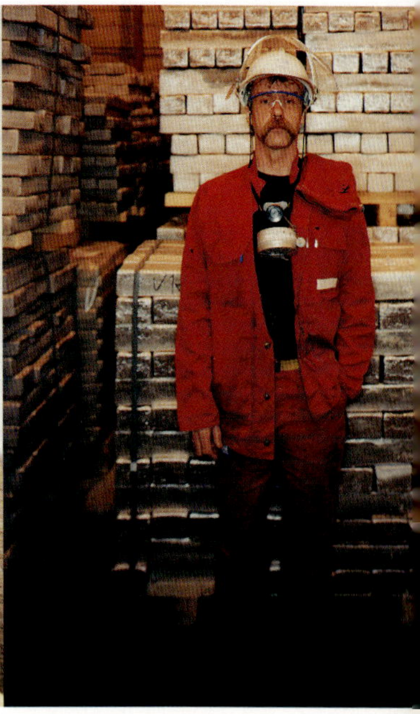

ZUBIN SHROFF

133 BROADWAY, SUITE 1610,

NEW YORK, NY 10010

TELEPHONE: 212 228-4071

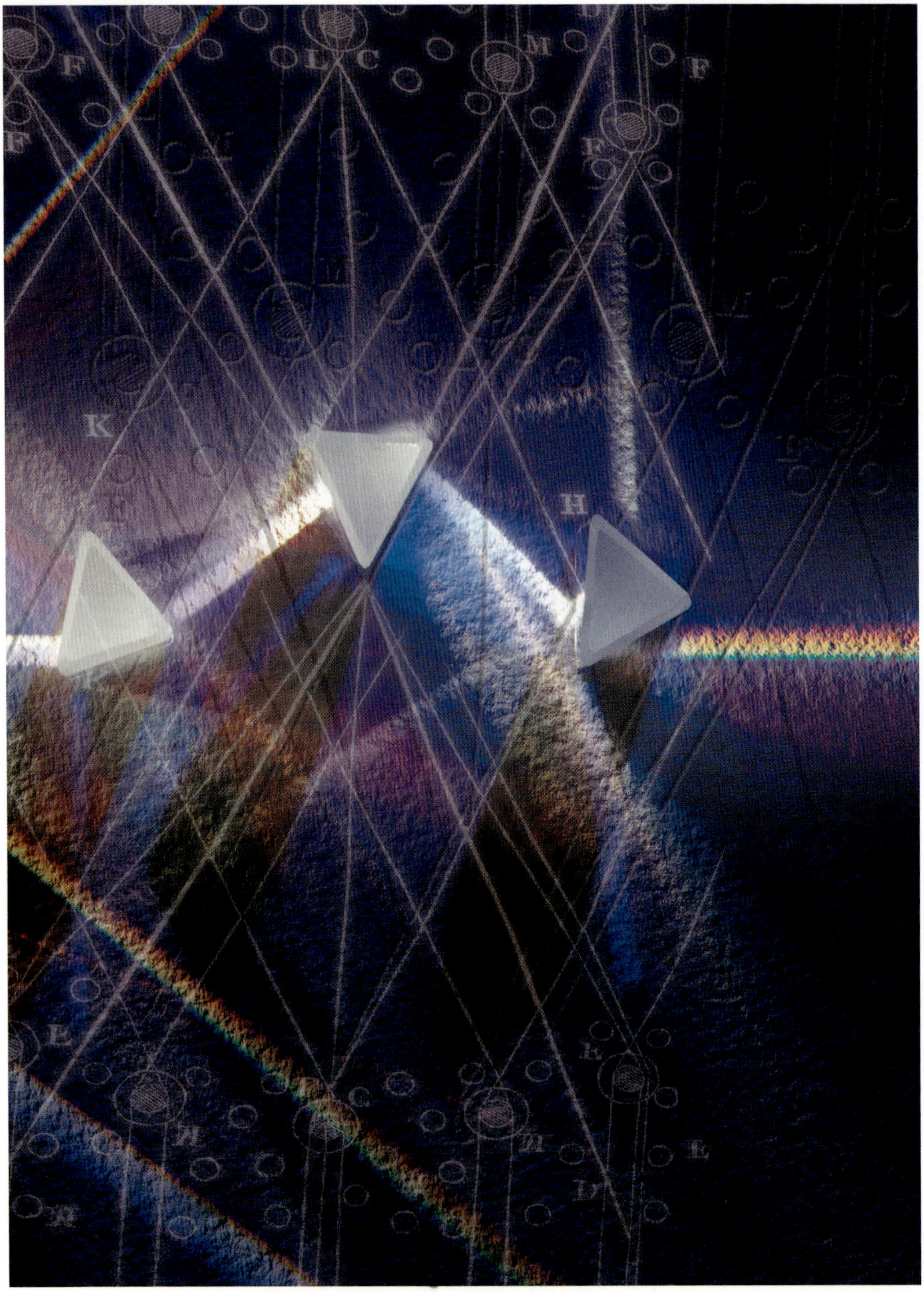
F
L C
M
F
F
F
K
H
E
E
L

Carlos Alejandro Photography
1155 Yorklyn Road
Yorklyn, DE 19736-0001
302.234.1100
carlos@caphoto.com
www.caphoto.com

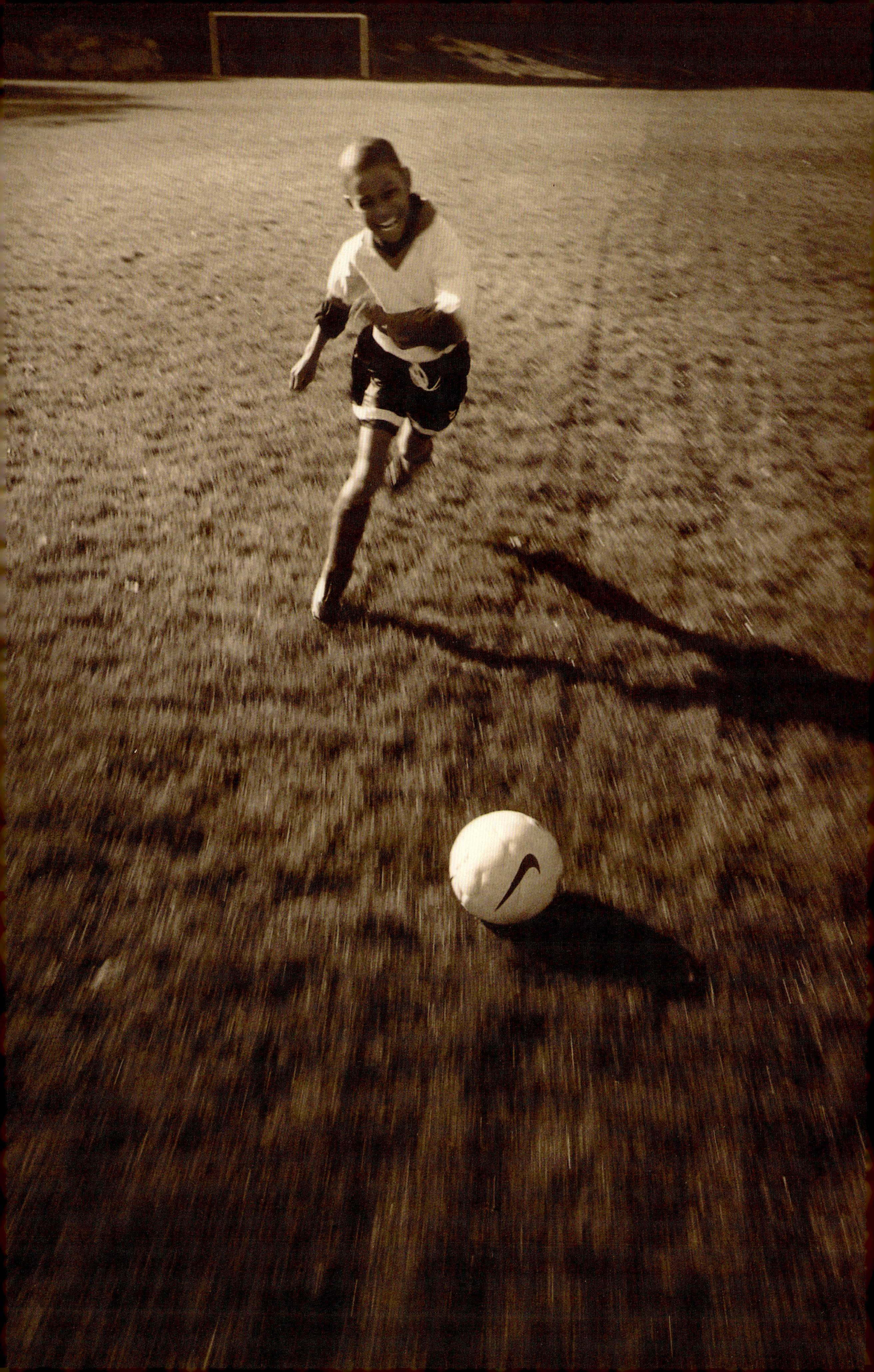

JIM FLYNN PHOTOGRAPHY   617.268.3627 / WWW.JIMFLYNNPHOTO.COM

DAVID SHOPPER PHOTOGRAPHY
www.davidshopper.com
888.820.3276

DAVID SHOPPER PHOTOGRAPHY
www.davidshopper.com
888.820.3276

Pepsi • AT&T • Camay • Canon • Carnival Cruise • Clairol • Columbian Coffee • Coty • Crest • Dupont • Eastman Kodak • Fruit Of The Loom • GTE • Gottex • Hue • Macy's • MCI • Minolta • No Nonsense Pantyhose • Olympus • Evista • Valtrex • Slimfast • Sprint • Tropicana • US Healthcare

nancy ney

nancyney.com

contact **vue** represents
ph 212.431.5780 • fx 212.431.9312

represented in **New York/AKA 212 . 620 . 4777** *and* **Los Angeles/Hamilton Gray 213 . 380 . 3933**

Michael Grecco Photography

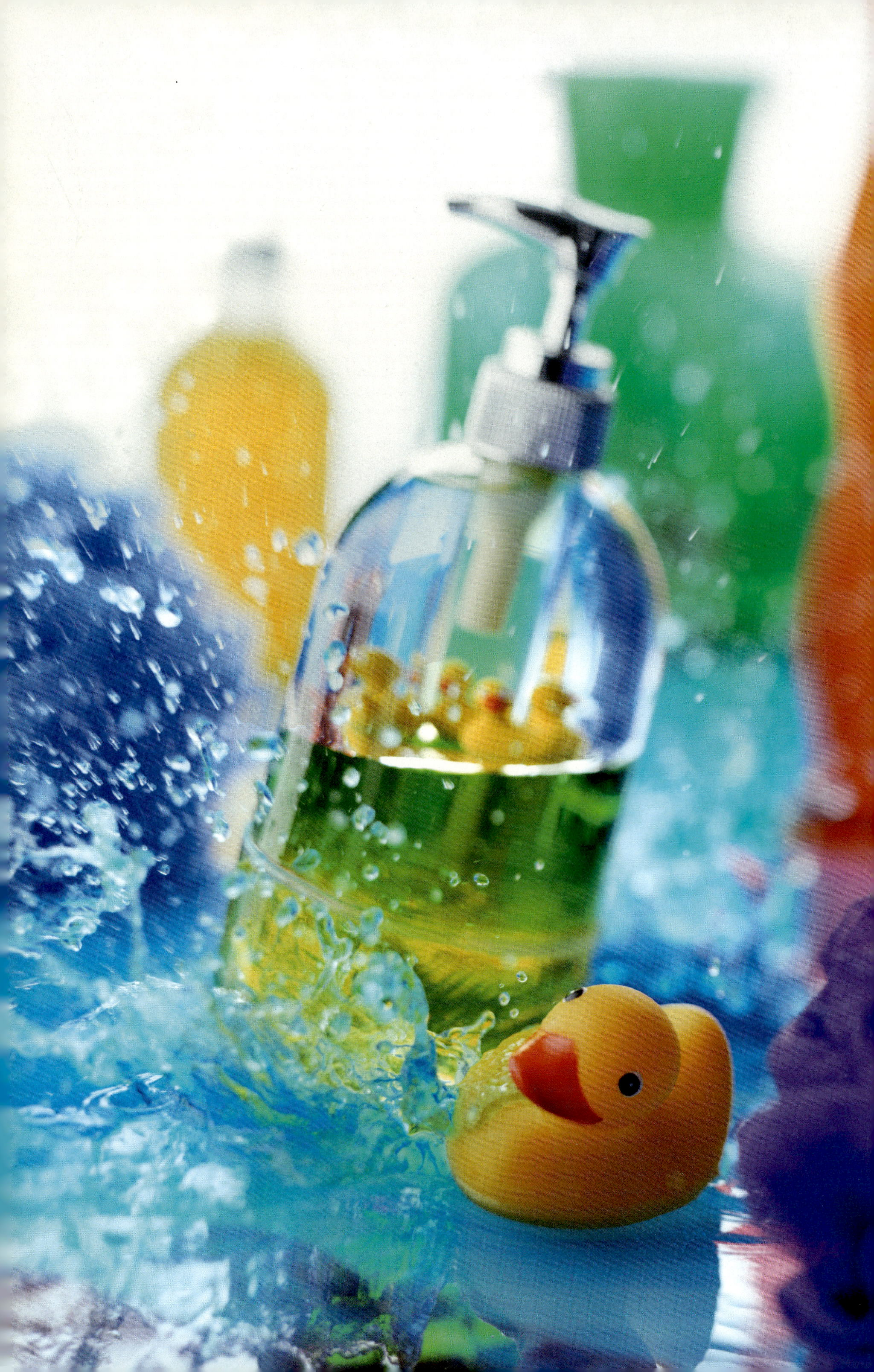

Katrina DeLeon Photography

286 FIFTH AVENUE   NEW YORK, NY 10001   212.279.2838 TEL   212.563.0402 FAX

Represented by Cynthia Held
phone 323.655.2979   fax 323.655.2134   studio 212.620.8115   www.gozoprod.com

GOZO

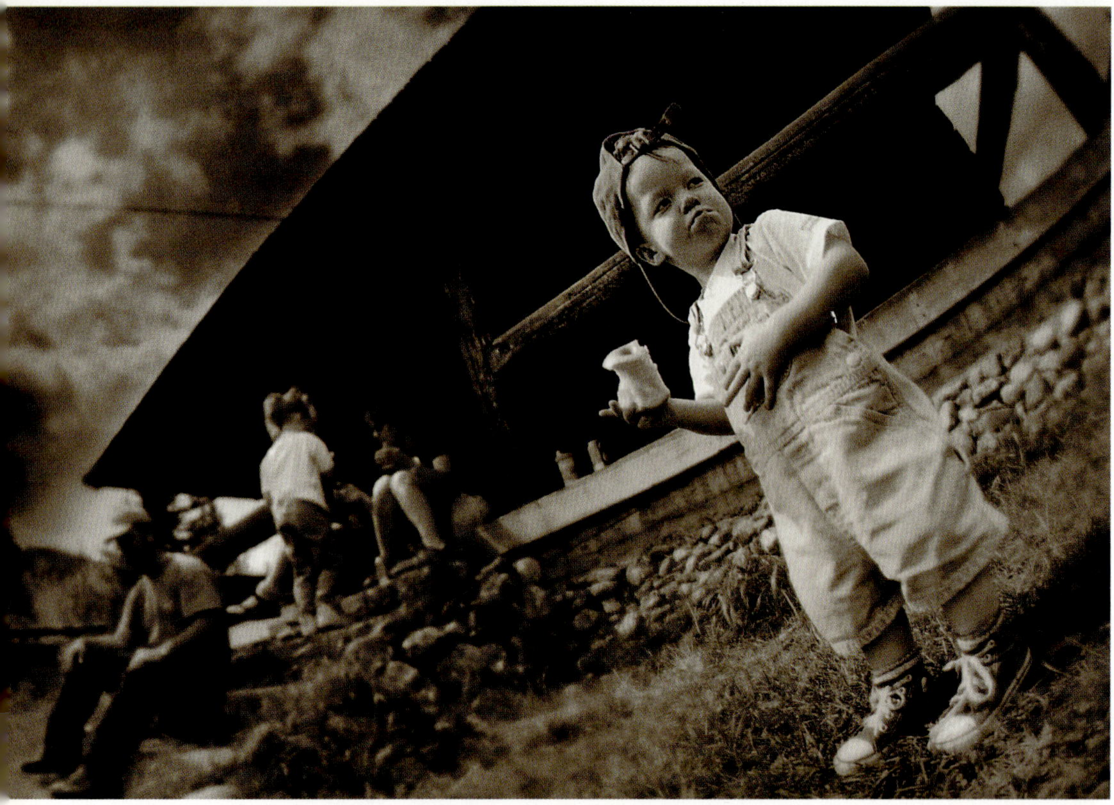

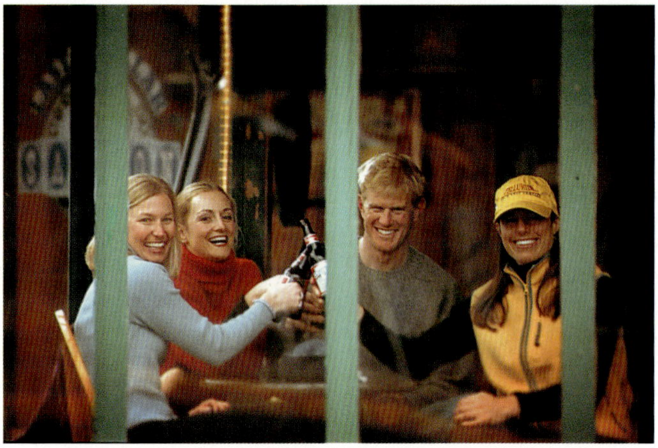

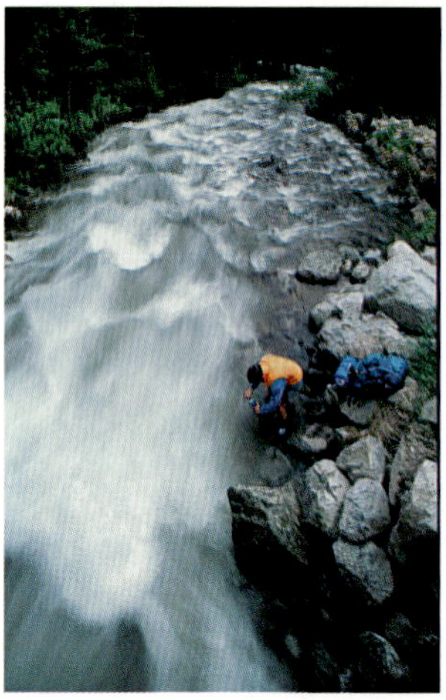

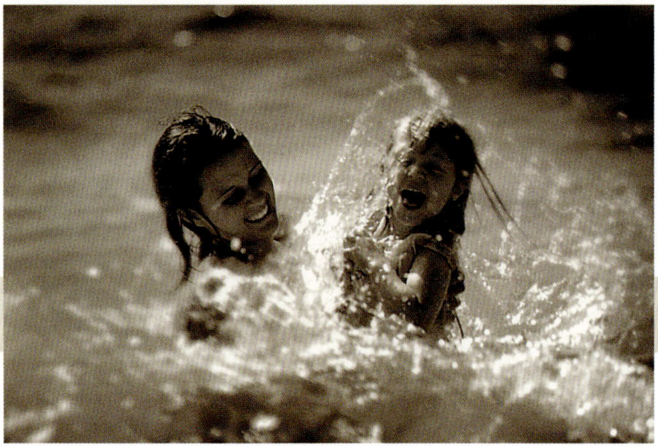

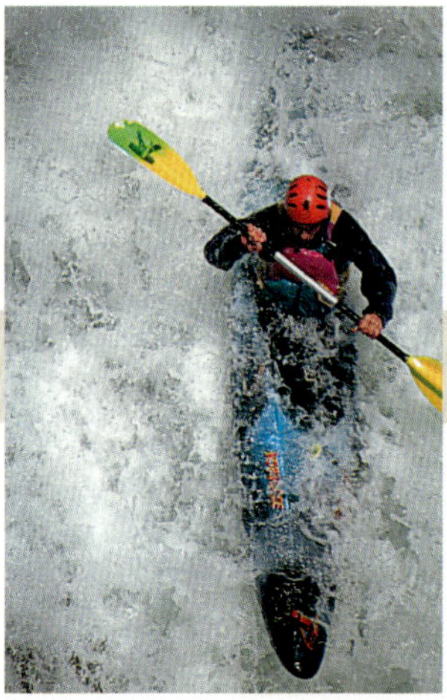

DEMIN

Tony Demin 406-222-1220
www.tonydemin.com
Represented by:
Jackie Page 212-772-0346

New York City
Jackie Page
212-772-0346
jackiepage@pobox.com

LANGONE ON LOCATION

Peter Langone Studio
954-467-0654
peterlangone.com   fax 954-522-2562

More in South Section Page 480

SOUTH

Randy Anderson Studio 498-499

Peter Barrett 486-487

Sue Barton Represents 474-475, 480-481

Sarah Whalen 484-485

Barbara Bowman 510-511

Robert Burke 520-521

Stewart Charles Cohen 506-507

Ryann Cooley 488-489

Crosby Stills 522

Cameron Davidson 510-511

Kevin Dodge 490-491

Denise Ford, Agent 506-507

John Gillan Photography, Inc. 505

Simon Griffiths 496-497

Michael Hart 516-517

Eric Haselton 493

Steve Hogben 508

Scott Keith 494-495

Bevil Knapp 509

Peter Langone 474-475, 480-481

Robert Latorre 500-501

James McEntee 98-99

Lisa Means 502-503

Tim Olive 518-519

Jackie Page 472-475, 480-481

Repfile, Inc. 488-489, 552-553

Michelle Roache Management Services 98-99, 474-475, 480-481

Dave Shafer 492

Brian Smith 482-483

Southlight Associates 486-487

The Hawkins Group 498-499, 516-517

Danny Turner 514-515

Bob Werre 504

White Light Images, Inc. 493

Jimmy Williams Productions 484-485

New York   Jackie Page   212-772-0346
California Sue Barton   415-457-3695
Florida   Michelle Roache   305-666-3545

Peter Langone Studio
954-467-0654
peterlangone.com fax 954.522-2562

LANGONĒ ON LOCATION

More in Northeast Section Page 474

alan greenspan

Miami Beach   305 534 3130   **Brian Smith** photography
New York   212 571 7719

dy margolis

photography Brian Smith 305 534 3130 Miami Beach
212 571 7719 New York

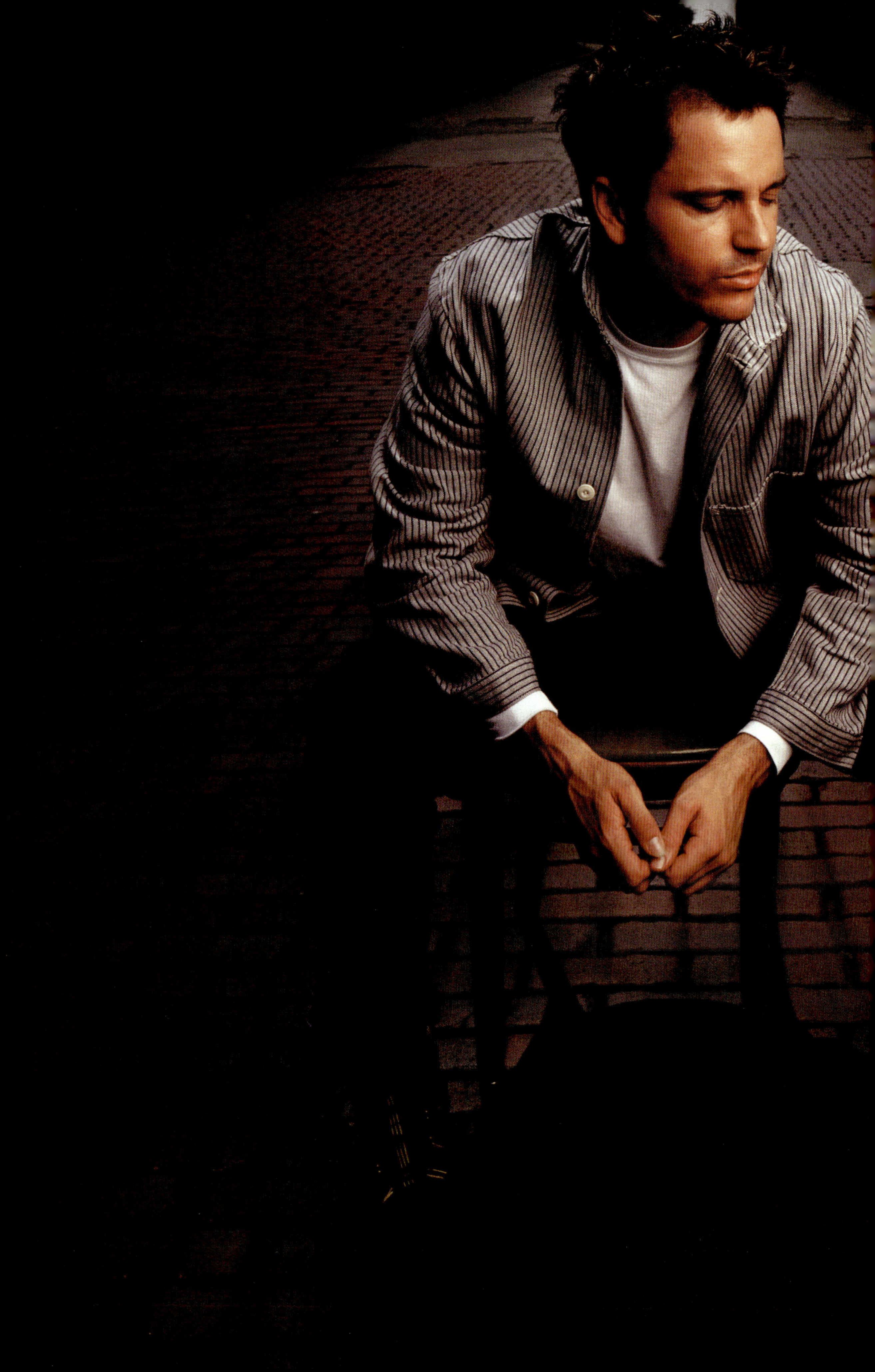

Jimmy Williams
919-832-5971

Jimmy Williams
919-832-5971

CLIENTS Ford Motor Company • Miller Brewing Company • Heineken • Coors Light • AeroMexico • Royal Caribbean Cruise Line • Westin Hotels • Radisson Hotels • The Island of the Bahamas • Carnival Cruise Line • Hilton Resorts • Superclubs

PETER BARRETT

phone (305) 557.0694
fax (305) 557.8885
www.petebarrett.com
represented in southeast by southlight associates
phone (561) 883.7768

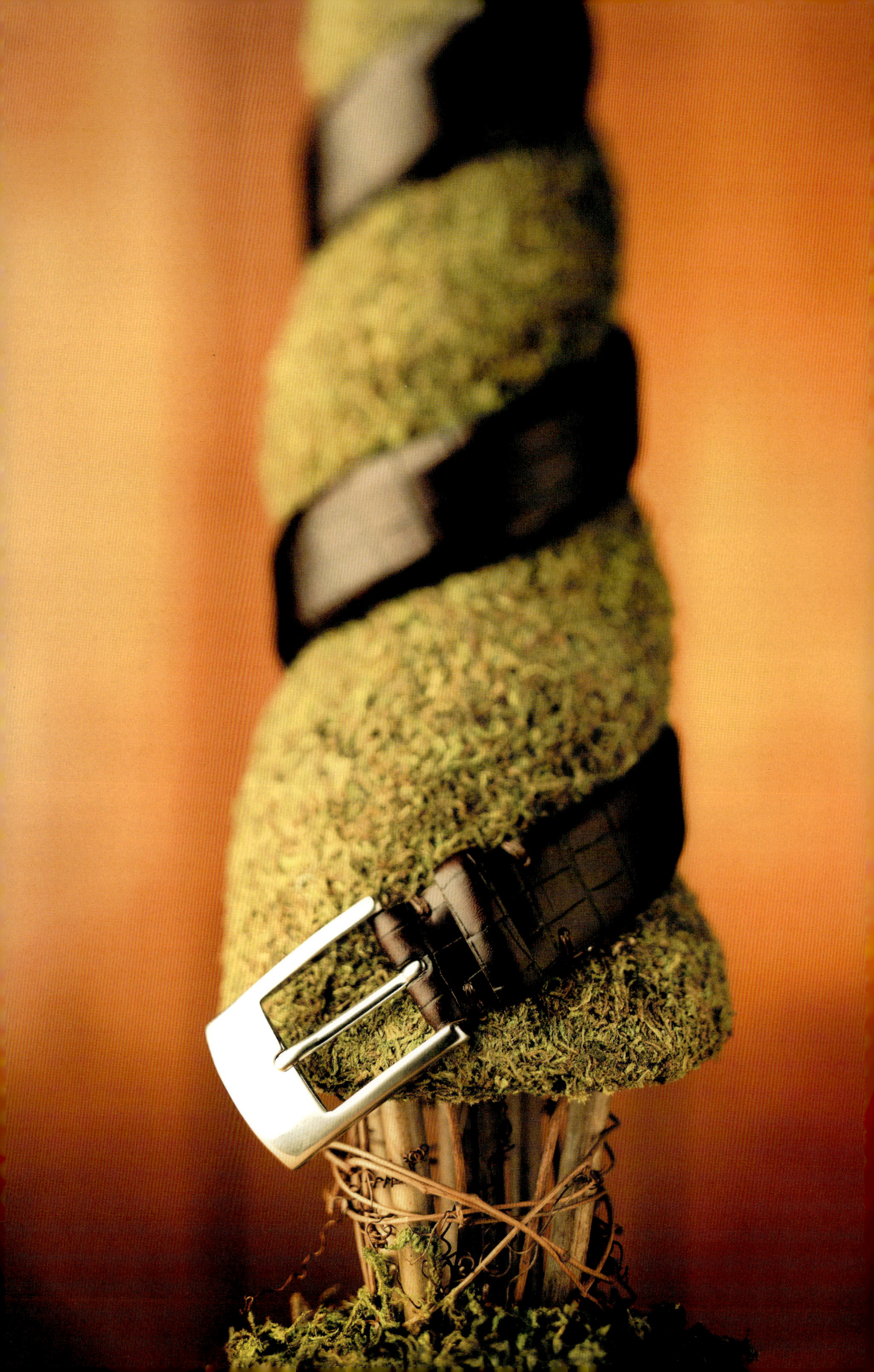

ryann cooley

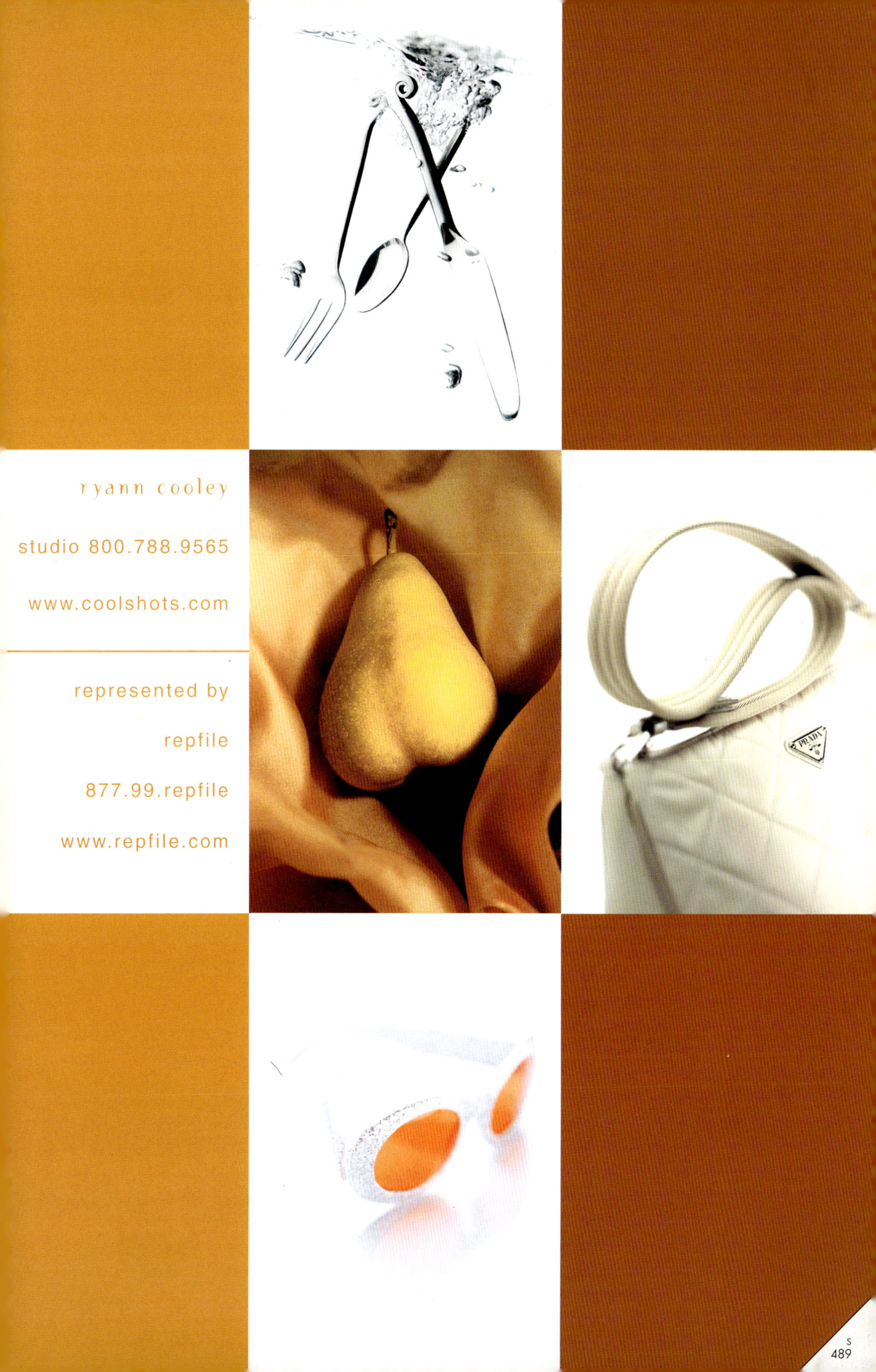

studio 800.788.9565

www.coolshots.com

represented by

repfile

877.99.repfile

www.repfile.com

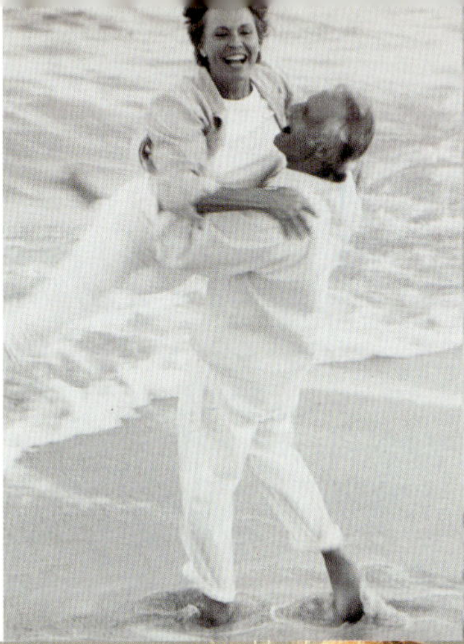

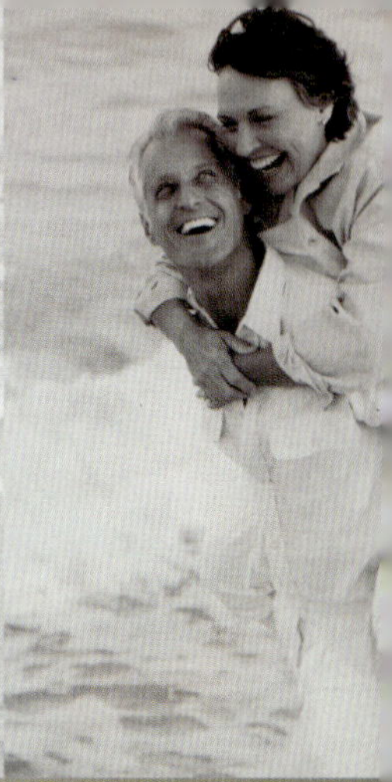

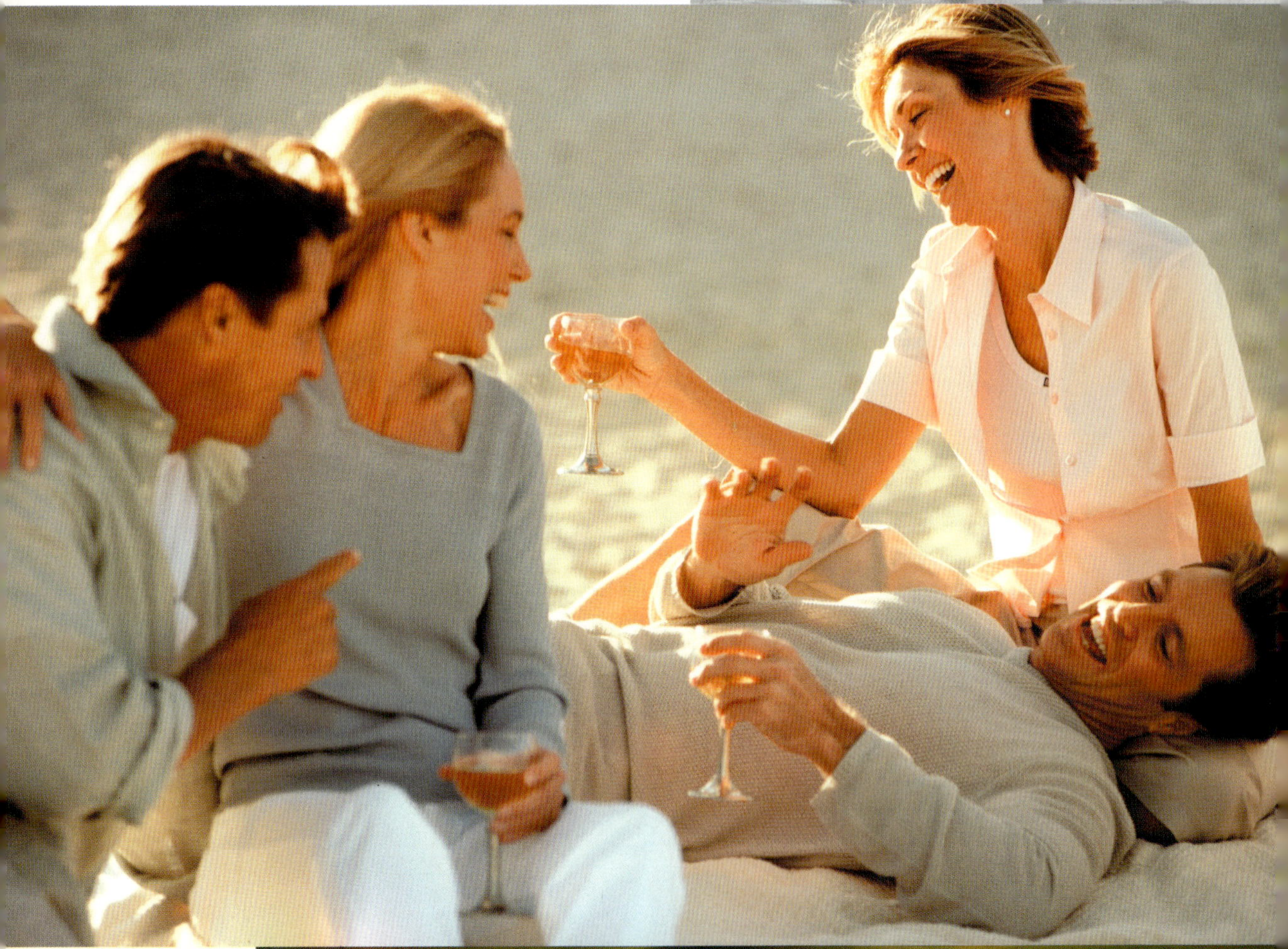

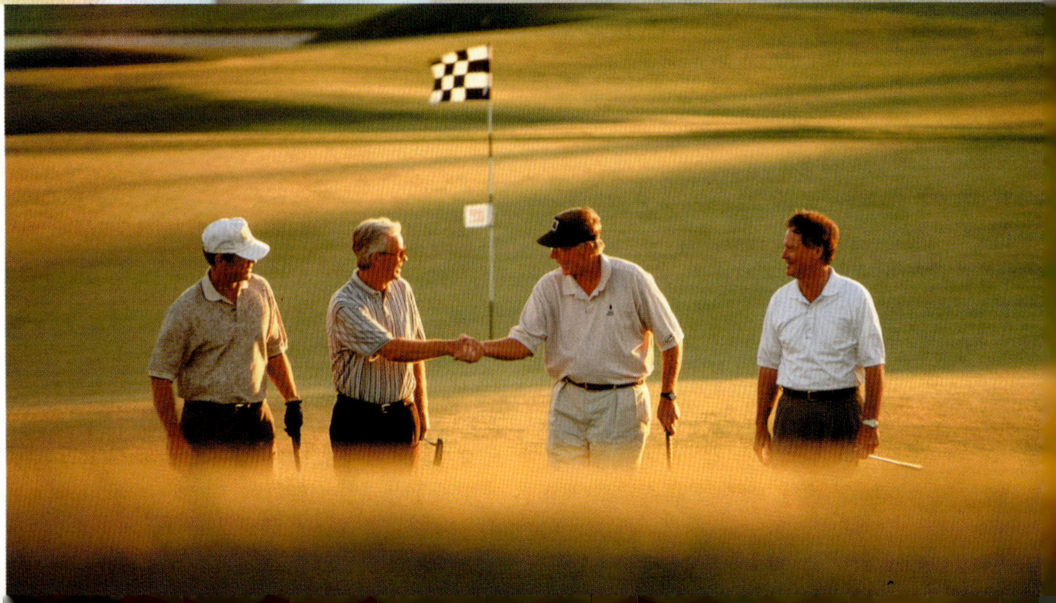

Kevin Dodge . Miami . 305.439.2658

CLIENT: KODAK   LOCATION: LAKE POWELL, UTAH

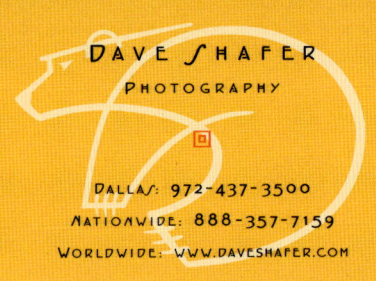

Dave Shafer
Photography

Dallas: 972-437-3500
Nationwide: 888-357-7159
Worldwide: www.daveshafer.com

CLIENT: THE SOURCE SPORTS   TALENT: BRIAN JORDAN, ATLANTA BRAVES

eric haselton
tel: 305.710.1952
fax: 305.859.2076

SCOTT KEITH
PHOTOGRAPHY

2124 Farrington Street

Suite 300

Dallas, Texas 75207

214.698.0646 Voice

214.744.4001 Fax

www.scottkeithphoto.com

7

S
495

simon

919.829.9109

simong.com

ANDERSON STUDIO

Represented by The Hawkins Group
214/327-6828
www.Hawkinsgroup.com/ra_thumbnails.html

ANDERSON STUDIO

Represented by The Hawkins Group
214/327-6828
www.Hawkinsgroup.com/ra_thumbnails.html

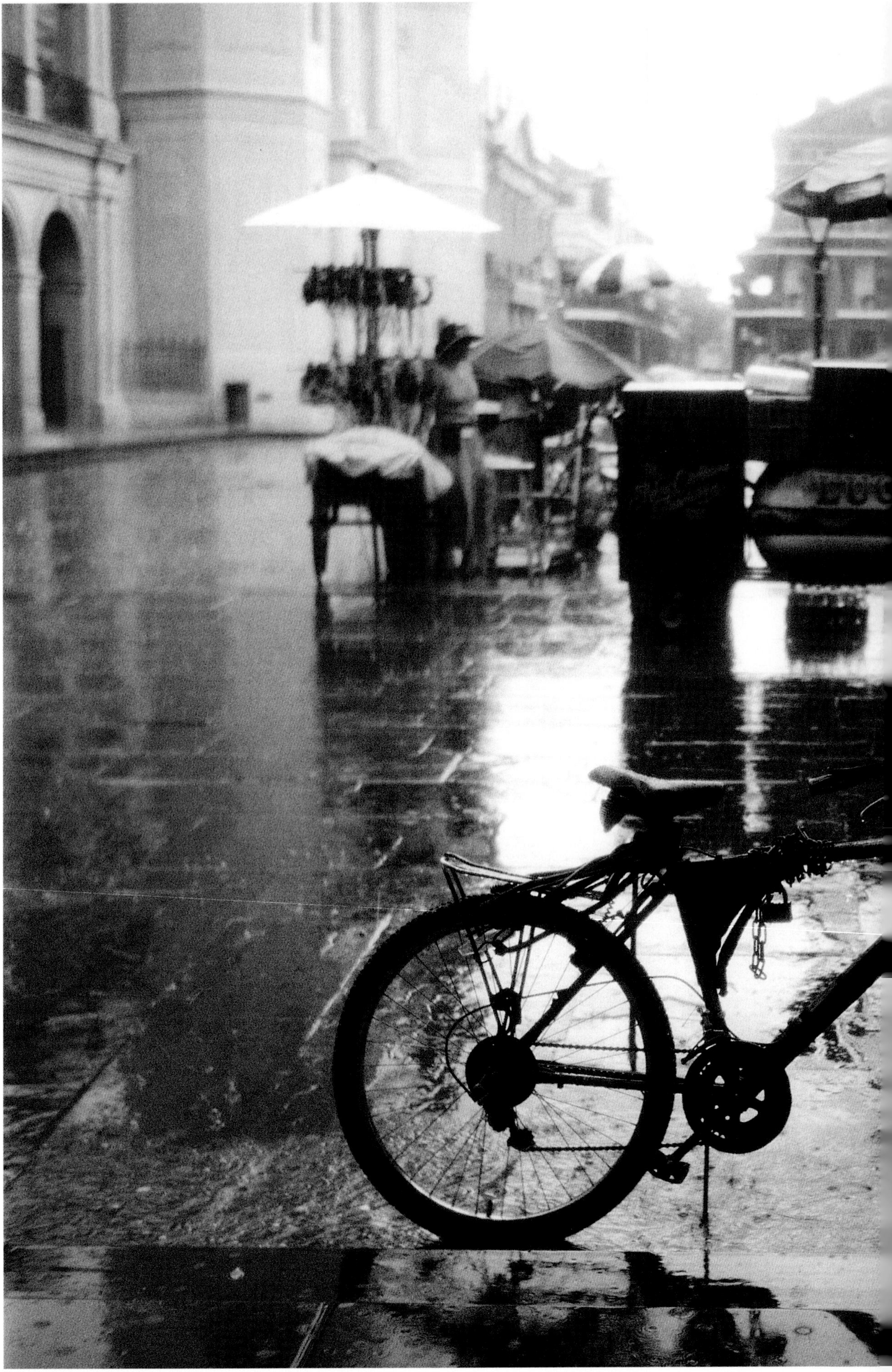

LATORRE

moving pictures

ROBERT LATORRE PHOTOGRAPHER DIRECTOR CINEMATOGRAPHER 5626 ALTA AVENUE DALLAS TEXAS 75206 PHONE 214.744.3474 FAX 214.824.7782 WWW.BIGFISH.NET HOME OF THE BIG FREEZE WWW.BIGFREEZE.COM

lisa means ∎ tel 214 826 4979 ∎ fax 214 826 4045
6711 dalhart lane ∎ dallas texas 75214 ∎ pgr 800 509 0703

lisa means ■ tel 214 826 4979 ■ fax 214 826 4045
6711 dalhart lane ■ dallas texas 75214 ■ pgr 800 509 0703

L M
photography

Studios in Houston, locations wherever

BOB WERRE Photograp

713.271.5904 • BobWphoto.cc

JOHN GILLAN PHOTOGRAPHY

BLACK BOOK 1999 • WWW.JOHNGILLAN.COM • BLACK BOOK 2000
REPRESENTED BY THERESA JAE • TEL: 954.236.3556 • FAX: 954.236.3996 • EMAIL: JJGILLAN@AOL.COM

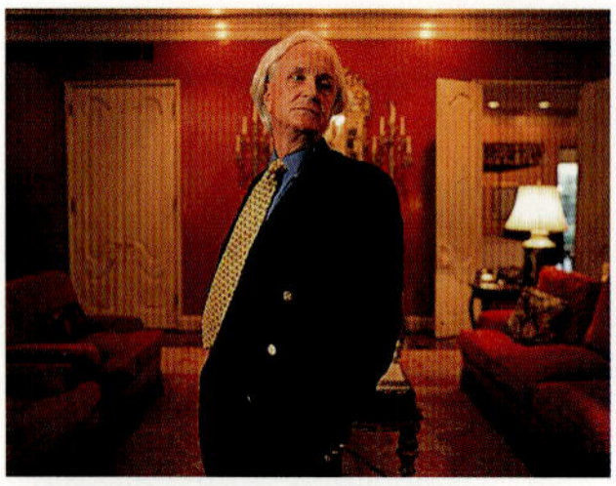
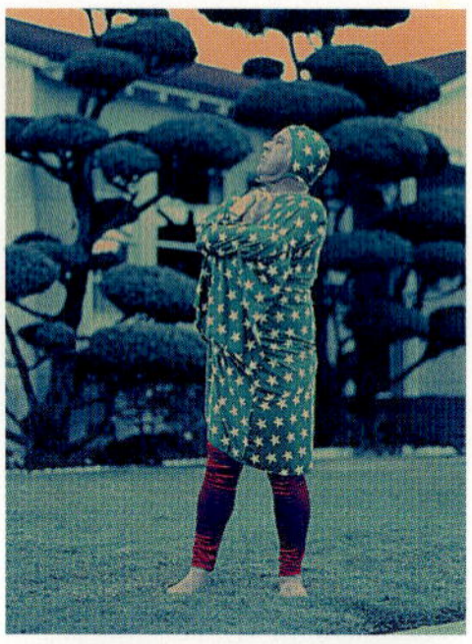
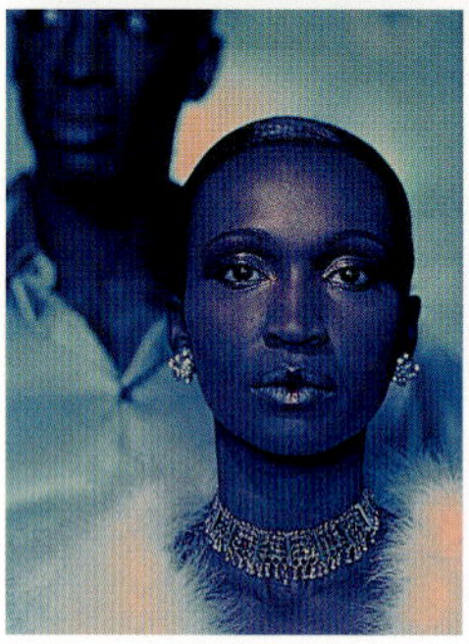
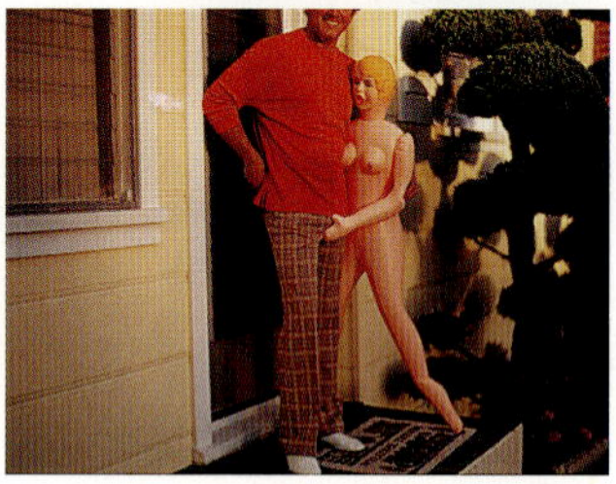

WWW.STEWARTCOHEN.COM

PHOTOGRAPHY
STEVE HOGBEN

WWW.STEVEHOGBEN.COM - (404) 266-2894 ATLANT

udio and location

bevil knapp
photographer

w orleans louisiana bevil@bevilknapp.com 504-831-1496 fax 504-832-1272

S 509

CAMERON DAVIDSON

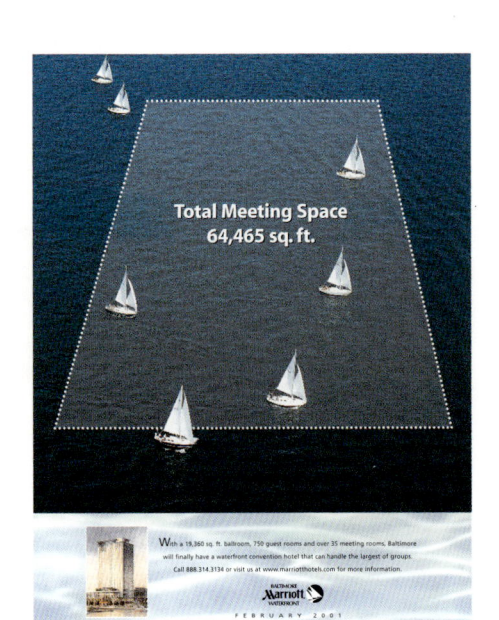

Dominion Resources

Total Meeting Space
64,465 sq. ft.

Grand Ballroom
3,100 Person Capacity

750 Water View Rooms

With 77,294 sq. ft. of meeting space, a 19,360 sq. ft. Grand Ballroom and over 35 meeting rooms, Baltimore will finally have a waterfront convention hotel that can handle the largest of groups. Call 888.314.3134 or visit us at marriotthotels.com for more information.

BALTIMORE
WATERFRONT
Marriott
FEBRUARY 2001

ph 703.845.0547   *fx* 703.845.9542
www.camerondavidson.com
agent: barbara bowman 415.243.0224

S
511

STEVE

www.cowboyphotographs.com

THORNTON

404-231-9900

PETER FORSBERG
Colorado Avalanche Center
Denver, Colorado
ESPN Magazine

JAMI UECKER
Pin-Up Girl
Dallas, Texas
Atomic Magazine

DANNY TURNER ~ *Photographer* ~ PH 214.559.0259 ~ FX 214.526.0289 ~ DANMAN.COM

STEVE VOLLMER
Computer Wizard
Las Vegas, Nevada
CIO Magazine

JASON SEHORN
New York Giants Cornerback
Newport Beach, California
ESPN Magazine

DANNY TURNER ~ *Photographer* ~ PH 214.559.0259 ~ FX 214.526.0289 ~ DANMAN.COM

REPRESENTED BY
THE HAWKINS GROUP
214-327-6828

HART

MICHAEL HART PHOTOGRAPHY
WWW.HARTPHOTO.COM

Tim Olive   404.872.0500

www.olive.com

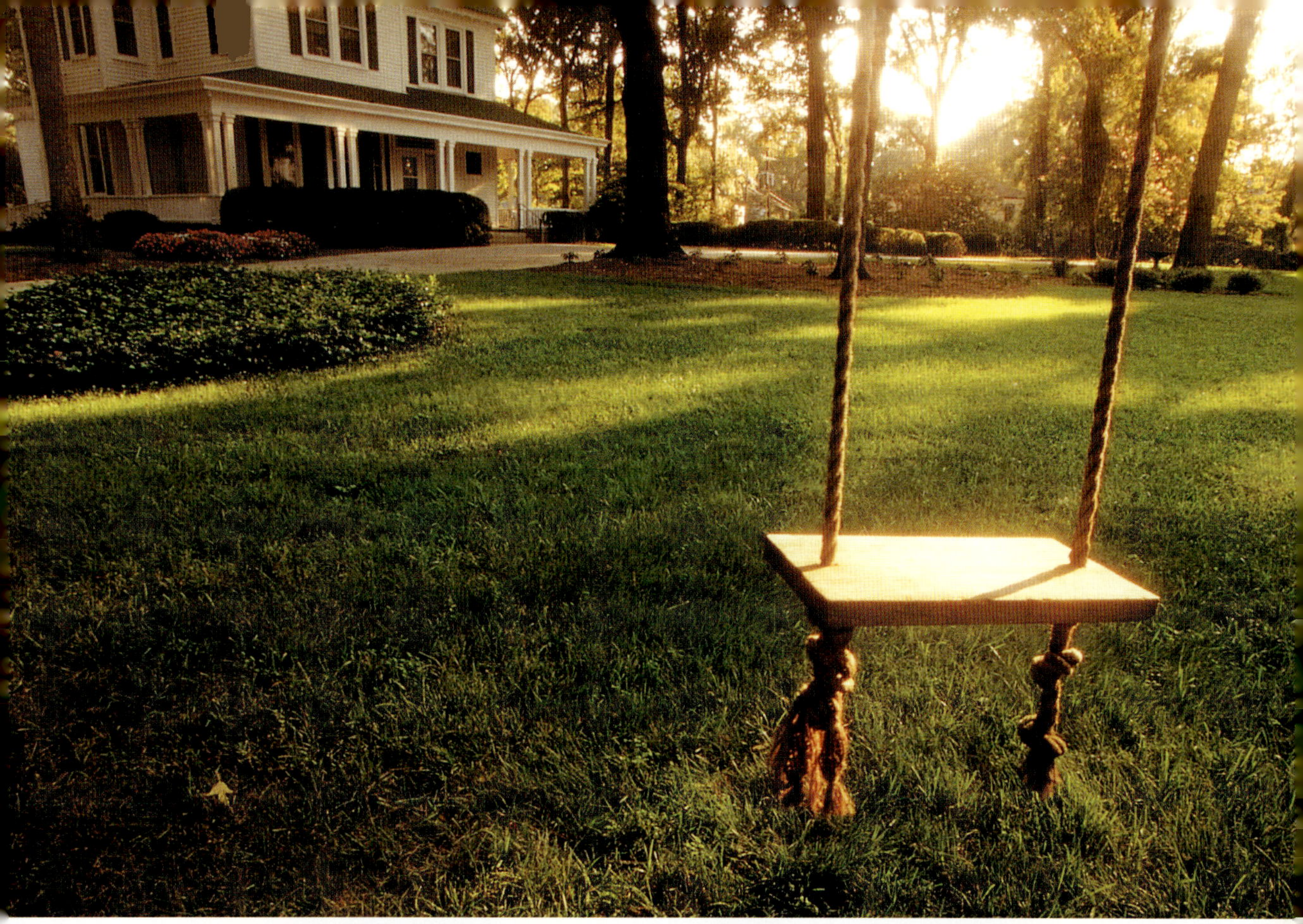
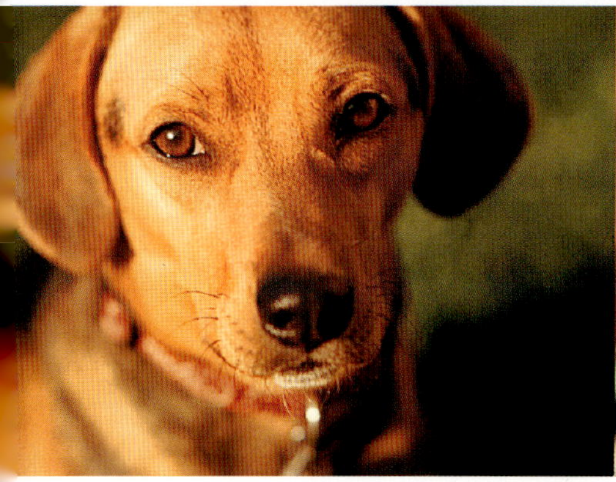
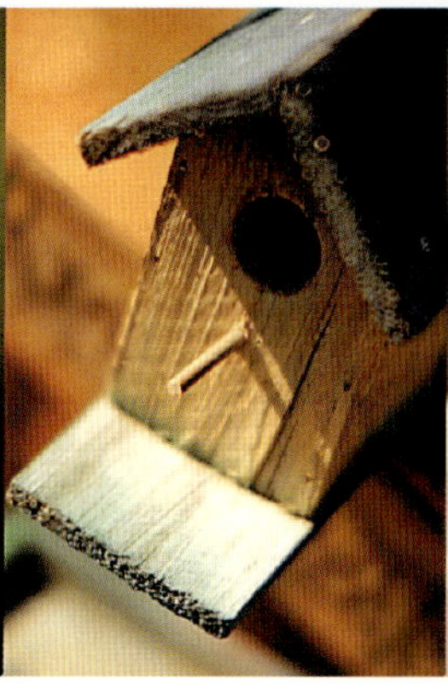
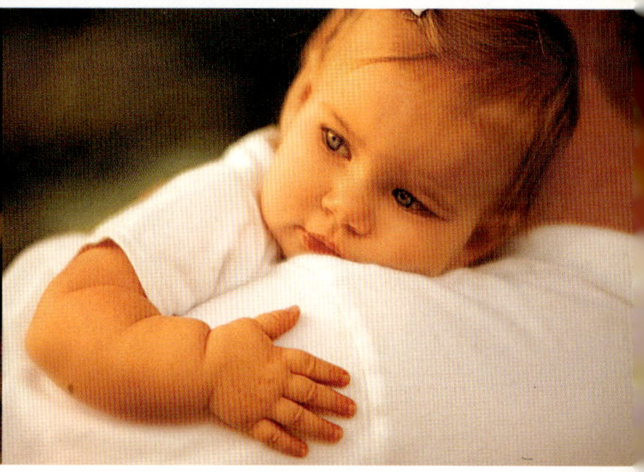
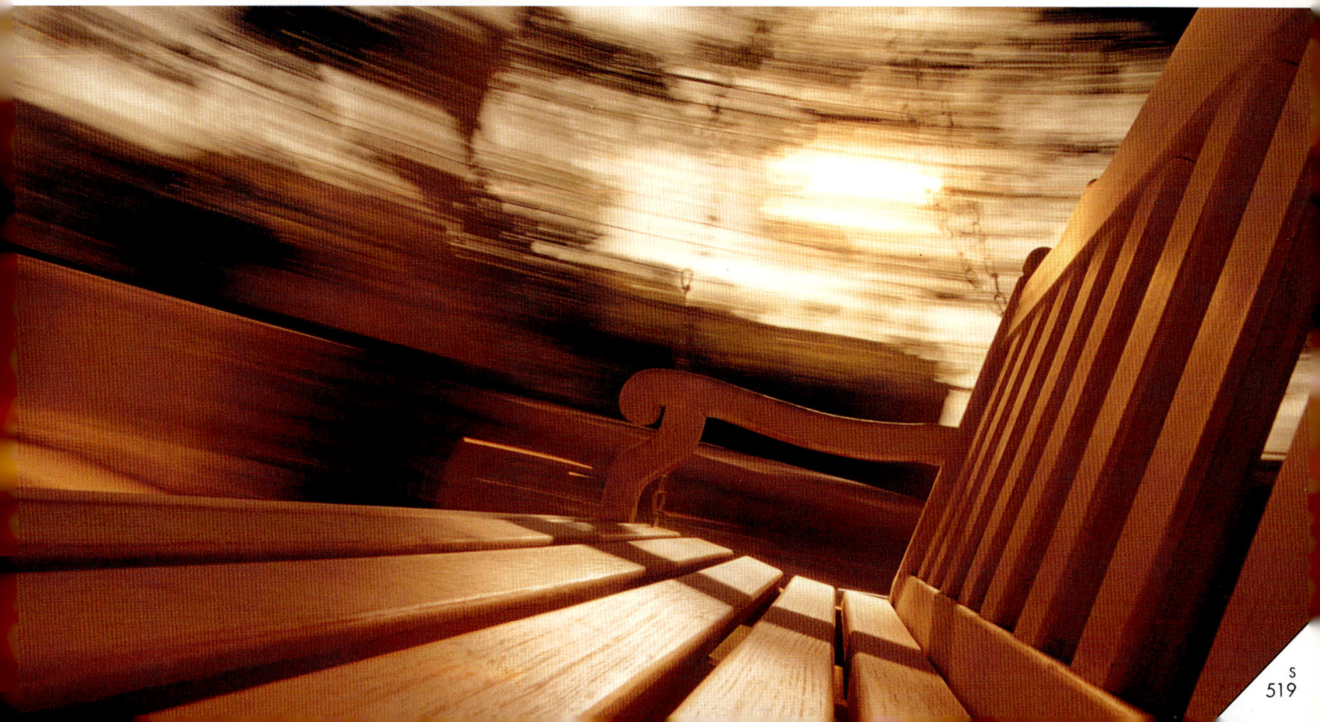

ROBERT BURKE

Baltimore, MD / Washington, DC

Tele [410.313.9671]   Fax [410.313.9672]

burkephotography.com

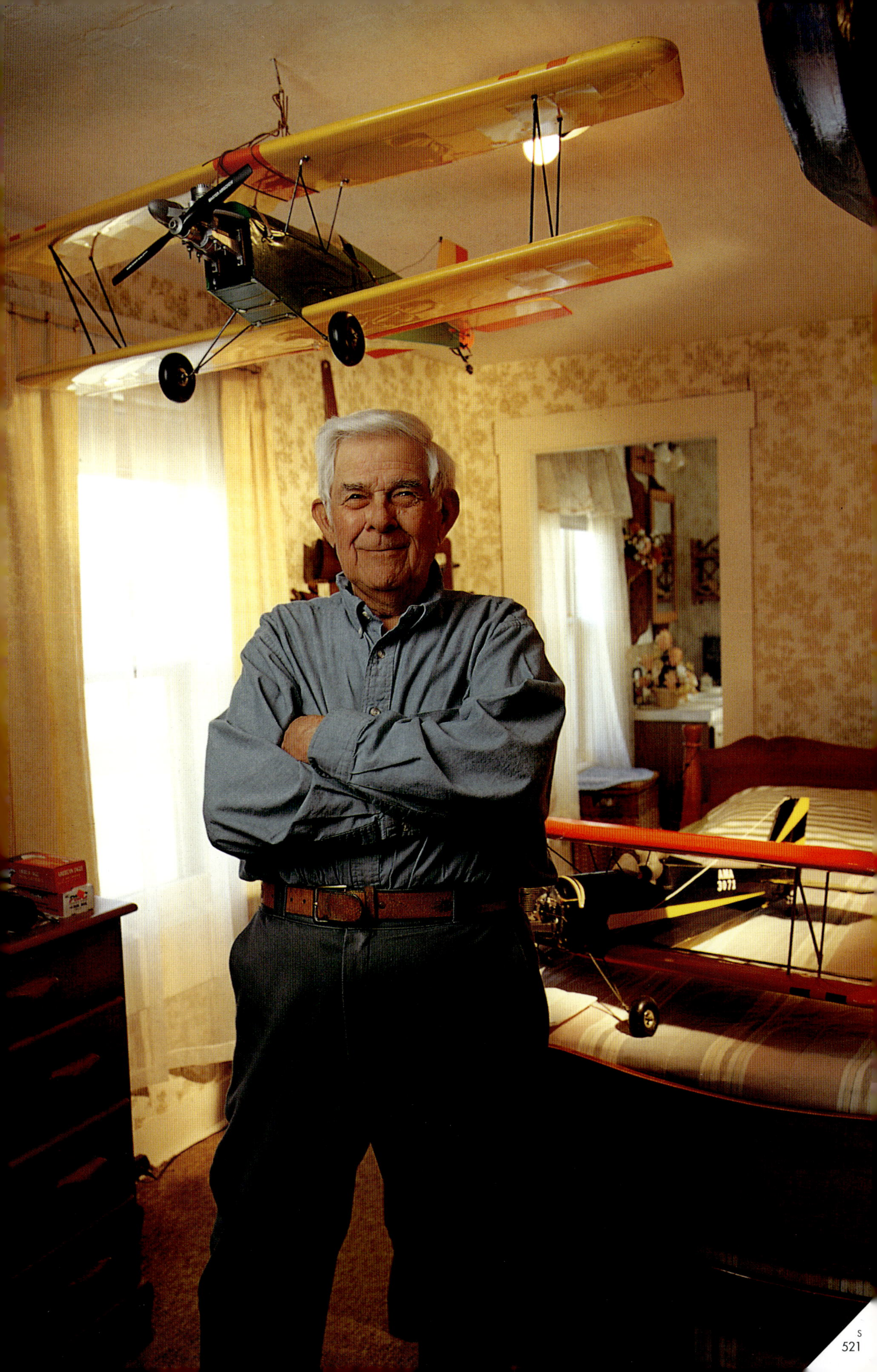

CROSBY
STILLS

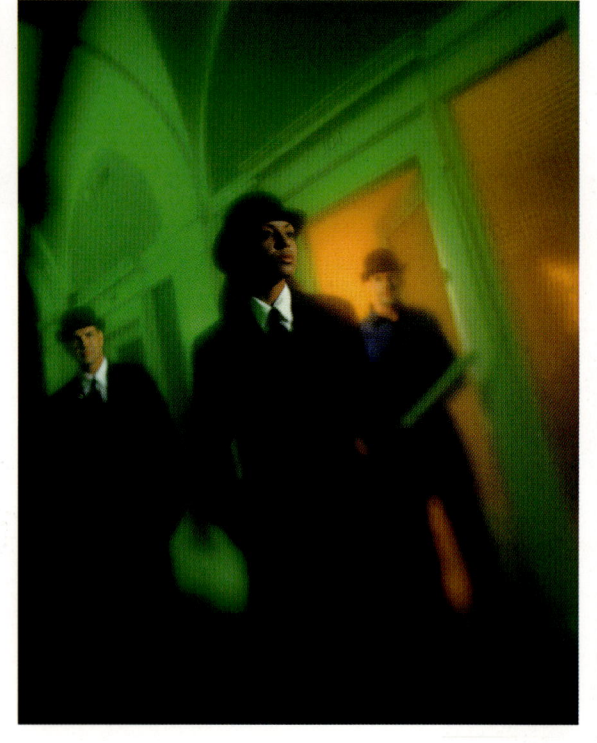

Commercial Photographers Shooting from the Southeast
Phone 864.232.4403 Fax 864.242.0773 • e.mail - david@crosbystills.com

www.crosbystills.com

MIDWEST

Jim Arndt 530-531

Paul Audia 540

Baartman Photography 596

Chris Bailey 262-263, 541

David Bentley 600-601

Jan Bugher 592-593

Desmond Burdon 224-225, 541

Tom Burkhart 562-563, 702-703

Burns Auto Parts 590-591

Creative Management/Randi Fiat 16-21, 682-683

Teri Campbell 534-535

Tony D'Orio 598-599

Peggy Day 562-563, 658-659

Thomas Drew 560-561, 767

Dublin Productions 596-597

Steve Ewert 541, 544-545

Brad Feinknopf 558-559

Ken Frantz Photography, Inc. 532-533

Paula Friedland Studio, Inc. 548-549

Eric Futran 573

Gregory Gaymont 556

Andy Goodwin 538-539

Steve Grubman Photography, Inc. 602-603

Holly Hahn & Company (H2 + Co.) 570-571, 576-577

Steve Henke 574-575

Denise Hopkins 552-553

Hurewitz Creative Partners 240-241, 598-599

James Imbrogno 578-579

David Joel 557

Don Johnston 562-563, 568-569

Joyce Photography, Inc. 594-595

Kalman & Pabst Photo Group 771

Karl Knize 588-589

John Lair Studio 586-587

Joe Lampi 597

Albert Leggett 529

Richard Mack Photography Ltd. 546-547

Steven McDonald 550-551

Judith McGrath & Associates 224-225, 262-265, 541-545

Robert Mead Associates 42-43, 554-555

Meoli Studio 552-553

Marc Norberg Studio, Inc. 580-581

Keith Philpott 584-585

George Pizzo 562-565

Repfile, Inc. 488-489, 552-553

Carolyn Somlo/Reptile Artists Agent 602-603

Ted Rice 590-591

Kate Roth 536-537

Frank Schiefelbein 572

Schumann & Co. 578-579

Jeff Sciortino 576-577

Charlie Simokaitis 541-543

Dick Spahr 592-593

Tom Strand Studio 582-583

Patti Sugano 532-533

U3-Agents For The Visual Arts 562-569,
    658-659, 702-703

Nick Vedros 554-555

Greg Whitaker 570-571

Dan White 604-605

Troy Wood 562-563, 566-567

Z Agency 606

Jodie Zeitler 236-237, 598-599

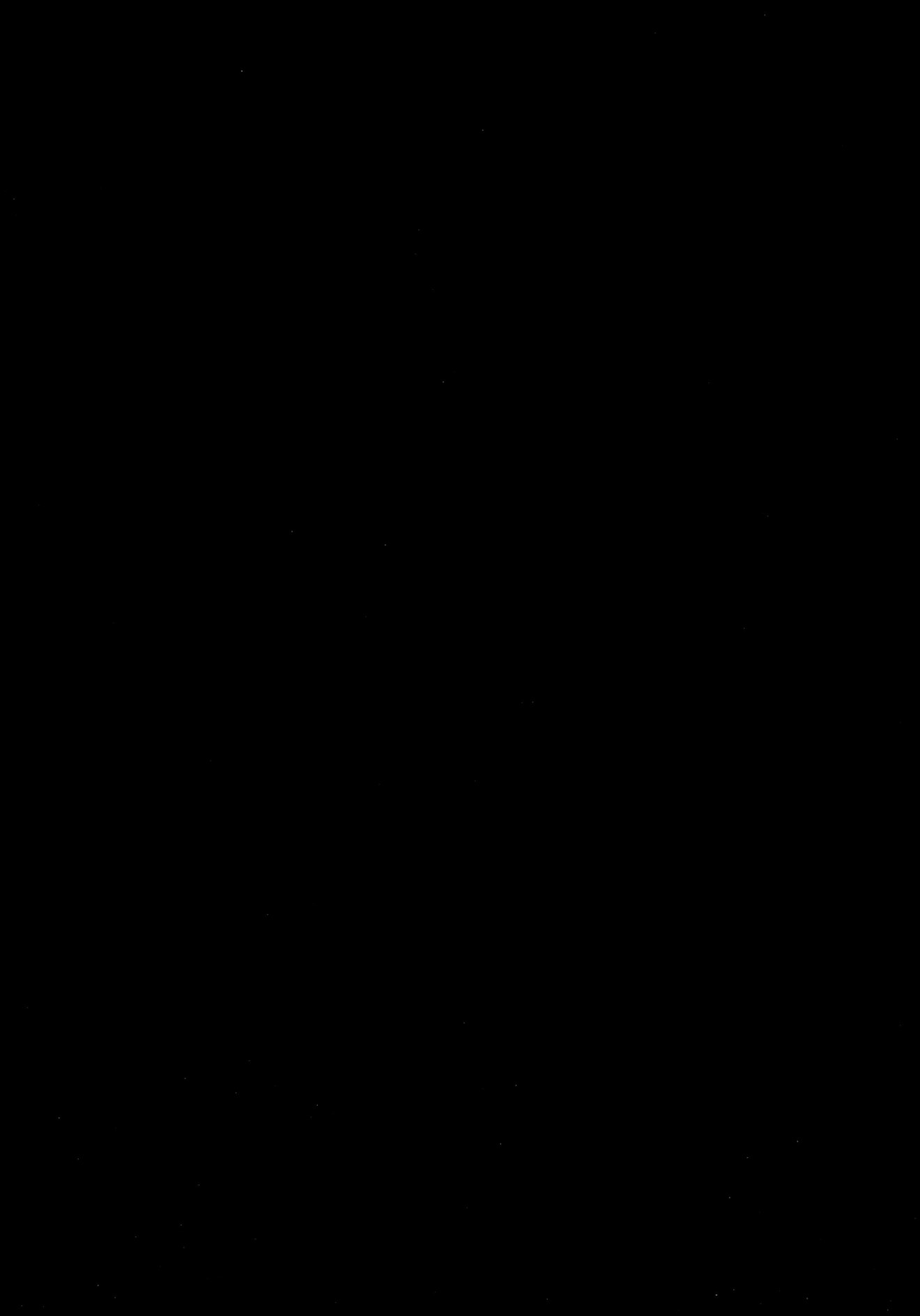

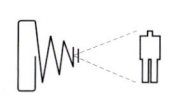

ALBERT LEGGETT
502.584.0255
www.leggettphoto.com

Used with permission of Philip Morris Incorporated

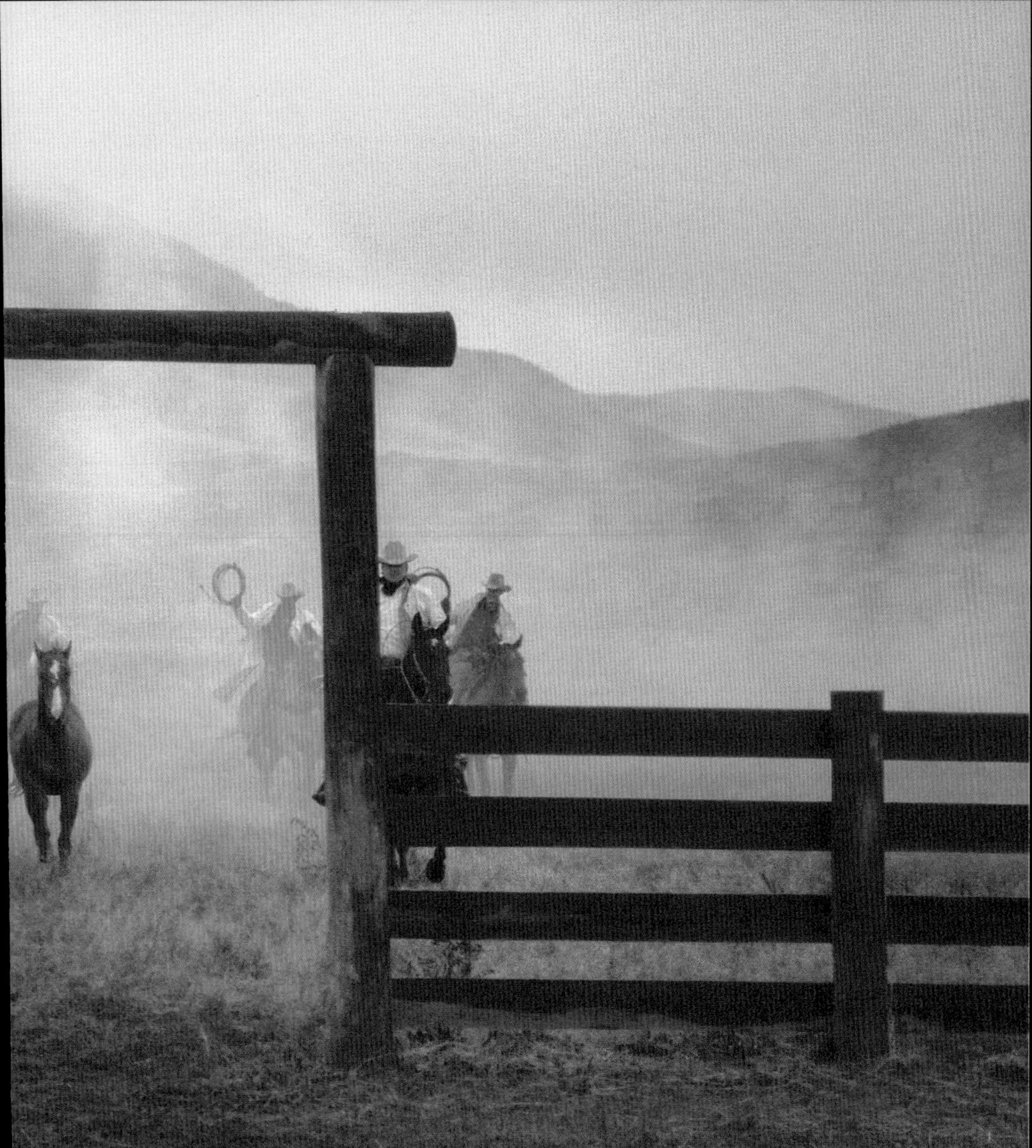

KEN FRANTZ
photography

VOX 312.951.1077 FAX 312.951.2903

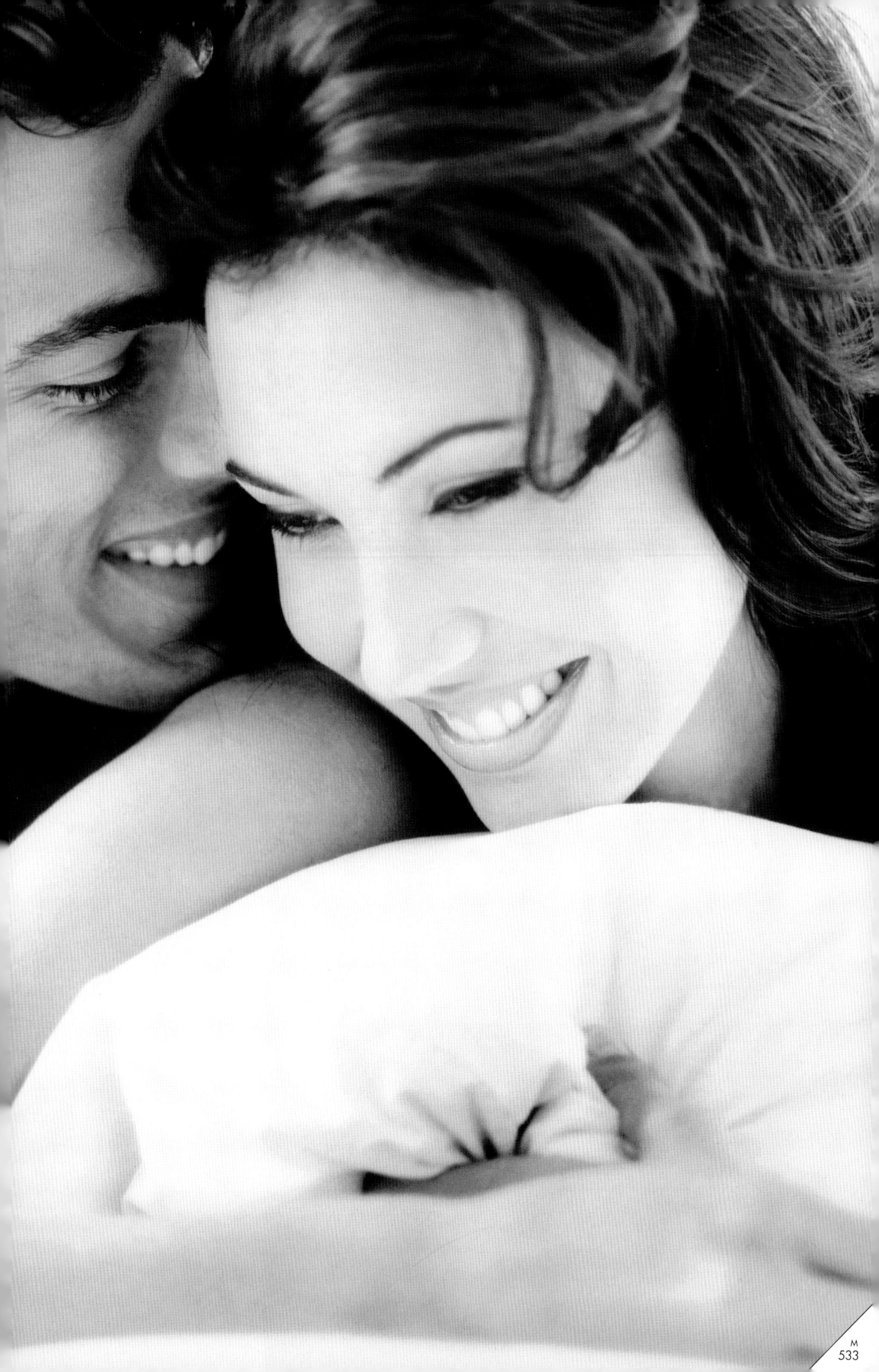

www.*terishootsfood*.com

888-784-9696

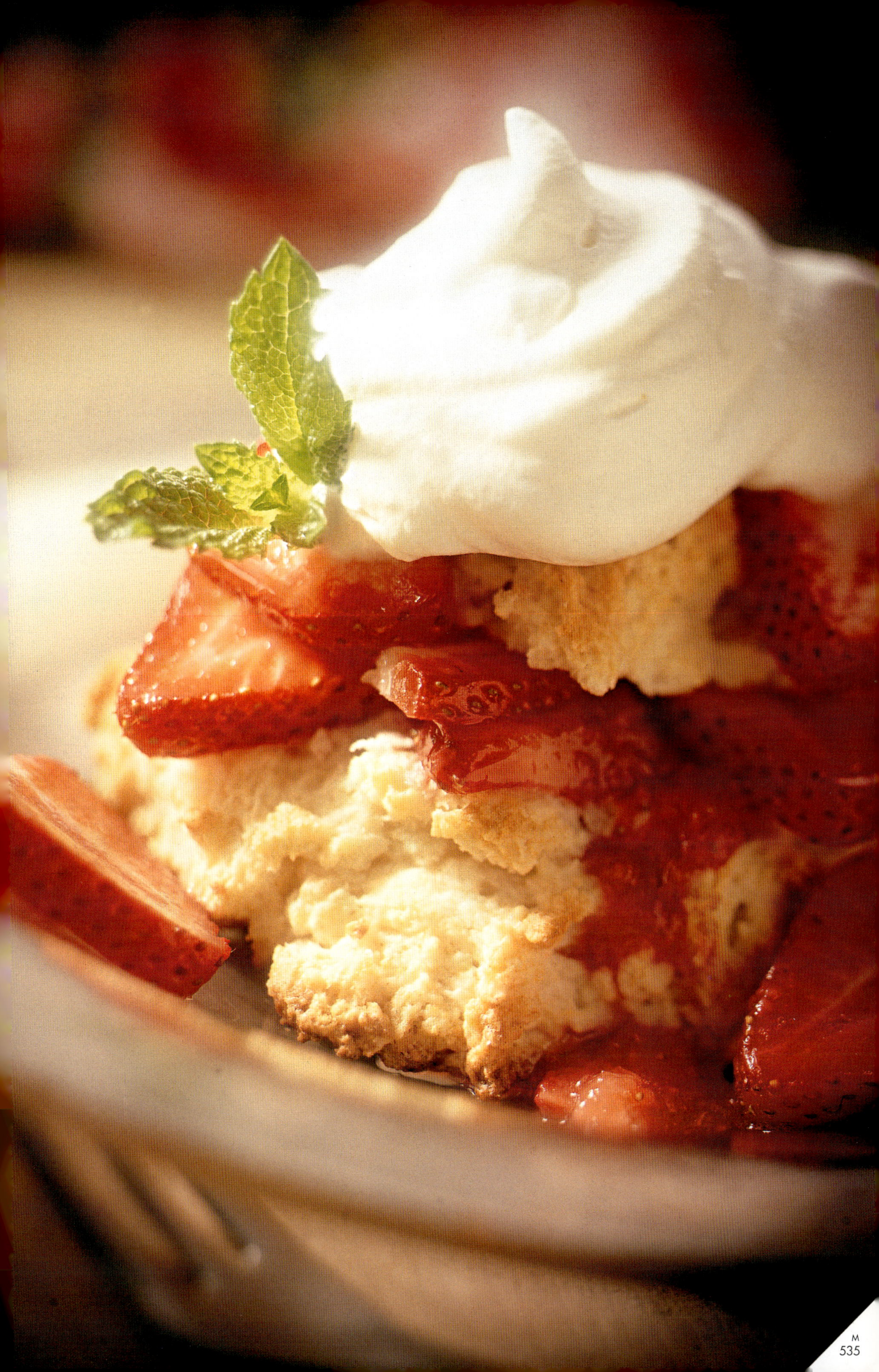

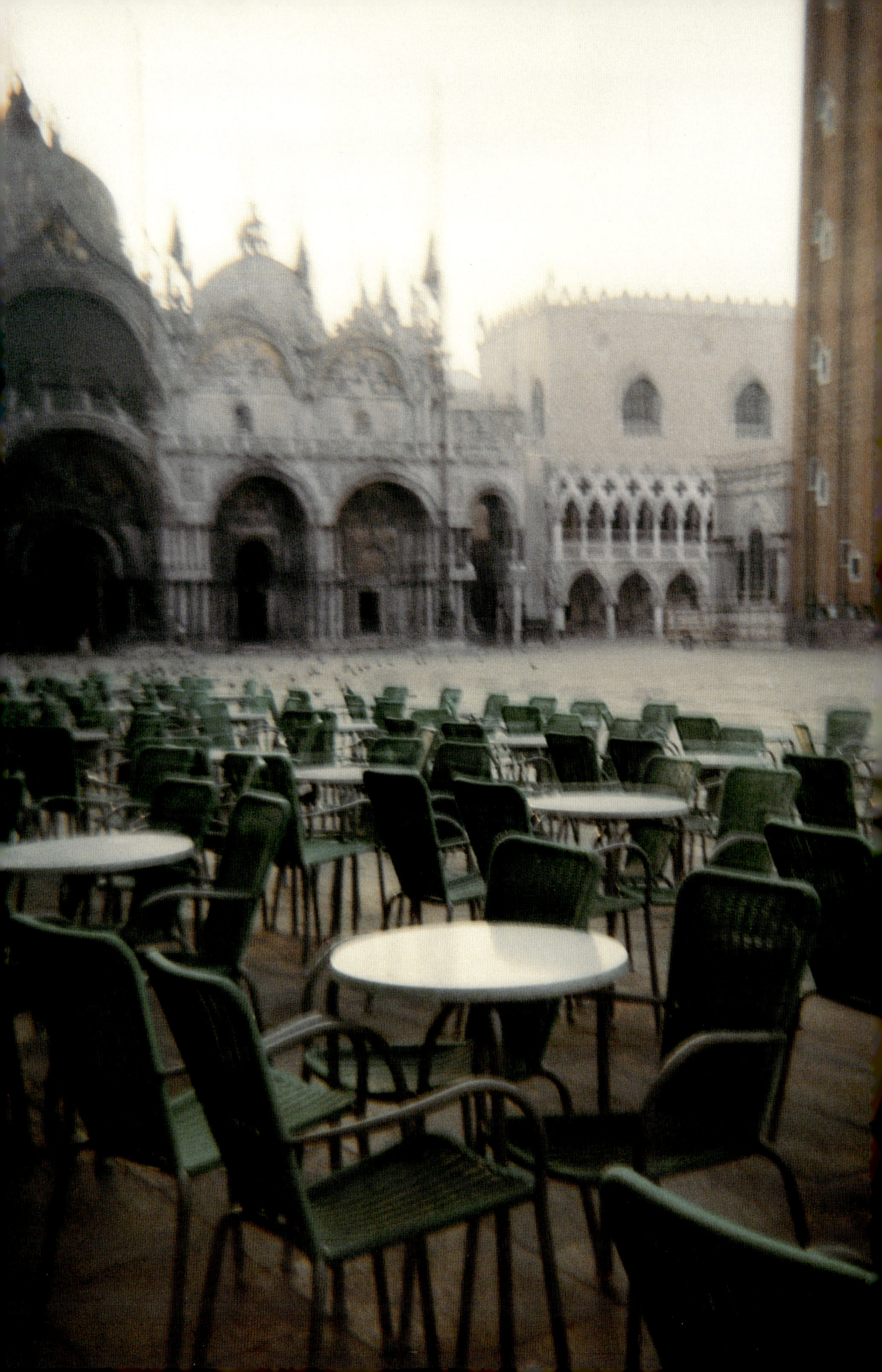

KATE ROTH studio **773 276 8751** agent **randi fiat** t **312 329 9800** f **312 329 7223**

Goodwin
PHOTOGRAPHY

GOODWIN
PHOTOGRAPHY

AUDIA PHOTOGRAPHY
REPRESENTED BY Z agency

Chicago 312.832.0418
800.626.0418
www.audia.net

CHRIS BAILEY

CHARLIE SIMOKAITIS

STEVE EWERT

DESMOND BURDON

TIM TURNER

NICK VEASEY

tel (847)866.8568 JUDITH McGRATH
ARTISTS
REPRESENTATIVE *fax (847)866.8067*

www.judymcgrath.net

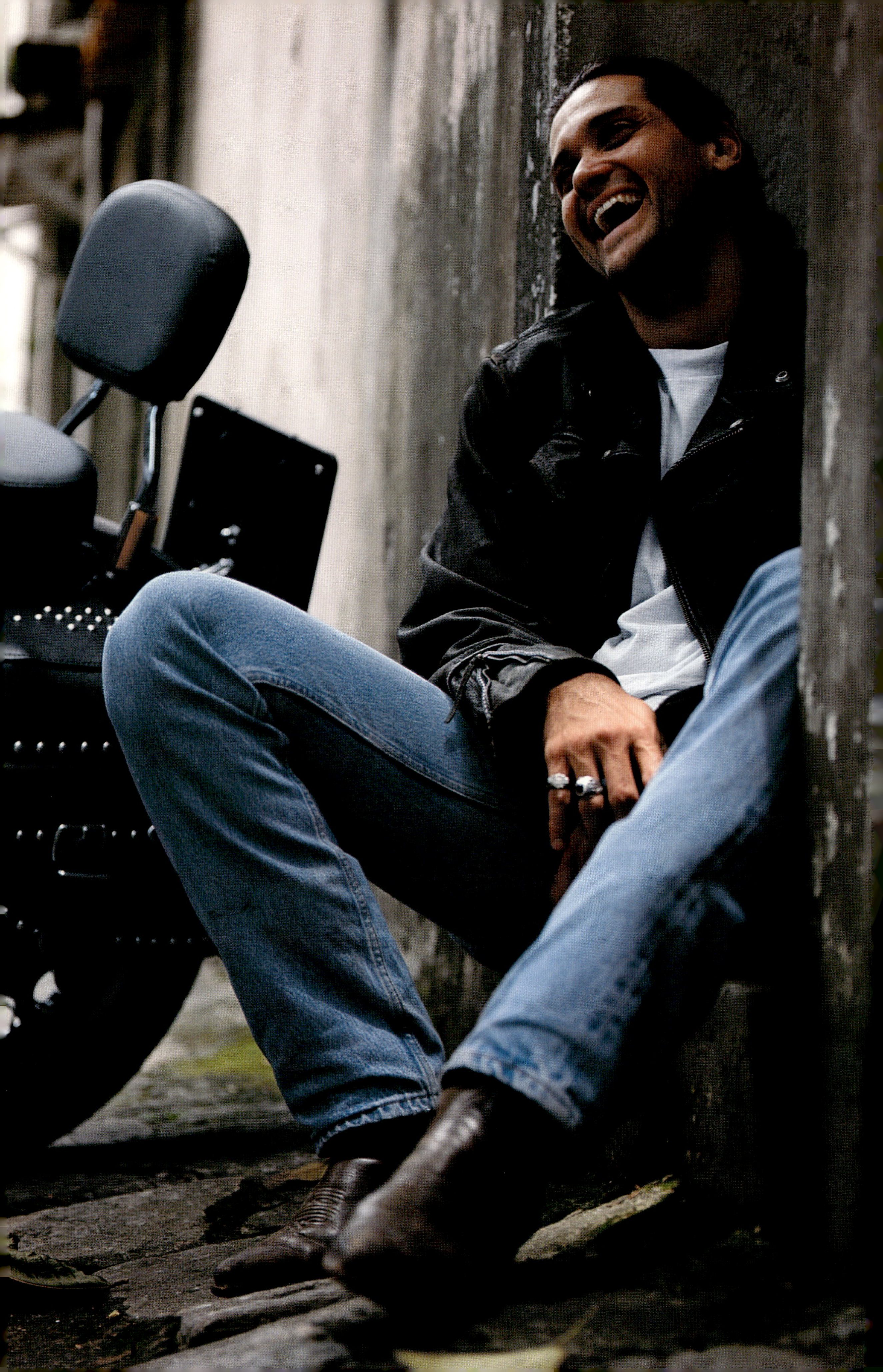

SIMOKAITIS
773 539 4644

REPRESENTED BY JUDY MCGRATH
847 • 866 • 8568

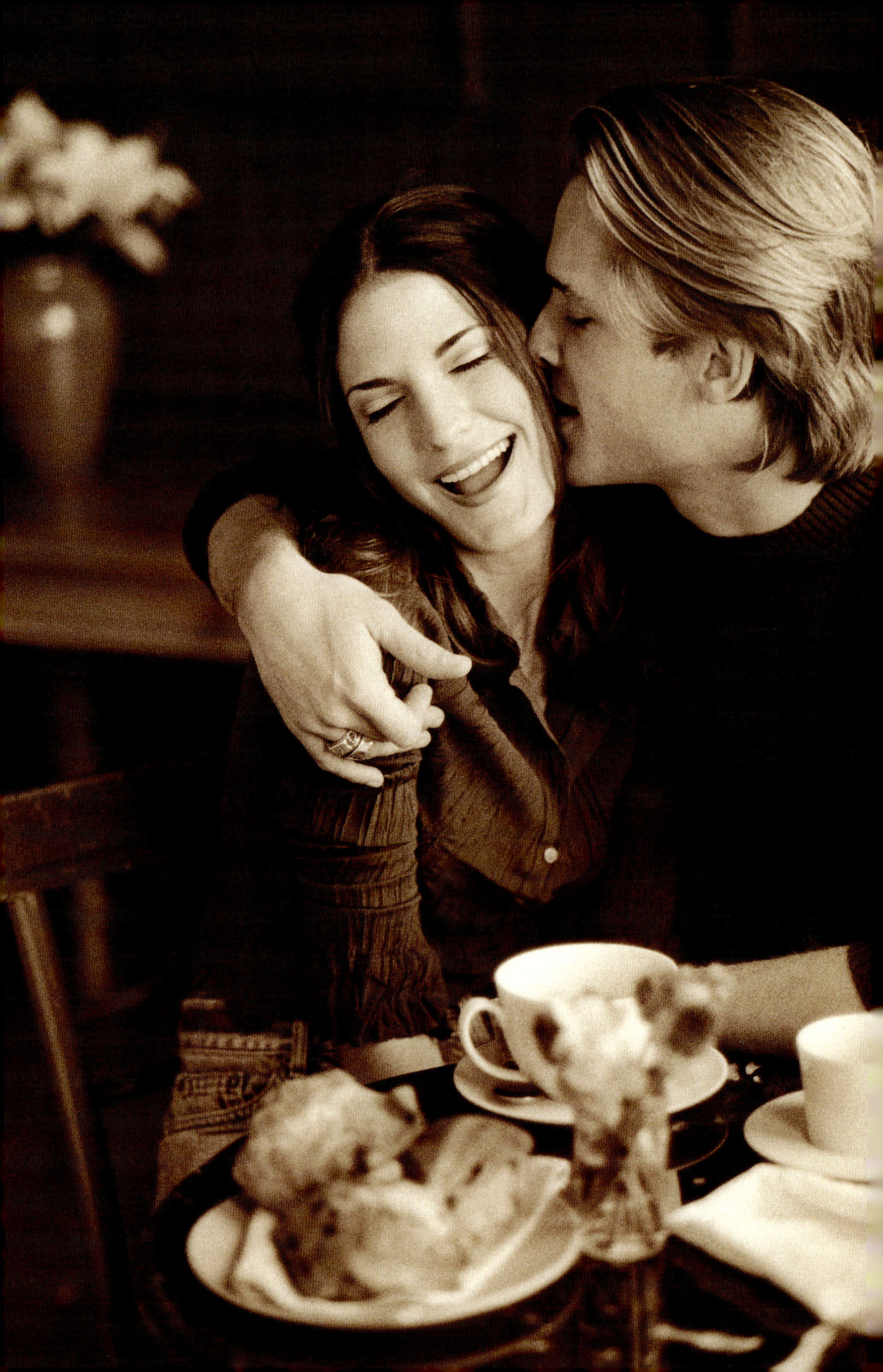

EWERT

STEVE EWERT PHOTOGRAPHY 17 North Elizabeth Street Chicago, Illinois 60607 T 312.733.5762 F 312.733.2202
portfolio and stock photography archive at www.ewertphoto.com
Represented in the Midwest by Judy McGrath 847.866.8568

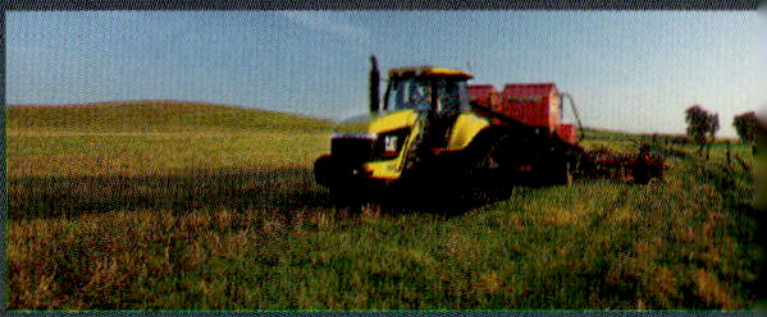

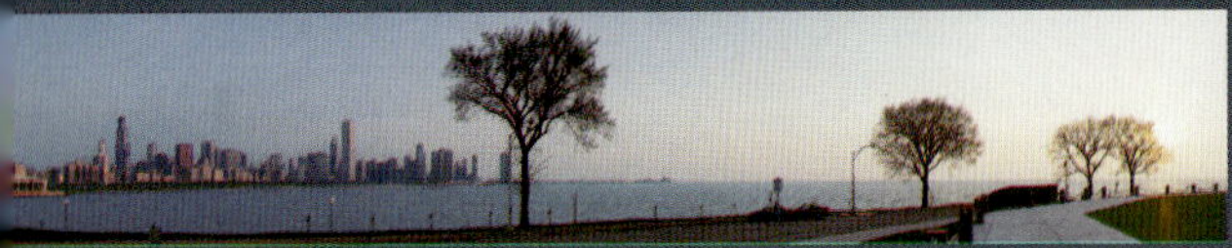

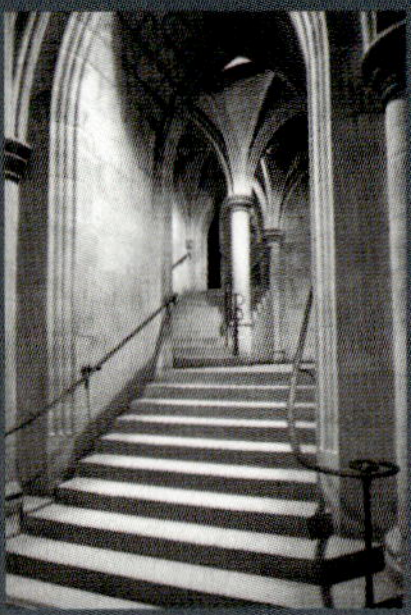

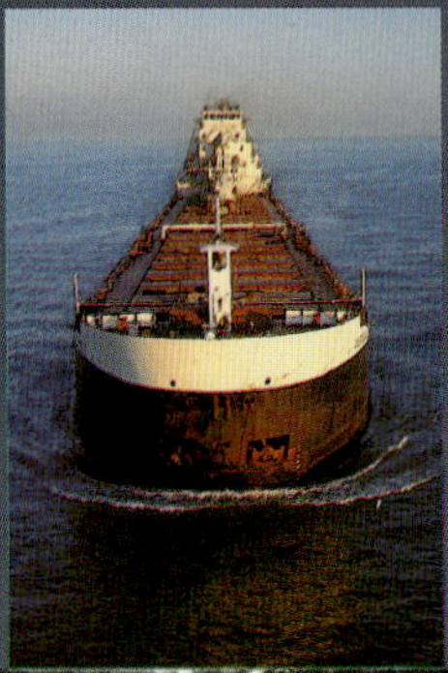

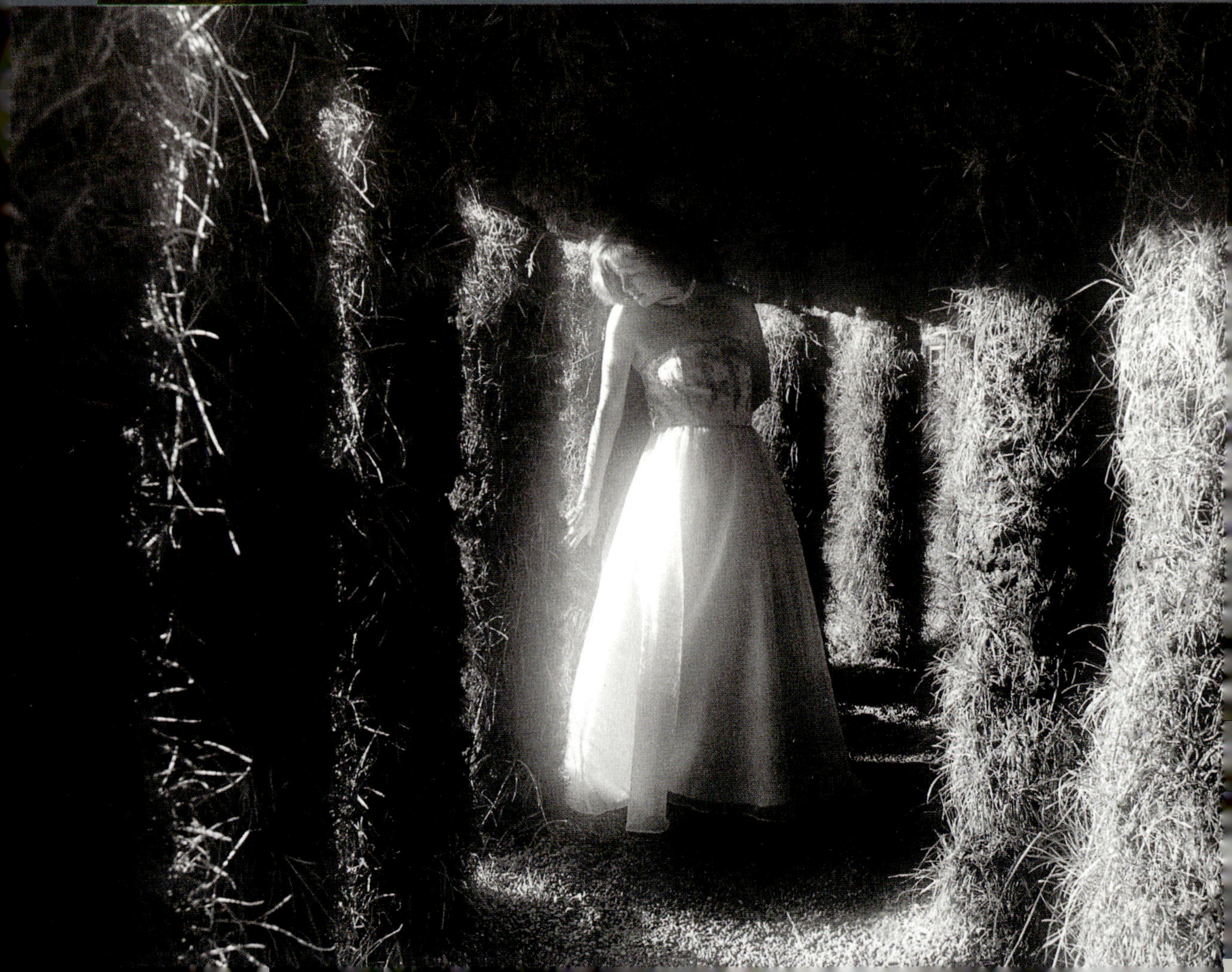

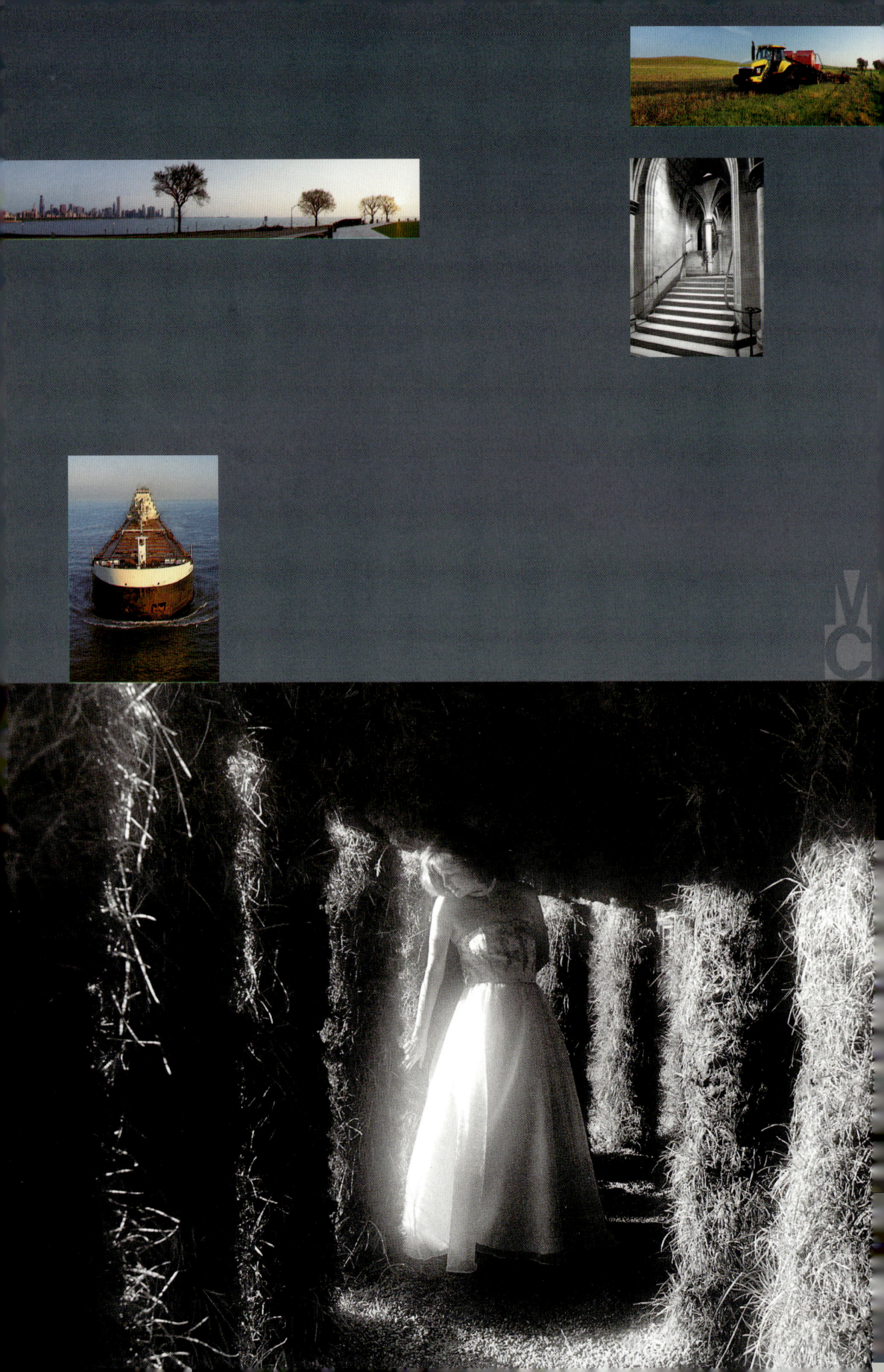

HARD MACK PHOTOGRAPHY LTD   847 869 7794   EVANSTON ILLINOIS   WWW.MACKPHOTO.COM

Paula FRIEDLAND STUDIO, Inc.

Tel: 402 345 2028
Fax: 402 345 9911

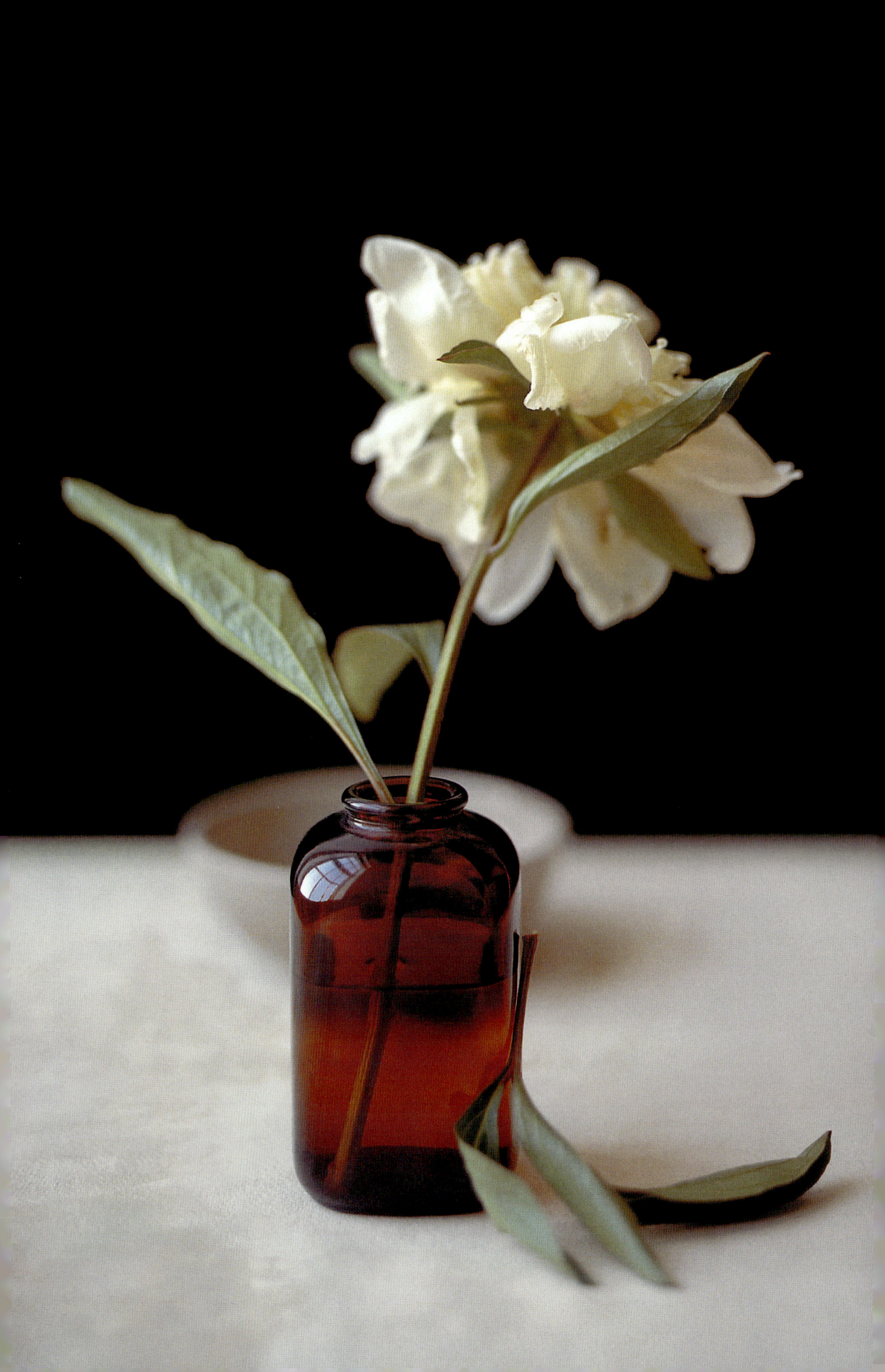

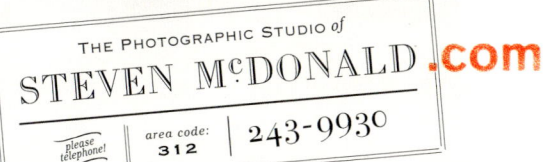

The Photographic Studio of
STEVEN M^cDONALD.com

please telephone! | area code: 312 | 243-9930

rick meoli

represented by denise hopkins 314.208.1602
in denver by repfile 1.877.99.repfile

meoli studio

314.752.5550

www.meolistudio.com

VEDROS

© Nick Vedros, Vedros & Associates 2000

PHOTOGRAPHY • DIGITAL IMAGING
Visit www.vedros.com FOR STOCK AND ADDITIONAL IMAGES

(816) 471-5488   FAX (816) 471-2666
IN THE EAST CALL ROBERT MEAD ASSOCIATES (800) 717-1994   (212) 688-7474

VEDROS

© Nick Vedros, Vedros & Associates 2000

PHOTOGRAPHY • DIGITAL IMAGING
VISIT www.vedros.com FOR STOCK AND ADDITIONAL IMAGES

(816) 471-5488   FAX (816) 471-2666
IN THE EAST CALL ROBERT MEAD ASSOCIATES (800) 717-1994   (212) 688-7474

GREGORY

GAYMONT

P 312-421-3146
F 312-421-3147

ggaymont@earthlink.net

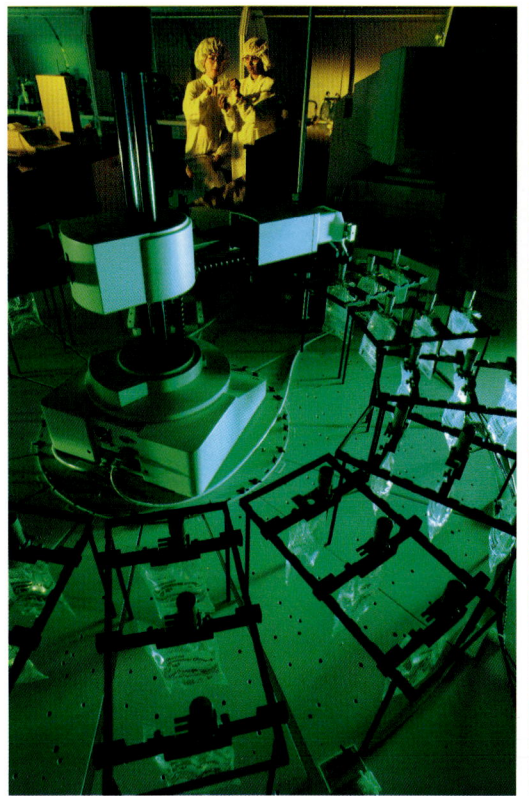

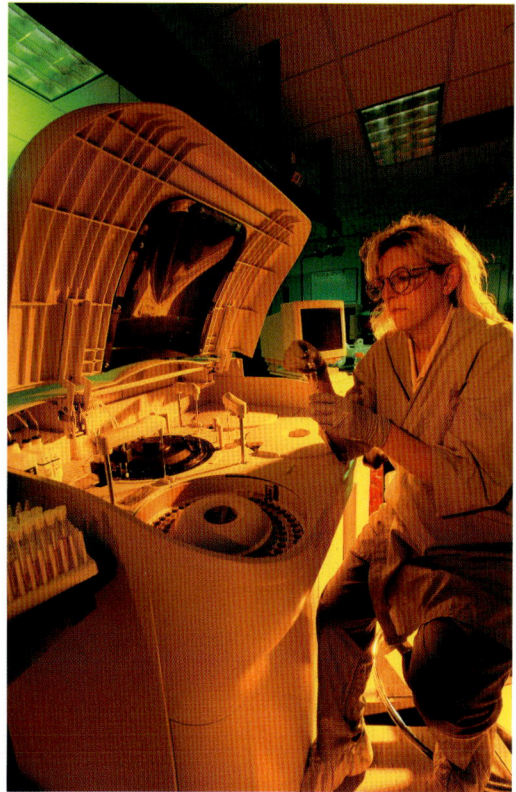

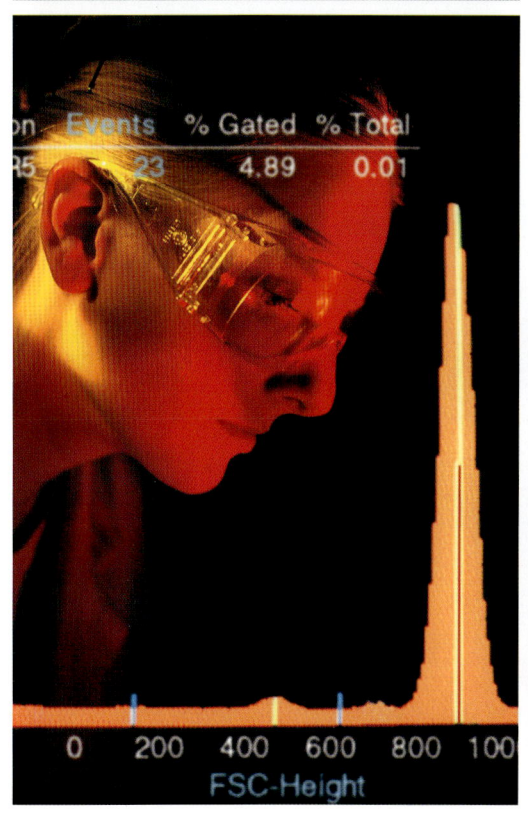

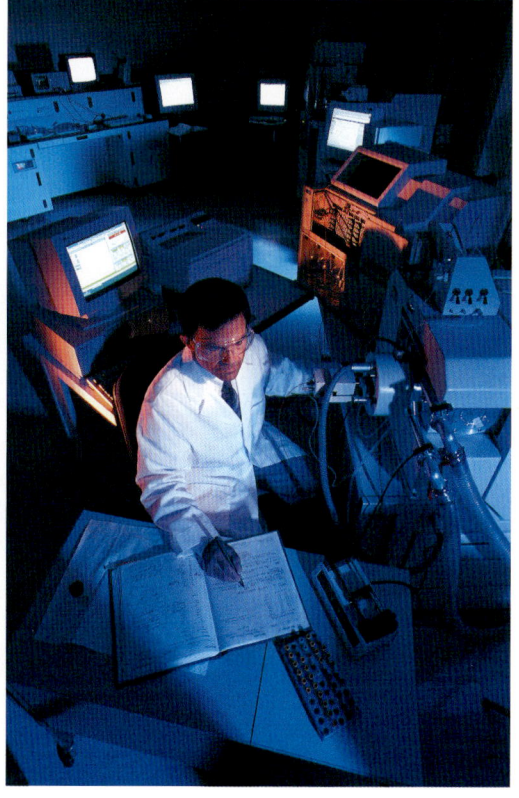

BAXTER INTERNATIONAL

ALLEGIANCE HEALTHCARE

US GYPSUM

CNA INSURANCE

AIR LIQUIDE CORPORATION

ASTRA MERCK

McCORMICK TRIBUNE FOUNDATION

SARA LEE

REYNOLDS METALS

AMERICAN NATIONAL CAN

CARDINAL HEALTH INC.

ATLAS VAN LINES

DAVID JOEL PHOTOGRAPHY

(Chicago Area)

PHONE: 800.211.2694

FAX: 847.251.1296

E-MAIL: david@davidjoel.com

WEB: www.davidjoel.com

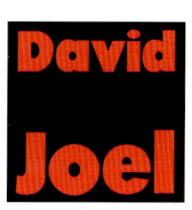

David Joel

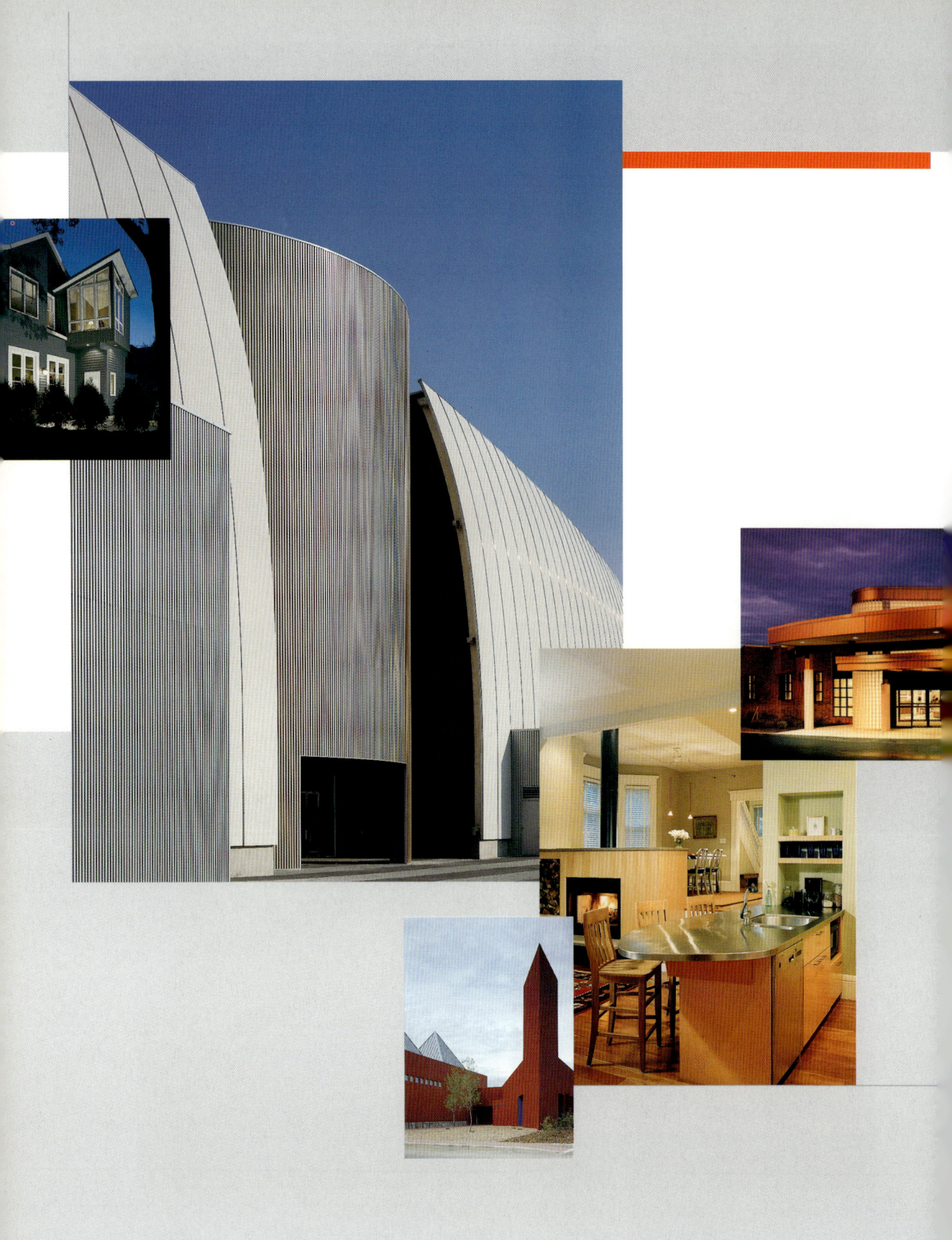

feinknopf

877-367-2120   www.feinknopf.com or www.planetpoint.com/brad_feinknopf

EXCELLENCE IN ARCHITECTURAL PHOTOGRAPHY
INTERIORS AND EXTERIORS

©2000 Thomas R.Drew

tom drew :photographer	black, white & color inc.	photography for advertising and design	810.795.4620

www.bwcphoto.com

PeggyDay

u.3
REPS
agents for the visual arts

Jake Wallis

Dave Schmitz

800.550.5583 | www.uthree.com | 248.975.8867 | agents@uthree.com

agents for the visual arts

u.3 REPS

George **Pizzo**

Don **Johnston**

Tom **Burkhart**

Troy **Wood**

800.550.5583 | www.uthree.com | 248.975.8867 | agents@uthree.com

GEORGE PIZZO PHOTOGRAPHY   DIGITAL AND ANALOG IMAGERY

represented by U3. 800/550/5583   STUDIO > 800/248/7856   FAX > 248/588/8273

PiZZO

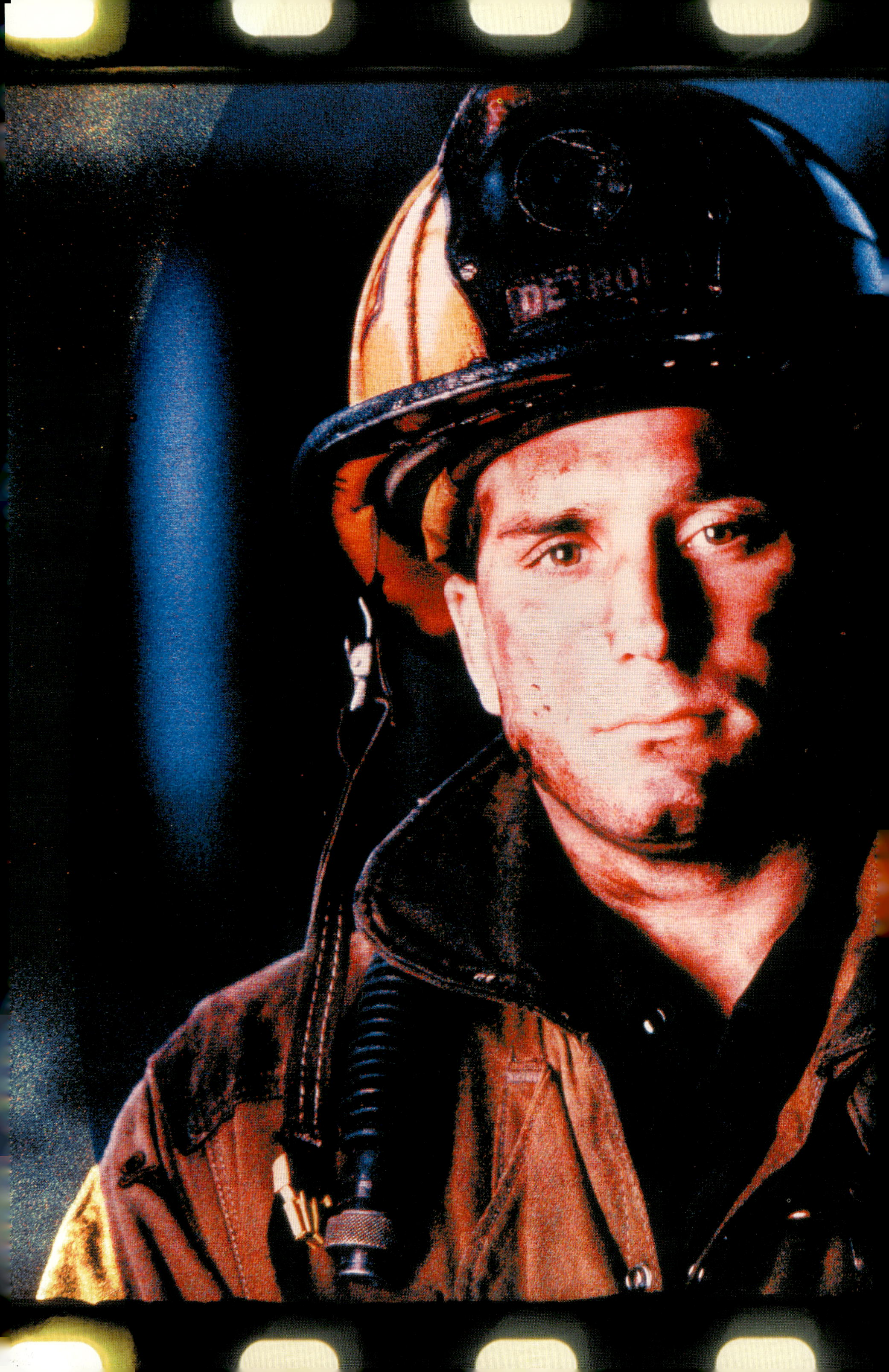

TROYWOOD
PHOTOGRAPHY

STUDIO 800/248/7856
FAX 248/588/8273

REPRESENTED BY U-3
800/550/5583

johnston

JOHNSTON

don johnston
USA 1-800-816-3404 • 248-969-6050 • FAX 248-969-0014 • www.johnston-images.com

Greg Whitaker

Represented by
Holly Hahn [H²+Co.]
312-633-0500
(f) 312-633-0484
www.hollyhahn.com

Studio
812-988-8808
www.gregwhitaker.com

Greg Whitaker

Represented by
Holly Hahn [H²+Co.]
312-633-0500
(f) 312-633-0484
www.hollyhahn.com

Studio
812-988-8808
www.gregwhitaker.com

Frank Schiefelbein

ASSIGNMENT • LOCATION • STOCK

Phone: 847•358•3626

Email: studio@frankschiefelbein.com

www.frankschiefelbein.com

Eric Futran/Chefshots
(773) 525-5020 • fax (773) 525-1305
www.chefshots.com
eric@chefshots.com

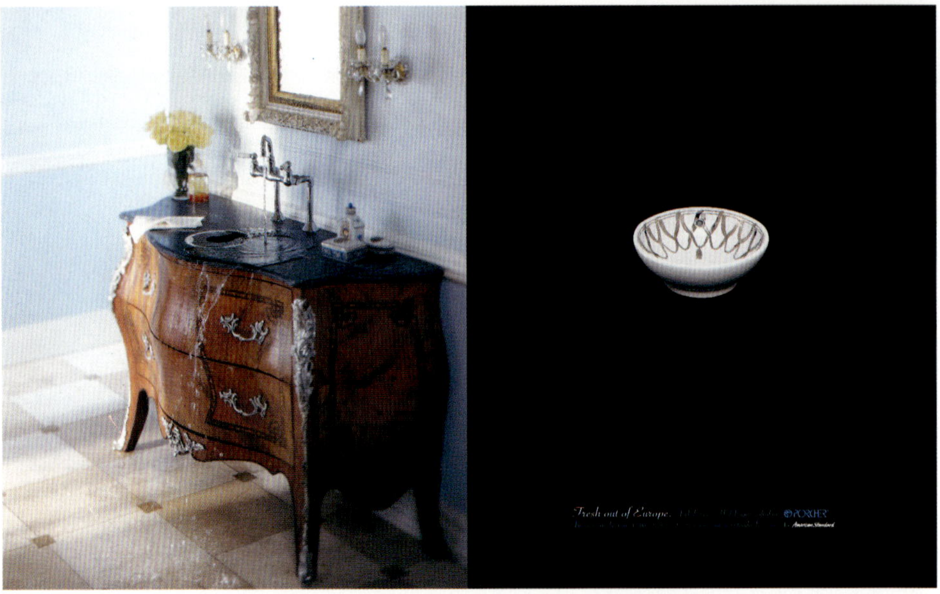

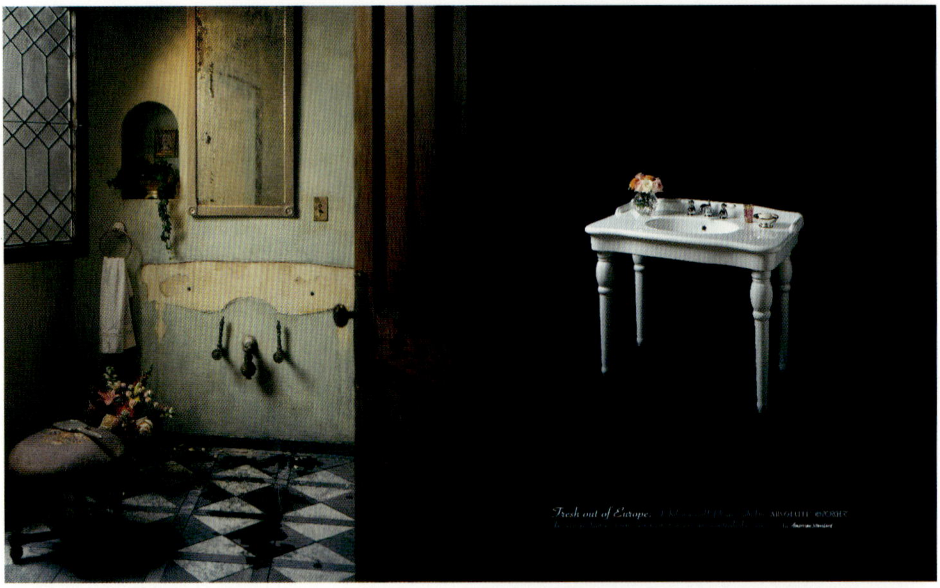

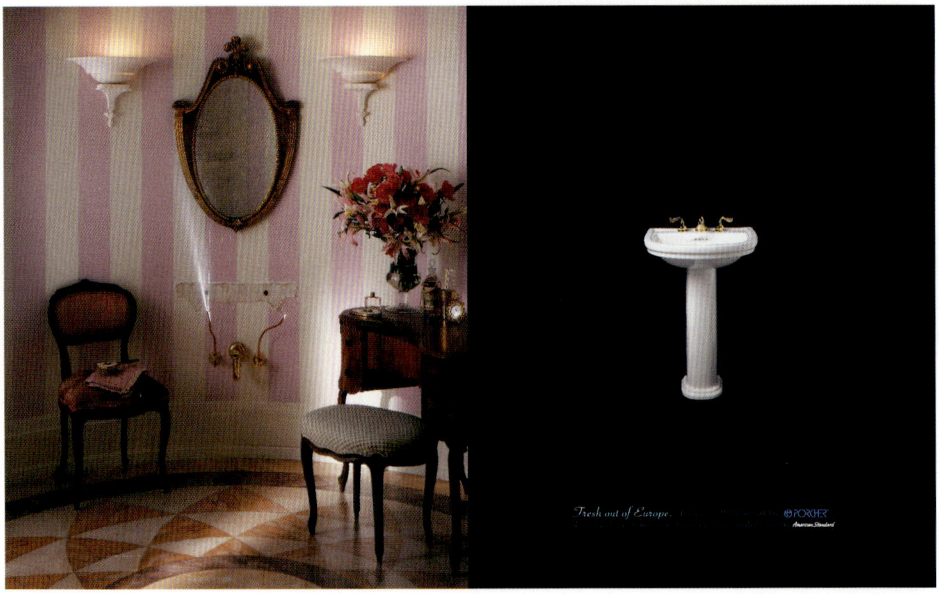

Steve Henke Studio

photography . set design . production   612.788.7777

Sciortino

Sciortino

REPRESENTED BY
Holly Hahn
TEL 312-633-0500
FAX 312-633-0484
WEB hollyhahn.com

STUDIO
Jeff Sciortino
TEL 312-829-6112
FAX 312-829-6113
WEB jeffsciortino.com

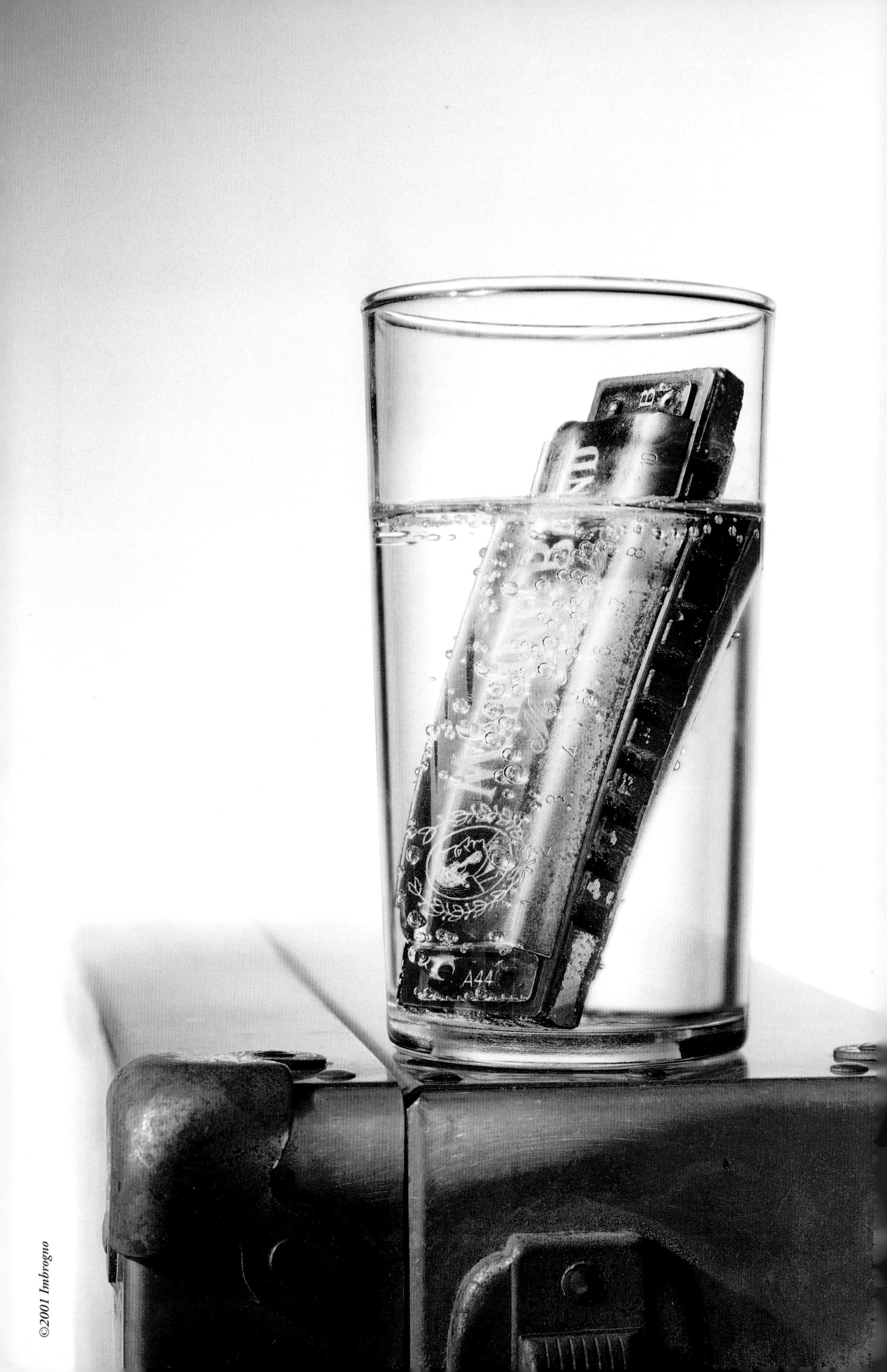

IMBROGNO PHOTOGRAPHY STUDIO (312) 733-3650

WWW.IMBROGNO.COM

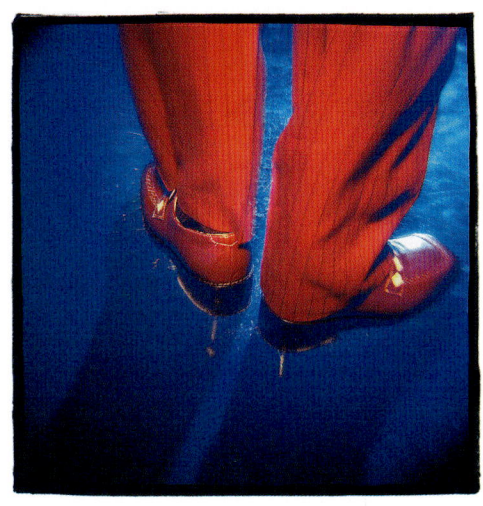

REPRESENTED BY SCHUMANN & COMPANY (800) 710-1969

marc norberg studio inc 612 340 9863 www.marcnorberg.com

Test results show almost anything is indeed better than a sharp stick in the eye.

NORBERG

No night life. No crime. No rush hour traffic.
Is it any wonder we find other people's problems so interesting?

Client: Primera
Agency: Colle & McVoy
AD: Tim Musta

THOMAS STRAND 612-333-4155

www.thomasstrand.com

philpott

www.keithphilpott.com
913.492.0715
kansas city

www.keithphilpott.com
913.492.0715
kansas city

UNTIL I FIND A REAL MAN, I'LL TAKE A REAL SMOKE.

LEAVE THE BULL BEHIND.

NO FAKE SMILES, NO HIDDEN AGENDAS, NO BULL.

LEAVE THE BULL BEHIND.

JUST GIVE IT TO ME STRAIGHT.

LEAVE THE BULL BEHIND.

H N   L A I R   S T U D I

5 0 2   5 8 9   7 7 7 9

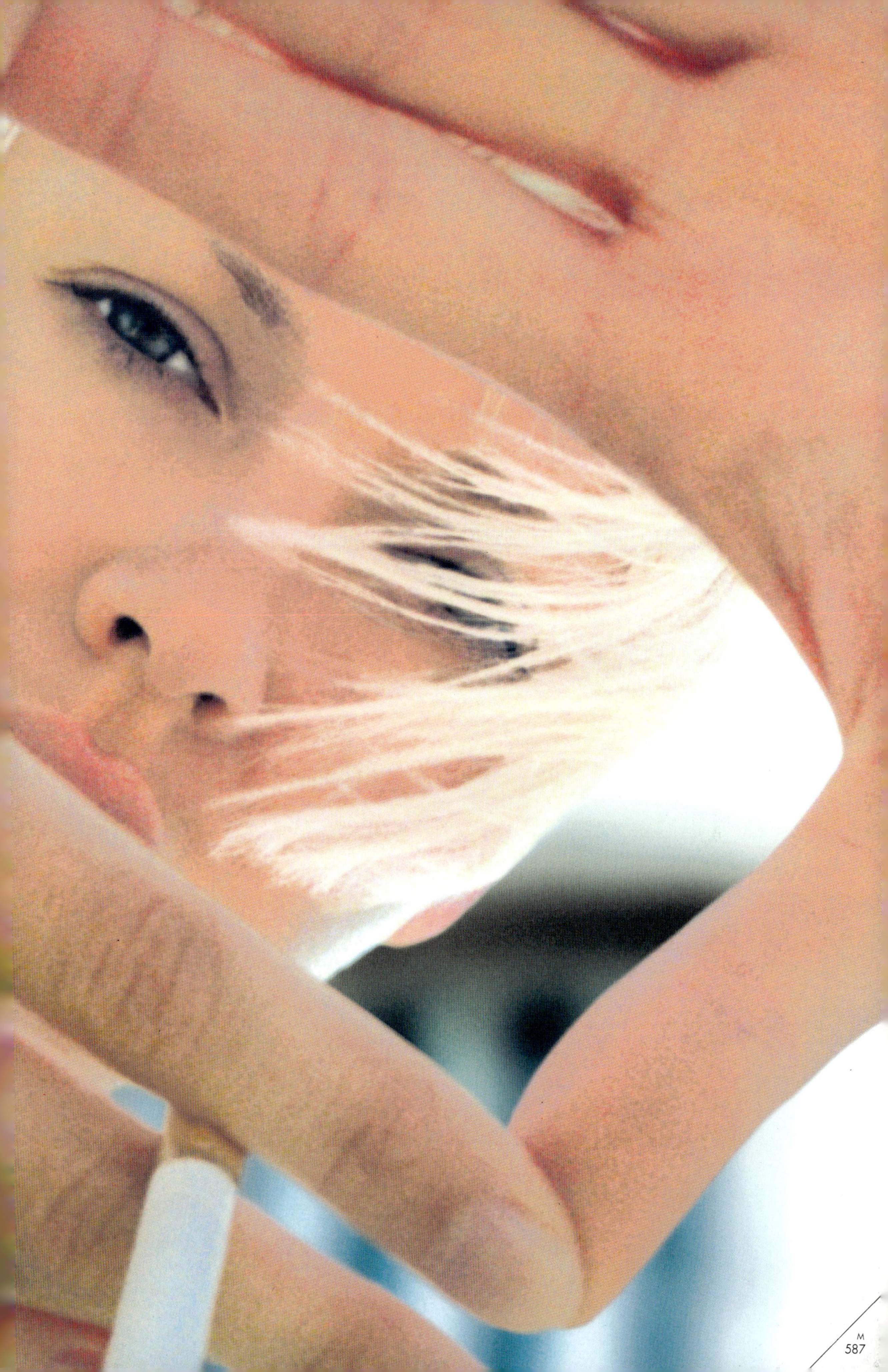

Karl **Knize**

(Niz)

773 . 477 . 1001

w w w . k a r l k n i z e . c o m

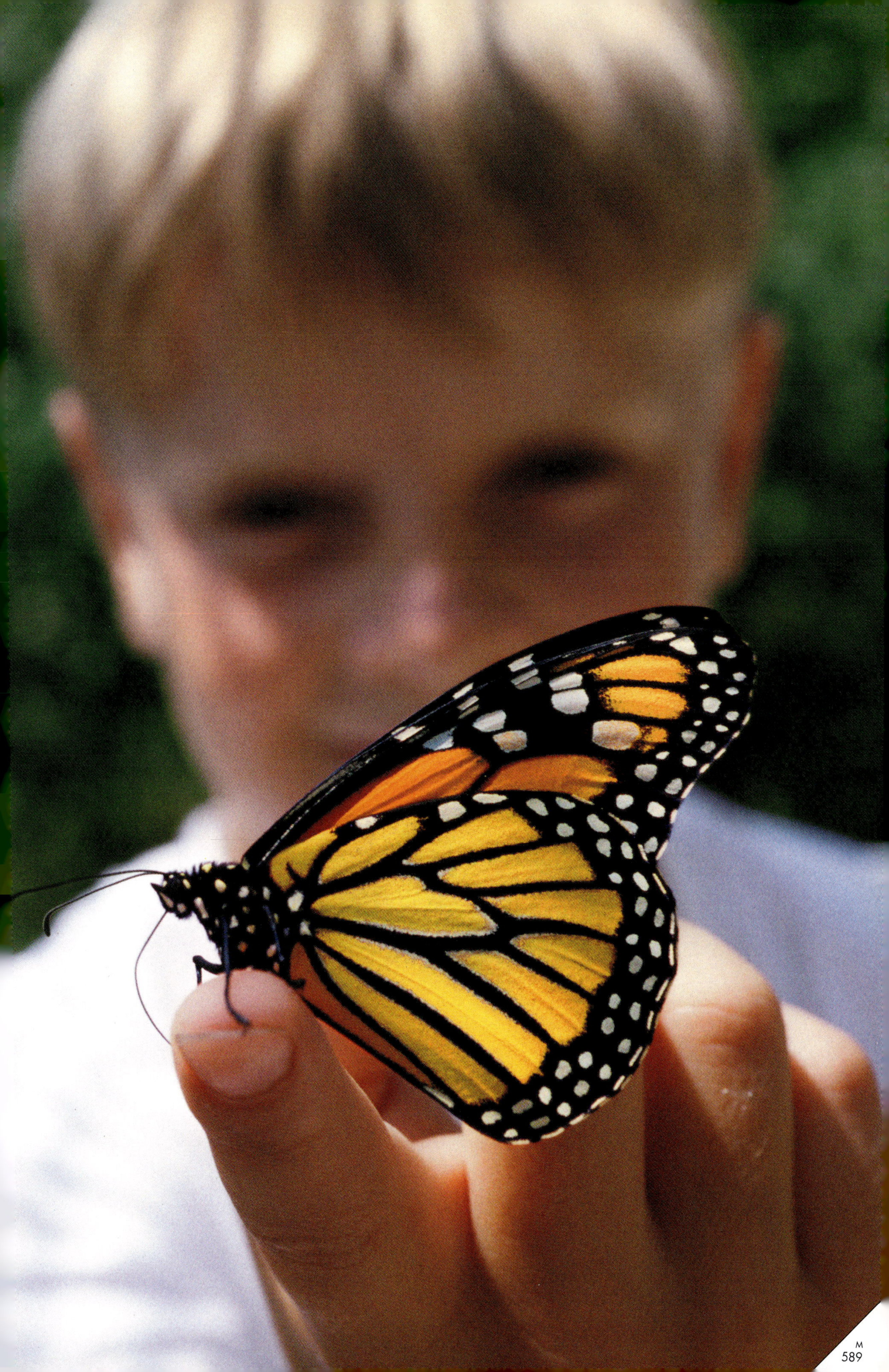

ted rice

columbus, ohio
tedrice@infinet.com
www.tedrice.com

trust intuition

represented by leslie burns
leslie@burnsautoparts.com
614.228.6727

rice

SPAhr pHotogRaphy

Dick Spahr *Telephone* 317.255.2400 *Fax* 317.255.2417

Represented By Jan Bugher 317.322.0450

SPAhr pHotogRaphy

Dick Spahr *Telephone* 317.255.2400 *Fax* 317.255.2417

Represented By Jan Bugher 317.322.0450

joyce
PHOTOGRAPHY

Todd Joyce
Joyce Photography
18 West 7th St. 8th fl
Cincinnati, Ohio 45202
phn 513-421-1209
fax 513-421-3880
joycepho@one.net
www.joycephotography.com

w w w . j o y c e p h o t o g r a p h y . c o m

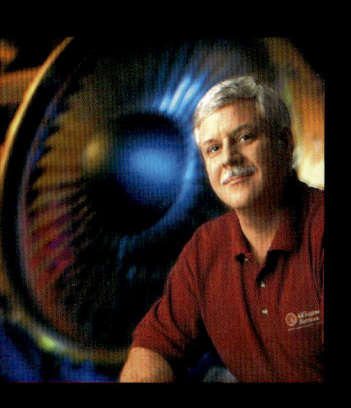

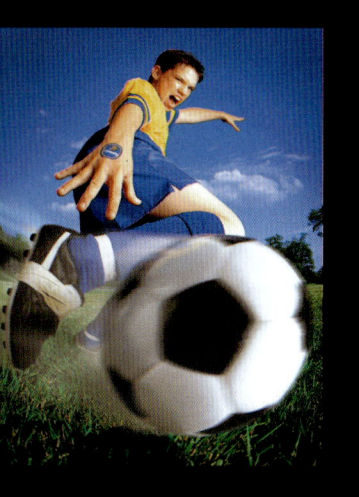

joyce

PHOTOGRAPHY

April 5, 2000

Memo to stockholders

Upon recently hearing about a radical new technology called a "search engine," we enlisted the services of one Dr. Olsrud. As soon as you inform us that you've lost something the good doctor catapults into action. He looks under things. He looks behind things. He stops and rests for awhile. His new artificial hip enables him to search far and wide with an elf-like quickness. There is no corner of our office that escapes the gaze of his mostly cataract-free left eye. And he only takes one short break every day around noon to have a small stroke.

WELCOME TO THE FUTURE. WELCOME TO DUBLINPRODUCTIONS.COM

dublinproductions.com

COLD AND LONELY?

WWW.TOOHOT.COM

TONY D'ORIO

Represented In Chicago by Jodie Zeitler 312 222-0504
Elsewhere by Hurewitz Creative Partners 212 682-2600
Studio 312 421-5532

BENTLEY

DAVID BENTLEY   2059 WEST GRAND AVENUE   CHICAGO, ILLINOIS   60612   312.829.2001 / 312.829.4050 fax

BENTLEY

DAVID BENTLEY   2059 WEST GRAND AVENUE   CHICAGO, ILLINOIS   60612   312.829.2001 / 312.829.4050 fax

GRUE

Steve Grubman Photography, Inc. 456 North Morgan, Chicago, IL 60622 Tel 312 226-2272

MAN.

587 www.grubman.com Represented by Reptile Artists Agent • Call Carolyn Somlo 773 477-5372

Ⓦ

DAN WHITE

STORY TELL

816.421.2400

HALLMARK · LEE JEANS · NORTHWEST AIRLINES · SEABOARD CORPORATION
SPRINT · EASTMAN KODAK   www.danwhite.com

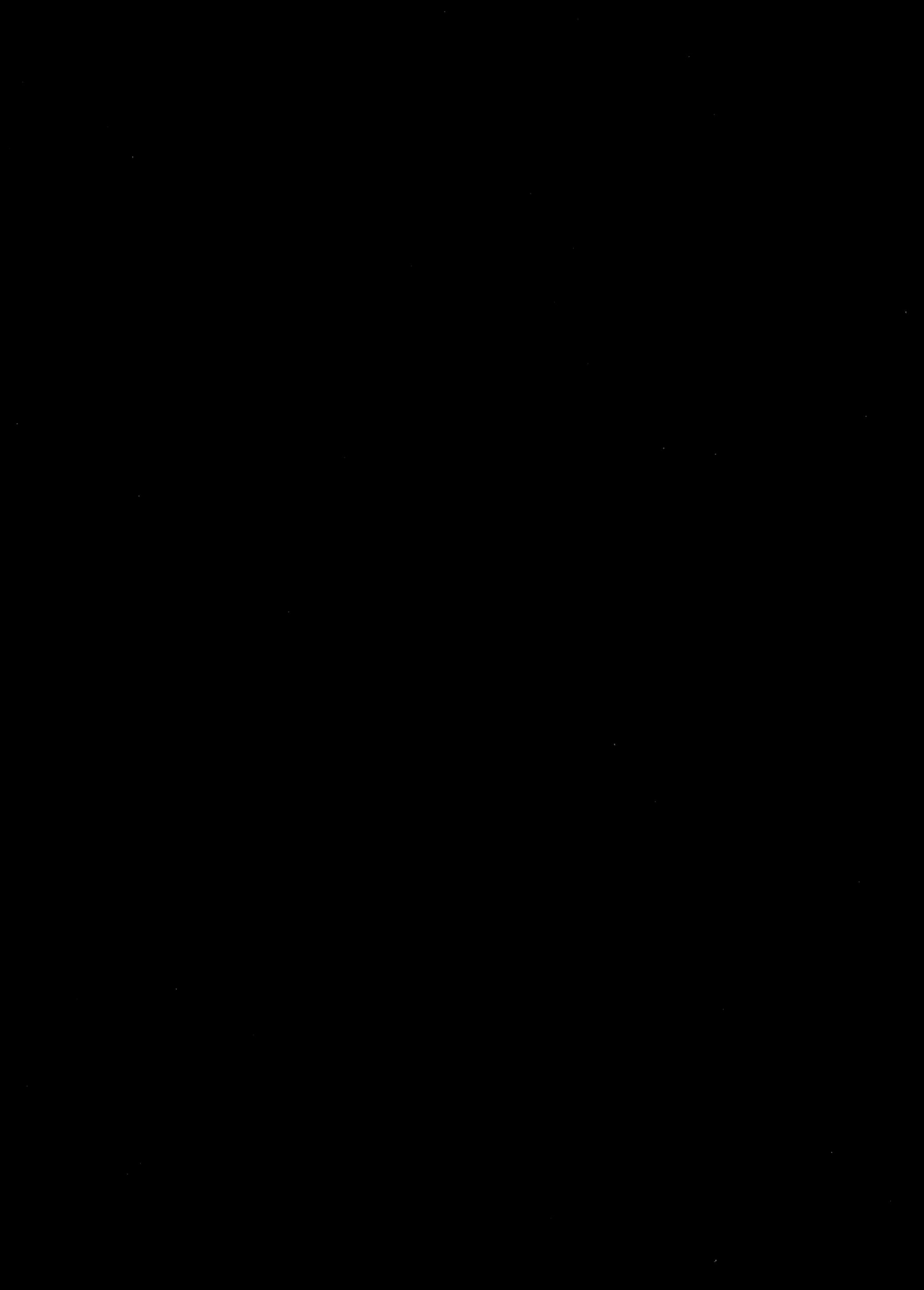

WEST

John Acurso 738-739
AKA Reps 696-697
Christopher Ayers 740-741
Deborah Ayerst Artists Agent 618-619
Jacques Barbey 750-751
Ellen Barnes 620-623
Andrew D. Bernstein Associates 718-719
Rick Bolen 624-625
Charlie Borland 664-665
Thomas Broening 748-749
Jeffrey Burke 696-697
Burke/Triolo Productions 696-697
Tom Burkhart 562-563, 702-703
Caesar Photo Design 694-695
Marianne Campbell Associates 314-315, 708-709
Joan Carelas 688-689
Marc Carter 722-723
Marge Casey & Associates 343-351, 742-743
Michael Conn 658-659
Cosmos Paris 666-667
Creative Management/Stephanie Menuez 16-21, 682-683
Damon Productions, Inc. 640-641
Patrick Darby 670-671
Brooke Davis 644-645

Peggy Day 562-563, 658-659
Deddens & Deddens 702-703
Ric Deliantoni 712-713
Walt Denson 644-645
Alan Dockery 613
Francoise Dubois/Dennis Represents 718-719
Dana Edmunds 734-735
Heather Elder 614-615
Lisa Ellison, Artist Representative 676-677
Rhoni Epstein Artists' Management 692-693, 706-707
Jim Erickson 682-683
Hunter Freeman 614-615
Joe Gibbs 638-639
Acey Harper 646-647
Tim Hawley 696-697
Robert Holley 728-729
Vic Huber 692-693
Terry Husebye 700-701
Illumini Productions 666-667
Bruce James 696-697
Joan Jedell Productions, Inc. 746-747
William Jones 732-733
Vincent Kamin & Associates 644-645, 666-667
Catherine Karnow 668-669
Lehmen/Dabney, Inc. 726-727

Mel Lindstrom 660-663

Brian Mahany 654-655

Tom Maloney 696-697

Tim Mantoani 636-637

Paul Markow/Markow Southwest, Inc.
  690-691

Joe McBride 744-745

Frank Meo 636-637

Scott Montgomery 688-689

John Morrison 686-687

Will Mosgrove 708-709

Stan Musilek, Inc. 618-619

Anthony Nex 706-707

Glenn Oakley 656-657

Roseanne Olson 726-727

Tim Pannell 746-747

David Papas 680-681

Gary Parker 720-721

Aaron Rapoport 714-715

Philipp Scholz Rittermann 684-685

Lew Robertson 696-697

Howard Rosenberg 628-631

John Russell 704-705

Sampsel & Preston 730-731

Robb Scharetg 648-653

Chris Schrameck 742-743

Freda Scott, Inc. 644-645

Karen Shell 724-725

Jay Silverman Productions 672-675

Mark Silverstein 736-737

Chip Simons 634-635

Gil Smith 666-667

Souders Studios 678-679

Maggie Storck 648-653

Jeremiah Sullivan & Associates 710-711

Team Russell 704-705

Lorraine Triolo 696-697

U3-Agents for the Visual Arts 562-569,
  658-659, 702-703

Randel Urbauer 642-643

Douglas E. Walker 632-633

Debra Weiss 632-633

Elyse Weissberg 690-691

Randy Wells 698-699

Glen Wexler 626-627

Byll Williams 676-677

Sam Yocum 716-717

Leslie Zahara – Zahara Productions 48-49,
  686-687

ALAN DOCKERY

photography
digital imaging
telephone 323 662 8153
fax 323 662 3787

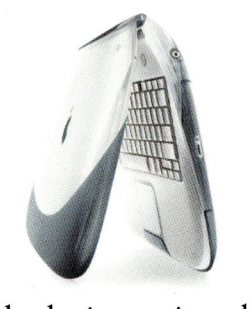

1 2 5   1 Pets.com
  3 4   2 United Airlines
         3 Apple Computer
         4 Victory Motorcycles
         5 Realcities.com

Hunter Freeman

152 Mississippi Street
San Francisco, CA 94107
415 252 1910 phone
415 252 1917 fax
www.hunterfreeman.com

Represented by
Heather Elder
415 285 7709 phone
415 285 7979 fax
www.heatherelder.com

JOHN SCHULZ PHOTOGRAPHY (SAN DIEGO) 1.888.447.8862 PHOTOPOP.COM

JOHN SCHULZ PHOTOGRAPHY (SAN DIEGO) 1.888.447.8862 PHOTOPOP.COM

MUSILEK 415.621.5336

AGENT: DEBORAH AYERST 415.567.3570

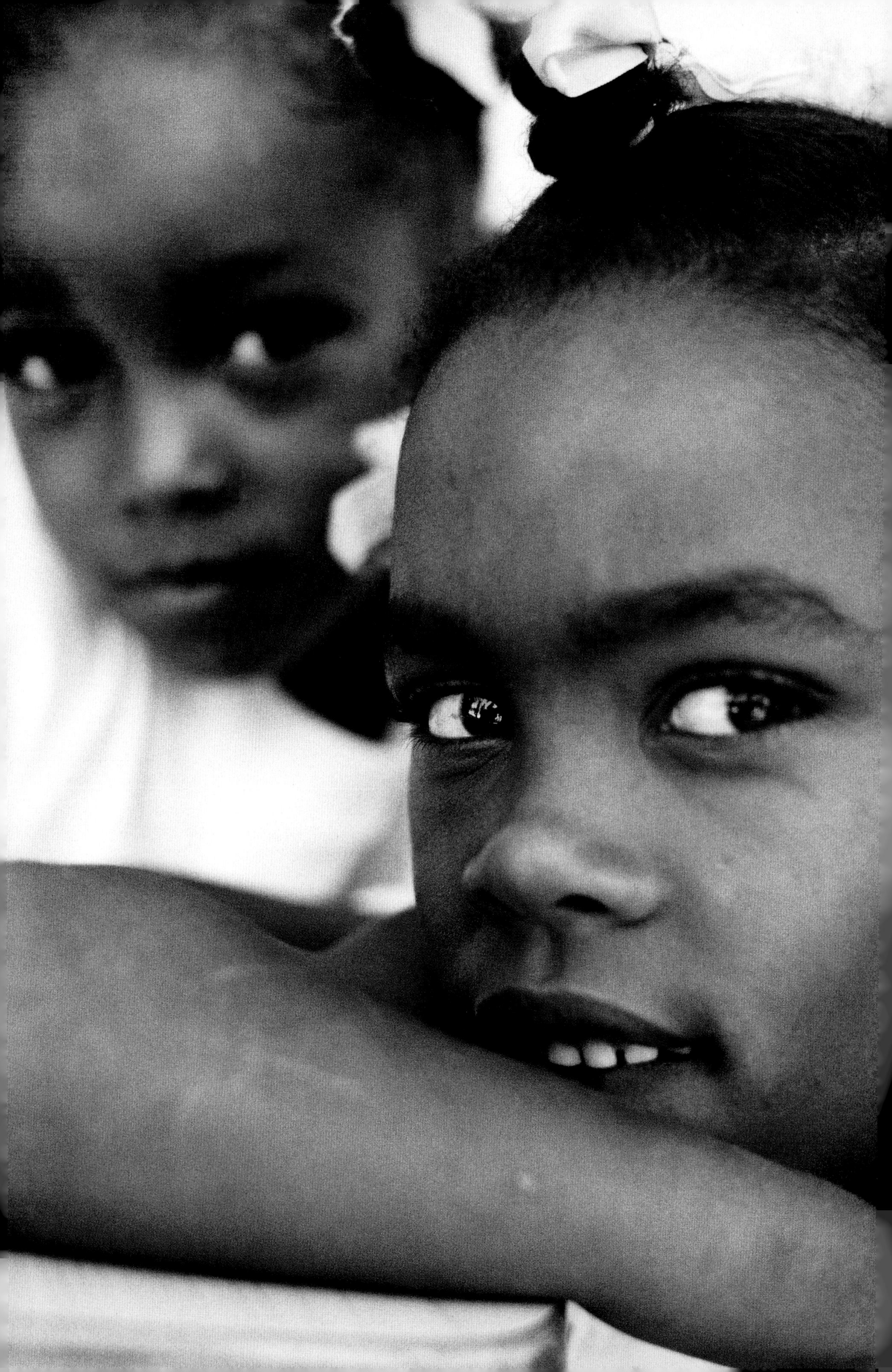

Ellen Barnes Photography | 480.940.9966 Phone 480.940.9977 Fax

eB

Ellen Barnes Photography | 480.940.9966 Phone 480.940.9977 Fax

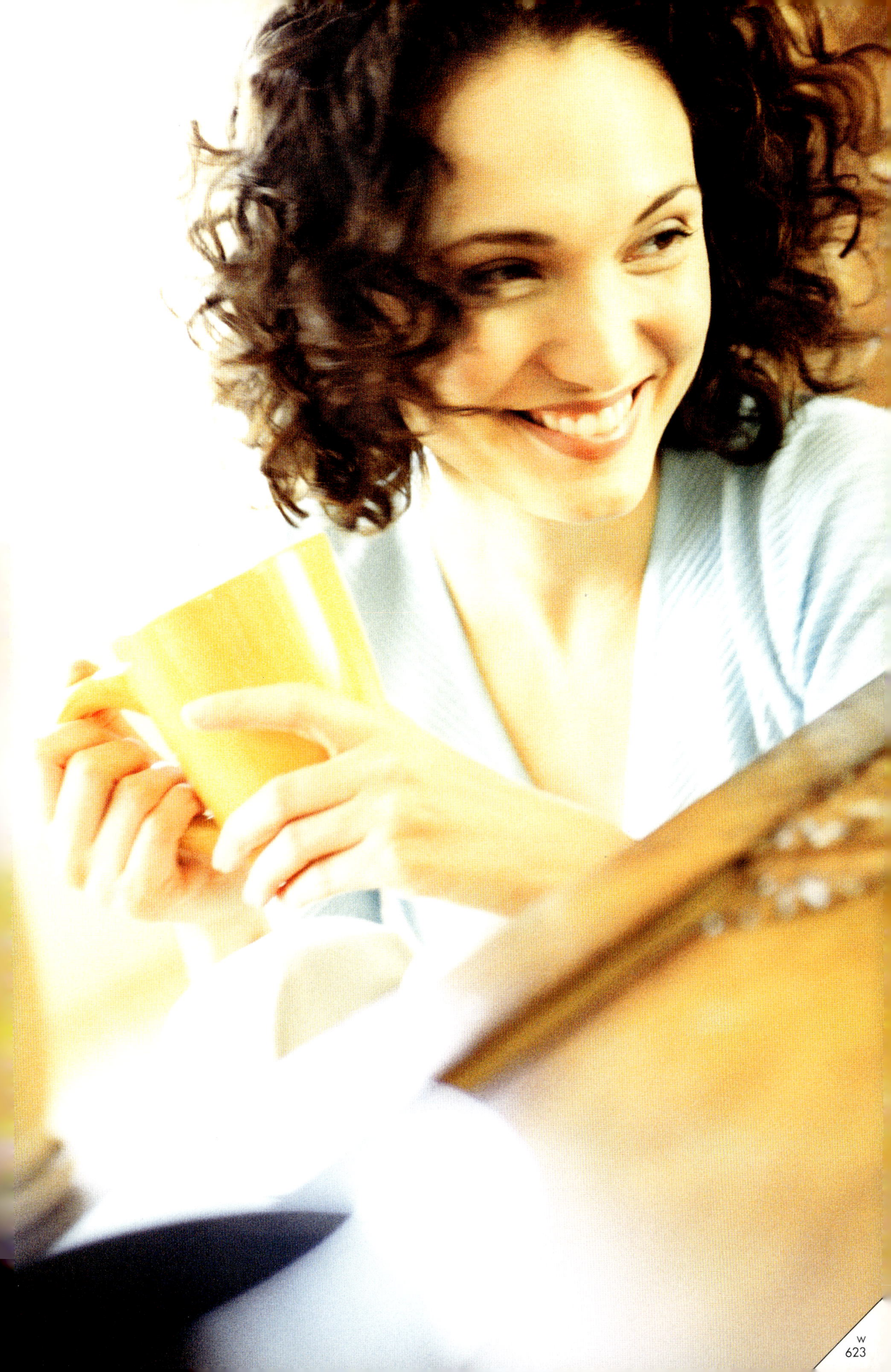

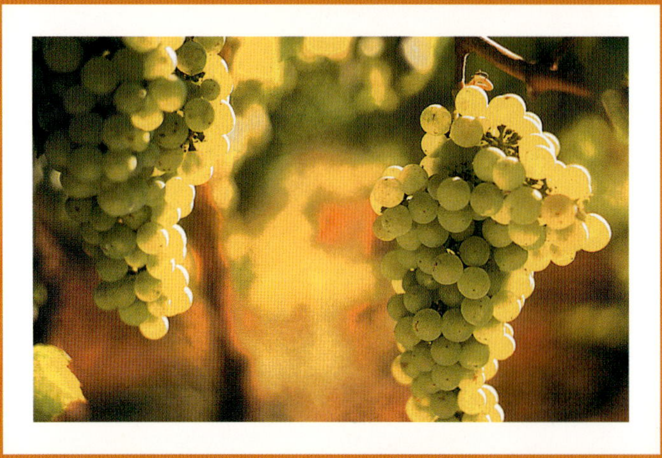
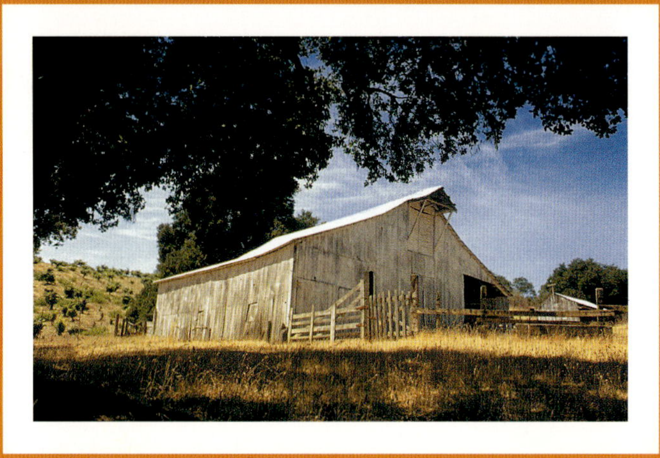
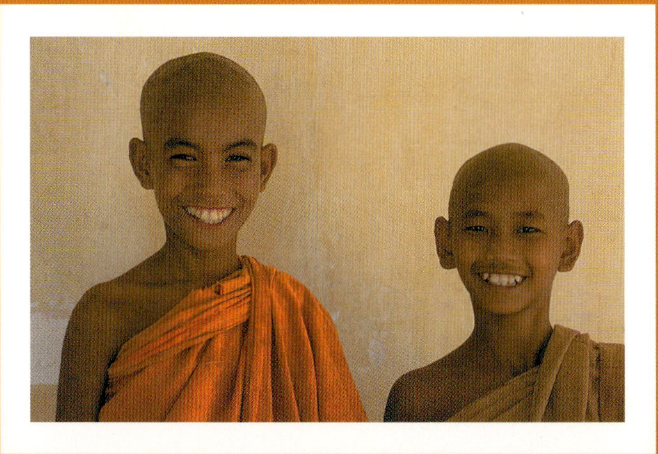

RICK BOLEN PHOTOGRAPHY

SONOMA, CALIFORNIA

707 933 0932

WWW.BOLENPHOTO.COM

GLEN WEXLER STUDIO   323 465.0268

agency: **Young & Rubicam/SF**   client: **Adobe Systems**

agency: **Suissa Miller**   client: **Acura**

agency: **Shafer Advertising**   client: **Fujitsu**

agency: **J Walter Thompson/NY**   client: **Qwest Communications**

agency: **Young & Rubicam/NY**   client: **Sony**

agency: **J Walter Thompson/NY**   client: **Qwest Communications**

GLEN WEXLER STUDIO   323.465.0268

HOWARD ROSENBERG PHOTOGRAPHY
213.484.0523

HOWARD ROSENBERG PHOTOGRAPHY
www.hrphoto.com

HOWARD ROSENBERG PHOTOGRAPHY
2 1 3 . 4 8 4 . 0 5 2 3

HOWARD ROSENBERG PHOTOGRAPHY
www.hrphoto.com

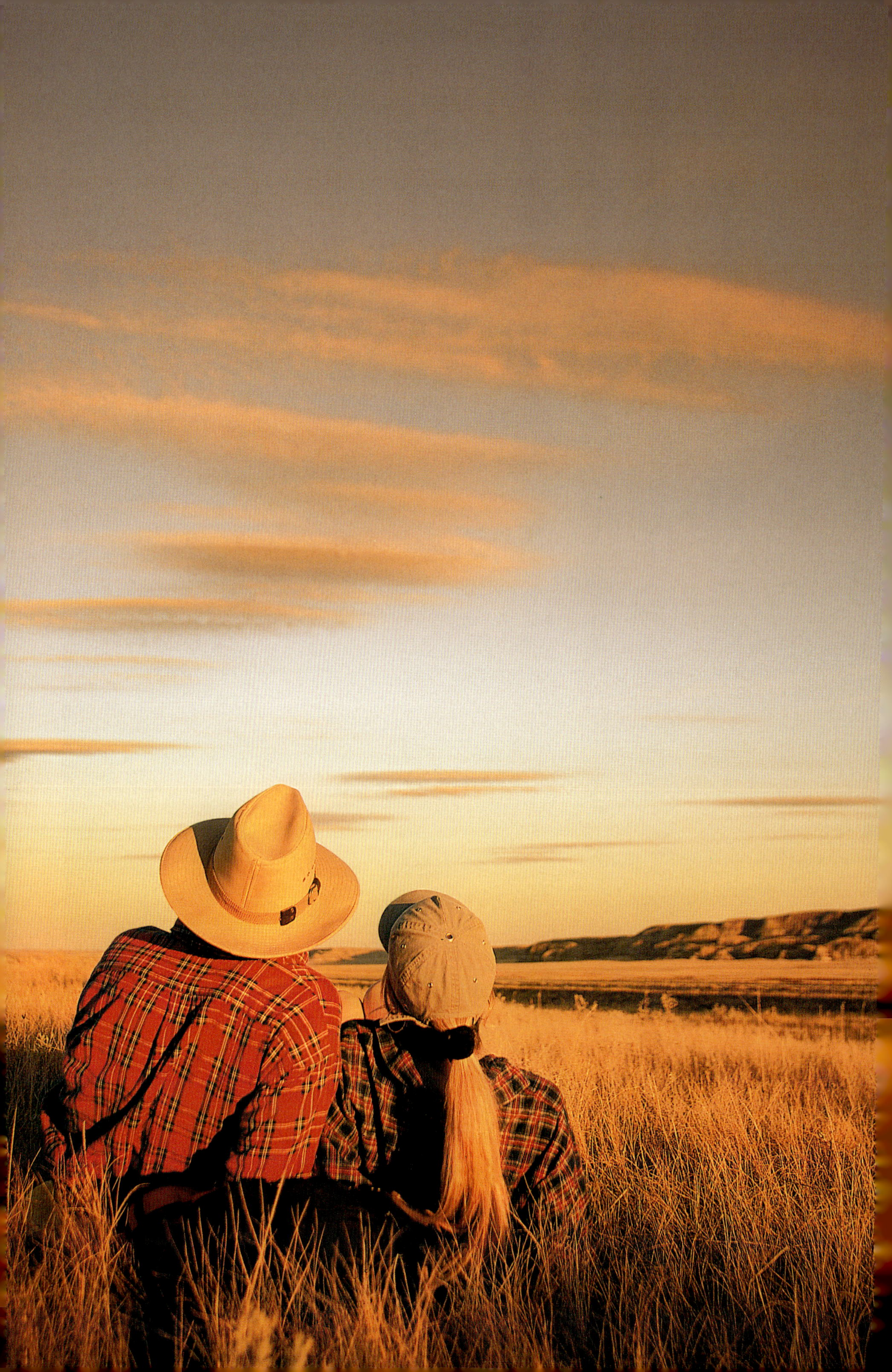

DOUGLAS E. WALKER

800.567.3707

REPRESENTED BY DEBRA WEISS 323.463.4060

CHIP SIMONS | PHOTOGRAPHY   TEL: [505]869.0344

FAX: [505]869.0944 WWW.CHIPSIMONS.COM

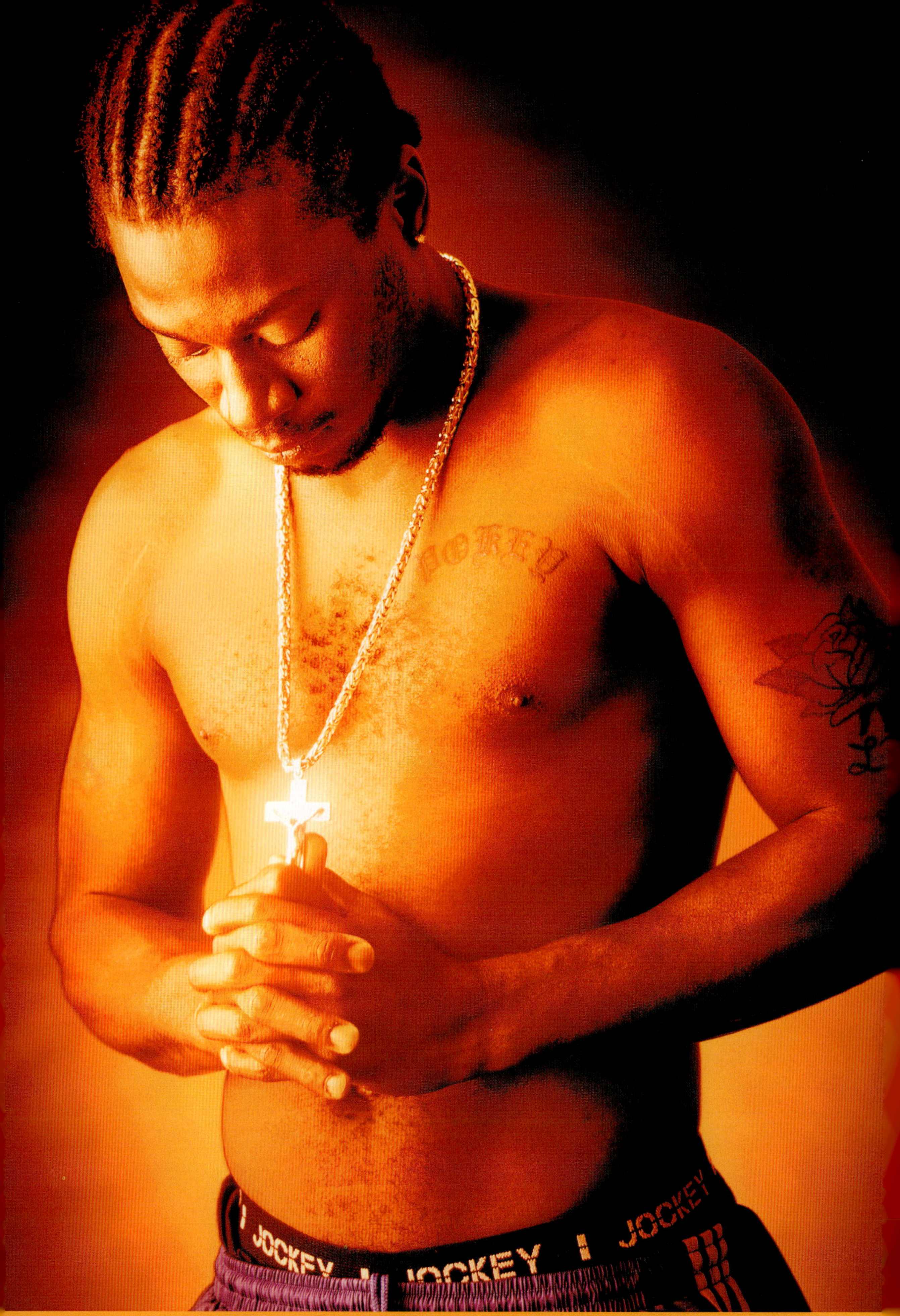
I JOCKEY I JOCKEY I JOCKEY

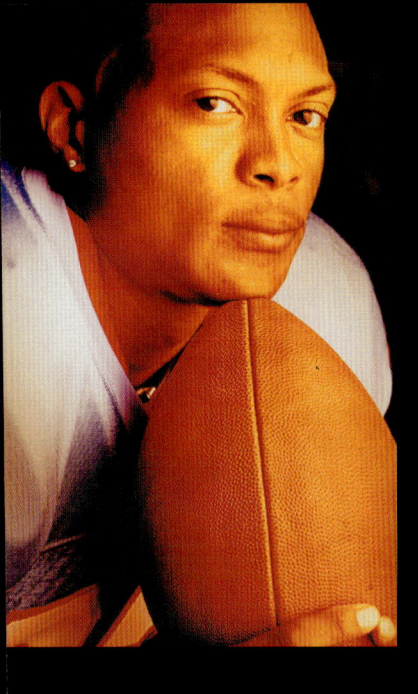

tim mantoani

800.543.9960 ✸ mantoani.com
represented by frank meo 212.643.7428

JGPHOTO.COM

STUDIO 415.241.9131

JOE
GIBBS PHOTO
GRAPHY

The Designory/Mercedes-Benz

w
641

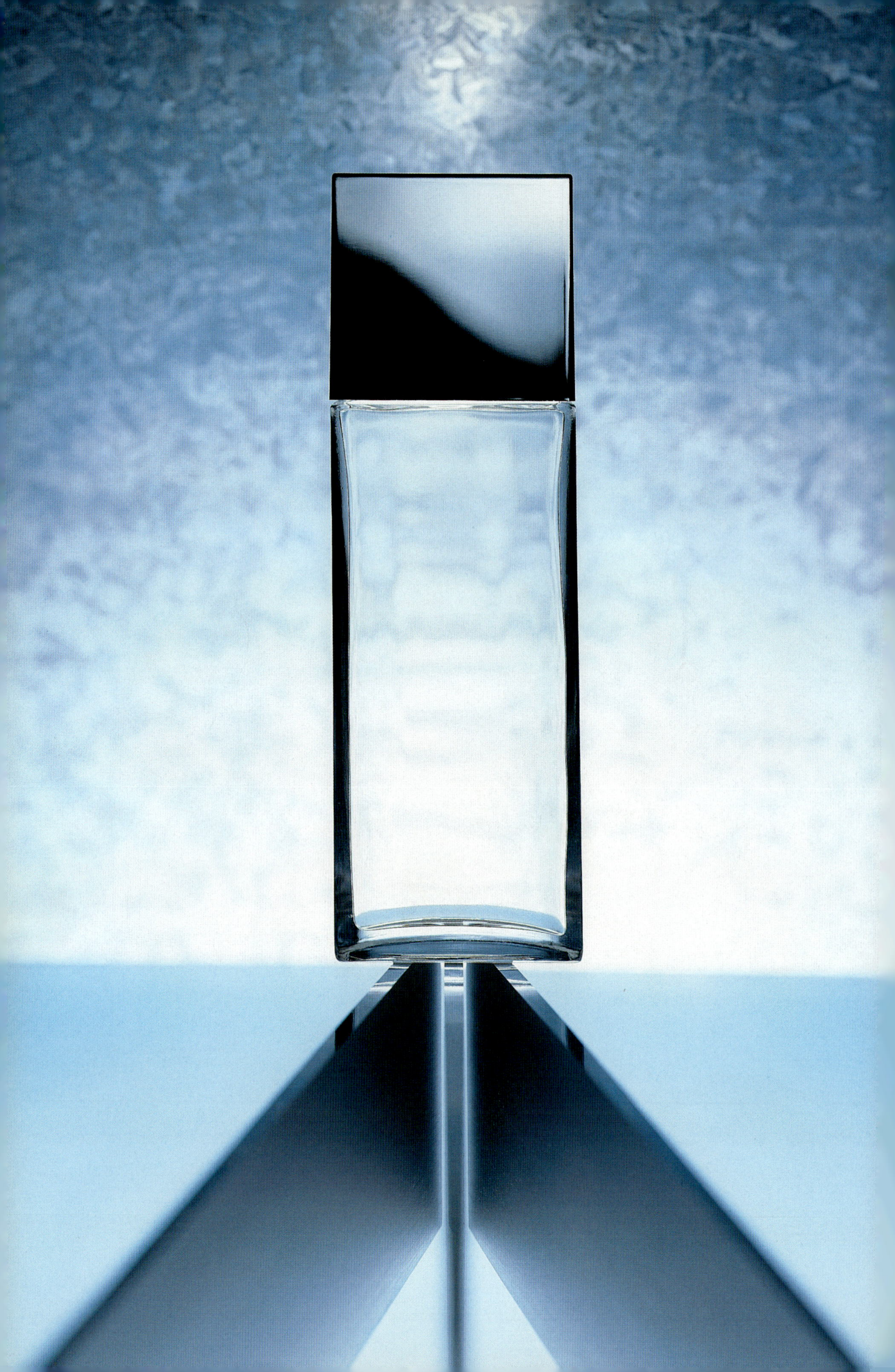

randel urbauer

studio 323 225 7622 fax 323 223 9737
www.ruphoto.com

w
643

Walt Denson | SAN FRANCISCO

Phone: 415.331.5555

West Coast: Freda Scott 415.398.9121   Midwest: Vince Kamin 312.787.8834   Southwest: Brooke Davis 214.352.9192   www.waltdenson.com

Walt Denson | SAN FRANCISCO

Phone: 415.331.5555

West Coast: Freda Scott 415.398.9121   Midwest: Vince Kamin 312.787.8834   Southwest: Brooke Davis 214.352.9192   www.waltdenson.com

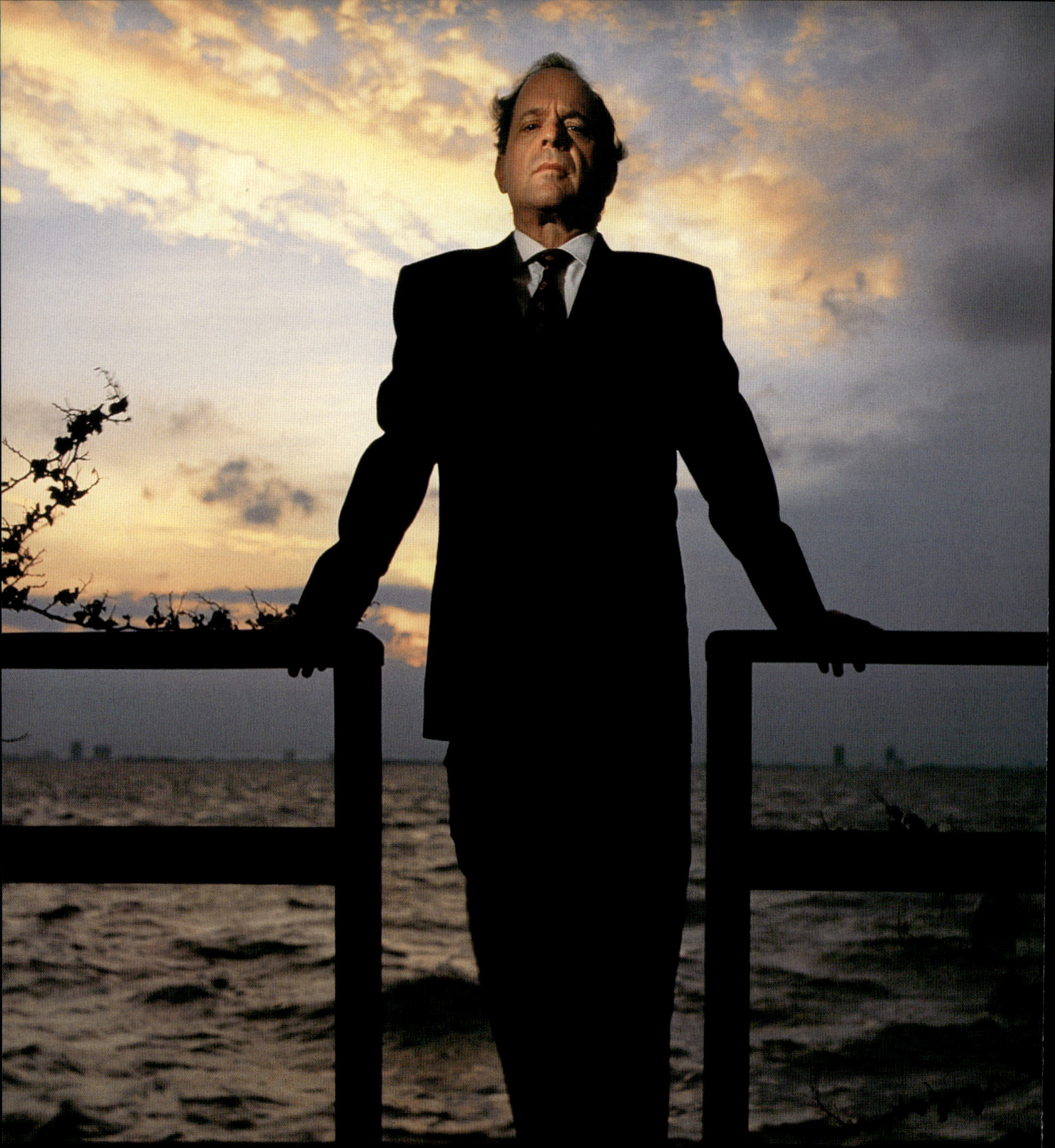

ACEY HARPER

PH. 415.383.4208
FX. 415.383.5603
www.aceyharper.com

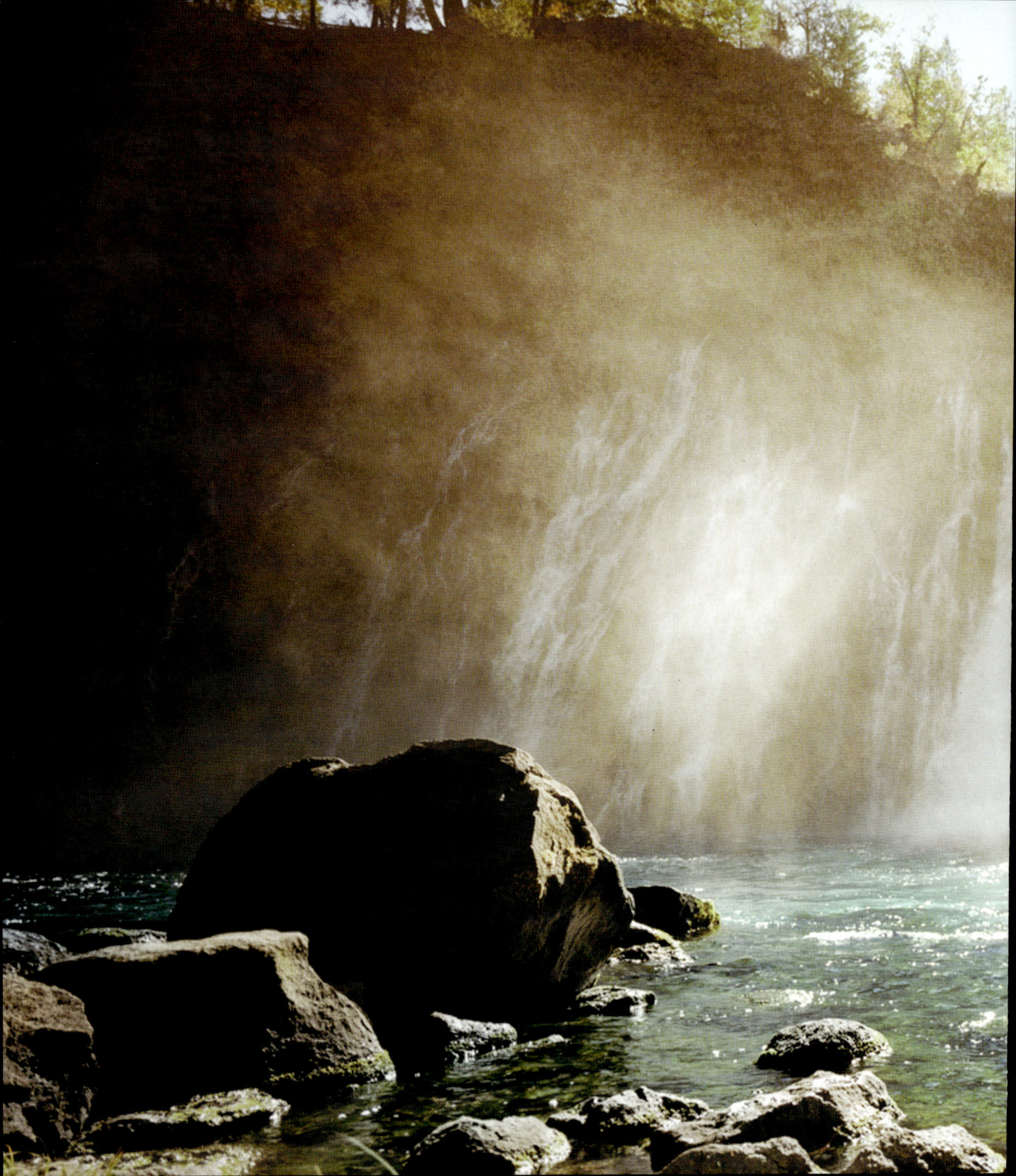

ROBB SCHARETG

[PICTURES]

PH: 415.751.0313   FX: 415.751.0314   WWW.SCHARETGPICTURES.COM

REPRESENTATION: MAGGIE STORCK/i2i PH: 212.925.5410

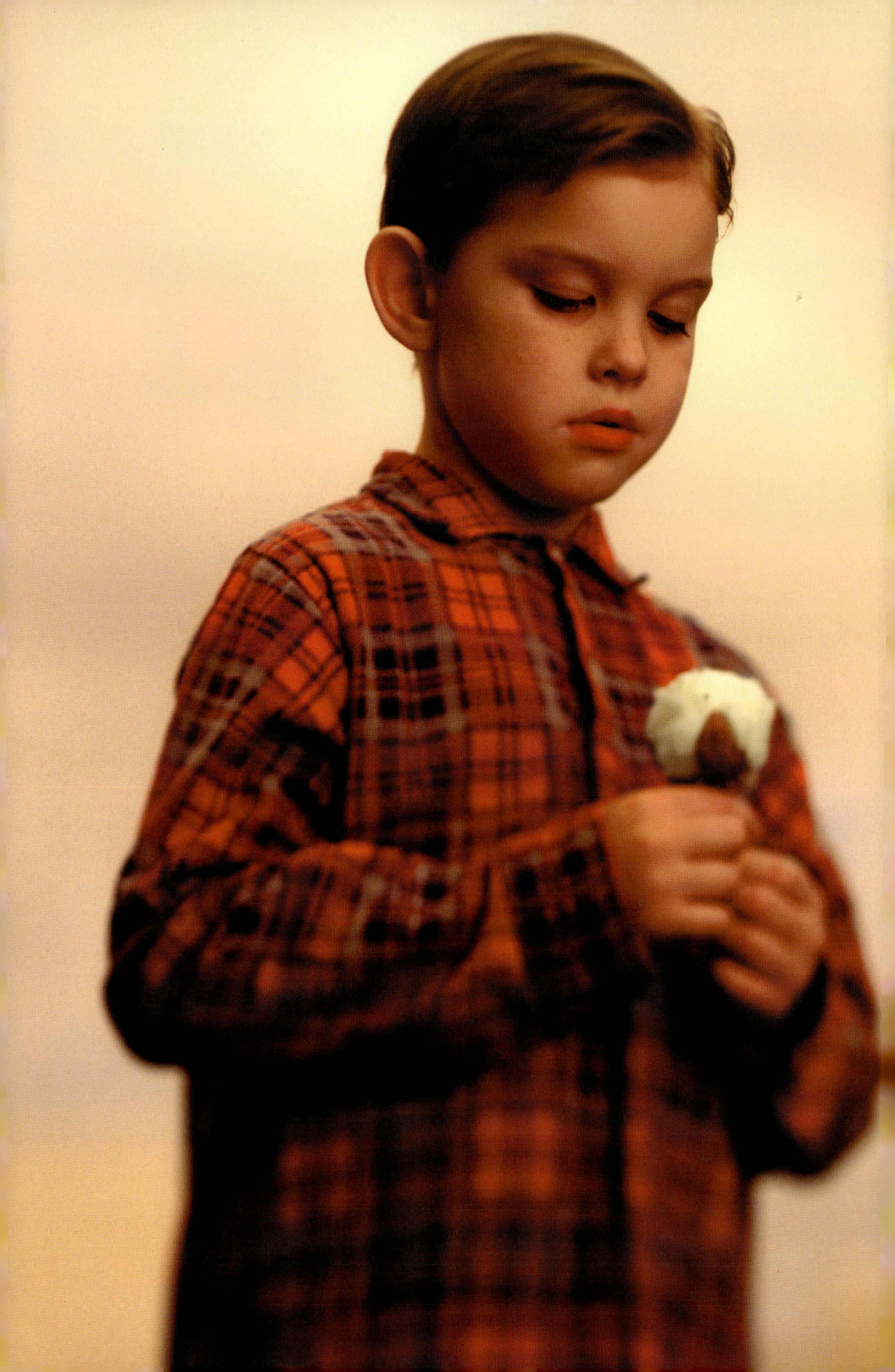

ROBB SCHARETG
[PICTURES]

PH: 415.751.0313   FX: 415.751.0314   WWW.SCHARETGPICTURES.COM

REPRESENTATION: MAGGIE STORCK/i2i PH: 212.925.5410

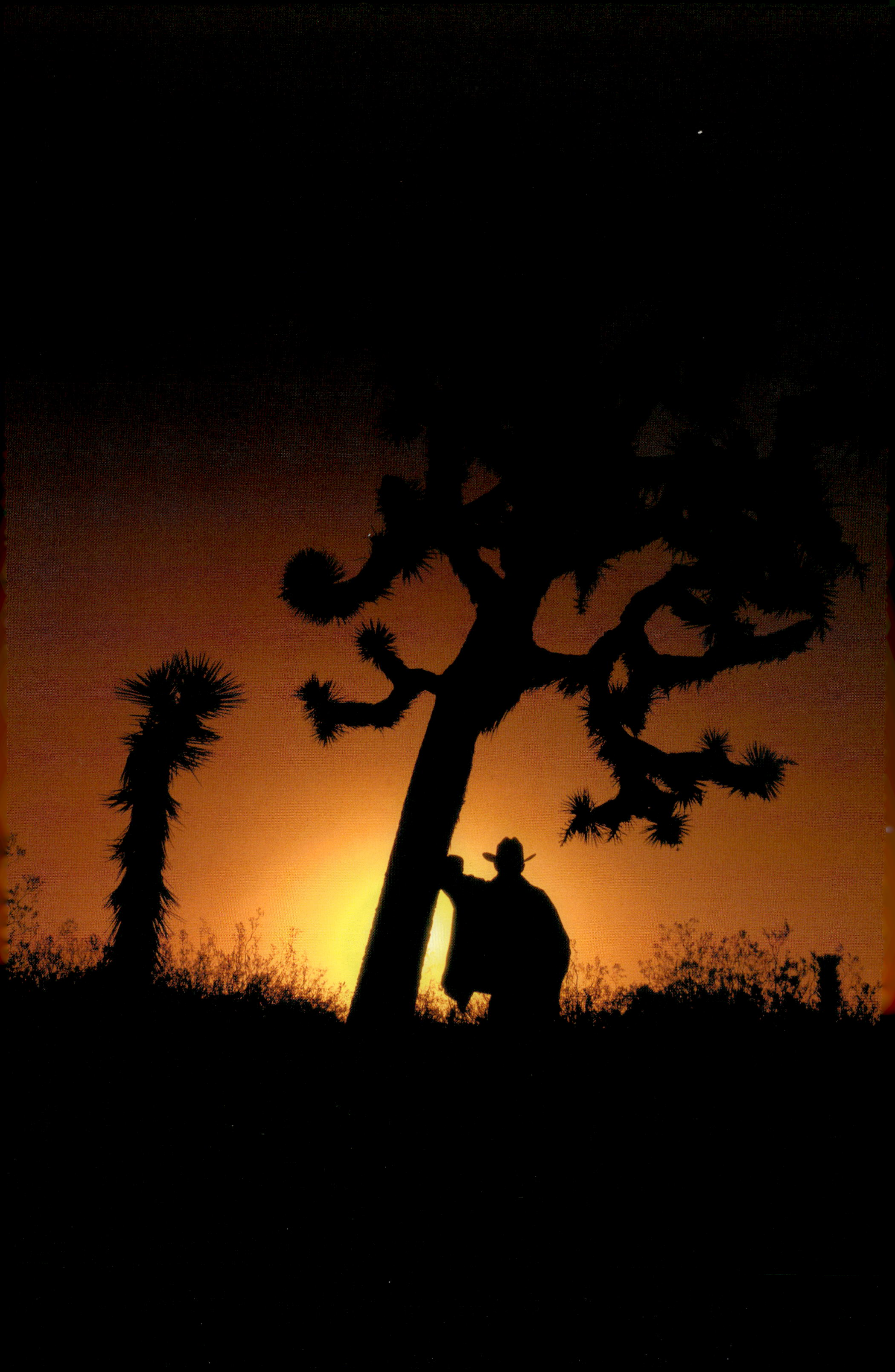

ROBB SCHARETG

[PICTURES]

PH: 415.751.0313   FX: 415.751.0314   WWW.SCHARETGPICTURES.COM

REPRESENTATION: MAGGIE STORCK/i2i   PH: 212.925.5410

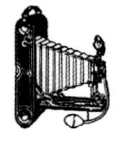

BRIAN MAHANY

610 22nd Street #305 San francisco California 94107

Tel: 415·552·8802   Fax: 415·552·1245

www.mahanyphotography.com

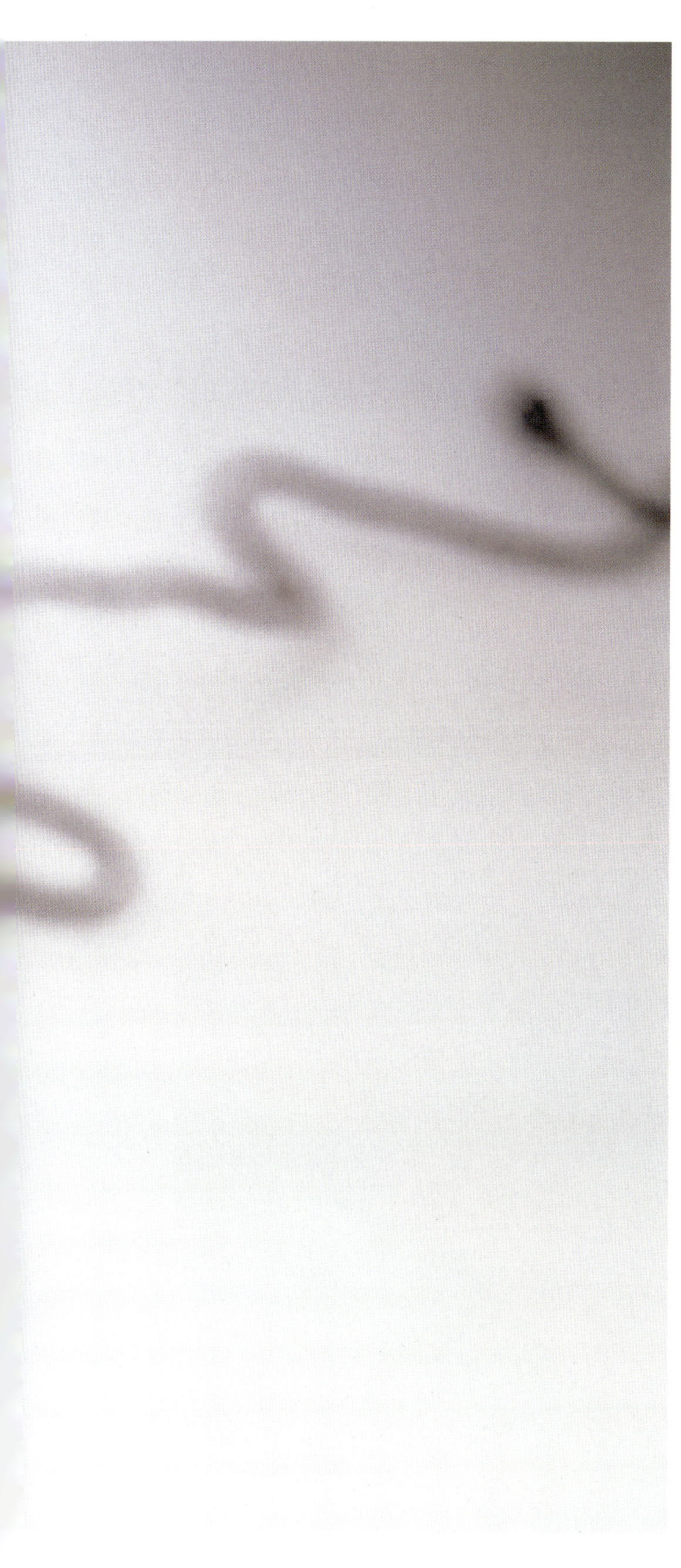

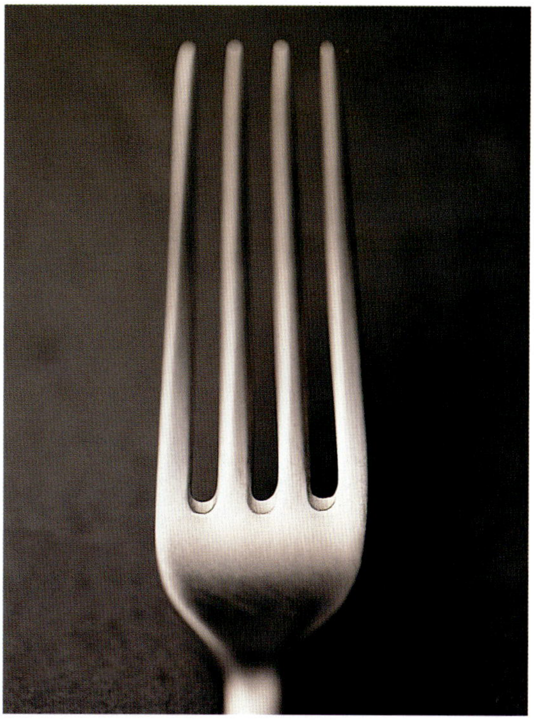

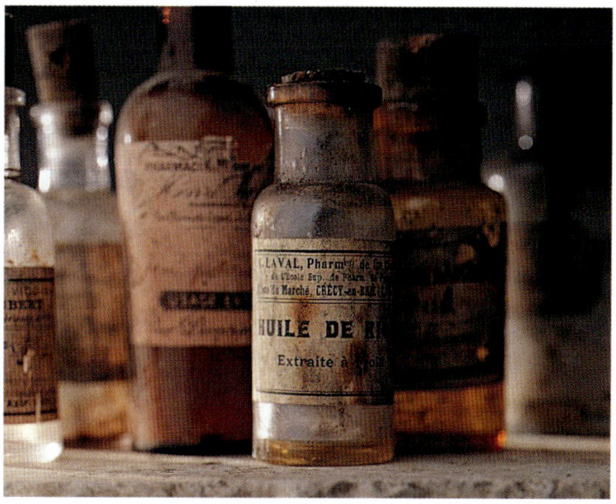
L. LAVAL, Pharm
HUILE DE
Extraite à

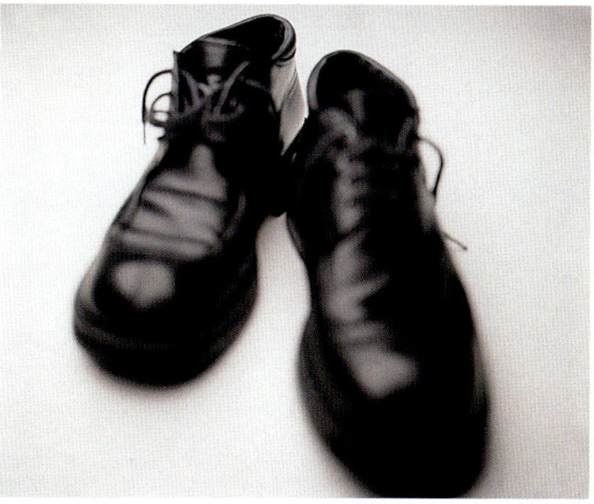

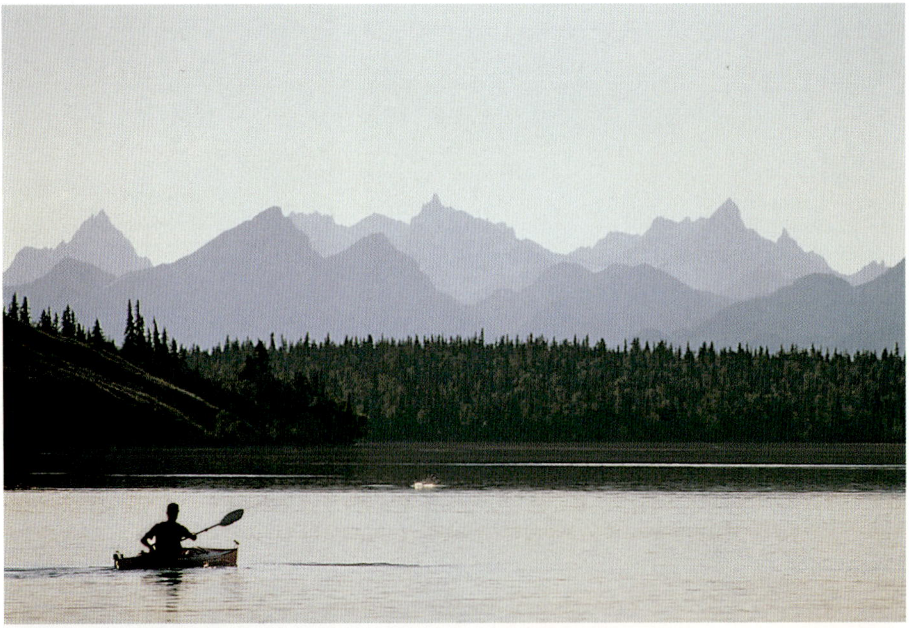
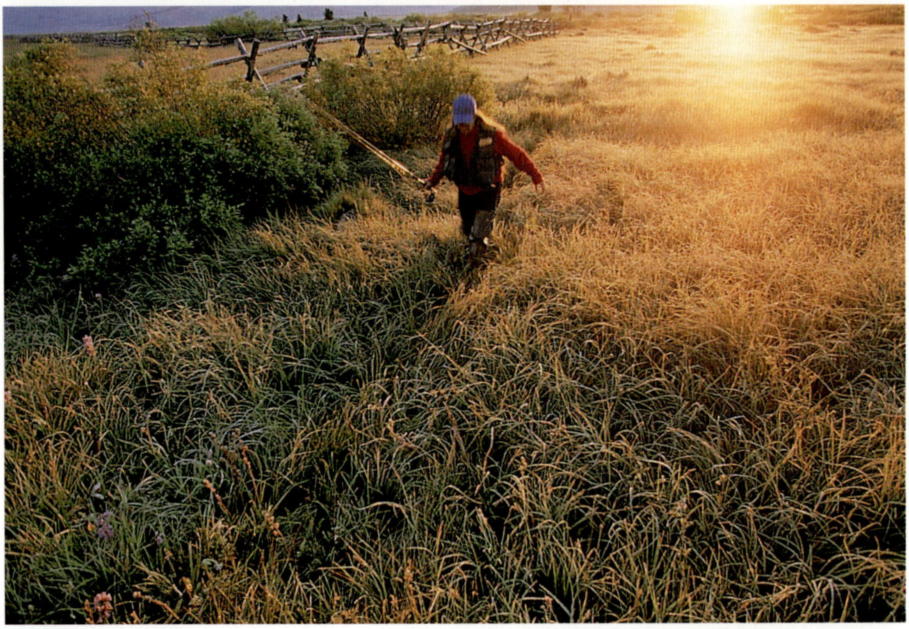
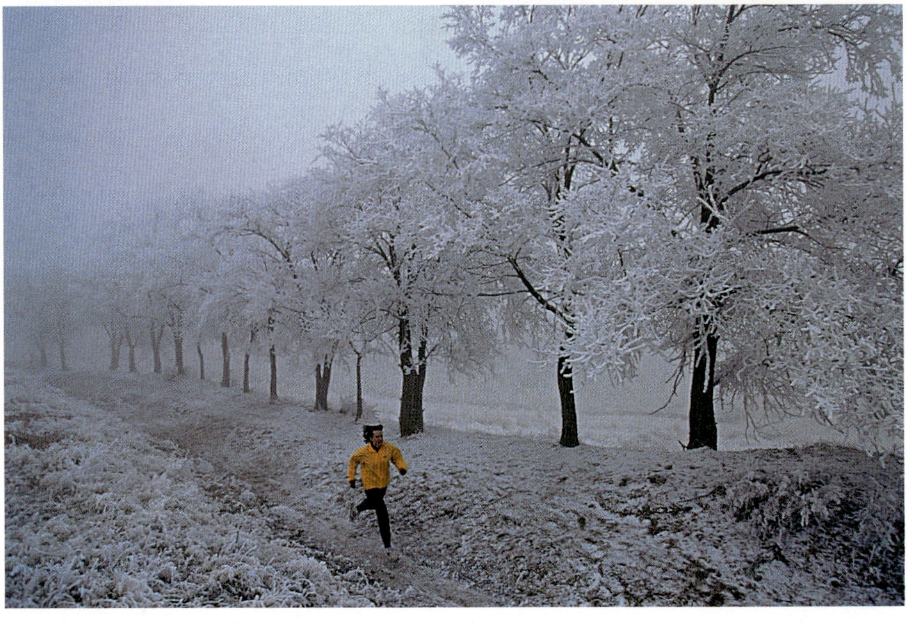

GLENN OAKLEY

208.383.9163
www.oakleyphoto.com
glenn@oakleyphoto.com

PEGGY DAY

800-728-7955

LINDSTROM

4 1 5 - 9 7 9 - 9 3 4 0

www.melphoto.com

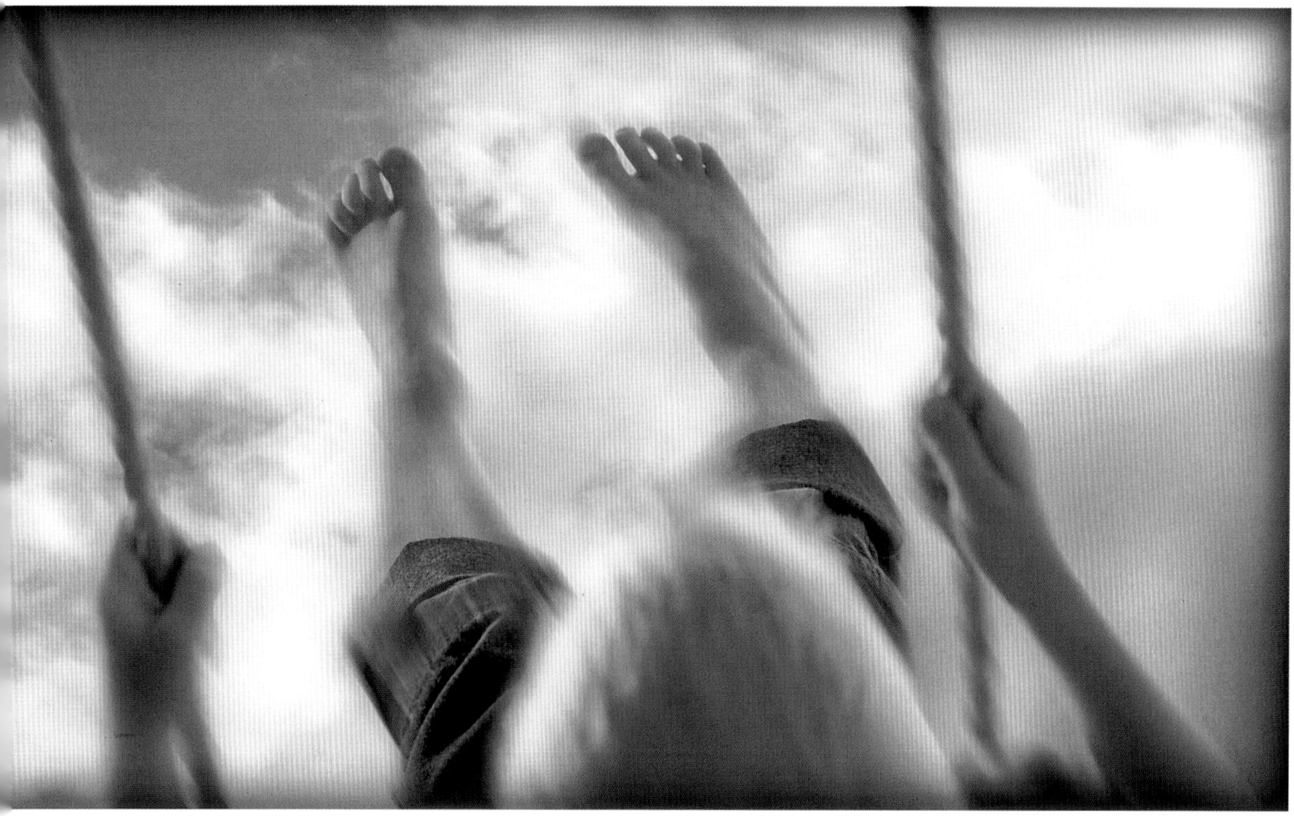

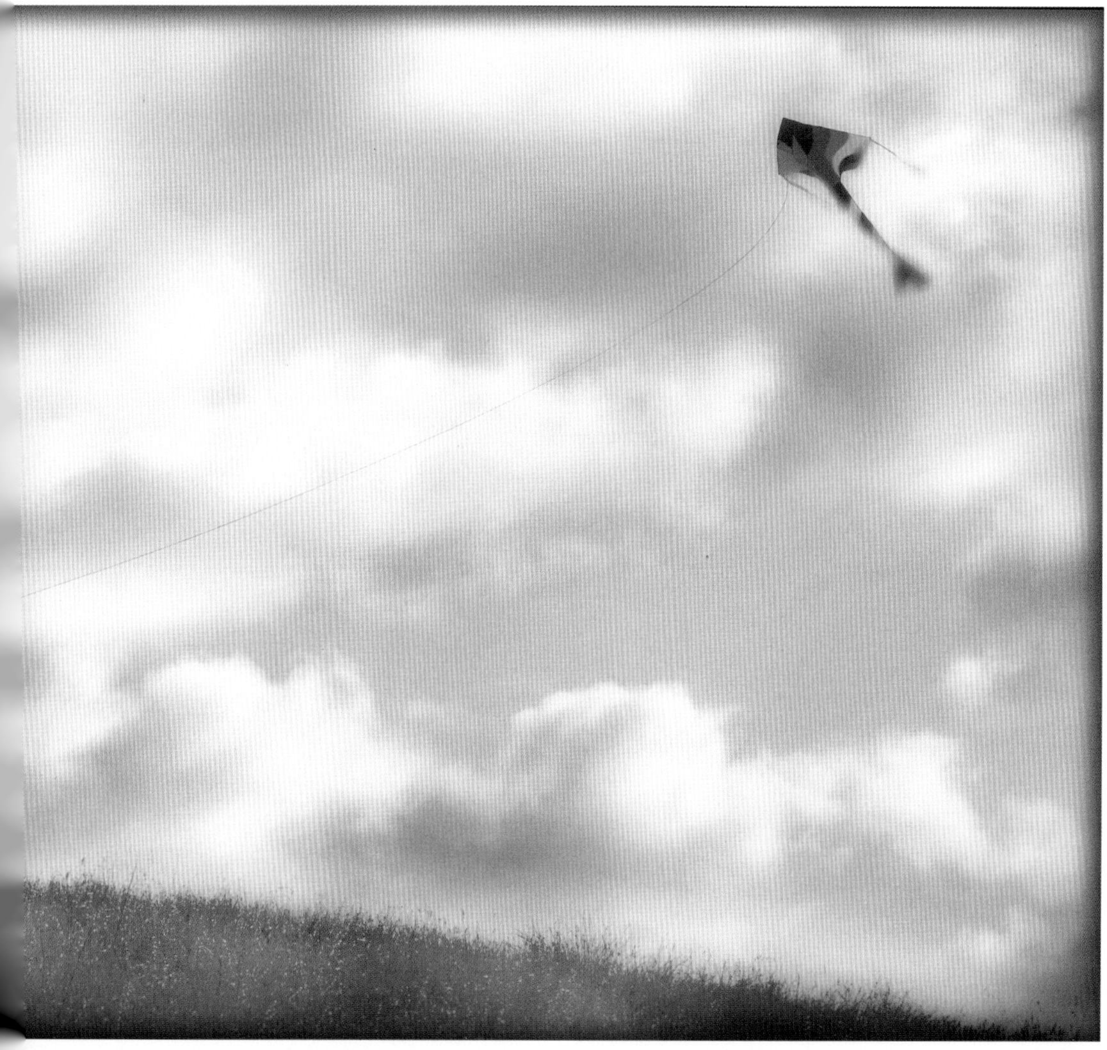

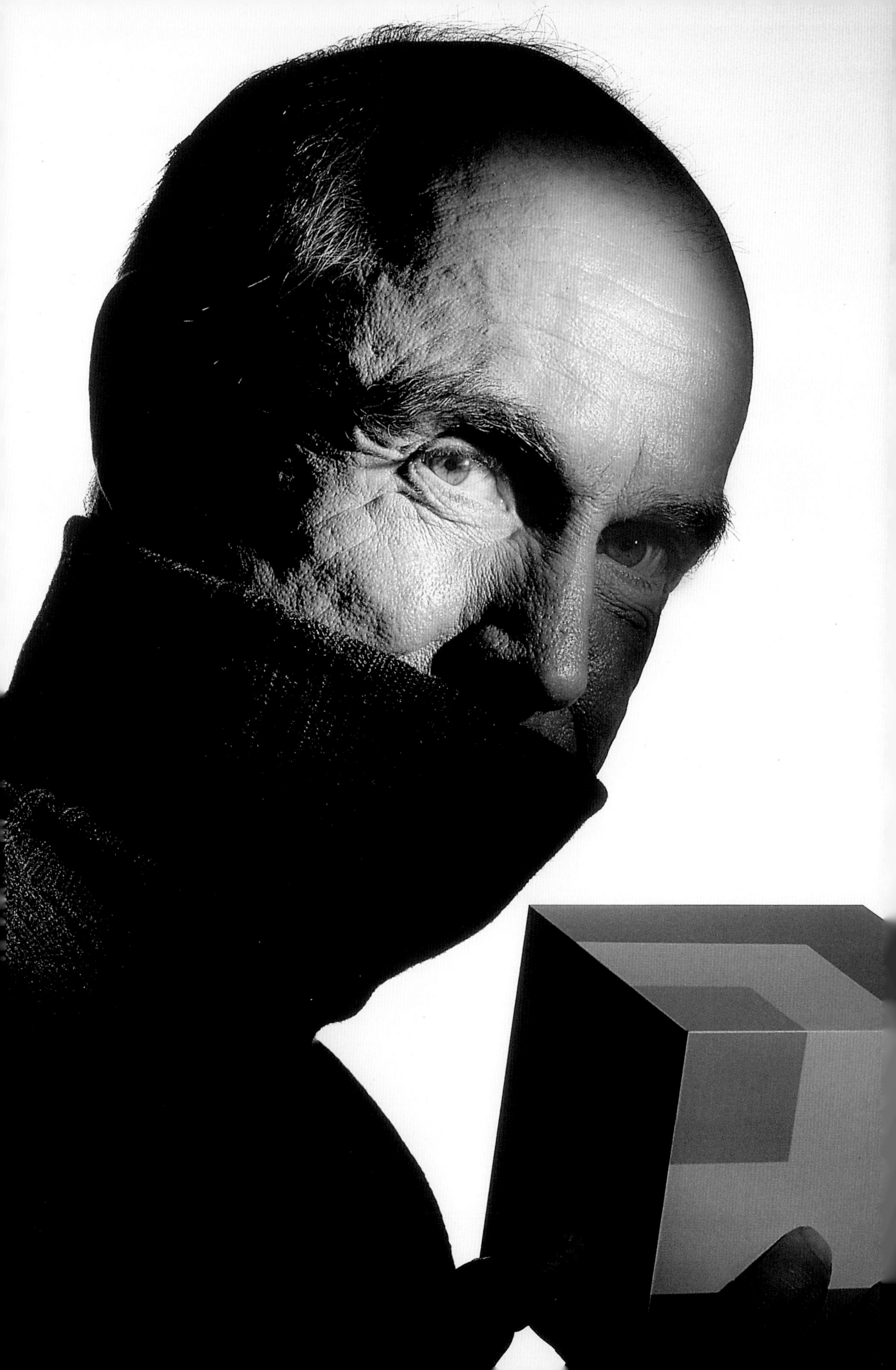

LINDSTROM

415 · 979 · 9340

www.melphoto.com

W 663

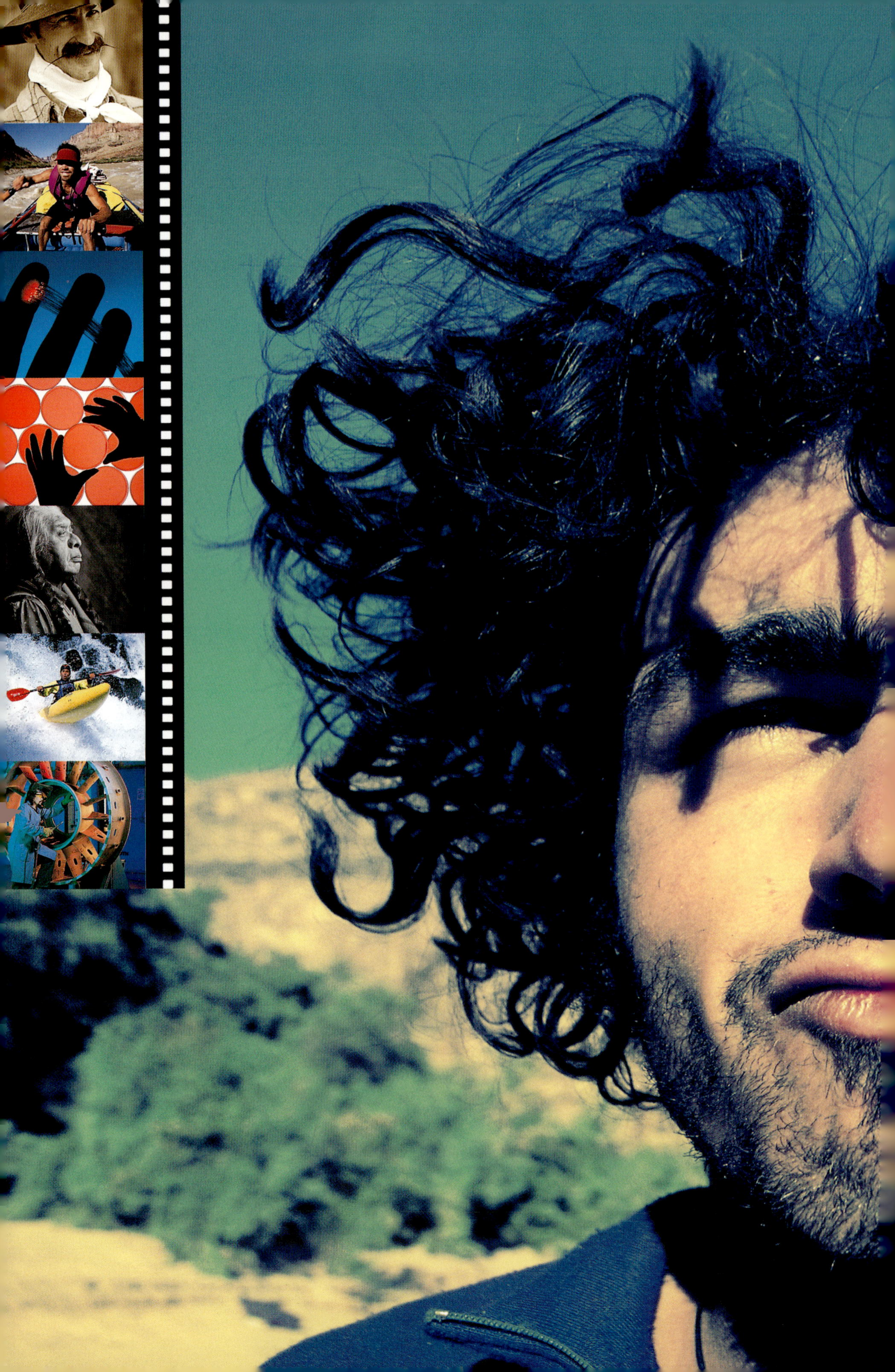

503.452.4700
borlandphoto.com
BORLAND

W 665

gil smith \studio/

T 213 384 1016 | F 213 384 1224 | 2865 West 7th Street Los Angeles, CA 90005 | gs@gilsmith.com | www.gilsmith.com

catherine karnow

photographer

415 928 3232

Smithsonian   Hertz
    Condé Nast   Seagram
Goldman Sachs
     National Geographic

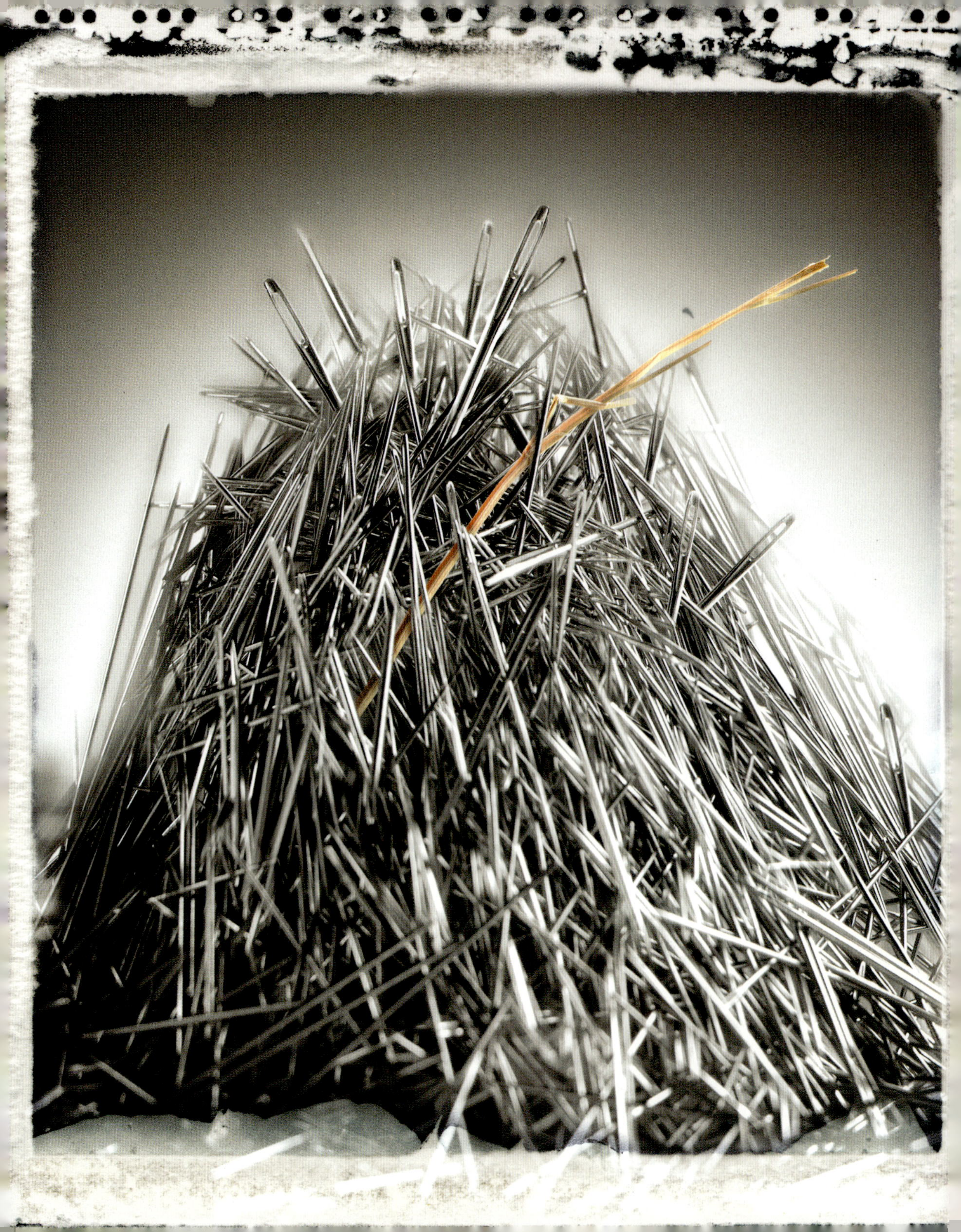

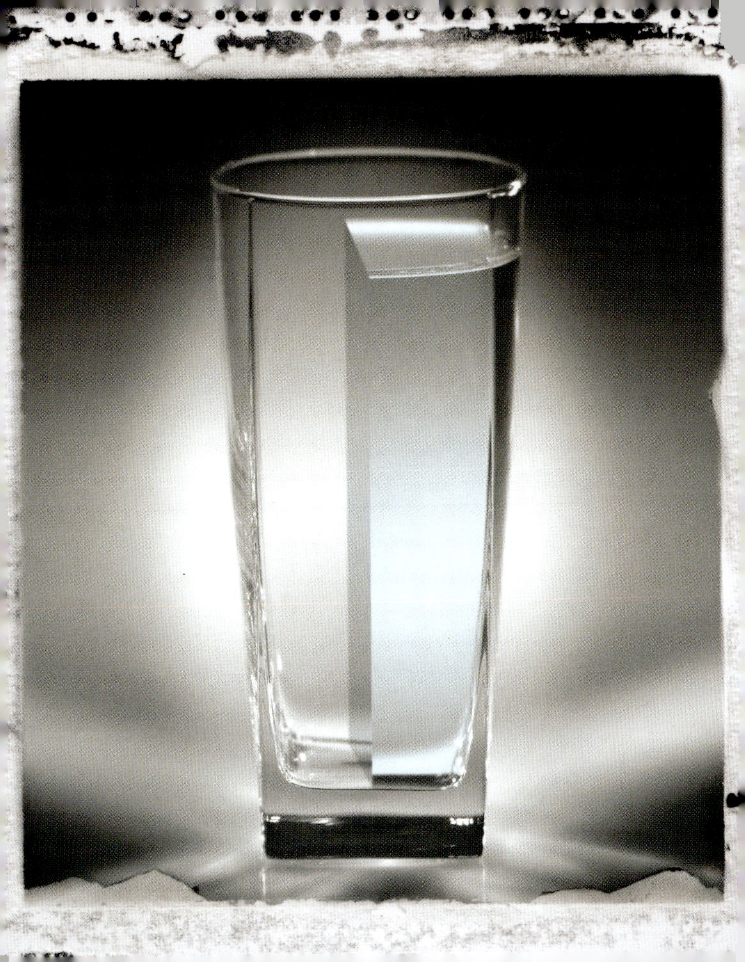

I Feel Your Thirst.

SILVERM*N
P R O D U C T I O N S

JAY SILVERMAN PRODUCTIONS
1541 NORTH CAHUENGA BOULEVARD
HOLLYWOOD, CALIFORNIA 90028
TEL: 323-466-6030 FAX: 323-466-7139
www.jaysilverman.com

CALL FOR OUR PORTFOLIO OR REEL
CONTACT: ANNE MEDCALF

Take it with you.

ESPN RADIO

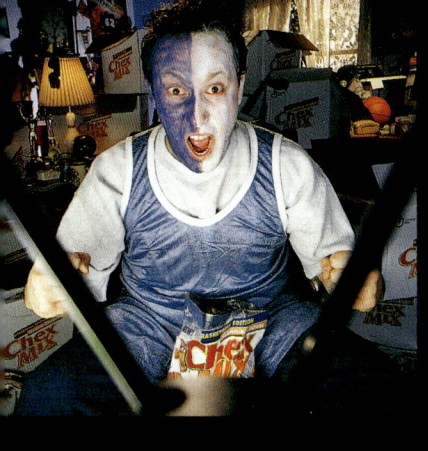

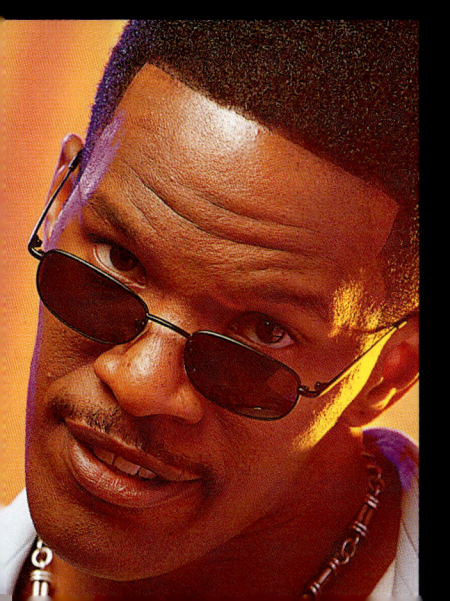

SILVERMAN
PRODUCTIONS

JAY SILVERMAN PRODUCTIONS
1541 NORTH CAHUENGA BOULEVARD
HOLLYWOOD, CALIFORNIA 90028
TEL: 323-466-6030 FAX: 323-466-7139
www.jaysilverman.com

CALL FOR OUR PORTFOLIO OR REEL
CONTACT: ANNE MEDCALF

BYLL WILLIAMS

Studio
818.341.9833

Represented by
Lisa Ellison
323.259.2400

W
677

Cold Drinks

SOUDERS STUDIOS

Denver, CO
1.800.900.333

Hot Foods

SOUDERS STUDIOS

Denver, CO
1.800.900.3330

www.papas.com

David Papas   415.648.7079

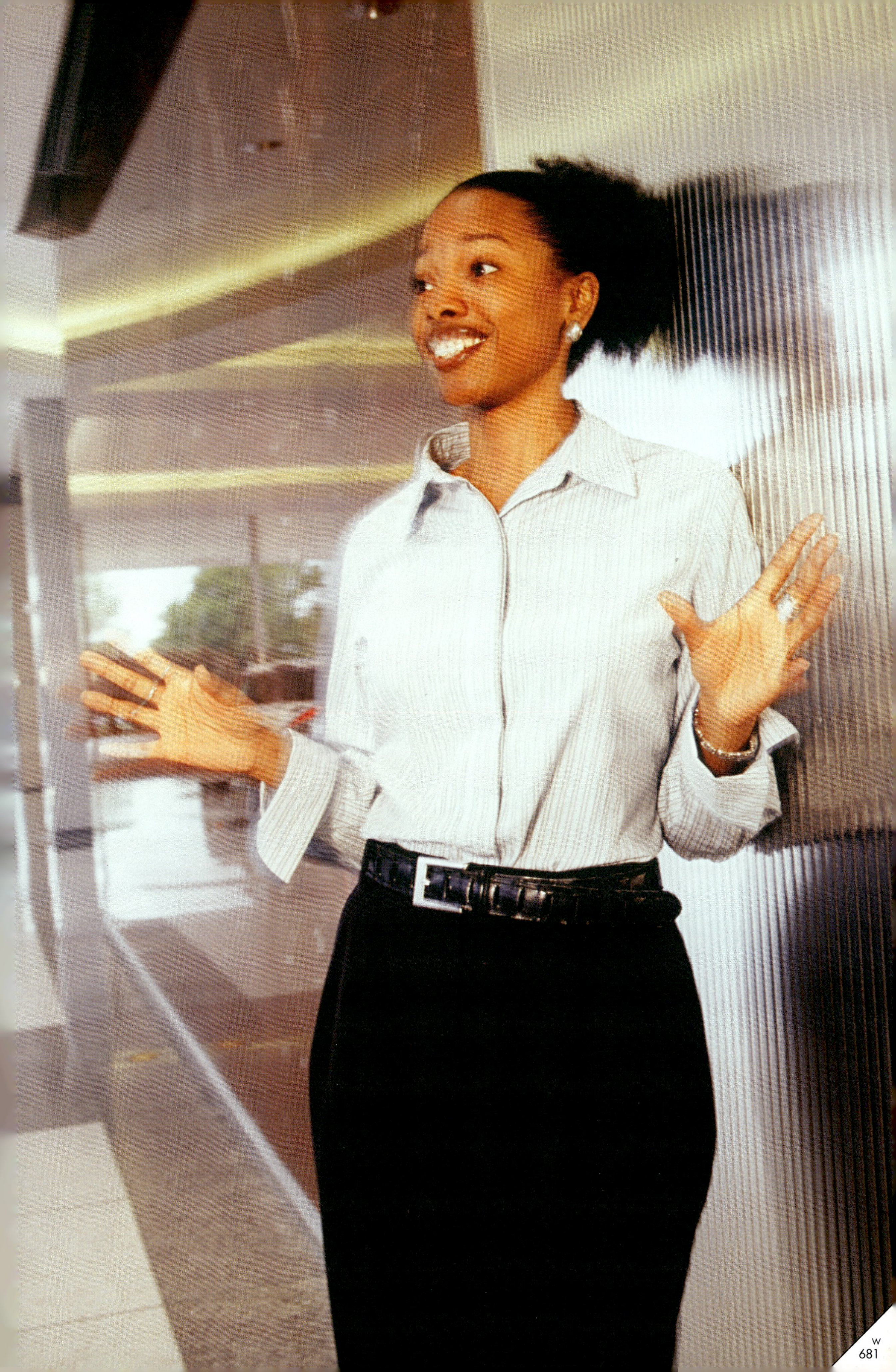

Erickson

www.JimErickson.com

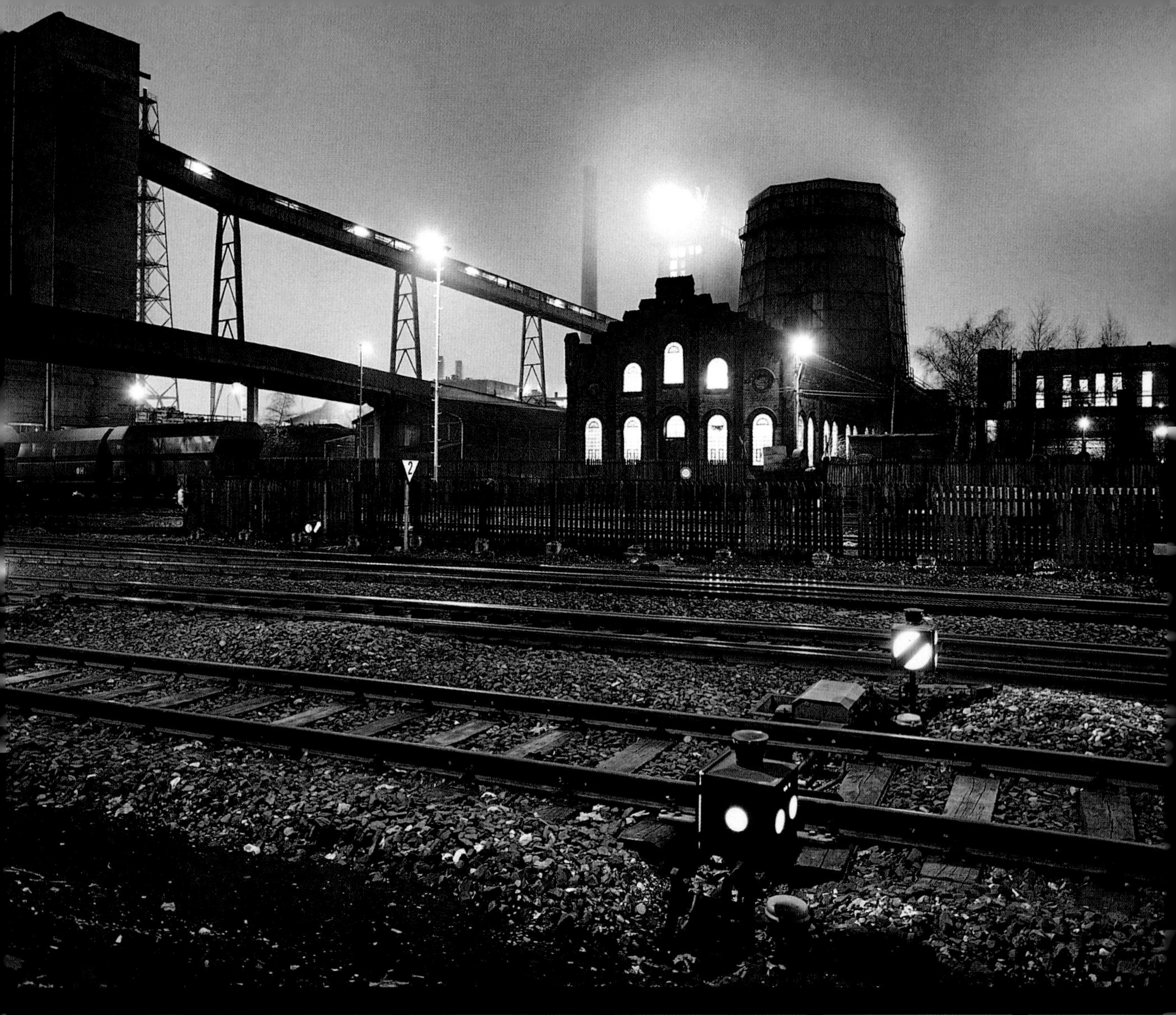
2

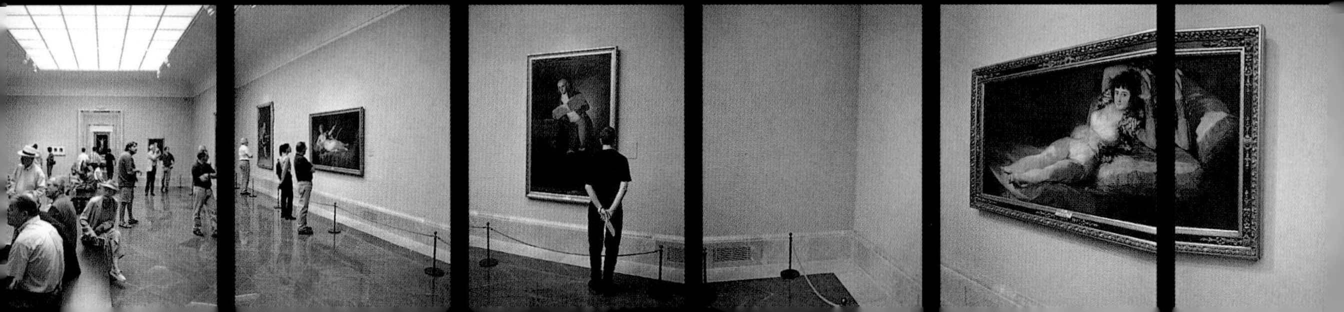

photography

PHILIPP SCHOLZ RITTERMANN

p: 619.702.7735

f: 619.702.7621

Craven "A"

BurlingtonGlobalDenim
BURLINGTON GLOBAL DENIM
handwoven constructions • bulky lightweights
ringspun multi-slub technology • crosshatch • natural

BurlingtonGlobalDenim
BURLINGTON GLOBAL DENIM
handwoven constructions • bulky lightweights
ringspun multi-slub technology • crosshatch • natural

©1993 R.J. REYNOLDS TOBACCO CO.
WinstonMenthol
Winston y Puerto Rico no hay nada mejor.
Winston
MENTHOL LIGHTS
9 mg. "tar", 0.8 mg. nicotine av. per cigarette by FTC method.

John Morrison

New York ~ 212.964.9296
West Coast ~ 707.987.4856 • Fax: 707.987.8297
Web: http://www.saber.net/~johnmorrison/

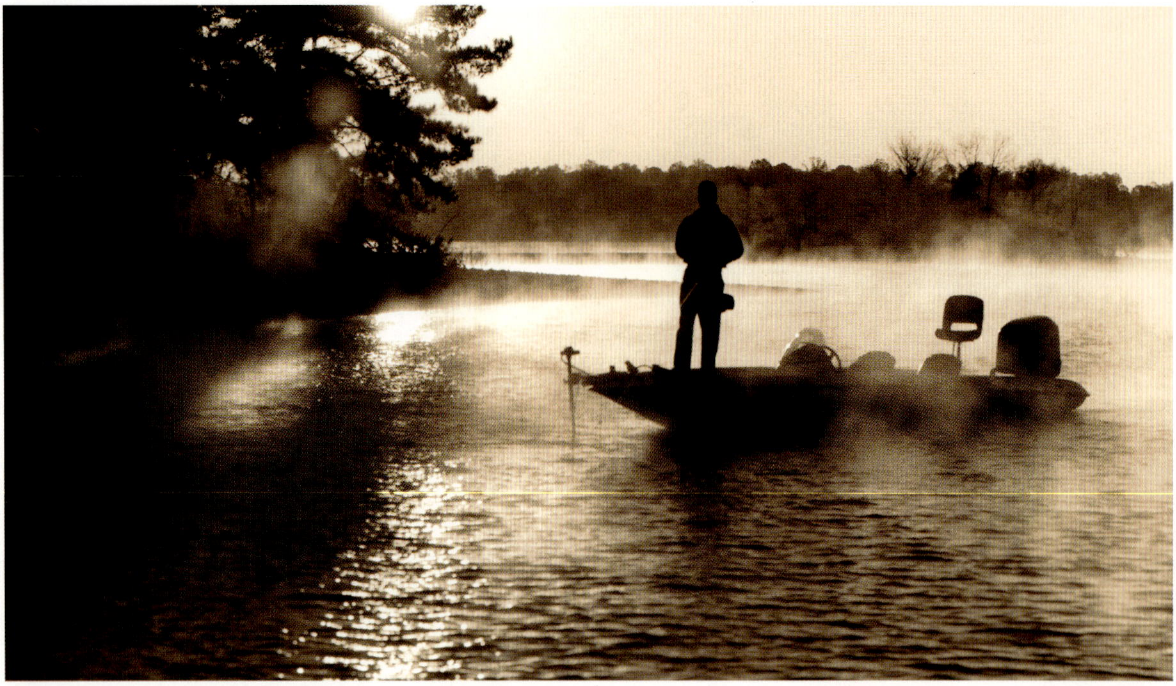

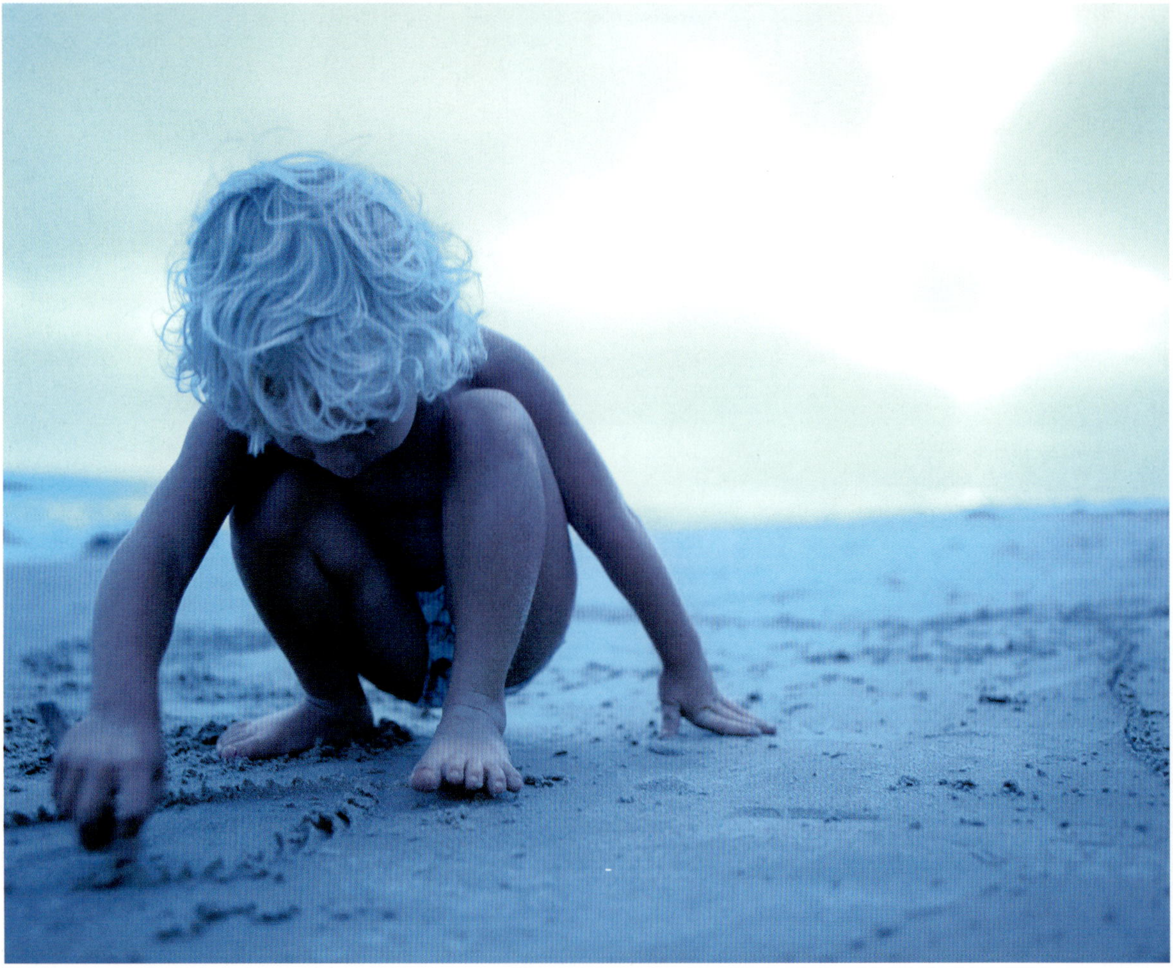

Scott Montgomery

Studio 800.621.1676 | www.smontgomery.com

paul markow   phx

az   888.273.7985

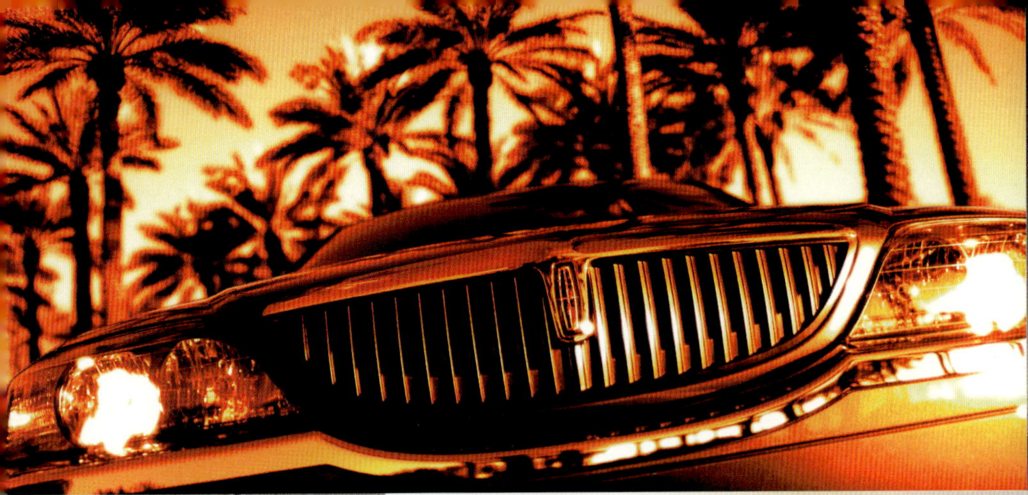

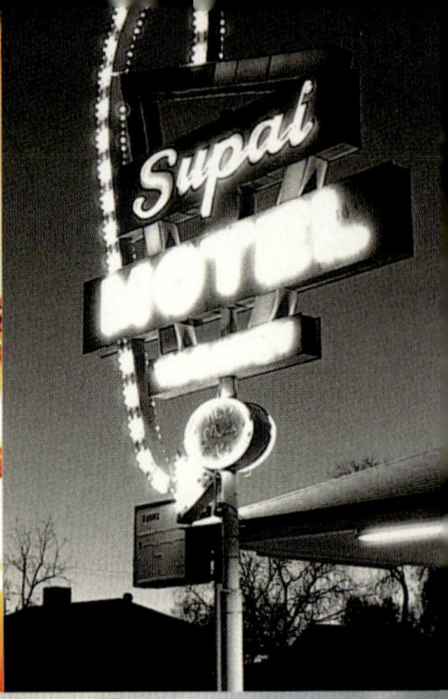
Supai
HOTEL

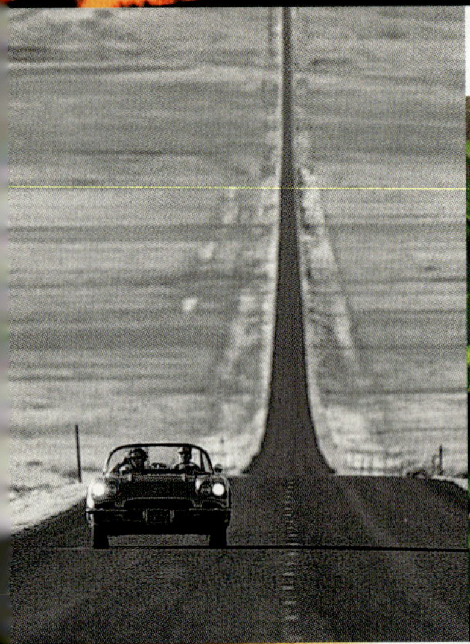

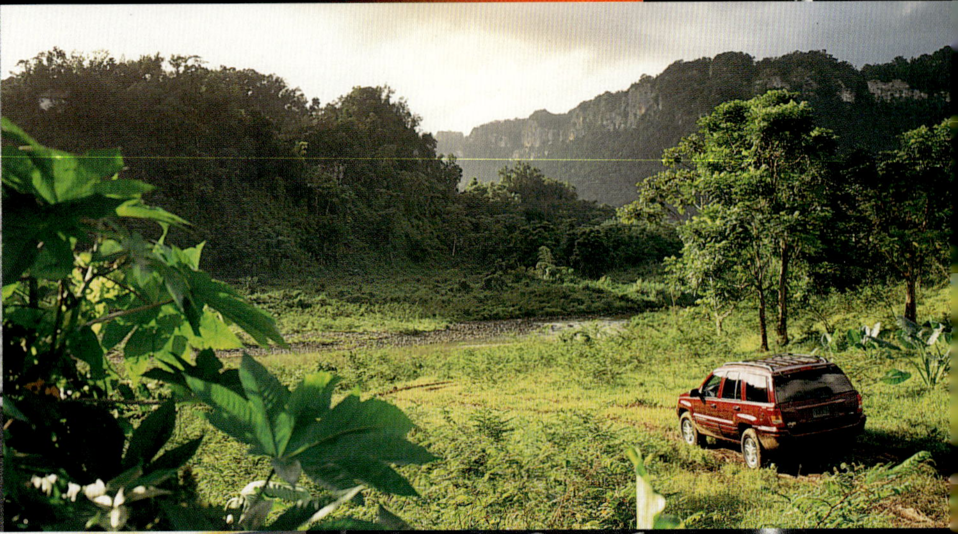

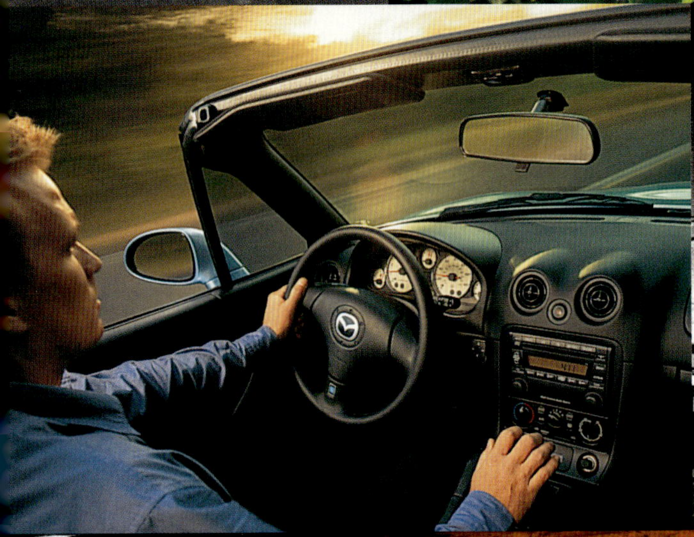

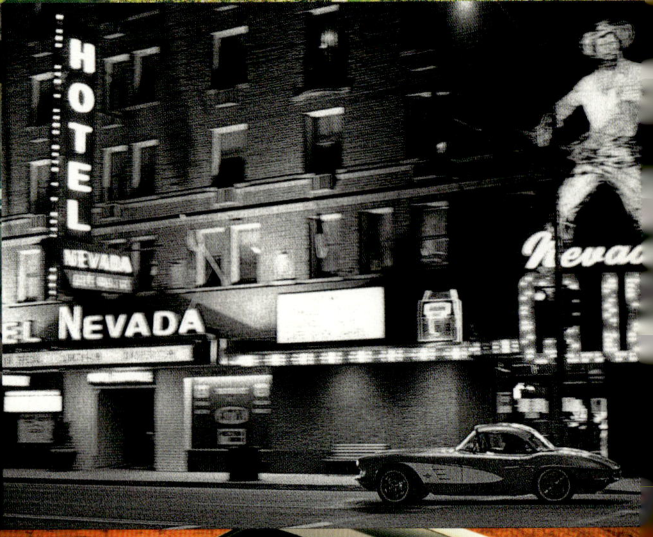
HOTEL
NEVADA
EL NEVADA

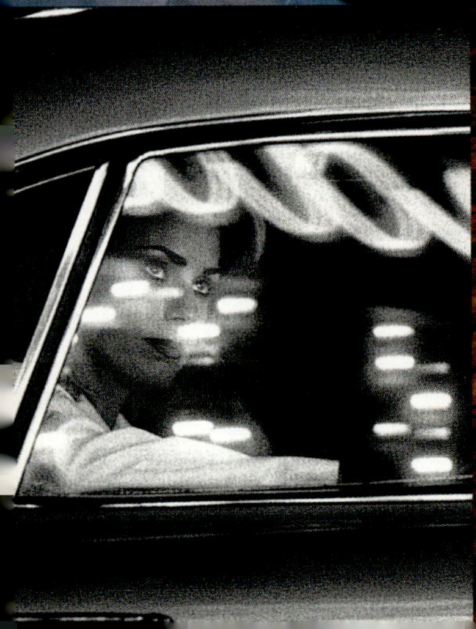

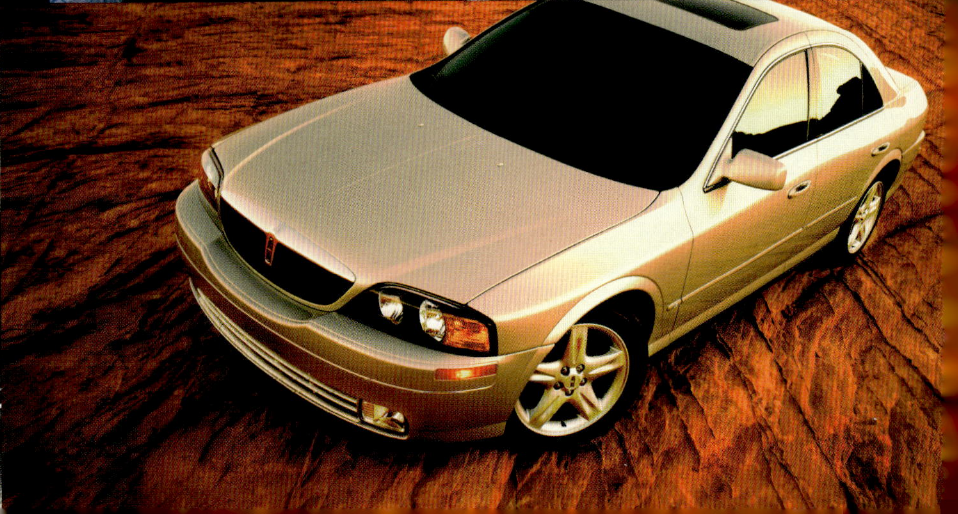

vic huber

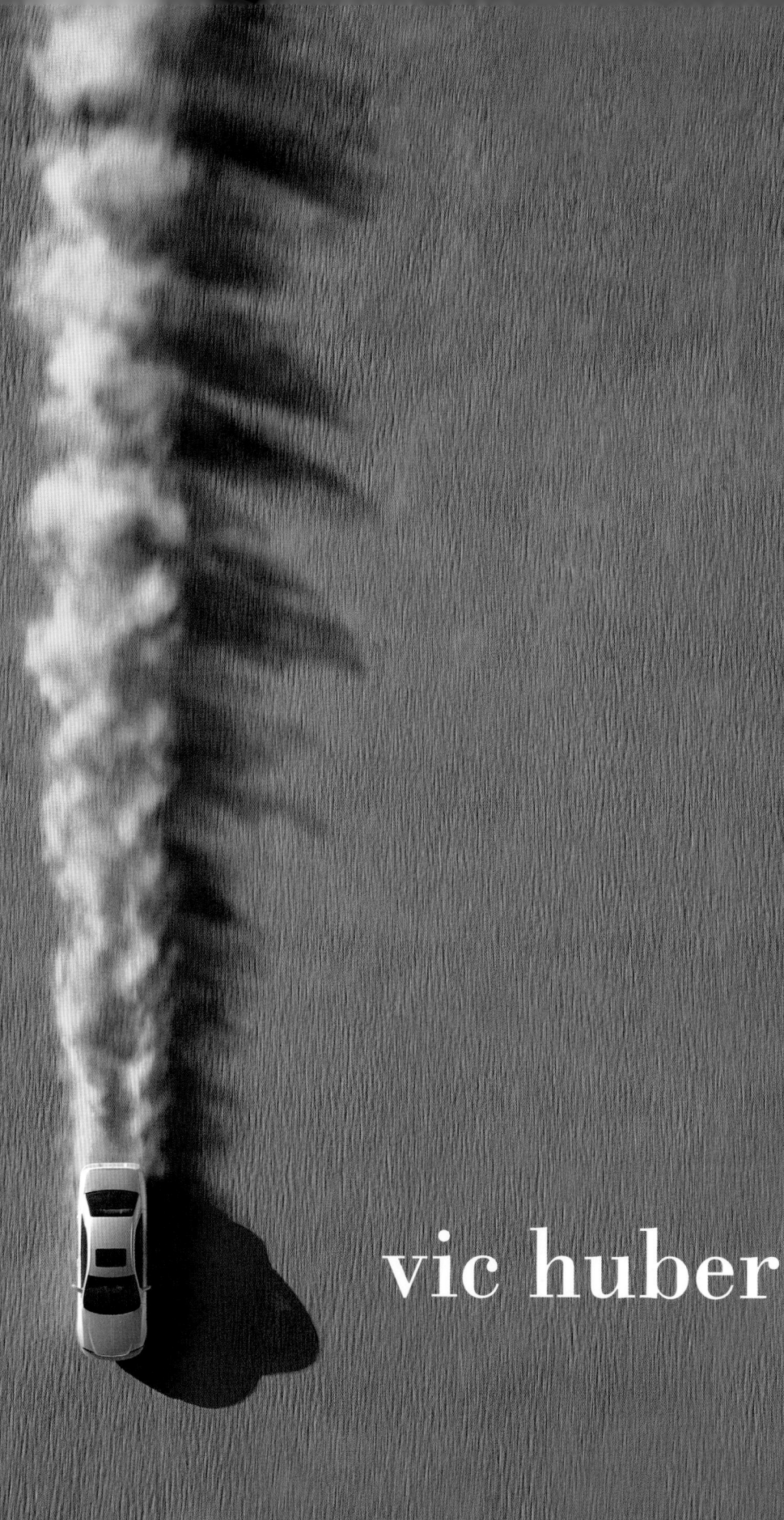

represented by shelly steichen 949-261-5844

©2001 Caesar Lima

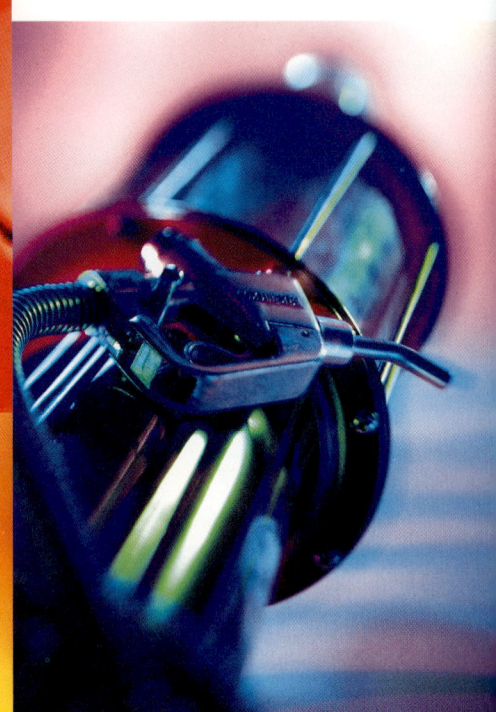

> WWW.CAESARPHOTO.COM

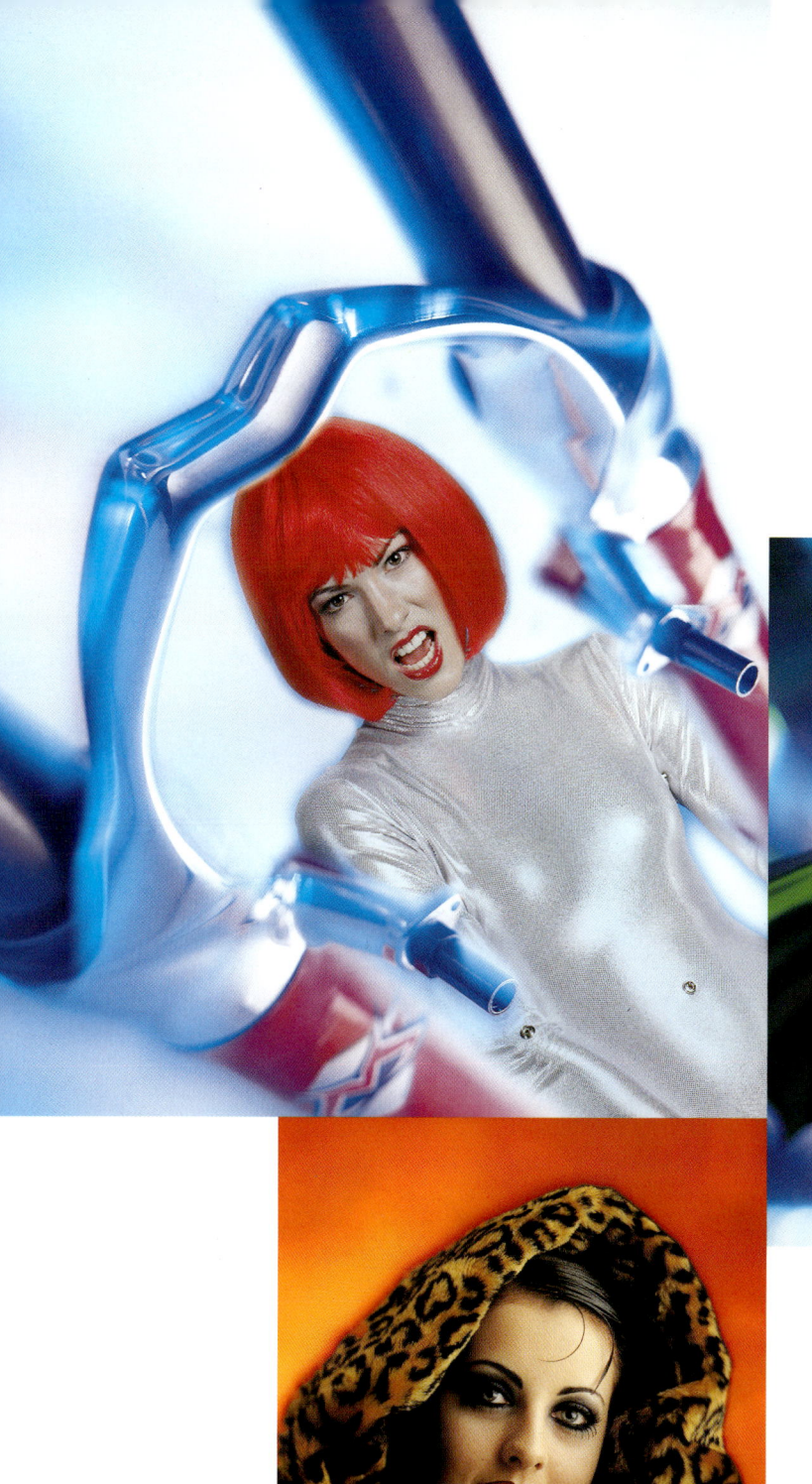

INFO@CAESARPHOTO.COM

> 800 > 8 CAESAR TF
> 818 > 223.8184 PH
> 818 > 223.8185 FX

caesarphoto C com

W
695

GIMME!

gimme

gimme

(oh c'm

Bruce **James**

Lew **Robertson**

Tim **Hawley**

Burke/Triolo Productions

LOS ANGELES STUDIO/ALISON ARMSTRONG 310.837.9900
EMAIL burketriolo@burketriolo.com
CHICAGO/TOM MALONEY 312.704.0500
www.burketriolo.com

425.644.6115

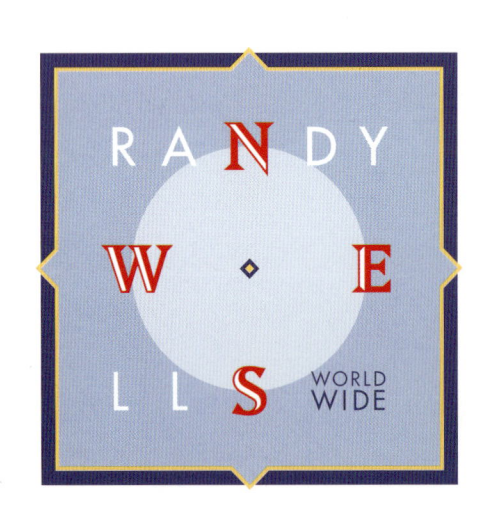

RANDY
W · E
LLS WORLD WIDE

WWW.RANDYWELLS.COM

Client:Disney CD: Dexter Fedor AD:Laura Della Sala

TERRY HUSEBYE PHOTOGRAPHY
415.444.5844   www.husebyephoto.com

Client:Procter&Gamble Agency:DMB&B AD:Ricardo Turcios

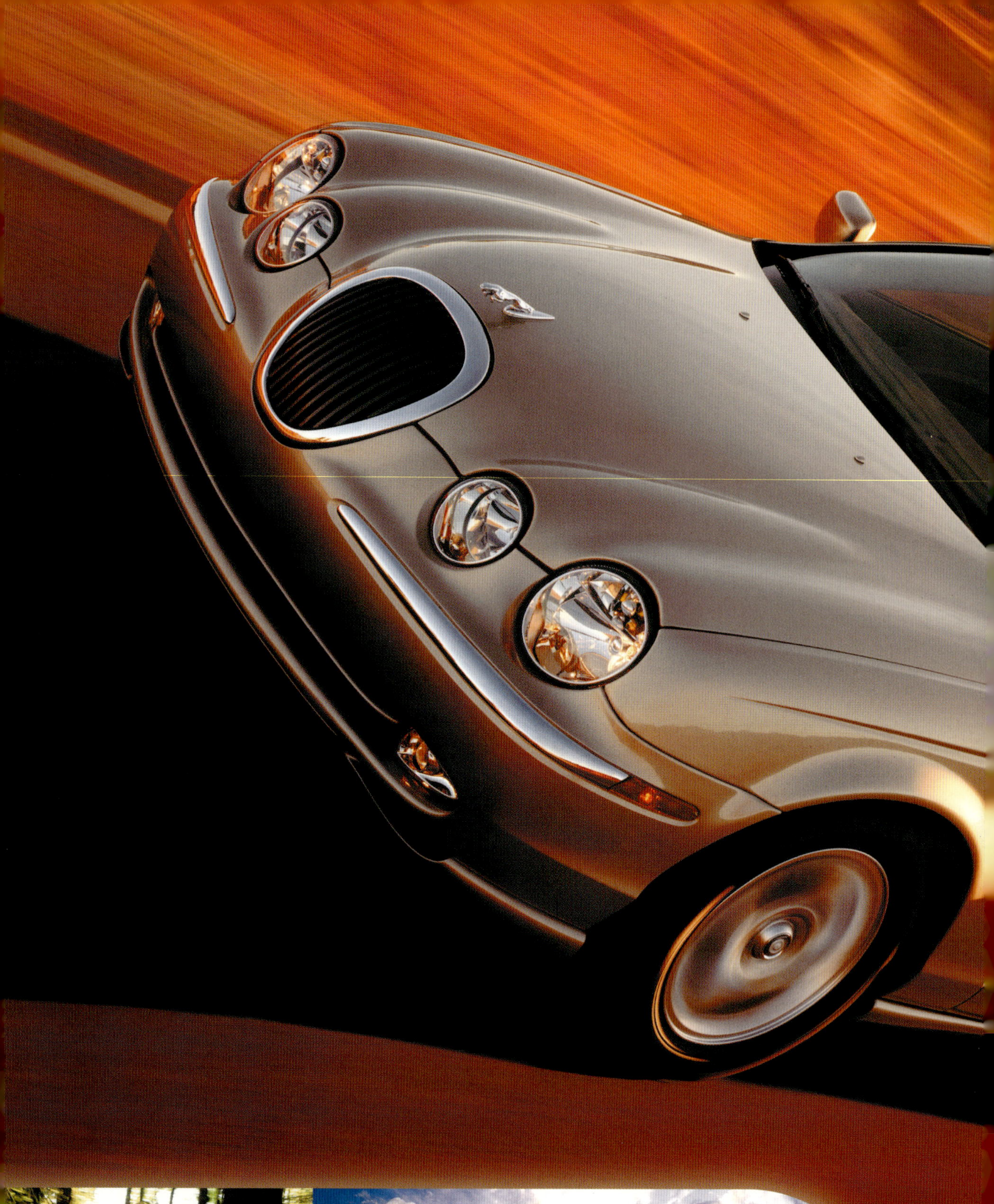
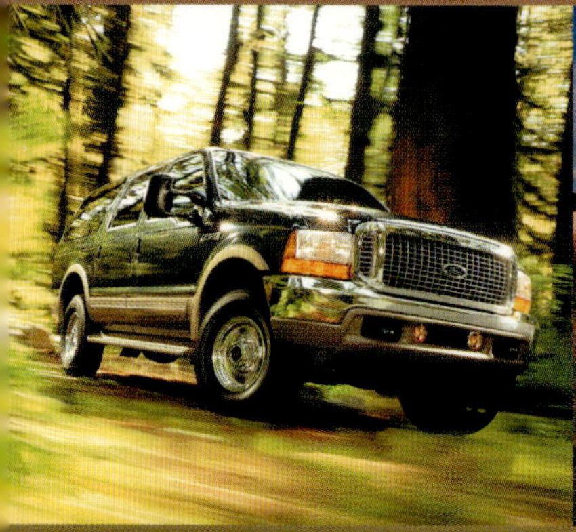
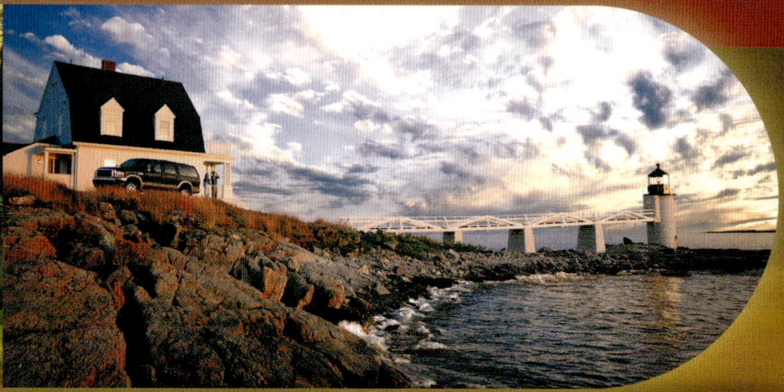

Tom Burkhart photography

WEST Deddens & Deddens . 310/203/9714   EAST U-3 . 800/550/5583   STUDIO . 800/248/7856   fax 248/588/8273

w703

John Russell

970.920.1431
Aspen.Hawaii

anthony **nex** photography

RHONI EPSTEIN ASSOCIATES 310 207 5937

www.anthonynex.com

LA 310 836 4357   NY 212 741 7934

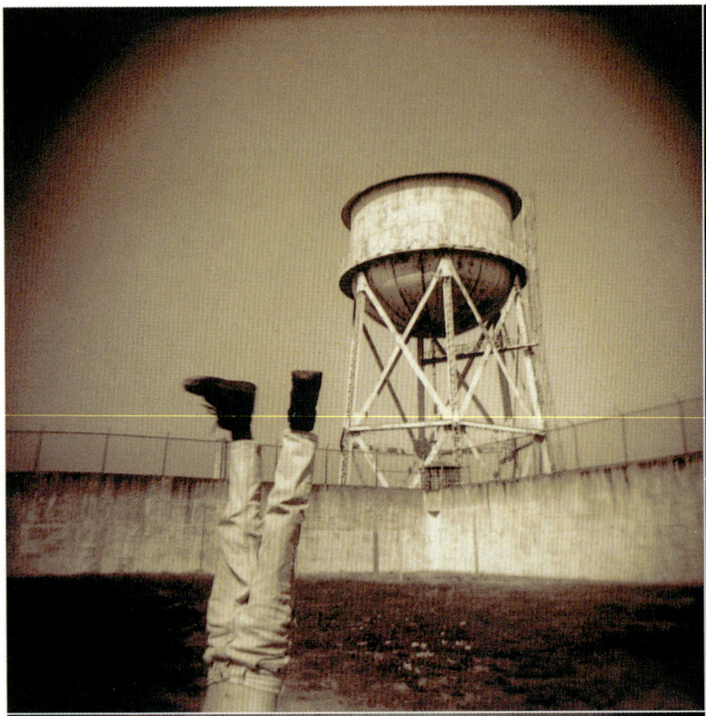
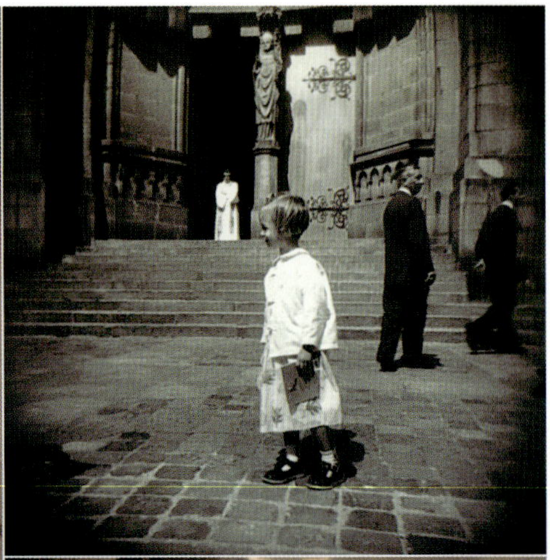
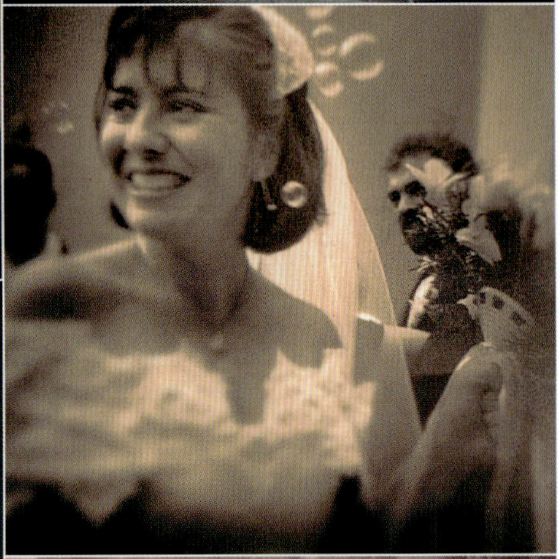
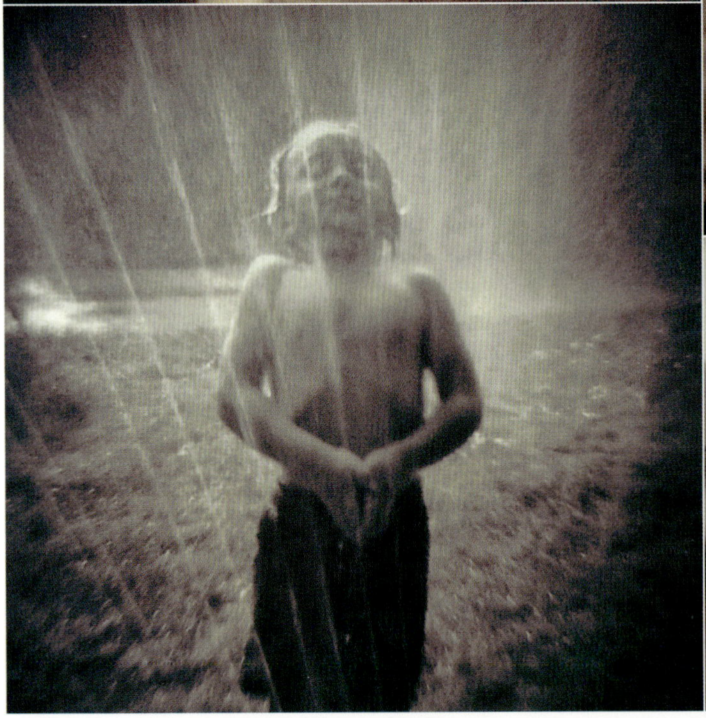
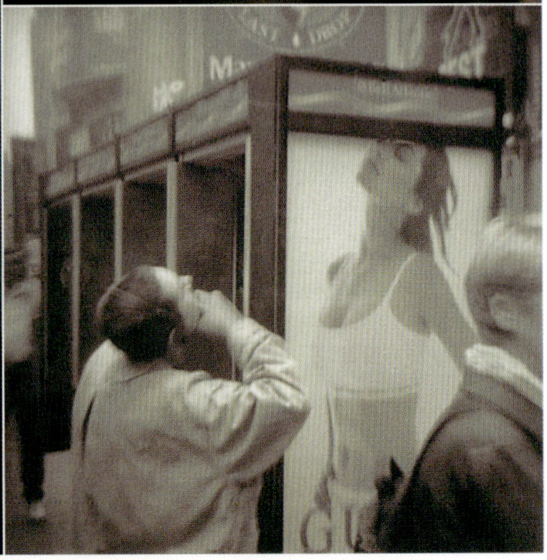

WILL MOSGROVE

SAN FRANCISCO

415 / 331 / 1526

seulement

votre

cœur

dit

la vérité

JEREMIAH SULLIVAN WEST 6

36.0711 EAST 212.969.0043

DELIANTONI
San Francisco
415-495-1115
planetpoint.com/deliantoni

Deliantoni
San Francisco
415-495-1115
planetpoint.com/deliantoni

Aaron Rapoport 323.883.0388

www.aaronrapoport.com

Yocum

www.yocum.net | 888.929.8878 | info@yocum.net

W
717

B

Andrew D. Bernstein
Associates
Photography, Inc.

DENNIS REPRESENTS • CONTACT FRANÇOISE DUBOIS
376-9738 PHONE • 805 376-9729 FAX • 310 710-7591 MOBILE • www.francoisedubois.com

GARY PARKER

SAN FRANCISCO / SILICON VALLEY

408-292-4916
gary@garyparker.com

WWW.GARYPARKER.COM

MARC CARTER
PHOTOGRAPHY

———

REPRESENTED BY AME SIMON
206 517 4965

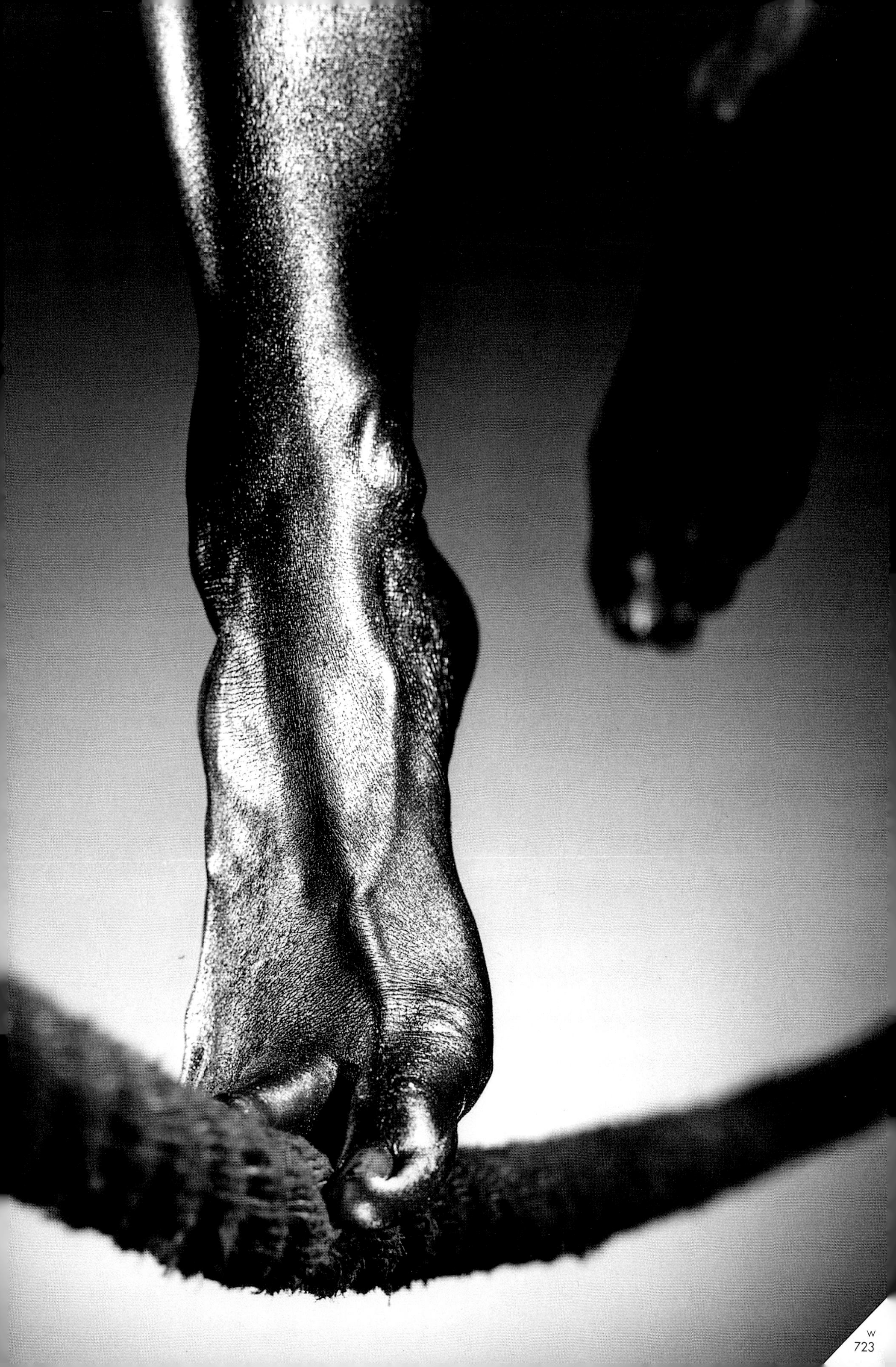

KAREN SHELL • Toll-Free: 877-464-0731 • Tel: 602-212-0471 • Fax: 602-212-0488 • www.shell-photo.co

mail: karen@shell-photo.com • 505 W. LaMar Rd., Phoenix, AZ 85013

SHELL
photographics

rosanne olson

PHOTOGRAPHY

t 206.633.3775   f 206.547.1986
rosanneolson.com

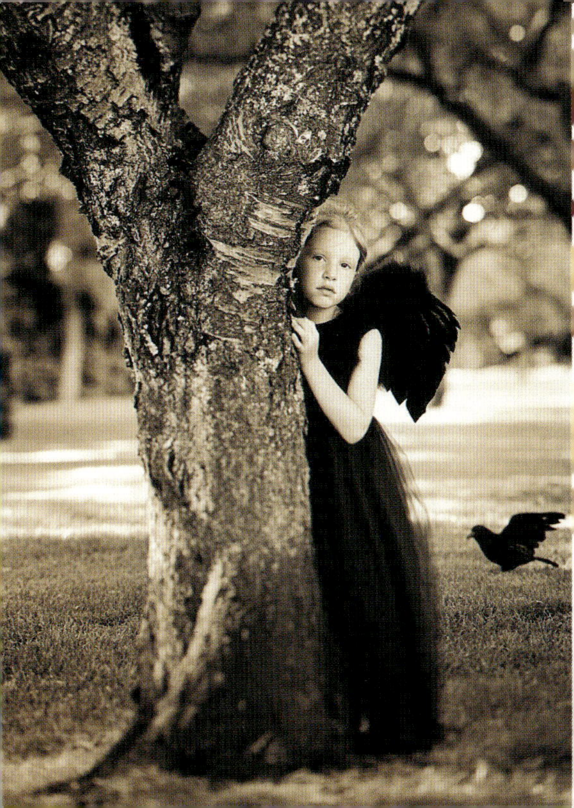

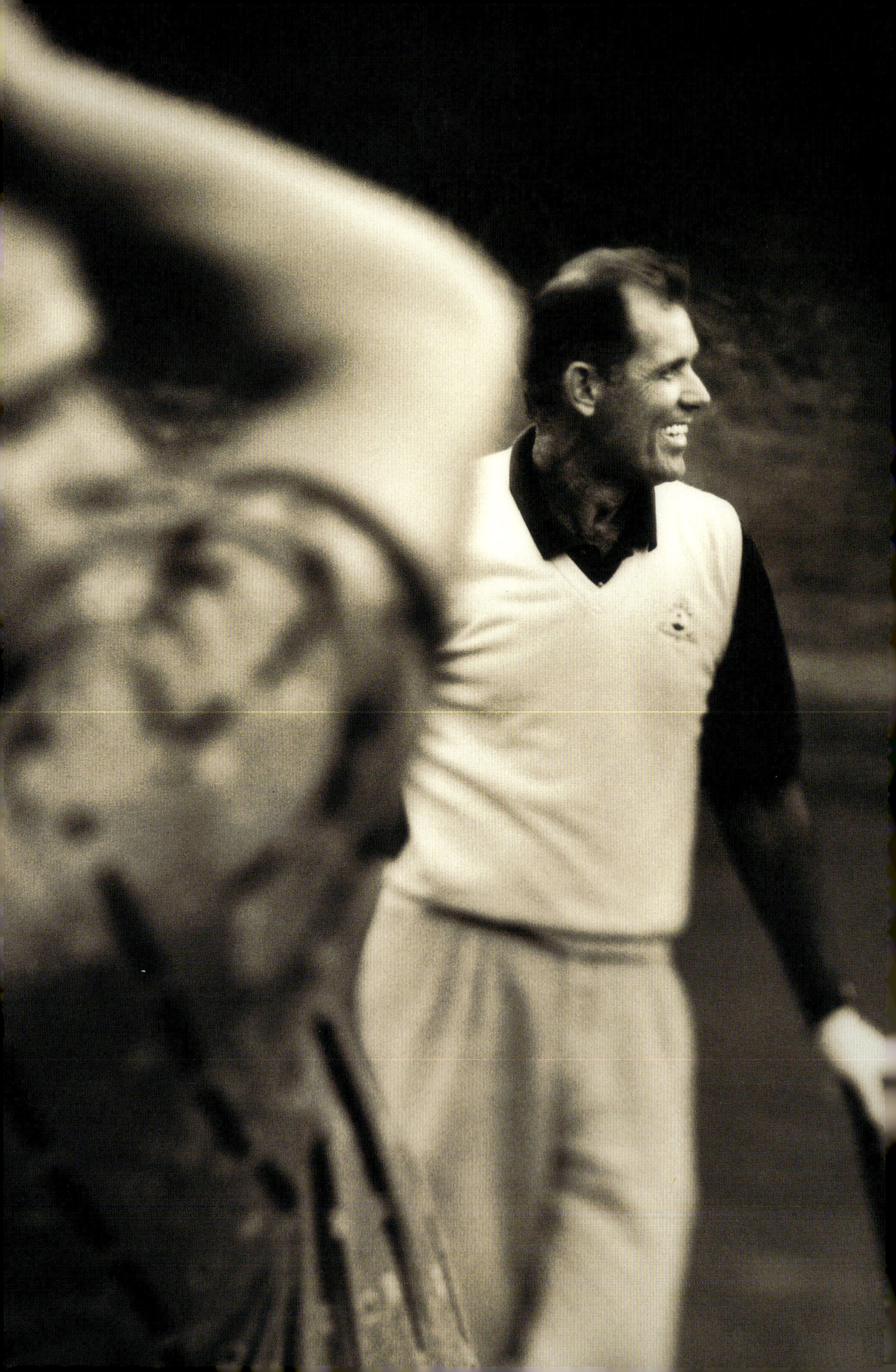

Robert Holley
PHOTOGRAPHY

LOS ANGELES · 310 748 4002

Sampsel-Preston

702-873-0094

www.sampselpreston.com

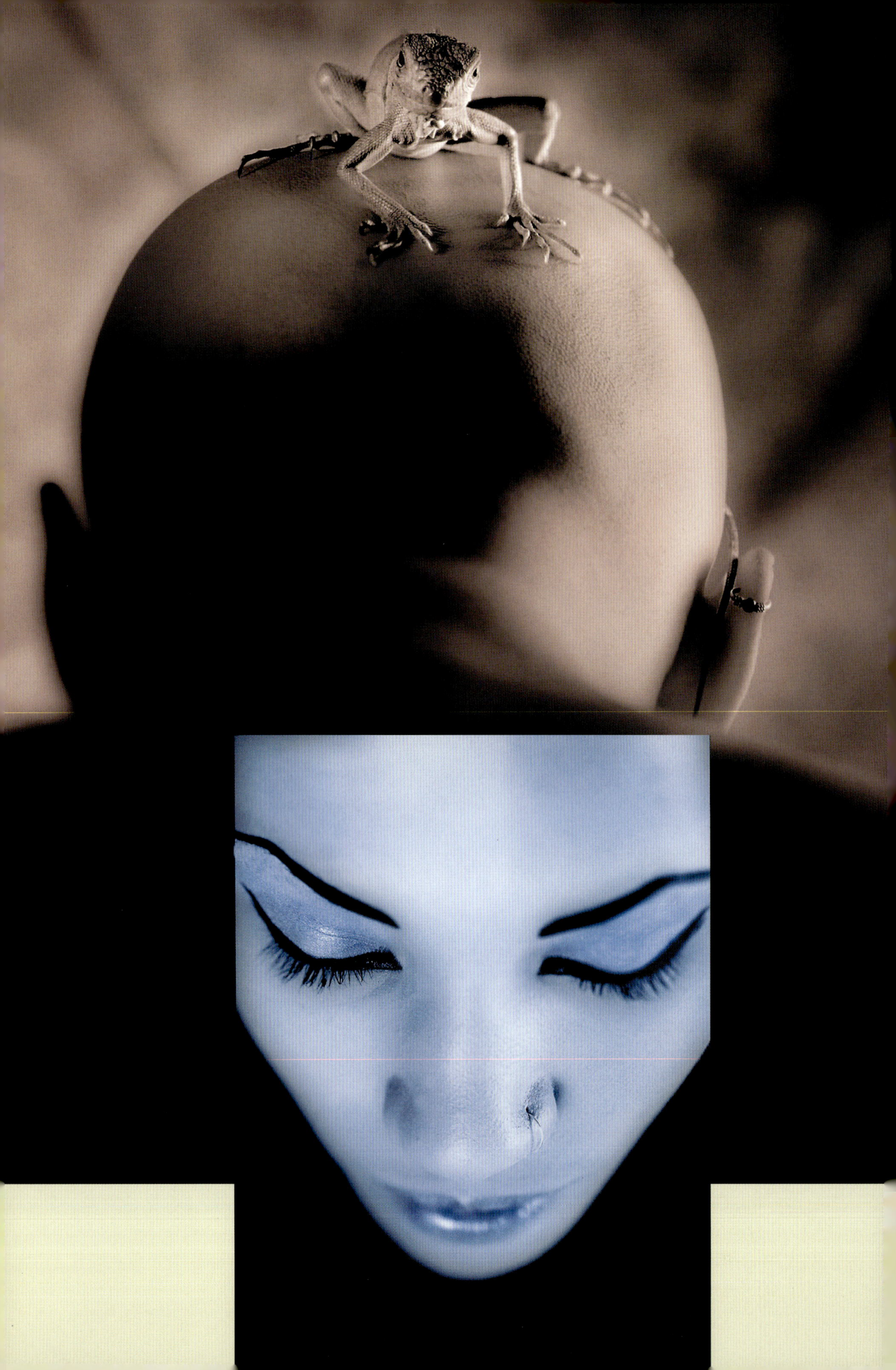

Jones

TEL (602) 244-1971 OR 1-800-758-6685

WEB SITE ~ "WILLJONESPHOTO. COM"

Dana Edmunds Photography 808.521.7711 www.danafoto.com

DANA

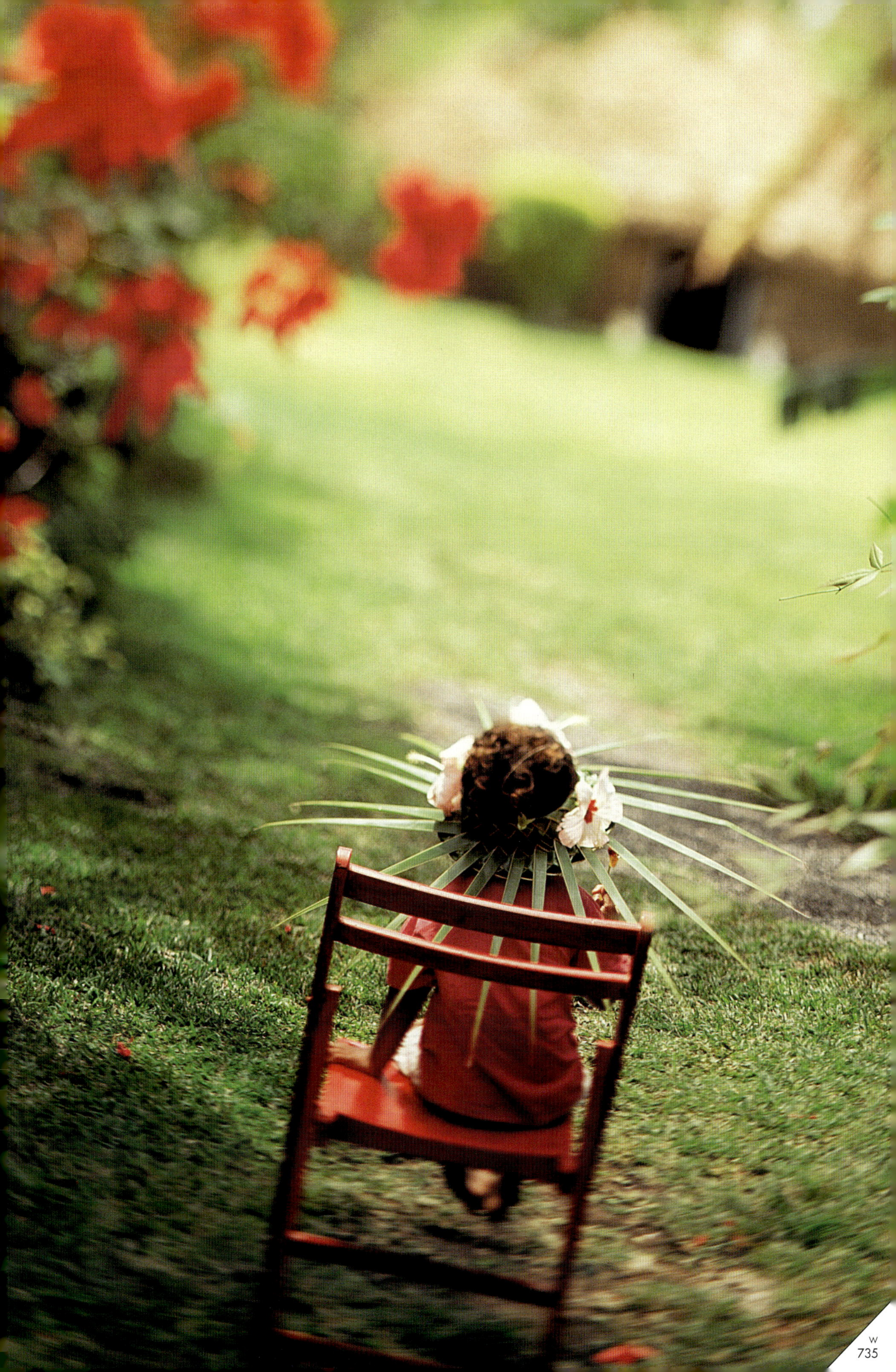

MARK SILVERSTEIN | 800.216.2083 323.223.4213

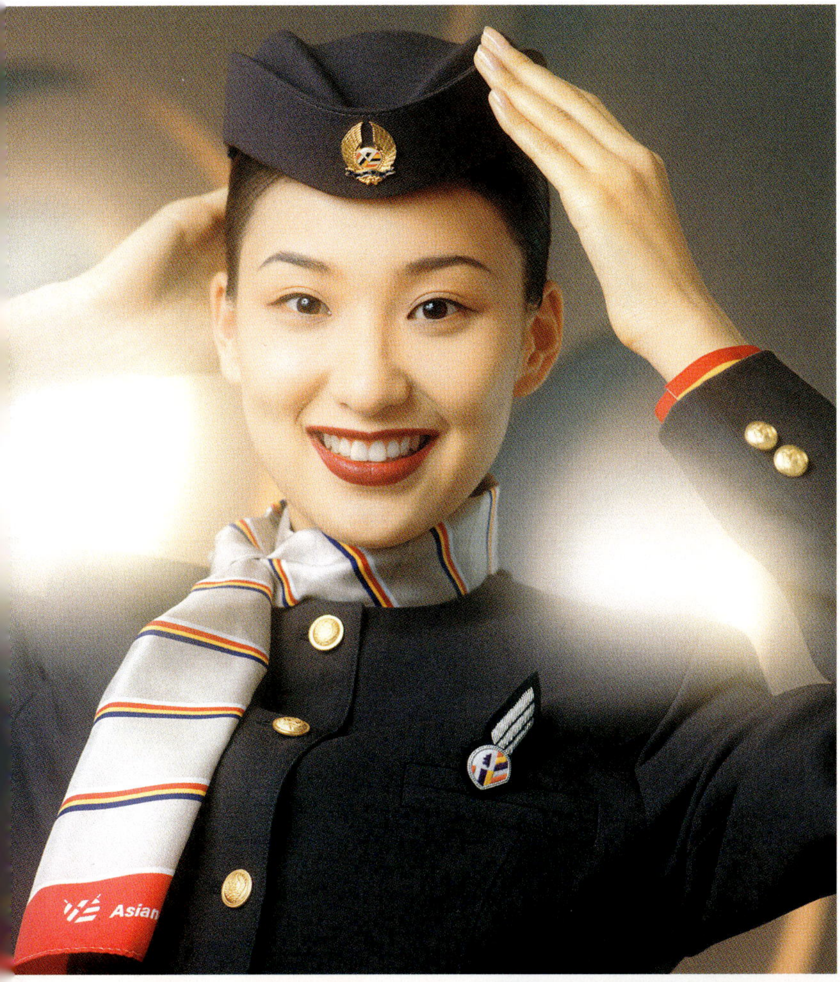
Asian

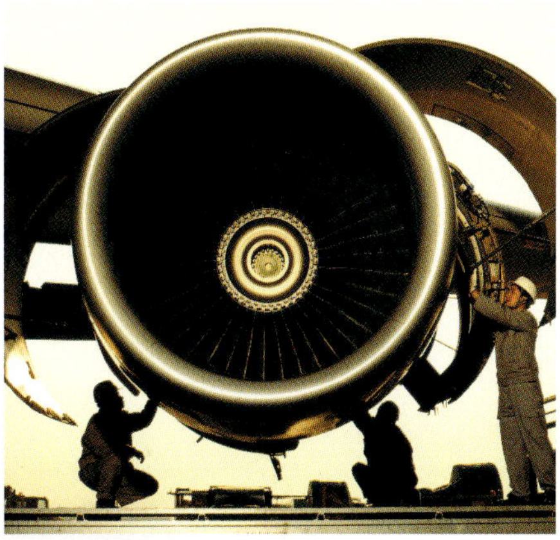

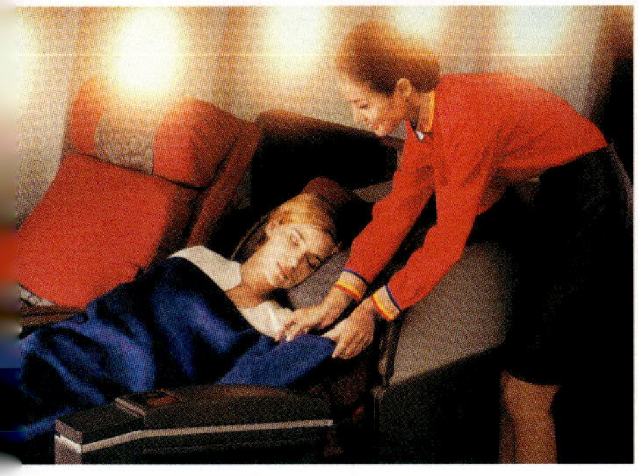

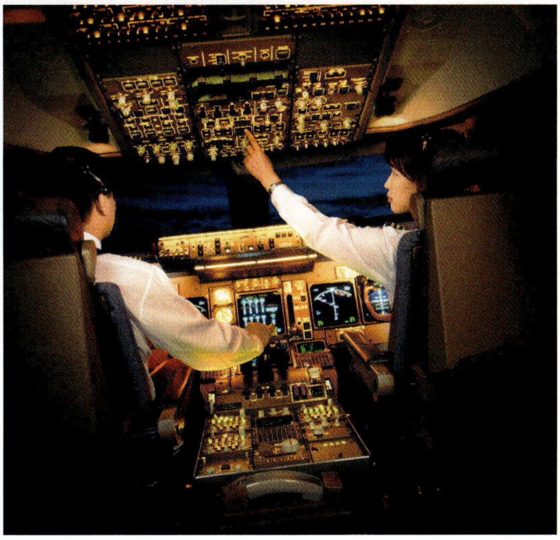

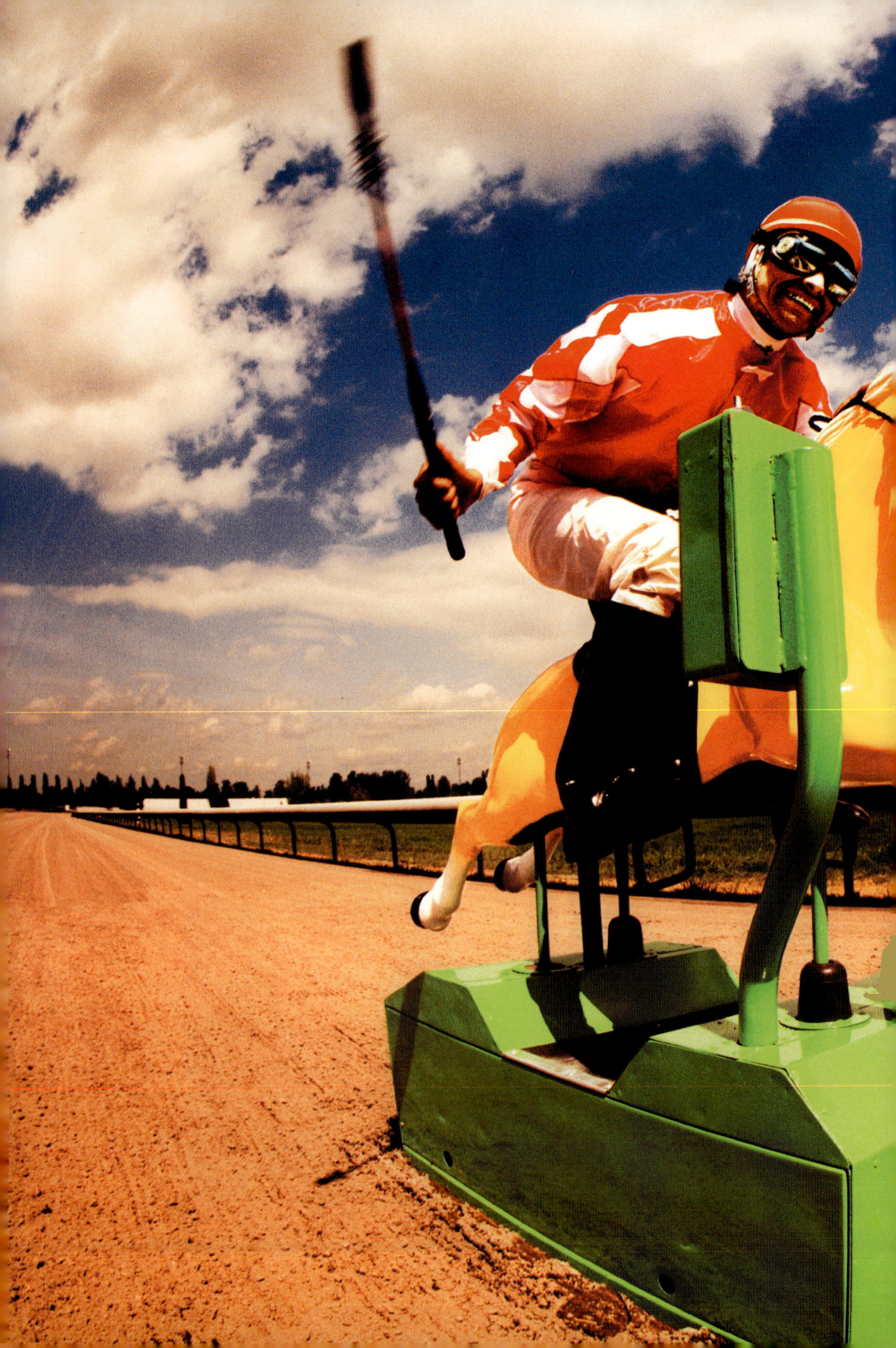

john acurso photography

portland **503.231.0551**

new york **877.201.3542**

www.**acurso.com**

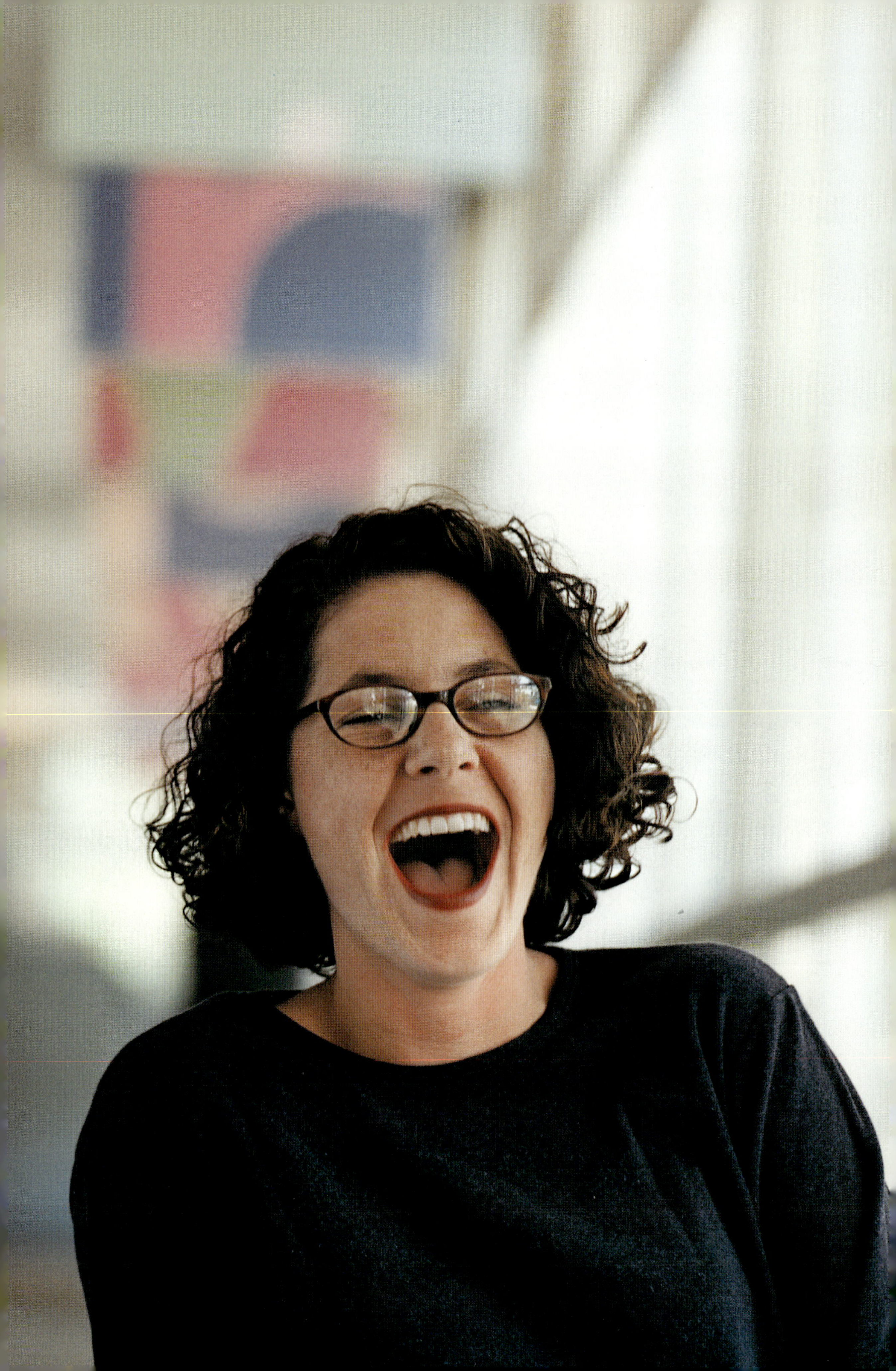

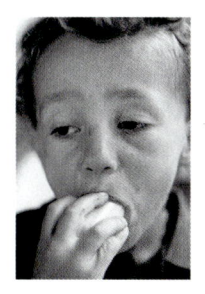

CHRIS AYERS
650.961-2700 888.644-2700
chris@ayersphoto.com

Chris Schrameck Photography
New York & Vancouver   800.319.8899
New York Agent : Marge Casey & Associates   212.929.3757

Chris Schrameck Photography

New York & Vancouver 800.319.8899
New York Agent : Marge Casey & Associates 212.929.3757

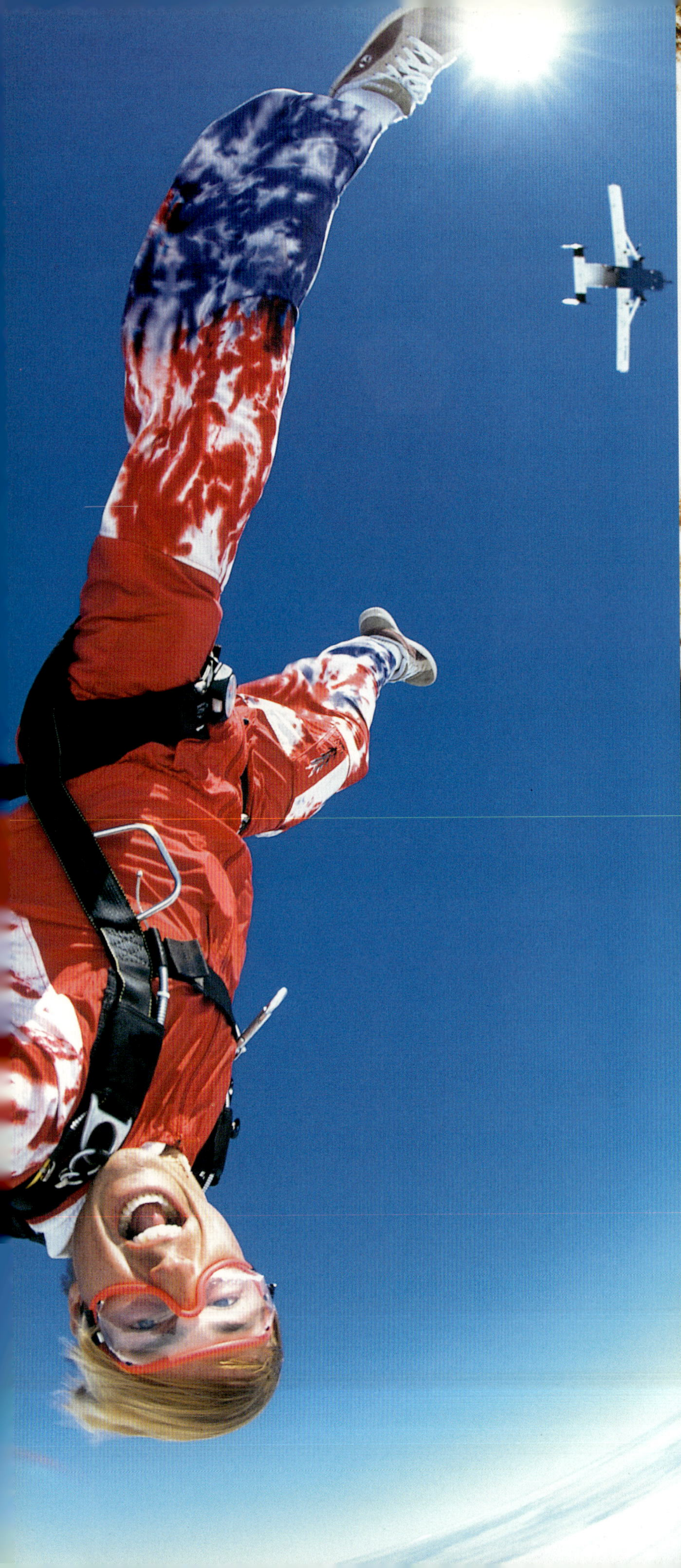
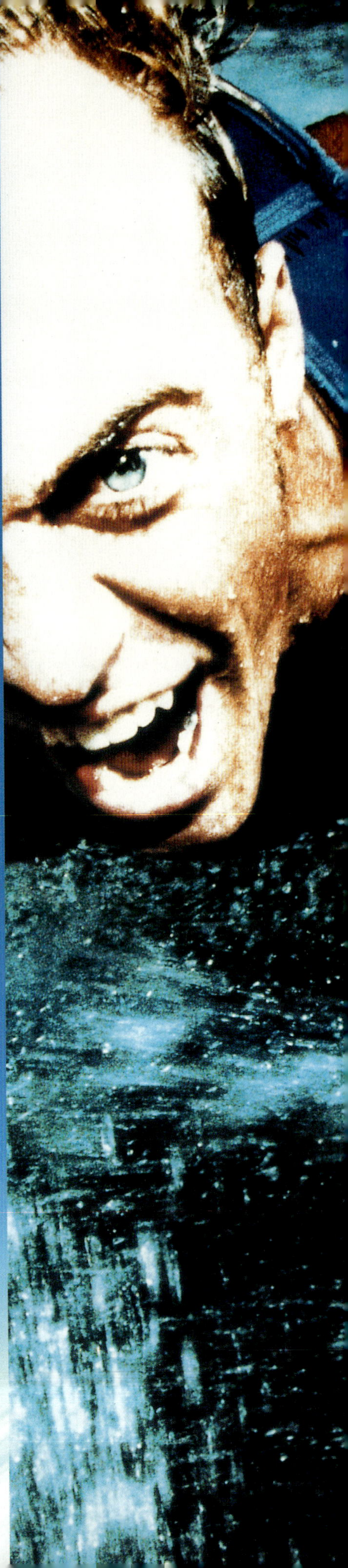

Joe McBride
PRODUCTIONS

949.240.9538 www.joemcbride.com

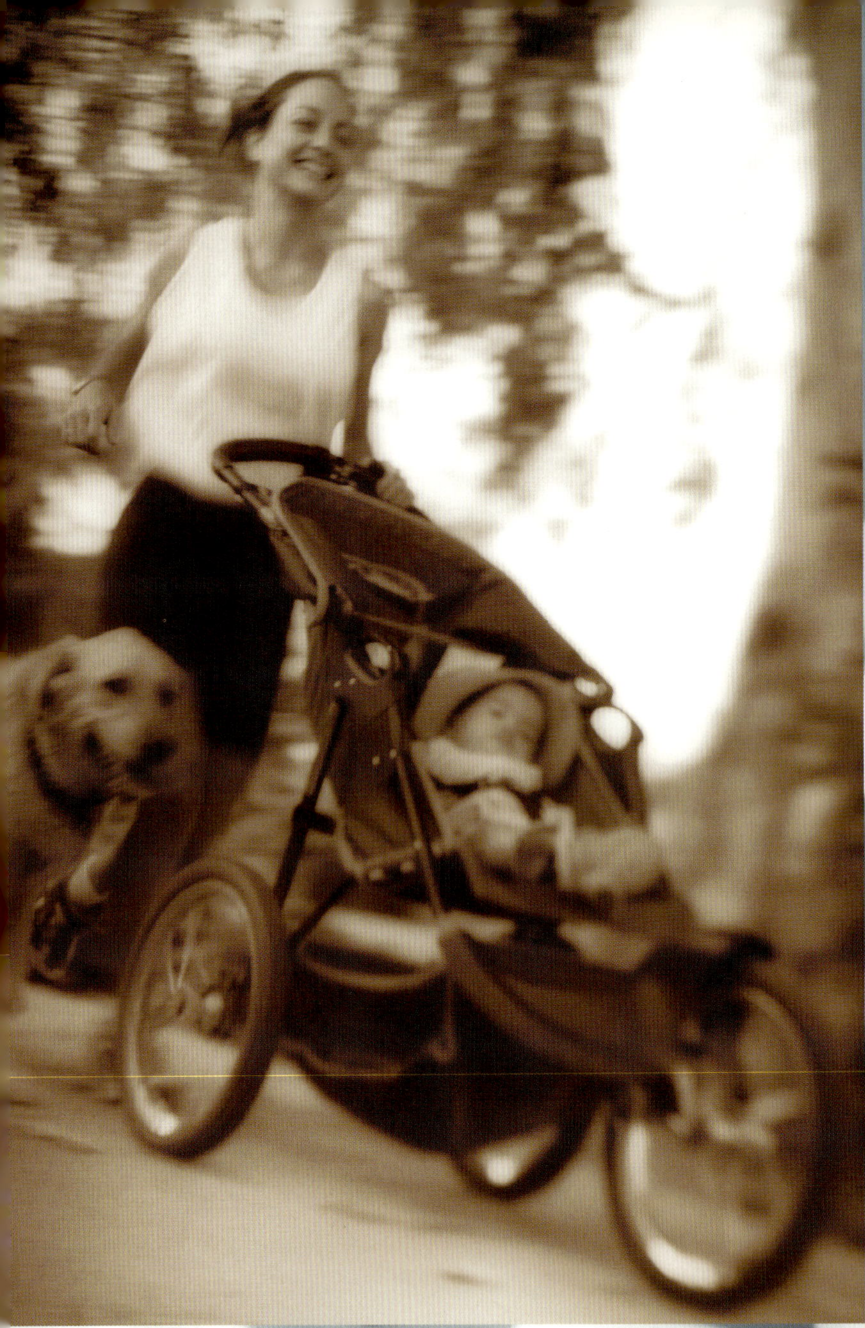
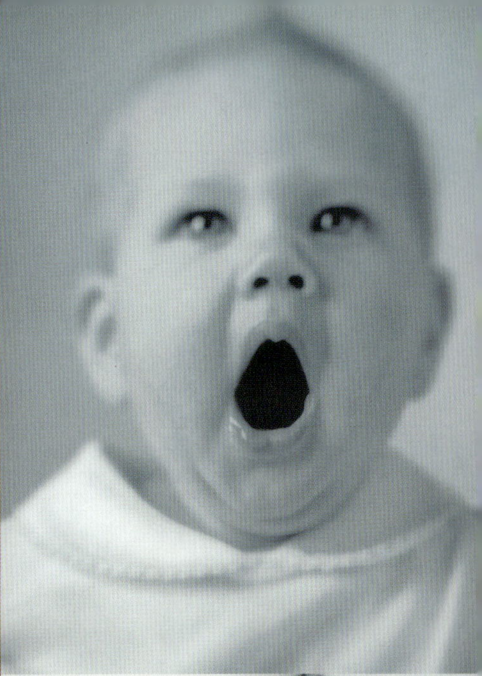
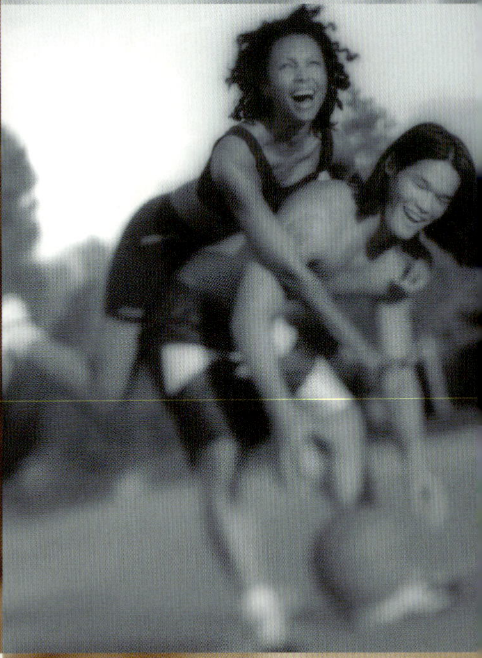
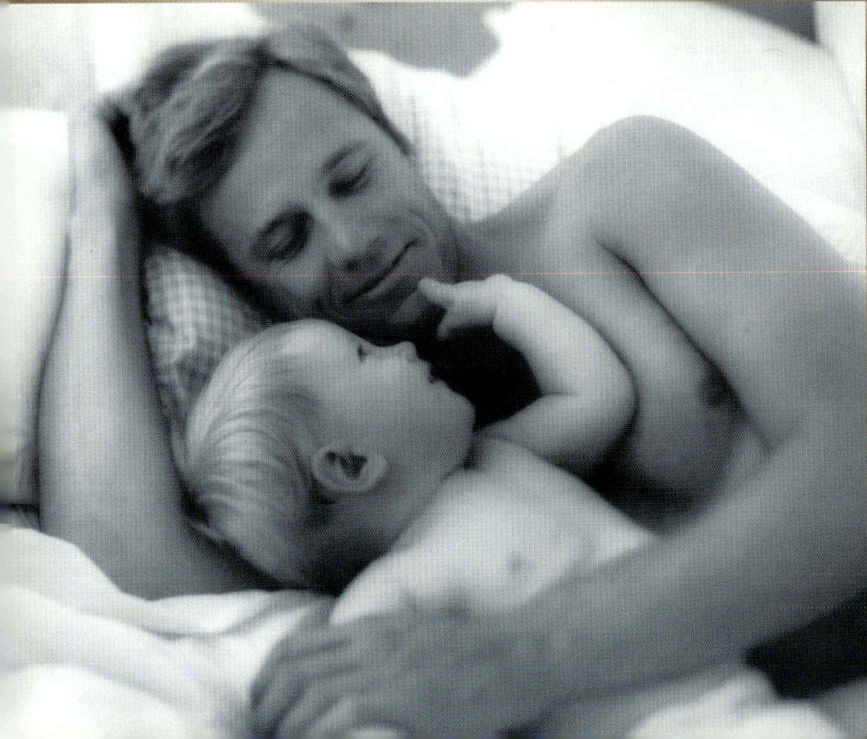
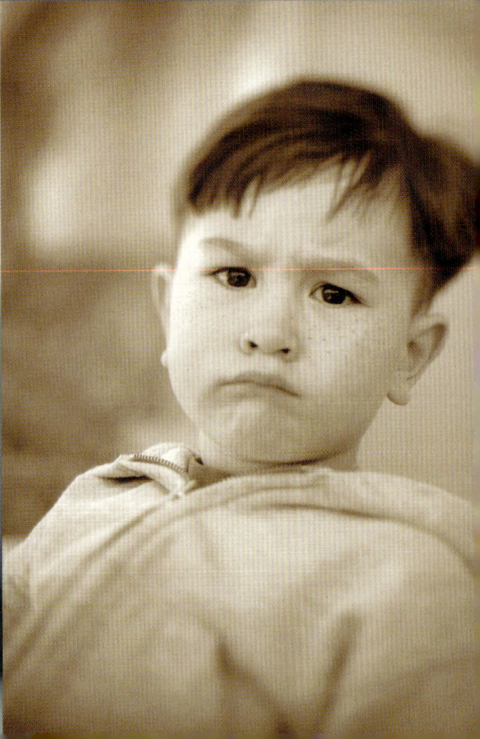

Tim Pannell Photography

p . 480.782.5544
f . 480.782.5545
www.timpannell.com

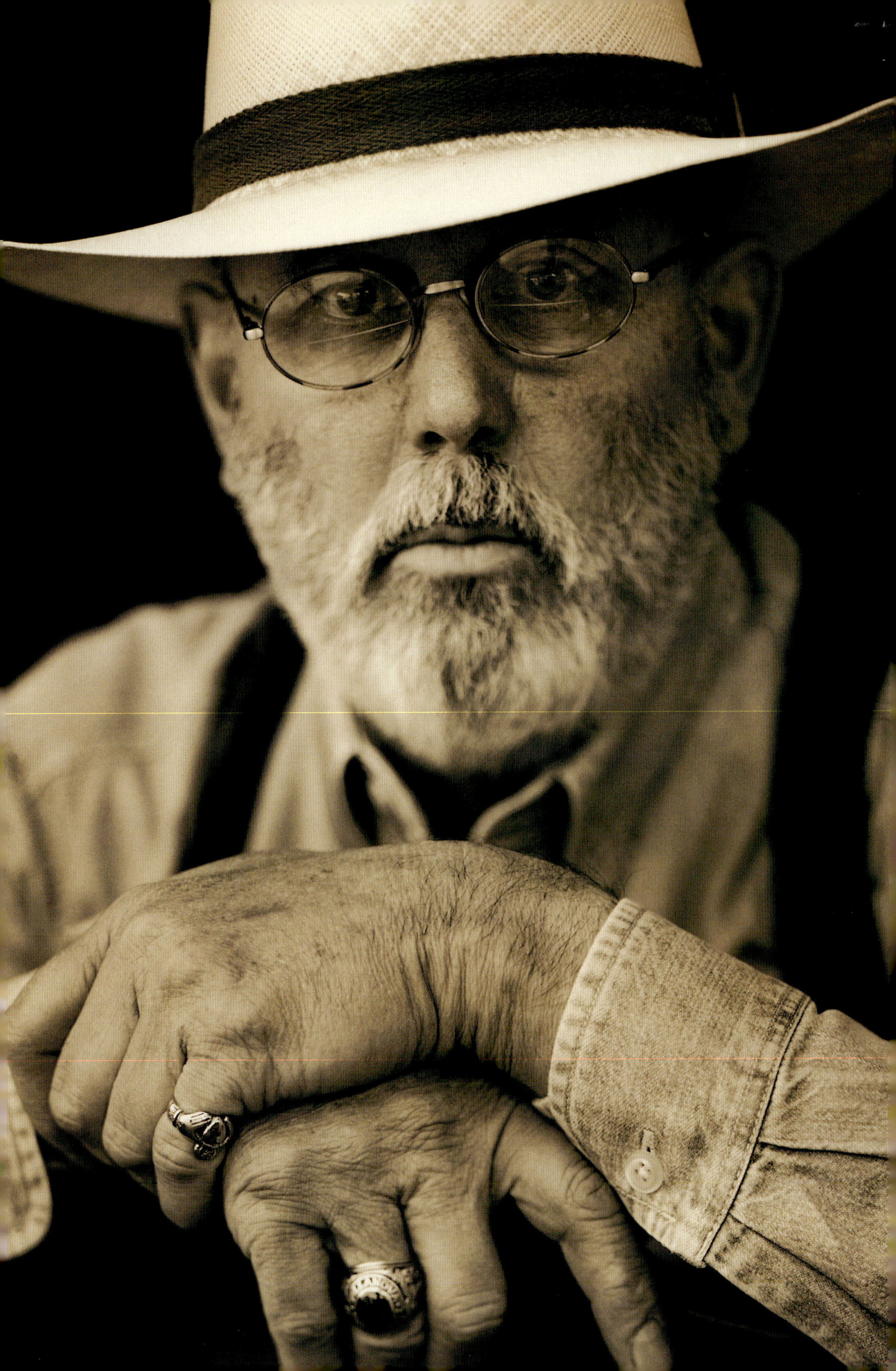

THOMAS BROENING

PHOTOGRAPHY

415.922.7946

JACQUES BARBEY

480.443.1274

©2000 Jacques Barbey

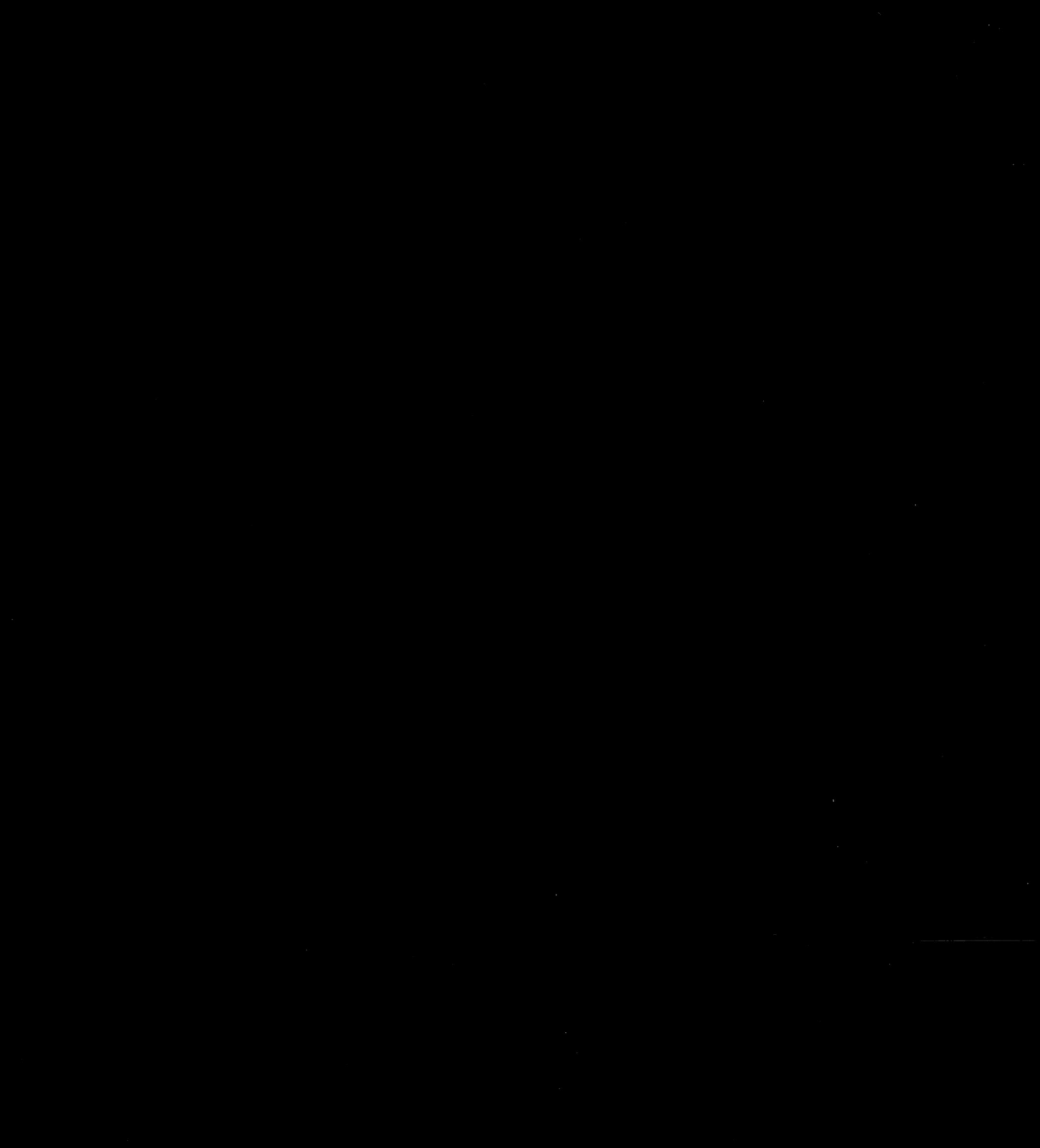

DIGITAL

Bender & Bender 756-757

Barry Blackman 765

Richard Bradbury 100-101, 108-109, 769

Clor Photography & Imaging 764

Davo Photographic 760-761

Don Dixon & Avner Levona 100-101, 106-107, 768

Thomas Drew 560-561, 767

Mike Iezzi 764

Kalman & Pabst Photo Group 771

Korman + Company 100-105, 108-113, 768-770

Mir Lada 762-763

Kent Lund 760-761

Carlo Pieroni 100-101, 110-111, 770

Philip Rostron 442-443, 766

John Still 758-759

We're Jammin' 100-101, 106-107, 768

BENDER • BENDER

CONTACT
CHAD BENDER
740•726•2470

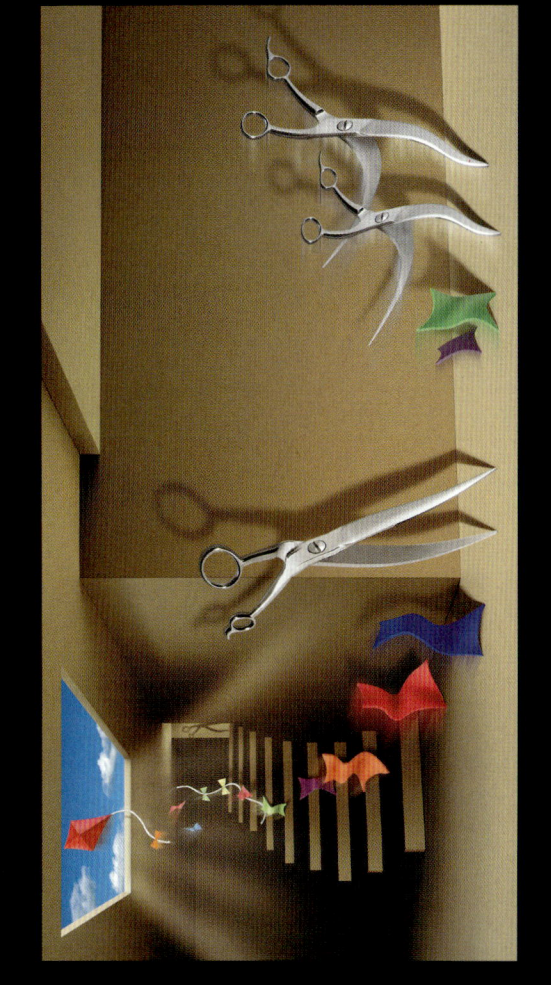

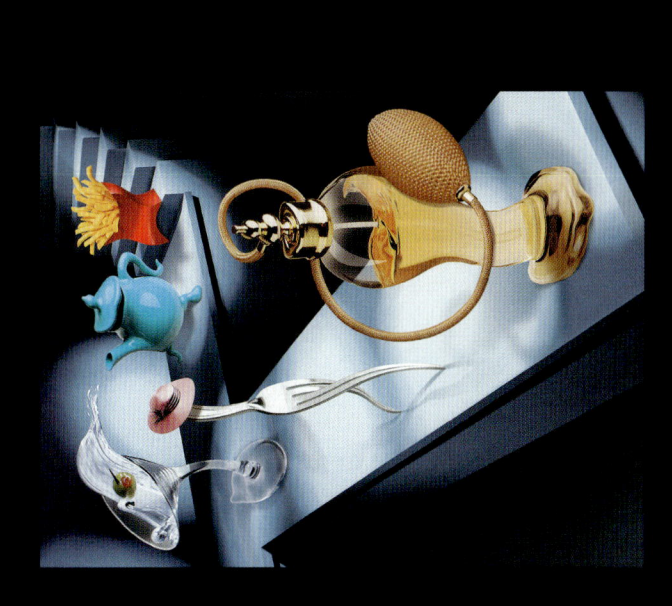

WWW.BENDERIMAGING.COM

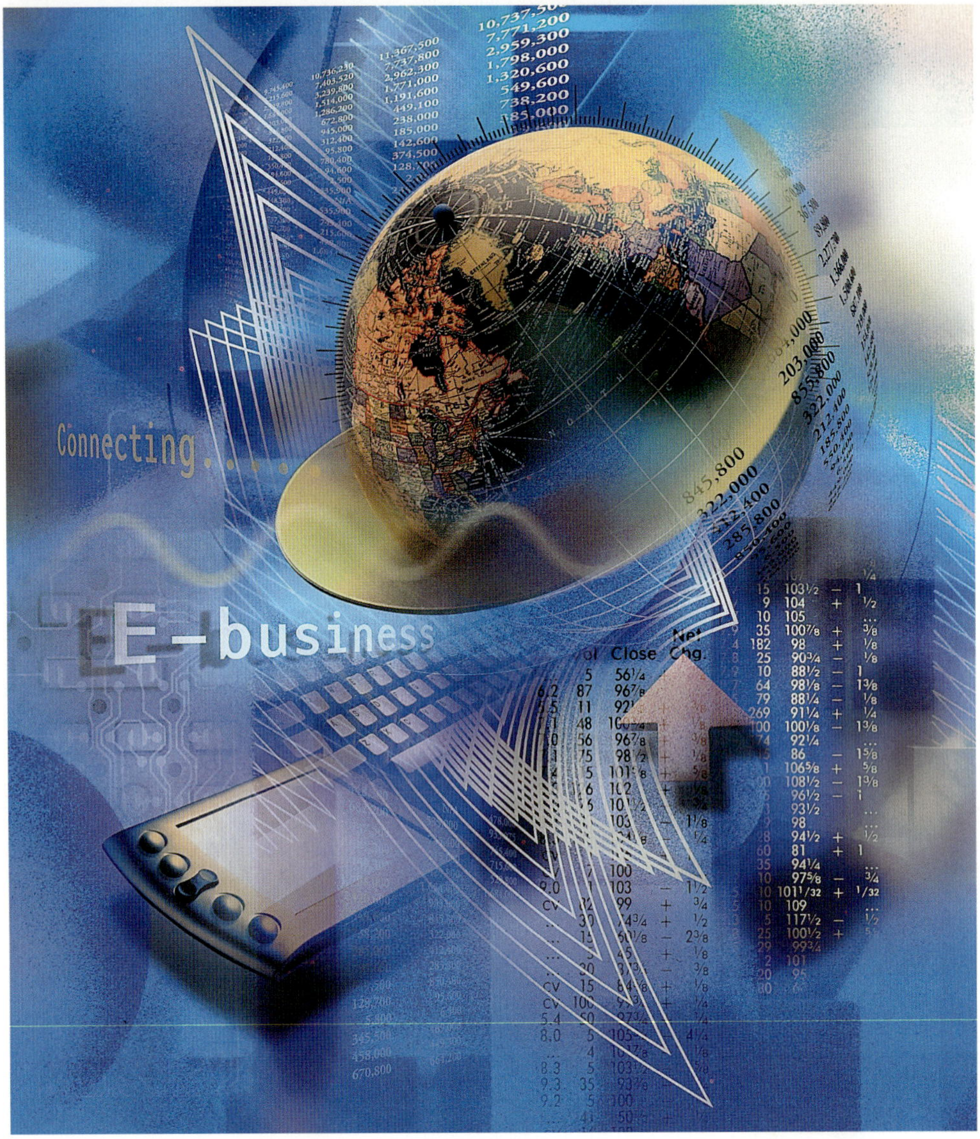

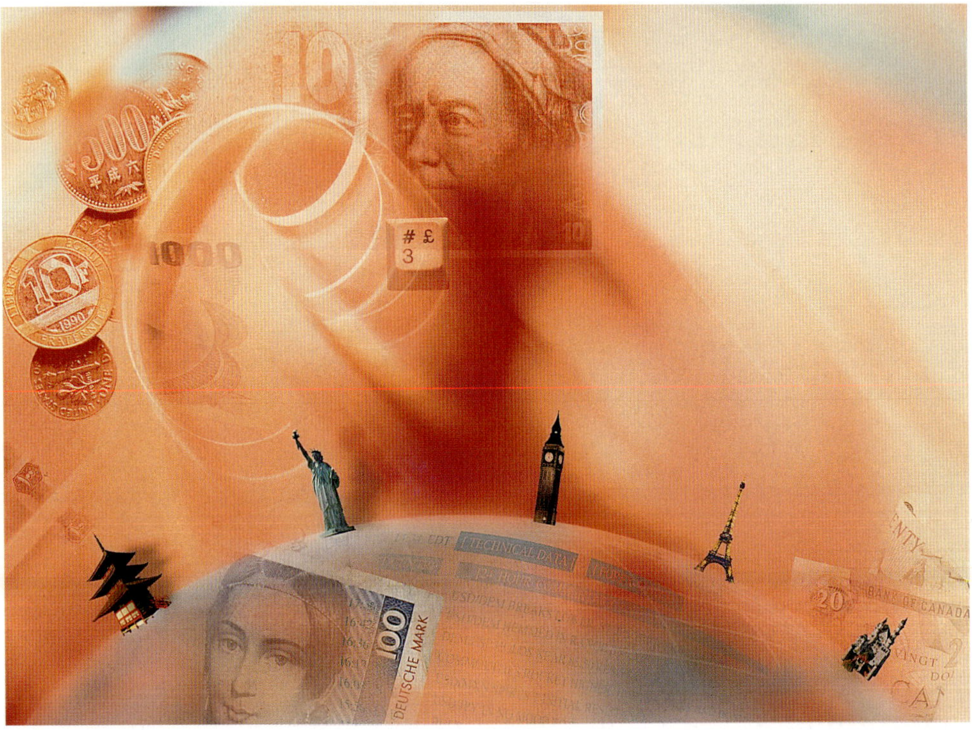

JOHN STILL

www.johnstill.com
info@johnstill.com
617.451.8178
fax 482.1826

SIMPLY

THE HIGHEST QUALITY VIRTUAL REALITY ON THE PLANET.

davo.com
Full **360°** views inside and out.
virtual reality · digital stills

DAVO PHOTOGRAPHIC
248 588 9600

represented by Kent Lund
248 433 2701

D
761

RESULTS MAY VARY

1.877
MIR LADA
.COM

RESULTS MAY VARY

MAX AIR GUM...BATES CANADA

D
763

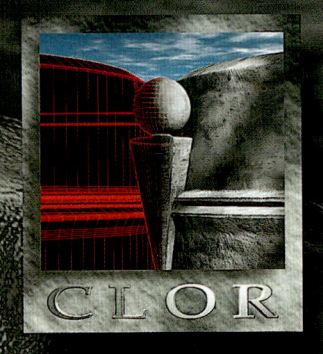

Digital Photography

Clor Photography & Imaging

1237 Chicago Road
Troy, MI 48083

Phone: 248.583.5540
Facsimilie: 248.583.3216

Represented by Mike Iezzi

3D-Illustration

Capabilities

Studio & Location Photography
Digital & Conventional

Computer Imaging
Composite & Retouching

3D-Illustration
Product & Virtual Sets

Animation
Web, Broadcast & Film

Digital Video
Studio & Location

3D-Animation

Digital Video/FX

Chris Clor: cclor@earthlink.net

Mike Iezzi: miezzi@earthlink.net

www.clorimages.com

BARRY BLACKMAN

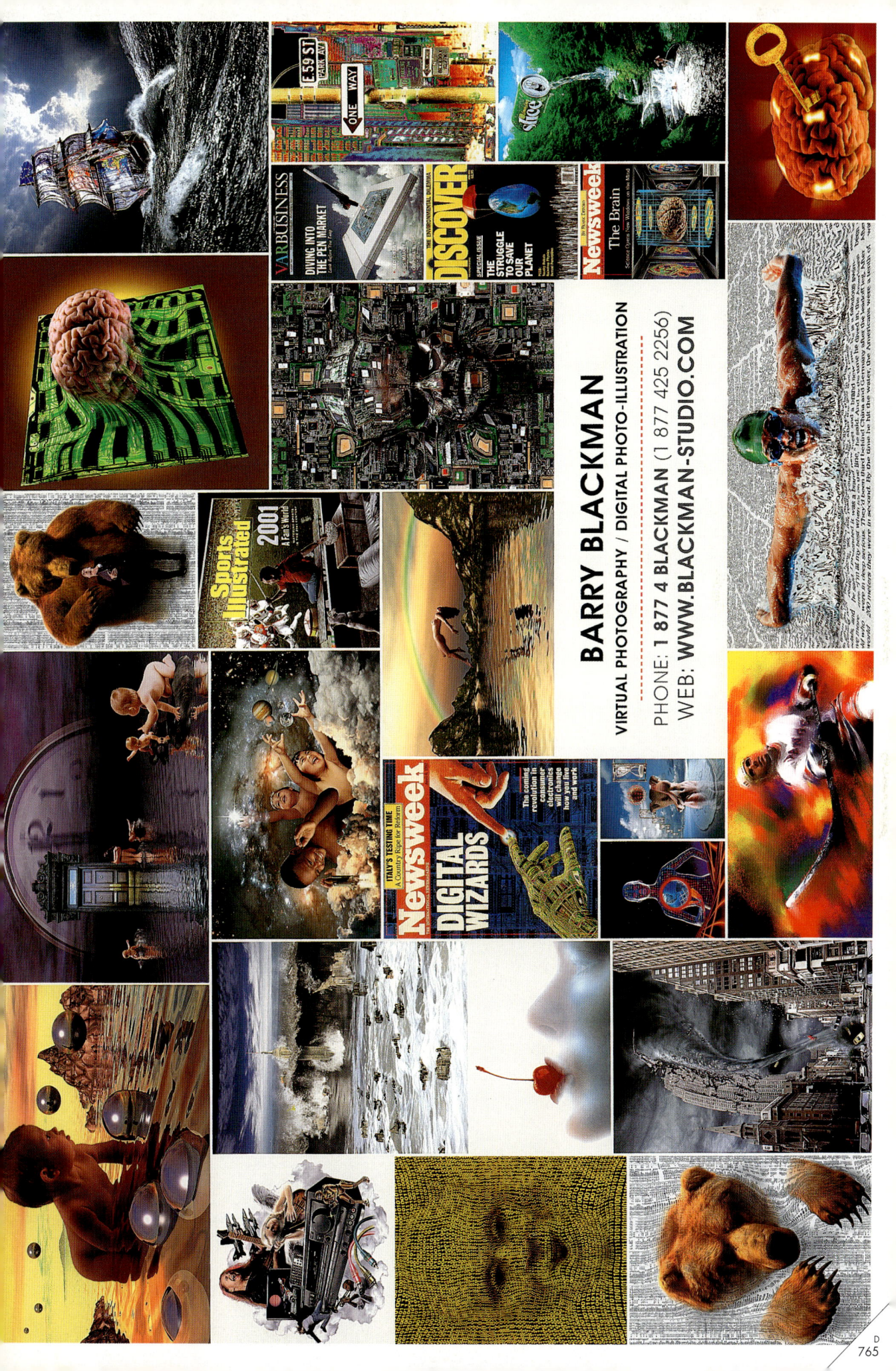

VIRTUAL PHOTOGRAPHY / DIGITAL PHOTO-ILLUSTRATION

PHONE: 1 877 4 BLACKMAN (1 877 425 2256)
WEB: WWW.BLACKMAN-STUDIO.COM

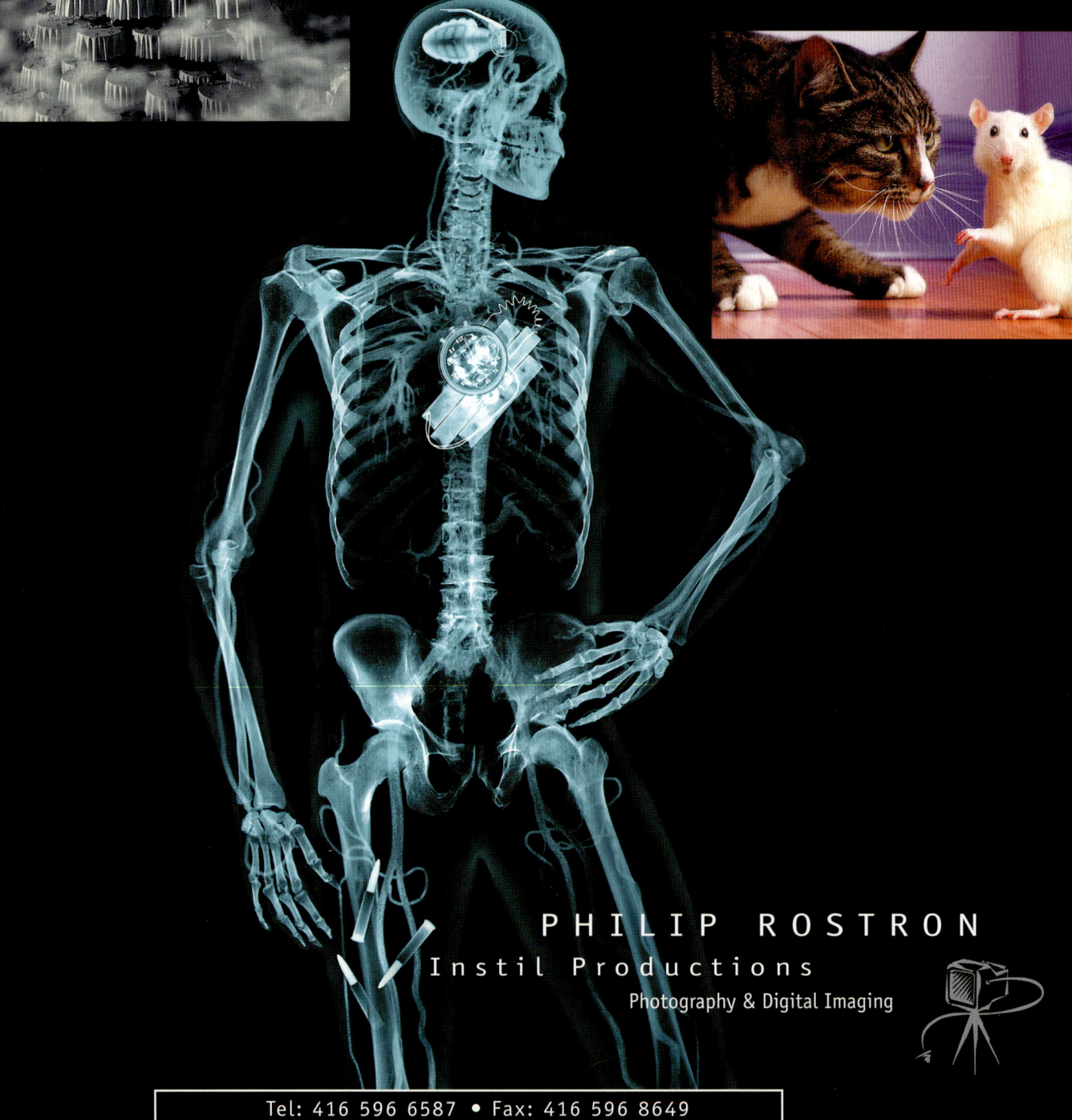

PHILIP ROSTRON
Instil Productions
Photography & Digital Imaging

Tel: 416 596 6587 • Fax: 416 596 8649

instil@interlog.com • www.instilproductions.com

tom drew :photographer   black,white & color inc.   photography for advertising and design   810.795.4620

www.bwcphoto.com

digital capture surpassing the quality of large format film.
really.

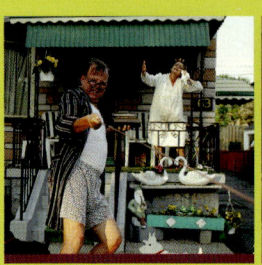

WE'RE JAMMIN',
team of Photographer Don Dixon
and Digital Artist Avner Levona
STUDIO: (416) 465-3634
www.were-jammin.com

represented by
KORMAN + COMPANY

korman + company

EAST: (212) 402-2450
WEST: (626) 583-1442

Please see additional work in the "East" section

Richard Bradbury

Photography & image manipulation

Representation:
US: Korman + Company
East: 212 402 2450
West: 626 583 1442

UK: Stan Cripps
+44 20 8838 0520

www.rbradbury.com

korman + company

Please see additional work in the "East" section

carlo pieroni

www.carlopieroni.com   e-mail: cp@carlopieroni.com

represented in the United States, Canada, Mexico by

korman + company

East Coast 212.402.2450   West Coast 626.583.1442
in France by Eskimo (+33) 06.16.23.28.66   Iin Italy by Kim Arena (+39) 02.70.10.67.75

Please see additional work in the "East" section

kalmn fabor
photogroup

we go wherever your imagination takes us.

3907 perkins avenue
cleveland, ohio 44114
fax: 216.426.9091
216.426.9090
www.kpphoto.com